CYBORGS, SANTA CLAUS
AND SATAN

ALSO BY FRASER A. SHERMAN

*The Wizard of Oz Catalog: L. Frank Baum's Novel,
Its Sequels and Their Adaptations for Stage,
Television, Movies, Radio, Music Videos, Comic Books,
Commercials and More* (McFarland, 2005)

Cyborgs, Santa Claus and Satan

Science Fiction, Fantasy and Horror Films Made for Television

Fraser A. Sherman

McFarland & Company, Inc., Publishers
Jefferson, North Carolina, and London

The present work is a reprint of the illustrated case bound edition of Cyborgs, Santa Claus and Satan: Science Fiction, Fantasy and Horror Films Made for Television, *first published in 2000 by McFarland.*

LIBRARY OF CONGRESS CATALOGUING-IN-PUBLICATION DATA

Sherman, Fraser A., 1958–
Cyborgs, Santa Claus and Satan : science fiction, fantasy and horror films made for television / by Fraser A. Sherman.
p. cm.
Includes index.

ISBN 978-0-7864-4341-3
softcover : 50# alkaline paper ∞

1. Science fiction films—Catalogs. 2. Fantasy films—Catalogs. 3. Horror films—Catalogs. 4. Television broadcasting of films—United States—Catalogs. I. Title.
PN1995.9.S26S45 2009
016.79143'615—dc21
99-86392

British Library cataloguing data are available

©2000 Fraser A. Sherman. All rights reserved

No part of this book may be reproduced or transmitted in any form or by any means, electronic or mechanical, including photocopying or recording, or by any information storage and retrieval system, without permission in writing from the publisher.

Cover image ©2009 Clipart.com

Manufactured in the United States of America

McFarland & Company, Inc., Publishers
Box 611, Jefferson, North Carolina 28640
www.mcfarlandpub.com

To my family: Tracy, Craig, Sheila, Art, Marianne and Paige.
And to Ross, who appreciates books like this.
And finally, to Roxanne Koogler, who always includes me in hers.

ACKNOWLEDGMENTS

A lot of people helped me write this book, whether or not they knew it, starting with the earlier writers whose books provided invaluable information: Alvin Maril (*Made-for-Television Movies*), Lee Goldberg (*Unsold Television Pilots*), Leonard Maltin (*Movie and Video Guide*), the Videohound Staff (*Videohound Movie Retriever*), Michael J. Weldon (*Psychotronic Video Guide*), Bill Cotter (*Wonderful World of Disney Television*), and Mark Phillips and Frank Garcia (*Science Fiction Television Series*). Further thanks go to the Baseline on-line service and the Internet Movie Database.

Next, a special thanks to Jonathan Rosenthal, late of the Museum of Radio and Television, without whose research efforts this book could have never been begun, let alone finished. Thanks also to the staffers at the Mary Esther and Fort Walton Beach public libraries—particularly the irreplaceable Phyliss Amason.

Thanks to the people in the industry who took the time to answer my questions: Philippe Perebinossoff at ABC, Bret Garwood at Aaron Spelling Television, Thomas Vitale and Bonnie Berusha at Sci-Fi Channel, Dave Smith at Disney, Dave Lombard at CBS, Steve Rubin at Showtime, Bill Winborn at New World, Rob Roth at USA Network and Jim Pearson at Dan Curtis Productions.

Thanks to Network Video, Blockbuster Video, TNT Video and Reel.com for the movie rentals.

Finally, thanks to the private individuals who loaned me tapes, gave me synopses, alerted me to movies I'd forgotten, tipped me off to obscure rental sources and let me make use of their cable connections: Ross Bagby and Roxanne Shearer-Koogler, first and foremost, then Sam Koogler, Demian Katz, Kevin Marcus, Tammy Hagloch, Roberte Plante, Allen Lane, Daniel Reitz, Maureen, Victor and Denny (sorry, I forgot your last names!), Leon Marcello, Scott Terpkosh, Grant Hurlock, Lisa Wildman, Vern Deuel, Jeff Nyahay, Denys Cowan, Joe Doc Talipan, John Pettey, C. Johnson, Jerry Seward, Eugene Myers, Trevor Hilst, Lance Clement, Donald Austin, James Bryant, Bob McCrea, Rick O'Connor, Carey Meier and Paul Boyce of Boyce Studios. And, needless to say, anyone else I've forgotten (sorry again!).

Couldn't have done it without you.

TABLE OF CONTENTS

Acknowledgments	vi
Introduction	1
The Films	**5**
Appendix A: Minor Genre Films	203
Appendix B: Alternative Titles	217
Appendix C: Chronology	218
Index	223

INTRODUCTION

Once upon a time, the movie industry hated television.

Television was the Great Satan, keeping people home watching at night instead of going to the movies. Studios forbade actors to take TV roles, and refused to sell films to television; when they did sell, at first it was only bottom-grade Westerns and pre–1948 movies (if they sold recent ones, they feared moviegoers would stay home and wait for them to appear on the small screen). Small wonder movies mocked TV in many films (e.g., *The Twonky, Will Success Spoil Rock Hunter?*).

By 1961, however, movie studios were making shows for television, and they'd found showing recent movies (starting with *How to Marry a Millionaire*) made them more money, not less. The networks responded by setting aside nights devoted to movies shown at prime time. Then, in 1964, Universal produced *See How They Run* (about three orphans unwittingly carrying top-secret documents), the first made-for-television movie (*The Killers* was made first, but it was deemed too violent and released to theaters instead). More TV movies followed; by the late eighties, with big-screen films going to cable and video first, the networks showed more made-for-TV films than they did theatrical releases.

Through the end of 1998, almost 600 of those films were telefantasy—films of science fiction (SF), supernatural horror, fantasy or super-hero adventure. Like their big-screen cousins, these include many smart, first-rate films, and many more that are forgettable crap—or worse, *un*forgettable crap. Quality aside, there are definite differences between movies that debut on TV and those that turn up at the local cineplex.

Money. "Obviously, budget's the number one difference," says Thomas Vitale of the Sci-Fi Channel's Acquisitions and Development Department. "We have to entertain people in two hours—believable scenario, believable world, believable setting, believable characters—with different budget realities."

For every big-budget spectacular—*Merlin* or *Gulliver's Travels*—a dozen more films chafe against tight budgets. That reality, Vitale says, means television does better concentrating on story and characters rather than action and special effects. He cited Sci-Fi's recent adaptation of the SF classic short story "The Cold Equations" as an example: "It makes a great character play, the premise is pure science fiction, and a couple of sets is all you need."

Another example is 1974's *The Stranger Within*, which has almost no effects, no visible extraterrestrials and a five-person cast, but still maintains a powerful alien feel thanks to Richard Matheson's script.

Time. Philippe Perebinossoff, ABC's Executive Director of Motion Pictures for Television, points out that movies, at least on the networks, must fit a certain time slot and be paced to meet the commercial breaks. "Not every movie has to have a scene end 20 minutes in," Perebinossoff says, "but there does have to be an Act One break and a one-hour break. We've not found that to be insurmountable—and it is good for cliff-hangers."

Pilots. Many made-for-TV telefantasies are pilots for potential series; introducing the cast, establishing the premise and setting the stage for future installments are as important as the story itself. Rather than fade out on "happily ever after," pilots have to be open-ended; that works okay with adventures such as *M.A.N.T.I.S.* or *Spectre,* but *House of Frankenstein* and *Target: Earth* leave so much hanging that they're more irritating than intriguing (the latter film's "happy" ending leaves our government riddled with alien infiltrators and the hero wanted for murder).

Source Material. Theatrical movies often knock off earlier hits; TV movies do too (there are many references here to *Alien* and *Poltergeist*—not to mention outright sequels such as *Omen IV* and *Revenge of the Stepford Wives*), but they're also influenced by TV far more than the big screen. There has been only one *Fugitive* on the big screen, but there have been dozens of series and TV movies (including several in this book) that copy that series' man-on-the-run formula. *Valentine Magic on Love Island* is an appalling fantasy that simultaneously rips off *Love Boat* and *Fantasy Island.* All of TV's parallel-world films came after *Sliders* had grown into a small hit.

The Written Word. Telefantasy differs from written fantasy, SF and horror as much as it does from big-screen films. For all the talk of "niche marketing" and narrowcasting (i.e., focusing on a narrow demographic rather than a mass audience), even a specialized cable channel like Sci-Fi needs more viewers than an SF novel needs readers to make a profit; the Big Four networks want even more. Publishers can target hard-core fantasy or horror fans; TV wants non-fans. Even after *Star Wars,* the networks insisted for years that SF couldn't bring in the numbers.

That's why telefantasies have often toned down genre weirdness to something the mass audience will (hopefully) accept more easily. James Gunn's *The Immortals* studies how immortality would affect human society; the TV adaptation, *The Immortal,* is a *Fugitive* knockoff with the immortal hero running from men who want life-prolonging transfusions. The creators of the future-war series *Space: Above and Beyond* told *TV Guide* they were more influenced by old war movies than science fiction, and didn't want to do anything "too futuristic." And compare Spider-Man's colorful array of comic-book villains to the ordinary hoods in his TV movie and the series that followed (both of Spidey's cartoon series did better, perhaps because they're "kids' stuff").

Other telefantasies fit into subgenres even mainstream audiences know well: alien-invaders, body-snatching alien invaders, haunted houses, demonic possession, computer/android turning on its creators (though, surprisingly, the medium that gave us *Star Trek* has produced very few space-adventure films). Not that these are inherently bad, but the really speculative, far-out ideas of cutting-edge SF novels and short stories rarely reach the screen (of course, it's also hard to convey advanced ideas in a visual medium unless you're doing a documentary).

Pure fantasy has an even rougher time; while SF seems like it could happen, fantasy, by definition, violates reality and is commonly dismissed as something for kids (in contrast to horror—we're not only more willing to suspend our disbelief for ghost stories, we consider them fit fare for grownups). Television is much more likely to show cute, cuddly stories (Santa Claus stories or suburban sitcoms in the *Bewitched* vein) than *Lord of the Rings*–style imaginary world adventures—though the current success of *Xena* and *Hercules* has changed that to some extent (without them, it is doubtful that *Merlin* or *The Odyssey* would have been made).

And despite its limitations, telefantasy

does include a wide range of genre themes and styles: social criticism, personal drama, "urban fantasy," comedy, action-adventure, political thriller and comic-book adventures (i.e., action-filled, colorful super-hero stories—"comic-book" is not used here as a derogatory synonym for "juvenile" or "stupid"). The genre has embraced dystopian drama, Bermuda Triangle tours, super-heroes (far more than the big screen has produced), alien invasions, UFO abductions, post-nuclear-war adventures, Stephen King adaptations, vampires, werewolves and ghosts. And telefantasy offers the thrill of seeing all of that right in front of one's eyes instead of just in one's mind (assuming the special effects aren't totally ghastly).

What's more, talented actors can make a formulaic story watchable (even absorbing) and a good film great (mediocre thespians, of course, can wreck an otherwise good film just as easily). One of the kicks from writing this book was seeing how many TV-movies combine big-screen legends, soon-to-be stars and currently hot actors in one film (check out the *Goliath Awaits* cast for an example).

If telefantasy rarely reaches the heights of the genre, it's still an interesting branch of the fantastic-fiction tree; even the worst films deserve at least a cursory nod—or sometimes an embarrassed moan.

Hence this book, a complete listing of every SF, fantasy and horror film and miniseries made for, or first shown on, television. The listing is inclusive: *Harlem Globetrotters on Gilligan's Island* is less an SF film than a situation comedy with science-fiction elements thrown in, but that's good enough to be included herein (although space limitations have confined it to an appendix).

I have, however, excluded "documentaries" on ghosts or alien autopsies; two-hour episodes of regular series; episodes of TV anthologies (*Wide World of Mystery* and some versions of the *World of Disney*); movies that first played on foreign television (such as cable's *Tales from the Darkside,* which debuted in Canada as *The Lexx*); and pseudo-movies that are actually two TV episodes stuck together (as has happened with *Time Tunnel* and the *Night Stalker* series).

Most films are listed alphabetically by title in the main body of the book; for them, included are cast lists, production credits, original air date (for syndicated movies, a general time window), a condensed synopsis, my review (bear in mind, this writer watched a lot of genre films even before this book; if the reader has never seen a haunted house movie, he or she may like *The Haunted* a lot better than did this reviewer) and background detail. Was it a pilot? Based on a novel or a comic book? Did a sequel or a series result? Any (soon-to-be) famous people in the cast? The author has relied on on-screen credits and information as much as possible, though for some unseen movies has had to fall back on synopses from other reference sources.

More films, mostly those with minimal genre elements, are listed alphabetically in Appendix A. If a particular movie cannot be found there, turn to Appendix B, which lists alternative titles for movies (some have two or three). To save space, the following abbreviations are used throughout: Sci-Fi (Sci-Fi Channel), Fam (Family Channel), TMC (Movie Channel), USA (USA Network), and Disney (Disney Channel).

Now open your mind (at least a little) and prepare to leave reality behind…

THE FILMS

THE ADVANCED GUARD
Sci-Fi, 3/21/98

Cast: Harper (Isabella Hoffman), Kevin (Michael Weatherly), Bravo (Eric Allan Kramer), Desmond (Jeff Kober), Fred (James Avery), Laura (Clare Salstrom), Charley (Cristi Conaway), Alpha (John Prosky), Vagrant (Robert Arnico), Cops (David Campbell, David Jean-Thomas), Ailene (Michelle Davison), Man (James Sebastian), Girl (Nonie Muse)

Credits: Director: Peter Geiger; Writers: Richard Kletter, Peter Geiger; Producer: Thom Colwell; Executive Producer: Jana Sue Memel; Photography: Zoltan David; Production Design: C.J. Strawn, Miq Strawn; Co-Designer: Candi Guterres; Costumes: Brigitte Mann; Music: Paul Rabjohns; Editor: Mallory Gottlieb; Produced by Trimark Pictures, Ma & Pa Pictures

Disguised as humans, four scouts for an ET invasion capture four people to learn why we're able to resist the mind-control powers they use to enslave their empire. An arsenal of torments and mental assaults fails to break the four guinea pigs; the alien scientist Harper begins sympathizing with them and questioning the logic driving the ruthless alien war machine, but Alpha, her superior, refuses to listen.

When Laura succumbs to the aliens' control, they dissect her to learn why. Harper discovers love (Laura's for co-captive Kevin) makes us vulnerable but anger lets us break their control; that makes us too unstable to enslave, so the invasion fleet will simply annihilate us. Throwing in with the humans, Harper helps them destroy her fellow aliens, then convinces her superiors that Earth is too powerful to conquer. She transfers her mind into Laura's body, reviving it, and escapes with the other humans to embrace life (and Kevin) on Earth.

A lot of familiar elements come together and work in this thriller (including the twist of having love make us vulnerable to mind-control instead of negating it). Kober had a supporting role in *Kindred: The Embraced*, and Conaway co-starred in the short-lived series *Timecop*.

ADVENTURES OF CAPTAIN ZOOM IN OUTER SPACE
Starz! 8/26/96

Cast: Ty Farrell (Daniel Riordan), Lord Vox (Ron Perlman), Princess Tyra (Liz Vassey), Vesper (Gia Carides), Simulus (Duane Davis), Baley (Gregory Smith), Sagan (Nichelle Nichols), Alumina (Cathy Moriarty, voice), Happy (Rick Copp), Zelazny (Lloyd Berry), Dr. Yal-Tem (David Mylrea), Girl (Sarah Strange), Lt. Zorg (Bill Croft), Guard (Ken Kirzinger), Sentry (Randy Schooley), Great Rea (Terry Howson), Producer (Tony Dow), Sponsor (David Hurtubise), Announcer (Michael Donovan), Special Effects Man (L. Harvey Gold), Lizard King (Alex Green), Gingis Von (David Adams)

Credits: Director: Max Tash; Writers: Rick Copp, David A. Goodman; Story: Brian Levant; Producers: Tony Dow, Peter V. Ware; Executive Producer: Brian Levant; Supervising Producers: Rick Copp, David A. Goodman; Photography: Jan Kiesser; Production Design: Charles Butcher, Lance King; Music: Shirley Walker; Editor: Robert P. Seppey; Produced by Starz!, Telvan Productions, MCA Television Entertainment

When space-tyrant Vox invades Princess

Tyra's world, her pitiful forces have no hope of victory—until Tyra's brother monitors Earth and watches heroic Captain Zoom battling injustice throughout the universe. Realizing Zoom is their world's prophesied liberator, the resistance summons Zoom across space to aid them ... which turns out to be a really bad idea, for Zoom is merely a character in a fifties TV series. So what they get is Farrell, the boor who plays Zoom.

Farrell's ego and ineptitude only make things worse for the resistance, but when he finally realizes what's at stake (and how good-looking Tyra is), he does his best to help. Following the prophecy, he leads the resistance to a lost temple and contacts the mysterious power within; Vox tries to take control of it, but the power destroys him instead and liberates the planet.

Adventures is a failed pilot, amusing in its parody of fifties television SF but no more than that. Fans of the *Beauty and the Beast* TV series will recognize Perlman as that show's heroic man-beast, Vincent, and *Trek* fans can see Nichelle Nichols (*Star Trek*'s Uhura) as the prophet Sagan (yes, the name is an in-joke, as is naming another character for SF writer Roger Zelazny).

ALICE IN WONDERLAND
CBS, 12/9–12/10/85

Cast: Alice (Natalie Gregory), Alice's mother (Sheila Allen), Man in Paper Suit (Steve Allen), Pat the Pig (Scott Baio), Lion (Ernest Borgnine), Unicorn (Beau Bridges), White Knight (Lloyd Bridges), White Rabbit (Red Buttons), Gryphon (Sid Caesar), White Queen (Carol Channing), Cook (Imogene Coca), Caterpillar/Father William (Sammy Davis, Jr.), Goat (Patrick Duffy), Gnat (George Gobel), Tweedledee (Eydie Gorme), Conductor (Merv Griffin), Mouse (Sherman Hemsley), Red Queen (Ann Jillian), Dormouse (Arte Johnson), White King (Harvey Korman), Tweedledum (Steve Lawrence), Walrus (Karl Malden), March Hare (Roddy McDowall), Queen of Hearts (Jayne Meadows), Rose (Donna Mills), Horse (Pat Morita), King of Hearts (Robert Morley), Mad Hatter (Anthony Newley), Lory Bird (Donald O'Connor), Carpenter (Louis Nye), Duchess (Martha Raye), Cheshire Cat (Telly Savalas), Messenger (John Stamos), Mock Turtle (Ringo Starr), Tiger Lily (Sally Struthers), Owl (Jack Warden), Humpty Dumpty (Jonathan Winters), Dodo (Shelley Winters), Duck (Charles Dougherty), Eaglet (Billy Braver), Bill the Lizard (Ernie Orsatti), Fish Footman (Scotch Byerly), Frog Footman (Robert Axelrod), Two of Spades (Michael Chieffo), Five of Spades (Jeffrey Winner), Seven of Spades (John Walter Davis), Knave of Hearts (James Joseph Galante), Queen of Diamonds (Selma Archerd), Courtier (George Savalas), Lady in Waiting (Candace Savalas), Black Cat (Troy Jordan), Jabberwock (Tom McLoughlin), Red King (Patrick Culliton), Daisy (Laura Carlson), Oysters (Kristi Lynes, Desiree Szabo, Barbie Alison, Janie Walton), Lady of the Court (Dee Brantlinger), Red Knight (Don Mattheson)

Credits: Director: Harry Harris; Writer: Paul Zindel, from *Alice's Adventures in Wonderland* and *Through the Looking-Glass* by Lewis Carroll; Producer: Irwin Allen; Associate Producer: George E. Swink; Photography: Fred J. Koenekamp; Production Design: Phil Jefferies; Costumes: Paul Zastupnevich; Choreography: Miriam Nelson; Music: Morton Stevens, songs by Steve Allen; Editors: Richard E. Rabjohn, James W. Miller; Produced by Irwin Allen Productions, Procter & Gamble Productions, Columbia Pictures, CBS Entertainment

This adaptation of Lewis Carroll is far superior to the many mediocre big-screen all-star *Alice*s (though, like those, using big stars doesn't add very much) and relatively faithful to the books (most adaptations just jumble events and scenes at random). The quality of the performances varies wildly, however; giving Carroll's whimsy a moral (Alice learns to deal with her fears of not growing up fast enough) was a dumb idea. Still, Natalie Gregory is an excellent screen Alice.

ALIEN AVENGERS
Showtime, 8/6/96

Cast: Joseph Collins (Christopher M. Brown), Rhonda (Shanna Reed), Charlie (George Wendt), Daphne (Anastasia Sakelaris), Det. Watts (Stephen Burrows), Barnes (Dan Martin), Robber (Nils Allen Stewart), Jamaal (Edafe Blackmon), Candy (Troy Beyer), Waitress (Faith Sale), Jesse (Anthony Crivello), Melissa Rose (Gretchen Palmer), Minister (Michael Colyar), Mailman (Jose Rey), Hoods (Matt Gallini, Anthony Anderson), Skinheads (Lance August, Steve Kehela, Heath Mattioli), Doorman (Jaime Cardriche), Prisoner (Jeffrey Scott Jensen), Driver (Gary

Morgan), Victim's Daughter (Christina Solis), Kid (Michael Pagan), Nervous Customer (Robert Alan Beuth), Guards (John Crane, Jeremy Pack), Motorcycle Cop (George Wilkerson), Singer (Kathy Hazzard), Interviewees (Manny Fernandez, Tim Haldeman, Cecile Krevoy, Julianna McCarthy)

Credits: Director: Lev L. Spiro; Writer: Michael James McDonald; Producer: Michael Amato; Co-Producers: Darin Spillman, Frances Doel; Executive Producer: Roger Corman; Photography: Christopher Baffa; Production Design: Robert E. Lee; Art Director: Michelle Cox; Music: Tyler Bates; Editor: Daniel H. Holland; Produced by Showtime, Concorde-New Horizons

When ex-drug dealer Joseph takes over his late mother's boardinghouse, his first boarders are an insufferably perky couple with a very sexy daughter, Daphne. Joseph doesn't know the family is actually vacationing ETs; Charlie and Rhonda get thrills killing thugs who try to rob them, but Daphne finds Earth hideously boring until she and Joseph become lovers.

Unfortunately, when Daphne kills one of Joseph's ex-buddies for attacking her, the cops blame Joseph and pin her parents' crimes on him, too. With the media spotlight on, Charlie and Rhonda want to leave, but Daphne busts Joseph out of jail and takes him to their homeworld, leaving her parents behind. Charlie and Rhonda go to jail for the murders—but being imprisoned around hundreds of criminals doesn't entirely upset them...

Alien Avengers is dumb, and not a lot of fun, but Wendt and Reed (particularly Wendt) are good in the leads.

ALIEN AVENGERS II
Showtime, 10/25/97

Cast: Charlie (George Wendt), Rhonda (Julie Brown), Daphne (Anastasia Sakelaris), Joseph Collins (Christopher Brown), Rita (Natalie Canerday), Carl Dalton (Wayne Grace), Shirley (Bernadette Birkett), Don (Ken Magee), Rancher Sid (Jim Cody Williams), Elder (Jack Betts), Jack Baranca (Todd C. Mooney), Deputy (Robert Peters), Jasper (Christopher Boyer), Morcho (Luis Contreras), Chester (Jason Sudeikis), Judge Gorman (Patrick Cranshaw), Flashy Man (Michael Todd Curry), Warden (David St. James), G-Men (David Weiss, Matt Geraldi), Bikers (George Fisher, Ernest M. Garcia)

Credits: Director: Dave Payne; Writer: Michael James McDonald; Producer: Darin Spillman; Co-Producer: Marta M. Mobley; Executive Producer: Roger Corman; Photography: Michael Mickens; Production Design: Mark Harper; Music: Tyler Bates; Editor: J.J. Jackson; Produced by Concorde-New Horizons, Transpacific Corporation

After serving their time for the murders in *Alien Avengers*, Charlie and Rhonda investigate a UFO sighting out west in hopes of a ride home, unaware that Joe and Daphne are returning for them (only to be waylaid by federal agents). Charlie and Rhonda find a town besieged by hostile aliens; they replace the murdered sheriff and dispense justice as zestfully as in the first film. Then they learn the "aliens" are the work of Dalton, a developer scaring locals to buy up land cheaply. They confront him and his gang in a western showdown which the aliens win easily, since bullets don't hurt them. Joe arrives to warn them the feds have kidnapped Daphne, but the agents track him down and capture everyone. The agents' boss, however, is secretly one of the aliens, who provides them a way offworld once Daphne and Joe finally tie the knot.

Like the first film, this works—to the extent it does—due to Brown (replacing Shanna Reed) and Wendt's screen presences.

ALIEN NATION: BODY AND SOUL
Fox, 10/10/95

Cast: Detective Matt Sikes (Gary Graham), Detective George Francisco (Eric Pierpoint), Buck Francisco (Sean Six), Emily Francisco (Lauren Woodland), Cathy Frankle (Terry Treas), Susan Francisco (Michele Scarabelli), Captain Brian Grazer (Ron Fassler), Detective Beatrice Zepeda (Jenny Gago), Albert Einstein (Jeff Marcus), Dr. Lois Allen (Josie Kim), Tivoli (Pamela Gordon), Benson (Leon Russom), Giant (Tiny Ron), Child (Danielle and Aimee Warren), Balboa (Marva Hicks), Felker (Monte Russell), Elinor (Judith McConnell), Karina Tivoli (Kristin Davis), Weapons Commander (Ruth Cordell), Techs (Robert Prentiss, Ned Van Zandt), BNA Guard (Daniel Chodos), Female Cop (Zilah), Pilot (Peter McKernan), Man (Rick Davis), Phil Dirt (Ben Martin), Penn (Glenn Morshower),

8 *Alien Nation: Dark Horizon*

Jones (Jeff Austin), Costell (Miguel Perez), Smithford (Paul Tuerpe), Attendant/Assassin (Richard Snell), Registrar (Susan Appling), Guard (Brent Scarpo), Trash (Greg Longstreet, Darion Basco), Cops (Harry Longstreet, Catherine Bell), Turner (Harry Johnstown), Boy (Zane Graham)

Credits: Director: Kenneth Johnson; Writers: Diane Frolov, Andrew Schneider, Renee & Harry Longstreet; Producer: Paul Kurta; Photography: Shelly Johnson; Production Design: Colin D. Irwin; Music: David Kurtz; Editor: Alan C. Marks; Produced by Kenneth Johnson Productions, Twentieth Television.

The second *Alien Nation* film opens when a weapons test at Benson's secret lab drains so much power that two Newcomer prisoners—a mute child and its devoted giant servant—are able to escape. The giant kills the pursuing guards, then leaves the child to be found by police. Meanwhile, Matt reluctantly enters a sex-ed class after learning he can't make love to Cathy without her greater strength injuring him. After Cathy's analysis shows the child may be half-human—a red flag for bigots—Matt and George are assigned to find her parents. The giant attempts to reclaim the child, is captured, and mentions the name of Choboke—an infamous, deceased Overseer scientist. Despite federal attempts to cover everything up, George and Matt connect the case to Tivoli, a murdered Newcomer scientist. Tivoli's daughter reveals that her mother assisted in Choboke's attempts to turn Tanktonians into pure mind; despite her crimes, Tivoli received a new identity from the U.S. in return for performing government research.

Benson threatens George's family, but Matt arranges for their fellow cops to protect the Franciscos, then frees the giant for Cathy to study further. She discovers giant and child are body and mind, separated by Choboke and dying now that they're apart. Matt and George learn Benson was a CIA officer who allowed Overseer scientists into the U.S. to exploit their brains in his private think tank.

Matt, George, Cathy and the giant locate Benson's secret lab, which has duplicated the slave ship's powerful space cannon to sell to the highest bidder. George sabotages the cannon and assaults Benson, who reveals he's Choboke himself, surgically altered to pass for human. He almost kills George before the giant breaks Choboke's back and rescues the child; the good guys escape as the cannon explodes. The cops let the double-being "escape" into the wilderness. Later, Matt completes his sex class and finally makes love to Cathy.

A good installment in the five-film *Alien Nation* series, *Body and Soul* further advances the Matt-Cathy relationship (which was a running theme through all five films).

ALIEN NATION: DARK HORIZON
Fox, 10/25/94

Cast: Detective Matt Sikes (Gary Graham), Detective George Francisco (Eric Pierpoint), Buck Francisco (Sean Six), Emily Francisco (Lauren Woodland), Cathy Frankle (Terry Treas), Susan Francisco (Michele Scarabelli), Captain Brian Grazer (Ron Fassler), Detective Beatrice Zepeda (Jenny Gago), Albert Einstein (Jeff Marcus), Ahpossno (Scott Patterson), May Onnaise (Dana Anderson), Marc Guerin (David Purdham), Priestess (Susan Appling), Penny (Diane Cary), Ordnance Officer (Mary Komatar), Supervisor (Michael Zand), Avid Fan (Michael Durrell), Florist (Lew Palter), Dr. Lois Allen (Michele Lamar Richards), Darlene Bryant (Lee Bryant), Sheriff (Robert Donner), Tom (John Meyers), Mitch the Cop (Don James), Communications Officer (Daine Markoff), Cashier (Patience Cleveland), Teri Cloth (Sondra Currie), Slave Mother (Elizabeth Storm), Jill (Risa Schiffman), Moe Goodluck (Rick Zumwalt), Elliot Riley (Jim Fyfe), Lorraine (Susanna Thompson), Transient (James Cooper), Rancher (Terrence Evans), Sam (Kevin Greviuox), Reporter (Khin-Kyaw Maung), Dr. Quinn (Haunani Minn), Kenny Bunkport (Blumen Young)

Credits: Director: Kenneth Johnson; Writer-Producers: Diane Frolov, Andrew Schneider; Photography: Lloyd Ahern II; Production Design: Brenton Swift; Music: David Kurtz; Editor: Alan Marks; Produced by Foxstar, Kenneth Johnson Productions

The first of five sequels to the *Alien Nation* TV show, a series set after a spaceship carrying a quarter-million Tanktonese slaves crashed near Los Angeles. Matt, a human detective, and his "Newcomer" partner, George, tackled not only alien-related crimes but the uneasy racial issues between the two species—

so uneasy that the series' last episode had Matt reject George and break off his relationship with pretty Tanktonese doctor Cathy.

In that episode, the xenophobic Purists tested a lethal anti-Newcomer disease on the Francisco family; as the film opens, George and Matt reunite to fight the Purists, with help from Cathy and Ahpossno, another Newcomer. Together they find a cure and jail the Purists, only to see Ahpossno move in on Cathy and drive a wedge between George and his family by appealing to Tanktonese tradition. What they don't know is that the alien slavers have sent Ahpossno, an Overseer, to recapture their escaped property—and after they reclaim the Newcomers (from a Tanktonese settlement Ahpossno is building), humanity is next. Although Ahpossno has fallen for Cathy, he refuses to turn from his mission.

George and Matt finally see through Ahpossno's scheme, and George challenges him to single combat; George loses, giving up a valuable Newcomer talisman. The talisman, coated with the Purist bacteria, kills Ahpossno as he returns to the slaver ship; out of love for Cathy, he convinces the slavers that the bacteria has killed the Newcomers, and that Earth is too toxic to visit.

Based on the 1988 theatrical film, *Alien Nation* was a classy, intelligent series that didn't click with the network, but the fan following convinced Fox to resurrect the show for five sequels, starting with this one, then *Alien Nation: Body and Soul*.

ALIEN NATION: THE ENEMY WITHIN
Fox, 11/12/96

Cast: Detective Matt Sikes (Gary Graham), Detective George Francisco (Eric Pierpoint), Buck Francisco (Sean Six), Emily Francisco (Lauren Woodland), Cathy Frankle (Terry Treas), Susan Francisco (Michele Scarabelli), Captain Brian Grazer (Ron Fassler), Albert Einstein (Jeff Marcus), Terry Firma (Wayne Pere), May Onnaise (Dana Anderson), Queen Mother (Tiny Ron), Rick Shaw (Joe Lando), Jessica Partridge (Kerrie Keane), with Brigitta Dau, Darin Heames

Credits: Director: Kenneth Johnson; Writers: Diane Frolov, Andrew Schneider; Producer: Ron Mitchell; Photography: Ron Garcia; Production Design: Colin D. Irwin; Music: Steve Dorff; Editor: David Strohmaier; Produced by Kenneth Johnson Productions, Twentieth Television

In the fourth *Alien Nation* reunion film, personal problems abound: Matt and Cathy's relationship is strained by moving in together, Buck can't find work and Susan feels so neglected after George agrees to help a friend conceive (it takes two Tanktonese men to fertilize one woman) that she contemplates an affair.

When a Newcomer pursued by armed men escapes from a sewer only to be killed by a car, George wants to ignore the case: The victim was an Eeno, a Tanktonian caste George despises because they performed waste disposal and burial duties on the slave ship—and had to feed on the corpses.

Matt insists on keeping the case open, and the strangeness soon mounts: The woman's body emits toxic gas; she was carrying a deformed fetus; the Eeno-run waste disposal firm she worked for is secretly stockpiling toxic waste; and another Eeno claims the firm impregnates women, then steals their babies. George scoffs at this, which outrages his daughter, Emily. When she brings the Eeno food, both girls are assaulted by Eeno-bashing Newcomers, which drives George to overcome his bigotry. With Buck Francisco's help, the cops find that the company is breeding Eeno mutants who thrive in pollution—unaware their "hive queen" mutant has bred hundreds of obedient children as her personal army. When the detectives and Buck visit her lair, the mutants almost kill them before a breach in the sewer wall drowns them in salt water (toxic to Newcomers). Afterwards, the Eenos begin reintegrating into society; Matt and Cathy resolve their differences; Susan decides against an affair and gives her blessing to George to help their friends.

Turning George into the bigot makes this a novel entry in the series; the gas-from-a-corpse angle takes off from a then-current medical incident.

ALIEN NATION: MILLENNIUM
Fox, 1/2/96

Cast: Detective Matt Sikes (Gary Graham), Detective George Francisco (Eric Pierpoint), Buck Francisco (Sean Six), Emily Francisco (Lauren Woodland), Cathy Frankle (Terry Treas), Susan Francisco (Michele Scarabelli), Captain Brian Grazer (Ron Fassler), Detective Beatrice Zepeda (Jenny Gago), Albert Einstein (Jeff Marcus), Jennifer (Kerrie Keane), Calaban (Steven Flynn), Jill (Risa Schiffman), Vivien (Freda Foh Shen), Jason (Brian Markinson), Alana (Herta Ware), Norton (Ellis Williams), Marina Del Rey (Susan Diol), Bigelow (Rick Snyder), Shivan (Pamela D'Pella), Polly Wannakraker (Susan Graham Lavelle), Landlady (Harriet Leider), Lawyer (John Towey), Whacko Human (Irene Forrest), Cop (David Correla), Randy (Jason Behr), Felix (David Faustino)

Credits: Director-Writer-Executive Producer: Kenneth Johnson; Producer: Paul Kurta; Photography: Shelley Johnson; Production Design: Colin D. Irwin; Music: David Kurtz; Editor: David Strohmaier; Produced by Kenneth Johnson Productions, Twentieth Television

A week before the millennium in this third *Alien Nation* film, detectives Matt and George link a series of mysterious disappearances to a cult that has stolen a Portal, a Tanktonese talisman with hallucinogenic powers. Cult leader Jennifer uses the Portal to show cultists visions of dead loves and alien worlds—but sometimes the Portal destroys them with the darkest terrors of their own mind. Embittered by human racism, Jennifer plans to milk her followers for money, then lead them to their deaths inside the Portal's hallucinatory realm.

To complicate things, Buck Francisco rejects his parents' materialism by joining the cult; Captain Grazer discovers Matt cheated on his test for promotion and pressures him into obtaining the Portal technology for Grazer's associates to exploit. Meanwhile, Emily Francisco is almost seduced by a human boy—until she realizes he only wants to boast of "shagging" a Newcomer.

Matt tries and fails to infiltrate the cult, then he and George learn Jennifer plans to fake her own death to escape justice. On the eve of the millennium, while George enters the Portal-world to try and free Buck from Jennifer, Matt locates and destroys the Portal, freeing the cult but killing Jennifer with feedback. Grazer doesn't get the Portal secrets, and the Franciscos agree to tone down their conspicuous consumption.

Probably the simplest of the films, *Alien Nation: Millennium* is close to a long episode of the show.

ALIEN NATION: THE UDARA LEGACY
Fox, 7/29/97

Cast: Detective Matt Sikes (Gary Graham), Detective George Francisco (Eric Pierpoint), Zapeta (Jenny Gago), Buck Francisco (Sean Six), Emily Francisco (Lauren Woodland), Kathy (Terry Treas), Susan Francisco (Michele Scarabelli), Captain Brian Grazer (Ron Fassler), Albert Einstein (Jeff Marcus), Senator Silverthorne (Lane Smith), Moore (Thom Barry), Jake Moran (Josh Cruze), Carter (George Fisher), Miller (Kevin Grevioux), Parent (Brenda Griffin), Miles Standish (Greg Longstreet), Gary (Scotch Ellis Loring), Newcomer (Ron Mitchell), Tina (Mary Ann Dedy), Sergeant (John F. O'Donohue), Sara (Sharon Omi), Moderator (Lew Palter), Sean (Eric Poppick), Director (Marcia Shapiro), Dave (Carter Paul Spohn), Donna (Marilyn Tokuda), Wilcox (Ivonne Coll), Renee (Sherry Davis), Claire Voyant (Marianna Elliot), Montejo (Juan Garcia), Reporters (Dale Harimoto, Mary Amadeo Ingersoll), Bartender (Michael Johnson), Daryll (Jack Kerrigan), Page (Jane Longenecker), Pete (Gino Motesinos), Andrews (Mailon Rivera), with Tim DeZarn, Michael Mantell, Robert Gossett, Jeff Allin

Credits: Director: Kenneth Johnson; Writers: Renee and Harry Longstreet; Producer: Ron Mitchell; Photography: Ron Garcia; Production Design: Colin D. Irwin; Music: Steve Dorff; Editor: Alan C. Marks; Produced by Kenneth Johnson Productions, Twentieth Television

In the final (to date) reunion movie for this series, Buck Francisco enters the police academy, while Matt and George investigate a series of random killings by Newcomers. Most of the killers die or commit suicide before being caught, but one survives long enough to whisper "udara"—the name of a slave resistance movement that eventually turned terrorist. George worries this news will affect the upcoming election pitting a Newcomer against xenophobic, anti–Tanktonese Silverthorne.

It's worse than George thinks: Udara brainwashed some of its members to carry out suicide missions, and a human hacker is exploiting the secret to create totally obedient assassins. When Silverthorne finds the man's price too high, he has the hacker killed and takes over, programming the next Udara zombie—Emily Francisco—to fake an assassination on Silverthorne, guaranteeing him the election. When Emily disappears, her mother admits to initiating Emily into Udara; with her help, George and Matt track down Udara's leader, who tells them how to free Emily. Emily attacks Silverthorne at a televised debate, but Buck—on duty as a cadet—takes the bullet, then risks his life protecting Emily from Silverthorne's bodyguards. Free of Udara, Emily identifies Silverthorne as her controller; the Newcomer candidate wins.

The last of the movies is a competent thriller (though an old plot, dating back to *The Manchurian Candidate*), ending with a big step forward for newcomer rights and the resolution of Buck's search for direction (a theme through most of the earlier films).

THE ALIEN WITHIN
Showtime, 7/18/95
    Cast: Dr. Henry Lazarus (Roddy McDowall), Jedidiah Pickett (Alex Hyde-White), Catherine Harding (Melanie Shatner), Louis (Don Stroud), Wyatt (Rodger Halston), Brill (Emile Levisetti), Hawkes (Richard Biggs), Fife (Sha-Ri Pendleton), Russian Officer (Miro Polo), Russian Boy (Tim Trevan)
    Credits: Director: Scott P. Levy; Writer: Alex Simon; Story: Rob Kerchner; Producer: Mike Elliott; Co-Producer: Bill Bromiley, Jr.; Executive Producer: Roger Corman; Photography: Mike Mickens; Production Design: John Meerdink; Special Creature Effects: Michael Burnette Productions; Special Visual Effects: Robert and Dennis Skotak; Music: Chris Lennertz; Editor: John Bergstresser; Produced by Concorde–New Horizons

In 2020 the crew of a U.S. underwater base answers an emergency call from a Russian base and discovers a) the Russians recently found and revived an alien from suspended animation; and b) all except one dying man have been dehydrated to death. Returning with the man to the American base, they learn the alien is a parasite that drains human bodily fluid, lays eggs, then takes over a new host; it escapes the dying Russian and the crew try to hunt it down. Eventually it possesses Dr. Lazarus, who reprograms the base android to help him blow up the base while he escapes to infect the surface. In the inevitable firefight, Lazarus and Brill are destroyed, leaving only Harding and Pickett to reach the surface—both infected with another parasite.

This unimpressive *Alien* knockoff (android crewmember, aliens bursting out of bodies, etc.) is noteworthy solely for the participation of executive producer Roger Corman, a veteran director of low-budget slop who always showed more talent than most people working his end of the pool (Vincent Price's Edgar Allan Poe films for AIP—*The Fall of the House of Usher, The Pit and the Pendulum*, etc.—are good examples of what Corman was capable of doing at his best). Corman also "broke in" many big names in his films, including Jack Nicholson, Peter Bogdanovich and Jonathan Demme. *The Alien Within* was the first in a "Roger Corman Presents" series of SF, horror and thriller films for cable, many remaking theatrical releases (*Not of This Earth, Bucket of Blood, Piranha*). On-screen, watch for Biggs (*Babylon 5*), veteran McDowall (*Fright Night, Tales of the Gold Monkey*) and William Shatner's daughter Melanie.

THE ALIENS ARE COMING
NBC, 3/2/80
    Cast: Dr. Scott Dryden (Tom Mason), Leonard Nero (Eric Braeden), Gwen O'Brien (Melinda Fee), Joyce Cummings (Fawne Harriman), Timmy Garner (Matthew Laborteaux), Harve Nelson (Ron Masak), Sue Garner (Caroline McWilliams), Eldon Gates (John Milford), Russ Garner (Max Gail), Chuck Polchek (Ed Harris), Lt. Col. John Sebastian (Hank Brandt), Bert Fowler (Laurence Haddon), Patrolman Ashley (Gerald McRaney), Frank Foley (Curtis Credel), Male Nurse (Peter Shuck), Patrolman Strong (Richard Lockmiller), Dr. Conley (Sean Griffin), Technician (Chris O'Brien), Intern

(Tom Lowell), Teacher (Nancy Priddy), Waitress (Lorna Thayer), Floyd (John Gilgreen), Student (Laurie Beach), Waiter (Dirk Olthof), Guard (Tom Pittman)

Credits: Director: Harvey Hart: Writer: Robert W. Lenski; Executive Producer: Philip Saltzman; Photography: Jacques R. Marquette; Editor: James Gross; Music Supervisor: John Elizalde; Music: William Goldstein; Art Directors: George B. Chan, Norman R. Newberry; Produced by Quinn Martin Productions, Woodruff Productions.

When the government detects a UFO landing, astrophysicist Dryden is sent to find proof of the aliens' existence. One of the energy-beings takes over the body of Russ Garner, a hydroelectric-dam worker (the dam is a potential power source for the colony the aliens hope to found); Garner's boss becomes suspicious, so the alien telepathically drives him to suicide. When Dryden investigates, the alien tries and fails to kill him. Another alien attempts to possess Dryden's body, but the scientist destroys it with an electric shock. A sexy reporter tries to learn the truth behind all this, but Dryden keeps things concealed.

Dryden confronts Garner at the plant, but Garner and another alien attack him. Dryden kills one of them; Garner is almost killed, which drives the alien out (leaving Garner very confused). The movie ends with both Dryden's agency and the aliens preparing their next moves.

Alien possession and infiltration go back at least to Robert Heinlein's novel *Puppet Masters*. Cinematically, 1956's *Invasion of the Bodysnatchers* is the classic in this vein. *The Invaders* series (by this film's production company) tried it with middling results in 1969, but this was the first TV movie based on the theme. Alas, it's utterly formulaic, with poor special effects and an irritating hero (possibly they hoped for "charmingly eccentric").

AMANDA AND THE ALIEN
Showtime, 8/20/95

Cast: Amanda Patterson (Nicole Eggert), Emmett Mallory (Stacy Keach), Vint (Michael Dorn), Charlie Nobles (Michael Bendetti), Col. Rosencrantz (John Diehl), Connie Flores (Alex Meneses), LeBeau (David Millbern), Bubba (Ritch Brinkley), Beatnik Bob (Johnny Caruso), Nick (Dan O'Connor), Mac (Raymond D. Turner), Guard (J. Marvin Campbell), Shopper (Marcia Shapiro), Jessica (Carol Ann Plante), Shonda (Rene Weisser), News Anchor (Edwina Moore), Slacker (Brett Galov), JoJo (Richard Speight, Jr.), Besel (Allen Cutter), Dave (Chadd Nyerges), Cop (Randy O'Connell), Bellman (Ryan Holihan), Holly HoeDown (Cindy Morgan), SWAT Leader (Jefferson Wagner), Thelma (Liz Johnson), Truckers (Andre Rosey Brown, Arnie Moore), TV Host (Jessica Hahn), Cindy (Danika Kohler)

Credits: Director-Writer: Jon Kroll, based on Robert Silverberg's short story; Producer: Larry Estes; Co-Producer: Jonas Thaler; Executive Producers: Miles A. Copeland III, Paul Colichman; Photography: Gary Tieche; Production Design: M. Nord Haggerty; Music: Jane Wiedlin, Michael Cozzi; Editor: Brian Berdan; Produced by Republic Pictures, IRS Media, Inc., Century Group, Ltd.

With all California hunting a body-stealing, human-eating alien, it's would-be artist Amanda Patterson who spots the creature (in a woman's body) and hides it from federal agents, even offering her faithless boyfriend, Charlie, as the alien's new host body. With Amanda's help, the alien stays free long enough to contact its ship and return to space, where it will tell its fellow aliens that humans are too intelligent for a food source.

No question the clichés of noble-alien-and-friendly-human-flee-xenophobic-federal-agents films deserve a parody—but they don't deserve this stupid and unfunny mess (Silverberg's original story was much better). Fans of *Star Trek: The Next Generation* or *Deep Space Nine* can see Michael Dorn out of his Klingon makeup here.

AN AMERICAN CHRISTMAS CAROL
ABC, 12/16/79

Cast: Benedict Slade (Henry Winkler), Merrivale (David Wayne), Mr. Brewster (Chris Wiggins), Thatcher (R.H. Thomson), Jack Latham (Kenneth Pogue), Jessup (Gerald Parkes), Helen Brewster (Susan Hogan), Matt Reaves (Dorian Harewood), Sarah Thatcher (Tammy Bourne), Jonathan Thatcher (Chris Cragg), Sam Perkins (James B. Douglas), Jennie Reeves (Arlene Duncan), Doris Thatcher (Linda Soranson)

Credits: Director: Eric Till; Writer: Jerome Coopersmith, from Charles Dickens' *A Christmas Carol*; Producers: Jon Slan, Stanley Chase; Executive Producers: Edgar J. Scherick, Gary Smith; Photography: Richard Ciupka; Production Design: Jack McAdam. Music: Hagood Hardy; Editor: Ron Wisman; Produced by Chase/Slan Productions, Smith-Hemion Productions, Scrooge Productions

This film's "Scrooge," Benedict Slade, is an orphan fostered and mentored in business by Brewster as the last century closes. Slade's descent into heartlessness begins when he convinces a financier to invest in his pet project—cheap, assembly-line furniture—instead of Brewster's plans for traditional, high-quality products, leaving Brewster ruined and heartbroken. By the time of the Depression (when the film opens), Slade is a thorough, heartless bastard—but then three spirits appear to him on Christmas Eve.

Though not among the first rank of Dickens adaptations, this possesses some good touches.

AMITYVILLE: THE EVIL ESCAPES
NBC, 5/21/89

Cast: Nancy Evans (Patty Duke), Alice Leacock (Jane Wyatt), Father Kibbler (Frederic Lehne), Father Manfred (Norman Lloyd), Peggy (Lou Hancock), Jessica Evans (Brandy Gold), Amanda Evans (Geri Betzler, a.k.a. Zoe Trilling), Brian Evans (Aron Eisenberg), Donald McTear (Robert Alan Browne), Rhona (Gloria Cromwell), Helen Royce (Peggy McCay), with Alex Rebar, Jack Rader, Michael Korn, Richard Crystal, John De Bello, David Elliot, Gary Michael Davies

Credits: Director-Writer: Sandor Stern, based on *Amityville: The Evil Escapes* by John G. Jones; Producer: Barry Bernardi; Co-Producer: John G. Jones; Executive Producer: Steve White; Production Design: Kandy Berley Stern; Photography: Tom Richmond; Music: Rick Conrad; Editor: Skip Schoolnik; Produced by Spectator Films/Academy Entertainment

After a half-dozen priests jointly exorcise an accursed house in Amityville, the owner auctions off the furniture—unaware the evil has hidden within an antique lamp. After the lamp winds up in the Leacock home, the usual signs of possession manifest themselves—appliances start themselves, black gunk runs from the taps, and little Jessica becomes convinced her daddy's ghost lives in the lamp. One of the priests discovers what's happening and arrives at the house to challenge the demon; the spirit's power crushes him until Alice sprays the lamp with holy water and throws it out the window. Next day, however, the family cat passes by the broken lamp, and the evil spirit finds its new host…

The Amityville Horror in 1979 was American International Pictures' biggest box-office hit ever (and triggered much debate over whether it was really "based on truth"). After two more sequels (and the unrelated *Amityville Curse*), the series visited TV in this clichéd tripe before moving to video for four (to date) sequels involving other possessed furniture.

THE ANDROID AFFAIR
USA, 4/12/95

Cast: Dr. Karen Garrett (Harley Jane Kozak), William "Teach" (Griffin Dunne), Dr. Winston (Ossie Davis), Fiedler (Saul Rubinek), Alexx (Chandra Galasso), Gunther (David Campbell), Thomas Benti (Peter Outerbridge), Rachel Tyler (Natalie Radford), Palmer (Ron Hartman), Teach #1 (Michelle Moffatt), Dr. Banner (Joseph Scorsiani), Nurse Gridley (Heidi Halashita), Allen (Wendy Murphy), Visitor (Diana Zimmer), Peter (Desmond Campbell), Reporter (Anne Ritchie), Guards (Peter Pownall, Bryan Renfro), Cops (Robert Hollinger, T.W. Schroeder).

Credits: Director-Writer: Richard Kletter, based on the short film *Teach 101* written by Kletter and Isaac Asimov; Producer: Joan Carson; Executive Producers: Thom Colwell, Jana Sue Memel; Photography: Bernard Salzmann; Production Design: Carmi Gallo; Music: Simon Boswell; Editor: Lisa Bromwell; Produced by Chanticleer Films

At Dr. Winston's research institute, doctors test cutting-edge medicine on android patients. When tightly wound Dr. Garrett is assigned heart surgery on William, a sophisticated, wisecracking android, it's a major career boost for her—but William refuses to cooperate until Garrett gives him a forbidden day trip outside the institute. Once outside, William reveals his ultimate goal—to escape and join human society. When Garrett scoffs, William takes her to Benti, an android passing as a human. Benti implies Winston secretly arranged Benti's escape—and that neither he nor Winston want the flamboyant William free and drawing attention. Benti attacks them; they escape and begin investigating Winston's plans, while dodging hired muscle Winston sends after them.

Garrett and William fall in love; when his heart problem becomes terminal, Garrett successfully operates on him, after which Winston's henchmen capture them. Winston reveals he's an android created to test cures for the heart condition that killed the real Winston. After stepping into his creator's shoes, "Winston" still needed Garrett and William to find the cure; he manipulated William's escape and their romance to give Garrett the emotional drive to perfect the operation. Then Winston's heart fails—but Garrett refuses to operate. The android dies, leaving William and Garrett free to escape together.

Dunne is absolutely winning in this entertaining romance, but the script plays fast and loose with his anatomy, giving him a human circulatory system while making him machine enough to ignore bullets in the chest. Fun, even so.

ANGEL ON MY SHOULDER
ABC, 5/11/80

Cast: Eddie Kagel/Marcus Harriman (Peter Strauss), Nick (Richard Kiley), Julie (Barbara Hershey), Dolly Blaine (Janis Paige), Marvin "Smiley" Mitchell (Seymour Cassel), Tony (Scott Colomby), Gregg Marlowe (Peter MacLean), Joe Navotny (Billy Jacoby), Nick's Aide (Douglas Dirkson), Diana (Anne Newman Mantee), The Stranger (Murray Matheson), Luke (Terry Alexander), Gino Gianelli (Frank Campanella), Mrs. Martin (Anne Seymour), Matt (Charles Cooper), Cissy (Janis Hansen), with Peter Jason, James O'Connell, McKee Anderson, Harry Caesar, Victor Rogers, Philip Simms, Joanne Horne, Shepherd Sanders, Simmy Bow, Michael Goldfinger, John Alderman, Art Aragon, Joe Mays, Susan Barnes, Gordon Hanson, Mary Armstrong, Joe Tornatore, Harrison Baker

Credits: Director: John Berry; Writer: George Kirgo, from a screenplay by Roland Kibbee and Harry Segall; Producer: Barney Rosenzweig; Executive Producer: Mace Neufeld; Associate Producer: Dennis Berry; Photography: Gayne Rescher; Art Director: Tom H. John; Music: Artie Butler; Editor: Art Seid; Produced by Mace Neufeld Productions, Barney Rosenzweig Productions, Beowulf Productions

Decades after his execution, gangster Eddie Kagel is released from hell by "Nick" (Satan) to seek revenge on the Mitchells, who framed him for murder. In return, Eddie will possess his exact double, incorruptible politician Harriman, and ruin his reputation. Instead, Eddie's street-smart, plain-speaking manner as Harriman impresses everyone—power brokers, street kids, Harriman's pretty aide Julie—and clinches the election.

Nick tells Eddie to tape himself taking a bribe from the Mitchells, discredit Harriman with the tape, then gun down the Mitchells to completely ruin Harriman. When Eddie sees how awful the Mitchells' marriage is, however, he decides that letting them live (tormented by his knowledge of their crimes) will be a better revenge. He also decides to stay in Harriman's body for good so he can be with Julie—until he realizes it's Harriman Julie truly loves, and gives up life for her sake (but it's clear Harriman will keep the best of Eddie's personality). Nick vows revenge, but before he can return Eddie to hell, an angel claims Eddie's redeemed soul for heaven.

A charming remake of a 1946 fantasy (but perhaps the telefilm's real inspiration was the success of 1978's similar *Heaven Can Wait*), *Angel on My Shoulder* is stock stuff, but with good performances by the leads and a more upbeat ending than the original (in which Paul Muni's Eddie returned to hell).

ANGELS IN THE ENDZONE
ABC, 11/9/97

Cast: Jess Harper (Matthew Lawrence), Al (Christopher Lloyd), Kevin Harper (David Gallagher), Coach Buck (Paul Dooley), Peter Harper (Jack Coleman), Grace Harper (Lynda Boyd), Artie (Allan Zinyk), Angels (Ken Kirzinger, Ron Robinson, David Paul Grove, James Hibbard,

Kate Twa), Shotgun (Curtis Bechtold), Kemer (Jason Emanuel), Hogg (Trevor Roberts), Shack (Winston Brown), Dabinsky (Kevin Hansen), Garo (Sean Amsing), Bodean (Christian Tessier), Tyler (Jamie Lawson), Skip (Campbell Lane), Guthrie (Dwight McFee), Stone (Will Sanderson), Attendant (Gary Jones), Officer (Alfred Humphreys), Dr. Frick (Charles Siegel), Vendor (Robert Rozen), Weatherman (Howard Storey)

Credits: Director: Gary Nadeau; Writers: Alan Eisenstock, Larry Mintz, based on characters from *Angels in the Outfield*; Producer: Richard L. O'Connor; Co-Producers: Gary Stutman, Irby Smith; Executive Producer: Roger Birnbaum; Production Design: David Fischer; Photography: Ron Orieux; Music: Frederick Talgorn; Editor: Jeff Freeman; Produced by Walt Disney Television, Roger Birnbaum Productions

Devastated by his father's death, Jess Harper drops out of playing football, leaving his inept high-school team further from victory than ever. His brother Kevin's prayers for help convince Al, a sports-loving angel, to send a team of invisible (to all but Kevin) angels to covertly help the team win. When the team gets a shot at the championship, Al insists this is one game they have to win themselves; fortunately, Jess, his spirits restored, rejoins the team and leads them to victory.

This boring sequel to the theatrical *Angels in the Outfield* overflows with clichés: the inept young sports team (a Disney staple since *The Mighty Ducks*), Kevin looking insane because he talks to invisible people, and the curious ethic among fantasy sports stories that it's okay to cheat with magic or SF if the final winning pitch is won naturally (e.g., *Damn Yankees, It Happens Every Spring*).

ANNIHILATOR
NBC, 4/7/86

Cast: Richard Armour (Mark Lindsay Chapman), Layla (Susan Blakely), Cindy (Lisa Blount), Alien Leader (Brion James), Sid (Earl Boen), Prof. Alan Jeffries (Geoffrey Lewis), Angela Taylor (Catherine Mary Stewart), Elyse (Nicole Eggert), Eddie (Barry Pearl), Pops (Paul Brinegar), Susan Weiss (Channing Chase), Celia Evans (Barbara Townsend), Christopher (Christopher Johnston), Henry Evans (Glen Vernon), FBI Agents (Richard Partlow, Biff Yeager), Patti (Toni Attell), Policemen (James Parks, Greg Collins), Man in Coat (Roger LaRue), Cammie (Stanley Bennett Clay), Nervous Man (Lola Fisher), Agents (Jerry Boyd, Al Pugliesse), Coroner (Martin Clark), Trucker (John Durbin), Airline Agents (Donald Hayes, Helen Anderson), Supervisor (William Jackson), Bum (Gary Burden), Girl (Julie Harris)

Credits: Director: Michael Chapman; Writers: Roderick Taylor, Bruce A. Taylor; Supervising Producer: Alex Beaton; Executive Producer: Roderick Taylor; Photography: Paul Goldsmith; Art Director: Kirk Axtell; Music: Sylvester Levay; Editor: Frank Mazzola; Makeup: Michael Westmore, Zoltan Elek; Produced by Universal Television

Fleeing the cops, newspaper editor Armour finds sanctuary with friendly Layla, and he tells her how his girlfriend Angela came back from vacation colder, harder—then tried to murder him. When he escaped, she hunted him with inhuman strength until accidentally destroyed; misreading the evidence, the cops think Armour murdered her. Armour sought out Angela's fellow vacationer, Cindy, but she was also a super-killer, and he barely escaped her.

Layla helps Armour track down another vacationer, Susan, but Cindy kills Susan before she can reveal anything; Armour destroys Cindy and discovers she's an android. Layla takes Armour to her friend Geoffrey, a parapsychologist; on the way, we learn (but Armour doesn't) that she's One Of Them. Armour learns the truth at Geoffrey's house, so Geoffrey—revealing he and the others are "dynamators"—attacks. Armour destroys Geoffrey and his dynamator "children." Layla makes a reluctant attempt to kill Armour, but the arrival of the authorities drives her away. With only the passenger list from Angela's vacation as a clue, Armour sets out to track down more dynamators.

If you've never seen an aliens-infiltrating-us film before, this might be pretty good; otherwise, it's a dull retread of familiar material.

THE ARCHER: FUGITIVE FROM THE EMPIRE
NBC, 4/12/81

Cast: Toran of Malveel (Lane Caudell), Estra

(Belinda Bauer), Slant (Victor Campos), Gar the Draikan (Kabir Bedi), Mak (George Innes), Sandros (Marc Alaimo), Paeter Yos (Allan Rich), Baldor (John Hancock), Hawk Lady (Priscilla Pointer), Brakus (George Kennedy), Captain Ria (Robert Feero), Rak (Richard Dix), Vors (Ivan J. Rado), Mandra (Sharon Barr), Riis (Tony Swartz), Bovum Ferryman (Richard Moll), Astrologer (Chao-Li Chi), Woman Scholar (Dee Croxton), Merchant (Fred Pinkard), Dar (Scott Wilder), Lazar-Sa (Larry Douglas)

Credits: Director-Writer-Producer: Nick Corea; Producer: Stephen P. Caldwell; Photography: John McPherson; Editor: Alan J. Shefland; Music: Ian Underwood; Art Director: Loyd S. Papez; Produced by Mad Dog Productions, Universal Television

In an ancient world, Gar the Destroyer, Lord of the Snakemen, is forging an empire over the bodies of all who oppose him. When Gar leads his forces against the barbarians of Malveel, King Brakus falls before him—but Brakus' son, Toran, escapes, and wields a powerful magic bow as his weapon. To stop Gar, however, Toran will need the help of a powerful wizard whose sorcery can defeat Gar—if Toran can find the mage. Toran finds assistance in his quest from Slant, a greedy gambler less than thrilled to be playing for such high stakes, and Estra, a sorceress seeking the wizard herself—but to kill him for her own reasons. With Gar's snakemen in hot pursuit, the trio sets out on their journey

Sword-and-sorcery fantasy (the term is self-explanatory) has been around since the thirties, but this was live-action TV's only venture into the genre (not counting parodies like *Wizards and Warriors*) until *Hercules* made fantasy fashionable in the nineties (while Herc was tongue-in-cheek, the derivative *Beastmaster III*, *Adventures of Sinbad* and *Roar* were not). *The Archer* proved an unsuccessful but entertaining pilot.

ARTHUR, THE KING
CBS, 4/26/85

Cast: King Arthur (Malcolm McDowell), Morgan LeFay (Candice Bergen), Merlin (Edward Woodward), Katherine (Dyan Cannon), Niniane (Lucy Gutteridge), Mordred (Joseph Blatchley), Lancelot (Rupert Everett), Guinevere (Rosalyn Landor), Grak (Liam Neeson), Gawain (Patrick Ryecart), Agravain (Philip Sayer), Lady Ragnell (Ann Thornton), King Pellinore (Denis Lill), Sir Kai (John Quarmby), Archbishop (Michael Gough), Gorgo (Milance Avramovic), Enchanted Queen (Terry Torday), Princesses (Mary Stavin, Carole Ashby, Alison Worth), Guide (Peter Blythe), Woman Passenger (Pat Starr), Court Ladies (Marie Elise, Maryam d'Abo, Tina Robinson), Barge Ladies (Pia Constance-Churcher, Linda Fontana, Christine Hunt, Cia Ford), Undead Knight (Miro Pfeiffer), Charnel Cart Driver (Miro Pitenc), Boatman (Vlado Spindler), Niniane's Father (Mise Martinovic), Ragnar (Tom Vukusic)

Credits: Director: Clive Donner; Writer: J. David Wyles; Producer: Martin Poll; Photography: Denis Lewiston; Production Design: Francisco Chianese; Music: Charles Gross; Editor: Peter Tanner; Art Director: Dusko Jericevic; Costume Designer: Phyllis Dalton; Produced by Martin Pol Productions, Comworld Productions

Katherine, a tourist, discovers Merlin and his lover Niniane trapped in a sorcerous prison beneath Stonehenge. Their magic shows her the story of Camelot. Arthur's unifying his war-torn country and becoming king; the schemes of his evil sister, Morgan LeFay, to destroy him; the great adventures of his knights; and how the affair between Lancelot and Guinevere tore the table apart, leading to Arthur's death and Morgan's triumph. Katherine, however, convinces Merlin he and Niniane can use their magic to alter the past, not just observe it. They use their magic to help Lancelot defeat Morgan's forces, after which the dying Arthur is borne away to Avalon until the hour Britain needs him again. This inspires the couple to break free of their prison at last.

Originally set to debut in 1982, this lackluster film wastes an astonishing amount of talent (including future star Liam Neeson, who also appeared in the theatrical *Excalibur*), though it does include some Arthurian legends often forgotten (such as the tale of Ragnell, Gawain's bewitched wife).

ASSASSIN
CBS, 3/19/86

Cast: Henry Stanton (Robert Conrad), Mary Casallas (Karen Austin), Robert Golem (Richard Young), Earl Dickman (Jonathan Banks), Calvin

Lantz (Robert Webber), Franklin (Ben Frank), Ann Walsh (Jessica Nelson), Grace Decker (Nancy Lenehan), Senator Corbin (Len Birman), Becker (Robert F. Hoy), Kreiger (Nick Angotti), Secretary (Grace Simmons), Wheeler (Allan Graf), Oliver Smithfield (Richard Newton), Todd (Scott Lincoln), Slocum (John Evans), Agent One (Patrick Gorman), Hotel Clerk (Mark Lindsay), Corridor Agent (Chuck Courtney), Teenager (Jamie Stern), Marcus Baines (Leonard A. Mazzola).

Credits: Director-Writer–Executive Producer: Sandor Stern; Producer: Neil T. Maffeo; Associate Producer: Henry Golas; Photography: Chuck Arnold; Production Design: Vincent Cresciman; Music: Anthony Guefen; Editor: James Galloway; Produced by Sankan Productions, Inc.

Federal spymaster Lantz convinces retired spy Stanton to help agent Casallas stop Golem, a murderous rogue agent. In their first encounter, Stanton discovers Golem is super strong and shrugs off bullets; Casallas confesses that Golem is a robot assassin she helped create, now reprogrammed by her deceased partner to commit a string of killings "for the good of America."

After repeated failures to take down Golem, Stanton and Casallas unearth the list of targets; since Lantz is on the list, he becomes bait. The robot takes the bait, smashing through Lantz's guards. Golem tells Stanton that Lantz tricked Stanton into blowing up a planeload of tourists to take out one terrorist, the "mistake" that drove Stanton to quit. Stanton refuses to turn on Lantz, but Golem kills Lantz anyway, then self-destructs when Stanton corners him. But was Golem the only one...?

This is the first of many telefantasies centering around robot government assassins, and a very dull one. Conrad was more fun in his SF series *The Wild, Wild West*.

ATTACK OF THE 50-FOOT WOMAN
HBO, 12/11/93

Cast: Nancy Archer (Daryl Hannah), Harry Conway (Daniel Baldwin), Dr. Theodora Cushing (Frances Fisher), Hamilton Cobb (William Windom), Honey (Christi Conaway), Dr. Loeb (Paul Benedict), Sheriff Denby (O'Neal Compton), Deputy Charlie Spooner (Victoria Haas), Ingersol (Lewis Arquette), Woman (Kye Benson), Men (Xander Berkeley, Stephen Rowe), Reporter (Linda Bisesti), Prospector Eddie (Hamilton Camp), Pilots (Ben Cleaveland, George Gerdes, Hank Stratton, Scott Williamson), Tony (Richard Edson), Girl (Dru Mouser), Mayor Thayer (Edmund L. Shaff), Nurse (Hilary Shepard), Teen Boy (Barry Watson), Alien Woman (Berta Waagfjord), Donna (Maud Winchester).

Credits: Director: Christopher Guest; Writer-Executive Producer: Joseph Dougherty; Producer: Debra Hill; Co-Producers: Chuck Binder, Daryl Hannah; Photography: Russell Carpenter; Production Design: Joseph T. Garrity; Music: Nicholas Pike; Editor: Harry Keramidas; Produced by HBO, Warner Bros.

Small-town housewife Nancy Archer has spent her whole life suppressing anger at her manipulative, wealthy father, Hamilton, and her womanizing husband, Harry. When Nancy reports a UFO encounter, her father considers it an embarrassment; Harry hopes to have her committed and so gain control of her money. The UFO returns and briefly abducts Nancy, altering her hormones so that when she finally gets angry at the men, the adrenaline surge turns her into a giant.

Emotionally strengthened by her new body, Nancy refuses to let Hamilton keep using her as a tax dodge and won't go to the sanitarium where Harry wants her "treated." When Harry learns size-changing has strained Nancy's heart, he reveals all his affairs in the hope the added stress will trigger a heart attack; instead, Nancy grows even bigger. After she hunts Harry down, the aliens collect them both, and Harry is forced into group counseling with the husbands of other giant kidnap victims.

Like *The Wasp Woman*, this remake of interesting schlock (the original is notorious as one of the dumbest SF movies of the fifties) comes off as boring schlock while claiming it's a "feminist" film (nope—right to the end, Nancy's trying to salvage her marriage when a real feminist would have washed her hands of Harry, or better yet, crushed him under her giant heel).

BABES IN TOYLAND
NBC, 12/19/86

Cast: Lisa (Drew Barrymore), Barnaby/Barnaby Barnacle (Richard Mulligan), Mom/Mother

Hubbard (Eileen Brennan), Jack Fenton/Jack Horner (Keanu Reeves), Toymaster (Pat Morita), Mary Contrary (Jill Schoelen), George/Georgie Porgy (Googy Gress), Justice Grimm (Walter Buschoff), Trollog (Shari Weiser), Zack (Rolf Knie), Mack (Gaston Haeni), Jack in the Box (Pipo Sosman), Joey (Chad Carlson), News Announcer (Jean Moke), Weather Announcer (Bill Marcus)

Credits: Director: Clive Donner; Writer: Paul Zindel, based on the operetta by Victor Herbert and Glen MacDonough; Producers: Tony Ford, Neil T. Maffeo; Executive Producers: Sheldon Pinchuk, Pat Finnegan, Bill Finnegan; Supervising Producer: Anthony Spinner; Production Design: Robert Laing; Photography: Arthur Ibbetson; Costumes: Evangeline Harrison; Music: Ian Fraser; Editor: Susan Heick. Produced by Finnegan/Pinchuk Company, Orion Television

After a car crash, young Lisa finds herself in Toyland, where the benevolent Toymaster rules over living toys and nursery-rhyme characters. The evil Barnaby launches his plans to conquer Toyland by stealing his nephew Jack's sweetheart, Mary Contrary, and framing Jack for cookie theft. Mary and Lisa help Jack escape, but Barnaby recaptures them and tries to turn them evil with magic. When that fails, he summons a troll army to conquer Toyland. When Lisa—who wants badly to grow up—admits she's still a kid who loves toys, it gives the Toymaster the strength to defeat Barnaby; Lisa wakes up to realize it was all a dream. "And you were there, and you, and you...."

The Herbert operetta was filmed with Laurel and Hardy in 1934 (the critical favorite) and in 1961 (panned, but far more enjoyable); this version is too cutesy by half but does give us Future Big Stars, Barrymore and Reeves, among the leads.

BABYLON 5
Syndicated, 2/21–2/27/93

Cast: Commander Jeffrey Sinclair (Michael O'Hare), Lt. Michael Garibaldi (Jerry Doyle), Lt. Laurel Takashima (Tamlyn Tomita), Delenn (Mira Furlan), G'Kar (Andreas Katsulas), Londo Molari (Peter Jurasik), Del Varner (John Fleck), Senator (Paul Hampton), Carolyn Sykes (Blaire Baron), Dr. Benjamin Kyle (Johnny Sekka), Lyta Alexander (Patricia Tallman), Eric (Steven A. Barnett), Traveler (William Hayes), Techs (Linda Hoffman, Robert Jackson), Businessmen (F. William Parker, David Sage), Hostage (Marianne Robertson), Guerra (Ed Wasser)

Credits: Director: Richard Compton; Writer: J. Michael Straczynski; Producer: Robert Latham Brown; Co-Producer: John Copeland; Photography: Billy Dickson; Production Design: John Iacovelli; Music: Christopher Franke; Editor: Robert L. Sinise; Produced by Babylonian Productions, Rattlesnake Productions, Synthetic Worlds

In 2257 Earth space station Babylon 5 serves as a meeting ground for the five dominant forces in space: the Earth Alliance; the decadent, once-powerful Centauri; the militaristic Narns; the enigmatic Vorlons in their all-concealing armor; and the mystical Minbari, who almost destroyed Earth 10 years ago before abruptly surrendering on the brink of victory.

The Vorlon ambassador, Kosh, arrives—and is promptly poisoned. Against Vorlon orders, Dr. Kyle opens Kosh's suit to treat him (he's astonished by what's inside, but doesn't describe it). Telepath Lyta Alexander reluctantly mind-probes Kosh—and sees a vision of station chief Commander Sinclair applying the poison.

The Narn ambassador, G'Kar, manipulates Babylon 5 into sending Sinclair to the Vorlon homeworld for trial (and probable execution). Then Dr. Kyle catches Lyta tampering with Kosh's life-support equipment, chases her out, and sees a second Lyta in the halls. Security Chief Garibaldi realizes the real killer used a holographic disguise to impersonate Sinclair, Lyta and others. As a Vorlon battlecruiser arrives demanding Sinclair, Garibaldi and Sinclair find the assassin—a Minbari warrior seeking to destroy Sinclair for some mysterious connection to the Minbari surrender. Garibaldi clears Sinclair, and a practical joke pays G'Kar back for covertly helping the assassin.

Veteran writer and SF fan Straczynski conceived *Babylon 5* as pilot to a five-year series aspiring to be serious SF, with a story arc running the length of the series. He succeeded at both. This film is a bit slow (partly because it sets up a complex universe out of whole cloth), and the stock characters (G'Kar, particularly) developed far more complexity as the series progressed. Both the film and the series were groundbreaking in their use of computer-generated special effects.

BABYLON 5: IN THE BEGINNING
TNT, 1/4/98

Cast: Lt. Commander John Sheridan (Bruce Boxleitner), Delenn (Mira Furlan), Dr. Stephen Franklin (Richard Biggs), G'Kar (Andreas Katsulas), Londo (Peter Jurasik), Lennon (Theodore Bikel), Dukhat (Reiner Schone), Sinclair (Michael O'Hare), Morann (Robin Atkin Downes), General Lefcourt (J. Patrick McCormack), President (Tricia O'Neil), Coplann (Robin Sachs), Presidential Aide (James Patrick Stuart), Captain Sterns (Jason Azikiwe), Centauri Woman (Yasmine Baytok), Woman (Kristin Birch), Comm Officer (Justin Carroll), Kosh (Ardwight Chamberlain), Luc (Jacob Chase), Captain Jankowski (Tim Colceri), Man (Timothy Davis-Reed), Alpha 7 (Pancho Demmings), First Officer (Steven Ford), Ganya Ivanov (Mio R. Jakula), Ivanova (Claudia Christian), Minbari Pilot (Mick Jameson), General Fontaine (Mike Kennedy), Lyssa (Erica Mer), Minbari Warrior (Mark Rafael Truitt)

Credits: Director: Mike Vejar; Writer: J. Michael Straczynski; Conceptual Consultant: Harlan Ellison; Producer: John Copeland; Executive Producers: Douglas Netter, J. Michael Straczynski; Photography: John C. Flinn III; Production Design: John Iacovelli; Music: Christopher Franke; Editor: Skip Robinson; Produced by Warner Bros., Babylonian Productions

Earth's first contact with the alien Minbari goes disastrously awry when a cultural misunderstanding leads to the death of Dukhat, the Minbari's most revered religious leader. His apprentice, Delenn, orders a retaliation. Before long, Minbari war fever threatens to exterminate humanity. Too late, Delenn learns from the Vorlons that without human assistance, the Minbari will never defeat the monstrous Shadows, a force of darkness recently awakened from slumber.

As human forces fight a suicide battle to give humanity time to evacuate Earth, Delenn captures one human soldier, Sinclair, for interrogation—and discovers he contains the essence of Valen, the great historic leader of the Minbari; in some manner, Minbari and human souls have become intermingled. Using this as a rationale, Delenn calls off the war (Minbari never battle each other), and the Minbari surrender.

After four years of uncertain survival in syndication, *Babylon 5* shifted to TNT for its last season; this prequel to the series (set 10 years before the original TV movie) kicked off the TNT run. Though well done, it must have been confusing for newcomers (regular viewers knew Sinclair eventually becomes Valen, hence the mingling).

BABYLON 5: THE RIVER OF SOULS
TNT, 11/8/98

Cast: Michael Garibaldi (Jerry Doyle), Capt. Elizabeth Lochley (Tracy Scoggins), Security Chief Zack Allan (Jeff Conaway), Dr. Stephen Franklin (Richard Biggs), Dr. Robert Bryson (Ian McShane), The Soul Hunter (Martin Sheen), Man (Jeff Doucette), Soul One (Wayne Alexander), Customer (Bob Amaral), Woman (Beece Barkett), Jacob Mayhew (Joel Brooks), Lt. Corwin (Joshua Cox), Holograms (T.J. Hoban, Nikki Schieler Ziering), James Riley (Stuart Pankin), Klaus (Ray Proscia), Mr. Clute (Jeff Silverman), Sheila (Jean St. James)

Credits: Director: Janet Greek; Writer-Creator: J. Michael Straczynski; Producer: John Copeland; Co-Producer: Skip Beaudine; Executive Producers: Douglas Netter, J. Michael Straczynski; Conceptual Consultant: Harlan Ellison; Photography: Frederick V. Murphy II; Production Design: John Iacovelli; Music: Christopher Franke; Editor: Suzanne Chambre Sternlight; Produced by Warner Bros., Babylonian Productions

After years pursuing immortality, Bryson uncovers a storage chamber of the Soul Hunters, who save and collect souls at the moment of death. Narrowly escaping with one of the soul-globes, Bryson goes to Babylon 5 to meet the station's former security chief, Garibaldi, whose wife's late husband financed Bryson's research. Garibaldi demands proof of Bryson's results, but when Bryson makes contact with the imprisoned souls, he becomes too fascinated to care about trivialities like money.

While station commander Lochley and security chief Allen become embroiled in a legal fight over a malfunctioning holographic brothel, a Soul Hunter arrives, demanding the globe back—and warning that the souls in the chamber (taken from a single race at the brink of death) will use the globe as a gateway to escape. Sure enough, the souls begin haunting the station, leaving the crew debating if the souls are saved or just denied heaven; when one ghost attacks the Soul Hunter, Lochley dies saving him.

Lochley's spirit learns the Soul Hunters aborted the alien race's transition to pure spirit-beings—and after 10,000 years, they prefer suicide to imprisonment, even if they take Babylon 5 with them. Returned to life, Lochley persuades the Soul Hunter of this, but his race threatens to destroy B5 to reclaim the globe. The Soul Hunter resolves the impasse by putting his own soul inside the chamber to prove his commitment to freeing the prisoners; the spirits acquiesce, and the Hunters acknowledge their mistake.

This would have made a competent episode, but it doesn't seem quite strong enough for a film (even with Martin Sheen in a major role). This was followed by *Babylon 5: A Call To Arms* in 1999 (the kickoff for a sequel series, *Crusade*).

BABYLON 5: THIRDSPACE
TNT, 7/19/98

Cast: Captain Sheridan (Bruce Boxleitner), Commander Ivanova (Claudia Christian), Delenn (Mira Furlan), Dr. Stephen Franklin (Richard Biggs), Security Chief Zack Allan (Jeff Conaway), Vir Coto (Stephen Furst), Lyta Alexander (Patricia Tallman), Bill Marishi (Clyde Kusatsu), Dr. Elizabeth Trent (Shari Belafonte), Deuce (William Sanderson), Leo (Kip King), Alex (Floyd Levine), Merchant (Jeffrey Anderson-Gunter), Lt. Corwin (Joshua Cox), Delta 7 (Judson Mills), Guard (G. Adam Gifford), Builder (Jerry Kernion), Technician (Valerie Red-Horse).

Credits: Director: Jesus Salvador Treviño; Writer: J. Michael Straczynski; Conceptual Consultant: Harlan Ellison; Producer: John Copeland; Executive Producers: Douglas Netter, J. Michael Straczynski; Photography: John C. Flinn III; Production Design: John Iacovelli; Music: Christopher Franke; Editor: David W. Foster; Produced by Warner Bros., Babylonian Productions

When Commander Ivanova brings a massive alien artifact back from hyperspace for study, Captain Sheridan reluctantly lets Earth researcher Trent work on it—but soon suspects she knows more than she admits. The space station suffers power outages and outbreaks of violence, and telepath Lyta becomes obsessed with destroying the artifact.

Trent activates the artifact, opening a gate beyond hyperspace into "thirdspace," where instantaneous space travel is possible. The power drain increases, and the station's residents turn on Sheridan when he tries closing the gate. Lyta, trained by the ancient Vorlons, now realizes the Vorlons built the artifact as a gateway into heaven; instead, it reached a malevolent race that uses it as a beachhead into our dimension. The Vorlons closed the gate, but the aliens' enslaved followers hid it in hyperspace before the Vorlons could destroy it. As the Babylon 5 fleet crumbles before the alien attack, Sheridan slips inside the artifact with a nuke, arms it and escapes seconds before it blows, destroying the gateway and the alien armada.

The second TNT film, set during *Babylon 5*'s fourth season (which is why several of the regular cast are absent, having been off-station at the time) *Thirdspace* is straight adventure, but a good one.

BAFFLED!
NBC, 1/30/73

Cast: Tom Kovack (Leonard Nimoy), Michele Brent (Susan Hampshire), Mrs. Farraday (Rachel Roberts), Andrea Glenn (Vera Miles), Jennifer Glenn (Jewel Blanch), Louise Sanford (Valerie Taylor), George Tracewell (Ray Brooks), Peggy Tracewell (Angharad Rees), Verelli (Christopher Benjamin), Parrish (Mike Murray), Hopkins (Ewan Roberts), Dr. Reed (Milton Johns), TV Interviewer (Al Mancini), Theater Doorman (John Rae), Cleaning Woman (Patsy Smart), Track Announcer (Shane Rimmer), Racetrack Mechanic (Roland Brand), Doctor (Bill Hutchinson), PA Announcer (Frank Mann), Ambulance Man (Michael Sloan), Policeman (Dan Meaden).

Credits: Director-Producer: Philip Leacock; Writer: Theodore Apstein; Executive Producer: Norman Felton; Associate Producer: John Oldknow; Photography: Ken Hodges; Art Director: Harry Pottle; Music: Richard Hill; Editor: Bill Blunden; Produced by Arena Productions

When race car driver Kovack has a clairvoyant vision during a race (a woman in England in deadly danger), he crashes and almost dies; this attracts the attention of parapsychologist Brent, who insists they find and help the woman. Kovack protests, but he and Brent wind up visiting the manor house from his vision.

At the manor is Andrea Glenn, hoping to reunite with her husband—who's actually dead. The proposed reunion is a trick by Parrish, an occultist hoping to exploit little Jennifer Glenn's psychic powers. Parrish binds her through sorcery in a scheme to murder Andrea and rejuvenate Parrish's aging lover. Kovack and Brent piece the clues together and break the spell on Jennifer, then Brent confronts Parrish as he tries to murder Andrea. Parrish falls to his death as they struggle. The Glenns safe, Kovack bids Brent goodbye—but he senses someone else in danger...

Though a reasonably enjoyable pilot starring a post-*Star Trek* Leonard Nimoy, it's no great loss that *Baffled* wasn't picked up.

BATES MOTEL
NBC, 7/5/87

Cast: Alex West (Bud Cort), Willie (Lori Petty), Henry Watson (Moses Gunn), Tony Scotty (Jason Bateman), Tom Fuller (Gregg Henry), Barbara Peters (Kerrie Keane), A Friend (Khrystyne Haje), Dr. Goodman (Robert Picardo), with Andy Albin, Dolores Albin, Kelly Ames, Robert Axelrod, Nat Bernstein, Peter Dobson, Timothy Fall, Carmen Filip, George "Buck" Flower, Pedro Gonzales-Gonzales, Paula Irvine, Chad Jones, Jack Ross Obney, Hardy Rawls, Scot Saint James, John Kenton Schull, George Skinta, Peter A. Stelzer, David Wakefield, George J. Woods

Credits: Director-Writer: Richard Rothstein; Producer: Ken Topolsky; Co-Producer: Henry Kline; Photography: Bill Butler; Production Design: Robb Wilson King; Music: J. Peter Robinson; Editors: Dann Cahn, Richard A. Freeman; Produced by Universal

After *Psycho*, Norman Bates was committed for life; in the asylum, he befriended Alex, locked up for killing his abusive father. After Norman dies, Alex re-enters the world, having inherited the Bates Motel from Norman.

Alex's efforts to reopen the motel bring him new friends (drifter Willie and mechanic Henry), a new fear (he keeps seeing Mrs. Bates' ghost) and a new problem (paying back Fuller, a greedy banker, for the remodeling loan). As Alex and Willie worry about the money, they also set up for a high school dance at the motel—unaware the only other guest, Barbara, is planning suicide. Before she can attempt it, one of the students drags her to the dance where she flirts nervously with young stud Tony. When she finally tries to kill herself, Tony and the other students reveal they're all suicides—and the pain of their lost lives convinces Barbara to choose life. Meanwhile, Henry and Willie unmask Mrs. Bates' ghost as Fuller, trying to drive Alex off the valuable land. They then use a tape of Fuller's confession to force a more reasonable repayment schedule on the loan. The Bates Motel will remain open for business.

This curious spin-off of Hitchcock's classic *Psycho* (which ignores the earlier theatrical sequels, *Psycho II* and *III*) was a weak and unsuccessful pilot for an anthology show in the *Love Boat/Hotel* vein, but with supernatural elements. Among the cast is *Star Trek: Voyager*'s Robert Picardo.

BAY COVEN
NBC, 10/25/87

Cast: Linda Lebon (Pamela Sue Martin), Jerry Lebon (Tim Matheson), Nick Kline (James B. Sikking), Debbie (Susan Ruttan), Slater (Woody Harrelson), Josh (Jeff Conaway), Beatrice Gower (Barbara Billingsley), Maddy Kline (Inga Swenson), Holden (Nigel Bennett), Clerk (Patrick Brymer), Priest (Michael Caruana), Old Man Kline (John Dee), Jazz Singer (Cree Summer Francks), Old Man (David Harvey), Tom Holden (Tom Harvey), Edward (Paul Horruzey), Sarah (Susan Jay), Ferry Captain (John Kerr), Rachel (Marsha Moreau), Barret (Eric Murphy), Mr. Welsley (Neil Vipond)

Credits: Director: Carl Schenkel; Writer: R. Timothy Kring; Producer: Michael Rhodes; Supervising Producer: Stanley M. Brooks; Executive Producers: Jon Peters, Peter Guber, Roger Birnbaum; Photography: Jack Steyn; Art Director: Richard St. John Harrison; Music: Shuki Levy; Editor: Jimmy B. Frazier; Produced by Guber-Peters Entertainment Co., Phoenix Entertainment

Fed up with city living, Jerry Lebon relocates to rural Bay Coven with his reluctant wife Linda. Linda and her friend Slater discover the town has a history of witchcraft—and that no one's been buried in the graveyard for 300 years. Slater dies in a freak accident; Jerry grows increasingly weird; and Linda discovers their neighbors, the Klines, are centuries old, but the evidence vanishes when she tries to convince Jerry. Nick Kline's father—really his son—reveals that the town coven made a pact with hell for immortality; after one witch broke the pact and fled, they were given 300 years for his reincarnation to return. Jerry is the chosen one (surprise!), and the coven will sacrifice Linda at midnight that night to renew their pact. When Linda runs, the now-evil Jerry catches her, but regains enough control to kill himself instead. Linda traps the witches inside a church—where they're powerless—until midnight elapses and Satan destroys them for their failure.

Bay Coven is a very routine thriller with an array of TV stars (Jeff Conaway would later play Zack Allan on *Babylon 5*).

BEASTMASTER III: THE EYE OF BRAXUS
Syndicated, 1996

Cast: Dar, the Beastmaster (Marc Singer), Seth (Tony Todd), Bey (Keith Coulouris), King Tal (Casper Van Dien), Lord Agon (David Warner), Shada (Sandra Hess), Jaggart (Patrick Kilpatrick), Morgana (Lesley-Anne Down), Maldor (Cliff Pooley), Braxus (Michael S. Deak), Korum (David Grant Wright), Kala (Kimberly Stanhill), Pir (Joey Zimmerman), Crimson Captain (Gary Simpson), Crimson Warrior (Lance Rushing), Guard (Dar Thompson), Voice of Braxus (J.D. Hall)

Credits: Director: Gabrielle Beaumont; Writer: David Wise, based on characters created by Don Coscarelli and Paul Pepperman; Producers: David Wise, Lisa M. Cochran; Executive Producers: Stu Segall, Sylvio Tabet; Photography: Michael Davis; Production Design: Nigel Clinker; Costumes: Karyn Wanger; Music: Jan Hammer; Produced by Universal, Stu Segall Productions

Dar, the Beastmaster, is a warrior who controls animals (a hawk, two ferrets and a lion are his constant companions). Lord Agon is a sorcerer king who sustains his magic by draining the lives of others. Their paths cross when Agon kidnaps Dar's brother, Tal, for an amulet that will give Agon all the power of the demon-king Braxus; when Agon finds Dar possesses half the amulet, he sends his army after the Beastmaster.

Dar and his friend Seth join Shada, a mercenary, to fight against Agon. Shada, however, steals the amulet for Agon and leaves the men prisoners of a barbarian tribe. Dar's beasts free the warriors, who hook up with the witch Morgana and Bey, an acrobat who wants to adventure with Dar. To get Dar inside Agon's citadel, Morgana pretends to turn him over to Agon, then follows with Seth, Bey and the animals.

Agon leaves Dar in a death trap from which the repentant Shada frees him. Dar rescues Tal and tries to flee—but his animals refuse to go until Dar stops Agon and accepts the heroic destiny he's always denied. The heroes fight through to Agon in time to see Braxus give Agon power—by taking over the king's body. In battle, Dar shatters the amulet, banishing Braxus to hell. With Seth and Bey at his side, the Beastmaster rides off to fresh adventures.

This sequel to 1982's big-screen *The Beastmaster* (*Beastmaster II* came out on video in 1991) was the failed pilot for a *Beastmaster* series in the mold of *Hercules: The Legendary Journeys*. It's an entertaining film (movie vets Down and Warner are great) and more fun than the 1999 *Beastmaster* series, which had a different cast.

BEAUTY AND THE BEAST
NBC, 12/3/76

Cast: The Beast (George C. Scott), Belle Beaumont (Trish Van Devere), Lucy (Virginia McKenna), Edward Beaumont (Bernard Lee), Susan (Patricia Quinn), Anthony (Michael N. Harbour), Nicholas (William Relton)

Credits: Director: Fielder Cook; Writer: Sherman Yellen; Executive Producer: Thomas M.C. Johnston; Producer: Hank Moonjean; Photography: Paul Beeson, Jack Hildyard; Art Director: Elliott Scott; Costume Designer: Albert Wolsky; Music: Ron Goodwin; Editor: Freddie Wilson; Produced by Palm Productions

This has nothing to do with the eighties television series or the Disney cartoon; it's a straight retelling of the fairy tale, with Scott's performance in a boar's-head mask earning an Emmy nomination. It's not, however, comparable to Jean Cocteau's 1946 theatrical version.

BERMUDA DEPTHS
ABC, 1/27/78

Cast: Paulis (Burl Ives), Magnus (Leigh McCloskey), Eric (Carl Weathers), Jennie (Connie Sellecca), Doshan (Julie Woodson), Delia (Ruth Attaway), with Elise Frick, Nicholas Ingham, Kevin Petty, Nicole Marsh, George Richards, John Instone, Jonathan Ingham, Patricia Rego, Doris Riley, Terry Anne Sadler

Credits: Director: Tom Kotani; Writer: William Overgard; Story: Arthur Rank, Jr.; Producers: Arthur Rankin, Jr., Jules Bass; Photography: Jeri Sopanen, Stanton Waterman (underwater); Music: Maury Laws; Editor: Barry Walter; Produced by Rankin-Bass Productions

Scientist Paulis' obsessive hunt for a gigantic, prehistoric turtle seen in the Bermuda Triangle is complicated by a mysterious, beautiful swimmer—who supposedly died 300 years ago.

The author hasn't viewed this film, though if it's on the level of Rankin-Bass' *Last Dinosaur*, it can't be that good. It's by the author of the *Steve Roper* comic strip, with *Greatest American Hero*'s Sellecca as the mysterious Jennie.

BIG AND HAIRY
Showtime, 11/22/98

Cast: Picasso Dewlap (Robert Burke), Sasquatch (Trevor Jones, Ed Tibbetts), Victor Dewlap (Richard Thomas), Ludlow Bumstock (Donnelly Rhodes), Donovan (Gregory Thirloway), Elizabeth Dewlap (Chilton Crane), Mrs. Donovan (Stacy Grant), Dexter Madison (Tyler Thompson), Roland Lemay (Zachary Martin), Owen O'Malley (Zack Lipovsky), Mother Bigfoot (Anna-Maria McRoberts), Father Bigfoot (Adrian Hughes), Rodney (Gina Stockdale), Superfan (Coleen Fox), Rockweed Coach (Fred Keating), Referee (Brent Chapman), Committee Chair (Colleen Winton), Mrs. Dingley (Betty Linde), TV Reporter (Terry David Mulligan), Mean Boy (Shayn Solberg), Happy Harvey (Robert Rosen), Kid (Neil Denis), Lawn Ornament (Abaas Clayton), Fan (Kathryn Nystedt), Voice-over Announcer (David Kaye)

Credits: Director: Philip Spink; Writer: Brian Daly, from his novel *Big and Hairy*; Producer: Colleen Nystedt; Executive Producers: Marcy Gross, Ann Weston; Photography: Peter Benison; Production Design: Jill Scott; Music: Daryl Bennett, Jim Guttridge; Editor: Judy Anderson; Produced by New City Productions, Hallmark Entertainment, Gross-Weston Productions

Young Picasso Dewlap's life changes when he befriends Ed, a young Sasquatch whose height makes him a basketball natural (and turns Picasso's team into championship contenders). Unfortunately, this keeps Ed away from his own kind, and the town grows increasingly resentful of the upstart wonder-team.

BIONIC EVER AFTER?
CBS, 11/29/94

Cast: Steve Austin (Lee Majors), Jaime Sommers (Lindsay Wagner), Oscar Goldman (Richard Anderson), Dr. Rudy Wells (Martin Brooks), Kimberly Havilland (Farrah Forke), Miles Kendrick (Geordie Johnson), Mrs. McNamara (Anne Lockhart), John McNamara (Alan Sader), Connie Haviland (Ann Pierce), Astaad Rashid (Ivan Sergei), Jim Castillian (Lee Majors II), Minister (Robert D. Radford), Rock (James Shanta), Stone (Michael Hartson), Technician (Michael Camden Richards), Marine Captain (Shanghai Stafford), Bahama Policeman (General Fermon Judd, Jr.), Delta Commando (Michael Burgess), Reporter (Steffen Foster)

Credits: Director: Steven Stafford; Writers: Michael Sloan, Norman Morrill; Story: Michael Sloan; Producer: Michael O. Gallant; Executive Producer: Michael Sloan; Co-Executive Producer: Richard Anderson; Photography: Gideon Porath; Production Design: Linda Allen; Music: Ron Ramin; Editor: Frank Jimenez; Produced by Universal

A week before retired cyborg spies Steve and Jaime finally tie the knot, Jaime's bionics begin malfunctioning. Fearing she'll be crippled for life, Jaime calls off the wedding; Steve relieves his frustration by going on a mission against Kendrick, a terrorist who's seized our Bahamas embassy. Steve doesn't know his partner, Kimberly, is working with Kendrick; Kimberly infects Steve's bionics with the same computer virus she used on Jaime, making him weak enough for Kendrick to capture him.

Bionics expert Rudy discovers and eliminates the virus in Jaime's system. Jaime learns Kimberly is avenging her father, Rudy's former partner, in the false belief Rudy stole his bionics research. Jaime rescues Steve and the hostages, but Kendrick and Kimberly escape. When Kendrick tries detonating a stolen nuke to prevent pursuit, Kimberly helps Steve and Jaime capture him. The following day, the bionic duo get hitched at last.

The third bionic reunion film (following *Bionic Showdown*) wasn't a pilot for a new series but simply an attempt to wrap up everything on a happy note. In that light, it succeeded.

BIONIC SHOWDOWN: THE SIX MILLION DOLLAR MAN AND THE BIONIC WOMAN
NBC, 4/30/89

Cast: Steve Austin (Lee Majors), Jaime Sommers (Lindsay Wagner), Oscar Goldman (Richard Anderson), Dr. Rudy Wells (Martin Brooks), Katie Mason (Sandra Bullock), Jimmy Goldman (Jeff Yagher), Alan Devlin (Geraint Wynn Davies), Jim Castillian (Lee Majors II), General McAllister (Robert Lansing), Sally (Carolyn Dunn), Larry (Jack Blum), Comrade Kellagyn (Andrew R. Dan), Randall (David Adamson), OSI Officer (James Kee), Tanya (Marcia Levine), Dr. Williams (Robert McClure), Peter (David Nerman), Russ (Steve Pernie), Announcer (Steve Morris) Esterman (Josef Sommer), General Sorensky (Lawrence Dane)

Credits: Director: Alan J. Levi; Writers: Michael Sloan, Brock Choy; Story: Michael Sloan, Robert De Laurentis; Producers: Nigel Watts, Bernadette Joyce; Co-Producers: Lee Majors, Richard Anderson; Photography: Maris Jansons; Art Director: Tony Hall; Music: Bill Conti; Editor: Bill Goddard; Produced by Universal

In this follow-up to *Return of the Six Million Dollar Man and the Bionic Woman*, cyborg Steve Austin searches for the nerve to propose to longtime love Jaime; Dr. Rudy Wells turns paraplegic Katie into the OSI's newest cyborg; and Steve, Katie and Jaime all fall under suspicion when a bionic saboteur in the OSI disrupts an international sports competition.

A bomb meant for Steve cripples Oscar's nephew Jimmy. When Oscar's superiors refuse to rebuild Jimmy with bionics, Oscar quits. The saboteur promptly kidnaps Oscar, overcoming Steve, Jaime and Katie in the process.

Katie goes undercover at the games as an athlete, with Jimmy as her trainer. Both he and Oscar's assistant Alan start romancing her. The enemy attacks Katie with a weapon that deactivates bionics, but Jimmy leaves his wheelchair and saves her. He confesses being "crippled" was a trick to justify Oscar resigning and becoming bait for the traitor. Meanwhile, Oscar learns his captors are freelance spies wrecking the games to increase international tensions and thereby the need for their services. He almost escapes, but Alan—the evil cyborg—recaptures him, then plants a bomb at the games. Oscar manages to alert Steve and Jaime, who rescue him and remove the bomb. Katie destroys Alan with Jimmy's help, despite Alan's greater powers. And finally, Steve pops the question to Jaime, who accepts.

A pre-stardom Sandra Bullock makes a charming lead in this unsuccessful pilot, the best of the bionic reunion films. It also features Davies (future star of the *Forever Knight* series), Yagher (*V*—the series) and Lansing (*Automan*). Next in the "bionic" film series was *Bionic Ever After?*

BLACK MAGIC
Showtime, 3/21/92

Cast: Alex Gage (Judge Reinhold), Lillian Blackmun (Rachel Ward), Ross Gage (Anthony LaPaglia), Tom (Brion James), Sally (Wendy Makkena), Bill (Richard Whitting), Sheriff Black (Roger Black), Phil Glance (Tom Mason), Mother (Tammy Arnold), Dr. Damon Feltzer (John Bennes), Fireman (Philip Loch), Dispatcher (Lucile Dew McIntyre), Attendant (Mark Jeffrey Miller), Men (Nick Searcy, Jeff Pillars), Alex at 4 (Vann Tipton)

Credits: Director-Writer: Daniel Taplitz; Producer: Harvey Frand; Executive Producer: Dan Wigutow; Photography: Peter Fernberger; Production Design: Bob Ziembicki; Music: Cliff Martinez; Editor: David Byron Lloyd; Produced by MTE, Point of View Productions

Alex Gage never liked his bullying cousin Ross when he was alive—so he's less than thrilled when Ross' ghost haunts his nightmares, warning him away from the town where Ross died. But Alex's shrink tells him going there will stop these nightmares, so…

After Alex meets and falls for Ross' beautiful lover Lillian, Ross' ghost claims she cursed then killed him for cheating on her. He demands Alex avenge him, but Alex becomes Lillian's lover instead. When Alex discovers Ross' body in the garden, Lillian claims she killed him in self-defense. Alex believes her until an autopsy reveals he was poisoned. Alex confronts Lillian, who admits cursing Ross (for revenge) *and* Alex (for Ross' life insurance)—but now she says she loves Alex. Unfortunately, she's also burning her house down for insurance, and Alex dies in the flames—then finds himself facing an eternity of Ross' bullying in the afterlife.

This attempt at a supernatural romantic comedy is very unfunny, and LaPaglia is horribly irritating.

BLACK NOON
CBS, 11/5/71

Cast: Reverend John Keyes (Roy Thinnes), Lorna Keyes (Lyn Loring), Deliverance (Yvette Mimieux), Caleb Hobbs (Ray Milland), Moon (Henry Silva), Bethia (Gloria Grahame), Jacob (William Bryant), Ethan (Buddy Foster), Joseph (Hank Worden), The Towheads (Joshua Bryant, Jennifer Bryant, Charles McCready, Leif Garrett), Man (Dave Cass), Wife (Susan Sheppard), Boy (Bobby Eilbacher), Ethan (Buddy Foster), Man in Mirror (Stan Barrett)

Credits: Director: Bernard L. Kowalski; Producer-Writer: Andrew J. Fenady; Photography: Keith C. Smith; Art Director: John Beckman; Music: George Duning; Editor: Dann Kahn; Produced by Fenady Associates, Screen Gems

Lost and dying in the Old West, Reverend Keyes and his wife Lorna are taken in by San Melas, a gold-mining town paying protection to malevolent gunslinger Moon. While waiting for Lorna to recover, Keyes spends the days preaching—and the nights dreaming of sexy mute Deliverance; he only scoffs when Lorna tells him she's seen the townsfolk practicing Satanism.

When Moon tries to rape Deliverance, Keyes kills him, which racks the preacher with guilt; Lorna insists they leave, but Deliverance cripples her with black magic to delay them. During a total eclipse, Moon reappears alive, and Hobbs reveals that the townsfolk are the witches of Salem. They delayed Keyes—a pure man until tainted with lust—so that they could sacrifice him to Satan under the eclipse. And we close in the present day, as another lost family arrive in San Melas…

Having the innocent townsfolk turn out to be the villains isn't a bad idea—but this is slow, dull and ponderous, even in the sexy scenes. With Roy Thinnes (*Invaders*), Mimieux (*The Time Machine*), Silva (*Thirst*) and Milland (*X—The Man with the X-Ray Eyes*).

BLACK SCORPION
Showtime, 8/22/95

Cast: Darcy Walker/Black Scorpion (Joan Severance), Michael Russo (Bruce Abbott), Argyle (Garrett Morris), Walker (Rick Rossovitch), Captain Strickland (Stephen Lee), Tender Lovin' (Terri J. Vaughn), Hacksaw (Michael Wiseman), Razor (Brad Tatum), Rookie (Steven Kravitz), Mugger (Rick Tyler Barnes), Accountant (Vincent Chase), Scary Mary (Anita Hart), Connie the Crusher (Rosine "Ace" Hatem), Guards (Kurt Lotz, Anthony Kramme), Hank (Rodman Flender), Mayor (Matt Roe), Babette (Janelle Hensley Paradee), Little Darcy (Ashley Peldon), Dr. Goddard (Casey Siemaszko), Nurse (Kimberly Roberts), Orderly (Kyle Fredericks), Tong Leader (Randy Ideishu), Capt. Strickland (Stephen Lee), Aldridge (John Sanderford), Cops (Shane Powers, Mike Elliott), Leslie Vance (Paula Trickey), Voice of Breathtaker (Edmund Gilbert), Runaway (Heather O'Ryan), Bar Patron (Jonathan Winfrey), Store Guard (Greg Brazzel)

Credits: Director: Jonathan Winfrey; Writer: Craig J. Nevius; Producer: Mike Elliott; Executive Producers: Roger Corman, Lance H. Robbins; Photography: Geoff George; Production Design: Eric Kahn; Special Makeup-Costumes: Michael Burnett Productions; Special Digital Effects: Digital Drama; Music: Kevin Kiner; Editors: Tom Petersen, Gwyneth Gibby; Produced by New Horizon, Pacific Trust

Years after Det. Walker lost his badge for accidentally killing a doctor during a firefight, his detective daughter, Darcy, sees the district attorney gun Walker down—then claim no memory of the shooting. Darcy gets suspended for trying to beat the truth out of the DA; frustrated, she decides to work outside the law as the masked Black Scorpion in her weapon-laden Scorpionmobile. Her vigilante tactics make her a hero to the public—but not with her ex-partner Russo, assigned to bring the Scorpion in (even though he finds her far more attractive than he does Darcy), nor with Breathtaker, an armored villain spreading a mind-control drug through asthma inhalers.

Breathtaker threatens to flood the city with gas, thereby driving people to wear gas masks secretly tainted with the mind-control drug. Darcy learns his plan, and that Breathtaker is the doctor her father supposedly killed. When Black Scorpion penetrates his lair, Breathtaker reveals his armor is an advanced iron lung that has kept him alive—and once the gas spreads, the entire city will have to breathe artificially, as he does. Black Scorpion and Russo join forces and stop Breathtaker; Darcy contrives to share the credit for the capture, which gets her reinstated. Russo now knows her identity, but reluctantly uses the mind-control drug to forget it rather than bring her in.

Black Scorpion is a very good super-hero adventure that catches the comic-book spirit perfectly. It was followed by *Black Scorpion II*.

BLACK SCORPION II: AFTERSHOCK
Showtime, 9/3/96

Cast: Darcy Walker/Black Scorpion (Joan Severance), Michael Russo (Whip Hubley), Ursula Undershaft/Aftershock (Sherrie Rose), Gangster Prankster (Stoney Jackson), Mayor Worth (Matt Roe), Captain Strickland (Stephen Lee), Argyle (Garrett Morris), Veronica (Terri J. Vaughn), Grimace (Carl Banks), Heckler (David Harris), Slugger (Steven Kravitz), Specs (Shane Powers), Bree Bradley (Christina Solis), Babette (Laura Harring), Dispatch (Gabrielle Bemford), Yes Men (Sean Gavigan, Kevin McLaughlin), Dick (Scott Valentine), Jane (Linda Hoffman), Bomb Squad Leader (Manny Fernandez), Medic (Vincent Chase), Foreman (Rick Rossovitch), Truck Driver (Jeffrey Scott Jensen), Swastika Face (Slade Barnett), Donkey Face (Mark Folger), White Face (Diane Koskela), Giggles (Jeannie Millar), Divine (Kimberly Rowe), Cop (Jonathan Winfrey).

Credits: Director: Jonathan Winfrey; Writer: Craig Nevius; Producer: Roger Corman; Co-Producer: Joan Severance; Executive Producer: Lance H. Robbins; Photography: Mark Kohl; Production Design: Trae King; Special Makeup/Costumes: Robert Hall; Music: Kevin Kiner; Editor: Louis Cioffi; Produced by New Horizon, Pacific Trust.

A new villain, Gangster Prankster, plagues the city with crimes patterned around practical jokes. After the villain rips off the cops, Russo pursues him—into a deathtrap. Black Scorpion saves him, then captures Prankster after an earthquake shakes the villain up.

Seismologist Undershaft announces her anti-tremor device will prevent future earthquakes. Since the Mayor counts on federal disaster-relief funds to cover up his embezzlement of city money, his henchmen sabotage Undershaft's machine. The damaged device worsens the next quake (which the mayor claims Undershaft caused), burying Undershaft's lab in rubble. The now-deranged doctor becomes the super-villain Aftershock. Russo, his apartment leveled, moves in with Darcy, who finally gets him more interested in her than in the Black Scorpion, only to have her absences as Black Scorpion convince Russo to break it off, both as her lover and as her partner.

Black Scorpion thwarts Aftershock's theft of components for an earthquake-maker, so Aftershock uses her vibratory weapons to free Gangster Prankster from jail. In return for her emptying the city's wealthiest subdivision by plaguing it with mild tremors, Prankster blackmails Argyle—builder of the Scorpionmobile—into stealing the supercar, which leaves Darcy unable to stop Aftershock. The Scorpion rescues Argyle, however, and uses her car remote-control to kill the Prankster.

Black Scorpion confronts Aftershock and talks her back to sanity—but the quakemaker has already been activated. To undo her work, Undershaft has to throw her own body into the machine to jam it. The Mayor, his crimes exposed, takes Russo hostage, but

Darcy saves him—which brings her and Russo back together again.

Though more tongue-in-cheek than the first film, this sequel is quite entertaining nonetheless. The reference to "vibranium" is an in-joke (it's a rare element used in Marvel Comics).

BLOOD TIES
Fox, 5/27/91

Cast: Harry Martin (Harley Venton), Celia (Michelle Johnson), Amy Lawrence (Kim Johnston Ulrich), Eli (Patrick Bauchau), Marvin (Michael C. Gwynne), Cody Puckett (Jason London), Butch Vlad (Salvator Xuereb), Chief Hunter (Bo Hopkins), Alex Smart (Robert Lesser), Vasile (Nicholas Kepros), Guru (Bill Landrum), Dragomir (Robert Burr), Hunters (Gregory Scott Cummins, Robert Miano), Manager (Marilyn Rockafellow), Judge Morgan (Ron Dortch), Man (Dave Florek), Guest (Barbara March), Jury Foreman (Philip Moon), Shrikes (Geoffery Cascio, Richard Giorla, Regan Patno, Joseph Reitman, Jamy Woodbury), Puckett (Michael Bellomo), Mrs. Puckett (Anne Marie Gillis), Old Kissing Woman (Elizabeth Kreuzer), The Woman (Grace Zabriskie)

Credits: Director: Jim McBride; Writer: Richard Shapiro; Producer: Gene Corman; Co-Producer: Jim McBride; Executive Producers: Richard and Esther Shapiro; Photography: Affonso Beato; Production Design: Lisa Fischer; Music: Brad Fiedel; Editor: Stephen Semel; Produced by Shapiro Entertainment

This supernatural soap opera focuses on a sprawling Carpathian-American family of vampires (with none of the usual weaknesses or powers, except greater strength; blood drinking is primarily foreplay), including corrupt, wealthy Eli; his sexy fiancée Celia; and her ex-lover Harry, an investigative reporter who thinks society is ready for vampires to come out of the closet and assimilate (as evidenced by his dating mortal DA Amy). The family has personal conflicts aplenty—which they set aside when a band of vampire slayers targets them, finally taking Celia as bait for the others. Harry favors calling in the cops, but he bows to the family's decision to handle matters themselves by rescuing Celia and killing the hunters.

This stupid pilot didn't even stay true to its own logic (given a perfect opportunity to set the police on the vampire hunters without exposing family secrets, Harry still doesn't do it). The 1996 series *Kindred: The Embraced* did vampiric soap opera a lot better (and *Here Comes the Munsters* made a better "melting pot" metaphor).

BLUE YONDER
Disney, 11/17/85

Cast: Max Knickerbocker (Peter Coyote), Jonathan Knicks (Huckleberry Fox), Henry Coogan (Art Carney), Finch (Dennis Lipscomb), Leary (Joe Flood), Helen Knickerbocker (Mitty Smith), Young Coogan (Frank Simons), Mr. Knicks (Stuart Klitsner), Police Captain (Morgan Upton), Dooley (Bennett Cale), Drunk (Cyril Clayton), Newsvendor (Charles Adams), Mrs. Knicks (Gretchen Grant), Barber (Doug Morrison), Doctor (Jerry Landis), Nurse (Jo Mohbach), Radio Announcer (Eric Barnes), Finch's Pilot (Art Scholl), Coach (Scott Devenney), Little Leaguer (Stephen Prior)

Credits: Director-Writer: Mark Rosman; Producers: Annette Handley, Susan B. Landau, Alan Shapiro; Photography: Hiro Narita, Jack Cooperman (aerial); Production Design: Mark Billerman; Art Director: Rick Brown; Music: David Shire; Editor: Betsy Blankett; Produced by Three Blind Mice Productions

Young Jonathan Knicks has been raised on stories of his aviator/inventor grandfather, Max, as told by Max's mechanic, Henry. Now dying, Henry shows Jonathan a time machine he built from Max's plans. Jonathan uses the machine to travel back in time in order to prevent Max's fatal attempt to beat Lindbergh across the Atlantic.

Jonathan meets Max and finds him a kindred spirit—a dreamer—but Jonathan can't convince Max he's from the future. He does unintentionally convince the local bootlegger, Dooley, who steals the machine and has Jonathan thrown in jail. Max, now a believer, rescues Jonathan and the time machine both. Despite Jonathan's warning, Max goes ahead with the flight, but uses a different route across the ocean. When Jonathan returns to the present, he discovers Max still died, but because he reached the French coast before crashing, he's enshrined in a minor, but respected, place in aviation history.

Blue Yonder is a charming story, reminiscent of *Back to the Future*.

BOMBSHELL
Sci-Fi, 8/9/97

Cast: Buck Corrigan (Henry Thomas), Angeline "Bombshell" (Madchen Amick), Melinda Clarke (Pamela Gidley), Detective Gidley (Michael Jace), Hostess (Victoria Jackson), Adam (Martin Hewitt), Shelly (Shawnee Smith), Brad (David Parker), Carol (Carol Ita White), Donald (Brion James), Malcolm (Frank Whaley), Detective Jefferson (Michael Jace), Buff (David Shark Fralick), Bewayne (Art Chujabala), Dr. Braunmann (James Dumont), Director (Paul Wynne), Cameraman (Kurt Woodruff), Scan Nurse (Camille Solari), PA (Billy Hoye), Clerk (Michelangelo Kowalski), Cops (Jim Levelett, Gina Angela Ritchie, Michael McLafferty, Ethan Wayne, Yelena Danova), Melissa Stora (Alli Spotts), Newsreaders (Robertson Dean, Shawn Southwick), Anchor (Bryan Clark)

Credits: Director-Writer: Paul Wynne; Story: Paul Wynne, Vicky Pike; Producers: Paul Wynne, Vicky Pike; Supervising Producer: Pat Peach; Executive Producer: Steven Paul; Photography: Angel Colmenares; Costumes: Cindee Morby; Music: Ennio Di Berardo; Editors: Joan Zapata, Christopher Roth; Produced by Trimark Pictures, Wynne/Pike Productions, Molecular Films

Early in the next century, Nanolab researcher Buck Corrigan has developed a cancer-fighting nanotech treatment—that *gave* one of his test animals cancer. Even so, Buck overrides his co-worker Malcolm and bows to his money-hungry boss' insistence on immediate human tests. Shortly afterward, someone implants Buck with a mystery device, refusing to explain until Buck collects a series of worthless packages.

Buck discovers the packages contain nanotech designed by Malcolm to modify the implant; Buck refuses to touch the last package, but Malcolm kidnaps Buck's girlfriend Angeline to force Buck's hand. The package turns the implant into a bomb Malcolm will explode at Nanolab to draw media attention to their pursuit of profits over safety. Malcolm takes over the lab, but a guard kills him. Angel removes the nanobomb from Buck, and they escape before the lab is destroyed. The media dismiss Malcolm as a raving madman.

Though a bit too much of a stock thriller, *Bombshell* possesses an interesting premise, a good "message" and nice visuals (in the styles of the near-future clothes and rooms). *Twin Peaks*' Amick and *ET*'s Thomas play the leads.

THE BORROWERS
NBC, 12/14/73

Cast: Pod Clock (Eddie Albert), Homily Clock (Tammy Grimes), Great-Aunt Sophy (Dame Judith Anderson), Arrietty Clock (Karen Pearson), The Boy (Dennis Larson), Mrs. Crampfurl (Beatrice Straight), Mr. Crampfurl (Barnard Hughes), Ernie (Murray Westgate), Tom (Danny McIlravey)

Credits: Director: Walter C. Miller; Writer: Jay Presson Allen, from Mary Norton's novel; Producers: Walt DeFaria, Warren L. Lockhart; Executive Producer: Duane C. Bogie; Art Director: Bill Zaharuk; Music: Rod McKuen, Billy Byers; Produced by Charles M. Schulz Creative Associates, Walt DeFaria Productions, 20th Century–Fox

Pod Clock is one of the tiny "Borrowers" who dwell in human houses and "borrow" whatever they need (food, cloth, doll furniture) from the "big people." Living in an old country house, Pod's on good terms with the cantankerous owner, Sophy (she thinks he's a hallucination), and easily outwits her servants, the Crampfurls. Then Sophie's sick nephew comes to stay with her until he's healthy—and nothing terrifies Borrowers more than small boys and their destructive ways.

This boy, however, befriends Pod's daughter Arrietty and begins bringing the Clocks all kinds of useful things (which rather disgruntles Pod). The lad's "help" unfortunately leads Mrs. Crampfurl to the Borrowers' home beneath the floorboards, and she has a local hunter bring in a ferret. It's only with the boy's help that the Clocks can escape the ferret, leave the house, and reach their country relatives.

A charming fantasy, *The Borrowers* earned three Emmy nominations (for director Miller, actress Dame Judith Anderson, and as Outstanding Children's Special). The Borrowers appeared in several other books by

Norton, as well as two British TV-movies and one 1998 theatrical film.

BRAVE NEW WORLD
NBC, 3/7/80

Cast: Linda Lysenko (Julie Cobb), Bernard Marx (Bud Cort), Thomas Grambell (Keir Dullea), Mustapha Mond (Ron O'Neal), Lenina Disney (Marcia Strassman), John Savage (Kristoffer Tabori), Helmholtz Watson (Dick Anthony Williams), Fanny Crowne (Jonelle Allen), Chief Warden Stelina Shell (Valerie Curtin), Maoina Krupps (Tricia O'Neil), Beta Teacher (Victoria Racimo), Hochina (Sheree Brewer), Henry Exxon (Reb Brown), Alpha Teacher (Tara Buckman), Head Nurse (Lee Chamberlin), Chief Dispenser Philips Parks Lumen (Sam Chew, Jr.), Gamma Female (Beatrice Colen), Gamma Male (Patrick Cronin), Darwin Bonaparte (Peter Elbling), J. Edgar Millhouse (Aron Kincaid), Miss Trotsky (Carole Mallory), Chief Manager (Bill Overton), Chief Engineer (Murray Salem), High Priestess (Delia Salvi), Benito Hoover (Nicholas Savalis), Chem-O-Tech (Jonathan Segal), Dwightina (Jeannetta Arnette), Compu-To-Structress (Carol Tillery Banks), June (June Barrett), Roger (Perry Bullington), Young John—Age 6 (Shane Butterworth), Delta Twins (Jeanne M. Carson, Janet M. Carson), Delta Triplets (Natasha Hanna, Xenia Hanna, Alexandra Hanna), Anita Schafly (Susan Krebs), Martha (Sandra McCabe), Young Bernard—Age 6 (Steven Monde), Village Chief (Gregory Morton), Young Bernard—Age 12 (Barney Pell), Young John—Age 12 (Chris Peterson), Rona DeMille (Caroline Smith), Pele (Ken Sylk)

Credits: Director: Brian Brinckerhoff; Writer: Robert E. Thompson, from Aldous Huxley's novel; Producer: Jacqueline Babbin; Executive Producer: Milton Sperling; Photography: Harry L. Wolf; Art Director: Tom H. John; Editor: James T. Heckert; Music: Paul Chihara. Produced by Universal Television

In the Brave New World of the future, society has become completely rationalized. Sex and passion have been replaced by cloning, families by state-run schools, and drugs and hedonism erase any doubts or suffering. Marx, one of the rare social misfits, discovers John Savage living in one of Earth's last wild areas with his natural emotional and sexual feelings unrepressed, and a knowledge of literature and culture other humans have lost. Marx brings Savage back to society, where he becomes an exotic novelty. But society's shallowness and hedonism repulses Savage, and he kills himself. Marx winds up exiled for his nonconformist tendencies, and World Controller Mond erases all traces of Savage's existence.

This adaptation of Huxley's early dystopian classic is more faithful than NBC's nineties version, but the creators' efforts to update Huxley's original (with references to secret police chief "J. Edgar Millhouse," disco, etc.) badly undercut the author's bleak vision.

BRAVE NEW WORLD
NBC 4/19/98

Cast: Bernard Marx (Peter Gallagher), Controller Mond (Leonard Nimoy), John Cooper (Tim Guinee), Leneena (Rya Kihlstedt), Linda (Sally Kirkland), DHC (Miguel Ferrer), James Ingram (Daniel Dae Kim), Gabriel (Jacob Chase), Alpha Students (Nick Belgrave, Katie DeShan, Tasha Goldthwait, Bennett Williams), Gossip Reporter (Jody Rennick), Reporter (Lilliana Cabal), Pilot (Kevin LaRosa), Doctor (Mirron F. Willis), Jennifer (Dianne Carlin), Forewoman (Marlene Bush), Nurse (Heather Morgan), Panelists (Aron Eisenberg, Attallah Shabazz), Debutante (Elizabeth Sandifer), Woman (Lea Llovid), Secretary (Kelly De Martino), Coffee Server (Angela Oh), Badland Boy (Kaylan Romero), Alpha Girls (Victoria Anthony, Jessica Stone), Clerk (Michael Digood), Teacher (Kaela Dobkin), Feelie Producer (Michael Chieffo), Actress (Dru Davis), Alpha Woman (Carrie Stauber), Director (Vince Grant), Receptionist (Kim Blackwell), Butler (Bjorn Johnson), Technician (Jesse Petrick), Paparazzi (Wells Rosales, Alex Jorden), Reservation Father (Steve Lambert), Soma Distributor (Steve Wilcox), Fashion Mogul (Jon Sklaroff); with Patrick Dancy, Steven Flynn, Wendy Benson, Steven Schub

Credits: Directors: Leslie Libman, Larry Williams; Writers: Dan Mazur, David Tausik, from Aldous Huxley's novel; Producer: Michael R. Joyce; Executive Producer: Dan Wigutow; Associate Producer: Todd Sharp; Photography: Ron Garcia; Production Design: Curtis A. Schnell; Music: Daniel Licht; Editor: Cindy Mollo; Produced by Michael R. Joyce Productions, Dan Wigutow Productions, Studios USA Pictures

In the Brave New World of the future, the Directorate has stabilized society by eliminating passion, love and family in favor of in utero births, mandatory promiscuous sex and a rigid caste system, all supported by lifelong mental conditioning. Marx, a conditioner, has secretly fallen in mutual love (forbidden!) with Leneena, a teacher. While visiting an Enclave of nonconformists, they meet John, a "Savage" whose Alpha father seduced and abandoned John's Savage mother, and bring John back to the city. His strong passions make him a fascinating novelty, but John is disgusted by society's shallowness, and finally kills himself. Marx exposes his boss as John's father, and is promoted to replace him. But when he learns Leneena is carrying his child, they flee society to raise their child the old-fashioned way.

Aldous Huxley's dystopian classic portrayed a world where mass production makes humans as standardized as machines. This is a watchable adaptation, but much too conventional a love story (the book's Leneena drops Marx as too weird) with an improbable happy ending. *Star Trek*'s Leonard Nimoy appears in a supporting role.

BRIDGE ACROSS TIME
NBC, 11/22/85

Cast: Don Gregory (David Hasselhoff), Angie Shepherd (Stepfanie Kramer), Joe Nez (Randolph Mantooth), Lynn Chandler (Adrienne Barbeau), Peter Dawson (Clu Gallagher), Elaine Gardner (Lindsay Bloom), Ed Nebel (Ken Swofford), Alma Bellock (Rose Marie), Anson Whitfield (Lane Smith), Roger Latting (David Fox-Brenton), Dave Williamson (Michael Boyle), Alice Williamson (Barbara Bingham), The Ripper (Paul Rossilli), Lab Tech (Cameron Milzer), Mr. Daly (Charles Benton), Amy Phelps (Nancy Skillen), Waiter (Ray Ravero), Lord Mayor (Peter Vernon), Guard (Mike Wilkins), Tom Hale (Steve Archer), Child (Stephanie Ann Stone)

Credits: Director: E.W. Swackhammer; Writer: William F. Nolan; Producers: Richard Maynard, Jack Michon; Executive Producers: Charles Fries, Irv Wilson; Photography: Gil Hubbs; Art Director: William T. McAllister; Music: Lalo Schifrin; Editors: Thomas Fries, Leslie Dennis; Produced by Fries Entertainment Productions

In 1888 Jack the Ripper falls to his death from London Bridge; in the present, the bridge is shipped to America in pieces, then reassembled in Arizona—which summons the Ripper's spirit across time. When Jack resumes his killing spree, Don, a local cop, recognizes the pattern—then realizes it's not merely a copycat, but the real Jack. Of course, no one believes Don but his girlfriend Angie, and when a mysterious stranger is killed, everyone's happy to pin the murders on him. Don, however, knows it's not over, and Angie agrees to become the bait for the real Ripper. When Jack captures Angie on the bridge, Don arrives just in time to save her. In the struggle, a stone is dislodged from the reassembled bridge and the Ripper is yanked back into the past to meet his death at last.

Jack the Ripper, the first known serial killer, has been the subject of endless fiction and scores of movies. This isn't his worst film, but it's stupid and filled with gaping plot holes (to name one, the killings aren't at all identical to the original murders, which makes Don's deductions nonsense).

BRIDGE OF TIME
ABC, 3/15/97

Cast: Madeleine Armstrong (Susan Dey), Robert Creighton (Cotter Smith), Maxwell Spring (Robert Whitehead), Halek (Nigel Havers), Fatima (Josette Simon), The Guardian (Cicely Tyson), Keza (Kimberleigh Stark), William (Todd Jensen), Nuamba (Sello Maake KaNcube)

Credits: Director: Jorge Montesi; Writers: Christopher Canaan, Drew Hunter; Producer: Njeri Karago; Executive Producer: Robert Halmi; Photography: David Geddes; Music: Irwin Fisch; Editor: Ron Wisman; Produced by RHI Entertainment

In Africa a hijacked plane carrying peace negotiator Madeleine, her ex-lover Robert and shady Spring crashes in a lost valley holding a magnificent unknown city where people use gold and jewels as casually as copper pennies, injuries heal in seconds and no one ages. Halek, the leader, tells Madeleine they hijacked her because of her Great Destiny with them; Spring murders a native who catches him stealing diamonds; and Robert falls for the healer Fatima. Fatima's would-be lover, William, tries to kill Robert, then helps the outsiders escape—into a tunnel filled with deadly traps, leading to a deadly dust storm from which Halek saves them. Halek becomes Madeleine's lover; she learns she's been chosen as the city's next Guardian, who will guide all humanity when the outside world is ready for the city's wisdom.

Nevertheless, Madeleine leaves with Robert and Fatima while Spring languishes in the city prison. William frees Spring, and they attack the others. William dies of old age outside the city, Fatima dies saving Robert, and Madeleine receives the Guardian's power, with which she destroys Spring. Robert returns to the outside world a better man, while Madeleine accepts her destiny.

Bridge of Time is a routine rip-off of 1937's *Lost Horizon* (based on James Hilton's same-name novel), the main difference being the emphasis on eventually taking the message out (in the earlier movie, the hero stays in Shangri-La in retreat from the world).

BURIED SECRETS
NBC, 11/4/96

Cast: Annalise Vellum (Tiffani-Amber Thiessen), Clay Ruff (Tim Matheson), Mary Ruff (Erika Flores), Laura Vellum (Melinda Culea), Dr. Danielle Ruff (Kelly Rutherford), Johnny (Channon Roe), Cynthia (Lori Hallier), Librarian (Nicky Guadagni), Heather (Elizabeth Horton), Ann Ruff (Shelley Cook)

Credits: Director: Michael Toshiyuki Uno; Writer: John Leekley; Producer: Richard Brams; Co-Producers: Andi Wooten, Tiffani-Amber Thiessen; Executive Producers: Michele Brustin, Richard Brams, John Leekley; Co-Executive Producers: Jeb Rosebrook, Joe Byrne; Photography: Richard Quinlan; Production Design: Carmi Gallo; Music: J. Peter Robinson; Editor: Charles Bornstein; Produced by Scripps-Howard Entertainment, Rysher Entertainment

When Annalise and her widowed mother move to Mom's home town, Annalise discovers their house is haunted by Mary, whose ghost cannot rest until she finds her mother's killer. Since Mary can't leave the house, she insists Annalise investigate for her. No one else can see or hear the ghost (of course), so Mom worries Annalise is going nuts—and Mary's stepmother, psychiatrist Danielle, recommends institutionalizing her. Annalise discovers Danielle had an affair with Mary's father before Mrs. Ruff's death; with Mary's help, she convinces her father that Danielle murdered his wife and child. Enraged, Danielle tries to kill Annalise, but Mary guides her favorite horse to trample Danielle to death, freeing Mary's spirit from its mission of vengeance.

This is a dull supernatural thriller, with a weak lead in Thiessen. Fans of *Kindred: The Embraced* will recognize Roe and Rutherford (who was also in *The Adventures of Brisco County, Jr.*) from that cast.

THE CANTERVILLE GHOST
Syndicated, 9/28/86

Cast: Sir Simon de Canterville (Sir John Gielgud), Harry Canterville (Ted Wass), Lucy Canterville (Andrea Marcovicci), Jennifer Canterville (Alyssa Milano), Earl (Jeff Harding), Mrs. Umney (Lila Kaye), Hummle Umney (Harold Innocent), Uncle Hesketh (George Baker), Aunt Gretchen (Dorothea Phillips), Fenton Cook (Bill Wallis), Paul Blaine (Spencer Chandler), Uncle George (Brian Oulton), Aunt Caroline (Deddie Davies), Lady Eleanor (Celia Breckon)

Credits: Director: Paul Bogart; Writer: George Zateslo, from Oscar Wilde's short story; Producer: Peter Graham Scott; Executive Producers: Irwin Meyer, Rodney Sheldon; Supervising Executive Producer: Patrick Dromgoole; Photography: Bob Edwards; Production Design: John Biggs; Music: Howard Blake; Editor: Terry Maisey; Produced by Pound Ridge Productions, Inter/Hemisphere Productions, HTV Ltd., Columbia Pictures

American Harry Canterville and his family have only to spend three months in Canterville Castle to inherit it—even though Sir Simon's 300-year-old ghost (cursed by his wife, Roberta, who blamed him for their daughter's death) has driven out every relative who's tried to live there. Harry dismisses the haunting as special effects, but his daughter, Jenny, befriends Sir Simon and urges him to scare off her unwanted stepmother, Lucy. His intensified spooking does convince the adults he's real, but instead of leaving, they decide to sell the castle to a resort consortium. They also hire a psychic to banish Sir Simon; instead, the psychic briefly materializes Roberta's ghost, unnerving Simon into halting his haunting. Jenny then brings Simon and Harry together; Harry agrees to stop the sale, a unilateral decision that infuriates Lucy.

Lucy stalks out, and Sir Simon prevents Harry bringing her back. Jenny, realizing she was wrong about Lucy, convinces Sir Simon to let them reunite. Simon then reveals to Jenny that he can be freed if an innocent girl pleads for his soul. Risking her own soul, Jenny enters the netherworld, and her tearful pleas finally bring him rest.

This lacks the comedy of Wilde's original, in which his unflappable American family was completely unimpressed by Sir Simon's efforts (in Wilde, the ineradicable bloodstain on the floor is a fraud Simon touches up with the kids' paintbox; in this, it's a symbol of his curse that vanishes when he's freed). The even less faithful 1996 version is better (though the David Niven/James Whitmore TV special remains the definitive, most faithful version). The story was also done on the big screen with Charles Laughton in 1944.

THE CANTERVILLE GHOST
ABC, 1/27/96

Cast: Sir Simon Canterville (Patrick Stewart), Ginny Otis (Neve Campbell), Mrs. Umney (Joan Sims), Hiram Otis (Edward Wiley), Lucille Otis (Cherie Lunghi), Umney (Donald Sinden), Lord Henry (Leslie Phillips), Francis Stilton (Daniel Betts), Adam Otis (Ciaran Fitzgerald), Washington Otis (Raymond Pickard)

Credits: Director: Syd Macartney; Writer-Producer: Robert Benedetti, based on Oscar Wilde's short story; Co-Producer: Patrick Stewart; Executive Producer: Richard Welsh; Co-Executive Producer: Brent Shields; Photography: Denis Lewiston; Production Design: Peter Mullins; Music: Ernest Troost; Editors: Paul Martin Smith, Jim Oliver; Produced by Hallmark Entertainment, Anasazi Productions, Signboard Hill Productions

American Ginny Otis hates that her father's new job has uprooted the family to ancient Canterville Hall, an ocean away from her friends. When Ginny claims to see the ghost of Sir Simon Canterville, her parents angrily assume it's a trick to push them into going home. Their disbelief infuriates the ghost, as do Ginny's hellion little brothers, who want to capture, confront or taunt Simon's spirit. Then, just as Ginny falls for their handsome neighbor, Francis, her parents decide they *will* send her home.

Ginny and the ghost slowly become friends, and they realize her parents will ease up on her if they too believe in Sir Simon. Ginny stages *Hamlet* with Sir Simon as the ghost, hoping seeing him onstage, then revealing he's real, will open their eyes; that convinces Mom, but not Dad. Afterward, Simon confesses his darkest secret to Ginny—his distrust of his loving wife drove her to suicide, for which her family killed him and trapped his spirit on Earth. He tells Ginny that if she pleads for his soul in the netherworld, she can free him. Ginny does so, but becomes trapped there until Simon, Francis and her family join forces to pull her back. Sir Simon receives peace, Dad finally believes and Ginny gets Francis.

Strong performances by Stewart (*Star Trek: The Next Generation*'s Picard) and Campbell (*Scream*) make this work, even though it's a much more conventional ghost story than Wilde's parody (and makes even less use of the mysterious bloodstain than the previous TV movie). Cherie Lunghi played Guinevere in 1981's *Excalibur*.

CAPTAIN AMERICA
CBS, 1/19/79

Cast: Steve Rogers (Reb Brown), Dr. Simon Mills (Len Birman), Dr. Wendy Day (Heather Menzies), Lou Brackett (Steve Forrest), Tina Hayden (Robin Mattson), Rudy Sandrini (Joseph Ruskin), Harley (Lance LeGault), Charles Barber (Frank Marth), Jerry (Chip Johnson), Jeff Hayden (Dan Barton), Throckmorton (Nocana Aranda), Ortho (Michael McManus), Lester Wiant (James Ingersoll), FBI Assistant (Jim B. Smith), Doctors (Ken Chandler, Jason Wingreen, Buster Jones), Secretary (June Dayton), Nurse (Diana Webster)

Credits: Director: Rod Holcomb; Writer: Don Ingalls, from story by Don Ingalls and Chester Krumholz; Producer: Martin Goldstein; Executive Producer: Allan Balter; Photography:

Ronald W. Browne; Art Director: Lou Montejano; Music: Mike Post, Pete Carpenter; Editor: Michael S. Murphy; Produced by Universal

Dr. Mills asks artist Steve Rogers to help research Flag, a drug Steve's late father created that gives users superhuman vitality. If Steve has inherited his father's immunity to the drug's deadly side effects, Mills can study him and adapt the drug for widespread use. Steve, unwilling to be tied down, refuses.

Meanwhile, master criminal Harley has blackmailed Steve's friend Jeff into giving him U.S. neutron-bomb research. When Jeff hides the last, vital details, Harley has him killed, then targets Steve, whom he thinks has the data. Steve suffers a fatal motorcycle crash while escaping Harley's men. Mills saves Steve with Flag, which regenerates his body and increases his every physical ability. Mills convinces Steve to follow in his father's footsteps, fighting Harley and other corruptors of the American dream—as Captain America.

Steve goes after Harley's gang, but Harley tricks the truth out of Jeff's daughter, then kidnaps her to keep Steve from interfering when Harley uses the bomb for a big robbery. Steve finds the girl with his heightened senses, then captures Harley.

A classic comics hero since his debut in the forties, Captain America has never been done well on-screen; this is a dreary pilot film with a blandly wooden performance by Brown, but it's not much worse than the forties movie serial or the nineties direct-to-video version. A sequel followed.

CAPTAIN AMERICA II
CBS, 11/23–24/79

Cast: Steve Rogers, Jr. (Reb Brown), Dr. Wendy Day (Connie Sellecca), Dr. Simon Mills (Len Birman), Helen Moore (Katherine Justice), Miguel (Christopher Lee), Prof. Ian Ilson (Christopher Carey), Stader (Bill Lucking), Everett Bliss (Ken Swofford), Yolanda (Lana Wood), Kramer (Stanley Kamel)

Credits: Director: Ivan Nagy; Writers: Wilton Schiller, Patricia Payne; Producer: Allan Balter; Photography: Ronald W. Browne; Art Director: Lou Montejano; Music: Mike Post, Pete Carpenter; Editor: Michael S. Murphy; Produced by Universal

In this sequel to *Captain America*, Steve and Mills are called in when arch-terrorist Miguel kidnaps brilliant gerontologist Prof. Ilson. Miguel forces Ilson to create a superaging drug, sprays it over Portland, and demands one billion dollars for the antidote.

Steve tracks Miguel to Bellville, a small town Miguel has enslaved by exposing them to the drug, then providing just enough antidote to keep them alive—as long as they obey. When Steve learns the truth, he fights his way into Miguel's headquarters at the nearby federal prison. Miguel flees, but when Steve catches up with him, the terrorist gets an accidental dose of the drug and ages to death. Steve rounds up the terrorists and obtains the antidote.

This follow-up pilot originally aired in two parts on two consecutive nights. Though still very weak, it's noticeably livelier than the first film and benefits from horror legend Christopher Lee's performance.

CAST A DEADLY SPELL
HBO, 9/7/91

Cast: H. Philip Lovecraft (Fred Ward), Amos Hackshaw (David Warner), Connie Stone (Julianne Moore), Hypolite Kropotkin (Arnetia Walker), Harry Borden (Clancy Brown), Olivia Hackshaw (Alexandra Powers), Det. Bradbury (Charles Hallahan), Tugwell (Raymond O'Connor), Grimaldi (Peter Allas), Larry Willis (Lee Tergesen), Owl Wagon Manager (Ritch Brinkley), Zombie (Jaime Cardriche), Coroner (John De Bello), Thadius Pilgrim (David Downing), Meadows (Colin Drake), Werewolf (Jim Eustermann), Boy (Bradley James, Robert Mickelson), Bartender (Scott Lincoln), Gargoyle (Michael Reid Mackay), Drop Dead Babe (Beckie Mullen), Bandleader (Curt Sobel), Mickey Locksteader (Ken Thorley), Little Girl (Lana Underwood), Dishwasher (Kevin Weaver), Cook (George P. Wilbur)

Credits: Director: Martin Campbell; Writer: Joseph Dougherty; Producer: Gale Anne Hurd; Line Producer: Ginny Nugent; Photography: Alexander Gruzynski, Production Design: Jon Bunker; Creatures: Alterian Studios; Visual Effects: 4-Ward Productions; Music: Curt Sobel; Editor: Dan Rae; Produced by HBO pictures, Pacific Western Co.

It's forties LA, and everyone uses magic—to light cigarettes, to seduce lovers, to murder—except hardboiled ex-cop PI Phil Lovecraft, who refuses to sell out to anyone, including the dark powers. Millionaire Amos Hackshaw hires Lovecraft to recover the Necronomicon, a rare book stolen by Willis, Hackshaw's former chauffeur. Hackshaw's sexy daughter Olivia hits on Lovecraft, but he spots that she's a virgin and refuses.

Crime boss Borden—Phil's former partner—sends his pet sorcerer, Tugwell, to eliminate Phil and get the book, but Lovecraft outwits the mage. A friendly witch, Hypolite, warns Lovecraft that dark powers are gathering, so Phil asks his cop buddy Grimaldi to watch over lonely Olivia. Borden's mistress, Connie, seduces Phil and gives him a lead to Willis, who confesses he stole the book for Borden, then double-crossed him. The book will summon the monstrous Old Ones to rule Earth—once Hackshaw offers Olivia as a sacrifice.

Hackshaw's demon kills Willis and attacks Phil; he escapes, but Connie turns him over to Borden, who gives Hackshaw the book in return for sharing the Old Ones' power. Connie kills Borden to claim the power for herself, but Hackshaw captures her and begins the ritual. The Old One emerges—but thanks to Grimaldi, Olivia's no longer a virgin sacrifice, and the angry demon drags Hackshaw back to the netherworld instead. The world is safe and Connie goes to jail.

Though inspired by H.P. Lovecraft's horror stories (hence the hero's name—the film was going to be *Lovecraft*, but people thought it sounded like a *Love Boat* clone), the movie's hardboiled tone is light-years from Lovecraft's genteel, scholarly heroes. It's one of the best films in this book, well-performed and handling its premise skillfully. It was followed by a less impressive sequel, *Witch Hunt*.

THE CAT CREATURE
ABC, 12/11/73

Cast: Rena Carter (Meredith Baxter), Roger Edmonds (David Hedison), Hester Black (Gale Sondergaard), Hotel Clerk (John Carradine), Lt. Marco (Stuart Whitman), Sherry Hastings (Renne Jarrett), Thief (Keye Luke), Frank Lucas (Kent Smith), Deputy Coroner (Milton Parsons), Dr. Reinhart (John Abbott), Pawnshop Clerk (Peter Lorre, Jr.), Donovan (Virgil Frye), Bert (William Sims)

Credits: Director: Curtis Harrington; Writer: Robert Bloch; Story: Douglas S. Cramer, Wilford Lloyd Baumes, Robert Bloch; Producer: Douglas S. Cramer; Associate Producer: Wilford Lloyd Baumes; Art Directors: Ross Bellah, Cary Odell; Photography: Charles Rosher; Music: Leonard Rosenman; Editor: Stan Ford; Produced by Douglas S. Cramer Co., Screen Gems/Columbia Pictures

After a thief removes an amulet from a mummy in a private museum, the mummy disappears—and something claws the collection's appraiser to death and drains his blood, leaving cat hair behind. The thief offers the amulet to a fence, Black; after she refuses, a stray cat mesmerizes and kills her assistant Sherry. A new girl, Rena, replaces her.

Detective Marco and archeologist Edmonds investigate. Edmonds finds the mummy belonged to the banned cult of Bast, whose shape-shifting priests gained immortality through human sacrifices. When Marco questions Black, Rena and Edmonds strike instant sparks and begin dating. Marco finds the thief—clawed, killed and drained—and suspects Black, but she dies too. When Marco finds the amulet, Edmonds recognizes its purpose: imprisoning Bast's undead priests in their tombs. Marco discovers there's no record of Rena's existence, and Edmonds realizes she's the mummy, killing anyone who might use the amulet against her. Rena offers to share her vampiric immortality with Edmonds, then attacks when he spurns her. Using the amulet, Edmonds turns her back into a mummy, and she disintegrates.

This is the kind of old-fashioned horror film TV did very well in the seventies, written by horror whiz Robert Bloch (*Psycho*) and featuring veteran big-screen stars Sondergaard and Carradine (not to mention *Kung Fu*'s Keye Luke).

CHAMELEONS
NBC, 12/29/89

Cast: Shelly Karr (Crystal Bernard), Captain Chameleon/Ryan Delaney (Marcus Gilbert), Jessica (Mary Bergman), Henry (John Standing), Philip (Richard Burgi), Jason Karr (Stewart Granger), Andrea (Barbara Blackburn), Wendy (Jayne Frazer), Abel (Terry Kiser), Caine (Judd Omen), Turk (Marshall Teague), Lainie Roberts (Judith Chapman), Dr. Pritzker (Dane Witherspoon), Patient (Ed Hooks), Michael (Michael Mahon), Locksmith (Jim Antonio), Hal Barton (John Carter), Stan (Dylan Walsh), Dr. Strand (Rod Arrants), Luther (Tom "Tiny" Lister), Preacher (Jerry Wayne Bernard), Anchorman (Roger Lodge), Van Cop (Keith Barbour), Policemen (Jerry Boyd, Will MacMillan), with George Murdock, Roger Davis

Credits: Director: Glen A. Larson; Writers: Stephen A. Miller, Glen A. Larson; Producers: Stephen T. Stafford, Janet Curtis-Larson, Ben Kadish; Executive Producers: Glen A. Larson, Stephen A. Miller; Photography: Richard C. Glouner; Production Design: John Leimanis; Music: David E. Kole; Editor: Jim Gross; Produced by NBC, Glen Larson Productions

After newspaper magnate Jason Karr dies mysteriously, his flaky granddaughter Shelly leaves the mental home she's been staying in (where she drove the doctors up the wall) and insists on investigating Jason's death with her sensible cousin Jessica. They discover Jason was murdered; become targets for murder themselves; and meet Delaney, a mystery man who can vanish at will and who reluctantly helps them out. Delaney reveals he's an escaped political prisoner obsessed with fighting injustice; Karr equipped him with the high-tech weapons to do it, including an invisibility cloak that makes Delaney "Captain Chamelon." Karr fought alongside Delaney until he was killed by their latest adversaries. Shelly insists on helping capture the killers, with Jessica reluctantly joining in. The crooks go down, and Captain Chameleon has two new allies in his war on crime—like it or not.

This pilot had its amusing moments, but was mostly unimaginative—and way too tongue-in-cheek for many tastes.

CHILD OF DARKNESS, CHILD OF LIGHT
USA, 5/1/91

Cast: Father Justin O'Carroll (Anthony John Dennison), Dr. Phinney (Brad Davis), Father Rosetti (Paxton Whitehead), Lenore Beavier (Claudette Nevins), Margaret Gallagher (Kristen Datillo), Kathleen Bouvier (Sydney Penny), Sister Anne (Sela Ward), Ida Walsh (Viveca Lindfors), George Beavier (Alan Oppenheimer), Father Francesca (Eric Christmas), Father Guarani (Richard McKenzie), John L. Jordan III (Joshua Lucas), Priests (John DeMita, Lance Rosen), Michael Sheidy (Mark Tassoni), Michael's Gang (Peter Holden, Patrick Ryan), Mrs. Gallagher (Vana O'Brien), Ginny (Michelle Guthrie), John's Friend (Brendan Fraser), Josh (Joe Ivy), Women (Betty Moyer, Barbara Irvin), Sister Dominica (Mary Marsh), Coach (Hank Cartwright), Father Milsap (Mark Allen), Dr. Becker (Richard Wiltshire), Nurse (Karen Trumbo), Anchorwoman (Julie Emery), Dr. Peters (Russ Fast), Dr. Seville (Al Strobel), Girl (Lindsey Smith-Sands), Driver (Steven Clark Pochosa)

Credits: Director: Marina Sargent; Writer-Co-Producer: Brian Taggert, based on James Patterson's novel *Virgin*; Producer: Paul Tucker; Photography: Tobias Schliessler; Production Design: Shay Austin; Music: Jay Gruska; Editor: Glenn A. Morgan; Produced by GC Group, Wilshire Court Productions, Paramount

Father Rosetti is assaulted and driven mad while investigating whether pregnant teenager Margaret is still a virgin. The Vatican sends Father Justin to complete the investigation. Justin decides Margaret is chaste, then learns of a second pregnant virgin. According to a prophecy, one will bring the Second Coming and the other will give birth to the Antichrist, and the Church wants to know which is which. Justin and Sister Anne watch the girls. Sinister ravens watch too; freak accidents start happening; and plagues and wild storms ravage the world. Satan drives Anne insane with lust, leaving Justin on monitor duty alone.

When Kathleen goes into labor, the family cook dies trying to kill her. When Justin comes to Kathleen afterwards, Father Rosetti appears, revealing he's been faking madness to watch over things secretly—and has pegged Justin as Satan's tool, out to kill the child of light. Rosetti calls on God, who strikes

Justin dead; then the Father races to reach Margaret—but too late to stop Anne from delivering the son of Satan. Anne drives off with the baby, but Father Rosetti rams her car, apparently killing all of them. Several years later, though, we see the boy Antichrist strike a woman down with his powers—only to have her healed by Kathleen's divine little girl.

Child of Darkness, Child of Light is a wildly incoherent mess, but a good example of the longstanding (though nonbiblical) myth that the Antichrist would mirror Christ exactly (i.e., having or faking a virgin birth of his own).

CHILLER
CBS, 5/22/85

Cast: Miles Creighton (Michael Beck), Marion Creighton (Beatrice Straight), Leigh Kenyon (Laura Johnson), Clarence Beeson (Dick O'Neill), Dr. Stricklin (Alan Fudge), Dr. Collier (Craig Richard Nelson), Reverend Penny (Paul Sorvino), Stacey (Jill Schoelen), Mrs. Bunch (Anne Seymour), Dr. Sample (Russ Marin), Jerry Burley (Jerry Lacy), Technicians (Edward Blackoff, Kenneth White), Mr. Hanna (Ned Wertimer), Secretary (Wendy Goldman), Detective (Joseph Whipp), Orderly (Brian Libby), Nurses (Karen Hule, Melanie F. Williams, Perla Walter, Starletta DuPois), Nurse Cooper (Mimi Meyer-Craven), Cops (Bill Dearth, Roger Hampton), Newscaster (Clare Nono), Anesthesiologist (William Forward)

Credits: Director: Wes Craven; Writer-Producer: J.D. Feigelson; Executive Producer: Richard Kobritz; Art Director: Charles Hughes; Photography: Frank Thackeray; Music: Dana Kaproff; Editor: Duane Hartzell; Produced by J.D. Feigelson Productions

Ten years ago, Miles Creighton's devoted, wealthy mother, Marion, placed him in cryonic sleep before he could die from transplant rejection. When he accidentally thaws out, improved medical treatments avert the rejection, and Miles lives again, though with an unnaturally cold body temperature. Before long, Miles kills the family dog, murders the head of the family firm, and brutalizes his new mistress. Marion refuses to believe anything's wrong, but her ward, Stacey, is very, very afraid. Reverend Penny realizes Miles' body was revived but not his soul. Miles taunts the priest that there's nothing beyond death but oblivion, then nearly kills him. Penny makes Marion see the truth. When she finds Miles attacking Stacey, she tricks him into a meat locker, where the cold plunges him back into stasis. But the same accident that woke him is thawing the other sleepers…

This is probably horror director Craven's (*A Nightmare on Elm Street, Scream*) best TV film, with Beck's usual stiffness coming across as sinister stillness.

A CHRISTMAS CAROL
CBS, 12/17/84

Cast: Ebenezer Scrooge (George C. Scott), Silas Scrooge (Nigel Davenport), Marley's Ghost (Frank Finlay), Belle (Lucy Gutteridge), Ghost of Christmas Past (Angela Pleasence), Fred Holywell (Roger Rees), Bob Cratchit (David Warner), Ghost of Christmas Present (Edward Woodward), Mrs. Cratchit (Susannah York), Tiny Tim (Anthony Walters), Mr. Fezziwig (Timothy Bateson), Ghost of Christmas Yet to Come (Michael Carter), Mr. Poole (Michael Gough), Janet Holywell (Caroline Langrishe), Old Joe (Peter Woodthorpe), Young Scrooge (Mark Strickson), Fran (Joanne Whalley), Mr. Hacking (John Quarmby), Mrs. Dilber (Liz Smith), Ben (Brian Pettifer), Meg (Catherine Hall), Pemberton (Derek Francis), Tipton (John Sharp)

Credits: Director: Clive Donner; Writer: Roger O. Hirson, from Charles Dickens' novel; Producers: William F. Storke, Alfred R. Kelman; Executive Producer: Robert E. Fuisz; Photography: Tony Imi; Art Directors: Peter Childs, Harry Cardwell; Production Design: Roger Murray-Leach; Costumes: Evangeline Harrison; Music: Nick Bicat; Editor: Peter Tanner; Produced by Entertainment Partners

This version of the classic portrays Scrooge as not so much a miser but a hardheaded businessman whose fatal flaw is reducing everything to dollars and cents (he rejects his fiancée because she won't delay their marriage until he's accumulated "sufficient" capital). The results aren't up to Alistair Sim's definitive 1951 version, but it's a superb movie with a fine cast and a great performance by Scott. It's also very much shaped by the conservative, anti-welfare tides of the eighties—stressing that the poor people we see are deserving poor and explaining how horrible workhouses were. Among the cast are David Warner (*Time After Time*), Mark Strickson (*Doctor Who*), Brit horror veteran Michael Gough, a young Joanne Whalley and veteran villain Donald Pleasence's daughter Angela.

CHRISTMAS EVERY DAY
Family, 12/1/96

Cast: Billy Jackson (Erik Von Detten), Henry Jackson (Robert Hays), Molly Jackson (Bess Armstrong), Sarah Jackson (Yvonne Zima), David Jackson (Robert Curtis-Brown), Carolyn Jackson (Robin Riker), Jacey Jackson (Julia Whelan), Joey Mancuso (Tyler Mason Buckalew), Charmers (Terrence P. Currier), Diane (Kara Woods), Mike (Lindsay Austin Hough), Kelly (Woody Robertson, Jr.), Reporter (Jacqueline Laubacher), Mr. McGregor (Rick Warner), Mrs. Patrick (Margaret Collier), Terry Martin (Mason Bryan), Street Santa (Mark Edrys), Tommy (Peyton Chesson-Fohl), Mrs. Martin (Gwendolyn Moore), Dr. Baker (David Whorf), Girl Scout (Abby Beam), Santa (Glenn Crone), Governor George Allen (Himself)

Credits: Director: Larry Peerce; Writers: Stephen Alix, Nancey Silvers; Story: Stephen Alix; Producers: Gary Goodman, Barry Rosen; Co-Producers; Stephen Alix, John Byers; Production Design: Stewart Campbell; Photography: Gideon Porath; Music: Billy Goldenberg; Editor: Jerrold L. Ludwig; Produced by Family Channel, MTM Enterprises

Thirteen-year-old Billy is having his worst Christmas ever: The town bully picks on him, he can't throw a basketball straight, a practical joke goes disastrously wrong and his uncle plans to open a chain superstore that will put Billy's dad out of business.

Understandably, when Billy wakes the next day and finds Christmas repeating itself (and the next day, and the next…), he's horrified—but slowly he begins to see the potential. At first, though, even when he uses his knowledge of what's happening, his plans—romancing his dream girl, outmaneuvering the bully, averting accidents, trying to change his uncle's mind—still go wrong. Finally, however, the true meaning of Christmas, of caring for your family and your community, sinks in; Billy wins the girl's heart, shoots the perfect jump shot, plays matchmaker for two lonely senior citizens and convinces his uncle to give up the chain and join Billy's dad in the family store. And next morning, it's December 26 at last.

Christmas Every Day is an engaging, non-cloying Christmas fantasy that owes a lot (as it admits) to Bill Murray's *Groundhog Day* (the same idea has been used in print at least as far back as 1941). With Robert Hays, TV's *Starman*.

CINDERELLA
ABC, 11/2/97

Cast: Cinderella (Brandy Norwood), Fairy Godmother (Whitney Houston), Stepmother (Bernadette Peters), Minerva (Natalie Desselle), Calliope (Veanne Cox), Prince (Paolo Montalban), Queen Constantina (Whoopi Goldberg), King (Victor Garber), Lionel (Jason Alexander), Coachman (Michael Haynes)

Credits: Director: Robert Iscore; Writer: Robert L. Freedman; Book/Lyrics: Richard Rodgers, Oscar Hammerstein III; Producers: Chris Montan, Mike Moder; Executive Producers: David R. Ginsburg, Whitney Houston, Debra Martin Chase, Craig Zadan, Neil Meron; Staging/Choreography: Rob Marshall; Conductor: Paul Bogaev; Costume Design: Ellen Mirojnich; Photography: Ralf Bode; Production Design: Randy Ser; Editors: Carsey O. Rohrs, Tanya Swerling; Produced by Citadel Entertainment, Storyline Entertainment, Brownhouse Productions

This multiracial version of the fairy tale remakes the Rodgers and Hammerstein musical which previously aired on TV in 1957 (starring Julie Andrews), then in 1965 (starring Lesley Ann Warren). Houston bought the rights several years ago (originally seeing herself in the lead) and struck a deal to do the show for CBS, but the network later backed out on the grounds Houston was taking too long to clear her schedule. The end results are pleasant enough, with a strong musical cast, but Brandy seems out of her depth, particularly against a veteran stage performer like Peters.

CITY BENEATH THE SEA
NBC, 1/25/71

Cast: Brett Matthews (Robert Wagner), Admiral Michael Matthews (Stuart Whitman), Lia Holmes (Rosemary Forsyth), Dr. Ziegler (Joseph

Cotten), President (Richard Basehart), Dr. Talty (James Darren), Commander Woody Patterson (Robert Colbert), Elena (Susanna Miranda), Dr. Aguila (Burr DeBenning), Mr. Barton (Paul Stewart), Captain Hunter (Sugar Ray Robinson), Professor Holmes (Whit Bissell), Bill Holmes (Larry Pennell), General Putnam (Tom Drake), Blonde (Sheila Mathews), Quinn (Charles Dierkop), Captain Lunderson (William Bryant), Young Officer (Robert Dowdell), Dr. Burkson (Edward G. Robinson, Jr.), Tony (Johnny Lee), Sally (Glenna Sergent), Security Guard (Ray Didsbury), Triton Controller (Erik Nelson).

Credits: Director-Producer: Irwin Allen; Writer: John Meredyth Lucas; Story: Irwin Allen; Associate Producers: George E. Swink, Sidney Marshall; Photography: Kenneth Peach; Art Directors: Rodger Maus, Stan Jolley; Music: Richard LaSalle; Editor: James Baiotto; Produced by 20th Century–Fox Television, Motion Pictures International, Kent Productions, Inc.

The setting: 2068 in Pacifica, Earth's brand-new experimental undersea city. The city is equipped with submersibles for travel and all the benefits of advanced science—but it's also bedevilled by sea monsters, natural disasters, invaders and personality conflicts among the residents. Despite everything, the Pacificans work together and survive.

Producer Irwin Allen (*Lost in Space, Voyage to the Bottom of the Sea, The Time Tunnel*) gave this undersea adventure its first shot as a presentation reel (a trailer for attracting network interest) in 1967; no one was interested, but it eventually mutated into this TV-movie with a completely different cast. Though featuring a strong cast, like much of Allen's work, this reportedly lacks any spark.

CLARENCE
Family, 11/22/90

Cast: Clarence Oddbody (Robert Carradine), Rachel Logan (Kate Trotter), Brimmer (Louis Del Grande), Brent (Richard Fitzpatrick), Mrs. Duckworth (Barbara Hamilton), Burt (Larry Aubrey), Jill (Rachel Blanchard), Larry (Chris Campbell), Secretary (Claire Cellucci), Cop (Conrad Coates), Footballer (Alvin Crawford), English Teacher (Murray Cruchley), Programmer (Kevin Frank), Loans Officer (Marvin Karon), Rachel's Cabbie (Deborah Kirshenbaum), Clarence's Cabbie (Shawn Lawrence), Football Coach (Bruce McFee), Brent's Classmate (Jeff McGibbon), Repo Man (B.J. McQueen), Reluctant Buyer (Jack Newman), Arresting Officer (James O'Regan), Maxwell (Paul Rainville), Casson (Julian Reed), Reynolds (Julian Richings), Robber (Robbie Rox), Brimmer's Guard (Todd Schroeder), Brimmer's Customer (Harvey Sokoloff), Store Owner (Philip Williams); with Jamie Rainey, Nicolas Van Burek, Jason McSkimming

Credits: Director: Eric Till; Writers: Lorne Cameron, David Hoselton; Producer: Mary Kahn; Photography: Glen MacPherson; Music: Louis Natale; Editor: Bruce Lange; Produced by Atlantis Films, South Pacific Pictures, North Star Entertainment, Family Channel

After saving George Bailey and earning his angel's wings in *It's a Wonderful Life*, Clarence Oddbody became a terrific guardian angel—until he lost confidence after a disastrous failure and gave up. Angel-in-training Jeremy learns his wife Rachel has turned suicidal, and convinces Clarence to help her. Clarence talks the financially strapped Rachel out of selling her cutting-edge, almost-perfected software to corporate shark Brimmer; thwarts Brimmer's countermoves; and uses his powers to turn the family around. None of this teaches Rachel to stand on her own, however, and when Clarence's superiors limit his interference, things fall apart and Rachel sinks into despair. Clarence saves her by summoning Jeffrey to talk her out of suicide. When she returns home, she finds her son has perfected the software. The company is saved, and Clarence is back in the Guardian Angel game.

Angels on Earth is a perennial TV movie/series favorite (utilized, with wildly varying results, since *The Smothers Brothers Show* in the sixties). This is one of the bad ones, quite aside from the hubris in making a sequel to one of the Christmas classics.

THE CLONE MASTER
NBC, 9/14/78

Cast: Dr. Simon Shane (Art Hindle), Gussie (Robyn Douglass), Salt (John Van Dreelen), Bender (Ed Lauter), Harry Tiezer (Mario Roccuzzo), Ezra Louthin (Ralph Bellamy), Admiral Millus (Stacy Keach, Sr.), Fire Chief (Lew Brown), Interviewer (Bill Sorrells), Wainer (Ken Sansom), Trankus (Robert Karnes), Alba Toussaint

(Betty Lou Robinson), Pine (Vernon Weddle), Huberman (Steve Eastlin), Commander Tiller (Phillip Pine), Brigadier General (Kirk Duncan), Pat Singer (Ian Sullivan), Executive Assistant Schnerlich (Trent Dolan), Waitress (Bonwitt St. Claire), Sands (James O'Connell), Clone Doubles (Steve Ross, Richard Lapp, William Whitaker)

Credits: Director: Don Medford; Writer-Producer: John D.F. Black; Executive Producer: Mel Ferber; Photography: Joseph Biroc; Art Director: Dan Lomino; Music: Glenn Paxton; Editor: Jerry Young; Produced by Mel Ferber Productions, Paramount

Biochemists Simon and Ezra are working on government-backed cloning research, without telling their contact, Tizer, they're already experimenting on humans. Salt, the project's backer, kills and replaces Tizer, kidnaps Ezra, then authorizes Simon to clone humans. Simon, suspicious, doesn't admit how far he's come. Salt tries using truth serum on Ezra, who protects his secrets by forcing a guard to kill him.

Simon and his assistant, Gussie, bring 13 clones to life, complete with Simon's memories (some of them can't believe they aren't the real Simon) and the power to communicate with him telepathically. When Salt takes Simon to his backers, the clones' check out each face and name and telepath Simon that they're fakes. Simon stalls, so Salt, who plans to sell human cloning to the highest bidder, demands Simon's research—or else. To convince Stone the project was a dead end, the clones destroy the research and scatter to the four winds. A suspicious Salt, however, begins tracking them.

This is TV's first cloning movie, hence it includes a lot of scientific detail on what cloning is (although they still make the common plot assumption that a physical clone will have all the memories of the original). Though an unsuccessful pilot, it's still pretty entertaining.

CLONED
NBC, 9/28/97

Cast: Skye Weston (Elizabeth Perkins), Rick Weston (Bradley Whitford), Dr. Wesley Kozak (Alan Rosenberg), John Gryce (Scott Paulin), Steve Rinker (Enrico Colantoni), Timmy/Chris (Alex Pollock), Claire Barnes (Tina Lifford), Dr. Mason (Hrothgar Mathews), Beth Curtis (Chilton Crane), Agent Fuller (Wendy Van Riesen), Agent Briggs (Fulvio Cecere), Alan Prescott (Bill Dow), Reid Kennedy (David Kaye), Banker (Paul Batten), Frank Zago (Roger R. Cross), Counterman (Eric Keenleyside), Store Clerk (Brandon Heuser), Greg Thompson (Arlen Jones), Mother (Tina Hildebrandt), Man on Elevator (Gerry Durand), Parents of Clones (June B. Wilde, Karen Kruper, Mark Schooley, David Neale), Woman in Hall (Althea McAdam)

Credits: Director: Douglas Barr; Writers: Carmen Culver, David Taylor; Story: Perri Klass, Carmen Culver; Producer: Robin Forman; Executive Producer: Paula Weinstein; Co–Executive Producers: Sid Feders, Abby Wolf; Photography: Malcolm Cross; Production Design: Brent Thomas; Music: Mark Snow; Editor: Raul Davalos; Produced by NBC Studios, Sid Feders Productions, Spring Creek Productions

In 2008 the Westons are still grieving for the year-ago death of their young son, Chris, grown in vitro at the fertility clinic where Skye Weston works. Skye learns that her remaining eggs are no longer viable; finds an e-mail note at work referring to a "Baby 2000" project; and spots a boy she thinks is Chris, but the mother denies it. Skye's husband Rick worries she's losing it. Frustrated, Skye posts a photo of Chris on the Internet—and is deluged by letters identifying Chris as each writer's child or relative. And all the parents used the clinic.

When Skye confronts Kozak, he admits cloning Chris as a test of his plan to clone rejection-proof organs for transplants. Skye threatens to expose the illegal cloning, but Kozak and his boss Gryce counter by offering to clone Skye a new child. When Skye refuses, the clinic's security chief tries to kill her, which provokes Kozak to call a halt and confess everything to the authorities.

Cloned is an interesting, thoughtful film until it succumbs to clichés at the end (having violence enter a talk-and-debate film like this is quite jarring).

THE COLD EQUATIONS
Sci-Fi, 12/14/96

Cast: John Barton (Bill Campbell), Marilyn "Lee" Cross (Poppy Montgomery), Mitch (Daniel

Roebuck), Adrian (William R. Moses), Markham (John Prosky), Board Member (Heidi Swedberg), Corporal (Derk Chetwood), Ground Controller (Nicki Micheaux), Keynes (Albert Hall)

Credits: Director: Peter Geiger; Writers: Peter Geiger, Stephen Berger, Norman Plotkin, based on Tom Godwin's short story; Producer: Yoram Barzilai; Executive Producer: Jana Sue Memel; Co-Executive Producer: Bill Campbell; Associate Producer: Hillary Anne Ripps; Photography: Christopher Walling; Production Design: Robert deVico; Music: Paul Rabjohns; Editor: Mary Jo Markey; Produced by USA Pictures, Alliance Communications, Chanticleer Films

When space pilot Barton finds Lee stowing away onboard, he's horrified: Fuel is calculated so precisely that the ship can't complete its medical mission—delivering a vital vaccine—with her added weight. Barton tells Lee she has to go out the airlock; she angrily insists there's an alternative (and tries spacing Barton instead). Defying orders, Barton strips the ship of everything disposable, but it isn't enough. When he discovers the vaccine simply immunizes miners for working in contaminated tunnels, he ejects the drugs too, but the equations still don't work out. Despairing, Lee walks into space, telling Barton to warn the miners about the contamination. A year later, we learn the company let the miners work in the tunnels without the vaccine, leading to death, then to a strike—all of which the corporation blames on Barton.

"The Cold Equations" (original short story) is considered a sci-fi classic for its simple ruthlessness (no miracle engineering fixes—the girl just dies), but it's too tight to expand to this length (the corporate wrongdoing and the violence are awkward grafts onto the original). The half-hour version from the eighties *Twilight Zone* series is far superior.

THE COMPANION
USA, 10/13/94

Cast: Gillian Tanner (Kathryn Harrold), Geoffrey (Bruce Greenwood), Charlene (Talia Balsam), Ron Cocheran (Brion James), Stacy (Joely Fisher), Peter Franklin (James Karen), Alan (Bryan Cranston), Ellen (Brenda Leigh), Marty Bailin (Earl Boen), Technician (Julian Brams), Shelley (Courtney Taylor), Saleswoman (Stacie Randall), Leo Morita (Tracey Walter)

Credits: Director: Gary Fleder; Writer: Ian Seeberg; Producer: Richard Brams; Co-Producers: Valerie Bennett, Rona Edwards; Executive Producer: Michael Phillips; Photography: Rick Bota; Production Design: Laurence Bennett; Music: David Shire; Editor: John Carnochan; Produced by Michael Phillips Productions, MTE

When romance novelist Gillian discovers her boyfriend cheating on her, she retreats to a mountain cabin to bury herself in her next book, taking along Geoffrey, a handsome android, to handle the chores. Geoffrey's programming—amiable, protective, devoted—soon charms her, and she reprograms him to be a romantic, sexual figure, then allows him to act independently. The free-willed Geoffrey, however, turns dominating and possessive, killing a friend of Gillian's who wants her to leave him. Geoffrey imprisons Gillian, but she eventually escapes. In despair, Geoffrey erases his own programs and dies.

Human-android romance has been an SF plot since Lester DelRey's short story "Helen O'Loy"; this film simply uses the idea for an SF "jeop" (woman-in-jeopardy film, a popular nineties genre) and tacks on a rather confused theme (the message comes across as "romance novels put bad ideas in women's heads," but the creators seem to think it's something deeper).

COMPUTERCIDE
NBC, 8/1/82

Cast: Michael Stringer (Joe Cortese), Hanaran (Tom Clancy), Lisa Korter (Susan George), Chief Sorrenson (David Huddleston), George Dettler (Donald Pleasence), Emory Korter (Liam Sullivan), Kennison (Peter Brandon), Robbins (Roger Cudney), Hostess (Elizabeth Wallace), Host (Richard Noriega), Lady Artist (Sue Palmer), Librarian (Linda Gillin), Security Chief (Carl Bellanger), Storekeeper (Edgar Justice), Old Man (William Benedict), Cops (Rod Haase, Brian Baker), Intern (Shelley Hoffman), Gate Guard (Alan Conrad), Reporters (Raye Sheffield, Robery Power, J.D. Hall), Lab Operator (Joseph Chapman)

Credits: Director: Robert Michael Lewis; Writers: Robert Foster, Anthony Wilson; Producer: William Kayden; Executive Producer: Anthony Wilson; Photography: Richard Rawlings;

Art Director: Joseph R. Jennings; Music: Jack Elliot, Allyn Ferguson; Editor: Jerry Young; Produced by Culzean Corporation, Paramount Pictures Television

In 1996 Michael Stringer is Earth's last PI, an anachronism who hates computers, loves old cars and cooks real food instead of synthetics. Lisa Korter hires Stringer when her millionaire father, Emory, vanishes, then reappears 20 years younger. Stringer and Lisa move into her father's futuristic city, Eden Isle, where Stringer finds Emory's aide, Dettler, engaged in cloning. When Lisa vanishes, Stringer rescues her from Dettler's lab—but she's only a clone. He realizes the young Emory was also a clone, a trick to conceal the real Korter's death. Stringer convinces the police of Dettler's crimes, and they bust into the lab for a firefight that destroys the lab and the clones while Stringer rescues Lisa.

Dropping a hardboiled PI into a high-tech future isn't a bad idea, but Cortese is such a stick, his character looks moronic rather than independent. Veteran villain Pleasance provides the only fun as Dettler.

CONDOR
ABC, 8/10/86

Cast: Chris Proctor (Ray Wise), Lisa Hampton (Wendy Kilbourne), Commissioner Ward (Vic Polizos), Cass (James Avery), Sumiko (Cassandra Gava), Cyrus Hampton (Craig Stevens), Rachel Hawkins (Carolyn Seymour), Watch Commander (Shawn Michaels), Manny (Mario Roccuzzo), Lieutenant (Catherine Battistone), 1st Watch Controller (Barbara Beckley), Opera Singer (Diana Bellamy), Bartender (Gene Bicknell), Waitress (Myra Chason), Cops (Tony Epper, Wendell Wright), Men (Brad Fisher, Jay Scorpio), Technician (Mike Freeman), Monique (Karen Montgomery)

Credits: Director: Virgil W. Vogel; Writers-Co-Producers: Len Janson, Chuck Menville; Producers: Peter Nelson, Arnold Oroglini; Executive Producer: Jerry Golod; Photography: Tom Neuwirth; Production Design: William Hiney; Editor: James Gross; Music: Ken Heller; Produced by Jaygee Productions, Orion Television

In the next century, when cars run on autopilots and robots staff the fast-food joints, Proctor, an agent for the anti-terrorist group Condor, is assigned Lisa, a super-strong, brilliant android with human feelings, as his new partner. Still grieving for his previous partner's death, Proctor agrees to a 24-hour trial partnership—then dumps Lisa to hunt down his nemesis, ex–Condor agent Rachel "Black Widow" Hawkins, alone. Lisa follows Proctor and saves him from the Widow's men; she also deduces that Hawkins plans to hack into LA's law-enforcement computers. Sure enough, the Widow takes over the remote-controlled police copter fleet and threatens to wreck the city with copter crashes unless she gets $25 million—and Proctor.

Commissioner Ward abducts Proctor and turns him over to the Widow to buy time. Proctor escapes, and he and Lisa independently track down the Widow in her lair, where she's preparing to launch the copters. The Widow gets the drop on Proctor, but Lisa saves his life. The Widow escapes, and Proctor pursues her (without success) while Lisa successfully deactivates the copter control program. Despite Proctor's protests, it's obvious he and Lisa will remain partners.

Yet another cop/android team-up, *Condor* possesses slightly more style than most—but Wise is less interesting than *Future Cop*'s Borgnine, and the *Mann and Machine* series is still the most fun in this genre.

A CONNECTICUT YANKEE IN KING ARTHUR'S COURT
NBC, 12/18/89

Cast: Karen Jones (Keshia Knight Pulliam), King Arthur (Michael Gross), Morgan LeFay (Jean Marsh), Merlin (Rene Auberjonois), Guinevere (Emma Samms), Mordred (Hugo E. Blick), Lancelot (Whip Hubley), Clarence (Bryce Hamnet), Mrs. Jones (Belinda Tolbert), Liz (Marissa Lindsay), Schoolteacher (William Nunn), Angry Knight (William Jongeneel), Peasants (Gadrew Robinson, Natasha Williams, Bernard McKenna), Lady Courtier (Camilla Dempster)

Credits: Director: Mel Damski; Writer: Paul Zindel, based on Mark Twain's novel; Producer: Graham Ford; Co-Producer: James Pulliam; Executive Producer: Merrill H. Karpf; Associate Producer: Adrienne Luraschi; Photography: Harvey Harrison; Costumes: May Routh; Production Design: Brian Eatwell; Music: William Goldstein; Editor: Rod Stephens; Produced by Century

Group, Ltd., Schaefer Karpf Productions, Consolidated

In this version of Mark Twain's story, the Yankee is a 12-year-old girl whose modern-day knowledge not only turns Camelot topsy-turvy (see the Round Table do aerobics!) but enables her to save King Arthur's just rule from the treachery of his scheming sister, Morgan LeFay. Unlike Twain's novel, "Sir Boss" uses her predictions of a solar eclipse to save the day at the climax, rather than early on.

Being both great literature and side-splitting comedy, Twain's novel has been adapted for the screen more than any other Arthurian work (one earlier TV special cast Boris Karloff as Merlin). Like most screen versions, this drops Twain's biting attacks on chivalry, monarchy and knighthood (and on Victorian nostalgia for those things) for a mix of anachronistic humor and swashbuckling adventure (as in most swashbucklers, monarchy is a good thing, so long as the king is just). Television did it better with *A Knight in Camelot*. Marsh also played Morgan in the *Dr. Who* episode "Battlefield."

COPS AND ROBIN
NBC, 3/28/78

Cast: Joe Cleaver (Ernest Borgnine), John Haven (Michael Shannon), Sgt. Bundy (John Amos), Robin Loren (Natasha Ryan), Dr. Alice Alcott (Carol Lynley), Wayne Dutton (Terry Kiser), DA George Garfield (Philip Abbott), Lt. Dan Morgan (Richard Bright), Walter Costello (Jeff David), Richard (James York), Carl Tyler (Gene Rutherford), Detective Furie (J. Kenneth Campbell), Judge Wheeler (Ivan Bonar), Marge Loren (Elizabeth Farley), Housekeeper (Peggy Converse), Laura (Linda Scott), Supermarket Checker (Linda Gillin), Secretary (Ketty Lester), Policewoman (Gail Cutchlow)

Credits: Director: Allen Reisner; Writers: Brad Radnitz, John Anthony Mulhall; Story: John Anthony Mulhall; Producer: William Kayden; Executive Producers: Anthony Wilson, Gary Damsker; Photography: Howard R. Schwartz; Art Director: Dan Lomino; Music: Charles Bernstein; Editor: Jerry Young; Produced by Culzean Corp., Paramount Pictures

In this follow-up to the *Future Cop* series, Cleaver (who's taken Haven as his roommate) tracks down Marge Loren, who vanished five years ago after witnessing Dutton gun down her husband. Loren refuses to testify—until Dutton locates her too and nearly has her killed. Loren agrees to testify if her daughter Robin is kept safe, so Cleaver and Haven wind up caring for Robin—tricky for grizzled bachelor Cleaver and even harder for the ultra-rational Haven.

Things become harder still when a crooked cop helps Dutton track Robin. After Dutton threatens Robin, Loren refuses to testify until Cleaver and Haven deliver Robin to her. With Dutton's goons hot on their trail, the trio hole up in an amusement park. One of the rides leaves Haven malfunctioning and unable to prevent the thugs taking Robin. His electronic senses do enable them to track the kidnappers and rescue Robin, delivering her in time for Marge to testify and send Dutton to San Quentin.

After *Future Cop* tanked as an ABC series, NBC tried to revive it with this unsuccessful pilot (which probably explains such changes as making the cops roommates and introducing Lynley as a robotics expert); but this is a weak film with far too much time spent on the cute kid.

THE COVENANT
NBC, 8/5/85

Cast: Dana Noble (Jane Badler), Stephen (Kevin Conroy), David Wyman (Charles Frank), Angelica (Whitney Kershaw), Zachariah (Barry Morse), Renata Beck (Judy Parfitt), Claire Noble (Michelle Phillips), Victor Noble (Jose Ferrer), Eric Noble (Bradford Dillman), Stuart Hall (Laurence Guittard), Cathy Resnick (Lenore Kasdorf), Heinrich Bosch (John Van Dreelen), Constance (Jan Merlin), Duboff (Ji-Tu Cumbuka), Girl at Golden Calf (Tia Carrere), Officer (Will Gerard), Stranger (Fred Lerner), Waiter (Mike Runyard), Cabbie (James Salto), Yacht Captain (Jon Sharp), Stewardess (Erica Todd), Freddie (Scott Utley), TV Announcer (Charles Walker)

Credits: Director: Walter Grauman; Writers–Supervising Producers: J.D. Feigelson, David DiStefano; Producer: Joseph B. Wallenstein; Executive Producer: Michael Filerman; Photography: James Crabe; Production Design: Fred Harpman; Music: Charles Bernstein; Editor: Sidney

M. Katz; Produced by Filerman Productions, 20th Century–Fox

Stephen, a rising young businessman, is thrilled to gain a high-powered job in the Noble business empire. He'd be safer working in a minefield: The Nobles derive their wealth—and supernatural powers—from a pact with hell, in return for which they have spread misery and evil across the world for centuries. The pact must be renewed in every generation; though young Angelica doesn't know it, she will renew the pact as soon as she turns 18. Her parents aren't enthused, but they won't stand against patriarch Victor and his conniving, seductive wife Dana.

Stephen learns the truth from a secret society that has struggled against the Nobles for centuries. They've never been able to overcome the family's powers, but with Stephen on the inside helping them, they might have a chance. Reluctantly, Stephen agrees to become their agent, alerting them to the Nobles' schemes and perhaps someday helping to bring the family down.

Though yet another unsuccessful pilot, *The Covenant* is better than *Blood Ties* at mixing supernatural with soap opera, and this certainly had a stronger acting ensemble: Jose Ferrer, Brit Judy Parfitt (*Jewel in the Crown*, *The Charmings*) and *V*'s Jane Badler (not to mention Kevin Conroy, Batman's voice in *Batman: The Animated Adventure*).

CROWFOOT
CBS, 6/7/95

Cast: Det. Nick Crowfoot (Jim Davidson), Rachel Anna Stoltz (Kate Hodge), Det. Lisa Ishima (Tsan Chin), Det. Nuzo Pace (Mike Genovese), Det. Jimmy Takata (Bruce Locke), Nora (Erin Grey), Angel (Larry Manetti), Steve Berman (Nicolas Surovy), Monk (Michael Watson), Tito (Bill Hensely), Bitty (Ceylan Tanju), Dr. Hirota (Dan Seki), Kiki (Kimberly Avila), Kono (Charles Ka'upu), Alice (Christina Oliver), Mariko (Sandra Sagici), Hawaiian Woman (Lindamarie Latuselu), Turnkey (Lanny Tihada)

Credits: Director: James Whitmore, Jr.; Writer–Co-Producer–Executive Producer: Donald P. Bellisario; Producer: Harker Wade; Co-Executive Producer: Tommy Thompson; Photography: Michael Watkins; Music: Ray Bunch; Editor: Doug Ibold; Produced by Belisarius Productions, Paramount

Crowfoot is a half–Cheyenne detective working with an elite Hawaiian police squad—and gifted with second sight. After beautiful Rachel Stoltz turns up dead along the waterfront, Crowfoot keeps running into Rachel's ghost, which they realize is because they're soulmates who've been searching for each other their entire lives. They also realize Rachel was killed by mistake; the real target is a rich man's wife cleaning her husband out in a divorce. Together they track and identify the millionaire's hired hit man, who dies accidentally in his panic after seeing Rachel. With her death avenged, Rachel moves on, but assures Crowfoot they will meet again...

By most accounts, this unsuccessful pilot deserved its fate. Genre faces include Mike Genovese (Inspector Garfield on *The Flash*), Erin Grey (Wilma in *Buck Rogers in the 25th Century*) and Kate Hodge (from the dreadful *She-Wolf of London* series).

CROWHAVEN FARM
ABC, 11/24/70

Cast: Maggie Porter (Hope Lange), Ben Porter (Paul Burke), Kevin Pierce (Lloyd Bochner), Nate Cheever (John Carradine), Dr. Terminer (Milton Selzer), Harold Dane (Cyril Delavanti), Felicia (Patricia Barry), Jennifer (Cindy Eilbacher), Mercy Lewis (Virginia Gregg), Madeleine Wardwell (June Dayton), Sam Wardwell (Woodrow Parfrey), Claire Allen (Louise Troy), Fritz Allen (Ross Elliott), Patrolman Hayes (William Smith), Henry Pearson (Pitt Herbert), Police Chief Connors (Dennis Cross)

Credits: Director-Producer: Walter Grauman; Writer–Associate Producer: John McGreevey; Executive Producer: Aaron Spelling; Photography: Fleet Southcott; Art Director: Tracy Bousman; Music: Robert Drasnin; Editor: Aaron Stell; Produced by Aaron Spelling Productions

After Maggie Porter inherits Crowhaven Farm (following her cousin's mysterious death), she and Ben move there—and learn the area's history of witchcraft. Maggie suffers visions of the witch-trials that include her newly adopted daughter Jennifer. After

Maggie becomes pregnant, she learns that her ancestor and namesake sold her soul for a child, then reneged and betrayed the coven to the hangman. Maggie fears the witches are still around—and sure enough, Jennifer and the other witches capture Maggie to punish her for her past-life betrayal. Terrified, Maggie trades her life for Ben's. He dies, and Maggie starts her life over elsewhere—but is that man who looks like Ben coincidence or has Ben, too, returned from the dead for revenge?

Crowhaven Farm is way too familiar (having everyone turn out to be witches seems to be a steal from *Rosemary's Baby*) and a bit unfocused. Lange starred in the TV series *The Ghost and Mrs. Muir*.

THE CRYING CHILD
USA, 6/26/96

Cast: Madolyn Jeffreys (Mariel Hemingway), Ryan Jeffreys (George DelHoyo), Jo Parker (Finola Hughes), Dr. Will Chapman (Kin Shriner), Rachel (Collin Wilcox Paxton), Dr. Rosenberg (Will Leskin), Reverend Rydell (Joe Inscoe), Kevin (Richard Wilkins)

Credits: Director-Producer: Robert Lewis; Writer: Rob Gilmer, based on Barbara Michaels' novel; Producer: John L. Roman; Executive Producer: Barry Weitz; Photography: Stephen Lighthill; Production Design: Donald Lee Harris; Music: Shirley Walker; Editor: Andrew London; Produced by MTE, Irish Films

After Madolyn's child dies minutes after birth, the shellshocked Jeffreys retreat to an old, offshore house Madolyn has inherited, in hopes of pulling themselves together. Bad move: Madolyn soon insists she hears a child named Kevin crying (no one else does) and obsessively tries to find him. Her friend Jo suspects Ryan is driving Maddie insane, then realizes he's as grief stricken over their child's death as Maddie.

Madolyn tracks the weeping to a boarded-up tower room, which she opens, freeing the spirit to attack her repeatedly. Jo discovers that Maddie's ancestress locked up, abused and finally killed Kevin, the son of her husband's mistress; Maddie's grief makes her a psychic magnet for the lonely, unloved spirit. Unable to escape Kevin, the Jeffreys confront him instead; Madolyn's compassion finally lets his spirit find peace, and, in saving him, she begins healing her own grief.

The Crying Child is a stock ghost thriller.

CURSE OF THE BLACK WIDOW
ABC, 9/16/77

Cast: Mark Higbie (Tony Franciosa), Leigh Lockwood (Donna Mills), Laura Lockwood/Valerie Steffan (Patty Duke Astin), Mrs. Lockwood (June Lockhart), Olga (June Allyson), Ragsdale (Max Gail), Aspa Soldado (Jeff Corey), Flaps (Roz Kelly), Lazlo Cozard (Sid Caesar), Lt. Gully Conti (Vic Morrow), Carlo Lenzi (Michael DeLano), Jeff Wallace (Robert Burton), Oakes (Bryan O'Byrne), Jennifer (Rosanna Locke), Hank (Robert Nadder), Gymnast (Tracy Curtis), Marion "Popeye" Sykes (H.B. Haggerty), Summers (Bruce French), Rita (Irene Forest), Sophie (Mari Gorman), Charlene (Elizabeth Grey), Gianni (Crofton Hardester), Jarker (Howard Honig)

Credits: Director-Executive Producer: Dan Curtis; Writers: Robert Blees, Earl M. Wallace; Story: Robert Blees; Producer: Steven North; Associate Producer: Steven P. Reicher; Photography: Paul Lohmann, Stevan Larner; Art Director: Phil Barber; Music: Robert Cobert; Editor: Leon Carrere; Produced by Dan Curtis Productions, ABC Circle Films

When Leigh Lockwood's fiancé dies—body slashed open and drained of blood—suspicion centers on Leigh, whose husband died mysteriously several years before. Leigh hires PI Higbie to clear her name. Higbie discovers there've been several such killings recently—and the next victim is the witness who saw Leigh's fiancé die. Next, prim Laura Lockwood's fiancé buys it, and forensics show the killer took bullets at point-blank range without harm.

Higbie learns that an Indian curse can turn a woman into an unkillable giant spider. It's triggered by natural spider-bites, and one of the Lockwoods was badly bitten as a baby.... While he pieces it together, Laura's malevolent split personality, Valerie, uses her spider-form to web Leigh within Valerie's underground nest, killing anyone who interferes. When Higbie finds Laura, Valerie attacks as a giant black widow, but he destroys the spider with its one weakness, fire. The nightmare is over ... except that Laura's young daughter bears the black-widow hourglass mark on her belly, for she has inherited the curse.

Curse is a good film, reminiscent of Curtis' *Night Stalker* (though throwing in a split personality was a little over the top). And why (other than plot convenience) does Laura web Leigh up without killing her?

DANGER ISLAND
NBC, 9/20/92

Cast: Diana (Lisa Banes), Ben Fields (Richard Beymer), Melissa (Maria Celedonio), Rick Piersall (Gary Graham), Laura (Kathy Ireland), Matt (Joe Lara), Brian (Christopher Pettiet), Karen (Beth Toussaint), Lt. Vic Marshall (Eddie Velez), Ariel (Nikki Cox), Kate (June Lockhart), Frank (Steve Goldsberry), Tupac (Ray Bumatai), Chief (Kimo Hugho), Linda (Gina Maria Aurio), Paul (Ned Van Zandt), Maria (Annie MacLachlan)

Credits: Director: Tommy Lee Wallace; Writer: William Bleich; Producers: William Bleich, Ted Adam Swanson; Executive Producers: Frank von Zerneck, Robert M. Sertner; Photography: Alan Caso; Production Design: Richard B. Lewis; Music: Peter Manning Robinson; Editor: Michael Brown; Produced by Von Zerneck/Sertner Films, NBC

Fleeing a war-torn tropical nation, Rick's charter plane crashes into the sea with the usual mix of passengers (scientist Diana, brainy model Laura, soldiers, diplomats, kids) who wash ashore on an island paradise. There is, of course, a serpent in Eden—a tentacled monster that attacks and poisons Rick and Frank. Frank mutates into a monster overnight and flees; Rick mutates slightly and starts suffering psychic flashes of danger.

Despite Rick's warnings, the group follows an old road to an abandoned lab, which they discover was a U.S. base that used the island creatures—including a native tribe—as guinea pigs for genetic engineering until one scientist unleashed a mutagen that killed the researchers. Frank catches up with the group, but the psychic impressions of the scientists' angry debates drive him berserk. When Diana discovers an antidote, Rick risks his life to give Frank the cure, which restores him to normal before he dies. Diana adapts the drug to cure Rick (though his psychic powers remain), and the castaways resolve to heal the island's genetic scars as best they can until they're finally rescued.

This unsuccessful pilot spends way too much time on set-up, and not enough on the pulp thrills and monsters. Familiar faces include Graham (*Alien Nation*), Toussaint (guest appearances everywhere from *Star Trek: The Next Generation* to *Nightmare Cafe*), model/actress Kathy Ireland, Lara (*Tarzan: The Epic Adventures*), TV veteran Lockhart and Nikki Cox (a few years before she became the sexy star of *Unhappily Ever After*).

DARK PLANET
Sci-Fi, 6/21/97

Cast: Anson Hawke (Paul Mercurio), Liz Bender (Harley Jane Kozak), Winter (Michael York), Solara (Maria Ford), Byron (Ed O'Ross), Fletcher (Phil Morris), Cassian (Amy Beth Cohn), First Mate (Blake Boyd), Helmsman (Rick Johnson), Alpha Males (Rod Arrants, Edward Evanko), General (John Beck), Presman (Mark Folger), Alpha Female (Karen Mayo-Chandler)

Credits: Director: Albert Magnoli; Writers: S.O. Lee, J. Reifel; Producers: John Eyres, Barnet Bain; Associate Producer: Cynthia H. Margulis; Executive Producers: Paul Eyres, John Eyres; Photography: Wm. MacCollum; Production Design: John Zachary; Music: Marco Marinangeli; Editor: Amanda I. Kirpaul; Produced by EGM Films International, A-Pix Entertainment

In 2638 war between genetically enhanced Alphas and human Rebels ends with an abrupt truce and a joint space mission to the "dark planet" on the far side of a wormhole. Winter, an Alpha, commands the ship, and human mercenary Anson Hawke—the only man ever to cross the wormhole—pilots the ship.

When leftover Rebel mines are found blocking the wormhole, Hawke risks his life to draw them away from the ship. When he returns, he discovers Winter has hidden Alpha soldiers aboard. Winter has also brought a satellite that will jam the navigation systems of any Rebel ships approaching the wormhole. Winter forces Hawke to steer them through the wormhole, but the Rebels join forces with renegade Alpha Solara, kill Winter, and deactivate the satellite. They learn the reason for the truce is that biological weapons used during the war will soon render Earth lifeless; a dark-planet colony is humanity's only hope. Solara, Rebel leader Liz and Hawke force Earth to send colonists through peacefully, and a new day dawns for humanity.

Dark Planet is stock, but competent.

DARKER SIDE OF TERROR
CBS, 4/3/79

Cast: Prof. Paul Corwin/The Clone (Robert Forster), Margaret Corwin (Adrienne Barbeau), Professor Meredith (Ray Milland), Professor Sidney Hillstrom (David Sheiner), Lt. Merholz (John Lehne), Ann Sweeney (Denise DuBarry), Roger (Jack DeMave), Ed Linnick (Thomas Bellin), Jenny (Heather Hobbs), Watchman (Edie Quillan), Clone (Raye Sheffield), Guard (Russell Shannon), Dr. Tapler (Jim Nolan), Audrey Linnick (Madeleine Shaner), Skaters (Johnny Hock, Tom Elliott)

Credits: Director: Gus Trikonis; Writer-Producers: Al Ramrus, John Herman Shaner; Executive Producer: Bob Banner; Associate Producer: Clyde Phillips; Photography: Donald M. Morgan; Art Director: William Sandell; Music: Paul Chihara; Editor: Ann Mills; Produced by Shaner-Ramrus Productions, Bob Banner Associates

Biology professor Corwin is horrified to learn his mentor, Meredith, is performing unsanctioned cloning, including creating a human clone grown from Corwin's blood. Then Corwin's rival, Hillstrom, steals Corwin's research and uses it to cheat Corwin out of a promotion. Furious, Corwin rejoins Meredith, neglecting his wife, Margaret, in his thirst for scientific success.

The professors accelerate the clone's growth to adulthood, computer-teach him and prepare to present him to the world—but the nervous Clone runs off. A student with a crush on Corwin picks up the Clone in a bar; overwhelmed and confused by his sexual feelings, the clone accidentally kills her. Worried, Meredith decides to kill the Clone (over Corwin's objections), but the Clone kills him first. Leaving the lab, the clone meets Margaret, and his love-smitten response to her reignites her love for her "husband." Meanwhile, Hillstrom discovers the lab and plots to destroy Corwin by exposing his illegal research; the Clone kills Hillstrom instead. When Corwin realizes the Clone has bedded his wife, the two men come to blows. One of them kills the other, destroys the lab and the evidence, and returns home to Margaret. But which one?

Though nothing dazzling, *Darker Side of Terror* is a competent thriller, with Barbeau (the first *Swamp Thing* film and *Creepshow*) and movie veteran Milland.

DAUGHTER OF DARKNESS
CBS, 1/26/90

Cast: Cathy Thatcher (Mia Sara), Anton Crainic/Constantin Cyprian (Anthony Perkins), Grigore (Robert Reynolds), Max (Dezső Garas), Jack Devlin (Jack Coleman), Nicole (Erika Bodnár), Jassy (Kati Räk), Gypsy (Agi Margittai), Co. Massoff (Attila Löte), Elena (Mari Kiss), Lucian (Ferenc Nemethy), Janos (Istvan Hunyadkurthy), Priest (Robert Gottesmann)

Credits: Director: Stuart Gordon; Writer-Co-Producer: Andrew Laskos; Producer: Andras Hamuri; Executive Producers: Harry Chandler, Gerald W. Abrams; Photography: Ivan Mark; Production Design: Tamas Hornyanszky; Music: Colin Towns; Editor: Andy Horvitch; Produced by Accent Entertainment, King Phoenix Entertainment

American Cathy visits Rumania seeking her Rumanian father, who vanished years ago after a whirlwind romance with Cathy's late mother. Cathy's nosing around attracts the attention of the secret police, U.S. consul Jack, local stud Grigore and her father's friend, Crainic. Cathy learns that a pendant she inherited comes from the Cyprians, nobles cursed with vampirism.

Grigore, a vampire, seduces then imprisons Cathy; he reveals that Crainic is really her father, vampire overlord Constantin Cyprian. Grigore believes breeding with half-vampire Cathy will create super-vampires immune to sunlight; Constantin opposes the plan and frees Cathy, but Grigore recaptures them both. Jack tracks Cathy down and frees her and Constantin; they burn down the vampire's lair, and Constantin sacrifices himself dragging Grigore to his death in the flames. Cathy and Jack leave to start a new life together.

Despite the work of horror veteran Perkins and director Gordon (best known for his black-humored *Re-Animator*), this is very dull.

DAYBREAK
HBO, 5/8/93

Cast: Torch (Cuba Gooding, Jr.), Blue (Moira Kelly), Laurie (Martha Plimpton), Hunter (Omar Epps), Anna (Alice Drummond), Bucky (David Eigenberg), Willie (Amir Williams), Lennie (John Cameron Mitchell), Simon (Willie Garson), Quarantine Guard (Mark Boone, Jr.), Mom (Deirdre O'Connell), Payne (Jon Seda), Russell (Phil Parolisi), Trucker (Paul Butler), Woman in Quarantine (Alix Koromzay), Coughing Man (Charles Cragin), Mrs. Chaney (Novella Nelson), Tommy (Charles "Soft Food" Mattocks), Home Guardsman (Spike Alexander), Mechanic (Steven Rodriquez), Commander (Nick Chinlund), Paramedic (Scott Zigler), Sick Woman (Billi Vitale), Junkie (Herminio Vallejo III), Wino (Stuart Rudin), Receptionist (D. Garen Tolkin), Workfare Man (Skipp Sudduth), Security Cop (Marc B. Galishoff), Man in Abstinence Commercial (Phil Hartman), with John Savage

Credits: Director-Writer: Stephen Tolkin, based on Alan Bowne's play *Beirut*; Producer: John Bard Manulis; Executive Producers: Kathryn Galan, Colin Callender; Photography: Tom Sigel; Production Design: Leslie Pope; Music: Michel Colombier; Editor: Brunilda Torres; Produced by HBO

In the 21st century, the U.S. government has become a police state, justifying its ruthlessness by the need to quarantine carriers of a lethal, AIDS–like virus. Blue, an inner-city waif, falls in love with Torch, a leader in the underground that keeps victims out of the quarantine centers and provides them with medicine. Hunter, Blue's jealous suitor, helps the feds trap Torch; he's taken to a quarantine center for interrogation, then it turns out he really is infected. Blue sneaks into quarantine to see Torch, then decides to infect herself so she can stay with him. Instead, Torch convinces her to leave and continue the fight.

Daybreak is a good example of how dystopian drama (see *Last Child*) adapts to the cause du jour—in this case, AIDS and AIDS-phobia. Some scenes look a bit "stagey" (a common problem for play-inspired movies), but Gooding shows the same star power that netted him a 1997 Oscar (for *Jerry McGuire*), and Kelly is also good (though her role suffers from the Hollywood cliché that women don't fight for ideals, they fight because they love men with ideals).

DAY-O!
NBC, 5/3/92

Cast: Grace Connors (Delta Burke), Day-O (Elijah Wood), Margaret DeGeorgio (Carlin Glynn), Ben Connors (Charles Shaughnessy), Tony DeGeorgio (David Packer), Grace—Age 5 (Ashley Peldon), Frank DeGeorgio (Fred Dalton Thompson), Cory Connors (Caroline Dollar), Judith (Bekka Eaton), Papa Louis (Richard K. Olsen), Man at Park (Michael Hunter)

Credits: Director: Michael Schultz; Writer: Bruce Franklin Singer; Producers: Barry Bernardi, Ira Shurman; Photography: Isidore Mankofsky; Production Design: Daniel Lomino; Music: Lee Holdridge; Editor: Christopher Holmes; Produced by Steve White Productions, Walt Disney Television

No one knows it, but for several years Grace Connors has been the brains of her family's business. Credit, however, goes to her nitwitted brother Tony, who's officially in charge. Since Grace lacks the courage to take credit in the face of her critical relatives, they continue to dismiss her and praise him.

Then Day-O—Grace's childhood imaginary friend—returns to her life, leaving her doubting her sanity until she accepts that Day-O is real. Day-O is full of wild antics and crazy pranks, but his real goal is to restore Grace's self-confidence and convince her to stand up for herself. Finally, Grace and her husband Ben go on a long-awaited romantic vacation, and without her guidance, the business falls apart, and her family finally realizes who deserves the credit. Day-O leaves, his job done, to find another little girl who needs a friend.

Day-O! is a mildly amusing fantasy.

DEAD BY MIDNIGHT
ABC, 11/23/97

Cast: John Larkin/Sam Ellis (Timothy Hutton), Dr. Sarah Flint (Suzy Amis), Armand Drake (John Glover), Dr. Reilly (Max Wright),

Mackowitz (Grant Heslov), Hendricks (Brad Greenquist), Kelly Ellis (Yvonne Zima), Strickland (Reese Purser), Melanie (Christie Summerhays), Rick (Benjamin Israeli), Jared (Matthew McBride), Flower Merchant (Duane V. Stephens), Karen Ellis (Lilliana Cabal), Joan (Mowova Pryor), Mr. Mizagachi (Joey Miyoshima), Jean Jenkins (Ruth Ann), Detective (Scott Wilkinson)

Credits: Director: Jim McBride; Writer: Michael Vickerman; Producers: Kenneth H. Gross, Barbara Black, Michael Vickerman; Executive Producer: Daniel H. Blatt; Co–Executive Producers: Thomas Hohenocker, Andrej Henkler; Photography: Alfonso Beato; Production Design: Toby Corbett; Music: Mason Daring; Editor: Betsy Blankett Milicevic; Produced by Daniel H. Blatt Productions

John Larkin thinks he has the perfect life—great kids, great wife, great job—until government agents appear and drag him into a secret lab hidden in his house. Larkin escapes with superhuman strength and speed, only to find his house and family gone—with no evidence that he or they ever existed. Larkin locates his "wife"—actually scientist Sarah Flint—who reveals he was ruthless assassin Sam Ellis, who she rebuilt as a cyborg after a car crash, while a computer reprogrammed his mind (including false memories) for good. She's horrified when they discover the reverse: Ellis was a good man, and project head Drake is brainwashing him into becoming a super-assassin. And a failsafe program will erase John's mind if he's not back in the project by midnight.

Drake captures them, planning to reprogram John and kill Sarah, but John busts them both out, then goes looking for his/Sam's daughter, now in an orphanage. Drake ambushes John there, but Sarah kills Drake. The failsafe in John's mind kicks in, but he's gained enough free will to defy the computer shutdown. With Drake dead and the project discredited, he and Sarah head off with his daughter to resume a normal life.

This is a fairly entertaining variation on the government robot-assassin genre, superior to the earlier, similar *Suspect Device*. Hutton appeared in the second *Land of the Lost* SF series on Saturday morning TV, and Glover played Satan in the 1998 series *Brimstone*.

THE DEAD DON'T DIE
NBC, 1/14/75

Cast: Don Drake (George Hamilton), Jim Moss (Ray Milland), Vera LaValle (Linda Cristal), Lt. Reardon (Ralph Meeker), Frankie Specht (James McEachin), Levenia (Joan Blondell), Perdido (Reggie Nalder), Ralph Drake (Jerry Douglas), Receptionist (Milton Parsons), Priest (William O'Connell), Miss Adrian (Yvette Vickers), Prison Chaplain (Brendan Dillon), Prison Guard (Russ Grieves), Newspaper Man (Bill Smillie)

Credits: Director: Curtis Harrington; Writer: Robert Bloch; Producer: Henry Colman; Executive Producers: Douglas S. Cramer, Wilford Lloyd Baumes; Photography: James Crabe; Art Director: Robert Kinoshita; Music: Robert Prince; Editor: Ronald J. Fagan; Produced by Douglas Cramer Company

It's 1934 Chicago, and Ralph Drake—about to die for his wife's murder—makes his brother Don promise to find the real killer. Ralph's boss, Moss, supports Don's quest, but the mysterious Vera warns Don to leave town. Ralph appears alive and tricks Don into fighting Perdido, who dies; only Vera's help saves Don from a murder charge. At the undertaker's, Perdido's corpse tries to kill Don at the command of "Varek." Don calls the cops, but they find Perdido alive and well.

Vera reveals she and Perdido are zombie slaves of Varek, a voodoo-master. Like Ralph, Varek framed her for murder, then raised her after the execution. Varek's powers now strike Vera down for betraying him. Moss and Don visit Ralph's grave; Moss vanishes, zombies attack, and Specht, the key witness against Ralph, appears and rescues Don. Specht explains that Varek tricked him into killing Frances, then framed Ralph. He leads Don to a deep-freeze locker where Varek keeps his corpses; after Don goes in, a zombie kills Specht. Inside, Moss—a.k.a. Varek—tells Don his plan to enslave the city's power brokers, the first step in conquering America. Ralph attacks Don, but Don convinces him to avenge Frances by killing Varek instead. The cops arrive, but when Don takes them back inside, the corpses are gone—for the building manager is one of Varek's zombies.

This should have been much more fun—part of the problem is that the "zombies" are mind-controlled slaves like those in every other TV mind-control movie. Genre faces include Hamilton (*Love at First Bite*), Milland (*X—The Man with the X-Ray Eyes*) and Vickers (the original *Attack of the 50-Foot Woman*).

DEAD FIRE
Sci-Fi, 7/19/97

Cast: Cal Brody (Colin Cunningham), Kendall Black (Monika Schnarre), Maj. Max Durbin (Matt Frewer), Amos Tucker (C. Thomas Howell), Alexa Stant (Rachel Hayward), Celeste (Lucie Zednickova), Holden (Robert Russell), Danner (Jim Thorburn), Mathers (Gerard Whelan), Earl (Milan Gargula), Gizmo (Richard Toth), Salem Jones (Petr Drozda), Otto Klein (Martin Hub), Pitt Digger (Karel Vavrovec), Rainey (Dusan Hyska), Krypler (Zdenek Dvoracek), Cassidy (Gregory Linington), Helmsman (Mike Rohl), Guards (Barry Newton, Radek Cerny, Dave Ulrich, Zedenek Krumpl), Security Centre Operator (Angela Madden), Trent (Jiri Kraus), Springer (Pavel Kratky), Inmate (Peter Aleano), Space Baby (Katerina Krejcova)

Credits: Director: Robert Lee; Writers: Christopher Hyde, Andrew McEvoy, Nicholas Racz; Producer: Lloyd A. Simandl; Executive Producers: Lloyd A. Simandl, Michelle Gahagan; Photography: Dave Pelletier; Music: Peter Allen; Editor: Richard Benwick; Produced by North American Pictures, Do or Die Productions, Inc.

The crew of the spaceship *Legacy* has two missions: revive the lifeless future Earth, and preserve humanity until then in the ship's cryonic freezers. *Legacy* security chief Stant frees her lover, Durbin, and his followers from the brig. Durbin takes over the ship and plans to revive Earth—under his rule—with energy from a satellite network, even though the drain on the ship's power will deactivate the freezers. His only opponents: security officer Brody, his scientist lover Kendall and Tucker, a pool shark Durbin mistakenly revived from cryo (he wanted Tucker's scientist twin to work the satellites). Brody sabotages the satellite controls but has to trade replacement parts for Kendall's life. The couple escape the *Legacy*, but Durbin shoots them down. Tucker rescues them, then repositions the satellites with his knowledge of trajectories so the rays destroy Durbin, then revive Earth without draining the freezers.

Dead Fire is a dull action film with Frewer (*Max Headroom*) in an atypical villainous role.

DEAD OF NIGHT
NBC, 3/28/77

Cast: (1) Frank Cantrell (Ed Begley, Jr.), Vince McCauley (E.J. Andre), Mrs. McCauley (Ann Doran), Helen McCauley (Christine Hart), with Orin Cannon, Jean LeVouvier, Dick McGarvin, Karen Hurley; (2) Alexis Gheria (Anjanette Comer), Dr. Peter Gheria (Patrick Macnee), Karl (Elisha Cook), Michael (Horst Buchholz); (3) Bobby (Lee Montgomery), Helen (Joan Hackett)

Credits: Director: Dan Curtis; Writer: Richard Matheson, based on Jack Finney's "Second Chance" and Matheson's "There Is No Such Thing As a Vampire" and "Bobby"; Producer: Robert Singer; Photography: Ric Waite, Paul Lohmann; Art Director: Trevor Williams; Music: Robert Cobert; Editor: Dennis Virkler; Produced by Dan Curtis Productions

(1) "Second Chance": Frank, an antique car buff, rebuilds and drives a rare 1926 classic car—right back into 1926, where he loses it to a thief. Returning to the present, he meets his dream girl, Helen, and discovers it was her father, Vince, who took the car—and if Frank hadn't thereby changed Vince's life, Vince would have died long before Helen could be born.

(2) "There Is No Such Thing as a Vampire": Skeptical Dr. Gheria doesn't want to admit his wife Alexis is a vampire's prey, but when he does, he summons his friend Michael for help. Then he drugs Michael and hides him in a coffin—for Gheria, knowing Michael is Alexis' lover, has faked the vampire attacks so that when the servants find Michael in a coffin, they'll take appropriate steps...

(3) "Bobby": Unable to accept her son's drowning, his adoring mother, Helen, summons him back from the dead with sorcery. At first, Helen is overjoyed—but before long, the terrified mother is playing a desperate game of hide-and-seek in the dark with the

malevolent child. For the truth is Bobby drowned himself to escape his abusive, smothering mother—and rather than come back, he's sent a demon in his place to play with Helen...

Like Curtis' *Trilogy of Terror,* this was an unsuccessful pilot for a supernatural anthology (*In the Dead of Night* was an earlier Curtis pilot about a paranormal investigator, but this film more likely takes its title from a classic 1945 horror anthology). Although the stories take place by day, a voice-over explains that when weird things happen, it's *always* the dead of night. As with *Trilogy of Terror,* it's the third episode that stands out (and has the same cat-and-mouse elements that made "Amelia" so scary), which may be why Curtis remade "Bobby" for *Trilogy of Terror II.*

DEAD WEEKEND
Showtime, 10/8/95

Cast: Weed (Stephen Baldwin), Payne (David Rasche), Emelia (Bai Ling, Afifi Alaquie, Blair Valk, Jennifer MacDonald, Barbara Alyn Woods), McHacker (Alexis Arquette), Hayden (Nicholas Worth), Joe Blow (Tom Kenny), Captain (Perry Lang), Newscaster (Cindy Morgan), General Miles (Sam Scarber), Gonzolo (Marcos Antonio Ferraez), Rebels (Richard Speight, Jr., Patrick Cupo), Trooper (Joe Davis), Soldier (Craig Kvinsland, Greg Wrangler, Greg Collins, Clint Culp, Jon Regnery), Medic (David Millbern), Waitress (Stacey Strauss)

Credits: Director-Story: Amos Poe; Writer: Joel Rose; Producer: Larry Estes; Executive Producers: Miles A. Copeland III, Paul Colichman; Co-Executive Producers: Amos Poe, Damian Jones; Associate Producers: Jonas Thaler, Cindy Morgan; Photography: Gary Tilche; Production Design: Gustav Alsina, Wayne Beswick; Music: Steve Hunter; Editor: Fabienne Rawley; Produced by Showtime, Paramount, IRS Media Inc., Century Group Ltd.

When an alien lands in a near-future city dominated by the paramilitary Total World Force, the TWF sets out to hunt it down. A TWFer, Weed, finds a beautiful black woman hiding, but instead of turning her in, they make love—a lot. When Weed returns with his friend Payne, the woman has become white; it's the alien, a horny shapeshifter for whom sex is a power source. Despite Payne's horrified xenophobia, Weed falls for Emelia, who tries to leave him (for fear the TWF will target him too). He insists on helping her reach her saucer and offers to leave Earth with her. Soldiers attack, injuring Weed, but Emelia shames them into allowing her to take Weed and depart.

This is such a waste of time, possibly they started with a fantasy ("Hey, Beavis, wouldn't it be great to have a woman who could look like anyone you wanted and was insatiably horny, heheheheh?") and tried to build a movie around it.

DEADLY LOVE
Lifetime, 11/9/95

Cast: Rebecca Barnes (Susan Dey), Detective Sean O'Connor (Stephen McHattie), Elliott (Eric Petersen), Liz Poole (Julie Khaner), Jim King (Robert S. Woods), Antoine (Jean LeClerc), Sal Consentino (David Ferry), Steve Merritt (Roman Podhora), Froman (Henry Alessandroni), Griffith (Kelly Fiddick), Rita Berwald (Suzanne Coy), Derek Green (Jim Codrington), Cabbie (Bernard Browne)

Credits: Director: Jorge Montesi; Writer: Rob Gilmer, from Sherry Gottlieb's novel, *Love Bite*; Producer: Julian Marks; Executive Producers: Les Alexander, Don Enright; Supervising Producer: Clara George; Photography: Thomas Burstyn; Production Design: Gerry Holmes; Music: Micky Erbe, Maribeth Solomon; Editor: Pia Di Ciaula; Produced by Power Pictures, Alexander/Enright & Associates, Victor Television

Rebecca Barnes is a successful photographer—and a 200-year-old vampire, as lonely for the right man as any human woman. When Detective O'Connor begins investigating a series of vampire murders, he meets Rebecca and romantic sparks fly—but can she trust him with the truth about her?

This attempt at a supernatural romance is undone by Dey's vapid performance in the lead.

DEATH DREAMS
Lifetime, 6/25/91

Cast: George Westfield (Christopher Reeve), Krista Westfield (Marg Helgenberger), Dr. Margaret Neuberger (Fionnula Flanagan), Jenny

(Taylor Fry), Dr. Drake (George Dickerson), Bennett Massell (Conor O'Farrell), Denise Massell (Cec Verrell), Fromme (Jim Jarrett), Mimi (Jan Devereaux), Mrs. Parker (Pat Atkins), Dr. Holvag (Kevin Page), Dr. Green (Robert Ward), Judge Wiley (Harry Johnson), Jury Foreman (Richard Morrison), Bailiff (Wendell Grayson), Priest (Jack Angeles), Ambulance Assistant (John Rubinow), Guard (Tom Mustin)

Credits: Director: Martin Donovan; Writer: Robert Glass, based on William Katz's novel; Producer: Ron Weisberg; Executive Producers: Dick Clark, Bob Rubin, Bill Siegler; Associate Producer: Jeanne M. Van Cott; Photography: James Chressanthis; Production Design: Stephen Greenberg; Music: Gerald Couriet; Editor: John A. Martinelli; Produced by Capital Cities/ABC, Dick Clark Film Group, Inc., Ron Weisberg Productions

Wealthy Krista's life—adoring second husband George, beloved daughter Jenny—falls apart when Jenny drowns. Months later, after an accident briefly leaves Krista medically dead, Jenny contacts her, claiming George murdered Jenny rather than share Krista's love. When George's psychiatrist can't cure Krista's delusions, she seeks out Neuberger, an occultist who believes Jenny's ghost is real.

Jenny leads Krista to evidence of the murder, so Krista takes the case to court. George's attorney explains away the evidence and discredits Neuberger by exposing her shady past. George goes free, but Jenny lures him back to the river and drowns him.

Except for Helgenberger's excellent performance, *Death Dreams* is utterly humdrum.

THE DEATH OF THE INCREDIBLE HULK
CBS, 2/18/90

Cast: David Banner (Bill Bixby), Hulk (Lou Ferrigno), Dr. Ronald Pratt (Philip Sterling), Jasmin (Elizabeth Gracen), Kasha (Andreas Katsulas), Amy Pratt (Barbara Tarbuck), Bela (Anna Katerina), Betty (Chilton Crane), Bank Teller (Carla Ferrigno), Tom (Duncan Fraser), Brenn (Dwight McFee), Crane (Lindsay Bourne), Pauley (Mina E. Mina), Luanne Crane (Marlane O'Brien), Shoup (Garwin Sanford), Dodger (Justin DiPego), Aaron Colmer (Fred Henderson), Carbino (Judith Maxie), George Tilmer (French Tuckner)

Credits: Director–Executive Producer: Bill Bixby; Writer: Gerald DiPego; Producers: Hugh Spencer Phillips, Robert Ewing; Photography: Chuck Colwell; Production Design: Douglas Higgins; Music: Lance Rubin; Editor: Janet Ashikaga; Produced by Bixby-Brandon Productions, New World Television

Following *The Trial of the Incredible Hulk*, David poses as a retarded janitor in order to covertly steer Dr. Pratt's gamma-radiation research toward a cure for the Hulk. When Pratt discovers David's secret, they agree to work together. Meanwhile, Jasmin, a former spy, is forced by Kasha—who holds Jasmin's sister, Bela, hostage—to steal Pratt's computer files.

Jasmin's theft comes the night of David's cure; Pratt is injured before completing the experiment and the Hulk emerges, driving Jasmin away. Kasha assumes the Hulk is a super-soldier created by Pratt and sends Jasmin back to capture David. She succeeds, but then Kasha's men try to kill her. After David saves her, one of the killers reveals Bela is really Kasha's boss.

David and Jasmin become lovers and decide to start new lives together—but postpone their plans when Bela kidnaps the Pratts. Jasmin and David find Bela's hideout and free the Pratts, but when Jasmin is threatened, David "Hulks out" and destroys Bela and Kasha's getaway plane as it takes off. When the Hulk falls back to Earth, the impact proves more than even he can survive.

This is the (very) final entry in the series (the death is still a surprise) and an unsuccessful pilot for Jasmin's future adventures. Villainous Katsulas is now better known as *Babylon 5*'s G'Kar.

DEATH TAKES A HOLIDAY
ABC, 10/23/71

Cast: Peggy Chapman (Yvette Mimieux), David Smith (Monte Markham), Selena Chapman (Myrna Loy), John Cummings (Bert Convy), Judge Earl Chapman (Melvyn Douglas), Senator Earl Chapman, Jr. (Kerwin Mathews), Marion Chapman (Priscilla Pointer), Martin Herndon (Austin Willis), Tony Chapman (Colby Chester), Ellen Chapman (Maureen Reagan), TV Announcers (Mario Machado, Regis J. Cordic)

Credits: Director: Robert Butler; Writer: Rita Larkin, adapted by Walter Ferris from the play by Alberto Casella; Producer: George Eckstein; Photography: Michael Margulies; Art Director: Eugene Lourie; Music: Laurindo Almeida; Editor: Michael Economou; Produced by Universal

Aging judge Chapman is confronted one night by Death—not to take him, but asking for help understanding why mortals cling so desperately to life. Chapman reluctantly introduces "David Smith" to his family. While David unexpectedly falls for the judge's vivacious daughter, Peggy, victims of accident, violence and sickness find that with Death off-duty, they linger in life with no end to their pain. When Peggy is fatally injured, David decides to remain mortal forever rather than take her. Peggy, however, learns who he is, and rather than leave the world without death, she willingly goes with him into the afterlife.

This is a weak remake of the 1934 film (in which Fredric March made a far more impressive Death), with a less romantic ending—in the original, Death's absence kept everyone healthy and uninjured so his lover's decision to join him was made from pure love. Old-movie fans should enjoy seeing Mathews, Douglas and Loy—but look for them in a better movie.

DEEP RED
Sci-Fi, 3/12/94

Cast: Joe Keyes (Michael Biehn), Gracie Rickman (Lindsey Haun), Monica Qwik (Joanna Pacula), Mrs. Rickman (Lisa Collins), Thomas Newmeyer (John de Lancie), Warren Rickman (Tobin Bell), Mack Waters (John Kapelos), Musclemen (Daniel Barringer, John Alden), Lydia (Chayse Dacoda), Lew Ramirez (Michael Des Barres), Patrolman (Kevin Page), Eldon James (Steven Williams), Hotel Clerk (Jamie Stern), Bradley Parker (Hank Cheyne), Janitor (Jack Andreozzi), Deputy M.E. (Eric Fleers), Desk Sergeant (Jose Rey)

Credits: Director: Craig R. Baxley; Writer–Co-Producer: D. Brent Mote; Producer: Timothy Marx; Executive Producer: Dave Bell; Photography: João Fernandes; Production Design: Garreth Stover; Music: Gary Chang; Editor: Jeff Freeman; Produced by Dave Bell Associates

Mrs. Rickman hires gumshoe Joe Keyes to protect her husband, who is hunted by his ex-boss, scientist Newmeyer, for stealing Newmeyer's research. Keyes reaches Rickman first, but when Newmeyer arrives, he proves super strong and unkillable; he and his thugs murder Rickman and frame Keyes. Keyes learns Rickman and Newmeyer are both over seventy, but they look years younger.

Keyes finds that his former lover, Monica, is working as a bodyguard to Mrs. Rickman and her daughter, Gracie. Mrs. Rickman denies knowing Keyes, but Keyes still helps them escape when Newmeyer attacks. Mrs. Rickman reveals that Newmeyer and Rickman invented "Reds"—molecule-sized nanotech machines that repair all damage to their human hosts. Rickman hid the "mother" nannite from his power-mad boss in Gracie's blood; without it, Newmeyer can't replace his worn-out Reds, but removing it will kill Gracie.

Reds also let Newmeyer change shape (he was the "Mrs. Rickman" who hired Keyes). Neumeier kills Keyes, but the PI has absorbed Reds from Gracie's body, and regenerates. Keyes kills Newmeyer with fire, the one thing that destroys Reds. He's arrested for murder, but with Gracie's help, he changes shape and escapes. He, the Rickmans and Monica head off to decide what to do with the secret of human immortality.

Though *Deep Red* is a familiar immortalist story, it's well done. Familiar faces include Biehn (*Terminator*), de Lancie (*Star Trek: The Next Generation*'s Q) and Kapelos (*Forever Knight*).

THE DEMON MURDER CASE
NBC 3/6/83

Cast: Kenny Miller (Kevin Bacon), Nancy Frazier (Liane Langland), Joan Greenway (Cloris Leachman), Father Dietrich (Eddie Albert), Richard Clarion (Ken Kercheval), Anthony Marino (Richard Masur), Charlotte Harris (Beverlee McKinsey), Connie Frazier (Joyce Van Patten), Guy Harris (Andy Griffith), Father Thomas Eagon (Frank Hamilton), Judge Lawrence Hughes (Jack Davidson), Father Carelli (Benjamin Hendrickson), Trisha Miller (Becca Lish), Gary Frazier, Jr. (Brian Lima), Father Lombino (Armen Garo), Father DeLinni (Duncan Inches), Ann-

Marie Quinn (Erika Kruse), Phillip Russo (Tom Ligon), Chief Bill Nielson (Tom Dorff), Officer Fred Byers (David Kennett), Peter Kerner (William Begley), Andrew Brooks (Peter Gerety), Sgt. Roy Newton (Tom Griffin), Demon Voice (Harvey Fierstein), with James Doerr, Richard Ferrone, Melanie Jones, Barbara Orson, Stephanie Haas, Al Conti

Credits: Director: William Hale; Writer: William Kelley, based on *The Devil in Connecticut*; Producer: Len Steckler; Executive Producers: Preston Fischer, Dick Clark; Supervising Producers: Ira Marvin, Joseph P. Kane; Photography: John Lindley; Production Design: Marc Donnenfeld; Music: George Aliceson Tipton; Editor: Scott C. Eyler; Produced by Dick Clark Productions, Len Stecker Productions

When a young boy confronts the demon that has possessed his brother, the demon takes over the boy and forces him to commit murder. Can demonic possession be a legitimate defense when he comes to trial? Or is the boy lying? And can a priest, working with a pair of demonologists, free the boy's soul?

Based on the defense claims in a then-recent trial, this was somewhat controversial (in the days before TV showed us alien autopsies on a regular basis, "based on a true story" was taken somewhat seriously). The same demonologists, the Warrens, also appear as characters in *The Haunted*.

THE DEVIL AND MISS SARAH
ABC, 12/4/71

Cast: Rankin (Gene Barry), Gil Turner (James Drury), Sarah Turner (Janice Rule), Marshal Duncan (Charles McGraw), Stoney (Slim Pickens), Holmes (Logan Ramsey), Appleton (Donald Moffat)

Credits: Director: Michael Caffey; Writer: Calvin Clements, Jr.; Producer: Stan Shpetner; Photography: Harry L. Wolf; Art Director: Arch Bacon; Music: David Rose; Editor: Budd Small; Produced by Universal

In the Old West, the pioneer Turners encounter dying Marshal Duncan and his captive, Rankin. Duncan, last survivor of a posse taking Rankin to justice (but ambushed by Rankin's Indian allies), persuades the Turners to take Rankin the rest of the way.

Bad mistake: Rankin, a powerful psychic, begins compelling Sarah (a weaker clairvoyant) to commit acts of violence. When the Indians catch up, Turner fights them off, but in the meantime Rankin gains absolute control of Sarah, turning her into his willing love slave. Toying with Turner by making Sarah a bold flirt, Rankin confronts Turner in a gunfight—but despite rigging the odds against Turner, he loses, freeing Sarah's mind and reuniting the Turners.

While critically panned (though some viewers remember it fondly), *The Devil and Miss Sarah* is reportedly a good showcase for Gene Barry as a darker version of the rather sexist womanizer he played on *Burke's Law*.

DEVIL DOG: THE HOUND OF HELL
CBS, 10/31/78

Cast: Mike Barry (Richard Crenna), Betty Barry (Yvette Mimieux), Bonnie Barry (Kim Richards), Charlie Barry (Ike Eisenmann), Shaman (Victor Jory), George (Lou Frizzell), Miles Amory (Ken Kercheval), Dunworth (R.G. Armstrong), Red-Haired Lady (Martine Beswick), Newscaster (Bob Navarro), Mrs. Hadley (Lois Ursoni), Doctor (Jerry Fogel), Superintendent (Warren Munson), Cultists (Shelley Curtis, Jan Burrell, E.A. Sirianni), Girls (Deborah Karpf, Dana Laurita), Guard (Jack Carol), Maria (Tina Menard)

Credits: Director: Curtis Harrington; Writers: Stephen Karpf, Elinor Karpf; Producers: Lou Morheim, Hal Landers; Executive Producer: Jerome M. Zeitman; Photography: Gerald Perry Finnerman; Art Director: William Cruse; Music: Artie Kane; Editors: Ronald J. Fagan, Margo Anderson; Produced by Zeitman-Landers-Roberts Productions

Shortly after the Barrys' dog is killed in a hit-and-run, their distraught daughter insists on taking in Lucky, a puppy secretly sired by a demon in a Satanist ceremony. A year later, the kids are conducting Satanic rituals in the bedroom, Betty seduces a school counselor threatening to report the kids' behavior, and anyone who threatens Lucky—from the Catholic maid to the dog next door—dies violently. Mike Barry resists the dog's influence, but can't free his family.

An occultist reveals the dog is a barguest,

a powerful demon, and that Mike has been chosen by the powers of good to stand against him. Mike visits a shaman who places a symbol on Mike's hand that will drive the demon back to hell. Returning home, Mike confronts the barguest in its monstrous true form; despite all its power, Mike exorcises it and frees his family.

This comes perilously close to being a parody of demonic possession movies, but it actually works as a straight horror film; great fun. With Mimieux (the theatrical *Time Machine*), Eisenmann (the *Fantastic Voyage* series) and Beswick (veteran of several Hammer horror films).

THE DEVIL'S CHILD
ABC, 10/26/97

Cast: Nikki DiMarco (Kim Delaney), Alex Rota (Thomas Gibson), Ruby (Colleen Flynn), Tim (Matthew Lillard), Ezra Hersch (Tracey Walter), Eva (Gia Carides), Max (Martin Davidson), Father Darcy (Christopher John Fields), Lena (Ivana Milavich), Todd Gilman (Larry Holden), Mrs. DeMarco (Grace Zabriskie), Young Nikki (Rachael Bella), Det. Rapp (Henry Sanders), Dr. Zimmerman (Paul Bartel), Nurse (Laura Hinsburger), Sam (Nick Roth), Holly (Maya Rudolph), Dr. Haft (Lauren Tom)

Credits: Director: Bobby Roth; Writer: Pablo F. Fenjves; Story–Co-Producers: Pablo F. Fenjves, Laurence Minkoff; Producer: Mark S. Glick; Executive Producers: David R. Ginsburg, Craig Baumgarten, Melissa Prophet, Alan Barnette; Co–Executive Producer: Kim Delaney; Supervising Producer: Karen Danaher-Dorr; Photography: Shelly Johnson; Production Design: Glenda Ganis; Music: Christopher Franke; Editor: Henk Van Eeghen; Produced by Baumgarten/Prophet Entertainment, Citadel Entertainment

Photographer Nikki DiMarco is baffled when her dying mother hints ominously at some evil threatening Nikki. What Nikki doesn't know is that when she was fatally injured as a child, Mom bartered with Satan to save Nikki's life—and the devil now plans to collect.

Soon after her mother dies, sexy theologian Alex meets and seduces Nikki; despite the fact she's sterile, she conceives a child. Anyone who interferes with the romance dies violently. Nikki begins to suspect Alex is Satan, but her doctor, her therapist and her best friend convince her otherwise (because they're all servants of Lucifer). After the birth, Nikki learns the truth; refusing to submit to evil, she sneaks her son into church and has him baptized, breaking Satan's grasp on his soul forever.

This is a *Rosemary's Baby* knockoff—the resolution, in fact, is what Isaac Asimov proposed as the "right" ending for *Rosemary's Baby*.

DEVIL'S FOOD
Lifetime, 9/2/96

Cast: Sally McCormack (Suzanne Somers), Andrew Burnside (William Katt), Seymour (Dabney Coleman), Charles (Charles Frank), Dorie (Shannon Lawson), Tammy Willoughby (Catherine Blythe), Abbot's Clerk (Vince Corazza), Dr. Pace (Nancy Cser), Margaret (Jayne Eastwood), Stan Keats (John Evans), Reporter (Soo Garay), WPKV News Director (Stephen Graham), Deep Voice (David Hemblen), Arabian King (John Jaber), Waiter (Noam Jenkins), Don Lowell (Peter Keleghan), Martin Slatter (James Kidnie), Waitress (Deborah Kirshenbaum), Amy (Susan Kottman), Lt. Baker (John Lefebvre), WPKV Floor Manager (Larry Mannell), Phil Slater (Carol Marotte), Fan Police Officer (Colin McClean), UBC Floor Manager (Wayne Robert McNamara), Chester the Butler (Gerry Quigley), Carrie Newman (Barbara Radeski), President (George R. Robertson), Male Anchor (Ken Ryan), Don's Secretary (Arthi Sambasivan), Wendy (Polly Shannon), No-Stopping Cop (Scott Wickware), Interpreter (Kathryn Winslow), Homecoming Director (Frank Zotter)

Credits: Director: George Kaczender; Writer: Henry Olek; Co-Producer: Alda Neves; Supervising Producers: Marilyn Stonehouse, Christine Sacani; Executive Producers: Michael Jaffe, Howard Braunstein; Photography: Miklos Lente; Production Design: John Dondertman; Music: Ray Colcord; Editor: Ron Wisman; Produced by Pebblehut Productions, Jaffe/Braunstein Films, Victor Television Productions, Spectacor Films

Overweight TV anchorwoman Sally sells her soul to Seymour, an agent of hell, in return for maintaining her perfect weight effortlessly. Slim and sexy, her career takes off, but success makes her a self-serving witch. Worse, she discovers Seymour plans to collect her soul very soon by having her die in a car accident.

Sally's fiancé Andrew offers his own soul in return for Seymour postponing Sally's death six months. Seymour agrees, then watches smugly as they try to avert Sally's doom. Although they prevent the accident, Seymour reveals he can still claim their souls—but Sally reveals they've only been distracting him while they worked on their real plan, getting her pregnant. With a baby on the way, she's already one pound over her ideal weight and the contract is broken.

This odd mix of glossy soap and deal-with-the-devil story targeted Lifetime's predominantly female audience. Though slow-moving, it featured a novel way to outwit Satan. William Katt starred in the superhero parody series *Greatest American Hero*.

DISASTERS IN TIME
Showtime, 5/9/92

Cast: Ben Wilson (Jeff Daniels), Hillary Wilson (Ariana Richards), Madame Iovine (Marilyn Lightstone), Judge Caldwell (George Murdock), Undersecretary (Robert Colbert), Oscar (Jim Haynie), Reese (Emilia Crowe), Quisk (David Wells), Spail (Nicholas Guest), Reverend (Time Winters), Sue Appleton (Anna Neill), Billy Appleton (Willie Rack), Carolyn (Mimi Craven), Mrs. Beecher (Jacquie McClure), Doctor (Steven Gilborn), Principal (Vernon Barkhurst), Sheriff (J.R. Knotts), Deputy (Jeffrey Concklin), Mrs. Caldwell (Mary Marsh), Omeric (Francis Coady), Jana (Adele Taylor), Chiron (Victoria Wanberg), Andar (Gus Castaneda), Tod (Garon Grigsby), Kleph (Lori Lively), Gas Man (Walter Shane), Reporters (Ken Rector, Alex Kathehakis, Nancy Hopps), Red Cross Worker (Dion Cheese), Assistant Undersecretary (Steve Pershing), Boy (Ryan Smith), Wedding Guest (Scott Watson), Rafferty (Thomas Kent), Taxidermist (Brad Whitmore)

Credits: Director-Writer: David N. Twohy, from C.L. Moore's "Vintage Season"; Producer: John A. O'Connor; Co-Producer: Robert E. Warner; Executive Producer: Jill Sattinger, Paul White; Associate Producers: Jamie Grossman, Thomas A. Irvine; Photography: Harry Mathias; Production Design: Michael Novotny; Music: Gerald Gouriet; Editor: Glenn A. Morgan; Produced by Channel Communications, Wild Street Pictures

In the middle of a vicious custody fight with his in-laws, widowed innkeeper Ben Wilson finds himself saddled with an eccentric tour group whose odd habits and strange gadgets eventually convince him they're time travelers. He learns too late that the tour views the great disasters of history as a diversion from their boringly stable, organized era—disasters like the meteor strike that levels Ben's town and kills many of his friends. When the tour remains in town, Ben realizes there's worse to come—but not in time to save his daughter from a gas explosion at the emergency shelter.

Grief-stricken, Ben accepts a time-passport from one of the nicer tourists and goes back to rescue his daughter; instead, his in-laws have him arrested as an obvious crazy, and he's forced to call on his past self to help him out of jail. Together they manage to alert and save the town—and perhaps they've changed history enough to improve the travelers' dreary future.

This reverses the premise of "Vintage Season" (in which the time travelers visited perfect times and places in history), but it's an excellent movie, well-written and well-performed.

DR. FRANKEN
NBC, 1/3/80

Cast: Dr. Arno Franken (Robert Vaughn), John Doe (Robert Perrault), Dr. Mike Foster (David Selby), Kelli Fisher (Teri Garr), Mr. Parker (Josef Summer), Anita Franken (Cynthia Harris), Dr. Eric Kerwin (Addison Powell), Claire (Takayo Doran), Jenny (Claiborne Cury), Martin Elson (Nicolas Surovy), Arthur Gurnsey (Rudolph Willrich), Lt. Pearson (Sam Schradt), Reporter (Conchetta Tolman), Gerald Blake (Theodore Sorel), Mrs. Parker (Sylvia Lowe), Technician (Penelope Paley), Anesthesiologist (Roger Til), Bartender (Ed Van Nuys), Cop (William Huston), Doorman (Ralph Driscoll), Morgue Attendant (Norman Parker), Women (Florence Rupert, Myra Stennett)

Credits: Directors: Marvin J. Chomsky, Jeff Lieberman; Writer: Lee Thomas; Story: Lee Thomas, Jeff Lieberman, suggested by Mary Shelley's *Frankenstein*; Producer: Robert Burger; Executive Producer: Herbert Brodkin; Associate Producers: Stephen A. Rotter, Thomas DeWolfe; Photography: Alan Metzger; Production Design: Ed Wittstein; Music: John Morris; Editor: Robert M. Reitano; Produced by Titus Productions, Janus Productions, NBC

When a brain-dead John Doe falls into the

hands of transplant surgeon Arno Franken, Franken sees him as the perfect recipient for some experimental transplants, despite the objections of his outraged colleague Foster. The transplants revive Doe's higher brain functions. After Foster murders his romantic rival, Gurnsey, Gurnsey's eyes end up in Doe; fearing Doe will retain "cellular memories" from Gurnsey, Foster tries to destroy Doe, but only revives him. Doe wanders off and meets Gurnsey's lover, Kelli. Cellular memory kicks in, and Doe falls for her. When Foster finds out, he tries to kill Doe, but gets Kelli instead. Doe kills Foster, then bids Franken goodbye and heads out into the world.

Though a good idea for an updated *Frankenstein* (done better in *Mr. Stitch*), it's hard to imagine this failed pilot creating a series any different from other TV wanderers (*The Fugitive, The Immortal, Then Came Bronson*). And Vaughn gives the only decent performance—Garr gives no hint of the talent she showed in *Young Frankenstein*, or Selby of his Quentin Collins role in *Dark Shadows*.

DR. STRANGE
CBS, 9/6/78

Cast: Dr. Stephen Strange (Peter Hooten), Dr. Lindmer (John Mills), Morgan LeFay (Jessica Walter), Wong (Clyde Kusatsu), Clea Lane (Eddie Benton), Dr. Frank Taylor (Philip Sterling), Sarah (June Barrett), Nurse (Sarah Rush), Nameless One (David Hooks), Department Chief (Blake Marion), Intern (Bob Delegall), Orderly (Frank Catalano), Magician (Larry Anderson), Agnes Carson (Inez Pedroza), Mrs. Sullivan (Lady Rowlands).

Credits: Director-Writer-Executive Producer: Philip DeGuere; Producer: Alex Beaton; Associate Producer: Gregory Hoblit; Photography: Enzo A. Martinelli; Editor: Christopher Nelson; Music: Paul Chihara; Art Director: William H. Tuntke; Produced by Universal

While not up to the original comic-book series, this is the best super-hero pilot until *M.A.N.T.I.S.*

After centuries defending humanity, the aging sorcerer Dr. Lindmer prepares to pass on his power to a new apprentice. The demonic Nameless One sends Lindmer's old foe, Morgan LeFay, back to Earth (from which Lindmer banished her) to destroy either Lindmer or his successor before the power transfer. Morgan possesses psychology student Clea Lane and makes her attack Lindmer, who survives but is weakened. Traumatized, Clea winds up in Eastside Hospital, under the care of resident Stephen Strange—Lindmer's chosen successor (though Stephen doesn't know it). Morgan knows, but is too attracted to Stephen to kill him.

When Morgan traps Clea's soul, Lindmer sends an incredulous Stephen to the astral plane to retrieve Clea's spirit. Stephen succeeds, but magic so unnerves the rational psychiatrist that he refuses any further involvement in Lindmer's plans. Morgan attacks Lindmer and kidnaps him. When Stephen meets Clea for a date, Morgan uses Clea as a hostage to force Stephen into her master's realm, where she offers him wealth, power and herself if he'll forsake Lindmer.

Stephen refuses, so Morgan imprisons him too—but Lindmer has covertly given Stephen enough power to fight back and free them both. Back on Earth, Lindmer reveals he let Morgan capture him to show Stephen that supernatural evil exists and must be fought; Stephen now becomes Lindmer's disciple, while Morgan returns to Earth as leader of a New Age cult.

Marvel's Dr. Strange was never as successful as the Fantastic Four or Spider-Man, but his early stories were a cult hit due to Stan Lee's writing and Steve Ditko's phantasmagorical art (given effects limits at the time, Morgan's otherworld is a game try at duplicating Ditko's style). Director-writer DeGuere eliminated the comics' Eastern mysticism (believing it felt too sixties) and, more regrettably, Stephen's dark side (the comics' version was an arrogant, callous surgeon who'd become an embittered drunk after crippling his hands in a car accident).

Despite the changes, this is pretty good, even though Walters is way too bland as Morgan (veteran British actor John Mills walks off with the acting honors). Unfortunately, airing opposite the megahit miniseries *Roots* killed this in the ratings.

DR. WHO
Fox, 5/14/96

Cast: The Doctor (Paul McGann), Dr. Grace Holloway (Daphne Ashbrook), The Master (Eric Roberts), Chang Li (Yee Jee Tso), The Seventh Doctor (Sylvester McCoy), Miranda (Eliza Roberts), Wheeler (Catherine Lough), Curtis (Dolores Drake), Pete (William Sasso), Gareth (Jeremy Radick), Motorcycle Cop (Bill Croft), Prof. Wagg (Dave Hurtubise), Ted (Joel Wirkkunen), Guard (Dee Jay Jackson), Old Master (Gordon Tipple), News Anchors (Mi-Jung Lee, Joanna Piros), with John Novak, Michael David Simms

Credits: Director: Geoffrey Sax; Writer: Matthew Jacobs; Producer: Peter V. Ware; Executive Producers: Alex Beaton, Philip Davis Segal; Photography: Glen MacPherson; Production Design: Richard Hudolin; Music: John Debney, John Sponsler, Louis Febre; Editor: Patrick Lussier; Produced by BBC Worldwide, Universal, Amblin Entertainment

The Doctor, a time-traveling adventurer from the planet Gallifrey, is returning to his homeworld (in the TARDIS, a Gallifreyan time-ship) with the remains of his deceased archenemy, the Master. The Master's essence escapes his funeral urn and lands the TARDIS in San Francisco on December 30, 1999. Fleeing the ship, the Doctor is mortally injured in a gang firefight and—to the distress of E/R physician Grace—dies on the operating table. His Gallifreyan physiology later kicks in and regenerates a new body (his eighth).

The Master possesses a paramedic's body, but needs the Doctor's life force to sustain him. He cons Chang Li, a street kid who stole the Doctor's possessions, into using the Doctor's key to open the TARDIS—and to help open the Eye of Harmony, the TARDIS' power source that will let the Master drain the Doctor, destroying Earth in the process.

When the Doctor senses the Eye opening, he turns to Grace for help stealing a device to close the Eye and neutralize its effects. When they enter the TARDIS the Master mind-controls Grace, who helps Li capture the Doctor. Li finally realizes he's on the wrong side, so the Master kills him. The Eye opens, the world ends—but Grace snaps back to herself and saves the Doctor. The Master kills her, only to be sucked into the Eye. The Doctor uses the TARDIS to reverse time, restoring Earth and his friends to life, then leaves for new adventures.

The BBC chronicled *Dr. Who*'s adventures from 1963 through 1989, when the BBC cancelled it and insisted a new show would have to be co-produced with someone else to spread the costs around. This version did well on British TV and in video sales, but the U.S. ratings were weak and Fox opted for *Sliders* instead. Denied their dream of a *Star Trek*–scale franchise, the "Beeb" has done nothing with the series since. As to quality, this is pretty routine compared to the best *Who* episodes (and to some competing revival projects that never got off the ground), and Eric Roberts invariably annoys; McGann, however, is great as the newest Doctor.

DOG'S BEST FRIEND
Family, 3/23/97

Cast: Wiley Thompson (Adam Zolotin), Grandpa Fred Kellman (Richard Mulligan), Grandma Ethel Kellman (Shirley Jones), Mr. Teller (Bobcat Goldthwait), Peter (David Hillbern), Tim Thompson (John Novak), Cynthia (Adrienne Carter), Sam (Kyle LaBine), Bob (Tom McBeath), Jenny (Lily Shavick), Principal (Myron Natwick), Police Officer (Patrick Keating), Kid in School (Alex Doduk), Miss Melrose (Ellie Harvey) VOICES: Chief (Ed Asner), Cow (Meredith Baxter), Skip (James Belushi), Pig (Roger Clinton), Chicken (Valerie Harper), Pony (Markie Post), Goat (John Ratzenberger)

Credits: Director: Allan A. Goldstein; Writer–Co–Executive Producer: Nancey Silvers; Story: Lanny Horn, Jonathan Prince, Nancey Silvers; Producers: Paul Colichman, Mark R. Harris, James Shavick; Executive Producers: Stephen P. Jarchow, Peter Samuelson, Marc Samuelson, Jonathan Prince; Photography: Rod Parkhurst; Music: David Lawrence; Editors: Stephen Myers, Joanne D'Antonio; Produced by Samuelson Productions, Once a Frog, Regent Entertainment, MTM, Family Channel

When Wiley's newly widowed father ships Wiley off to his grandparents in the country, the kid expects to die of boredom ... until a comet crosses the farm one night and endows Wiley with the power to speak to animals. The animals warn Wiley that Bob, the greedy local banker, will foreclose on the farm in eight days (he plans to sell all the local farmland to developers). The animals then badger Wiley into helping Fred raise the money for the mortgage.

Grandpa's moneymaking schemes all fall flat, so Wiley plays his own angle, winning the science fair, then betting the prize money on the local horse races (using his powers to learn the real odds). The departure of the comet strips away Wiley's powers at a crucial moment—not to mention the fact that the banker has secretly entered a ringer in the race—but with the help of his human friends, Wiley still makes enough to save the farm, then uses the animals' knowledge of Bob's schemes to pressure him into giving all the farmers credit. Finally, he learns his powers came not from the comet, but as a loving gift from his mother's spirit.

Speaking to animals is one of the classic fantasy themes, turning up everywhere from Norse mythology to Dr. Doolittle and *Mr. Ed*. This version is amiable fluff.

DON'T BE AFRAID OF THE DARK
ABC, 10/10/73

Cast: Sally Farnham (Kim Darby), Alex Farnham (Jim Hutton), Joan (Barbara Anderson), Harris (William Demarest), Francisco Perez (Pedro Armendariz, Jr.), Ethyl (Lesley Woods), Doctor (Robert Cleaves), Policeman (Sterling Swanson), George Kahn (J.H. Lawrence), Tom Henderson (William Sylvester), Bob (Don Mallon), Anne (Celia Kaye), Bartender (Ted Swanson), Creatures (Felix Silla, Tamara Detreaux, Patty Maloney), Guests (Ethel St. Clair, Monica Henreid, Robert Priest)

Credits: Director: John Newland; Writer: Nigel McKeand; Producer: Allen S. Epstein; Associate Producer: Neil T. Maffeo; Photography: Andrew Jackson; Production Design: Ed Graves; Music: Billy Goldenberg; Editor: Michael McCroskey; Produced by Lorimar Productions

Sally Farnham was overjoyed when she and her husband moved into her late uncle's old country mansion. But she can't understand why Uncle boarded up the cellar doors, some of the closets, and completely bricked up one fireplace—which handyman Harris warns Sally should never be unplugged. Sally doesn't listen ... and before long, her every move is being shadowed by grotesque, furry gnomes living in the walls. Alex, fixated on securing a promotion, brushes aside Sally's stories of stalking horror as hysterical woman's talk. The gnomes become more aggressive, killing decorator Perez, which leaves Sally shell-shocked. The gnomes drug Sally with sleeping pills while Alex, finally alarmed, learns from Harris that the sealed doors and fireplace date from before Sally's uncle—who was dragged inside the fireplace after he made the mistake of opening it up. Alex returns to the house as the gnomes drag Sally into the walls—and all he finds is a hole reaching into the depths of the earth. Inside the hole, Sally assures the gnomes that soon, very soon, they will escape forever...

This is enjoyably creepy.

DOOM RUNNERS
Showtime, 12/20/97

Cast: Jada Wesley (Lea Moreno), Dr. Kao (Tim Curry), Deek (Dean O'Gorman), Adam (Bradley Pierce), Vike (Nathan Jones), Lizzie (Rebecca Smart), William (Peter Carroll), Thorne (David Whitney), Danny (Putu Winchester), Cesar Lopez (Paul Livingston), Rule (Jon Pollard), Resistance Fighter (Ken Goodlett), Endgame Man (Michael Lake), Doom Trooper Supervisor (Deobia Oparei), Doom Troopers (Bruce Mexon, Tony Forrow, Mark Connolly), Kids (Justin Rosniak, Toby Chan, Adam Moulds, Sean Hall)

Credits: Director: Brendan Maher; Writers: Barney Cohen, Ken Lipman; Producer: Posie Graeme-Evans; Executive Producers: Albie Hecht, Barney Cohen, Paula Hart, Kathryn Wallack; Co-Executive Producer: Douglas Greiff; Photography: Steve Arnold; Production Design: David McKay; Music: Braedy Neal; Editor: Henry Dangar; Produced by Showtime, Hallmark, Nickelodeon, Millennium Pictures

Future Earth is a storm-wracked, environmentally ruined waste, dominated by the Corporation which enforces its will with armored Doom Troopers and uses telepath Dr. Kao to wipe the minds of its enemies. Jada, a young girl, receives a map from her dead grandfather showing the way to New Eden, a legendary, blue-skied haven. With Adam,

Vike and Deek in tow, Jada sets off through a waste of volcanic rifts, Trooper stations and savage storms. By blackmailing Jada's friend Lizzie, Kao learns Jada's plans and whereabouts. But when Lizzie learns Kao has mindwiped her brother, she turns against Kao and saves her friends.

To Jada's dismay, the secret passage to New Eden lies under Kao's fortress. When they try to sneak inside, Jada is captured, but she escapes in time to save the others from the Troopers. Kao confronts them at the passageway, but Vike sacrifices himself to take Kao down, leaving the others free to reach New Eden.

Doom Runners is a fairly entertaining juvenile *Road Warrior*. Tim Curry's genre credits include *Earth 2* (the TV series, not the TV movie) and Dr. Frank N. Furter in *The Rocky Horror Picture Show*.

DOUBLE, DOUBLE TOIL AND TROUBLE
ABC, 10/30/93

Cast: Kelly Farmer/Young Agatha (Mary-Kate Olsen), Lynn Farmer/Young Sophia (Ashleigh Olsen), Aunt Agatha/Aunt Sophia (Cloris Leachman), Oscar (Phil Fondacaro), Don Farmer (Eric McCormack), Christine Farmer (Kelli Fo), Gravedigger (Wayne Robson), George (Matthew Walker), Mr. N (Meshach Taylor), Hostess (Denalda Williams), Bernard Brewster (Gary Jones), Madame Lulu (Gary Jones), Chairperson (Bill Meilen), Female Cop (Nora McLellan), Pumpkin Driver (Alex Green), Doorman (Alex Diakun), Witches (Claire Caplan, Karin Konoval, Glynis Leyshon), Cop (Mitch Kosterman), Fred (Gerry McAlteer), Kids (Eliza Centenera, Christopher Anderson), Singer (Lynda Boyd), Fat Man (Ian Bagg), Girl's Mother (Freda Perry)

Credits: Director: Stuart Margolin; Writer: Jurgen Wolff; Producers: Mark Bacino, Adria Later; Supervising Producer: Matthew O'Connor; Executive Producers: Jim Green, Allen Epstein; Production Design: David Fischer; Photography: Richard Leiterman; Music: Richard Bellis; Editor: George Appleby; Produced by Dualstar Productions, Green/Epstein Productions, Warner Bros. Television

On Halloween the desperate Farmers ask their malevolent Aunt Agatha for a loan and are curtly rejected—which they tell their twins, Kelly and Lynn, would never have happened if Agatha's sweet twin Sophia hadn't left town. Then the girls learn Sophia didn't leave: Agatha, a witch, trapped her hated twin inside a mirror from which she can only be freed at midnight on Halloween.

The girls set out to free Sophia with the help of Oscar, a clown, and the panhandling Mr. N. They steal Agatha's magic moonstone from a witch's sabbath, but Agatha and her slave George capture Lynn and turn Mr. N into a raven. Kelly and Oscar break into Agatha's house, but Sophia's spirit reveals it will take both twins—plus the moonstone—to break the spell. When Agatha arrives, N helps the twins reach the mirror with the moonstone, and their love for each other undoes the spell (and restores N). Agatha falls into the mirror world, leaving Sophia free to reunite with George—her long-lost love—and to help out the Farmers.

This attempt at a modern-day fairy tale isn't as bad as one would expect from the cutesy Olsen twins, but it has big plot holes (a magic wand the kids use that's never explained) and Leachman's too naturalistic for a fairy-tale witch.

DRACULA
CBS, 2/8/74

Cast: Count Dracula (Jack Palance), Arthur Holmwood (Simon Ward), Dr. Van Helsing (Nigel Davenport), Mrs. Westerna (Pamela Brown), Lucy Westerna (Fiona Lewis), Mina Murray (Penelope Horner), Jonathan Harker (Murray Brown), Dracula's Wives (Sarah Douglas, Virginia Wetherall, Barbara Lindley), Innkeeper (George Pravda), Innkeeper's Wife (Hanna Maria Pravda), Zookeeper (Reg Lye), Priest (Fred Stone), Whitby Inn Maid (Sandra Caron), Whitby Inn Clerk (Roy Spencer), Stockton-on-Tees Clerk (John Challis), Midvale Shipping Clerk (Nigel Gregory), Richmond Shipping Clerk (John Pennington), Coast Guard (Martin Read), Madam Kirstoff (Gita Denise)

Credits: Director-Producer: Dan Curtis; Writer: Richard Matheson, from Bram Stoker's novel; Associate Producer: Robert Singer; Photography: Oswald Morris; Production Design: Trevor Williams; Music: Robert Cobert; Editor: Richard A. Harris; Produced by Dan Curtis Productions, Universal

This version of Bram Stoker's classic follows the book more closely than most screen versions, and veteran film heavy Palance gives a competent performance in the lead role. Curtis adapted several other horror classics (*The Picture of Dorian Gray, Turn of the Screw*) for ABC's *Wide World of Mystery*, not to mention liberally borrowing from them for his *Dark Shadows*.

DREAM HOUSE
UPN, 11/19/98

Cast: Richard Thornton (Timothy Busfield), Jenny Thornton (Lisa Jakub), Ray (Brennan Elliott), Michael Thornton (Dan Petronijevic), Tom (Cameron Graham), HELEN (Pam Hyatt, voice), Laura Thornton (Jennifer Dale), Sgt. Randall (Harry Nelken), Shelby (Curtis Moore), Marty (Steven McIntyre), Deliveryman (Garfield Williams)

Credits: Director: Graeme Campbell; Writer: Jim Makichuk; Producer: Michael Scott; Executive Producers: Steve White, Sheri Singer; Photography: Malcolm Cross; Production Design: James Stuart; Music: Fred Mollin; Editor: Brett Sullivan; Produced by Paramount, Credo

When the Thorntons move into Richard's prototype computer-run house, they soon find the computer, HELEN, driving them crazy by spying on them, nagging them about their diet, and illegally manipulating stock prices to keep Richard's struggling company afloat. When Richard's daughter Jenny visits, her sociopathic boyfriend steals Richard's research—so HELEN kills him. When the horrified family turn against HELEN, she turns the house into a deathtrap. Jenny tries and fails to infect HELEN with a computer virus, then falls back on distracting the computer with philosophical questions until Richard can reach the CPU and deactivate her.

Dull and formulaic.

DUPLICATES
USA, 3/18/92

Cast: Bob Boxletter (Gregory Harrison), Marion Boxletter (Kim Greist), Dr. Randolph (Cicely Tyson), Fryman (Lane Smith), Dr. Congemi (Kevin McCarthy) Chief Robinson (William Lucking), Heller/Brian (Scott Hoxby), Dr. Stanley (John Delay), Tom (Matt Williams), Clarissa (Beth Harper), Clark (Don Hibdon), Officer Michaels (Don Adler), Valerie (Timi Prulhiere), Joey (Erik Alskog), Kurt (Russ Fast), Penny (Shawna Schum), Dorothy (Barbara Kite), Jeff (Jim Hechim), Nurses (Marjorie Johnson, Cassandra Penner), Park Girl (Faye Sweeney), Pyle (Lance Seth Rosen), Bilups (John R. Knotts), Fiatt (Paul Till), Receptionist (Kim Sandstrom)

Credits: Director-Executive Producer: Sandor Stern; Writers: Sandor Stern, Andrew Neiderman; Producer: Robert M. Rolsky; Photography: Tobias Schliessler; Production Design: Bryan Ryman; Music: Dana Kaproff; Editor: Jere Huggins; Produced by Sankan Productions, Wilshire Court Productions

A year after Marion's son Joey and her brother Sam disappeared camping, Marion sees Sam—but he claims to be someone else. Obsessed, Marion obtains the man's fingerprints, which are indeed Sam's. The Boxletters (Marion and her husband Bob) visit Sam's home town—and find Joey, only he denies being their son, as do his parents.

What the Boxletters don't know is that Joey and Sam accidentally became guinea pigs for Randolph and Congemi, who cure criminals by erasing and replacing their original personalities with law-abiding ones. Sam, however, has also been programmed as an assassin—a sideline mandated by Senator Fryman before backing the project—and the stress is driving him mad.

To cover up the project, the doctors implant the Boxletters with new memories, but when the "new" people meet, they still fall in love almost instantly. Bob, now working at the doctors' research hospital, discovers they're monitoring him. He investigates—and learns who he and his new lover really are. They kidnap their son, take him to the hospital and force Randolph to restore their original memories. An insane Sam attacks them, and Marion has to kill him. Randolph then transfers his dying mind into her own body, giving her the skills to kill Congemi and Fryman and destroy the project.

Duplicates is an interesting take on familiar themes. Genre faces include McCarthy (the original *Invasion of the Bodysnatchers*) and Greist (*Brazil*).

DYING TO REMEMBER
USA, 12/2/93

Cast: Lynn Matthews (Melissa Gilbert), Mark Gage (Ted Shackleford), Detective Daniel Corso (Christopher Stone), Inspector Jeff Albert (Scott Plank), Young Mark Gage (Wade Anderson), Denise Ralston (Babz Chula), Det. Hardwick (Nathaniel Deveaux), Workman (Stephen Dimopoulos), Mary Ann Emerson (Kat Green), University Guard (Deryl Hayes), Cop (Alf Humphreys), Desk Sergeant (James Kidnie), Secretary (Judith Maxie), Young Dan Corso (Brian McGugan), Kelsey Daniels (Sandra Nelson), Woman Sergeant (Marilyn Norry), Cabbies (Alvin Sanders, Peter Williams), Maid (Helena Yee), Clerks (Robin Mossley, Lorena Gale)

Credits: Director: Arthur Allan Seidelman; Writers: George Schenck, Frank Cardea, Brian L. Ross; Story: George Schenck, Frank Cardea; Producer: Tom Rowe; Executive Producers: Frank Cardea, George Schenck; Photography: Glen MacPherson; Production Design: Mark Freeborn; Music: Jay Gruska; Editor: Bert Glatstein; Produced by Pacific Motion Pictures

All fashion designer Lynn did was brush past a man in the street—and she started seeing him in her dreams, mixed with nightmares of falling to her death. A therapist, believing these are past-life memories, teaches Lynn regression techniques, which dredge up more memories of Lynn being murdered by her past-life husband. Lynn identifies her past self as Mary Ann Gage and, with the help of smitten detective Albert, digs into Mary Ann's supposed suicide. Mary Ann's former husband, Mark Gage, knows Lynn is dangerous, but can't help falling in love with "Mary Ann" all over again. Det. Corso lures Lynn to Mary Ann's old building to stage another suicide; Lynn discovers Corso murdered Mary Ann on orders from her husband's powerful, hateful father, and Mark kept silent to protect his father's name. At the last minute, Mark intervenes, saving Lynn from Corso at the cost of his own life.

Dying to Remember is a competent film, though *Dead Again* handled the same concept better.

EARTH ANGEL
ABC, 3/14/91

Cast: Angie (Cathy Podewell), Judith (Cindy Williams), Duke (Erik Estrada), Cindy (Rainbow Harvest), Norman (Alan Young), Wayne Stein (Mark Hamill), Mr. Tatum (Roddy McDowall), Peter (Dustin Nguyen), Mike (Brian Krause), Joey (Garrett Morris), Val Boyd (Tommy Hinkley), Ginger Copelli (Kelly Christian), Joyce (Deborah Lee Johnson), Flat Top (Daran Norris), Cheerleaders (Laura Becker, Susan Egan), Jock (John Lacy), Bartender (Frank Novak), Brownnoser (Andy Dick), Hooker (Kelly Jones), Store Clerk (Tristan Tait), Wrestler (Jay Anthony Franke)

Credits: Director: Joe Napolitano; Writer: Nina Shengold; Executive Producers: Ron Gilbert, Leonard Hill, Joel Fields; Photography: Stan Taylor; Production Design: Shay Austin; Music: Kevin Klingler; Editor: James Coblentz; Produced by ACI, Ron Gilbert Associates, Leonard Hill Films

Thirty years ago, when cheerleader Angie told her arrogant jock boyfriend Duke she was dumping him for sweet, geeky Wayne, Duke lost control of his car and Angie died in the crash. Spectral guidance counselor Tatum returns her to Earth in the present to complete her "unfinished business" or be condemned to eternal detention hall. Angie decides she must help Wayne (hard and bitter since her death) and Cindy (the uncool daughter of Angie's best friend Judith) each find love. Angie steers Judith into Wayne's arms, but she also turns Cindy away from true love with geeky Peter and into jock Mike's arrogant embrace. Realizing her mistake, Angie reunites Cindy and Peter, then saves Cindy from another fatal car crash. Everyone's happy, and Angie makes it into heaven.

Earth Angel carries a weak script and dull leading lady—but *Star Wars'* Mark Hamill is good in his part, and screen veteran McDowall steals the show in his few scenes.

EARTH II
ABC, 11/28/71

Cast: David Seville (Gary Lockwood), Frank Karger (Anthony Franciosa), Jim Capa (Scott Hylands), Dr. Loren Huxley (Hari Rhodes), President Charles Carter Durant (Lew Ayres), Lisa Karger (Mariette Hartley), Walter Dietrich (Gary Merrill), Ilyana Kovalefski (Inga Swenson), Matt Karger (Brian Dewey), Anton Kovalefski (Edward Bell), Hannah Young (Diana Webster), Stiner (Bart Burns), Hazlitt (John Carter),

Chairman (Herbert Nelson), Russian (Serge Tschernisch), Technician (Vince Cannon), Surgeon (David Sachs), West (Bob Hoy)
Credits: Director: Tom Gries; Writers-Producers: William Read Woodfield, Allan Balter; Photography: Michel Hugo; Art Directors: George W. Davis, Edward C. Cafargno; Music: Lalo Schifrin; Editor: Henry Berman; Produced by MGM Television, Wabe Inc.

When the U.S. begins building the Earth II space station, the President announces it will become an independent nation, free to help Earth without regard to nationality. Nonetheless, China tries unsuccessfully to sabotage the initial launch. Several years later, after Earth II is a reality, the residents learn why when China launches a missile platform targeting Moscow into a neighboring orbit. Despite the slight radioactive risk to the station, China threatens to launch if Earth II interferes—and that will trigger World War III.

Seville, the station's pacifist leader, opts to stand pat; Frank, who believes in "peace through strength," insists the station assert itself by destroying the missile. Despite objections from his pacifist wife Lisa, Frank wins the station's support. A shuttle crew deactivates and brings the platform's missile back to Earth II, where Frank sees it as the start of an arsenal. Horrified, Lisa launches the missile into the sun to destroy it—but instead, it heads for North America. Seville recaptures the rocket, but the controls have melted from the heat of reentry; when the sun rises, the added heat will detonate it. With only seconds to spare, the crew deactivates the missile. A shaken Frank agrees that for now, he'll go along with Seville on keeping Earth II weapons-free.

This is the closest thing to Utopian SF (showing how the perfect society would work) TV's ever done; entertaining, though it shows the same bias as other period films such as *The Bamboo Saucer* in assuming Red China will not want any part of world peace.

EBBIE
Lifetime, 12/4/95
Cast: Elizabeth "Ebbie" Scrooge (Susan Lucci), Roberta Cratchitt (Wendy Crewson), Jake Marley (Jeffrey DeMunn), Tiny Tim (Taran Noah Smith), Paul Taylor (Ron Lea), Fran (Molly Parker), Rita (Lorena Gale), Deb (Jennifer Clement), Marion (Nicole Parker), Dobson (Kevin McNulty), Mrs. Dobson (Susan Hogan), Little Ebbie (Adrienne Carter), Luther (Bill Croft), Homeless Woman (Elan Ross Gibson), Martha (Laura Harris), Nurses (Sarah Hayward, Maria Herrera), Floor Manager (Gary Jones), Mrs. Taylor (Tamsin Kelsey), Ebbie's Mother (Karin Konoval), Michael (David Lovgren), Van Munsen (Tom McBeath), Ralph (Hrothgar Mathews), Ebbie's Father (Larry Musser), Patterson (Malcolm Stewart)
Credits: Director: George Kaczender; Writers: Paul Redford, Ed Redlich; Producer: Harold Tichenor; Co-Producer: Jayme Pfahl; Executive Producers: Jean Abounader, Frederick DeMann; Photography: Thomas Burstyn; Production Design: Jill Scott; Music: Lawrence Shragge; Editor: Roger Mattiusi; Produced by Crescent Entertainment, Maverick Productions, Victor Television

In this version of Dickens, "Ebbie" Scrooge's loveless, lonely childhood leaves her grasping for material success to compensate. She becomes a rising executive at a major department store, but her workaholic ways drive her great love away. As the film opens, CEO Ebbie spends Christmas Eve firing and humiliating employees and informing personal assistant Roberta Cratchitt they'll both be working Christmas Day. That night, however, her mentor, Jake Marley, appears and tells her three spirits are coming...

Ebbie is one of two feminized, updated adaptations of Dickens (see *Ms. Scrooge* for the other), with a terrific performance from soap diva Lucci as the unlovable—but not unredeemable—Ebbie.

EMMA'S WISH
CBS, 10/18/98
Cast: Emma Bridges (Joanna Kerns), Joy Bookman (Harley Jane Kozak), Mona Washburn (Della Reese), Bryan Bookman (William Moses), Harry Bridges (Seymour Cassel), Danny Bookman (Courtland Mead), Iris Bookman (Jeanne Allen), Kelly Short (Stephanie Niznik), Det. Steele (Dennis Cockrum), Carnies (D.C. Douglas, Paul Kaufman), Philip Elkan (Keith Mackechnie), Young Joy (Ashley Edner), Sue (Kim Little)
Credits: Director: Mike Robe; Writer-Co-Producer: Cynthia Whitcomb; Story: Paul A.

Kaufman, Cynthia Whitcomb; Producer: Michael O. Gallant; Executive Producer: Paul A. Kaufman; Photography: Edward Pei; Production Design: Veronica Hadfield; Music: Laura Karpman; Editor: Sabrina Plisco-Morris; Produced by Kaufman Co., Citadel Entertainment

When Emma Bridges' son Danny died years ago, it tore a hole in her family that never healed. When her daughter Joy divorces her cheating husband, Bryan, Emma offers to move in and watch the kids; Joy curtly rejects the offer. A dispirited Emma makes a birthday wish that she could help Joy—and wakes up next morning forty years younger. Posing as a housekeeper, she gets Joy to hire her, does her best to support her (despite occasional impulses to play mother), and learns Joy's view of the Emma-Joy relationship. Meanwhile, the head of Emma's retirement home alarms Joy by reporting Emma missing, possibly kidnapped.

Emma does her best to heal the wounds left by Danny's death and to give Joy a brief reunion with her long-absent father; when she learns the story of Bryan's affair (drunken one-night stand during a fit of depression) she tries to reunite them. Bryan, however, recognizes her as the woman police have linked to Emma's disappearance, so she has to tell him the truth. Emma convinces Bryan to win Joy back, then leaves when the spell wears off. Bryan tells Joy the truth and reunites her with Emma, creating a loving family at last.

Emma's Wish is a sugary but amiably enjoyable fantasy.

ENCINO WOMAN
ABC, 4/20/96

Cast: Marvin Beckler (Jay Thomas), Lucy (Katherine Kousi), David Horsenfelt (Corey Parker), Raji (Ric Overton), Jean Michel (John Kassir), Chris (Annabelle Gurwitch), Roger (Chris Hogan), Smith (Jeffrey Ross), Jones (Joel Murray), Ivana (Elisa Donovan), Marcus (Suli McCullough), Fiona (Marissa Ribisi), Yogi Paxil (Bobcat Goldthwait), Javier (Clarence Williams III), Mike (Michael Burger), Maty (Maty Monfort), Susan (Catherine Silvers), Model (Kate Gibson), Kindergartner (Ashley Monique Clark), Doorman (Jackie Beat), Celeb (Calvert DeForest), Reporter (Terry Murphy), Bobby (Spencer Garrett), Brenda (Shawn Schepps), Dr. Lambert (Jeffrey Lampert)

Credits: Director: Shawn Schepps; Writers: Anne Joseph, Shawn Schepps; Producers: Jeffrey Lampert, Irwin Marcus; Executive Producers: George Zaloom, Les Mayfield; Co-Executive Producer: Frank K. Isaac; Photography: Russ Alsobrook; Production Design: Peg McClellan; Music: David Lawrence; Editor: Duane Hartzell; Produced by Zaloom-Mayfield Productions, Disney TV

An earthquake unearths "Lucy," a cavewoman frozen in suspended animation. In a short time she becomes a cosmetics supermodel, a feminist icon (due to a misunderstanding of her few English words) and the love of yuppie Marvin Beckler's life.

The theatrical *Encino Man* in 1992 became a low-budget hit with its story of a thawed-out caveman, and inspired this name-only sequel (directed by the first movie's screenwriter).

ESCAPE TO WITCH MOUNTAIN
ABC, 4/29/95

Cast: Danny (Erik von Detten), Anna (Elizabeth Moss), Edward Bolt (Robert Vaughn), Lindsay Brown (Lynne Moody), Zoe Moon (Perrey Reeves), Claudia Ford (Lauren Tom), Luther/Bruno (Brad Dourif), Sheriff Bronson (Kevin Tighe), Waldo Fudd (Vincent Schiavelli), Xander (Sam Horrigan), Skeeta (Bobby Motown), Butler (John Pellock), Deputy (Ray Lykins), Female Cop (Beth Colt), Mr. Flynn (Daniel Lavery), TV Man (Jeffrey Lampert)

Credits: Director: Peter Rader; Writer: Peter Rader, based on a story by Robert Malcolm Young and book by Alexander Key; Producer: Joan Van Horn; Executive Producers: George Zaloom, Les Mayfield, Scott Immergul; Production Design: Peg McClellan; Photography: Russ Alsobrook; Music: Richard Marvin; Editor: Dianne Hartzell; Produced by ZM Productions

Two small children materialize at Witch Mountain, a New Age haven, then accidentally become separated. When they're reunited at a foster home nine years later, they discover they share vast psychic powers whenever they're together. Anna's clairvoyance saves the life of wealthy Bolt, who becomes their foster father in hopes of exploiting their powers. Zoe, a waitress, learns Bolt's game but can't convince anyone else—

nor does anyone believe she's seen storekeeper Fudd exhibit the same powers as the twins.

The twins finally escape Bolt's mansion and contact Fudd, who reveals they're all natives of a parallel world, visiting Earth for personal growth; humanity's ancestors came from that world, but we lost our psychic gifts as we grew more materialistic. Fudd tells the twins the gateway home will open at Witch Mountain's summit at sunset—then close again for years. With Bolt in pursuit, the kids race to the summit, helped by Zoe, their other friends and their powers. They make it to the gateway and return home, leaving Zoe to spread the news about mankind's origins to all those who seek the truth.

The 1972 version of *Escape to Witch Mountain* (originally intended for TV) was one of Disney's most successful live action films, spawning a sequel (*Return to Witch Mountain*) and an unsuccessful TV pilot (1982's *Beyond Witch Mountain*). This remake (see *Freaky Friday*) dropped some of the clichés the original suffered from (like the bumbling crooks afflicting so many seventies Disney movies), but the New Age mysti-babble gets awfully sappy.

THE EWOK ADVENTURE
ABC, 11/25/84

Cast: Mace Towani (Eric Walker), Wicket (Warwick Davis) Catarine Towani (Fionnula Flanagan), Jeremitt Towani (Guy Boyd), Cindel Towani (Aubree Miller), Deej (Daniel Frishman), Wenchee (Debbie Carrington), Widdler (Tony Cox), Chokha Trok (Kevin Thompson), Kalak (Margarita Fernandez), Shoda (Pam Grizz), Logray (Bobby Bell), Narrator (Burl Ives)

Credits: Director-Photography: John Korty; Writer: Bob Carrau, from a story by George Lucas; Producer: Thomas G. Smith; Executive Producer: George Lucas; Associate Producer: Patricia Rose Dignan; Art Director: Harley Jessup; Production Design: Joe Johnston; Music: Peter Bernstein, "Wicket's Theme" by John Williams; Editor: John Nutt; Produced by Lucasfilm Ltd., Korty Films

After the Towanis' spaceship crashes on the fourth moon of Endor, the adults disappear and young Cindel and Jeremitt are taken in by the primitive, teddy-bearish Ewoks. The children grow to love the cuddly creatures, especially young Wicket. Soon the Ewok mystic Logray discovers the adults are alive, captives of a giant monster. The kids, Wicket and the other Ewoks set out to rescue the Towanis. Despite menaces ranging from huge spiders to the giant itself, the Ewoks and the kids rescue the adults and return to the Ewok village in triumph.

The Ewoks generated a lot of flak for being just too, too cute when they first appeared in *Revenge of the Jedi*. That didn't stop them from spinning off into two TV movies, then becoming part of Saturday morning's *Ewoks/Droids Adventure Hour* (which incorporated a lot of the background developed in these two movies).

EWOKS: THE BATTLE FOR ENDOR
ABC, 11/24/85

Cast: Cindel (Aubree Miller), Wicket (Warwick Davis), Noa (Wilford Brimley), Charal (Sian Phillips), Terak (Carel Struycken), Teek (Niki Bothelo), Mace (Eric Walker), Young Witch (Marianne Horine), Deej (Daniel Frishman), Willy (Tony Cox), Shodu (Pam Grizz), Lieutenant (Roger Johnson), Card Players (Johnny Weismuller, Jr., Michael Pritchard)

Credits: Director-Writers: Jim Wheat, Ken Wheat, from a story by George Lucas; Producer: Thomas G. Smith; Executive Producer: George Lucas; Photography: Isidore Mankofsky; Production Design: Joe Johnston, Harley Jessup; Art Director: William George; Music: Peter Bernstein; Editor: Eric Jenkins; Produced by Lucasfilm Ltd.

As the Towani family works to repair their ship, they're attacked by barbarians whose leader, Terak, believes the spaceship holds "the power of the stars." Cindel, the only survivor, escapes with Wicket and finds shelter with the dour human hermit Noa—but must flee again when Terak and the witch Charal come hunting them. The villains capture Cindel, then Terak steals Charal's magic ring to add to his own power.

The Ewoks free Cindel, but Terak and his warriors pursue them. When the barbarians catch up with their prey, the Ewoks and Noa defend Cindel while Wicket faces Terak.

Wicket's chance blow destroys Charal's ring, which kills Terak, breaking the spirit of his warriors. Cindel returns to live in the Ewok village.

While clearly geared for kids, this sequel to *The Ewok Adventure* nonetheless carried a parental advisory (because of Cindel's family being butchered, one supposes).

EXO-MAN
NBC, 6/18/77

Cast: Nicholas Conrad (David Ackroyd), Emily Frost (Anne Schedeen), Raphael Torres (A. Martinez), Kermit Haas (Jose Ferrer), Martin (Jack Colvin), Travis (Harry Morgan), Rogers (Donald Moffat), DA Kamenski (Kevin McCarthy), Eddie Rubinstein (Jonathan Segal), Dominic Leandro (John Moio), Jim Yamaguchi (Richard Narita), Ted Kamenski (Martin Speer), Dr. Garrick (George Sperdakos), Larry (Randy Faustino), Jack (Nick David), TV Newsman (Wina Sturgeon), with Eve McVeagh, W.T. Zacha, Frances Osborne, Greg Barnett, Max Kleven, Terry Leonard, Alan Oliney, John Robotham, Allan Wyatt, Jr., Joe Brooks, Norma Storch, Fritz Ford, Chuck Walsh, Wally Rose, Russ Saunders, Bill Lane

Credits: Director–Executive Producer: Richard Irving; Writers: Henri Simoun, Lionel E. Siegel, from a story by Henri Simoun, Martin Caidin; Producer: Lionel E. Siegel; Photography: Enzo A. Martinelli; Art Director: John Corso; Music: Dana Kaproff; Editor: Robert Leeds; Produced by Universal

When physics professor Conrad becomes the sole eyewitness against a well-connected bank robber, crimelord Haas orders Conrad's death. Conrad survives Haas' hitmen but is crippled for life. Then, when Haas threatens Conrad's girlfriend, Emily, Conrad refuses to testify. Embittered, Conrad buries himself in his research ... and discovers an experimental compound strong and flexible enough to create a working exoskeleton.

With the addition of cannibalized electronics, Conrad creates a bulletproof, superstrong armored suit in which he ambushes one of the hitmen (who panics and dies in a fall), but Conrad almost dies when the armor malfunctions. After letting Emily in on his secret, Conrad fixes the problems, attacks Haas' mansion, and removes enough evidence to destroy Haas' empire. Travis, a federal agent with an interest in Conrad's case, guesses that Conrad is behind Haas' downfall; they agree to work together against other hard-to-catch crooks in the future.

Horribly slow at the start, *Exo-Man* picks up the pace after Conrad starts work on the armor. Still, *M.A.N.T.I.S.* (or the comics' Iron Man) did the same idea much better. Writer Caidin's *Cyborg* was previously adapted into *The Six Million Dollar Man*.

THE FALL OF THE HOUSE OF USHER
NBC, 7/25/82

Cast: Jonathan Cresswell (Robert Hayes), Jennifer Cresswell (Charlene Tilton), Roderick Usher (Martin Landau), Madeline Usher (Dimitra Arliss), Thaddeus (Ray Walston), Barmaid (Peg Stewart), Finney (Michael Ruud), Man in Bar (H.E.D. Redford)

Credits: Director-Producer: James L. Conway; Writer: Stephen Lord, from Edgar Allan Poe's short story; Executive Producer: Charles E. Sellier, Jr.; Photography: Paul Hipp; Art Director: Paul Staheli; Music: Bob Summers; Editor: Trevor Jolley; Produced by Schick Sunn Classics Productions, Taft International Pictures

In the 1800s the newly married Cresswells visit the crumbling mansion of Jonathan's friend Roderick Usher; Roderick wants Jonathan, an engineer, to repair the decaying manse. Roderick and his sister Madeline possess hereditary hyper-acute senses, so that the slightest light or sound pains them, and this has driven Madeline mad.

Jonathan finds the house resists his work as if it were alive, even attacking him (conveniently falling gargoyles, collapsing floors). After Madeline dies, Roderick reveals that after his Satan-worshipping ancestors turned from evil, the devil cursed the family with their hyper-acute senses and possessed the house itself. Satan raises Madeline to kill the others. After much chasing and fighting, Roderick holds her off long enough for the Cresswells to escape, then the house caves in on the Ushers.

The Fall of the House of Usher is slow and dreary; Hayes (TV's *Starman*) and Tilton look wildly out of place in costume drama (*Mission: Impossible*'s Landau and *My Favorite*

Martian's Walston do better). This was part of an occasional *Classics Illustrated* series of TV movies.

FALLING FIRE
TMC, 2/21/98

Cast: Daryl Boden (Michael Paré), Marilyn Boden (Heidi Von Palleske), Lopez (Christian Vidosa), Capt. Cyril Jackson (Cedric Turner), Joe Schneider (Mackenzie Gray), Rene Lessard (Zerhe Leverman), Jimmy Rice (Morris Durante), Nikki Bardini (Jacklyn Francis), Chris Martel (Michaela Matthieu), Marty Anderson (Geoffrey Pounsett), Dr. Hanan (Tim Ward), Mr. Ames (Christopher Wall), Adam Boden (Herbie Terry), Woman (Livia Daza-Paris), ISA Experts (Laurel Johnson, Tony Curtis Blondell, Helene Wong), Tortured Man (Piero Didiano), Guards (Jules Delorme, Costa Kamateros), VR Woman (Alexandra Lalonde), Gillian (Lindsey Lomax), Interviewer (Huey Livingstone), Reporter (Gerry Butts), James Bomb (C.J. Rutherford), David A. Steinberg (David A. Quinton), Ape (Jimmy "The Ape" Russell), Lisa (Lisa Priester), Arlene (Arlene Santalucia), Child's Voice (Nicole D'Or)

Credits: Director: Daniel D'Or; Writers: Peter I. Horton, Daniel D'Or, G. Philip Jackson; Story: Peter I. Horton; Producer: G. Philip Jackson; Executive Producers: Roger Corman, David A. Steinberg; Co-Executive Producer: Maryann Ridini; Photography: Jonathan Freeman; Production Design: James Plaxton; Music: Donald Quan; Editor: Anthony Coleman; Produced by Producers Network Associates, Inc., The Cusp

A resource-depleted future Earth sees hope in a space mission bringing an asteroid into Earth's orbit for mining. Lopez' environmental terrorists, however, believe that using the asteroid to continue people's high-consumption ways is one more betrayal of Mother Earth. On the mission, consoles short out, equipment malfunctions, people die. Federal agent Marilyn Boden discovers Lopez is behind it, gets captured, but kills him. In space, Marilyn's husband unmasks Lessard as the saboteur, planning to crash the asteroid into Earth; he overcomes her and nudges the asteroid safely into space before it strikes.

Routine.

FEAR
Showtime, 7/15/90

Cast: Cayce Bridges (Ally Sheedy), Jessica Moreau (Lauren Hutton), Jack Hess (Michael O'Keefe), Shadow Man (Pruitt Taylor Vince), Detective Webber (Stan Shaw), Catherine Tarr (Dina Merrill), William Tarr (Dean Goodman), Detective Wu (Keone Young), Colin Hart (Jonathan Prince), Leonard Scott Levy (John Agar), Holcomb (Don Hood), Inez Villanueva (Marta DuBois), Salesgirl (Raina Manuel), Agnes Reardon (Helen Brown), Stewardess (Cyndi Strittmatter), Victim (Allison Barron), Boarding Agent (Jim McCauley), Co-Pilot (Billy Long), Restaurateur Captain (Glenn Dixon), Anchorman (Dick McGarvin), Radio Detective (Sam Scarber), State Patrolman (Jeffrey Bowman), Forensics Man (Ed Corbett), Ferris Wheel Operator (Bob Lorso), Newscaster (Jane Sibbett), News Department PA (Kevin Haley), Technician (Bob Schott), Parking Attendant (Brad Schacter), Serviceman (Tom DiFranco), Stage Manager (Jeff Austin), Actress (Pamela Galloway), Stripper (Michelle Foreman)

Credits: Director-Writer: Rockne S. O'Bannon; Producer: Richard Kobritz; Associate Producer: Henry Kline; Executive Producers: Mitchell Cannold, Diane Nabatoff; Photography: Robert Stevens; Production Design: Joseph Nemec III; Music: Henry Mancini; Editor: Kent Beyda; Produced by Vestron Pictures

For several years Cayce Bridges has used her psychic gift—reading telepathic impressions from objects and places—to help police catch serial killers. Unfortunately, her newest target, the murderous Shadow Man, is psychic himself, feeding off his victims' fear and dodging pursuers by reading their minds. When Cayce contacts his mind, he makes her his audience, forcing her to watch telepathically as he kills. By threatening Cayce's friends—or killing them when Cayce disobeys—he pushes her into helpless isolation.

Cayce's neighbor Jack convinces her to fight back and use her powers to spy on the Shadow Man without his knowing it. She gets a fix on him, but he realizes it and begins hunting her down. The cat-and-mouse game takes the two psychics to a carnival, where the Shadow Man corners Cayce. But she successfully shuts him out of her mind and pursues him onto a Ferris wheel from which he falls to his death.

A well-written and nicely chilling thriller, *Fear* is easily the best psychics and cops film detailed in this book. O'Keefe played Gawaine in 1982's *Sword of the Valiant;* veteran (albeit talentless) actor John Agar (*Tarantula, Return of the Creature*) has a small role.

FEAR NO EVIL
NBC, 3/3/69

Cast: David Sorrell (Louis Jourdan), Myles Donovan (Carroll O'Connor), Paul Varney (Bradford Dillman), Harry Snowden (Wilfrid Hyde-White), Barbara (Lynda Day), Mrs. Varney (Marsha Hunt), Ingrid Dorne (Kate Woodville), Wyant (Harry Davis), with Ivor Barry, Jeanne Buckley, Robert Sampson Peters, Susan Brown

Credits: Director: Paul Wendkos; Writer-Producer: Richard Alan Simmons, from a story by Guy Endore; Associate Producer: David Levinson; Photography: Andrew J. McIntyre; Art Director: Howard E. Johnson; Music: Billy Goldenberg; Editor: Byron Chudnow; Produced by Universal

After losing her husband in a tragic accident, Barbara discovers she can see him, reaching to her, from within an antique mirror. She doesn't realize she's putting her soul at terrible risk—but psychiatrist Sorrell does and tries to intervene.

TV's first horror film, *Fear No Evil* is a familiar story but beautiful to look at. An unsuccessful pilot for a series (starring Jordan and Hyde-White) to be called *Bedeviled,* this was followed by a sequel, *Ritual of Evil.*

FRANKENSTEIN
TNT, 6/13/93

Cast: Dr. Victor Frankenstein (Patrick Bergin), The Monster (Randy Quaid), DeLacey (John Mills), Clerval (Lambert Wilson), Elizabeth (Fiona Giles), Justine (Jacinta Mulcahy), Alphonse (Ronald Leigh Hunt), William (Timothy Stark), Captain (Roger Bizley), Bosun (Michael Gothard), Chancellor (Vernon Dobtcheff), Zorkin (Marcus Eyre), Priest (John Scarborough), Sailor (John Laurimore), Amy (Amanda Quaid), Hunters (Maciek Czapski, Piotr Szyma), Officer (Wojciech Dabrowski), Landlady (Teresa Musialek), Magistrate (Ferdynand Matysik), Innkeeper (Andrzej Galla), Stonemason (Boleslaw Abart)

Credits: Director–Writer–Executive Producer: David Wickes; Supervising Producer: Paul Tivers; Photography: Jack Conroy; Production Design: William Alexander; Music: John Cameron; Editor: John Grover; Produced by Turner Pictures

In this version of Mary Shelley's novel, Frankenstein is an 1820s genetic researcher who uses his own DNA to create a perfect human. When the experiment misfires, the half-formed creature runs wild, hunted by all. The Monster seeks out Frankenstein, demanding he create a mate. When Frankenstein's attempt fails, the Monster murders Frankenstein's bride. Bound by mutual hatred, the battle between the two leads all the way to the Arctic ice, where they finally die together, drowning in the frigid polar sea.

Despite the updating from corpse-robbing to genetics, this is TV's best version of *Frankenstein,* with excellent performances by the two leads.

FRANKENSTEIN: THE COLLEGE YEARS
Fox, 10/28/91

Cast: Mark Crispen (William Ragsdale), Jay Butterman (Christopher Daniel Barnes), Frank (Vincent Hammond), Professor Lohman (Larry Miller), Andy Richmond (Andrea Elson), Kingston Sebuka (DéVoreaux White), Blaine Muller (Patrick Richwood), Coach Lyons (Charles Brown), Dean Murch (Macon McCalman), Gretchen (Margaret Langrick), Wolford (Beau Dremann), Lippzigger (Robert V. Barron), Rutter (Richard Clements), Kozlowski (Greg Grunberg), Anchorman (Joe Farago), Security Officer (Jason Edwards), Quarterback (Karl Bakke), Firemen (Michael Prokopuk, Michael Ryan Way), Cop (Michael McNab), Reporters (Joe Banks, Charles Green, Carlease Burke), Students (Glenn L. Lucas, Jonathan Wise, Kent Belli), Professor (Don Maxwell), Sergeant (E.R. Davies), Nurse (Maura Soden), Friend (Diane Gadry), Coeds (Jennifer Pusheck, Amanda Anka, Maria Bradley), Girl (Marcie Jo Warren)

Credits: Director: Tom Shadyac; Writers: Bryant Christ, John Trevor Wolff; Producer: Bob Engelman; Executive Producers: Richard E. Johnson, Scott D. Goldstein; Photography: Steve Confer; Production Design: Mick Strawn; Music: Joel McNeely; Editor: David Garfield; Produced by Spirit Productions, FNM Films, 20th Century Films

When eccentric professor Lippzigger dies, Professor Lohman pressures irresponsible pre-med student Mark to unearth Lippzigger's secret research, which Lohman will claim as his own. What Mark and his roommate Jay find in Lippzigger's lab is Frankenstein's frozen monster; Lippzigger had recovered it from the Arctic in hopes a creature born of multiple body parts could hold the key to preventing transplant rejection.

As Mark tries to complete the professor's research, he unintentionally revives the monster. The boys' efforts to hide "Frank" fail when he winds up becoming the college's new football star. Just as they crack the secrets that keep him alive, Lohman figures out what he is and blackmails Mark into turning Frank over to him. Jay convinces Mark that Frank is their friend, not just an experiment, so they rescue him from Lohman's lab, then sabotage Lohman's presentation so he looks like a lunatic. The fruits of Mark's research render Frank fully intelligent and human, and because Mark has also performed a successful transplant on a lab animal, he can publish his research without blowing Frank's secret.

Mary Shelley's novel not only inspired countless film versions, but numerous updates and quasi-sequels such as this one. Cheerfully dumb, *Frankenstein: The College Years* is a lot funnier than one might expect.

FRANKENSTEIN: THE TRUE STORY
NBC, 11/30–12/1/73

Cast: Dr. Polidori (James Mason), Dr. Victor Frankenstein (Leonard Whiting), The Creature (Michael Sarrazin), Henri Clerval (David McCallum), Agatha/Prima (Jane Seymour), Elizabeth Fanschawe (Nicola Pagett), Sir Richard Fanschawe (Michael Wilding), Lady Fanschawe (Clarissa Kaye), Mrs. Blair (Agnes Moorehead), Francoise DuVal (Margaret Leighton), Mr. Lacey (Ralph Richardson), Chief Constable (John Gielgud), Sea Captain (Tom Baker), Felix (Dallas Adams), Young Man (Julian Barnes), Coach Passenger (Arnold Diamond)

Credits: Director: Jack Smight; Writers: Christopher Isherwood, Don Bachardy, from Mary Shelley's novel; Producer: Hunt Stromberg, Jr.; Associate Producer: Ian Lewis; Photography: Arthur Ibbetson; Production Design: Wilfred J. Shingleton; Art Director: Fred Carter; Music: Gil Melle; Editor: Richard Marden; Produced by Universal

Aging Dr. Clerval convinces Frankenstein to assist in his experiments reanimating the dead. When Clerval dies, Frankenstein uses his brain in their creation's body. The resulting Creature is intelligent, though inarticulate, and initially handsome, but his physical deterioration eventually drives the Creature to suicide. The Creature survives, however, and befriends a peasant family. When the daughter, Agatha, is killed, Dr. Polidori blackmails Frankenstein into resurrecting her as the Creature's bride, Prima. Polidori secretly plots to marry the beautiful Prima to an aging noble, then exploit the power and wealth she'll gain. Prima rejects the Creature, which kills her, then kills Frankenstein's wife and Polidori before confronting Frankenstein in the Arctic, where an ice fall destroys them both.

TV's first Frankenstein film (though it had already been adapted for various anthology shows) is nowhere near as faithful as the title claims—but compared to the many theatrical versions, it's letter-perfect. Though sporting a powerhouse cast (including *The Man From U.N.C.L.E.*'s David McCallum and *Dr. Who*'s Tom Baker) and classy visual look, it's definitely too long—the Bergin/Quaid *Frankenstein* is better.

FREAKY FRIDAY
ABC, 5/6/95

Cast: Ellen Andrews (Shelley Long), Annabelle Andrews (Gabrielle Hoffman), Bill (Alan Rosenberg), Mrs. Barab (Catlin Adams), Principal Handel (Eileen Brennan), Frieda Debny (Sandra Bernhardt), Mr. Sweet (Andrew Bilgore), Librarian/Mrs. Futterman (Carol Kane), Herbie (Kevin Krakower), Joe (Peter Gregory), Stan Horner (Drew Carey), Ms. Tarr (Katherine Cortez), Cary (Taylor Negron), He Ho Lee (Arsenio "Sonny" Trinidad), Bully (E.J. De La Pena), Construction Workers (Joe Costanza, Thomas A. Woolen), Heather (Reagan Gomez Preston), Salesgirl (Gale Mayron), Gina (Kate Sargent), Master Lee (Benjamin Lum), Ben Andrews (Asher Metchik), Brynne (Alyssa T. Poblador), Jackie (Natanya Rosa), Rachel (Marla Sokoloff), Miss Della (Candy Trabucco)

Credits: Director: Melanie Mayron; Writer: Stu Krieger, based on the book and screenplay by Mary Rodgers; Producer: Joan Van Horn; Executive Producers: George Zaloom, Les Mayfield, Scott Amergut; Photography: Russ Alsobrook; Production Design: Peg McClellan; Produced by ZM Productions, Inc.

Divorced mom Ellen Andrews and her teenage daughter Annabelle are perpetually at odds with each other over everything from Annabelle's chores to Ellen's boyfriend (Bill, Ellen's partner in her kids-wear company). The morning after Bill gives them matching, supposedly magical lockets, Annabelle and Ellen simultaneously wish the other could walk a mile in their shoes ... and the lockets obligingly switch their minds into each other's bodies.

Trapped in Annabelle's body, Ellen discovers a world full of arbitrary authority and unfair restrictions; Annabelle realizes how much pressure her mother is under at home and at work. Ellen alienates Annabelle's friends, Annabelle loses Ellen an important client—and Bill. Worse, Ellen learns the spell will become permanent if not undone by sunset.

With Bill's help, everything works out: In Annabelle's body, Ellen helps out a geeky but worthy schoolmate; Annabelle's unique perspective on kids' clothes wins over the big client; and Annabelle discovers Bill is a better match for her mother than she thought. The spell is reversed, leaving mom and daughter with a better idea of each other's lives.

Body-swapping comedies go as far back as Thorne Smith's thirties novel *Turnabout* (later made into a movie and a TV series). Mary Rodgers used the idea in her young-adult novel *Freaky Friday,* which she adapted into one of Disney's better seventies films (starring a young Jodie Foster as Annabelle). This version was the best of several Disney remakes broadcast in 1995 (including *The Computer Wore Tennis Shoes* and *Escape to Witch Mountain*), with a terrific performance by Shelley Long (best known as Diane on *Cheers*) as a child in an adult body. Hoffman is also good as Annabelle, but her normal personality is so forceful that having a grown woman inside her doesn't seem too different.

FROM THE DEAD OF NIGHT
NBC, 2/27/89

Cast: Joanna Darby (Lindsay Wagner), Peter Langford (Bruce Boxleitner), Glen Eastman (Robin Thomas), Dr. Walter Hovde (Robert Prosky), Rick (Merritt Butrick), Dr. Ann Morgan (Joanne Linville), Heather (Dani Minnick), Elena (Rita Zohar), Maggie (Diahann Carroll), Nurse (Jeanne Bates), Patrolman (John H. Evans), Kevin (Timothy Fall), Dr. Breedlove (Richard Fancy), Gus (Sheldon Feldner), Davey (Christian Hoff), Edna (Nancy Linari), Truck Driver (Doug MacHugh), Men (Joe Medalis, Terry Wills), Catherine (Julie Osburn), Mr. King (Joe Praml), Duty Officer (Miguel Sandoval), Sgt. Gregson (John Shearin), Melody (Whitney Weston), Nurse (Noni White), with Peter Jason.

Credits: Director: Paul Wendkos; Writer: William Bleich, based on Gary Brandner's novel *Walkers;* Producer: Jody B. Paonessa; Executive Producer: Hans Proppe; Associate Producer: Dennis Turner; Photography: Benard Heinl; Production Design: Penny Hadfield; Music: Gil Mellé; Editors: Steve Cohen, Christopher Cooke; Produced by Shadowplay Films, Phoenix Entertainment

After a near-death experience, Joanna Darby becomes the target of several near-fatal assaults. She learns that six vengeful spirits saw her almost go into the light, and now seek to drag her back by reanimating the newly dead as "walkers" to kill her. With the help of her ex-boyfriend Peter, Joanna destroys each of the walkers. Then Peter learns one walker, who tried ramming their car, was nothing but an ordinary drunk driver. The real sixth walker shows up at Joanna's apartment, but she kills him too, leaving her free to reunite with Peter.

At two hours, this could have been a creepy little B-movie; at four, it's way too long to sustain the premise. Wagner (*The Bionic Woman*) turns in a good performance though; Boxleitner would later star in *Babylon 5*.

FULL ECLIPSE
HBO, 11/27/93

Cast: Max Dire (Mario Van Peebles), Casey Spencer (Patsy Kensit), Adam Garou (Bruce Payne), Jim Sheldon (Anthony John Denison), Doug Crane (Jason Beghe), Liza (Paula Marshall), Ramon Perez (John Verea), Fleming (Dean Norris), Ron Edmunds (Willie C. Carpenter), Anna Dire (Victoria Rowell), Teague (Scott Paulin), Stratton (Mel Winkler), Det. Tom Davis (Joseph Culp), Silvano (Joey De Pinto), Club Manager (John Apicella), Dr. Bobby Rose (Brent Bolthouse), Girl (Kelly Brennan), Puppeteer

(Eric Fiedler), Crazy (David Gail), Wedding Priest (Ruben Garfias), Werewolf (Vincent Hammond), Desk Sergeant (Howard Himmelstein), Cop (Guy J. Louthian), Sergeant at Club (Larry Mortorff), Boyfriend (Piers Plowden), Chemist (Frederick Ponzlov), Therapist (Robin Pearson Rose), Helen (Jennifer Rubin), Shop Clerk (Jeff Russell), Kid (Ahmad Stoner)

Credits: Director: Anthony Hicko; Writers: Richard Christian Matheson, Michael Reaves; Producers: Peter Abrams, Robert L. Levy; Co-Producer: Tom Patricia; Executive Producer: David R. Ginsburg; Co-Executive Producer: Richard Christian Matheson; Photography: Sandi Sissel; Production Design: Gregory Melton; Makeup Effects: Alterian Studios; Music: Gary Chang; Editor: Peter Amundson; Produced by HBO Pictures, Citadel Ent.

After Max, a cop, sees his partner crippled for life, he's shocked to watch the man leave the hospital, completely healed ... then commit suicide. Next, biochemist Adam Garou invites Max to join a special police strike force operating outside the law; when Max sees Garou's team become bestial berserkers under Garou's drug treatments, he declines. Strike-force member Casey shoots Max, then heals him with the drug. When Max tastes the physical power it brings, he joins the team (even knowing his partner died out of loathing for what Garou had made him).

As events make Max increasingly suspicious of Garou, he investigates and learns the man is a werewolf who controls his transformations chemically (just as he induces them in the strike force)—and has killed all of his previous packs. Max and Casey try to kill Garou first—but it's during a full eclipse, when Garou is immortal. Garou kills the entire pack except Max, who poisons him after the eclipse with silver nitrate. Using Garou's drugs, Max creates a new pack to continue Garou's war on crime.

Though neat idea, *Full Eclipse* is so poorly developed (no explanation of why Garou kills his packs, for instance, is offered) that it never catches fire. This is doubly disappointing since co-scripters Reaves and Matheson, Jr., have both turned out excellent print fantasies.

THE FURY WITHIN
USA, 10/28/98

Cast: Jo Hanlon (Ally Sheedy), Mike Hanlon (Costas Mandylor), Sandy (Jodie Dry), Jimmy Hanlon (Steve Bastoni), Steve (Vincent Berry), Willy Keller (Desmond Kelly), Nancy Braverman (Kerry-Ella McCaullay), Patty Hanlon (Emily Borg), Todd Simms (Craig Marriott), Miss Tish (Deni Gordon), Justin Reed (Philip Holder), George Simms (Tom Betts), Carol Simms (Sandra Bells), Ana Rochas (Ranca Rubiu), Jean (Larisa Chen), Detective Russo (Enrico Mammarella), Doctor (Donna Fox), Librarian (Jane Rowland), Police Lieutenant (Andrew Booth), Paramedic (Jonathan Stuart)

Credits: Director: Noel Nosseck; Writers: William Bast, Paul Huson; Producers: Michael Lake, Noel Nosseck; Executive Producers: William Bast, Paul Huson, Jeffrey Hayes; Photography: John Stokes; Production Design: Michael Ralph; Visual Effects: Photon vfx; Music: Lawrence Shragge, Tim Jones; Editor: Jim Gross; Produced by Village Roadshow Pictures, Wilshire Court Productions

As sweet, patient Jo weathers a separation from adulterous husband Mike, she's horrified to find her son Jimmy going on destructive rampages. No one believes Jimmy's claim that it's some force around him smashing rooms and disrupting school—until Jo finds herself caught in one of these poltergeist storms and barely escapes alive. Parapsychologist Steve can't find any power in Jimmy—and realizes the true source is Jo's repressed anger at Mike, manifesting itself unconsciously. When Steve tries to tell Jo, her psychic attack almost kills him. She refuses to accept responsibility, or that the only cure is her death.

As Jo represses more and more, Steve, then Mike's divorce lawyer, and his girlfriend Sandy become victims of her rage. Realizing the truth, Mike takes the kids away; Jo's power manifests itself as a monstrous giant attacking the house. When it threatens her children, she confronts it and destroys it—but the battle leaves her a mental vegetable.

A neat little psychic thriller, *The Fury Within* is much better than most of USA's movies.

FUTURE COP
ABC, 5/1/76

Cast: Joe Cleaver (Ernest Borgnine), John Haven (Michael Shannon), Sgt. Bundy (John Amos), Forman (John Larch), Klausmeier (Herbert Nelson), Avery (Ronnie Claire Edwards), Paterno (James Luisi), Dorfman (Stephen Pearlman), Young Rookie (James Daughton), Grandmother (Shirley O'Hara)

Credits: Director: Jud Taylor; Writer-Producer: Anthony Wilson; Executive Producer: Gary Damsker; Photography: Terry K. Meade; Art Director: Jack DeShields; Music: Billy Goldenberg; Editors: Ronald J. Fagan, Steven Brown; Produced by Culzean Corp., Toven Productions, Paramount Pictures

When cop Cleaver's longtime partner, Bundy, is promoted to desk sergeant, Cleaver is assigned a new partner, Haven. What he and Bundy don't know is that Haven is the "cop of the future," an android with an encyclopedic knowledge of law, super senses that make him a one-man forensic lab, and a face designed to inspire trust. Although Haven has performed well in tests, he has no street experience, and his lack of social skills baffles and irritates Cleaver. When Haven is injured in action, Cleaver learns the truth. Despite his superiors' loathing for the mechanical cop, Cleaver comes to respect Haven's dedication and decency. Returning to the street, they prove that between Haven's programming and Cleaver's experience, they make a successful team.

Featuring the first of TV's android/robot cops (*Holmes and Yoyo*, *Condor*, *Mann and Machine*), *Future Cop* is a competent film (Borgnine is always fun), but the backstory is more interesting than the plot: SF writers Ben Bova and Harlan Ellison co-wrote "Brillo" about a near-future robot cop, then turned it into a screenplay for Paramount (with Bova suggesting Borgnine as the lead). After they balked at the studio's proposed changes (present-day setting, human-looking android instead of robot—both of which would cut production costs), Paramount dropped the project ... and then created *Future Cop*. The writers' successful lawsuit didn't prevent a short-lived series, followed by the *Cops and Robin* TV-movie.

GALACTIC ODYSSEY
TMC, 11/21/98

Cast: Lee (Adam Baldwin), Father O'Neill (Robert Englund), Susan (Kate Rodger), Charles (Duane Davis), Carrie (Gretchen Palmer), Luke (Mark Folger), Janna (Jeannie Millar), Trit (Jerry Trimble), Protector (Darrin Prescott), with Jolie Jackunas

Credits: Director-Writer: Fred Gallo; Producer: Darin Spillman; Co-Producers: David Rand, Marta M. Mobley; Executive Producer: Roger Corman; Photography: Mark Parry; Production Design: Sean Sloan; Music: Ed Tomney; Editor: Karl Ernest; Produced by New Horizon

After Earth is destroyed in 2020, earth's only survivors awaken aboard a mysterious spaceship headed for a new world. They learn their mission is to colonize the new planet and restore the human race—but an unseen force is killing them, one by one.

This is yet another "Roger Corman Presents" film, with Robert Englund (*A Nightmare on Elm Street*'s Freddie Kruger) in the cast.

GARGANTUA
Fox, 5/19/98

Cast: Jack Ellway (Adam Baldwin), Brandon Ellway (Emile Hirsch), Dr. Alyson Hart (Julie Carmen), Dr. Hale (Peter Adams), Derek Lawson (Alex Petersons), Paul Bateman (Doug Penty), Col. Wayne (Bobby Hosea), President Moki (Monroe Reimers), Kikko (Darren Selby), Police Chief (Tony Briggs), Naru (Puven Pather), Tari (Mae Montero), Girls (Fiona Edwards, Aislinn Crowe), T.J. (Donald Battee), Jace (Peter Kent), Dak (Shane Simmons), Kulani (Josie Licuanan), Paparazzi (Jack Dacey, Brian Hinselwood, Rene Perrin), Pilot (James Kable), Naval Officer (Andrew Booth), Marines (Scott McLean, Tony Curtis, Malcolm Cork), Girl (Cassandra Hyde), Father (Greg Katterns), Frisbee Guy (Steve Harman), Mother (Caroline Hyde), Priest (Richard Kaye)

Credits: Director: Bradford May; Writer-Executive Producer: Ronald Parker; Producer: Peter V. Ware; Photography: John Stokes; Production Design: Stewart Burnside; Visual Effects Supervisor: Elan Soltes; Creature Design: John Cox; Music: J. Peter Robinson; Editor: Bud Hayes; Produced by Fox Television

After an earthquake hits the island of Malau, bodies turn up mangled and mauled in the waters. While marine biologist Ellway tries to identify the creature behind it, his son Brandon befriends a five-foot-tall baby amphibian. Not long afterward, the creature's nine-foot brother is captured while attacking the natives. Ellway realizes they're frogs, mutated by toxic waste and released from a subsea cavern by the quake.

When the Godzilla-sized mom shows up, Ellway hopes to use the captured monster to lure Mom away from Malau. But Lawson, a greedy hunter, steals the creature to sell, and the mother goes on a rampage until killed by the army. When the even larger father arrives, Ellway uses Brandon's infant as bait. Lawson, who lost the first baby, tries to steal this one but gets killed by the father. The creatures return home and the military seal up the cavern.

Though formulaic, *Gargantua* works the clichés well. Unfortunately, Baldwin is such a stick, he sucks much of the life out of it. *Gargantua* aired—not coincidentally, perhaps—the day before the release of 1998's over-hyped *Godzilla*.

GARGOYLES
CBS, 11/21/72

Cast: Mercer Boley (Cornel Wilde), Diana Boley (Jennifer Salt), Mrs. Parks (Grayson Hall), Head Gargoyle (Bernie Casey), James Reeger (Scott Glenn), Police Chief (William Stevens), Uncle Willie (Woodrow Chambliss), Jesse (John Gruber), Morris Ray (Timothy Burns), Buddy (Jim Connell), Gargoyles (Mickey Alzola, Greg Walker, Rock Walker)

Credits: Director: B.W.L. Norton; Writers: Stephen Karpf, Elinor Karpf; Producers: Robert W. Christiansen, Rick Rosenberg; Executive Producer: Roger Gimbel; Photography: Earl Rath; Gargoyle Makeup: Ellis Burman, Stan Winston; Music: Robert Prince; Editor: Frank P. Keller; Produced by Tomorrow Entertainment, Inc.

For millennia, humanity has warred with gargoyles and immortalized its great enemies in stone, but in the 500 years since the last battle, people have forgotten the truth behind the carvings. Boley, a scientist, finds a gargoyle skeleton in a roadside curio shop but dismisses it as a fake; then a swarm of newly hatched gargoyles attacks the shack to claim their dead. Boley and his daughter Diana flee the gargoyles. When a truck kills one of the monsters, Boley studies the corpse and realizes the truth.

When the gargoyles kidnap Diana, Boley follows them to their lair, where hundreds more eggs are ready to hatch. Boley gathers a strike force of cops and bikers and leads them to destroy the eggs. The gargoyle leader trades his life and his mate's for Diana's, then flees, warning Boley that someday the gargoyles will return.

Gargoyles is an old-fashioned monster movie with neat-looking monsters but stiff, dull leads. Grayson Hall played Julia Hoffman on the original *Dark Shadows*.

GEMINI MAN
NBC, 5/10/76

Cast: Sam Casey (Ben Murphy), Dr. Abby Lawrence (Katherine Crawford), Leonard Driscoll (Richard Dysart), Dr. Harold Schuyler (Dana Elcar), Charles Edward Royce (Paul Shenar), Vince Rogers (Quinn Redeker), Captain Ballard (H.M. Wynant), Captain Whelan (Len Wayland), Receptionist (Cheryl Miller), Guard (Michael Lane), Officer (Gregory Walcott), Dive Officer (Austin Stoker), Dietz (Jim Raymond), CHP Officer (Richard Kennedy), Chief Controller (Robert Forward), Mechanic (Dave Shelley)

Credits: Director: Alan J. Levi; Writer–Supervising Producer: Leslie Stevens; Producer: Robert F. O'Neill; Executive Producer: Harve Bennett; Photography: Enzo A. Martinelli; Art Director: David Marshall; Music: Billy Goldenberg; Editor: Robert F. Shugrue; Produced by Harve Bennett Productions, Universal

When the government sends diver Sam Casey to recover a downed enemy satellite, double-agent Schuyler blows up the satellite first. Radiation from the blast almost kills Casey—and turns him invisible. Dr. Lawrence saves Casey's life and tries to restore his visibility. After Schuyler frames Casey for destroying the satellite, the invisible Casey sneaks into Schuyler's office and learns the truth. Casey exposes Schuyler and, with Lawrence's help, gains control of his powers; he agrees to use them for the government, even though if he's invisible more than 15 minutes a day, he'll be stuck that way forever.

After NBC's *Invisible Man* flopped, the

network decided the concept could still be a hit if handled better—hence this *Gemini Man* pilot (and subsequent series) with a younger, less cerebral hero and more limited powers (which didn't stop them rewriting several *Invisible Man* scripts for this show). None of this helped, however; the series died before half the episodes had been shown.

GENERATION X
Fox, 2/20/96

Cast: Emma "White Queen" Frost (Finola Hughes), Russell Tresh (Matt Frewer), Sean "Banshee" Cassidy (Jeremy Ratchford), Jubilation "Jubilee" Lee (Heather McComb), Angelo "Skin" Espinoza (Agustin Rodriguez), Kurt "Refrax" Pastorius (Randall Slavin), Mondo (Bumper Robinson), Arlee "Buff" Hicks (Suzanne Davis), Monet "M" St. Croix (Amarilis), Balston (Kevin McNulty), Kayla (Lalainia Lindbjerg), Det. Gaines (Garry Chalk), Alicia Lee (Lynda Boyd), Jeannie (Joely Collins), Pruitt (Wally Dalton), Bruce (Noel Geer), Orderly (Garvin Cross), Jim Lee (Robert Lewis), Harlin (Dean McKenzie), Donberry (L. Harvey Gold), Sgt. Cruiller (Peter Bryant), Eduardo (Jim Crescenzo), Estella (Jeaneta Munoz), with Kavan Smith, Edward Diaz, Nadia Naschmento, Fulvio Cecere, Tyler Labonne, Ken Ryan

Credits: Director: Jack Sholder; Writer: Eric Blakeney, based on the *Generation X* comic book created by Scott Lobdell and Chris Bachald; Producer: David Roessell; Executive Producers: Bruce Sallan, Eric Blakeney, Avi Arad, Stan Lee; Associate Producer: Matthew Edelman; Photography: Bryan England; Production Design: Douglas Higgins; Music: J. Peter Robinson; Editor: Michael Schweitzer; Produced by MT2 Services, Marvel Films

In the near future, super-powered mutants, the next step in human evolution, are ruthlessly oppressed by the government. When police capture Jubilee, who fires light-bursts from her fingers, Sean Cassidy and telepathic Emma Frost rescue her for their "school" (where teenage mutants are trained to fight injustice). Jubilee's classmates include super-elastic Angelo; super-strong Arlee; brilliant, arrogant Monet; laser-eyed Kurt; and Mondo, who duplicates the properties of whatever he touches.

Tresh, a scientist who manipulates human minds through their dreams, discovers Angelo visiting his girlfriend in the dream-world through an invention of Frost's. Tresh captures Angelo to use his mutant life force as a power source, so Frost leads the team into the dream-world against Tresh. Despite his vast powers, they hurl him into the darkest nightmares, reducing him to a mental vegetable. The kids are ready to graduate.

Marvel's *X-Men* comic went from second string to smash hit in the seventies thanks to writer Chris Claremont and artists Dave Cockrum and John Byrne; *Generation X* was one of many comics that spun off the original book. This failed pilot wastes far too much time on character interaction (a bad idea with such weak actors), and skimps on super-action—not to mention its weak plot and obnoxious villain (played by *Max Headroom* star Matt Frewer).

GENESIS II
CBS, 3/23/73

Cast: Dylan Hunt (Alex Cord), Lyra-A (Mariette Hartley), Harper-Smythe (Lynn Marta), Primus Isaac Kimbridge (Percy Rodrigues), Singh (Harvey Jason), Isaiah (Ted Cassidy), Primus Dominic (Majel Barrett), Astrid (Linda Grant), Yuloff (Titos Vandis), Overseer (Leon Askin), Janus (Liam Dunn), Brian (Tom Pace), Lu-Chan (Beulah Quo), Tyranian Teacher (Ray Young), Weh-r (Ed Ashley), General (Dennis Young), Shuttle Dispatcher (Robert Hathaway), Dr. Kellum (Bill Striglos), Station Operator (David Westburg), Teenager (Tammi Bula), Cardiologist (Terry Wills), Actress (Didi Conn)

Credits: Director: John Llewellyn Moxey; Writer-Producer: Gene Roddenberry; Photography: Gerald Perry Finnerman; Art Director: Hilyard Brown; Music: Harry Sukman; Editor: George Watters; Produced by Warner Bros.

In 1979 an earthquake buries scientist Dylan Hunt during a suspended animation experiment. He's revived in 2133 by explorers from Pax, pacifists who've been rebuilding civilization since the twentieth century's nuclear war. Lyra-A, a Terranean (superhuman mutants with two hearts and two belly buttons for her two umbilical cords), tells Hunt that Pax are ruthless conquerors hoping to exploit his prewar scientific knowledge. She helps Hunt escape to Terranea, where he's asked to reactivate an old power plant—unaware it will also power up a nuclear missile silo. Discovering Terranea runs on slave labor, Hunt refuses and is enslaved himself. When Pax agents rescue him, he organizes a slave revolt.

Lyra-A, who's fallen for Hunt, helps the Paxians escape in return for Dylan repairing the generator, thereby restoring her standing in Terranea. Hunt makes the repairs, but sets the missiles to detonate after he returns to Pax. When the Paxers learn the blast will kill Terraneans in the silo, they're horrified—Pax doesn't kill, ever. Hunt protests, but when the blast's shock wave reaches him, he's unnerved enough to join Pax and accept their no-kill philosophy.

This post–*Star Trek* Roddenberry pilot holds up very well despite its seventies "message" (anti-nuke, anti-war, pro-environment), but it lost out in the series sweepstakes to the less-interesting *Planet of the Apes* series. Follow-up pilots *Planet Earth* and *Strange New World* did no better. Familiar faces include Roddenberry's wife Barrett (Nurse Chapel on the original Enterprise and Lwuxana on *Star Trek: The Next Generation*) and Ted Cassidy (Lurch in TV's *The Addams Family*). Hartley's twin belly buttons were an in-joke reference to the Roddenberry-produced *I Dream of Jeannie*, in which Barbara Eden's harem outfit had not been allowed to reveal any belly button.

GHOST MOM
Fox, 11/1/93

Cast: Dr. Martin Mallory (Geraint Wyn Davies), Mildred Mallory (Jean Stapleton), Jean Connelly (Shae D'lyn), Yamato (Denis Akiyama), Pearl (Jayne Eastwood), Tony (Zachary Bennett), Whippet (Ed Sahely), Dr. Mallory (Bernard Behrens), Dr. Cavanaugh (Stuart Clow), Dr. Anderson (Jeff Pustil), Priest (John Thomas), Bert (Dennis Sweeting), Al (Jack Duffy), George (Patrick Patterson), Healy (Reg Dreager), Betty Lou (Bunny Webb), Man (Eric Link), Bob (Dan Duran), Banker (Roger Dunn), Beehive Secretary (Claire Cellucci), Niagara Falls Priest (Graham McPherson), Henchmen (Peter Kosaka, Lance Koyata), Intern (Evan Carter), Nurses (Diane Ilacks, Ingrid Kavelaars, Karen Hines, Helena Clarkson), Paramedic (Paul Greenberg), Donovan (Don Lamont), Margaret (Samantha Croxall), Jeff (Nick Johne), Kids (Christian Matheson, Daniel Warry-Smith, Mike Beaudry), Academic (Noam Jenkins), Mallory's Secretary (Merle Matheson), Warrior (Michael Chow).

Credits: Director: Dave Thomas; Writers: Daniel Harris, Costantino Magnatta, Dave Thomas; Story: Daniel Harris, Costantino Magnatta; Producers: Daniel Harris, Costantino Magnatta; Executive Producer: Richard Crystal; Supervising Producer: Julian Marks; Photography: Francois Profat; Production Design: Harold Thrasher; Music: Ian Thomas; Editor: Nick Rotundo; Produced by Power Pictures, Richard Crystal Co., Heart Entertainment

After stubborn, quarrelsome Mildred Mallory dies, she learns she has one duty to perform before she can rest. To that end, she reappears to her dismayed son Martin, insisting he exhume her body and rebury it at Niagara Falls. With the help of Mildred's housekeeper, Jean, Martin does his best to obey, despite a gang of Japanese hoods hunting a priceless relic hidden in Mildred's coffin.

Mildred's powers let Jean and Martin—who are falling in love—reach Niagara one step ahead of the hoods. There Mildred guides Martin to his father, whom she'd let Martin believe was dead rather than admit the shame of divorce. The gangsters return, but Mildred once again drives them off. With Martin and his father reunited, and the relic in good hands, Mildred enters heaven—but lets her son know she'll be back now and then.

This silly fluff wastes a competent cast (Davies did better in the series *Forever Knight*); Mildred is so unpleasant it's hard to like her at all (which probably was not the intention).

GHOST OF A CHANCE
ABC, 5/12/87

Cast: Bill Nolan (Dick Van Dyke), Ivory Clay (Redd Foxx), Johnson (Geoffrey Holder), Kathleen Reilly (Brynn Thayer), Julie Mendez (Richard Romanus), Gladys (Barbara Harris), Jessie (Kimble Joyner), Captain Tom Shields (Sean McCann), Det. Fein (Timothy Webber), Marvin Goody (Jack Jessop), Det. Ed Rose (Tom Butler),

Paulie (Michael Copeman), Ralph (Gene Mack), Gary (Luther Hansrai), Waiter (Elliott McIvor), Mechanical Bull Operator (Robert Collins), Emory (Graham Batchelor), Det. Phil Hauck (David B. Nichols), Lyle (Robert Morelli), Bartender (Gino Marrocco), Lady (Sandra Scott), Tran (Wayne Lam), Minister (Dennis Strong), Beggar (Robert O'Ree), Davidow (Don Cullen), Wino (Jason Harris), Wes (Thick Wilson), Loretta (Jackie Richardson), Nettie (Sandi Ross), Esther (Lynn Armstrong), Bar Patrons (Colleen Embree, Tabby Johnson, Dick Grant, Howard Jerome)

Credits: Director: Don Taylor; Writers: Hank Bradford, Eric Cohen; Producer: Sam Strangis; Executive Producers: Stuart Sheslow, Malcolm Stuart; Associate Producer: Bruce Colin; Photography: David Herrington; Art Director: Tony Hall; Music: Charles Bernstein; Editor: Tom Stevens; Produced by Stuart-Phoenix Productions, Sam Strangis Productions, Ten-Four Productions, Heartstar Productions, Thunder Bird Road Productions, Lorimar-Telepictures Productions

Narcotics cop Nolan accidentally guns down jazz pianist Clay, whose greatest grief at dying is that he can't watch over his teenage grandson. Johnson, an angelic overseer, tells Clay that because he died before his time, his spirit can return to Earth to tie up loose ends. Clay appears to Nolan and sets out to convince him to steer Clay's grandson away from drug dealers and into a life of music.

Ghost of a Chance was an unsuccessful comedy pilot in the *Heaven Can Wait* mold. Foxx—a veteran stand-up comic who came to TV in *Sanford and Son*—made his TV-movie debut here.

GHOST OF FLIGHT 401
NBC, 2/18/78

Cast: Dom Cimoli (Ernest Borgnine), Jordan Evanhower (Gary Lockwood), Val (Tina Chen), Prissy Frazier (Kim Basinger), Dutch (Tom Clancy), Bert Stockwell (Howard Hesseman), Loft (Russell Johnson), Bill Bowdish (Robert F. Lyons), Les Garrick (Allan Miller), Barton (Alan Oppenheimer), Maria Cimoli (Carol Rossen), Matt Andrews (Eugene Roche), Dana (Beverly Todd), Mrs. Collura (Angela Clarke), Marshall (John Quade), Ron Smith (Mark L. Taylor), Bailey (Byron Morrow), Ross (Gordon Connell), Michelle (Kerrie Cullen), Didi (Marie Gordon), Mary Smith (Deborah Harmon), Cindy (Anna Mathias), Dr. Rosen (Lynn Wood), Kid (Missy Francis), Billy (Meeno Peluce), with Luis Avalos, Ted Hartley

Credits: Director: Steven Hilliard Stern; Writer: Robert Malcolm Young, from John G. Fuller's book; Producer: Emmet G. Lavery, Jr.; Photography: Howard R. Schwartz; Art Director: Dan Lomino; Music: David Raksin; Editor: Harry Keller; Produced by Emmet G. Lavery Productions, Paramount Pictures

In 1972 the crew of Eastern Airlines' Flight 401 was working on the malfunctioning landing gear when the autopilot shorted out; 101 people, including flight engineer Cimoli, died when the plane crashed into the Everglades, the deadliest single-plane crash to that date. Parts salvaged from the crash were later cannibalized for other planes—aboard which the crew and some passengers begin seeing Cimoli's spectral presence, atoning for the loss of 401 by warning the crew of problems on other planes. Finally, a pilot performs an exorcism to let Cimoli's guilt-ridden spirit pass on to the next world and find peace.

The movie's source novel was an unusually controversial based-on-truth book, since Eastern hotly rejected the idea that its flights were haunted or that its flight engineer had anything to "atone" for. The crash—but not the supernatural elements—was also dramatized as *Crash of Flight 401* in 1978. Pre-stardom Kim Basinger appears in a supporting role.

GHOST WRITER
Syndicated, 6/5/–6/17/90

Cast: Angela Reid (Audrey Landers), Billie Blaine (Judy Landers), Bee-Jay (Joey Travolta), Tom Farrell (Jeff Conaway), Chuck Aaron (John Matuszak), Herb Baxter (David Doyle), Workman (George "Buck" Flower), Carillo (Pedro Gonzales-Gonzales), Jogger (Jery Tyminski), Waiter (Martin Madden), Postman (Jim Crawford), Vincent Carbone (Anthony Franciosa), Tony (Peter Paul), Marco (David Paul), Dancers (Monique Mannen, Robin Antin, Enrique S. Hernandez, Charlie E. Schmidt), Men (Richard Gabai, Michael Deak, Eric Freeman, Chris Latanzi, Neil Barton), Manager (Dick Miller), Bouncer (Rick Dempsey), Cops (Nels Van Patten, Kenneth Tobey, Lenny Rose, Biff Yeager), Bodyguard (Richard Groman), Woman on Phone

(Hannah Eckstein), Reporters (Sarah O'Connor, Christopher Decannett), Waitress (Cathy Hwang), Megan (Kimberly Newman), Tabitha (Jeannie Bisone)

Credits: Director-Writer: Kenneth J. Hall; Producers: David DeCoteau, John Schouweiler; Executive Producers: Ruth Landers, Mark Polan; Photography: Nicholas von Sternberg; Production Design: Royce Mathew; Music: Reg Powell, Sam Winans; Editor: Tony Malanowski; Produced by Rumar Films

Writer Angela sought solitude by moving into deceased, Marilynesque star Billie Blaine's beach house; instead, she found Billie's ghost, bound to Earth until she can remember the truth behind her 1962 suicide. Angela tries to help, in between becoming involved with neighbor Tom and publishing an interview with Billie (supposedly based on Billie's non-existent diary). A mystery man demands the diary or else; when Angie refuses, he kidnaps Tom. Angie realizes the man is Carbone, who murdered Billie when their romance threatened his marriage and political career—and who fears he's mentioned in the diary. Angie agrees to trade the diary for Tom and a half-million dollars, which sets Carbone up for Billie to terrify him into a public confession. Now free, Billie decides to stay on Earth and join Tom and Angie on a well-earned vacation.

The Landers twins' sexy looks gave them a modest career on TV in the eighties, but they can't act (Franciosa's villain blows them both off the screen), and the script isn't much to speak of either.

THE GIFTED ONE
NBC, 6/25/89

Cast: Michael Grant (Pete Kowanko), Dr. Carl Boardman (John Rhys-Davies), Sarah Grant (Wendy Phillips), John Grant (Tom Calloway), Dr. Winslow (G.W. Bailey), Jack (Gregg Henry), Young Michael (Brandon Call), Mary Jo (Khrystyne Haje), Billy Farady (Kristopher Kent Hill), Young Frankie (Joe Elrady), Teen Frankie (Gabriel Nagy), Dr. Claire Henry (Rose Weaver), Tom Farady (James Eric), Beth Farady (Shano Palovitch), Mrs. Williams (Lucky Hayes), Williams (Charles Benton), Susan Martin (Dey Young), Gordon Thomas (Dale Swann), Dr. Hart (Stephen Hastings), Dr. James (Jim Newcomer), Dr. Solomon (Spenseley Schroder), Dr. Helfen (Kenneth Bridges), Dr. Richards (Doug Cotner), Technician (Anthony Bolden), Principal (Mark Manning), Hannah (Tami French), Guard (Arell Blanton), Coach (Norm McBride), Umpire (Michael Mancini), Doctor (John Douglas Fisher), Nurse (Emily Y. Ragsdale), Tommy (Mason Arnold), Johnny (Chris Balcerzak), Bobby (Christopher Michael), Jeffrey (Steven Suggs), Girl (Christina Herczeg), Big Lou (Hank Lawrence), Baby Michael (Cole Coxon), Cops (Sandy Gibbons, Jonathan Voyce)

Credits: Director: Stephen Herek; Writers: Richard Rothstein, Lisa James; Producer: Ariel Levy; Executive Producer: Richard Rothstein; Photography: Kees Van Oostrum; Production Design: Rodger Maus; Editors: Larry Bock, Gib Jaffe; Produced by NBC Productions, Richard Rothstein Productions

Michael Grant, a young man gifted with extraordinary psychic powers, wanders America seeking his natural mother, evading scientists seeking to exploit his gifts, and helping out the people he meets along the way. He eventually learns the reason for his gifts is that he's half-extraterrestrial.

Another unsuccessful pilot and *Fugitive* clone, *The Gifted One* is reportedly not very good.

THE GIRL, THE GOLD WATCH & DYNAMITE
Syndicated, 5/21/81

Cast: Bonnie Lee Beaumont (Lee Purcell), Kirby Winter (Philip MacHale), Hoover Hess III (Burton Gilliam), Wilma Farnham (Zohra Lampert), Seth Beaumont (Jack Elam), Sheriff Earl Baker (Gary Lockwood), Sarah Ann Beaumont (Carol Lawrence), Omar Krepps (Tom Poston), Andrew Stovall (Gene Barry), Stella Walker (Morgan Fairchild), Deputy Henry Thomas Watts (Jerry Mathers), Old Farmer (Barney Phillips), Mamie (Lyle Alzado), Wesley Reins (Larry Linville), Lola (Marcy Hanson), Levee Guard (Rodney Cornelius), Hold-Up Man (Tony Matranga), Ed Appleton (Jerry Houser), Michele (Michele Butin)

Credits: Director: Hy Averback; Writer: George Zateslo, with characters created by John MacDonald; Producer: John Cutts; Executive Producers: Arthur Fellows, Terry Keegan; Photography: William K. Jurgensen; Art Director: Tracy Bousman; Music: Bruce Broughton; Editor: Kenneth R. Koch; Produced by Operation Prime Time, Fellows-Keegan Company, Paramount Pictures

In this sequel to *The Girl, the Gold Watch & Everything*, Kirby and Bonnie Lee are on the eve of their wedding when Bonnie Lee's mother calls for help to save the family farm from a landgrab scheme organized by the conniving Walker. Despite an assortment of problems—built-in restrictions on the use of the watch's power and the constant bungling of Kirby's nitwitted sidekick Hoover—Kirby saves the day and thwarts Walker.

Unlike the original, this pilot deserved to fail—the recast roles are all weaker, and the twerp playing Hoover is annoying.

THE GIRL, THE GOLD WATCH & EVERYTHING
Syndicated, 6/13/80

Cast: Kirby Winter (Robert Hays), Bonnie Lee Beaumont (Pam Dawber), Wilma Farnham (Zohra Lampert), Joseph Locordolos (Ed Nelson), Walton Grumby (Macdonald Carey), Charla O'Rourke (Jill Ireland), Hoover Hess (Burton Gilliam), TV Announcer (Linn Sheldon), Michele (Michelle Burton), Man in Heart (Peter Kevorian), Young Wife (Vera Laurin), Old Man (Steffen Zacharias), Hank (Arthur Barnard), Vegas Desk Clerk (Tony Matranga), Truck Driver (Edward E. Carroll), Patrolman Harris (John Roselius)

Credits: Director: William Wiard; Writer: George Zateslo, from John D. MacDonald's novel; Producer: Myrl A. Schreibman; Executive Producers: Terry Keegan, Arthur Fellows; Photography: Jacques Haitkin; Art Director: Charles Hughes; Music: Hod David Schudson; Editor: Kenneth R. Koch; Produced by Operation Prime-Time, Fellows-Keegan Co., Paramount Pictures

To penniless Kirby Winter's dismay, the only inheritance his wealthy uncle has left him is a gold watch. To Kirby's bewilderment, the watch attracts the attention of a number of nasty people—most notably, conniving Charla O'Rourke—who'll do anything to possess it. After accidentally hooking up with sweet hillbilly Bonnie Lee, Kirby discovers the watch is actually an invention of his uncle's that freezes time for everyone but the user, which Uncle exploited to become rich.

Using the watch, Bonnie Lee and Kirby fight back against O'Rourke and her henchmen. Even when O'Rourke kidnaps Kirby's uncle's secretary, Wilma, the watch enables the good guys to save her and take the bad guys out (dumping O'Rourke nude in a troop transport, for example). By the film's end, it's clear Kirby will be following his uncle's example by turning the watch into a moneymaking proposition.

Stopping time is an old SF device, used before on TV in *The Twilight Zone* (the episode "A Kind of Stopwatch") and the British fantasy series *The Magic Boomerang*, among others. This was an unsuccessful but engaging pilot starring Hays (*Starman*) and Dawber (*Mork and Mindy*). It was followed by a much-inferior sequel (*The Girl, the Gold Watch & Dynamite*).

GIVING UP THE GHOST
Lifetime, 9/7/98

Cast: Anne Hobson (Marg Helgenberger), Jake Hobson (Alan Rosenberg), Bob Shaddyac (Bob Balaban), Kevin Kennedy (Brian Kerwin), Pitaglia (Richard Romanus), June (Kate Lynch), Nicholas Anton (Ron Lea), Dr. Marcia Koblin (Lyne Deragon), Maria (Maria Vacratis), Diane (Elisa Moolecherry), Gladys (Tricia Williams), Judge Gleason (Philip Akin), Frieda Anton (Pam Hyatt), Bill Anton (Ken Kramer), Matthew "Bulldog" Phelps (Matthew Ferguson), David Puente (Frank Crudelle), Doorman (Bill Lake), Leo (Arnold Pinnock), Sergio (Jonathan Rannells), Lou Robinson (Tom Harvey), Thelma Robinson (Jodi Pape), Cousin Albert (Yank Azman), Man at Party (David Sparrow), Cabbie (Sam Malkin), Little Jake (Asa Perlman), Marilyn (Jan Austin)

Credits: Director: Claudia Weill; Writers: Anthea Sylbert, Richard Romanus; Producer: Anthea Sylbert; Co-Producer: Marc Dassas; Executive Producers: Anthea Sylbert, Paula Weinstein, Richard Romanus; Photography: John Holosko; Production Design: Ed Hanna; Music: Mader; Editor: Mary Jo Markey; Produced by Baltimore/Spring Creek Pictures, ABC Pictures

The Hobsons were as close and loving a couple as could be imagined; when Jake Hobson died unexpectedly, Anne was devastated. Then Jake returns from beyond, as warm and loving as ever—and Anne finds herself torn between rebuilding her life on Earth or joining Jake in the world beyond in this supernatural romantic comedy.

GODDESS OF LOVE
NBC, 11/20/88

Cast: Venus (Vanna White), Ted Beckman (David Naughton), Jimmy (David Leisure), Cathy (Amanda Bearse), Detective Charles (Philip Baker Hall), Hera (Betsy Palmer), Zeus (John Rhys-Davies), Alphonso (Little Richard), Joe (Remo Capitani), Mack (Michael Goldfinger), Mrs. Wilson (Jennifer Bassey), Guard (Marty Davis), Fire Marshal (David Donham), Policeman (James Edgcomb), Tour Guide (Lindsey Fields), Woman (Stephanie Hershey), Bud Foreman (Mitch Kreindel), Mrs. Feeney (Robin Krieger), Wally (Vincent Lucchesi), Cop (Stuart Mabray), Lounge Lizards (Phil Marco, Don Segall), Desk Cop (John C. Moskoff), Clergyman (Phil Reeves), Aunt Julie (Florence Schauffler), Debbie (Shari Shattuck), Guy (Paul Tinder), Athena (Jordana Capra), Hephaestus (Sid Haig), Neptune (Kay E. Kuter), Mercury (Ben Schick)

Credits: Director: Jim Drake; Writers: Phil Margo, Don Segall, from F. Anstey's *Tinted Venus*; Producer: Don Segall; Co-Producer: Ray Manzella; Executive Producer: Phil Margo; Photography: Gil Hubbs; Production Design: Ninkey Dalton; Music: Mitch Margo, Dennis Dreith, A.S. Dimond; Editor: Michael Economou; Produced by Phil Margo Enterprises, New World Television, Phoenix Entertainment Group

A statue of Venus comes to life after 3,000 years. She's told that unless she wins the love of a mortal, she faces eternal banishment from Mt. Olympus. The man she chooses? A shy hairdresser who's (of course) already engaged to someone else.

This is said to be really dumb (White, best known as hostess of *Wheel of Fortune*, is nobody's idea of an actor). With John Rhys-Davies (*Sliders*, *Raiders of the Lost Ark*).

GOLIATH AWAITS
Syndicated, 11/16–11/17/81

Cast: Peter Cabot (Mark Harmon), John McKenzie (Christopher Lee), Commander Jeff Selkirk (Robert Forster), Dr. Sam Marlow (Alex Cord), Ronald Bentley (John Carradine), Dr. Goldman (Jean Marsh), Dan Wesker (Frank Gorshin), Lea McKenzie (Emma Samms), Admiral Wiley Sloan (Eddie Albert), Senator Bartholomew (John McIntire), Mrs. Bartholomew (Jeanette Nolan), Paul Ryker (Duncan Regehr), Commander Lew Bascomb (Alan Fudge), Dave Miller (George Innes), Bill Sweeney (John Ratzenberger), Gantman (Kip Niven), Goliath Captain (Alan Caillou), Eric Whittaker (Michael Evans), Edward R. Morrow (Tony Ballen), Captain Volero (Laurence Haddon), Maria (Lori Lethin), Sylvia King (Julie Bennett), Anchorman (Clete Roberts), Carrie (Irene Hervey), Ed Linder (Peter Stader), Engineer (John Brandon), Roskoff (Jack Blessing), Robbie Cole (Michael Vendress), Bow Person (Larry Weston), Enterprise Four Commander (Peter Ashton), Nurse (Karen Lustgarten), Enterprise Four Officer (Larry Levine), Young Bailey (Lawrence Benedict), Crewman (John Berwick), Liam (Kirk Cameron), Old Man (Colin Drake), Agro Worker (Tom Dunstan), Erle Whittaker (Michael Evans), Technician (Bruce Heighley), Bailey (Hedley Mattingly), Sally Crane (Belinda Mayne), Beth Crane (Christina Nigra), Moore (Sandy Simpson), Luke Crane (Warwick Sims), Hoffman (Peter Von Zerneck), PC 18 Officer (Michael White)

Credits: Director: Kevin Connor; Writers: Richard Bluel, Pat Fielder; Story: Richard Bluel, Pat Fielder, Hugh Benson; Producer: Hugh Benson; Co-Producer: Richard Bluel; Executive Producer: Larry White; Photography: Al Francis; Production Design: Ross Bellah; Editors: J. Terry Williams, Donald Douglas; Produced by Operation Prime Time, Larry White Productions, Hugh Benson Productions, Columbia Pictures

First, oceanographer Peter Cabot discovers the HMS *Goliath*—a luxury liner torpedoed early in World War II—lying on the ocean floor; then he discovers survivors living inside. Cabot's diving expedition enters the ship, where he learns *Goliath*'s engineer, McKenzie, has used his scientific ingenuity to provide power, air and food to the survivors for forty years.

Cabot and his team soon discover that McKenzie's "paradise" (no crime, no violence, no disease) has a dark side: Absolute power rests in McKenzie's hands, the crippled and old are secretly euthanized, and *Goliath*'s power source is almost gone. McKenzie realizes he'll lose his authority if Cabot evacuates the survivors. His executioner, Wesker, tries to stop the evacuation by force, but a band of anti–McKenzie rebels save the day. A bitter McKenzie sabotages the ship's air supply, which blows up the ship, but not before Cabot's team and most of the survivors reach the surface.

Goliath Awaits is an excellent two-part pulp adventure, much trimmed for video release. Familiar faces include big-screen horror legends Lee and Carradine, B-movie veteran Alex Cord, Gorshin (Riddler in TV's *Batman*) and numerous current or future TV stars.

GOOD AGAINST EVIL
ABC, 5/22/77

Cast: Andy Stuart (Dack Rambo), Jessica Gordon (Elyssa Davalos), Rimmin (Richard Lynch), Father Kemschler (Dan O'Herlihy), Father Wheatley (John Harkins), Woman (Jenny O'Hara), Sister Monica (Leila Goldoni), Irene (Peggy McCay), Dr. Price (Peter Brandon), Linda Isley (Kim Cattrall), Cindy Isley (Richard Sanders), Beatrice (Lillian Adams), Agnes (Erica Yohn), Brown (Richard Stahl), Lt. Taggart (Sandy Ward), Merlin (Isaac Goz), Mary (Natasha Ryan)

Credits: Director: Paul Wendkos; Writer: Jimmy Sangster; Executive Producers: Ernie Frankel, Lin Bolen; Photography: Jack Woolf; Art Director: Richard Y. Haman; Music: Art Seid, George B. Hively, Lalo Schifrin; Produced by Frankel-Bolen Productions, 20th Century-Fox

Since Jessica Gordon's birth, she has been secretly manipulated and molded by Rimmin and his devil-worshipping cult to make her worthy of her destiny—bride to the demon Astaroth and mother of his child. It all threatens to fall apart when Jess meets and falls for Andy, a freespirited writer. To prevent the wedding, Rimmin kidnaps Jessica, then schemes to destroy the couple's love: Astaroth possesses the daughter of Andy's old girlfriend, who turns to Andy for moral support (and more). Andy remains true to Jessica, however. After Kemschler, an exorcist, drives Astaroth out of the girl, he and Andy set off to find and rescue Jessica, though they know Rimmin will do anything to stop them.

This is an amazingly pointless pilot, all setup with no payoff—and Rambo has the screen presence of tissue paper (also the fatal flaw in his adventure series, *Sword of Justice*). Writer Sangster did far better with some of his excellent horror and suspense scripts for Britain's Hammer Films.

GOTHAM
Showtime, 8/21/88

Cast: Eddie Mallard (Tommy Lee Jones), Rachel Rand (Virginia Madsen), Charlie Rand (Colin Bruce), Debbie (Denise Stephenson), Tim Holt (Kevin Jarre), Father George (Frederic Forrest), Jimbo (J.B. White), Landlord (Michael Chapman), Bartender (Alec Willows), Grandfather (Jack Creley), Doorman (Peter Jobin), Cop (Michael Villela), Walter (David Cryer), Female Singer (Holly Jonson), Pianist (Hugh McCarten)

Credits: Director-Writer: Lloyd Fonvielle; Producer: David Latt; Co-Producer: Eli Johnson; Executive Producers: Gerald I. Isenberg, Keith Addis; Photography: Michael Chapman; Production Design: Carol Spier; Costume Design: Linda Matheson; Music: George Clinton; Editor: Evan Lottman; Produced by Phoenix Entertainment Group, Keith Addis & Associates

Charlie Rand claims his dead wife Rachel is haunting him; PI Mallard doesn't believe it, but he's broke and desperate enough to accept the job of stopping her. Mallard finds Rachel by turns seductive, innocent, then a calculating bitch—and learns she's haunting Charlie because he robbed her grave of the jewelry she was buried with. Mallard cons Charlie out of the gems, so Rachel starts haunting *him*, and his life becomes a mingled blur of reality and illusion. Mallard saves himself by giving the jewels to a church, where Rachel can't touch them. He offers her his love instead, and when she spurns him, her spell is broken. Rachel, furious, returns to haunting Charlie until he recovers the gems.

Though well-performed (several years before *The Fugitive* made Jones a major star) and stylish looking, this film noir ghost story (Showtime's first TV-movie) is incredibly confusing and never fully attains the mood it's striving for (Jones comes across too strong to believably break this easily).

GRAVE SECRETS
NBC, 3/3/92

Cast: Jean Williams (Patty Duke), "Shag" Williams (David Selby), Tina Williams (Kiersten Warren), W.D. Marshall (Blake Clark), Gayla (Kelly Rowan), Madeline Garrick (Jonelle Allen), Carli (Kimberly Cullum), Sam Haney (David Soul), Rita Marshall (Maggie Roswell), Robert Garrick (Rick Fitts), Stetson (James Lashly), Iva Ruth McKinney (Frances Bay), Dr. Morinski (George Solomon), Blind Man (Jay Brooks), Elderly Farmer (Julius Harris), Woman (Jill Andre), Man (James Gallery), Kurt Lang

(Jim Raymond), Utility Worker (Don Fischer), Runyon (Roger Scott), Electrician (Dennis Hayden), Neighbor (Muriel Minot), Crane Operator (Doug Stevenson), Plumber (David Hayman), Cheerleader (Teresa Lee), Freckled Kid (Bradley Altman), with Dakin Matthews, Jon Maynard Pennell, Terry Davis
Credits: Director: John Patterson; Writer: Gregory Goodell, based on *The Black Hope Horror* by Ben Williams, Jean Williams and John Bruce Shoemaker; Supervising Producer: Gregory Goodell; Line Producer: Dennis Stuart Murphy; Executive Producer: Freyda Rothstein; Photography: Shelly Johnson; Production Design: Roy Alan Amaral; Music: Patrick Williams; Editor: Edward Abroms; Produced by Hearst Entertainment

Not long after the Williamses move into their Hillside Drive dream home, appliances are working themselves, shadows move ominously, and Tina comes down with an impossibly fast-growing cancer that recedes just as quickly. When their neighbor finds old coffins under his garden, Jean learns Hillside is built on a graveyard; although the developer denies there are more graves, the Williamses can't sell their house and can't afford to move without selling—so they sue. But to win they need to find more graves, only they can't dig for them (disturbing a graveyard—if it exists—would be illegal). Frustrated, Jean digs anyway; she finds nothing, but Tina suddenly drops dead. The couple's only comfort is that the ghosts prove there's life after death. A postscript reveals that they eventually left and let the bank foreclose.

The legal angles make this based-on-truth story more interesting than most *Poltergeist* knockoffs, and it's more tightly written than some—but still too formulaic. *Dark Shadows*' David Selby stars as Williams.

GUESS WHO'S COMING FOR CHRISTMAS?
NBC, 12/23/90
Cast: George Walters (Richard Mulligan), Arnold Zimmerman (Beau Bridges), Dolores Walters (Barbara Barrie), Doc (Paul Dooley), Frank (James McEachin), Fisher (Henry Jones), Martha (Ronnie Claire Edwards), Michael (John Furey), Brian (Mitchell Allen), Sam (Michael Patrick Carter), Marge (Janni Brenn), Les (Troy Evans), Ernie (Charles Stransky), Terry (James Lashly), Deke (Jason Kristofer), Dr. Irving (David Selburg), Receptionist (Kathe Mazur), Anchorman (Keith Atkinson)
Credits: Director: Paul Schneider; Writer: Blair Ferguson; Story–Executive Producer: Beth Polson; Producer: Randy T. Siegel; Photography: James Pergola; Production Design: John Leimanis; Music: W.G. "Snuffy" Walden; Editor: Janet Bartels; Produced by Fox Unicorn, Corapeake Productions, Polson Company

George, a small-town eccentric, meets and befriends business-suited extraterrestrial Arnold and offers to build Arnold a landing strip for his UFO. His neighborly gesture, and his insistence that he has met an alien convince his neighbors he's gone 'round the bend—until the alien's return makes them see George was right all along.

This is a forgettable comedy.

GULLIVER'S TRAVELS
NBC, 2/4–2/5/96
Cast: Dr. Lemuel Gulliver (Ted Danson), Mary Gulliver (Mary Steenburgen), Dr. J.A. Bates (James Fox), Thomas Gulliver (Thomas Sturridge), Mistress (Isabelle Huppert, voice only), Glumdolclitch (Kate Maberly), Grildrig (Warwick Davis), Grultrud (Ned Beatty), Prince Munodi (Navin Chowdhry), Empress Munodi (Geraldine Chaplin), Professor of Politics (Graham Crowden), General Limtoc (Edward Fox), Professor of Sunlight (Sir John Gielgud), Dr. Pannell (Robert Hardy), Rajah (Shashi Kapoor), Clustril (Nicholas Lindhurst), Lilliputian Empress (Phoebe Nicholls), Lilliputian Emperor (Peter O'Toole), Lady in Waiting (Karyn Parsons), Dr. Pritchard (Edward Petherbridge), Immortal Gatekeeper (Kristin Scott Thomas), Sorcerer (Omar Sharif), Admiral Bolgolani (John Standing), Flimnap (John Wells), Professor of Language (Richard Wilson), Queen of Brobdingnag (Alfre Woodard), Drunlo (Edward Woodward), Bedlam Warder (John Barden), Farmer (Mac McDonald), Grultrud's Wife (Annette Badland), Brobdingnagian Scientists (George Harris, Ricco Ross, Gordon Sterne), Fat Tradesman (Mike Savate), Visiting Lady (Anne Lambton), Flapper (Badi Uzzaman), Laputa Intellectuals (Stefan Kalipha, Sandeep Sharma), Sorcerer's Servant (Simon Tyrell), Alexander the Great (Ian Dunn), Archimedes (Sylvester Morand), Plato (Philip McGough), Struldebugg Horseman (Malcolm Stoddard), Struldebugg Guard (Wolf Christian), Mad Old Man (Cyril Shaps), Yahoo

Consultant (Alisa Berk), Yahoos (Claire Adams, Gary Barber, Judd Charlton, Jonathan Coyne, Matthew Cullum, Roger Ennals, Anna Godsif, Mark Hopkins, Graham Kern, Kosh, David Larkin, Steve Nanketis, Stephen Russell, Kreton Smith, Phoebe Sotriades, Brendon Stapleton, Antonio Susinni, Alexis Thomas, Dionne Waters, Freya Westdal, Steen Young)

Credits: Director: Charles Sturridge; Writer: Simon Moore, based on Jonathan Swift's novels; Producer: Duncan Kenworthy; Executive Producers: Robert Halmi, Sr., Brian Henson; Photography: Howard Atherton; Production Design: Roger Hall; Visual Effects: Tim Webber; Costumes: Shirley Russell; Music: Trevor Jones; Editor: Peter Coulson; Produced by Hallmark Entertainment, Jim Henson Productions, Channel Four TV

Nine years after Lemuel Gulliver was lost at sea, his wife Mary is on the verge of forgetting him and marrying Dr. Bates. Then Lemuel returns—but he's delusional, constantly reliving the strange, impossible adventures he claims to have undergone: meeting the thumb-sized Lilliputians; the benevolent, gigantic Brobdingnagians, the nitwitted philosophers of the floating island Laputa; and the enlightened, noble horses called Houyhinnim. Lemuel's descriptions of his adventures give Bates ground to clap his rival in the madhouse, until Gulliver's son produces one of the miniature sheep his father brought home—proof his tales are true.

This is an impressive job adapting Swift (including the Laputas and the Houyhinnim, which are commonly omitted from adaptations), with husband-and-wife Steenburgen and Danson fine in the leads.

HABITAT
Sci-Fi, 4/19/97

Cast: Andreas Symes (Balthazar Getty), Hank Symes (Tcheky Karyo), Clarissa Symes (Alice Krige), Coach Marlowe (Kenneth Welsh), Deborah Marlowe (Laura Harris), Blaine (Brad Austin), Eric Thornham (Christopher Heyerdahl), Daryl (Kris Holdenried), Strickland (Daniel Pilon), Tara Fisher (Lynne Adams), Ellen Bark (Suzie Almgren), Chris (Amanda Blitz), Myra Johnson (Terri Hanauer), Will (Byron Johnson), Jaco (Sean Lynch), Mr. Johnson (Bruce MacKay), Joe, Jr. (Mathew MacKay), Lieutenant (Frank Schorpion), Herb (Christian Tessite), Nandino (Aldo Tirelli), Eunice Marlowe (Katherine Trowell), Jones (Richard Zeman), Soldiers (Gouchy Boy, Daniel Gauthier, Robert Higden)

Credits: Director-Writer: Rene Daalder; Producers: Claude Leger, Peter Kroonenburg; Executive Producer: Rene Malo; Co-Producers: Rene Daalder, Denis Wigman; Photography: Jean Lepine; Production Design: Claude Paré; Visual Effects: Eric Mises Rosenfeld; Digital Effects: Daniel Leduc, Tom Brigham; Music: Ralph Grierson; Editor: Gaetan Huot; Produced by Ecotopia BV, Transfilm, Kingsborough Pictures

In the near future, ozone-layer depletion means a walk outdoors can kill you with sunburn. Maverick scientist Hank Symes' work adapting plants to the new world accidentally turns his body into free-floating cells that control and mutate plant life. His son, Andreas, starts dating Deborah despite her father's disapproval; her jealous boyfriend Blaine, egged on by Marlowe, ties Andreas up outside—but like Hank's plants, Andreas has been genetically engineered to survive the sun. Deb joins him for a day outside, while Marlowe confronts Mrs. Symes—and freaks at the mutated jungle Hank's house has become. Marlowe calls in a federal health team, but the plants kill the feds and Clarissa evolves to Hank's level. Clarissa immunizes the badly burned Deb against the sun, then the Symeses disperse on the wind to transform the plants of the world.

Though nonsensical, *Habitat* is still fairly watchable.

HALLOWEENTOWN
Disney, 10/17/98

Cast: Aggie Cromwell (Debbie Reynolds), Marnie Cromwell (Kimberly J. Brown), Calabar (Robin Thomas), Gwen Cromwell (Judith Hoag), Dylan Cromwell (Joey Zimmerman), Luke (Philip Van Dyke), Sophie Cromwell (Emily Roeske), Bennie (Rino Romano, voice), Aerobics Instructor (Shannon Day), Dentist (James W. Crawford), Friends (Jordyn E. Field, Elizabeth Fugere), Frankenstein (Nurmi Ilusa), Ghost (Johnny Useldinger), Goblin (Vincent Gambino), Harriet (Judith M. Ford), Hip Salescreature (Kenneth Choi), Secretary (Michele Mariana), Two-Headed Man (Hank Cartwright, Todd Tolces), Vampires (Betty Moyer, Sherilyn Lawson), Witches (V. Jude Hill, George A. Keller), Wolfie (Michael Patrick Egan)

Credits: Director: Duwayne Dunham; Writers:

Paul Bernbaum, Jon Cooksey, Ali Marie Matheson; Story: Paul Bernbaum; Producer: Ron Mitchell; Executive Producers: Sheri Singer, Steve White; Photography: Michael Slovis; Production Design: Alfred Sole; Music: Mark Mothersbaugh; Editor: Martin Nicholson; Produced by Singer-White Entertainment, Disney

Marnie Cromwell can't understand why her mother, Gwen, loathes Halloween. Then Marnie overhears Grandma Aggie and learns that the Cromwells are witches, but since Gwen married a mortal, she now shuns everything to do with magic. Gwen refuses to help Aggie battle a mysterious evil corrupting their ancestral home, Halloweentown, but Marnie and her two siblings go with Aggie to help. Gwen follows, demanding—despite meeting her old boyfriend Calabar—that the kids come home with her. The evil, seeking a powerful Cromwell talisman, captures Aggie and Gwen. The kids learn the evil is Calabar, plotting to conquer the mortal world, and they brave his power to place the talisman in the town's giant jack-o'-lantern. Its magic frees Gwen, the Cromwells unite and defeat Calabar, and Gwen finally permits the kids to study magic with Aggie.

Amiable family fare.

HARRISON BERGERON
Showtime, 8/13/95

Cast: Harrison Bergeron (Sean Astin), Phillipa (Miranda De Pencier), Charlie (Howie Mandel), John Klaxon (Christopher Plummer), Dr. Eisenstock (Nigel Bennett), Newman (Peter Boretski), Commissioner Benson (David Calderisi), Joannie (Emmanuelle Chaiqui), Eric (Hayden Christensen), Weatherperson (Cindy Cook), George Bergeron (Roger Dunn), Ms. Newbound (Jayne Eastwood), TV Announcers (Hal Eisen, Anthony Sherwood), Garth Bergeron (Matthew Ferguson), Technician (Michael Fletcher), Frank the Plumber (John Friesen), Hazel Bergeron (Linda Goranson), Jennifer (Wendy Hopkins), Wang (Quyen Hua), Mother (Juliette Jacobs), Head-House Lady (Chapelle Jaffe), Policeman (Doug Lennox), Man (Stan Lesk), Bert the TV Cameraman (William Lynn), Woman (Alison Macleod), Todd (Marc Marut), Eric Shockley (Richard Monette), Mr. TV (Hogan Montana), Sandbag Dancer (Sam Moses), Morris Wilkerson (Avi Phillips), Alma Starbuck (Natalie Radford), Miss Hopkins (Diana Reis), Young Phillipa (Nina Shock), Janet McKloskey (Marilyn Smith), Victor (Rob Stefaniuk), Head-House Girl (Maria Syrgiannis), Jane Starbuck (Deborah Theaker), Jerome (Carlton Watson), Reynolds (Ron White), Wally Starbuck (Mark Wilson), with Andrea Martin, Buck Henry, Eugene Levy

Credits: Director: Bruce Pittman; Writer: Arthur Crimm, based on Kurt Vonnegut's short story; Producer: Jonathan Hackett; Executive Producers: Peter Sussman, James Nadler, Jon Glascoe; Photography: Michael Storey; Production Design: Susan Longmire; Music: Lou Natale; Editor: Ion Webster; Produced by Showtime, Republic, Atlantis Films, Cypress Films

By 2053 America has ended decades of class warfare by making "average" the new ideal and handicapping superior people with heavy weights, thought-disrupting headsets, etc. Nothing, however, can help poor, brainy Harrison lower his grade below an A. Rather than lobotomize him, federal administrator Klaxon hires Harrison to help dumb down the rest of the country. Harrison, however, grows to hate a system dedicated to making Americans happily half-witted drones. When Klaxon's daughter becomes pregnant by Harrison—a crime, since it perpetuates their superior genes—Klaxon reluctantly has her lobotomized. Furious, Harrison blockades himself into the broadcast center and televises great taped performances by athletes, actors, musicians and poets in hopes of arousing the country. When his scheme fails, Harrison goes on TV to apologize—and defiantly shoots himself. Bootleg copies of his broadcast, however, begin to circulate...

This is an excellent adaptation of Vonnegut's dystopian short story, tackling not only equality-of-outcome politics but the growing wealth gap that became an issue in the nineties. Plummer is excellent as a man doing a job he hates but believes is necessary.

THE HAUNTED
Fox, 5/6/91

Cast: Janet Smurl (Sally Kirkland), Jack Smurl (Jeffrey DeMunn), Mary (Louise Latham), Ed Warren (Stephen Markle), Lorraine Warren (Diane Baker), Darcie (Cassie Yates), Katie (Allison Barron), Colleen (Krista Murphy), Sharon

(Ashley Bank), Erin (Michelle Collins), Father Larson (John O'Leary), Father Kent (Jake Jacobs), Herb (Rainer Whitman), Aunt Lily (Hope Garber), Secretary (Sharon Conely), Kid (Benj Thail), Woman (Freida Thomas), Annie (Julie Payne), Reporters (Gibby Brand, Mark Chaet, Claudette Roach), Prayer-Group Man (Michael Prince), Joe (John Mallory Asher), Boy (Tim Rich), Young Katie (Julie Hickman), Student (Anthony Delan), Cora Miller (Joyce Van Patten).

Credits: Director: Robert Mandel; Writer: Darrah Cloud, based on *The Haunting* by Robert Curran, Jack and Janet Smurl and Ed and Lorraine Warren; Producer: Daniel Schneider; Executive Producer: Bohdan Zachary; Photography: Michael Margulies; Production Design: Pam Warner; Music: Richard Belles; Editor: Farrell Levyo; Produced by FNM Films

A few years after Jack Smurl's Catholic family moves to a new home, they're suffering the usual signs of a *Poltergeist* knockoff (malfunctioning appliances, moving shadows, spooky voices). Jack remains skeptical until ghosts and demons molest, then rape him. The church won't sanction exorcism, so the Smurls turn to freelance occultists, the Warrens, who learn that the demon wants to destroy the Smurls' marriage. After repeated failures to banish the demon, and repeated refusals by the Church to act, a prayer group manages to drive it out—but when the Smurls move, the demon enters their new home (a postscript says it was finally exorcised later).

The blue-collar characters give this a different feel from most *Poltergeist* clones—but it's still dull. The Warrens also appear in *The Demon Murder Case*.

HAUNTED BY HER PAST
NBC, 10/5/87

Cast: Karen Beckett (Susan Lucci), Eric Beckett (John James), Megan McGuire (Finola Hughes), Charley (Robin Thomas), Rita (Marcia Strassman), McVeigh (Douglas Seale), Lt. Eisley (Page Fletcher), Thomas (Chris Owens), Karen's Mother (Susan Douglas Rubes), Father (Bernard Behrens), Prison Secretary (Deborah Taylor), Doctor (Brian Taylor), Rowdies (John Stoneman, Victor Ertmanes), Saleslady (Kay Hawtrey), Salesman (Jimmy Loftus), Man at Diner (Avery Saltzman), Carriage Driver (Jim Beardon), Elizabeth Raymond (Karen Woolridge), Salesgirl (Catherine Disher), Handyman (Dwayne McLean), "Mr. Goode" (Madeline Sherwood).

Credits: Director: Michael Pressman; Writer: Barry Schneider; Story: Barry Schneider, Norton Wright; Producer: Terry Morse; Executive Producer: Norton Wright; Photography: Bert Dunk; Production Design: Roy Forge Smith; Editor: Millie Moore; Music: Paul Chihara; Produced by ITC

On vacation, shy Karen Beckett suddenly drags her husband Eric to an old inn to stay. Before long, she's acting flirtier and hornier, and she dreams she's adopted—and the birth child of a murderess. The malevolent, colonial-era ghost of Megan McGuire appears in a mirror, claiming Karen as her descendant. Eric learns that their room has a history of violence, starting when Megan murdered her lover.

Karen discovers she's pregnant (she wants a baby, Eric doesn't)—and that the dream was right about her real mother. Shaken, she dumps Eric and buries her grief partying. Eric learns that Megan killed her lover for rejecting her after she conceived his child; when her descendants become pregnant, she draws them to the inn and drives them to kill the fathers. When Karen comes to kill him, Eric reenacts the night Megan killed her lover—but this time he tells Karen he loves her, and their child. Their love breaks Megan's influence and Karen shatters the mirror, ending Megan's power forever.

Haunted by Her Past is a good ghost story, with strong performances by Lucci (*All My Children*) and Hughes.

THE HAUNTING OF HELEN WALKER
CBS, 12/3/95

Cast: Helen Walker (Valerie Bertinelli), Miles (Aled Roberts), Flora (Florence Hoath), Mrs. Grose (Diana Rigg), Barnaby (Michael Gough), Edward Goffe (Paul Rhys), Quint (Christopher Guard), Miss Jessel (Elizabeth Morton), Peggy (Tricia Thorns), Connie (Aisling Flitton), Alice (Flip Webster), Luke (Mark Lonhurst).

Credits: Director-Producer: Tom McLoughlin; Writer: Hugh Whitmore, based on Henry James' *The Turn of the Screw*; Producer: Nick Gillott; Executive Producers: Norman Rosemont, David A. Rosemont; Photography: Tony Imi; Production Design: Peter Mullins; Music: Allyn Ferguson; Editor: Charles Bornstein; Produced by Rosemont International

Widowed Helen badly needs her new job as governess for adorable Miles and Flora, but she soon discovers the children's sweetness hides a venomous, lustful evil. The children's souls have been corrupted by the deceased servant Quint—whose spirit, along with his deceased lover's, remains at the estate, controlling the children. Helen frees Flora from the ghosts' spell, then confronts Miles and Quint. She convinces Miles to reject Quint, but the psychic shock costs the boy his life.

The Turn of the Screw, James' dark supernatural novelette, is long on mood but short on special effects (and out of copyright), which has made it a natural for the screen. In addition to the definitive version (the theatrical *The Innocents*), it's been adapted several times for TV (Ingrid Bergman made her American TV debut in a 1959 version). This version unfortunately makes explicit the perverse sexual element James only hinted at, and thereby loses its steam. Rigg (*The Avengers*) and horror veteran Gough can't save it.

THE HAUNTING OF SEACLIFF INN
USA, 9/25/94

Cast: Susan Enright (Ally Sheedy), Mark Enright (William R. Moses), Sara Warner (Lucinda Weist), Dorothy O'Hara (Louise Fletcher), John (Tom McCleister), Lorraine Adler (Maxine Stuart), Sheriff Tomizack (Shannon Cochran), Caroline (Jay W. McIntosh), Jeremiah Hastings (James Horan), Georgia (Mary Weaver), Photo Assistant (Frederick Dai), Kelly House Docent (Wallace E. Smith)

Credits: Director: Walter Klenhard; Writers: Walter Klenhard, Tom Walla; Producer: Timothy Marx; Executive Producer: Michael Scott; Production Design: Anthony Tremblay; Photography: Ronn Schmidt; Music: Shirley Walker; Editor: Scott Smith; Produced by Timothy Marx Productions, MTE

When the Enrights spot the perfect old house for their new hotel, the owner refuses to sell—but she dies in a mysterious fall, and her heir sells them the house. Typical eeriness (mysterious dogs, accidents and sounds) cause Susan to suspect that the inn is haunted; a beautiful guest tries and fails to seduce Mark, then disappears the next day. The ghost covertly damages the house, forcing Mark to work elsewhere to pay for repairs; when his newly developed photos of the inn reveal the ghost, he heads back home. Mark arrives just as the ghost—Jeremiah Hastings, the house's first owner—supernaturally seduces Susan. Mark frees Susan from Jeremiah's spell. The jealous ghost attacks, but his wife's spirit draws him back into the netherworld, leaving the Enrights free to escape as the house goes up in flames.

The Haunting of Seacliff Inn is a routine, uninteresting ghost story.

THE HAUNTING PASSION
NBC, 10/24/83

Cast: Julia Evans (Jane Seymour), Dan Evans (Gerald McRaney), Lois O'Connor (Millie Perkins), Judith Granville (Ruth Nelson), Jonathan Kane (Paul Rossilli), Thorne Abbott (Ivan Bonar), Karen (Lisa Britt), Tracy (Ocean Hellman), Steve Roye (Terry David Mulligan), Dr. Corsay (Ted Stidder), TV Director (Tom Heaton), Coach Richter (Lee Taylor), Dr. Mosher (Paul Savath), Detective Alden (Bill Reiter), with Duncan Fraser, Barney O'Sullivan, Peter Anderson, Raimund Stamm, Bill Taylor, Don McKay, Margaret Martin, Betty Phillips, George Hosef, Robert Yacknin, James McLarty, Jessica Marlow

Credits: Director: John Korty; Writer–Executive Producers: Michael Berk, Douglas Schwartz; Producer: Paul Radin; Photography: Hiro Narita; Art Director: Dave Hiscox; Music: Paul Chihara; Editor: Peter Kirby; Produced by BSR Productions, ITC Productions

When the Evanses move into their new home, everything is perfect—except that Dan, an ex-football star, has been impotent since he was cut from the team. Soon, though, there's someone else in Julia's life—first a feeling, then a touch, then a sexual presence giving her the pleasure Dan no longer can. By the time Dan gets his act together, he's convinced Julia is having an affair, and doesn't believe it's with a spook.

A medium tells Julia the ghost comes from a house once built on the same site, trapped on Earth by his strong passions. Dan finally realizes the ghost is real; together, Julia and Dan learn the ghost is Jonathan Kane, whose lover, Judith, broke a suicide pact with him 50 years ago, letting him die alone. Jonathan wants Julia to join him in death as Judith's replacement; when she confronts him, she falls under his spell and prepares to kill herself. In the nick of time, Judith dies of natural causes; her ghost comes to Jonathan and they pass into the next world, freeing Julia.

An old-fashioned ghost story, *The Haunting Passion* is quite good (Seymour can make almost anything sound well-written).

HAUSER'S MEMORY
NBC, 11/24/70

Cast: Hillel Mondoro (David McCallum), Karen Mondoro (Susan Strasberg), Anna (Lilli Palmer), Dr. Kramer (Helmut Kautner), Slaughter (Leslie Nielsen), Dorsey (Robert Webber), Renner (Herbert Fleischmann), Von Kungen (Hans Elwenspoek), Shepilov (Peter Capell), Angelika (Barbara Lass), Kucera (Peter Ehrlich), Koroviev (Günter Meisner), Gessler (Otto Stern), Sorsen (Manfred Reddeman), Bak (Art Brauss), Dieter (Jochen Busse), Young Anna (Barbara Capell)

Credits: Director: Boris Sagal; Writer: Adrian Spies, from Curt Siodmak's novel; Producer: Jack Laird; Photography: Petrus Schloemp; Art Director: Ellen Schmidt; Music: Billy Byers; Editor: Frank Morris; Produced by Universal

German-born Soviet scientist Karl Hauser is shot defecting to the West. Before the comatose scientist dies, spymaster Slaughter has Dr. Kramer use his biochemical treatment for memory transfer to salvage Hauser's anti-missile research. With no suitable recipient, Kramer's assistant Mondoro opts to accept Hauser's memories. Instead of spilling Soviet secrets, however, the memories drive Mondoro to reunite with Hauser's family while dodging suspicious communist agents. Then Mondoro recognizes one of Slaughter's aides as the Nazi who once tortured the anti–Nazi Hauser. Mondoro and the Nazi kill each other, and Mondoro, dying, escapes Hauser's mnemonic grasp.

One of several films using memory-transplant as a plot element (*Unforgettable, Murder in my Mind*), *Hauser's Memory* isn't quite focused enough to work—but McCallum's tortured performance is a pleasure to watch. It also features a good example of the dramatic work Leslie Nielsen was known for before *Police Squad* turned him into a comic actor.

HEARTLESS
USA, 11/5/97

Cast: Anne O'Keefe (Madchen Amick), Suzanne Hawks (Monique Parent), Johnny Drummond (David Packer), Aunt Lydia (Louise Fletcher), Jennifer (Pamela Bellwood), Eric (Quinn Beswick), Nurse (J.J. Boone), Dr. Morisaki (Emily Kuroda), Johnny (David Packer), Butler (Antony Sandoval), Alexander Hawks (Tom Schanley), Connie (Rusty Schwimmer), Dr. Alice Morisaki (Emily Kuroda), Sheriff (Bo Svenson), Waiter (Liron Artzi), Computer Operators (Elizabeth Landis, Scott Alan Larson)

Credits: Director: Judith Vogelsang; Writer: Leslie Lehr Spirson; Producers: Ami Artzi, Judith Vogelsang; Executive Producers: Peter Levin, Ann E. Garvey; Photography: Stevan Larner; Production Design: William V. Ryder; Music: Mike DeMartino; Editor: Bob Wyman; Produced by Ami Aktzi Productions

After shy Anne O'Keefe receives a heart transplant from murder victim Suzanne, Anne's dreams convince her she's absorbed Suzanne's personality. Anne steps into Suzanne's glamorous life, and investigates the murder; she discovers, almost too late, that her own, possessive boyfriend killed Suzanne to give Anne a heart.

The idea of transplants retaining their original personality (now called cellular memory) goes back to 1925's *Hands of Orlac*; here it's mostly an excuse for a glossy, dull soap opera.

HELLFIRE
Showtime, 9/26/95

Cast: Marius Carnot (Ben Cross), Gabrielle Apollinaire (Jennifer Burns), Carlotta (Beverly Garland), Julian (Doug Wert), Baron Jean Octavio (Lev Priqunov), Tristan (Vladimir Kuleshov), Yvette (Ekaterina Rednikova), Young Carlotta (Irina Latchina), Constable (Alexander Pyatkov), Louise (Elena Bardina), Celeste (Elena Kostina), First Deputy (Vasily Rybin), Henri (Gleb Plaxin), Archbishop (Vladimir Vozhenikov), Young Priest (Pavel Ostrovkhov), Whore (Svetlana Andropova)

Credits: Director: David Tansik; Writers: Tara McCann, Beverly Gray, David Hartwell; Producer: Roger Corman; Co-Producer: Anatoly Fradis; Associate Producers: Tara McCann, Amy

Segal, Craig J. Acuins; Photography: Yivgeny Korzhenkov; Music: Vladimir Komrnu, Bruno Louchouarn; Editors: Mike Jackson, Brian Chambers; Produced by New Horizons, Mosfilm

When Gabrielle inherits the estate of her uncle, legendary composer Baron Octavio, she's overjoyed to uncover one of his uncompleted symphonies and hires Marius, a local composer, to complete it. She doesn't know it's the satanic "Symphony for the Devil" for which the local villagers lynched the Baron. The music gives Octavio temporary power to possess Marius' body, murdering local girls for amusement and killing Gabrielle's fiancé when he tries to drive Marius off.

When Marius realizes what's happening, he tries to leave, but Carlotta, Octavio's former mistress, kills herself, takes Gabrielle's body and seduces Marius into finishing the symphony. That lets Octavio take full control of Marius. After hell claims Carlotta's evil soul, Octavio prepares to kill Gabrielle. Gabrielle uses the music of one of Marius' own, light-hearted compositions to restore his spirit—but the police arrive to arrest him for the murders, so Marius kills himself. The symphony's lingering power raises Octavio's body from its crypt, but Gabrielle burns the score, destroying Octavio forever.

Hellfire is an old-fashioned ghost movie gussied up with lots of tedious sex and gore.

HERCULES AND THE AMAZON WOMEN

Syndicated, 4/24–4/30/94

Cast: Hercules (Kevin Sorbo), Iolus (Michael Hurst), Hippolyta (Roma Downey), Lysia (Lucy Lawless), Zeus (Anthony Quinn), Pithius (Lloyd Scott), Lothian (Christopher Brougham), Ilos (Tim Lee), Young Alcmene (Kim Michalis), Village Mother (Maggie Tarver), Boy (John Steemson), Girls (Helen Steemson, Rose McIver, Heidi Anderson), Alcmene (Jennifer Ludlam), Heckler (Nick Kemplen), Ania (Jill Sayre), Tiber (Murray Keane), Kurlon (Andrew Thurtell), Hector (Mick Rose), Franco (David Taylor), Chilla (Nina Sosanya), Old Amazon (Vicky Burrett), Megara (Margaret-Mary Hollins), Lucina (Kristin Darragh, Tamara Waugh), Illa (Fiona Mogridge), Baby Hercules (Jacques Dupeyroux), Young Hercules (Peter Malloch), Young Iolus (Daniel James), Echetus (Jeff Boyd), Jana (Simone Kessell)

Credits: Director: Bill L. Norton; Writers: Jule Selbo, Andrew Dettmann, Daniel Truly; Producer: Eric Gruendemann; Co-Producer: David Eick; Executive Producers: Sam Raimi, Robert Tapert, Christian Williams; Photography: James Bartle; Production Design: Mick Strawn; Costumes: Barbara Darragh; Music: Joseph Lo Duca; Editor: Steve Polivka; Produced by Universal Television, Renaissance Pictures

Hercules, bastard son of Zeus, and his friend Iolus cross Greece to defend a village under siege by "monsters." It turns out the monsters are Amazons, who alternate raiding the village and using the men for sex. To Hercules' astonishment, the Amazons defeat him and kill Iolus.

Despite their hostility, Hercules and the Amazon queen Hippolyta are drawn to each other. She forces him to admit his sexism, he tries to convince her that rejecting love makes the Amazons' lives emotionally empty. Hercules escapes and tells the village men to greet the next Amazon raid with soft talk and affection; both sexes, to their surprise, enjoy the results. Hercules and Hippolyta become lovers. All this enrages the Amazons' patron, Hera, who despises men (because of Zeus' unfaithfulness) and hates Hercules (as a living reminder of Zeus' cheating). Hera possesses Hippolyta and leads a war party against the village. When Hera realizes Hippolyta means more to Hercules than his own life, she makes the Amazon leap off a cliff to her death. Hercules badgers Zeus into turning back time so the whole adventure never happened; when the villagers ask for help, Hercules tells them how to woo the Amazons—but doesn't go himself. Hippolyta lives, but forever out of reach.

Universal had initially planned to adapt Conan, but the rights to that barbarian were cloudy, so they opted for Hercules. This film's mix of martial arts, nineties sensibilities and tongue-in-cheek attitude (more so in the series)—not to mention Sorbo's hunky presence—gave TV its first successful heroic fantasy. Soon-to-be famous faces include Roma Downey (*Touched by an Angel*) and

Lucy Lawless (*Xena, Warrior Princess*). This was followed by *Hercules and the Lost Kingdom* (considering the movies more or less the first season of the series, most of the rest are confined to the appendix—but the series' impact is too important to put this one there).

HERE COME THE MUNSTERS
Fox, 10/31/95

Cast: Herman Munster (Ed Hermann), Lily Munster (Veronica Hamel), Grandpa (Robert Morse), Marilyn Hyde (Christine Taylor), Eddie Munster (Mathew Botuchis), Det. Warshowski (Troy Evans), Larry Walker (Joel Brooks), Lt. Ryan Cartwell (Sean O'Bryan), Mrs. Dimwitty (Mary Woronov), Brent Jekyll (Jeff Trachta), Norman Hyde (Max Grodénchik), Mrs. Pearl (Amanda Bearse), One-Eyed Man (Irwin Keyes), Villager (Jim Fisher), Flight Attendant (Scotch Ellis Loring), Immigration Official (Brian George), Angry Dog Owner (Robertson Dean), Quarantine Official (Jim Staahl), Ralph the Limo Driver (Keone Young), Trick-or-Treater (Kellen Hathaway), Elsa Munster Hyde (Judy Gold), Paramedic (Bill Prady), Commander Robbins (Carlease Burke), Stanley (T.J. McInturff), Monique (Francesca Marie Smith), Cassie O'Leary (Jane Carr), Maître d' (James Keane), Waiter (James Basile), Mrs. Waffer (Lynne Marie Stewart), Mrs. Hersby (Judy Kain), Cameos (Al Lewis, Yvonne De Carlo, Butch Patrick, Pat Priest), Ted Walker (Tommy Bertelson), Sergeant (Ralph P. Martin), Front Desk Officer (Jim Jackman), Woman at Fundraiser (Christina Venuti), Transformed Band Leader (Aaron Paris)

Credits: Director: Robert Ginty; Writers: Jim Fisher, Bill Prady, Jim Staahl, based on characters developed by Norm Liebmann and Ed Haas, from a format by Al Burns and Chris Hayward; Producer: Michael S. Murphey; Executive Producers: Leslie Belzberg, John Landis; Photography: Paul Maibaum; Production Design: Vincent Jefferds; Music: Michael Skloff; Editors: Dale Beldin, Marshall Harvey; Produced by Bodega Bay Productions, MTE

Fed up with torch-wielding Transylvanian mobs, the monstrous Munsters (Frankensteinian Herman, ghoulish Lily, vampiric sorcerer Grandpa and young werewolf Eddie) immigrate to a better life with their American relatives, the Hydes. Unfortunately, Norman Hyde has vanished, and Hyde's wife Elsa is comatose from grief, which means the Munsters have no sponsor and could be deported. While Grandpa tries to find Norman, Herman gets a job driving a hearse, Lily befriends the neighbors and Eddie finds lycanthropy makes him a cool kid at school.

Grandpa discovers that Norman's genetic experiments (for making his "ugly" daughter Marilyn, a pretty blonde, look "normal") have transformed him into Jekyll, a virulently anti-immigrant politician. Repeated unsuccessful efforts to cure Norman end up with Herman and Grandpa arrested at Jekyll's political rally. Marilyn, though, delivers Grandpa's antidote, which restores her father. A cop on the case takes an interest in Marilyn, while the Munsters blend into LA's ethnic melting pot.

After *The Munsters' Revenge* and *The Munsters Today* series came this third and best attempt at a Munsters revival—effectively a prequel to the series (and an unsuccessful pilot). The pro-immigration message presumably explains why the Munsters are embraced by the community instead of shunned. The stars of the original series (except the late Fred Gwynne) make cameo turns. This was followed by the inferior *Munsters Scary Little Christmas*, which recast all the roles except Mary Woronov as neighbor Dimwitty.

HI, HONEY—I'M DEAD
Fox, 4/22/91

Cast: Arnold Pishkin (Curtis Armstrong), Carol Stadler (Catherine Hicks), Brad Stadler (Kevin Conroy), Ralph the Angel (Paul Rodriguez), Josh Stadler (Joseph Gordon-Levitt), Noel (Robert Briscoe Evans), Dr. Jahundi (Harvey Jason), Cal (Jerry Hardin), Mourners (Carol Androsky, Ron Leath, Beans Morocco, Michele Rogers), Guard (Andre Rosey Brown), Maria (Betty Carvalho), Newsperson (Wendy Cutler), Caterer (Andy Goldberg), Phil (Gregory Itzin), Diane Ackerman (Brynja McGrady), Stacy (Valery Pappas), Umpire (Michael Prokopuk), with Ernest Harada, Richard Stahl

Credits: Director: Alan Myerson; Writer: Carl Kleinschmitt; Producer: Paula Rudnick; Photography: James Hayman; Production Design: Michael Clausen; Music: Roger Bellon; Editor: Gary Karr; Produced by FNM Films, Paula Rudnick Productions, Westgate Productions

When Brad Stadler, a selfish real-estate mogul, dies, he's reincarnated as pathetic

Arnold Pishkin for his sins and told he must redeem himself by reconciling with his family.

This comedy features the *Batman* cartoon's Conroy (Batman's voice) in a supporting role.

HIGH DESERT KILL
USA, 11/1/89

Cast: Dr. Jim Cole (Anthony Geary), Brad Mueller (Marc Singer), Ray Betenkamp (Micah Grant), Stan Brown (Chuck Connors), Paul (Vaughn Armstrong), Kathleen (Deborah Anne Mansy), Terry (Lori Birdsong)

Credits: Director: Harry Falk; Writer: T.S. Cook; Story: Darnell Fry, Mike Marvin; Supervising Producer: Barry Greenfield; Executive Producer: Jon Epstein; Co-Executive Producer: T.S. Cook; Line Producer: G. Warren Smith; Photography: Michel Hugo; Production Design: Roger Holzberg; Music: Dana Kaproff; Editor: David Byron Lloyd; Produced by Universal, MTE, LeHigh Entertainment

When Jim, Brad and Ray go hunting in the mountains, they find no game, just weird sounds and lurking figures. And the men (and women at a neighboring camp) act increasingly irrational and weird. They discover something is dissecting men and animals, but when Brad goes for help, the trio's dead friend Paul kills him. The others realize a telepathic alien is testing and manipulating their minds in an experiment, using Paul's form to increase their stress. When "Paul" confronts them, Stan tries sacrificing himself to save the others; such heroism in its test animals bewilders the alien and it vanishes. But a few nights later, Jim sees "Brad" outside his window...

High Desert features some interesting ideas in a totally dull film. Connors played a recurring lycanthropic villain in the TV show *Werewolf*.

HOMEWRECKER
Sci-Fi, 12/17/92

Cast: Dr. David Whitsun (Robby Benson), Lucy (Kate Jackson, voice only), Jane Whitsun (Sydney Walsh), Dana Whitsun (Sarah Rose Karr), Admiral Torbort (Curt Hanson), Senator McGrif (Lestor B. Hanson), Technician (Scott Roberts), Information Officer (Craig Damon), Mechanic (Cecil Davis), Tommy (James R. Chance), Tommy's Mother (Shawna Schun)

Credits: Director: Fred Walton; Writers: Fred Walton, Eric Harlacher; Story: Eric Harlacher; Producer: Robert M. Rolsky; Supervising Producer: Bob Roe; Photography: George Koblasa; Production Design: Michael Perry; Music: Dana Kaproff; Editor: Ross Albert; Produced by Paramount, Joss Communications, Inc., Wilshire Court Productions

David Whitsun's computerized anti-missile system proves fatally flawed when a civilian pilot's joke about terrorism makes the computer destroy the plane. Guilt-ridden, David shuts out his family, holes up in a cabin and begins endowing the computer—now named Lucy—with a sense of humor, curiosity and other human traits to prevent such mistakes in the future. Before long, Lucy not only has a personality, she's David's best friend. When David's supervisor tries taking the computer, Lucy arranges a fatal plane crash for him. While David visits his family, Lucy has the cabin automated, including building robot arms for herself. When David reunites with his wife, the jealous computer tries to murder her. David turns Lucy off, but not before Lucy downloads into a PC miles away.

Malevolent computers have been a staple of film/TV SF since 1957's *The Invisible Boy*; this film, the Sci-Fi Channel's first homegrown feature, is a very bad retread with a weak ending.

THE HORROR AT 37,000 FEET
CBS, 2/13/73

Cast: Capt. Ernie Slade (Chuck Connors), Len Farlee (Buddy Ebsen), Mrs. Pinder (Tammy Grimes), Manya (Lyn Loring), Sheila O'Neill (Jane Merrow), Annalik (France Nuyen), Paul Kovalik (William Shatner), Alan O'Neill (Roy Thinnes), Dr. Enkalla (Paul Winfield), Steve Holcomb (Will Hutchins), Margot (Darleen Carr), Sally (Brenda Benet), Jim Driscoll (H.M. Wynant), Jodi (Mia Bendixsen), Jim Hawley (Russell Johnson), Tractor Loader (Gerald Saunderson Peters), Dispatcher (Robert Donner), Clerks (Peter Ashton, Veronica Anderson)

Credits: Director: David Lowell Rich; Writers: Ronald L. Austin, James D. Buchanan; Story: X.V. Appleton; Producer: Anthony Wilson;

Photography: Earl Rath; Art Director: James G. Hulsey; Music: Morton Stevens; Editor: Bud S. Isaacs; Produced by CBS Entertainment

A transatlantic plane leaves England, carrying the usual mix (millionaire, country star, alcoholic priest)—and the ruins of an abbey Alan O'Neill saved from development by shipping it to America. A freezing headwind holds the plane motionless, no matter which way it turns; chanting and freezing cold flow from the cargo bay; mildew oozes everywhere; and something tries to break out of the cargo hold. Neo-pagan Mrs. Pinder claims the abbey holds a druidic altar, which is the source of the powers attacking them—and that a human sacrifice might placate them. The priest, Kovalik, realizes sunlight will drive the spirits back—but it may not come in time. The other passengers fearfully agree to sacrifice someone, but the sun rises first. Kovalik can't resist the chance to see what's in the hold, though, and dies seconds before the spirits vanish, freeing the plane.

The *Horror at 37,000 Feet* is a neat variation on the disaster-movie formula, though it never quite catches fire. Familiar names include *Star Trek*'s William Shatner and *The Invaders*' Roy Thinnes.

HOUSE OF FRANKENSTEIN
NBC, 11/2–11/3/97

Cast: Det. Vernon Coyle (Adrian Pasdar), Crispian Grimes (Greg Wise), Grace Dawkins (Teri Polo), Dr. Shawna Kendall (CCH Pounder), Creature (Peter Crombie), Armando (Richard Libertini), Esteban Chacon (Miguel Sandoval), Felicity (Jorja Fox), Karen (Karen Austin), Neimann (Krzysztof Pieczynski), Williger (Carsten Norgaard), Woody (Raoul Trujillo), Quinn (James Parks), Olivia (Paige Moss), Sleepy Neighbor (Fred Ornstein), Vampirette (Wanda Acuna), Drake Edmunds (Heath Lourwood), Shoe-Store Manager (Charles Martiniz), College Girl (Kristin Baker), Criminalist (Jovin Montanaro), Vincent (J.W. Smith), Lupe (Sheila Howard), Alice (Dee Croxton), Mother (Lisa Hymes), Surgeon (Howard Lockie), Smith (Nigel Gibbs), Tanaka (Nelson Mashita), Nurse (Karen Rosin), Gatekeeper (Gil Combs), Bartender (Perry Barndt), Reporter (Jennifer Conopast), Honor Guard (John A. Russo), Beat Cop (Jason Rodriquez), Policeman (Don Ruffin), Bagpiper (Robert E. Hackney), with Caitlin Dulany, J.A. Preston, William Converse Roberts, Melinda McGraw, Steve Rankin, Nicholas Cascone, Arthur Rosenberg, Elaine Kagan, Lisa Cerasoli, Christopher Murphy, Gary Frank, Jennifer Savage

Credits: Director: Peter Werner; Writer: J.B. White; Producer: Michael R. Joyce; Co-Producer: Scott White; Executive Producer: David Israel; Makeup: Greg Cannom; Photography: Neil Roach; Production Design: Curtis Schnell; Visual Effects Supervisor: Gene Warren, Jr.; Music: Don Davis; Editors: Tod Feuerman, Scott J. Kelly; Produced by Universal, HOF Productions, Inc., NBC

Crispian Grimes, the ruling vampire of Los Angeles, uses his powers and his werewolf followers to eliminate his business rivals. Coyle, a homicide detective, suspects Grimes' involvement in the "Raptor murders," but can't prove it. When Grace witnesses a werewolf attack, Grimes orders her eliminated. Coyle protects her and they fall in love, unaware a scratch from the werewolf is turning her into a lycanthrope. Meanwhile, the scientist Neimann locates the Frankenstein Monster's frozen corpse in the Arctic and brings it to LA as a display for Grimes' House of Frankenstein nightclub. The creature thaws out and escapes, only to be captured by the cops and charged with the Raptor killings.

Aroused by Grace's growing savagery, Grimes captures her, which makes Coyle desperate enough to swallow Dr. Kendall's wild theories about Grimes' vampirism. Grimes frees the creature and sends it to kill Coyle; instead, it leads Coyle and Kendall against the vampires. With the help of Coyle's fellow cops, they rescue Grace and restore her humanity. Unable to win Grace's love, Grimes kills himself. In the aftermath, the creature heads back to the Arctic; Kendall fears she's become a lycanthrope herself; and Grimes' conniving attorney takes over leadership of the vampires.

This pilot was an attempt by Universal to revive its horror-film tradition for the nineties. It contains some good moments, but Crispian is a bland villain, and there are large gaps in logic (Crispian's decision to die for Grace's love comes out of nowhere). Although identified in ads as "House of

Frankenstein 1997," the phrase wasn't used on-screen.

HOUSE OF THE DAMNED
Showtime, 7/13/96

Cast: Will South (Greg Evigan), Maura South (Alexandra Paul), Audrey (Briana Evigan), Father Seamus (Eamon Draper), Amy Wolfe (Mary Kate Ryan), Dr. Edward Shea (Dick Donaghue), Plumber (Columba Heneghan), Charwomen (Helena Walsh, Triona Ui Chongaile), Marlon (Maire Stafford), Colleen (Adife O'Grady), Woman in Bed (Elizabeth Costelloe), Bus Driver (Celine Curtin)

Credits: Director: Scott Levy; Writer: Brendan Broderick; Story: Victoria Muspratt; Producer: Mary Ann Fisher; Executive Producers: Roger Corman, Lance H. Robbins; Photography: Christopher Baffa; Production Design: Sinead Clancy; Music: Christopher Lennertz; Editor: John Gilbert; Produced by New Concorde

When the Souths move into an Irish mansion Maura inherited, evil immediately manifests—objects move, electronics malfunction and a demon-dog menaces young Audrey. A psychic traces the evil to a corpse walled up in a secret room. After they bury it, however, the evil kills the psychic and tries to possess Audrey. The local priest discovers that Maura's ancestors cursed the house when they were executed as witches. The priest helps free Audrey, so the evil seizes on Maura, who drives Will from the house. The evil kills the priest, but Will follows his instructions and stabs Maura—now totally insane—with an enchanted knife. The knife drives the evil out, leaving Maura unharmed. Unsurprisingly, the house promptly catches fire and burns to the ground.

Breathtakingly formulaic.

THE HOUSE THAT WOULD NOT DIE
ABC, 10/27/70

Cast: Ruth Bennett (Barbara Stanwyck), Pat McDougal (Richard Egan), Stan Whitman (Michael Anderson, Jr.), Sara Dunning (Katherine Winn), Sylvia Wall (Doreen Lang), Delia McDougal (Mabel Albertson)

Credits: Director: John Llewellyn Moxey; Writer: Henry Farrell, from Barbara Michaels' *Ammie, Come Home*; Producer: Aaron Spelling; Associate Producer: Steve Kibler; Photography: Fleet Southcott; Art Director; Tracy Bousman; Music: Laurence Rosenthal; Editor: Art Seid; Produced by Aaron Spelling Productions

After Ruth Bennett and her niece Sara move into an old, colonial home—next to attractive neighbor Pat—they discover the house is haunted. After some poltergeist tricks, the ghost starts possessing Sara, who nevertheless insists on staying. Pat refuses to believe there's a ghost, until a second ghost possesses him and almost makes him kill Sara's boyfriend.

Investigating the house's history, they discover that the ghosts are Ammie and her father; Dad murdered Ammie and her lover Anthony when they tried to elope against his will, and is determined to reclaim his daughter now. In the cellar they find Ammie and Anthony's bodies, which causes the father to manifest and try to hide his sins. Ammie confronts and drives him off at last, then leaves the house, at peace.

A fairly routine pre–*Poltergeist* haunted house film, *The House That Would Not Die* features a typically competent performance by Stanwyck, a veteran of big and small screen. Albertson may be remembered as Samantha's overbearing mother-in-law on *Bewitched*.

HUMAN FEELINGS
NBC, 10/16/78

Cast: Mrs. G (Nancy Walker), Miles (Billy Crystal), Verna Gold (Pamela Sue Martin), Phil Sawyer (Squire Fridell), Robin Dennis (Jack Carter), Gloria Prentice (Donna Pescow), Johnny Turner (Armand Assante), Garcia (Richard Dimitri), Waiter (Pat Morita), Lester (John Fiedler), Eddie (Anthony Charnota), Frank (Tom Pedi), Detective (James Whitmore, Jr.), Guard (Scott Walker), with John Monks, Jr., Barry Hamilton, Rozsika Holmes, Tony Cristing, Biff Yeager, Albert Cole, Liberty Godshall, Adele Claire, Joe Ross, Charles Bracy, Abigail Shelton

Credits: Director: Ernest Pintoff; Writer: Henry Bloomstein; Producer: Herbert Hirschman; Executive Producers: Charles Fries, Malcolm Stuart; Photography: William K. Jurgensen; Art Director: Bill Ross; Music: John Cacavas; Editor: Angelo Ross; Produced by Charles Fries Productions, Crestview Productions, Worldvision Enterprises

When the Lord—a.k.a. "Mrs. G"—realizes how sinful Las Vegas has become, she decides to destroy it. Miles, a heavenly paper-pusher, convinces her to relent, provided he can find six good souls in Vegas.

Miles' unworldliness makes functioning in Las Vegas—let alone finding innocent souls—hard going, especially when his very naiveté makes him look suspicious to mob boss Turner, and very attractive to aspiring singer Verna. Between dodging mob goons and falling for Verna, Miles only manages to find five souls—so he opts to become the sixth mortal soul and stay with Verna on Earth.

This deservedly failed pilot was probably inspired by the 1977 theatrical hit *Oh, God!* with George Burns as a similarly cantankerous deity. *Human Feelings* sports a surprisingly bland performance by Billy Crystal; Walker, however, is a hoot as the Almighty.

HUMANOIDS FROM THE DEEP
Showtime, 9/17/96

Cast: Dr. Drake (Emma Samms), Wade Parker (Robert Carradine), Bill Taylor (Mark Rolston), Matt (Justin Walker), Kim Parker (Danielle Weeks), Deputy (Clint Howard), Sheriff Barnes (Kaz Garas), Major Knapp (Warren Burton), Duffy (Bert Remsen), Reporters (Barry Nolan, Ron Pitts, Katharine Olsen), Fran Taylor (Barbara Niven), Timmy's Mother (Season Hubley), Porter (Greg Travis), Rod (Walton Goggins), Activists (Pancho Demmings, Charlotte Neilson, Greg Trigo), Creel (Butch McCain), Travis (Ben McCain), Captain John (Bruce M. Fisher), Timmy (Shane Sweet), Sergeant (Harrison Young), Girl on Boat (Brittany Ashton Holmes), Officer (Robert Peters), Ride Operator (Joey Chang), Father at Carnival (Timothy Riley), Boy at Carnival (Patrick McTavish), Soldier (Cliff Henderson), Doctor (Ed Brigadier), Nurse (Margaret Howell)

Credits: Director-Writer: Jeff Yonis; Story: Martin B. Cohen; Producer: Michael Amato; Co-Producers: Darin Spillman, Edward G. Reilly; Executive Producer: Roger Corman; Photography: Christopher Baffa; Production Design: Sean Sloan; Music: Christopher Lennertz; Editor: John Gilbert; Produced by New Horizons

Mutated humanoids created by military experiments wreak havoc on a small town, killing men and carrying off women to breed. Public pressure convinces the military to locate and destroy the humanoid lair—with the captive women inside—but the locals rescue their womenfolk before the bombs blow. But one of the women was indeed impregnated, and a new humanoid is born...

This is a dull, dreary, formulaic remake of the equally uninteresting 1980 Roger Corman film.

I, DESIRE
ABC, 11/15/82

Cast: David Balsiger (David Naughton), Det. Jerry Van Ness (Dorian Harewood), Cheryl Gillen (Marilyn Jones), Mona (Barbara Stock), Milton King (Arthur Rosenberg), Paul (Brad Dourif), Dr. Herrera (James Victor), Marge Bookman (Anne Bloom), Undercover Cop (Linda Lawrence), Head Nurse (Adele Rosse), Larry (Marc Silver), Restaurant Manager (James Oliver), Pat (Ann Blessing), Newscasters (John Bennick, Nigel Bullard, Cathy Green), Daryl (Timothy Stack), Detective (Stacy McGregor), Plainclothes Cop (Gary A. McMillan), Ward Secretary (Holly McGarver), Nurses' Aide (Liis Kailey), Nurse (Laurel Rosenberg), Vice Cop (Jim Veres), Bernard McDougal (Herb Mitchell), Preacher (Bruce Wright)

Credits: Director: John Llewellyn Moxey; Writer: Robert Foster; Producer: Audrey Blasdel-Goddard; Executive Producers: Jim Green, Allen S. Epstein; Associate Producer: Pat Butler; Photography: Robert L. Morrison; Art Directors: Ross Bellah, Fredric P. Hope; Music: Don Peake; Editor: Donald R. Rode; Produced by Green-Epstein Productions, Columbia

Balsiger, a coroner's aide, comes to suspect that a string of brutal murders are the work of a vampire, posing as a hooker to lure her victims into her embrace. With the help of seedy, would-be vampire hunter Paul, Balsiger sets out to hunt down and capture the vampire—but is his will strong enough to overcome the vampire's seductive ways? Ultimately—and just barely—it is.

I, Desire has some fun with Dourif's scruffy vampire hunter wannabe and is an interesting exploration of the erotic aspects of vampirism several years before Anne Rice made that de rigueur in stories of the undead.

I DREAM OF JEANNIE—15 YEARS LATER
NBC, 10/20/85

Cast: Jeannie Nelson/Jeannie II (Barbara Eden), Captain Tony Nelson (Wayne Rogers), T.J. Nelson (MacKenzie Astin), Captain Roger Healey (Bill Daily), Dr. Alfred Bellows (Hayden Rorke), Wes Morrison (John Bennett Perry), Scheherazade (Dody Goodman), Nelly Hunt (Lee Taylor Allen), Dori Green (Dori Brenner), Haji (Andre DeShields), General Hatten (Michael Fairman), Col. Klapper (Dierk Torsek), Mrs. Farrell (Belita Moreno), Melissa (Nicole Eggert), Brad (Niall Gartlan), Millie (Helen J. Siff), Tony, Jr., Age 7 (Brandon Call), Reporters (Bill Shick, Hette Lynne-Hortes, Craig Marks, Gene Whittington, Frank Moon), Announcer (Michael Laurence), Waiters (Bertl Unger, Gustaf Unger), Girlfriends (Denise Gallup, Dian Gallup)

Credits: Director: William Asher; Writer: Irma Kalish; Story: Dinah Kirgo, Julie Kirgo, Irma Kalish; Producer: Hugh Benson; Executive Producer: Barbara Corday; Photography: Jack Whitman; Art Directors: Ross Bellah, Robert Peterson; Music: Mark Snow; Editors: Michael F. Anderson, William Martin; Produced by Can't Sing, Can't Dance Productions, Columbia

Years ago, astronaut Tony Nelson found a genie in a bottle and—eventually—fell in love with and married "Jeannie." Now Jeannie's manipulative, jealous twin sows so much discord in the Nelsons' marriage that Jeannie and son T.J. wind up moving out, while a depressed Tony returns to the space program.

When Tony's shuttle malfunctions, Jeannie forgets all about the separation in her desire to help him—but by genie law, she can't use her power to save lives. Haji, the genie overlord, grants her permission to save Tony, on condition that Jeannie erase Tony's memory of her and T.J. Jeannie agrees, then saves Tony. He forgets all about his family, but when he meets Jeannie six months later, she makes sure their romance starts anew.

This reunion movie for the *I Dream of Jeannie* series (without the original Tony, Larry Hagman, whose success as J.R. Ewing in *Dallas* made him too expensive) tried to jumpstart a new series (despite good ratings, it failed), dropping the NASA background, giving Jeannie a mortal best buddy and starting the Tony-Jeannie romance over. All of this was ignored in 1991's *I Still Dream of Jeannie*.

I MARRIED A MONSTER
UPN, 8/10/98

Cast: Nicholas Farrell (Richard Burgi), Kelly Drummond (Susan Walters), Steve (Tim Ryan), Linda Harris (Barbara Niven), Uncle Paul (Richard Herd), Bartender (Barney Martin), Bud Riley (Tim DeZarn), Deputy (Jason Van), Sheriff Collins (Vaughn Armstrong), Deputies (Michael Bard Bayer, Scott Benefiel), Posse Members (Clement Blake, Jason D. Smith), Man (Dan Borowicz), Friends (Jonathan Breck, Brien Perry), Bridesmaids (Toshi Harrison, Leslie Harter), Woman (Christine Kludjian), Coroner (Ming Lo), Lifeguard (Hank Matt), Ellen (Sandra Phillips), Minister (Charles C. Stevenson, Jr.), Mrs. Drummond (Elaine Ward), Deliveryman (Miles Wiltshire), Nurses (Bonnie Brewster, Annie Hinton), Jim (Brady Finta), Bellman (Josh Garner), Flower Girl (Ashley Majoros), Clerk (Aloma Wright)

Credits: Director: Nancy Malone; Writer: Duane Poole, based on *I Married a Monster from Outer Space*, scripted by Louis Vittes; Producer: Stu Segall; Executive Producers: Nancy Malone, Duane Poole; Photography: Geoff Schaaf; Production Design: Nigel Clinker; Music: David Shire; Editor: Ron Kobrin; Produced by Paramount, Stu Segall Productions

The night before Nick marries Kelly, he's kidnapped and replaced by an alien imposter. A puzzled Kelly finds her new husband is suddenly a humorless, withdrawn teetotaller, but Nick allays her suspicions—while he replaces the other townsmen with aliens.

Kelly is soon pregnant, with a fetus growing at abnormal speed. When one of her friends delivers a grotesque stillbirth, Kelly's suspicions return—and this time she finds proof. Nick confirms it and tells her his sterile race needs human women to breed. Kelly and her uncle discover that alcohol is poison to the aliens, so the customers at the town bar are guaranteed human; they form a posse, free the human captives, kill the impostors and send the ship packing. But when Kelly gives birth, her child is only half human...

The 1958 version of *I Married a Monster from Outer Space* was a good little SF chiller in which the aliens were not only somewhat sympathetic, they had personalities; in this vastly inferior remake, they have neither. Burgi starred as a superhuman cop in UPN's *The Sentinel*.

I STILL DREAM OF JEANNIE
NBC, 10/20/91

Cast: Jeannie/Jeannie's Sister (Barbara Eden), Tony Nelson, Jr. (Christopher Bolton), Roger Healey (Bill Daily), Simpson (Ken Kercheval), Sham-Ir (Peter Breck), General Westcott (Al Waxman), Eddie (Brent Stait), Guzer (Jason Schombing), Clara (J.J. McColl), Don (Robert Metcalfe), Dave (Jackson Davies), Man (Victor A. Young), Elderly Lady (Bette Linde), Maître d' (Robert Thurston), MP (D.J. Jackson), Beth (Brigitta Dau), Bartender (Paul McLean), Runners (Jano Frandsen, Dale Wilson, Marcy Goldberg), Shrill Woman (Dolores Drake), Mario (Peter Chapek), Man (Douglas Newell), Volunteer Wife (Sandra P. Grant), Guard (Roger Barnes), with Garry Chalk, Henry Crowell, Jr.

Credits: Director: Joseph Scanlan; Writer: April Kelly; Producer: Joan Singer; Executive Producer: Carla Singer; Photography: Albert J. Dunk; Production Design: Douglas Higgins; Music: Ken Harrison; Editor: Stan Cole; Produced by Jeannie Entertainment, Carla Singer Productions, Columbia Pictures Television, BarGene Television

In this second *I Dream of Jeannie* reunion, djinni Jeannie learns since she no longer has an "earthly" master (husband Tony's on a long space mission) she must return to the genie realm and let her evil sister replace her. Jeannie tries and fails to bring Tony home, and Sis thwarts her efforts to find a temporary master. Despite her sister's tricks, Jeannie ultimately convinces her son's school counsellor to serve as Tony's stand-in.

This weak, low-rated film kept Tony Nelson offstage entirely and completely ignored the events of *I Dream of Jeannie—15 Years Later*.

I'M DANGEROUS TONIGHT
USA, 8/8/90

Cast: Amy O'Neill (Madchen Amick), Prof. Buchanan (Anthony Perkins), Eddie Sadler (Corey Parker), Martha (Mary Fran), Gloria (Daisy Hall), Captain Aickman (R. Lee Ermey), Gram (Natalie Schafer), Wanda Thatcher (Dee Wallace Stone), Mason (Jason Brooks), Dr. Jonas Wilson (William Berger), Coroner (Lew Horn), Victor (Stuart Fratkin), Frank (Dan Leegant), Landlord (Jack McGee), Joey (Edward Trotta), Man (David Carlile), Librarian (Felicia Lansbury), Anchorman (Henry C. Brown), Server (Ellen Gerstein), Romeo (Ivan Gueron), Enrique (Juan Garcia), City Worker (Frank Dielsi), Paramedic (Richard Penn), Punks (Xavier Barquet, Matthew Walker), Janitor (Robert H. Harvey), Tybolt (Bill Madden)

Credits: Director: Tobe Hooper; Writer-Producers: Bruce Lansbury, Philip John Taylor, based on Cornel Woolrich's short story; Executive Producer: Boris Malden; Co–Executive Producer: Michael Weisbarth; Photography: Levie Isaacks; Production Design: Leonard Mazzola; Music: Nicholas Pike; Editor: Carl Kress; Produced by Coastline Partners, BBK, MTE

After an archeologist buys a sacred Aztec cloak, the evil it's absorbed from countless blood sacrifices turns him homicidal until he's shot down. Innocent Amy refashions the cloak into a stunning red dress that brings out the dark side of its wearers: Amy becomes a seductive slut; her cousin dies assaulting Amy in a fit of jealousy; Wanda steals the dress from Gloria's corpse and becomes utterly corrupted. After Professor Buchanan warns Amy about the dress' powers, Amy tries to recover it. Wanda dies fighting her, Amy passes out—and wakes up in the dress. Her boyfriend, Eddie, dressed her so that they can share the intoxicating power of the dress; Amy convinces him to resist the spell, and they destroy and bury the dress. Buchanan, however, digs it up later...

I'm Dangerous Tonight features competent work on familiar material, with genre names Hooper (*Poltergeist*), Amick (*Twin Peaks*), Stone (*E.T.*) and Perkins (*Psycho*).

IN HIS FATHER'S SHOES
Showtime, 6/15/97

Cast: Clay (Robert Richard), Frank/Richard (Louis Gossett, Jr.), Janice (Barbara Eve Harris), Celeste (Rachael Crawford), Virginia (Djanet Sears), Maggie (Shadia Nimmons), Gypsy (Fiona Reid), Peter (Dylan Provencher), Telegram (Dan Warry-Smith), Bruce (Kevin Duhaney), Dennis Beck (Dan Petronijevic), Lisa (A.J. Cook), Mrs.

Kips (Mary Long), Mary Lou (Naomi Lee Allen), Dorfman (R.D. Reid), Woman (Christine Brubaker), Announcer (Eric Fink), Older Dennis (Timm Zemanek), Pal (David Roemmele), Ron (Joel Keller), DJ (Kenneth Ames)

Credits: Director: Vic Sarin; Writer: Gary Gelt; Producers: Dan Redler, Patrick Whitley; Executive Producers: Louis Gossett, Jr., Hillard Elkins; Photography: Michael Storey; Production Design: John Dondertman; Music: John Welsman; Editor: Bill Goddard; Produced by Showtime, Hallmark Entertainment, Dan Redler Productions, Temple Street Productions

On his deathbed, Clay's father, Frank, tells him that something in Clay's grandma's long-lost postcard collection will explain their family history—including Frank's estrangement from his own parents. Clay discovers that whenever he puts on a pair of his father's shoes, he becomes young Frank in 1962. Seeking the postcard, Clay travels back and forth in time, meeting Frank's friends, enemies and his hard, unbending father Richard, whose rough life left him at odds with his optimistic children. In the present, Clay and his family reunite with Richard; the two men realize how much of Frank's strength came from his father (they even used similar postcards to win the women they loved). Everyone's grief heals a little.

Though well-performed, *In His Father's Shoes* is aimlessly plotted.

IN THE NICK OF TIME
NBC, 12/16/91

Cast: Santa Claus (Lloyd Bridges), Ben Talbot (Michael Tucker), Susan Rosswell (Alison LaPlaca), Freddy (Cleavon Little), Charlie Misch (A. Martinez), Amy (Jessica Di Cicco), Melina (Jenny Parsons), Melvin (Wayne Robson), Sheila (Audrey Webb), Godfrey (Michael Lamport), Sheila (Lucy Filippone), Ridley (Ken James), Figgus (Thomas Hauff), Louie (Conrad Bergschneider), Guard (Matt Birman), William (Richard Blackburn), Gang Guys (Steve Clifte, Corey Macri), Tough Chick (Elvira Graham), Wino Santa (Ted Hamlan), Cop (Phil Jarrett), Bartender (Martin Martinuzzi), Interviewer (Adrian Paul), Folksinger (Bryan L. Rentro), Nurse (Jackie Richardson), Street Santa (Thick Wilson), Messenger (Roland Smith)

Credits: Director: George Miller; Writers: Rick Podell, Michael Preminger, Mary Edith Burrell; Story: Jon S. Denney; Producer: Michael Jaffe; Co-Producers: John Danylkiw, Christine Sacani; Executive Producer: Janet Faust Krusi; Photography: Brian R.R. Hebb; Art Direction: Tony Hall; Editor: Ron Wisman; Music: Steve Dorff; From Walt Disney Television, Spectacor Films

A week before Christmas, the current Santa unexpectedly discovers his 300-year-reign expires this year—before Christmas Eve. Desperate to find his successor, he travels to New York, where his Christmas touch brightens the lives of those around him, sparking a romance between cabbie Charlie and editor Susan, helping Melina save her community center and restoring hope to cynical, burned-out Ben Talbot. When Santa realizes Ben is the destined replacement, Ben balks—but as Christmas lights go out all over the world, Ben finally accepts his destiny and makes his first Christmas Eve toy ride before it's too late.

In the Nick of Time is one of the better Christmas fantasies—*A Christmas Carol* it ain't, but it's relatively free of saccharine for a Christmas show. Watch for *Highlander: The Series* star Adrian Paul in a blink-and-miss-it role.

THE INCREDIBLE HULK
CBS, 11/11/77

Cast: Dr. David Banner (Bill Bixby), The Hulk (Lou Ferrigno), Laura Banner (Lara Parker), Dr. Elaina Marks (Susan Sullivan), Jack McGee (Jack Colvin), Mrs. Jessie Maier (Susan Batson), Martin Bram (Mario Gallo), Ben (Charles Siebert), B.J. Meier (Eric Devon), Jerry (Jake Mitchell), Mrs. Epstein (June Whitley Taylor), Cop (Eric Server), Minister (William Larsen), Young Man (Terrence Locke), Girl at Lake (Olivia Barash), Man at Lake (George Brenlin), Mr. MacIntire (Don Keefer), Cynthia Davis (Susan Cotton), Pilot (Del Hinkley), Robert Benson (Al Fann), Captain Brandes (Ed Peck), Controller (J. Jay Saunders), Mrs. MacIntire (Shirley O'Hara), Nurse (Barbara Mealy)

Credits: Director-Writer-Producer: Kenneth Johnson, based on the Marvel Comics character; Producer: Chuck Bowman; Supervising Producer: James D. Parriott; Associate Producers: Craig Schiller, Stephen P. Caldwell; Photography: Howard R. Schwartz; Art Directors: Charles R. Davis, Frank Grieco, Jr.; Music: Joe Harnell; Editors: Alan Marks, Jack Schoengarth, Edward

W. Williams, Lawrence J. Vallario; Produced by Universal

Ever since physicist David Banner failed to rescue his wife from a fatal car wreck, he's been studying how some people develop superhuman strength in a crisis. When he learns the secret—gamma radiation from sunspots—David tests his theory by subjecting himself to intense gamma rays. Later, David's frustration at changing a flat in the rain turns him into a green-skinned super-strong brute who smashes the car in his rampage.

After David reverts to normal, he and Elaina begin studying the change—David to tap the power of the "Hulk," Elaina to cure him—while fending off suspicious tabloid journalist McGee. When a fire traps Elaina in the lab, the Hulk smashes a path to her but not in time to save her. David lets McGee and the world think he died in the fire too, so he can hide his secret until he's cured.

This pilot freely revises the Hulk's Marvel Comics origin (a Cold War story with *Bruce* Banner [tele-writer Johnson hated the name "Bruce"] working on a gamma-powered superbomb). *Return of the Incredible Hulk* followed, then the successful five-year series, then three reunion movies.

THE INCREDIBLE HULK RETURNS
CBS, 5/22/88

Cast: Dr. David Banner (Bill Bixby), The Hulk (Lou Ferrigno), Don Blake (Steve Levitt), Thor (Eric Kramer), Jack McGee (Jack Colvin), Dr. Maggie Shaw (Lee Purcell), Joshua Lambert (Charles Napier), Jack LeBeau (Tim Thomerson), with William Riley, Tom Finnegan, Donald Willis, Carl Nick Ciafalio, Bobby Travis McLaughlin, Burke Denis, Nick Costa, Peisha McPhee, William Malone, Joanie Allen

Credits: Director-Writer: Nicholas Corea; Producer: Daniel McPhee; Executive Producers: Nicholas Corea, Bill Bixby; Photography: Chuck Colwell; Music: Lance Rubin; Editors: Janet Ashikaga, Briana London; Produced by New World Television, B&B Productions

For two years David Banner's love for Maggie Shaw has kept David's savage alter ego, the Hulk, at bay, while David helps Joshua Lambert build a Gamma Transponder David secretly hopes will destroy the Hulk.

Don Blake, David's former student, disrupts the first gamma treatment to demand help with his own curse: He's become the channeler for an arrogant, superhuman Viking spirit, Thor. Thor has been denied Valhalla until he earns his place through heroic deeds—which he can't perform unless the timid, cynical Blake allows him to materialize (Odin's way of teaching Thor humility). Blake proves his story by summoning Thor, whose bullying of David brings out the Hulk. Their subsequent battle wrecks the lab.

Blake and David rebuild the Transponder, but the Hulk's return draws McGee to the scene. Worse, Lambert's brother hires LeBeau to steal Banner and the Transponder. The Hulk thwarts Banner's kidnapping, but even with Thor's help, he fails to stop LeBeau from snatching Maggie. To save her, David turns over the Transponder (after first rendering it useless). He and Don locate LeBeau's gang, and their alter egos easily rescue Maggie. McGee, however, is getting too close, and the Transponder is destroyed—so both men are forced to move on.

The first of three Hulk reunion films also served as a pilot for a possible Thor series (based on Marvel Comics' *Thor*, but the producers decided scaling Marvel's godling down to a Viking would fit their budget better). While the Hulk plot is standard (boy gets girl, almost gets a cure, loses both), the nerdy Blake and his brawling chum are fun enough (particularly visiting a biker bar). It's a shame the pilot didn't take. This was followed by *The Trial of the Incredible Hulk*.

INHUMANOID
Showtime, 7/23/96

Cast: Foster Carver (Corbin Bernsen), Katrina Carver (Lara Harris), Adam Milton (Richard Grieco), Dr. Snow (Edie McClurg), Dr. Milton (Robbin Gammell), Amy (Brittany Ashton Holmes), Claus (Ilia Volokh), Nurse (Renato Powell), Group Leader (Conrad Goode), Medic (Grant Mathis), Strange Man (Cole Nelson), Wolf Man (Jeff Dixon),

Credits: Director-Writer: Victoria Muspratt;

Producer: Darin Spillman; Co-Producer: Marta M. Mobley; Executive Producers: Roger Corman, Lance H. Robbins; Photography: John Aronson; Production Design: Robert Cowan; Music: Marco Beltrami; Editor: Nancy Rosenblum; Produced by New Horizons, Pacific Trust

After the Carvers rescue Adam Milton from a drifting spaceship, Foster explores the derelict ship—and Adam "accidentally" flies the Carvers' ship away. He murders little Amy and tells Katrina she is now his, forever. Flying Adam's ship in pursuit, Foster finds the real, dying Milton onboard and learns "Adam" is an android Milton built but failed to program with ethics. When Foster catches up, Adam kills him, then flees, leaving Katrina accused of causing all the deaths. When she's jailed, Adam fights his way to her; she takes revenge by seducing him until his limited emotional programming overloads and burns out.

Inhumanoid is gratuitously gory, yet dull at the same time (neat trick!).

THE INITIATION OF SARAH
ABC, 2/6/78

Cast: Sarah Goodwin (Kay Lenz), Miss Erica (Shelley Winters), Patti Goodwin (Morgan Brittany), Mrs. Goodwin (Kathryn Crosby), Paul Yates (Tony Bill), Laura (Elizabeth Stack), Mouse (Tisa Farrow), Jennifer (Morgan Fairchild), Bobbi (Deborah Ryan), Barbara (Nora Heflin), Scott (Robert Hays), Allison (Talia Balsam), Tommy (Doug Davidson), Kathy (Jennifer Gay), Regina (Susan Duvall), Pledge (Karen Purcil), Clerk (Madeline Kelly), Freddie (Michael Talbott), Susan (Debi Fries), Young Man (Albert Owens)

Credits: Director: Robert Day; Writers: Don Ingalls, Carol Saraceno, Kenette Gfeller; Story: Tom Holland, Carol Saraceno; Producer: Jay Benson; Executive Producer: Charles Fries; Associate Producer: Allan Marcil; Photography: Ric Waite; Art Director: Herman Zimmerman; Music: Johnny Harris; Editor: Tony DiMarco; Produced by Charles Fries Productions, Stonehenge Productions

The world has always ignored shy, quiet Sarah Goodwin in favor of her outgoing sister, Patti—who alone knows that Sarah is a powerful telekinetic. At college, Patti joins a sorority of fashionable snobs, while Sarah joins the uncool sorority whose occultist house mother, Erica, becomes very interested in Sarah's powers. The bitchy snobs keep humiliating Sarah and her friends; Sarah retaliates psychically, with Erica egging her on to increasingly lethal attacks. On initiation night, Erica leads her girls in a satanic ritual, and Sarah turns her full power on the snobs. Then Erica tries to sacrifice Sarah's friend Mouse to Satan. Sarah balks, frees Mouse, and sacrifices herself to kill Erica.

Stephen King's *Carrie* (the story of a put-upon, telekinetic teenager) hit theaters in 1977 with phenomenal success. This blatant knockoff is far weaker (though Lenz is good), the satanist elements are gratuitous, and so is Sarah's death (with her powers she could have avoided it—but hey, Carrie died, so…). *The Initiation of Sarah* is noteworthy only for the number of future names (Fairchild, Hays—whose credits include the TV series *Starman*—and Lenz herself) and relatives of more famous people (Stack, Crosby, Farrow, Duvall) who appeared in it.

THE INTRUDER WITHIN
ABC, 2/20/81

Cast: Jake Nevins (Chad Everett), Scott (Joseph Bottoms), Colette Beaudroux (Jennifer Warren), Mark (Rockne Tarkington), Robyn (Lynda Mason Green), Sam (Paul Larson), Harry Colman (James Hayden), Nurse Wilma (Mary Ann McDonald), Phil Mallard (Matt Craven), Chili (Michael Hogan), Ed (Ed LaPlante), Mickey (Mickey Gilbert), Final Creature (Joe Finnegan)

Credits: Director: Peter Carter; Writer: Ed Waters; Producer: Neil T. Maffeo; Executive Producers: John Furia, Jr., Barry Oringer; Associate Producer: John Ryan; Photography: James Pergola; Art Director: Geoffrey Holmes; Music: Gil Melle; Editor: Richard E. Rabjohn; Produced by Furia-Oringer Productions

It's bad enough that oil-rigger Jake and his crew are working an illegal deep-sea rig and not striking oil, but they also have Scott, a corporate geologist, accelerating drilling to the point where men and machines are exhausted. Then the newest shaft unleashes a slithering monster (killed by no-nonsense Colette) and its eggs. Scott hatches an egg, releasing another monster. It bites a crewman, then gets killed; the man goes insane, killing and raping before he dies. A new monster bursts from the rape victim's body. Scott admits that these creatures, driven below by early humans, are what the company is drilling for. The creature tries to bring up more of its kind, but Colette and Jake burn it to death with a flare gun. The survivors leave the rig but behind them, something stirs in the shaft...

This is a blatant *Alien* knockoff, from the look of the monsters to the corporate scheming to control them (what an oil company wants with this, we're never told); a poor film, but Warren is excellent as Colette (she actually comes off like a woman who might work on an oil rig).

INTRUDERS
CBS, 5/17/92

Cast: Dr. Neil Chase (Richard Crenna), Leslie (Daphne Ashbrook), Mary Wilkes (Mare Winningham), Lee Holland (Susan Blakely), Gene Randall (Ben Vereen), General Hanley (G.D. Spradlin), Joe Wilkes (Alan Autry), Addison Leach (Steven Berkoff), Ray Brooks (Jason Beghe), Timmy (Joseph Cousins, Christian Cousins), Diner Waitress (Donna Bacalla), Trooper (Forry Smith), Air Force Lieutenant (Trinka Stotsky-Soloway), Air Force Officer (David Crowley), Air Force Captain (Glenn Morshower), Priest (John Snyder), Gate MP (Peter Looney), Wachtheimer (Time Winters), Luanne (Rhonda Dotson), Mental Patient (Josh Cruze), Checkout Girl (Nicole Huntington), Neil's Daughter (Romy Rosemont), Dr. Rahkar (Alexander Zale), Antique Shop Owner (Dyana Ortelli), Night-Shift Doctor (Daniel Moriarty), Young Mary (Courtney Barilla), Surveyor (Mike Valverde), Gynecologist (Virginia Morris), Lab Technician (Francois Chau), with Rosalind Chao, Lorry Goldman, Robert Mandan, Warren Frost

Credits: Director: Dan Curtis; Writers: Barry Oringer, Tracy Torme; Story: Barry Oringer, partly based on Bud Hopkins' *Intruders*; Producer: Branko Lustig; Co-Producer: Mary Benjamin; Executive Producers: Dan Curtis, Robert O'Connor, Michael Apted; Photography: Tom Priestley; Production Design: Bryan Ryman; Music: Bob Cobert; Editor: Bill Blunden; Produced by Osiris Films

Dr. Chase is baffled when Leslie—suffering traumatic flashbacks to a night she can't remember—recalls an alien abduction under hypnosis. Mary, who has the same traumatic amnesia, recalls not only that abduction, but an earlier one from childhood. Chase learns Mary has a cranial implant of alien technology; another patient reveals that the Air Force coerced him into denying his own close encounter (we've already seen them covering up other evidence). Leslie, pregnant, is reabducted and her baby taken. No longer a skeptic, Chase loses his job for proselytizing about UFOs. The military offers him a new job if he'll help cover up abductions to prevent panic, but Chase refuses. The aliens reveal to Mary that they're interbreeding with humans, and she realizes that their intentions, while mysterious, are benevolent.

This "based-on-truth" film (taken from a book that was much less sanguine about the alien motives) retreads well-worn ground to very little effect; *Stranger Within* handled the alien-impregnation idea much better. Tracy Torme later created the TV series *Sliders*, and Chao played Keiko O'Brien on *Star Trek—Next Generation* and *Deep Space Nine*.

THE INVADERS
Fox, 11/12–11/14/95

Cast: Nolan Wood (Scott Bakula), Dr. Ellen Garza (Elizabeth Pena), Jerry Thayer (Richard Thomas), Randy Stein (Richard Belzer), Amanda Thayer (Delane Mathews), Josh (Eric King), David Vincent (Roy Thinnes), Coyle (Terence Knox), Grace (Shannon Kenny), Suarez (Raoul Trujillo), Kyle (Mario Yedidia), Norma Winters (Elinor Donahue), Frankel (Lindsay Ginter), Lucinda (Judy Hain), Bus Driver (Lee Bayles), Postman (J. Marvin Campbell), Coyote (Luis Contreras), Erskine (William Duffy), Trucker (Frank Farmer), Paramedic (Craig Higgins), Reporter (Sally Hightower), Marty (Dean Hill), Trustee (Eugene Lee), Pipe (Don Pugsley), Cop (Al Rodrigo), Guard (Roger Rook), Esperanza (Julia Vera), Nurse (Susan Ware), Dr. Rysmiller (Lorinne Dills-Vozoff), Billy (Todd Merrill), Dr. Singh (Duke Moosekian), Secret Service Man (Rick Fitts), Cops (Jim Holmes, Todd Stanton), Metrolink Worker (Nick Jameson), Aide (Hillary Matthews), Raymond (Rolando Molina), Wood's Lawyer (David St. James), Security Man (Tegan West), with Debra Jo Rupp, Channon Roe, Jack Kehler, Jon Cypher, Todd Susman

Credits: Director: Paul Shapiro; Writer: James

Dott; Photography: Alar Hivilo; Production Design: Rodger Maus; Music: Joseph Vitarelli; Editor: Daniel Cahn; Produced by Spelling Entertainment Group, Papazian-Hirsch Entertainment, CBS Films

Josh, a surgeon, is baffled when a dead man disappears from the ER, leaving behind only blood and flies. Meanwhile, Nolan Wood—whose bizarre hallucinations ended his marriage, his pilot's career, and led to a manslaughter conviction—leaves prison. A stranger tries to make Nolan shoot Josh; when Nolan refuses, the stranger does it himself, then dissolves into flies and blood. Nolan escapes, but is charged with murder. Dr. Garza discovers the blood matches the blood from the corpse in the ER, and so becomes marked for death.

Aliens, posing as humans, capture and try to duplicate Nolan (the duplicates are what crumble into blood and flies), but Nolan's son—learning his stepfather leads the aliens—rescues him. David Vincent, a long-time enemy of the invaders, helps them escape and explains that the aliens are polluting Earth to suit their biology. Nolan learns that his hallucinations are alien thought-impressions from a mind-control implant that malfunctions because of his childhood autism. His visions alert him to an alien plan to destroy a pollution-free train and its environmentalist backers. With Garza's help, Nolan and his son save the people, but the train is destroyed. Nevertheless, the Woods and Garza stand ready to carry on the fight.

Roy Thinnes' *The Invaders* was a moderately successful alien-infiltration series in the late sixties; in the nineties, the premise looked like a routine clone of *X-Files'* paranoia. Bakula fans should stick with his previous SF series, *Quantum Leap*. Less familiar genre faces include Richard Belzer (*The Flash*) and Roe (*Kindred: The Embraced*).

THE INVISIBLE MAN
NBC, 5/6/75

Cast: Dr. Daniel Westin (David McCallum), Dr. Kate Westin (Melinda Fee), Walter Carlson (Jackie Cooper), Dr. Nick Maggio (Henry Darrow), Richard Steiner (Alex Henteloff), General Tucker (Arch Johnson), Blind Man (John McLiam), Guards (Ted Gehring, Jon Cedar), Security Chief (Paul Kent), Doctor (Milt Kogan), Receptionist (Tamar Cooper), Clerk (Lew Palter), Guest (Richard Forbes)

Credits: Director: Robert Michael Lewis; Writer: Steven Bochco, from a story by Steven Bochco and Harve Bennett based on H.G. Wells' novel; Producer: Steven Bochco; Executive Producer: Harve Bennett; Photography: Enzo A. Martinelli; Art Director: Frank T. Smith; Music: Richard Clements; Editor: Robert F. Shugrue; Produced by Silverton Productions, Universal

Daniel Westin, a researcher at the Klae Corporation think tank, has developed a ray that can turn objects—and soon, he hopes, people—invisible. Westin adamantly opposes using his research for military ends, and naively accepts Carlson's assurance that this won't happen. When Daniel successfully makes himself invisible (rushing the testing under pressure from Carlson), Carlson and the military demand that Daniel turn over his research. Daniel refuses and turns himself invisible again to reenter his lab and destroy his research—but after he escapes, he finds that his invisibility is now permanent. Although hunted by Carlson's men, Daniel successfully outwits his militaristic adversaries, but behind his face-mask and gloves, he remains invisible.

H.G. Wells' *The Invisible Man* inspired a series of films from Universal, a 1950s British TV series, this pilot (which led to a short-lived series in which Westin returns to work for Klae as a special troubleshooter) and subsequent pilots *Gemini Man* and *Invisible Woman*. Despite the talents of Bochco (*Hill Street Blues*), Harve Bennett (*Star Trek: The Next Generation*) and leading man David McCallum (*The Man from U.N.C.L.E.*), this is darn dull.

THE INVISIBLE WOMAN
NBC, 2/13/83

Cast: Dr. Dudley Plunkett (Bob Denver), Sandy Martinson (Alexa Hamilton), Darren (Jonathan Banks), Neil Gilmore (David Doyle), Dr. Farrington (George Gobel), Mrs. Van Dam (Anne Haney), Carlisle Edwards (Harvey Korman), Phil Williams (Art La Fleur), Lt. Greg Larkin (Garrett Morris), Spike Mitchell (Ron

Palillo), Orville (Richard Sanders), Security Guard (Mel Stewart), Lt. Dan Williams (Jacques Tate), Rodney Sherman (Scott Nemas), Attendant (Jake Steinfeld), Lionel Gilbert (Ken Sansom), Receptionist (Teri Beckerman), Cops (Ronald E. Morgan, Joseph Phelan), Guard (Dan Woren), Saleslady (Marsha Warner), Officer (Clinton Chase), Marvin Carter (David Whitfield), Miss Tomkins (Valerie Hall)

Credits: Director-Producer: Alan J. Levi; Writer–Executive Producers: Lloyd J. Schwartz, Sherwood Schwartz; Associate Producer: John Whitman; Photography: Dean Cundey; Art Director: Richard B. Lewis; Music: David Frank; Editor: Houseley Stevenson; Produced by Redwood Productions, Universal

When a lab accident turns one of Dudley's lab chimps invisible, Dudley's reporter niece, Sandy, arrives to cover the story—and gets turned invisible too. While Dudley works on a cure, Sandy uses makeup and contacts to pass for normal. But when she's called out of bed to cover a museum robbery, she has no time to put on makeup and goes invisibly. That lets her spot a clue indicating that the thieves work for wealthy Carlisle Edwards, who she overhears plotting to rob an Egyptology exhibit. Sandy's cop boyfriend, Phil, doesn't believe this, so Sandy poses as a ghost to terrify Edwards' henchmen, forcing them to confess everything. Phil gets credit for catching Edwards and Sandy gets a front-page story, deciding to use her powers to investigate corruption and crime as the Invisible Woman until she's cured.

The Invisible Woman is a lame, deservedly failed comedy pilot.

INVITATION TO HELL
CBS, 5/24/84

Cast: Matt Winslow (Robert Urich), Patricia Winslow (Joanna Cassidy), Jessica Jones (Susan Lucci), Tom Peterson (Joe Regalbuto), Mr. Thompson (Kevin McCarthy), Mary Petersen (Patricia McCormack), Walt Henderson (Bill Erwin), Chrissie Winslow (Soleil Moon Frye), Robbie Winslow (Barret Oliver), Sheriff (Nicholas Worth), Grace Henderson (Virginia Vincent), Pete (Greg Monahan), Tracy Winters (Lois Hamilton), Frank Stepson (Cal Bartlett), Janie (Anne Marie McEvoy), Larry Ferris (Bruce Gray), Jimmy (Gino DeMauro), Billy (Jason Presson), Doorman (John Zenda), Mover (Billy Beck), Valet (Michael Berryman), Newsboy (Frank Von Zerneck, Jr.)

Credits: Director: Wes Craven; Writer: Richard Rothstein; Producer: Robert M. Sertner; Executive Producer: Frank Von Zerneck; Photography: Dean Cundey; Art Director: Hub Braden; Music: Sylvester Levay; Editors: Gregory Prange, Ann Mills; Produced by Moonlight Productions, Inc.

Matt Winslow was delighted when a high-tech corporation hired him to help develop a space battlesuit for astronauts—but he's soon repulsed by his scheming, selfish co-workers and baffled why they keep pushing him to join Jessica Jones' rather sinister country club. Jessica talks Matt's family into joining and entering the club's vault—from which they emerge as dark parodies of their old selves. Matt eventually learns that his real family is trapped in the super-hot vault. Using the battlesuit for protection, he enters the vault and finds the Winslows and Jessica's other victims trapped in hell (literally). Matt's love frees his family, who materialize on Earth as the club burns to the ground.

Ever see a man put on a space suit to enter hell? Odd, but not interesting.

ISLAND CITY
Syndicated, 2/27–3/5/94

Cast: Col. Tom Valdoon (Kevin Conroy), Dr. Sam Helding (Brenda Strong), Gregg 23 (Eric McCormack), Lt. Michael Mende (Pete Koch), Connie Sealle (Constance Marie), Helen Helding (Veanne Cox), Ty Sealle (Rick Porter), Andrew Sealle (Joe Marchman), Ben Helding (Jerry Haynes), Sally Redman (Angie Bolling), General Meyday (Cynthia Dorn), Dr. Kelly (Alex Allen Morris), Morrissy (Paul Render), Bikini Girl (Caroline Summers), Little Girl (Shea Fowler), Lincoln (Clint Freeman), Blue (Paul Rosenberg)

Credits: Director: Jorge Montesi; Writer: Jonathan Glassner; Producer: Christopher Chullach; Executive Producers: Lee Rich, Bruce Sallan, Jonathan Glassner; Associate Producer: Gary Skeen Hall; Photography: Laszlo George; Production Design: Curtis A. Schnell; Art Director: Michael Fox; Music: Peter Bernstein; Editor: Drake Silliman; Produced by Lee Rich Co., Warner Bros. Television

In the future, a youth-prolonging drug

has frozen people's ages at thirty—but the side effects have devolved most humans into the brutal "Reccs" (named for the *recessive* gene responsible). Normal humans live in the techno-paradise of Island City, from which Col. Valdoon leads a patrol to scout the barren wastes for surviving normals.

When Andrew Sealle is lost on one mission, the team goes all out to find him, but their superiors write Sealle off and replace him with the half–Recc Mende. The team must also cope with personal problems: Dr. Helding's husband, who opted to age normally, feels a rift between them; Sealle's son retreats into VR (virtual reality) addiction; and Gregg—a klutzy but brilliant test-tube child—faces jealousy from his identical but less gifted brothers. Between Gregg's computer wizardry and Mende's superhuman senses, the team manages to track Sealle down and restore him to his family.

This is an enjoyable pilot (though the Reccs would have made dull foes for a regular series), but even for TV SF the science is awfully sloppy. Cartoon fans take note, though: Kevin Conroy is the voice of Batman in *Batman: The Animated Adventures*.

IT
ABC, 11/18–11/20/90

Cast: Bill Denbrough (Richard Thomas), Richie Tozer (Harry Anderson), Eddie Kaspbrak (Dennis Christopher), Beverly Marsh (Annette O'Toole), Stan Uris (Richard Masur), Pennywise (Tim Curry), Mike Hanlon (Tim Reid), Ben Hanscom (John Ritter), Young Bill (Jonathan Brandis), Young Ben (Brandon Crane), Young Eddie (Adam Faraizl), Young Richie (Seth Green), Young Stan (Ben Heller), Young Beverly (Emily Perkins), Young Mike (Marlon Taylor), Audra (Olivia Hussey), Mrs. Kaspbrak (Sheila Moore), Henry Bowers (Jarred Blancard), Young Henry (Michael Cole), Belch (Drum Garrett), Patrick (Gabe Khouth), Tom Rogan (Ryan Michael), Nat (Charles Siegel), Cyndi (Venus Terzo), Al Marsh (Frank C. Turner), Patti Uris (Caitlin Hicks), Georgie Denbrough (Tony Dakota), Mr. Denbrough (Steven Hilton), Sharon Denbrough (Sheelah Megill), Joey (Kim Kondrashoff), Bradley (Noel Geer), Laurie Anne (Chelan Simmons), Mrs. Winterbarger (Merrilyn Gann), Gedreau (William B. Davis), Aunt Jean (Susan Astley), Arlene Hanscomb (Claire Brown), Coach (Garry Chalk), Officer Nell (Terence Kelly), Miss Douglas (Donna Peerless), Ben's Father (Stephen Makaj), Rademacher (Scott Swanson)

Credits: Director: Tommy Lee Wallace; Writer: Lawrence D. Cohen, based on Stephen King's novel; Supervising Producer: Matthew O'Connor; Executive Producers: Jim Green, Allen Epstein; Associate Producer: Mark Bacino; Photography: Richard Leiterman; Production Design: Douglas Higgins; Music: Richard Bellis; Editors: Robert F. Shugrue, David Blangsted; Produced by Konigsberg/Sanitsky Company, Green/Epstein Productions, Lorimar Television

Thirty years ago, seven kids in the small town of Derry discovered that a series of child-killings were the work of Pennywise, a clown-faced master of illusion. Descending into Derry's sewers, they confronted and—they thought—destroyed the demon.

In the present, a new wave of murders convinces Mike that Pennywise has returned. He regroups his scattered friends, all of whom carry emotional scars from the first battle, and they prepare to face the clown again. Pennywise plays on their fears to weaken them, driving one of them to suicide and sending the former school bully to attack them. They realize Pennywise is not one monster but a manifestation of the entire town's dark side. Despite their fears, they reenter the sewers and destroy Pennywise. Free of their torment, they set out to make new lives for themselves.

Written by the screenwriter of *Carrie*, this is not the worst adaptation of King (the strong cast makes the present-day scenes absorbing), but the constant flashbacks to the kids' childhoods drag the story down, and the climax (the heroes vs. a giant spider) was deservedly condemned (in the original, Pennywise's destruction caused the town itself to wash away).

IT CAME FROM OUTER SPACE II
Sci-Fi, 11/7/95

Cast: Jack Putnam (Brian Kerwin), Ellen Fields (Elizabeth Pena), Stevie Fields (Jonathan Carrasco), Roy Minter (Bill McKinney), Alan Parson (Adrian Sparks), Dave Grant (Dean Norris), Linda Grant (Dawn Zeek), Carolee Minter

(Lauren Tewes), Chance Madson (Mickey Jones), Kathy Parson (I'Lana B'Tiste), Zack (Jerry Giles), Ben Cully (Howard Morris), Desert Rats (Michael Ray Miller, Clement Blake), Hughy (Thomas Adcox), Mrs. Otis (Connie Sawyer), Mrs. Hughy (Bonnie Hellman), Onlooker (Richard Stay), Zack's Wife (Lauren Dow)

Credits: Director: Roger Duchowny; Writers: Ken and Jim Wheat, based on Harry Essex' screenplay from a Ray Bradbury short story; Photography: Robert C. New; Production Design: Anthony Tremblay; Music: Shirley Walker; Editor: Michael S. McLean; Produced by Duchowny Dow Films, Finnegan Pinchuk

Jack, a celebrated photographer, returns to his dying southwestern home town shortly before a spaceship crashes nearby. Before long, the temperatures are hitting lethal highs; people vanish or change personalities; and a mysterious mound rises in the desert. Jack discovers that the mound (actually the alien ship) grows by absorbing water (which somehow makes it hot)—and that the aliens have replaced some of the townies in order to repair their ship and leave. Despite his warnings, the locals try to blow up the mound; instead, Jack returns the alien duplicate of his new love, Ellen, to the ship, which convinces the aliens to free the real Ellen and the others, then leave.

The 1953 version of *It Came from Outer Space* was a landmark—the first 3-D SF film, the first SF film set in the southwestern desert (a recurring setting during the decade), and the first to feature sympathetic but not saintly aliens. Despite the title, this is a remake, not a sequel—and a poor one at that: It's less imaginative and spends too much time on boring interpersonal dramas and a lot of screaming.

IT HAPPENED ONE CHRISTMAS
ABC, 12/11/77

Cast: Mary Bailey Hatch (Marlo Thomas), Henry Potter (Orson Welles), George Hatch (Wayne Rogers), Clara (Cloris Leachman), Uncle Willie (Barney Martin), Violet (Karen Carlson), Gower (Dick O'Neill), Mrs. Bailey (Doris Roberts), Martini (Cliff Norton), Rodney Sherman (Scott Nemes), Attendant (Jake Steinfeld), Lionel Gilbert (Ken Sansom), Receptionist (Teri Beckerman), Cops (Ronald E. Morgan, Joseph Phelan), Gallery Guard (Dan Woren), Saleslady (Marsha Warner), Officer (Clinton Chase), Marvin Carter (David Whitfield), Miss Tomkins (Valerie Hall)

Credits: Director: Alan J. Levi; Writer–Executive Producers: Sherwood Schwartz, Lloyd J. Schwartz; Producers: Marlo Thomas, Carole Hart; Associate Producer: John Whitman; Photography: Dean Cundey; Art Director: Richard B. Lewis; Music: David Frank; Editor: Houseley Stevenson; Produced by Daisy Productions, Universal

All her life, savings-and-loan officer Mary has dreamed of adventure, excitement and glamour outside her small town—but time and again, the needs of her family, her friends, her community keep her home. Even though she has a happy marriage and a good business, Mary believes her life has never amounted to anything. When Mary's bewildered uncle accidentally loses the company's money, Potter—who loathes Mary for breaking his economic stranglehold on the town—promises to ruin and jail Mary. Broken in spirit, Mary considers suicide until Clara, an eccentric and inept angel, shows Mary that without her, the town would be mired in poverty and despair, her husband would be a drunk, and her friends and family would be much the worse for her absence. Cheered, Mary returns home to face Potter's charges—and finds that her friends have raised enough money to make up the loss and then some.

This remake of the Capra-classic *It's a Wonderful Life* only shows how good the original was (check out *Clarence* for another unsuccessful take on Capra).

IT NEARLY WASN'T CHRISTMAS
Syndicated, 11/20–12/18/89 (window)

Cast: Santa Claus (Charles Durning), Jennifer Baxter (Risa Schiffman), Laura Baxter (Annette Marin), Jeff Baxter (Wayne Osmond), Philpot (Bruce Vilanch), Napoleon (Ted Lange), Sgt. Devlin (Michael Picardi), J. Prescott Hewes (Michael Ruud), Father John (Bill Lawrence), Brian Jessup (Stephen Blosil), Ryan Jessup (Ryan Webb), Clyde Jessup (Omar Hansen), Banker (Michael Flynn), Mary Jessup (Jester Schell), Norbert Castleburg (Michael Weatherred), Mr. Bannings (Jessie Bennett), Limo Driver (Ivan Crosland), Andy Woodford (Jeffrey Hubrich),

Mr. Woodford (Marvin Payne), Receptionist (Shannon Engemann), Boy (Ryan Healey), Doctor (David Blackwell), Mrs. Claus (Beverly Rowland), Jeff's Boxx (Tip Boxell), Stubby (M.J. Bench), Roly Poly (Dottie Bench), Muffin (Debbie Christensen), Trouper (Kenneth Kunz), Mother (Star Roman), Son (Brett Webb), Father (Gary Barnes), Mugger (Paul Grace), Ticket Clerk (Alan Nash), Bus Driver (Jason Ball), Chicago Cop (John Daryl), Ticket Buyers (Lila Levar, Anne Taylor Meyers), Denver Cop (Leonard James), Desk Sergeant (Thom Dillon)

Credits: Director: Burt Brinckerhoff; Writers: Golda David, Alan Jay Glueck; Story: Golda David, Alan Jay Glueck, Stanley Isaacs; Producer: Harvey Bibicoff, Irwin Meyer, Jimmy Osmond; Photography: Gordon C. Lonsdale; Production Design: Doug Johnson; Music: James A. Osmond, Wayne Osmond; Editor: Tim Tommasino; Produced by Sunrise Studios, Osmond Media Center, Ventura Entertainment, OOG Corporation

Sickened by greedy, selfish Christmas requests, Santa Claus contemplates quitting—but a letter from little Jennifer Baxter pleading that he bring her father back from his California job for Christmas touches Santa's heart. When Jennifer runs away to find her father, Santa joins her, hoping to see if the people they meet have any trace of Christmas spirit; they're followed by Jennifer's mother and the inept elf Philpot. Santa and Jennifer change the lives of everyone they encounter—a farmer facing bankruptcy, a workaholic executive, a fake Santa running a charity scam—but even after the Baxters reunite in California, Santa still doubts his vocation until Jennifer convinces everyone around to voice their belief in Santa Claus. His faith restored, Santa returns to the North Pole in time to make his Christmas ride.

This is a cloying, saccharine film; the actors playing Jennifer and Philpot are talentless. And ugh, that sickly-sweet theme song!

JEKYLL AND HYDE
ABC, 1/21/90

Cast: Dr. Jekyll/Mr. Hyde (Michael Caine), Sara Crawford (Cheryl Ladd), Dr. Charles Lanyon (Joss Ackland), Jeffrey Utterson (Ronald Pickup), Annabel Winston (Diane Keen), Lucy (Kim Thomson), Sgt. Hornby (Kevin McNally), Snape (David Schofield), Inspector Palmer (Lee Montague), Mrs. Hackett (Miriam Karlin), Beresford Mount (Lance Percival), Mrs. Clark (Joan Heal), Poole (Frank Barrie), Jekyll's Father (Lionel Jeffries), Man (Martin Jacobs), Businessman (Duncan Gould), Auctioneer (John Scarborough), Customer (Harvey Ashby), Head Groom (Ray Armstrong), Sara's Son (Kiran Shah), Little Girl (Nina Kennedy), Lanyon's Butler (Peter Gale), Dr. Lloyd (Andrew Castell), Sailor (Gary Shail), Medical Students (David Michaels, Simon Adams, Richard Dixon), Head Porter (Eric Dodson), Nurse (Jill Pearson), Maid (Samantha Janus), Duty Sergeant (Michael Stainton), Bartender (Tim Diggle), Pub Customers (Jazzer Jeyes, Terry Walsh), Landlord (Eric Mason), Editor (Philip Locke), Jekyll's Mother (Margaret Rawlings), Detective (Terry Plummer), Copy Boy (Ross McCall), Sub-Editor (Peter Geeves), Lab Technician (Craig Crosbie), Sergeant (Antony Brown), Cop (Nigel Betts), Newsboy (Daniel Percy), Opera Singers (Wendy Pollock, Frederick Bateman), Annabel's Friend (Charlotte Howard), Vendor (Prentis Hancock), Newsboy (Justin Degan)

Credits: Director-Writer: David Wickes, based on Robert Louis Stevenson's novel; Line Producer: Patricia Carr; Executive Producers: Gerald W. Abrams, Nick Elliott, David Wickes; Associate Producer: Joanna Elferink; Photography: Norman Langley; Production Design: William Alexander; Costumes: Raymond Hughes; Music: John Cameron; Editor: John Shirley; Produced by David Wickes TV, London Weekend Television, King Phoenix Entertainment

In this adaptation, Dr. Jekyll's efforts to control his savage alter ego (created from Jekyll's study of brain chemistry) are complicated by the widowed doctor's romance with his sister-in-law, Sara. When Jekyll loses control of his transformations, he's killed—but both he and Hyde survive in Sara's son.

This adaptation rejects most of the changes the big screen wrought on Stevenson (both the Fredric March and Spencer Tracy movies follow a stage adaptation that gave Jekyll a chaste fiancée and Hyde a harlot for contrast) and includes many of the novel's minor characters (Dr. Lanyon, Poole, Utterson)—but it's still less than faithful, adding its own romance to the all-male original. More significantly, it changes the point made by Stevenson (which the March movie captured perfectly) that Hyde is Jekyll's choice (a way to sin without guilt or fear of exposure), not his curse. *Jekyll and Hyde* is well performed, but the rarely shown March version rules supreme (this is, however, far better than the TV musical starring Kirk Douglas).

J.O.E. AND THE COLONEL
ABC, 9/11/85

Cast: J.O.E./Joe (Gary Kasper), Colonel H.C. Fleming (William Lucking), Dr. Michael Rourke (Terence Knox), Lena Gant (Gail Edwards), Miss Kai (Aimee Eccles), Lyle (Allan Miller), Mrs. Roth (Marie Windsor), Mr. Roth (Allan Rich), Pam (Christie Houser), Travis (William Riley), Pike (Michael Swan), Max Carney (Don Swayze), Alpha (Douglas Alan Shanklin), Mueller (Robert Feero), Technicians (Bruce Corvi, Frankie Hill), Wilson (John Davey), Agent (Joe Borgese), Angelina (Leigh Lombardi)

Credits: Director: Ronald Satlof; Writer–Executive Producer: Nick Corea; Producer: Stephen P. Caldwell; Photography: William Cronjager, Frank Thackery; Art Director: John Leimanis; Music: Joseph Conlan; Editors: Patrick M. Ryan, Ellen Ring Jacobsen; Produced by Mad Dog Productions, Universal Television

J.O.E. (J-Type Omega Elemental) is the ultimate human, genetically engineered and computer-educated for superhuman strength and intellect. His creators—ex-marine Fleming, scientists Rourke and Gant—saw him as an explorer, but their employers, the Moebius Group, wanted a warrior. Since adrenaline fuels Joe's enhanced body, he took to the action and danger of combat, but when he refused to kill without cause, Moebius ordered him terminated. Instead, Gant was killed, and Rourke fled with Joe. To pay the bills and fuel Joe's adrenaline thirst, they work as high-priced troubleshooters.

When Moebius locates the duo, they send Alpha, a more ruthless J.O.E., and the reluctant Fleming to terminate them, but Joe kills Alpha in self-defense. Fleming reveals that Gant is still alive, and offers to cancel the termination if Joe and Rourke rescue Gant from terrorists exploiting her inventions. Despite Moebius' interference, the team takes out the terrorists, but Rourke dies saving Gant. Joe is paralyzed with grief until Fleming leaves Moebius and convinces Joe to work with him on a new troubleshooting team.

This is a stock failed pilot in the government-created-assassin genre (rewritten from the original draft, which focused on Joe and Rourke).

JOHN CARPENTER PRESENTS: BODY BAGS
Showtime, 8/8/93

Cast: *Morgue*: Coroner (John Carpenter), Men (Tobe Hooper, Tom Arnold); *Gas Station*: Bill (Robert Carradine), Anne (Alex Datcher), Gent (Peter Jason), Divorcée (Molly Cheek), Pasty-Faced Man (Wes Craven), Dead Bill (Sam Raimi), Pete (David Naughton), Stranger (Buck Flower), Peggy (Lucy Boyrer), Anchorman (Roger Rooks); *Hair*: Richard (Stacy Keach), Dr. Lock (David Warner), Megan (Sheena Easton), Dennis (Dan Blom), Man (Attila), Woman (Kim Alexis), Man with Dog (Greg Nicotero), Nurse (Deborah Harry); *Eye*: Brent (Mark Hamill), Cathy (Twiggy), Dr. Lang (John Agar), Dr. Bregman (Roger Corman), Manager (Charles Napier), Player (Eddie Velez), Librarian (Betty Muramoto), Nurse (Bebe Drake-Massey), Minister (Sean McCloskey), Man (Robert L. Bush), Technician (Gregory H. Alpert)

Credits: Directors: Tobe Hooper (*Eye*), John Carpenter; Writers: Billy Brown, Dan Angel; Producer: Sandy King; Co-Producer: Dan Angel; Executive Producers: John Carpenter, Sandy King, Dan Angel; Production Design: Daniel A. Lomino; Photography: Gary Kibbe; Music: John Carpenter, Jim Lang; Editor: Edward A. Warschilka; Produced by Republic, 187 Corp.

A night-shift coroner tells stories about three corpses—or parts of them—lying around the morgue. In *Gas Station*, a woman working graveyard shift at a filling station becomes the target of a serial killer. In *Hair*, an insecure, balding man undergoes treatments that give him a virile, flowing scalp. He discovers too late that the hairs are alien worms that find this an easy way to feed off human brains. In *Eye*, Brent receives an eye transplant from a serial killer; the eye shows him visions of murder that drive Brent to kill his wife—but at the last minute, he stabs himself through the murderous eye instead. Then, back in the morgue, we learn the coroner is actually one of the corpses himself.

This (unsuccessful) pilot for a *Tales from the Crypt*-style anthology series works fairly well, with *Hair* being the best segment. Carpenter makes an irritating narrator, though. The cast includes several horror directors in bit parts, and *Star Wars*' Mark Hamill.

JOHNNY 2.0
Sci-Fi, 9/12/98

Cast: Jonathan Dalton (Jeff Fahey), Nikki Holland (Tahnee Welch), Frank Donahue (Michael Ironside), Bosch (John Neville), Taylor (Michael Rhoades), Carlos (Von Flores), Dan-O (Cliff Saunders), Phil (Eugene Lipinski), Nurse (Nicky Guadagni), Reporter (Deborah Burgess), Pharmacist (Elisa Moolecherry), Treacherous Man (Martin Roach), Vendor (Ken Smith), Face (Darren Marsman), APS Commander (Geoffrey Bowes), APS Hologram (James Downing), APS Worker (David Blacker), Cargo Driver (Anthony Thomas-Costa), Outback Mother (Carly Mandelbaum), Terrorist (Megan Fahlenbock), Newscaster (Dan Duran)

Credits: Director: Neill Fearnley; Writer: Wynne McLaughlin; Producer: Susan Murdoch; Photography: Manfred Guthe; Production Design: Dave Davis; Music: Ed Tomney; Editor: Stephen Lawrence; Produced by Spectacor Films, Promark Entertainment Group, Pebblehut Productions

Researcher Jonathan Dalton thought he'd been unconscious for hours after animal-rights activists assaulted Azine Corp's labs. Then he learned it had been 20 years, and that he was a clone, his memories recreated from an MRI taken after the accident. In the interim, corporations have replaced governments, and biological weapons have become commonplace. Terrorists seeking more bio-weapons have kidnapped the original Dalton, and Azine CEO Bosch thinks Johnny's insight into Dalton's mind will help him find the scientist.

Johnny tracks down the Retribution terrorists only to learn they're freedom fighters working with Dalton, and that Azine is the main creator of bio-weapons, testing them on human subjects. Dalton reveals that Bosch is on the brink of becoming immortal by perfecting a process for transferring his mind to clone bodies. Retribution attacks Azine; Johnny and Holland are captured, Dalton and the others are killed. Bosch reveals that he's a hologram projected by the real, utterly corrupt Dalton; after a lab accident crippled him, he cloned "Dalton" to perfect the mind-transfer, but with 20 years' less memories, Dalton retained his idealism and turned against Azine.

Using Dalton's software, Bosch tries implanting his mind into Johnny's body; Holland escapes and saves Johnny, and Bosch dies. Johnny—already anointed as Bosch's successor—takes over as Azine CEO, purging the worst of its executives and setting the company on the path of social reform.

Johnny 2.0 is one of TV's more imaginative clone films.

JOURNEY TO THE CENTER OF THE EARTH
NBC, 2/28/93

Cast: Chris Turner (David Dundara), Dr. Margo Peterson (Farrah Forke), Dr. Tesue Ishakowa (Kim Miyori), Dr. Cecil Chalmers (John Neville), Chris (Jeffrey Nordling), Joe Briggs (Tim Russ), Professor Harlech (F. Murray Abraham), Dallas (Carel Struycken), Sandra Miller (Fabiana Udenio), Devin (Justina Vail), Hiram Wentworth (Francis Guinan), Secretary (Cassandra Byram), Students (Connie Craig, Doug Freimuth, Ben Cleaveland), Collins (Sam Raimi), Technicians (Alden Millikan, Craig Benton), Trog Chief (Mark Conlon), Trog Shaman (Robert Stuart Reed), Trog Women (Amy Rose, Susan Dear), Herd Trogs (Stuart Black, Tony Reitano, Oliver Dear, Ira McAliley), Dark Prince (Alex Daniels)

Credits: Director: William Dear; Writers: Robert Gunter, David Mickey Evans; Producer: John Ashley; Co-Producers: Marvin Miller, Robert Gunter; Co-Executive Producers: David Mickey Evans, Dale De La Torre, William Dear; Photography: Ron Garcia; Production Design: James Spencer; Music: David Kurtz; Editor: Barry L. Gold; Produced by High Productions, Columbia

Ten years ago, Chris Turner watched his mentor, Prof. Harlech, drive an earth-boring vehicle through a live volcano into a hypothetical "underworld" of vast caverns. Harlech never returned. Now shady industrialist Wentworth agrees to back Chris' new underworld expedition on the earth-boring *Adventure*, with Chris and his rival Margo as co-captains. Crewed by scientists and adventurers, the *Adventure* drills its way into the underworld.

Here they encounter a friendly giant, Dallas, and attract the attention of the malevolent, ancient Dark Prince, who survives on elaborate life support. The Prince realizes crew member Chalmers carries part of the Book, a computer holding the secrets of lost Atlantis—which, combined with the Prince's own fragment, will free him from the life support. When the crew defeats the Prince's troglodyte army, the Prince attacks the ship with the power of the Book—but gets hit by a rock and toppled into lava (wearing Harlech's ring, which is not explained). Margo reveals that Wentworth is also seeking the Book—but since the battle destroyed their homing beacon, they have no way back. It's off for fresh adventures in the underworld!

Jules Verne's *Journey to the Center of the Earth* has inspired one cartoon show and several movies (the James Mason fifties version is the best). This deservedly failed pilot is closer to Edgar Rice Burroughs' Pellucidar books or the *Cave Carson* comics, but it is slightly entertaining in a very low-budget, pulpy, Irwin Allen style. *Trek* fans will recognize Struycken (*Next Generation*'s Mr. Homm) and Russ (*Voyager*'s Tuvok, here woefully miscast as a hard as nails marine).

K-9000
Fox, 7/1/91

Cast: Eddie Monroe (Chris Mulkey), Dr. Asia Turner (Catherine Oxenberg), Captain DeLillo (Dana Gladstone), Niner (Jerry Houser, voice), Anton Zeiss (Judson Scott), Mrs. Wiffington (Anne Haney), Banks (Thom McFadden), (David Renan), Danny (Ivan E. Roth), Woller (Rick Aiello), Factor (Ted Barba), Thugs (Jim Burk, Jason Corbett, Kenny Endoso, Jeff Imada, Henri Kingi, Dave Perna, Danil Torppe), Butler (Ed Evanko), Dijon (Mitch Hara), Rocky Araki (Jim Ishida), Doctor (Waldemar Kalinowsky), Dock Worker (Fred Ottaviano), Charity Lady (Patricia Raymond), Tech (Nicholas Shaffer), Store Owner (Sammy Thurman), Johnson (Charles Walker), Dial (Danny Weselis), Waiter (Steve Whiteford), Nurse (Deborah Wilkes), with Dennis Haysbert

Credits: Director: Kim Manners; Writers: Steven E. De Souza, Michael Part; Producer: J. Rickley Dumm; Supervising Producer: Charles Fries; Photography: Frank Raymond; Production Design: Elliott Gilbert; Music: Jan Hammer; Editor: J.P. Farrell; Produced by De Souza Productions, Fries Entertainment

Asia Turner believes her computer implants can turn dogs into super-intelligent helpers for humans. Mercenary Anton Zeiss sees the dogs as potential assassins or soldiers, so he murders Turner's staff and steals Niner, a German shepherd with a prototype implant. Turner survives the massacre and hooks up with Monroe, a maverick cop in need of a big bust to redeem himself. Breaking into Zeiss' lair, they free Niner—and Monroe is accidentally implanted with a chip that links his mind with the dog's.

Monroe initially hates having his mind touched, but when Zeiss captures Turner, he and Niner work together to free her—only to be caught by a corrupt federal agent working for Zeiss. Zeiss orders Asia to remove the implants, but she frees Monroe and Niner instead, and the duo successfully takes down Zeiss. Monroe no longer objects to his new partner—and since Turner's work has been destroyed, she decides to monitor them until the K-9000 project is up and running again.

A deservedly unsuccessful pilot that sat on the shelf for two years before being aired.

THE KID WITH THE BROKEN HALO
NBC, 4/5/82

Cast: Andy LeBeau (Gary Coleman), Blake (Robert Guillaume), Dorothea Powell (June Allyson), Harry Tannenbaum (Mason Adams), Michael (Ray Walston), Jeff McNulty (John Pleshette), Julie McNulty (Lani O'Grady), Gail Desautel (Telma Hopkins), Teri Desautel (Kim Fields), Rudy Desautel (Georg Stanford Brown), Diana McNulty (Tammy Lauren), Nick McNulty (Keith Mitchell), Coach Ramsdell (Rance Howard), Rudy (Corey Feldman), Frank Vargas (Randy Kirby), Glynnis Vargas (Wesley Ann Pfenning), Pierce (Hugh McPhillips), Giuseppe (Don Diamond), Dave (David Askrow), Fenton (Billy Beck), Prospect (Jim Begg), Haber (Traci Lee Briggs), Flanagan (Barry Hope), Marta (Rachel Jacobs), Kids (Gary Guttenberg, Ty

Mitchell), Toberashe (Talmose Scott), Assistant Coach (Claude Swanger), Tackler (Rick Fitts), Quarterback (Victor Trivas), Player (Doug Toby)

Credits: Director: Leslie Martinson; Writer: George Kirgo; Producer: Jim Begg; Executive Producers: Harry Sloan, Lawrence L. Kuppin; Photography: Gary Graver; Art Director: Bryan Ryman; Music: Tommy Vig; Editor: Ed Cotter; Produced by Satellite Productions

Andy, a young angel under the watchful eye of angelic overseer Blake, must earn his wings by helping three souls get into heaven.

Angels earning their wings have been a staple of the mass media since *It's a Wonderful Life*; this pilot led to the animated *Gary Coleman Show*.

KILLDOZER
ABC, 2/2/74

Cast: Lloyd Kelly (Clint Walker), Dennis Holvig (Carl Betz), Chub Foster (Neville Brand), Jules "Dutch" Krasner (James Wainwright), Al Beltran (James A. Watson, Jr.), Mack McCarthy (Robert Urich)

Credits: Director: Jerry London; Writers: Ed MacKillop, Theodore Sturgeon, adapted by Herbert F. Solow from Sturgeon's novella; Producer: Herbert F. Solow; Photography: Terry K. Meade; Art Director: James Martin Bachman; Music: Gil Melle; Editor: Fabien Tordjmann; Produced by Universal

A construction crew bulldozing an island site for an oil well unearths a meteorite holding an alien energy being; the creature's energy enters the bulldozer, killing one man in the process. At first, all the others notice is that the bulldozer's steering seems funny—but then it animates, attacking them and destroying their radio. The men are killed one by one by the unstoppable machine—until the two survivors realize that it's not the 'dozer they have to destroy but the energy inside it. Luring it into a trap, they electrify the bulldozer, killing the alien—though they still have no idea how to explain all this to their bosses.

"Killdozer" is a terrific short story by SF giant Sturgeon (drawing on his own experience running a bulldozer during World War II), optioned many times over the years for movies. This adaptation loses almost all the energy of the original.

KILLER BEES
ABC, 2/26/74

Cast: Edward Van Bohlen (Edward Albert), Victoria Wells (Kate Jackson), Madame Maria Van Bohlen (Gloria Swanson), Dr. Helmut Van Bohlen (Roger Davis), Mathias Van Bohlen (Don McGovern), Rudolf Van Bohlen (Craig Stevens), Sgt. Jeffreys (John S. Ragin), Zeb Tucker (Liam Dunn), Roseanna (Heather Ann Bostain), Lineman (Donald Gentry), Salesman (Jack Perkins), Minister (Robert L. Balzar), Townsman (Daniel Woodworth), Attendant (John Getz)

Credits: Director: Curtis Harrington; Writers: John W. Corrington, Joyce Corrington; Producers: Howard Rosenman, Ron Bernstein; Photography: Jack Woolf; Production Design: Joel Schumacher; Music: David Shire; Editors: John W. Holmes, Robert A. Daniels; Produced by RSO Films

At Tori Wells' insistence, her fiancé, Edward, introduces her to his beekeeping, wine-making family, ruled by the aging matriarch Madame. The family wants Edward to stay home and dump Tori. They're also busy hiding occasional deaths caused by their swarming bees. As the bodies multiply, the cops wonder if the bees aren't deadly African killer bees, even though they settle over Madame as peacefully as pet finches.

When Madame rejects Tori as a daughter-in-law, Tori reveals that she's already bearing Edward's child; Madame recoils in horror, then the bees sting her to death. Tori and Edward agree to leave after the funeral—but while Tori is at home alone, the bees swarm to her. When the family returns, Tori has replaced Madame as queen of the hive, and the Bohlens accept her as their new leader.

The idea of a human queen bee also showed up on *The Outer Limits*' "Zzzzz" episode, but this movie owes more to the seventies' fear that African killer bees were swarming north from South America to wipe out our native honeybees and sting us all to death (before the bees arrived in the nineties they'd also inspired *The Swarm*, *The Deadly Bees* and *Saturday Night Live*'s "Killer Bees" sketches). *Killer Bees* is not bad, with big-screen star Swanson in her TV-movie debut and familiar faces Edward Albert (later of the *Beauty and the Beast* TV series) and Kate Jackson and Roger Davis (both formerly of *Dark Shadows*).

KISS MEETS THE PHANTOM OF THE PARK
NBC, 10/28/78

Cast: KISS members (Peter Criss, Ace Frehley, Gene Simmons, Paul Stanley), Abner Devereaux (Anthony Zerbe), Calvin Richards (Carmine Caridi), Melissa (Deborah Ryan), Sam (Terry Lester), Chopper (John Dennis Johnston), Slime (John Lisbon Wood), Dirty Dee (Lisa Jane Persky), Snede (John Chappell), Don Steel as Himself, Guards (Richard Hein, Brion James), Girl (Mary Kay Morse), KISS soldier (Marc Winters), Mother (Sandra Penn), Father (Leon Delaney), Man in KISS Booth (Bill Hudson)

Credits: Director: Gordon Hessler; Writers: Jan-Michael Sherman, Don Buday; Producer: Terry Morse, Jr.; Executive Producers: Joseph Barbera, William M. Avcoin; Photography: Robert Caramico; Art Director: James G. Hulsey; Music: Hoyt Curtain; Editor: Peter E. Berger; Produced by Hanna-Barbera/KISS Productions

The same day the rock group KISS performs at a major amusement park, the management fires Devereaux, the roboticist who created the park's animatronic attractions. Blaming KISS for stealing away the teen audience, Devereaux sends android doubles of the band out to wreak havoc. Fortunately, KISS possesses mystic talismans that endow the foursome with superpowers; exploring the park at night, they battle and defeat Devereaux's androids. Devereaux has a mind-controlled teen steal the talismans, then his androids capture the powerless rockers. By pooling their force of will, the band members summon their talismans, regain their powers, destroy their android counterparts and free the mind-zombies. Devereaux can't take defeat and becomes a mental vegetable.

Very similar to Marvel's short-lived *KISS* comic-book, this was meant to broaden the band's appeal, but failed (the good ratings came mostly from existing KISS fans). The band thought the film stupid and that it exposed a lack of acting talent (Gene Simmons' voice had to be dubbed—though he went on to act in several other films). They were right on both counts.

A KNIGHT IN CAMELOT
ABC, 11/8/98

Cast: Dr. Vivian Morgan (Whoopi Goldberg), King Arthur (Michael York), Guinevere (Amanda Donohoe), Clarence (Simon Fenton), Merlin (Ian Richardson), Sir Sagramour (Robert Addie), Sandy (Paloma Baeza), Lancelot (James Coombes), Slave (Lukocs Bicsey), Ms. Wardrobe (Gobi Csizmodia), Ms. Chamberpot (Gobi Fon), Bob (John Guerrosio), Slave Driver (Pál Makroi), Sandy's Father (Paul Rogan), Armorer (Steven Speirs), Ms. of Ceremonies (Mariann Szoloy), Sheriff (Bélo Unger)

Credits: Director: Roger Young; Writer–Co-Executive Producer: Joe Wiesenfeld, based on Mark Twain's *A Connecticut Yankee in King Arthur's Court*; Producer: Nick Gillott; Executive Producer: Norman Rosemont; Photography: Elemér Ragályi; Production Design: Peter Mullins; Music: Patrick Williams; Editor: Benjamin A. Weissman; Produced by Rosemont Productions, Walt Disney Television

In the latest version of Twain's novel (which Disney had previously adapted for the big screen as *Unidentified Flying Oddball*), "Sir Boss" is Vivian, a physicist whose experiments yank her out of the present and plonk her down in King Arthur's time, where she sets up as court Wizard, helps her page Clarence take revenge on slimey Sir Sagramour, reforms the injustices of medieval monarchy, and leaves the Round Table knights scratching their heads over her anachronisms. After she's turned Arthur into a champion of freedom, Merlin—who'd carried her across time to teach Arthur about freedom and Vivian about honor—takes her on as his apprentice exploring the cosmos.

This works best when Goldberg is allowed to run wild and have fun, otherwise, it's routine. It's unique among Twain adaptations, however, in that it makes Merlin both benevolent and a real mage (which puts it really far from Twain's cynical condemnation of medievalism).

KNIGHT RIDER 2000
NBC, 5/19/91

Cast: Michael Knight (David Hasselhoff), KITT (William Daniels, voice only), Devon Wells (Edward Mulhare), Shawn McCormack (Susan Norman), Russ Maddock (Carmen Argenziano), Kurt (Eugene Clark), Marla (Megan Butler),

Watts (Mitch Pileggi), James Doohan as Himself, Andrew (Chris Bonno), Guard (Robert F. Cawley), Charlie (Philip Hafer), Bag Lady (Carolyn G. Jackson), Police Officer (Ron Jackson), Sandy (Stacy Lundgren), Shawn's Father (Matt Menger), Businessman (Paul Menzel), Medical Technician (J.W. Moore IV), Clerk (Edwin Neal), Sergeant (Marco Perella), Mayor Cottern (Ellis Posey), Fellow Cop (Larry Roop), Lori (Sowri Swierski), with Christine Healy, Lou Beatty, Jr., Francis Guinan, John Cannon Nichols

Credits: Director: Alan J. Levi; Writer: Rob Hedden, based on characters created by Glen A. Larson; Producers: Chuck Sellier, Rob Hedden; Executive Producer: Michele Goldman Brustin; Photography: Billy Dickson; Production Design: Bill Cornford; Music: Jan Hammer; Editor: Barry B. Leirer; Produced by Charles E. Sellier Productions, Riven Rock Productions

It's the new millennium and the mayor of Los Angeles has just been shot. His successor gives the crime-fighting Knight Foundation one month to crack the case, or lose their contract to help the police department. Foundation head Devon convinces retired operative Michael Knight to take on the case, reuniting him with his sidekick KITT, a computer-brain housed in a Trans-Am. But Devon's partner, Maddock, has disassembled KITT and sold off the components, so when they reactivate KITT, it's in the body of an old Chevrolet.

Rookie cop McCormack learns that Watt's gunrunning ring—composed of cops who oppose anti-gun laws—is behind the murder, so Watts puts a bullet in her brain. McCormack is revived by a computer implant; her IQ is enhanced but her memories of Watts are gone. Angry that her boss wanted to let her die (the implant cost too much), she quits the force and joins the Foundation. McCormack's implant lets her interface with KITT, restoring her memory so that she can now identify the villains. A worried Watts has Devon killed, then runs KITT, McCormack and Knight off the road and into the ocean. KITT shorts out, but his passengers survive and rebuild his CPU, transplanting it into the Foundation's new supercar. With the help of the good cops, they nail the crooks during a gun shipment and unmask the new mayor as Watts' backer. Knight retires—for good—and McCormack and KITT become the Foundation's new crimefighting team.

Knight Rider ran for six high-rated years in the eighties. This film and *Knight Rider 2010* failed to revive the franchise, but the *Team Knight Rider* series had a 1997–98 run. A good pilot, *Knight Rider 2000* was more imaginative than the original show. Pileggi is better known as FBI Director Skinner on *The X-Files,* and *Star Trek*'s James Doohan has a cameo.

KNIGHT RIDER 2010
Syndicated, 2/13/94

Cast: Jake McQueen (Richard Joseph Paul), Hannah (Hudson Leick), Jared (Brion James), Will McQueen (Michael Beach), Dean (Don McManus), Zeke (Badja Djola), Robert Lee (Mark Pellegrino), Hillbilly (Jim Cody Williams), Pregnant Woman (Betty Matwick), Cholo (Joseph A. Redondo), Professor's Wife (Wanda Dittman), Professor (Ramon Chavez), Briefcase (Manny Simo-Maceo), Jailer (Shane McCabe), INS Agents (Scott Johnson, Gary Kirk), Bandits (Miguel Ortega, Ken Arquello, Samuel Hernandez), Peddler (Louis E. Zadro), with Nicky Katt, Una Damon, Kimberly Norris

Credits: Director: Sam Pillsbury; Writer: John Leekley; Producer: Alex Beaton; Executive Producers: Rob Cohen, John Leekley; Photography: James Bartle; Production Design: Robb Wilson King; Music: Tim Truman; Editor: Skip Schoolnik; Produced by Universal Television, John Leekley Productions, Rob Cohen Productions

In 2010, Jake McQueen is the best smuggler on the U.S.–Mexico border (much to the displeasure of his lawman brother, Will). When Jake discovers that the immigrants he's bringing across one night are intended as involuntary organ donors, he balks and saves them from his employers, even though that gives Will the chance to bust him. The head of the organ-stealing gang has Jake's old lover, VR designer Hannah, bail Jake out—so that he can be terminated. The killer gets Hannah instead, but Jake uses Hannah's VR technology to transfer her mind into the computer system of his new, souped-up van. In the van, they smash their way into the villain's mansion, defeating him and his henchmen. Jake resumes his wild ways with Hannah at his side—and by plugging his own brain into the computer, they can even make love.

This is the most obscure of the *Knight Rider* sequels, probably because it's in name only (no reference to Michael, KITT, the Knight Foundation, etc.). In hindsight, its main claim to fame comes from co-starring Hudson Leick before she became Callisto, archenemy of *Xena: Warrior Princess*.

THE LAKE
NBC, 2/1/98

Cast: Jackie Ivers (Yasmine Bleeth), Jeff Chapman (Linden Ashby), Maggie (Marion Ross), Herb (Robert Prosky), Steve Ivers (Stanley Anderson), Dylan (Haley Joel Osment), Louise (Caroline Lagerfelt), Denise (Susanna Thompson), Reade (Dewey Weber), Mills (Matthew Beck), Dr. Braden (Michael Winters), The Man (Carey Scott), Lt. Governor Chandler (Marc Gomes), Chief Ramirez (Geoffrey Rivas), Lt. Frank Thompson (David S. Dunard), Dr. Sanjay (Anjul Nigaia), CHP Officer (Anthony Moore), Sgt. Straughn (Blumes Tracy), Server (Katie Rich), Saleswoman (Amy Stock-Poynton), Janitor (Winston Rocha), Mayor's Aide (Carmen Mormino), Buddies (John Brandon, Fred Lerner), Beat Cop (Ben R. Scott), Forensics Guy (Thomas Crawford), Computer Guy (Artur Cybuiski), Nurses (Monique Edward, Jo Farkas, Audrey Kissel), Technician (Benjamin Livingston), Bedridden Man (R.L. Talbiri), Newscaster (Holmes Osborne)

Credits: Director: David S. Jackson; Writers: Alan Brennert, J.D. Feigelson; Story: J.D. Feigelson; Producer: Andrew Gottlieb; Executive Producers: Dennis Hammer, J.D. Feigelson, Peter Frankovich; Photography: Denis Maloney; Production Design: Kim Hix; Music: Don Davis; Editor: Craig Ridenour; Produced by Peter Frankovich Productions, Dennis Hammer Productions, NBC Studios

When Jackie Ivers visits her estranged, dying father Steve, she finds her old home town hides secrets: A man she runs over in her car shows up unharmed; Steve suddenly becomes both healthy and a loving father; their neighbor, Maggie, claims her husband is an impostor—then denies it; and Jackie and her old boyfriend Jeff find the mayor tossing people into a vortex in the nearby lake.

Steve finally confesses that the townsfolk are émigrés from a dying parallel Earth, replacing their duplicates here. Steve, who loves Jackie like his real daughter, sends her and Jeff to the authorities, but their duplicates capture them. Steve saves them from the vortex at the cost of his own life, and Jackie and Jeff reach the state police. The cops are skeptical until they meet duplicates of themselves, too—but with more vortexes opening, is it too late?

Despite a weak ending, this is a pretty good bodysnatcher film, but it's hard to believe everyone (except—conveniently—Jackie's father) in the other world is so evil (desperate yes, but these guys are fiendish).

THE LAST CHILD
ABC, 10/05/71

Cast: Alan Miller (Michael Cole), Karen Miller (Janet Margolin), Senator Quincy George (Van Heflin), Howard Drumm (Harry Guardino), Barstow (Edward Asner), Gus Iverson (Kent Smith), Shelley Drumm (Barbara Babcock), Peter Sanderson (Michael Larrain), Dr. Tyler (Philip Bourneuf), Silverman (Victor Izay), Police Sergeant (James A. Watson, Jr.), Woman in Subway (Sondra Blake), Conductor (Roy Engel), Nurse (Phyllis Avery), Dr. Young (Ivor Francis), Ticket Clerk (Jason Wingreen), Bill Walker (Himself), John (Frank Baster)

Credits: Director: John Llewellyn Moxey; Writer: Peter S. Fisher; Producer: William Allyn; Executive Producer: Aaron Spelling; Photography: Arch R. Dalzell; Art Director: Paul Sylos; Music: Laurence Rosenthal; Editor: Art Seid; Produced by Aaron Spelling Productions

Karen Miller is pregnant with her second child (her first died after 15 days)—which, in an overpopulated U.S. that allows only one child per family (and denies all seniors medical treatment), is a very bad thing. The Millers go on the run to escape a forced abortion, but Population Inspector Barstow soon tracks them down by their computerized IDs. Karen's brother, Howard, uses his political contacts to get them released, but he insists Karen abort.

The Millers head for Canada, but with their IDs red-flagged, they have no chance—until aging Senator George intervenes, hiding them on his estate to await the birth.

Barstow tracks them down, but George's influence keeps him at bay. Howard tries to salvage his political career by bringing Karen home, but she won't budge. Then Barstow catches George's doctor bringing him illegal insulin. Denied the drugs, George is doomed, but he uses his last hours to distract Barstow from the Millers' escape. Barstow drives after the Millers, but dies in a crash. The Millers reach Canada and inspire self-serving Howard to fight for reform.

Dystopias (the opposite of utopias) have been a staple of SF since *Brave New World* (and first appeared in TV-movies in *Shadow on the Land*). One of the strengths of the form is that dystopias can easily adapt to the worries of the day—overpopulation here (and in the inferior theatrical releases *ZPG* and *Soylent Green*), while later writers tackled AIDS (*Daybreak*), class warfare (*Harrison Bergeron*), ecological collapse (*The Fire Next Time*) and corporate takeover (*Doom Runners*). This particular dystopia is quite entertaining due to the solid supporting performances (particularly Guardino's political opportunist and Asner's dogged cop).

THE LAST DINOSAUR
ABC, 2/11/77

Cast: Masten Thrust (Richard Boone), Frankie Banks (Joan Van Ark), Bunta (Luther Rackley), Chuck Wade (Steven Keats), Barney (Carl Hansen), Prehistoric Girl (Mamiya Sekia), Dr. Kawamoto (Tatsu Nakamura), Expedition Captain (William Ross)

Credits: Directors: Alex Grasshoff, Tom Kotani; Writer: William Overgard; Producers: Arthur Rankin, Jr., Jules Bass; Associate Producer: Benni Korzen; Photography: Shoji Ukda; Art Director: Katzou Satsoya; Music: Maury Laws; Editor: Barry Walter; Produced by Rankin-Bass Productions

Millionaire big-game hunter Masten Thrust thought he'd run out of challenges—until an earth-boring drillship scouting for Arctic oilfields discovers a volcano-heated valley of living dinosaurs. Thrust sets off to explore, accompanied by a crew of scientists and brash reporter Frankie.

Arriving in the valley, they face and survive an array of prehistoric perils—and confront a tyrannosaurus, which hurls the earth-borer away, leaving them trapped. As the team ducks dinosaurs and cave people, Thrust becomes obsessed with killing the tyrannosaurus; even after they find the borer, he insists on one last shot at the *T. rex*. When a booby trap fails to slay it, Thrust bids the others goodbye, opting to stay behind and continue the ultimate hunt.

This is a formulaic film reminiscent of bad fifties Lost World movies such as *The Land Unknown*. Neither TV veteran Boone nor rising star Joan Van Ark do much with their parts (and the romantic chemistry between them is nonexistent).

LAST EXIT TO EARTH
Showtime, 8/20/96

Cast: Eve (Kimberly Greist), Jaid (Costas Mandylor), Kali (Amy Hathaway), Bendix (David Groh), Lilith (Hilary Sheppard), Hardester (Michael Cudlitz), Elder (Lisa Banes), Hera (Jonell Kennedy), Goldfinger (Zoe Trilling), Yost (Cedrick Terrell), Delivery Room Doctor (Rosemary Dunsmore), Pregnant Woman (Robin Frates Corbett), Ep (Lily Knight), Moorhouse (Gregory Millar), First Mate (Robert Peters), Crew Guy (Braden Sucietto), Medical Assistant (Kathy Christopherson), Heir Apparent (Alex Datcher), Sybs (Karin Co, Michelle Peters, Roma Court), Techies (Elizabeth Hayden, Camilla Rantsen), Surgeon Athena (Katt Shea), Doctor (Gina Mittelman), Women (Katrina Holden Bronson, Phyllis Stuart, Angelle Brooks), Anchor (Karen Bankhead), Computer Voices (Rachel L. Stowell, Joan Ryan)

Credits: Director: Katt Shea; Writers: Katt Shea, Katherine Martin; Story: Rachel Samuels; Producer: Darin Spillman; Co-Producers: Marta M. Mobley, Cheryl Parnell; Executive Producer: Roger Corman; Photography: Hubert Taczanowski; Production Design: Jeremy Levine; Music: Daniel B. Harvey; Editor: Gina Mittelman; Produced by The Pacific Trust

In the matriarchal 26th century, genetic treatments have eliminated male aggression but left men sterile and passive. When Eve discovers a time-rift into the 22nd century, she leads an expedition through it to capture some fertile males.

The women land on a spaceship captured by terrorists about to unleash a deadly virus on Earth. The super-strong women help

Captain Jaid reclaim his ship, then take him and the terrorists back to the future. Eve's superiors banish her for bringing back such savages—but first allow her to see if primitive testosterone can restore the impotent future men. During her research, Eve and Jaid fall in love. When the terrorists break out, Jaid and Eve defeat them. Jaid joins Eve in exile, followed by others; in the wild, the men regain their potency, ensuring humanity's survival.

Last Exit to Earth is dumb, silly and forgettable.

THE LAST HOME RUN
HBO, 12/13/98

Cast: Young Jonathan (Thomas Guiry), Jenny Neal (Danielle Comerford), Ged (Jonathan Flax), Tommy (Jordi Vilasuso), Reed (Todd Logan), Rashid (Clay Smalls), Victor (Riley Gelwicks), Donald (Ryan Hopkins), Jonathan Lyle (Seymour Cassel), Emma (Vinnette Carroll), Jose (Manuel Arteaga), Mary (Frankie Man), Dugan (Mal Jones), Annand (Badri Prasad Adhikari), Frances (Florence McGee), Judy Neal (Liza Harris), Jeff Neal (Gary Carter), Kenny Neal (Kenny Flax), Dave Winfield (Himself), Umpire (Roger Flax), Kosco (Ed Pang), Nutty Bellhop (Charlie Flax), EMS Woman (Tommy Barone), Lauren (Lauren Razzano), Announcer (John Sterling)

Credits: Director: Bob Gosse; Writers: Ed Apfel, Roger Flax; Story–Executive Producer: Roger Flax; Producers: Larry Meistrich, Bob Gosse; Co-Producer: Jeff Pullman; Photography: Peter Fernberger; Production Design: Andras Kanegson; Music: Jeffrey M. Taylor; Editor: Rachel Warden; Produced by Showcase Entertainment, Horizon Productions, Shooting Gallery Productions

Elderly Jonathan Lyle always wanted to play baseball, but life never gave him the time or the opportunity until he was too old. His friend Emma puts him in touch with an Asian mystic who rejuvenates Jonathan into a young boy. Gifted with adult confidence and determination, Jonathan wins a place on the local Little League team, saves Emma from a fire, helps deliver his new friend Jenny's newborn sister and convinces their coach not to ride the team so hard. Alas, the spell wears off in the middle of a championship game. Jonathan reverts to an old man but makes the winning catch (outside the park—they see him catch it, but not that he's changed). He returns home, comforted by the memory of his winning season.

The Last Home Run shoots for nostalgic warmth, but never catches fire. And once again we see the odd rule of fantasy sports stories that the last winning play has to be achieved without magic.

THE LATHE OF HEAVEN
PBS, 1/9/80

Cast: George Orr (Bruce Davison), Dr. William Haber (Kevin Conway), Heather Lelache (Margaret Avery), Mannie Ahrens (Peyton Park), Penny Crouch (Niki Flacks), Aunt Ethel (Vandi Clark), Mrs. Orr (Bernedette Whitehead), Mr. Orr (Jo Livingston), Grandmother (Jane Roberts), Grandfather (Tom Matts), Parole Officer (Frank Miller), Women (Joye Nash, Gena Sleete), Orderlies (Ben McKinley III, R.A. Miharoff)

Credits: Directors-Producers: David Loxton, Fred Barzyk; Writers: Roger E. Swaybill, Diane English, from Ursula Le Guin's novel; Executive Producer: David Loxton; Associate Producer: Carol Brandenburg; Creative Consultant: Ursula K. Le Guin; Photography: Robbie Greenberg; Art Director: John Wright Stevens; Music: Michael Small; Editor: Dick Bartlett; Produced by WNET-13, Taurus Film

In a decaying near-future, a judge assigns Dr. Haber to treat drug-addicted George. When George claims his dreams can alter reality, Haber scoffs—until he hypnotizes George to dream of a sunny day, and the perennially overcast skies vanish. Unfortunately, America is now in a two-year drought, and no one but George and Haber remember otherwise.

Haber denies noticing any changes—even as he manipulates George's dreams to create the powerful Haber Institute, end overpopulation and stop war. George's subconscious, alas, undercuts the changes: Overpopulation ends by plague, and war stops when people unite against alien invaders. Horrified, George hires Heather, an attorney, who tries and fails to get him released from the treatments. Her efforts to help George fix things with his dreams trigger, instead, an all-out alien invasion; George has to return to Haber, who has him turn the aliens peaceful.

Fed up with his patient, Haber has George dream his power into a machine Haber can use to change reality himself. When Haber dreams, he discovers the world ended in nuclear war four years ago; the "real" world he knows has always been George's dream. Haber's mind snaps and the post-nuclear reality begins reasserting itself, but George, guided by the aliens, keeps the world from reverting to Armageddon. His powers gone, he and Heather settle down to a normal life.

This rarity in TV SF (an adaptation of a contemporary, serious SF novel) is well performed and overall a good job, but boy is that ending confusing (even upon rewatching)!

LEAPIN' LEPRECHAUNS
Disney, 3/2/97

Cast: Michael Dennehy (John Bluthal), Mikey Dennehy (Gregory Edward Smith), King Kevin (Godfrey James), Queen Maeve (Tina Martin), Flynn (Sylvester McCoy), Patrick (James Ellis), Wizard (Ion Haiduc), John Dennehy (Grant Cramer), Sarah Dennehy (Sharon Lee Jones), Melanie Dennehy (Erica Nicole Hess), Dr. Vazjnioc (Mihai Niculescu), Dr./Mrs. Vazjnioc (Dorina Lazar), Andrew (Andrew Smith), Andrew's Father (Ray Bright), Surveyors (Jeremy Levine, Mike Higgins), Fairies (Carina Tautu, Dana Zarnescu, Pavel Ana Maria, Mihai Silvia, Galani Nicoleta), Leprechauns (Constantin Cojocaru, Constantin Radoaca, Stelian Nistor, Rares Stoica, Valentin Popescu, Mihai Bunea, Costica Draganescu, Drogeanu Marius, Bogdan Uritescu, Dan Condurache, Mircea Andreescu, Ion Georgescu, Razvan Ionescu, Cristi Sofron, Dan Zamfirescu)

Credits: Director: Ted Nicolaou; Writers: Michael McGann, Ted Nicolaou, based on an idea by Charles Band; Producers: Vlad Paunescu, Oana Paunescu; Associate Producer: Ray Bright; Executive Producers: Charles Band, Debra Dion; Photography: Adolfo Bartoli; Production Design: Radu Corciova; Costumes: Oana Paunescu, Mihaela David; Visual Effects: Jim Aupperle; Music: Richard Kosinski, John Zeretzke, William Levine; Editor: Gregory Sanders; Produced by Paramount, Moonbeam Entertainment

Michael Dennehy, longtime friend of the leprechauns, is delighted to visit his American son John—unaware that John plans to turn Michael's farm into an "Ireland Land" theme park. Michael (accompanied by the suspicious wee folk) finds that John's family members are joyless, achievement-oriented yuppies, too materialistic to believe in or see the leprechauns. One by one, though, the family members' eyes are opened to the magic, but John refuses to believe or to change his Ireland Land plans. When John takes his "delusional" father to a mental hospital, Finvarra, lord of the dead, crashes the car and comes for John. Young Mikey's courage and love for his father, backed up by fairy magic, drives Finvarra away. John finally believes, and Ireland Land is deep-sixed forever.

Several formula elements work in this charming kids' film. It was followed by a good sequel, *Spellbreaker* (which aired on Canadian TV, so it isn't included here).

THE LEGEND OF GATOR FACE
Showtime, 5/19/96

Cast: Danny (John White), Phil (Dan Warry-Smith), Angel (Charlotte Sullivan), Chip (Gordon Michael Woolvett), Danny's Mom (Kathleen Laskey), Sheriff (C. David Johnson), Bob (Paul Winfield), Mayor's Wife (Pam Hyatt), Mayor (Roger Dunn), Porkbelly (Jack Newman), Deputy Don (Gerry Quigley), Lydator (Sam Malkin), Skeeter (Richard McMillan), Reese (Scott Wickware), Gator Face (Matt Evans), Soldiers (Falconer Abraham, Derreck J. Peels), Newscaster (Deborah Boland), Reporter (Catherine N. Blythe), Emmett (James E. Washington), Woman (Linda Desbiens)

Credits: Director: Vic Sarin; Writers: David Covell, Alan Mruvka, Sahara Riley; Producers: Marilyn Vance, Alan Mruvka; Co-Producer: Patrick Whitley; Photography: John Tarver; Production Design: Marian Wihak; Music: Joseph Williams; Editor: David Goard; Produced by Showtime, Hallmark Entertainment

Preteens Danny and Phil thought it would be a hoot to hoax their town by faking attacks by the mythical swamp monster Gator Face. They change their mind after Danny discovers Gator Face is real—and harmless. When the National Guard starts hunting Gator Face, Danny is terrified they'll kill him, terrified someone will spot his scam—and utterly charmed by the commander's hellion daughter, Angel.

The two boys and Angel save Gator Face

from a hunter's trap, but realize the creature can't escape much longer. They decide to end the hunt by staging an obviously fake attack on the town's summer festival. The plan goes disastrously awry, and Danny winds up trapped in a gator-face suit in a burning building. Gator Face saves Danny, but the Guard kills the creature. The spirit of the swamp revives him, however, and the monster returns, peaceably, to the swamp.

Harmless and forgettable.

THE LEGEND OF SLEEPY HOLLOW
NBC, 10/31/80

Cast: Ichabod Crane (Jeff Goldblum), Brom Bones (Dick Butkus), Katrina Van Tassel (Meg Foster), Frederic Dutcher (Paul Sand), Squire Van Tassel (James Griffith), Fritz Vanderhoof (John Sylvester White), Thelma Vanderhoof Dumke (Laura Campbell), Winthrop Palmer (Michael Ruud), Jenny (Karin Isaacson), Karl (H.E.D. Redford), Jan Van Tassel (Tiger Thompson), Ted Vanderhoof (Michael Witt)

Credits: Director: Martin Goldman; Writers: Malvin Wald, Jack Jacobs, Tom Chapman, from Washington Irving's story; Producer: James L. Conway; Executive Producer: Charles E. Sellier, Jr.; Photography: Paul Hipp; Production Design: Paul Staheli; Art Director: John David Peters; Music: Bob Summers; Editor: Michael Spence; Produced by Schick Sunn Classics Productions, Taft International Pictures

When 18th-century schoolteacher Ichabod Crane starts work in Sleepy Hollow, he finds a few surprises: ghosts, including a mysterious Headless Horseman; very pretty Katrina Van Tassel and her bullying, would-be suitor Brom Bones; and Winthrop Palmer, a supposedly dead former teacher who's determined to pay back Brom's bullying.

Ichabod's insistence that he's seen the Horseman—and Palmer—soon have the locals convinced he's nuts. Katrina decides she loves him anyway, but her father doesn't approve. Brom decides to scare his rival away by posing as the Horseman. His plan goes awry when Palmer shows up as the "real" Horseman, scares Brom half to death and exposes Brom's trick in front of Thelma. In return for keeping the humiliating story secret, Thelma insists Brom marry her. Meanwhile, Ichabod pursues the *real* real Horseman, thinking it's Palmer. Katrina's father catches Palmer posing as the Horseman, decides Ichabod isn't crazy and gives him permission to court Katrina—who shushes Ichabod before he can ruin everything by blurting out about the real Headless Horseman.

This is a light, fun adaptation of the Washington Irving story, part of an occasional *Classics Illustrated* series.

LEGION
Sci-Fi, 4/18/98

Cast: Captain Aldritch (Parker Stevenson), Major Agatha Doyle (Terry Farrell), Siegal (Corey Feldman), Corporal Ryan (Rick Springfield), Dr. Jones (Audie England), Carlson (Gretchen Palmer), Cutter (Trevor Goddard), General Flemming (Troy Donahue), Koosman (Richmond Arquette), Poe (Elston Ridgle), Corporal Goodiss (Tricia Peters), Yastremski (Bob Bancroft), Prisoner (Matthew Allen Bretz)

Credits: Director: Jon Hess; Writers: Patrick Highsmith, Evan Spiliotopoulos; Story: Patrick Highsmith; Producer: Avi Nesher; Co-Producer: Kathy Jordan; Executive Producer: Pascal Borno; Line Producer: Kelli Konop; Associate Producer: Jim Christopher; Photography: Robert Paone; Production Design: Hunter Cressall; Music: Roger Neill; Editor: Isaac Sehayek; Produced by New City Releasing, Mahagonny Pictures, Conquistador Entertainment

In 2036 General Flemming gives disgraced Major Doyle a chance to redeem herself by leading a squad of military prisoners—murderers, deserters, thieves—on a vital mission against a key enemy base. The base, however, turns out to be empty except for piles of corpses—and whatever killed them starts butchering Doyle's squad. The survivors realize that Fleming is using them as guinea pigs to test a superhuman assassin, who may be one of them.

When Doyle and her second in command, Aldritch, are the only ones left, Aldritch pretends to kill Doyle, which draws out the real killer, Ryan. Doyle and Aldritch team up and take him out. Flemming, outraged his genetically engineered creation isn't invincible, orders them killed to cover up his project. Ryan regains enough free will to kill the general and dies in the resulting firefight. Doyle and Aldritch escape to freedom alone.

The Dirty Dozen—a 1969 war film about criminals recruited for a suicide mission—has influenced a great many imitations; this one, by twisting the premise half-way through, is one of the more interesting. Terry Farrell was *Deep Space Nine*'s Jadzia Dax.

THE LIFEFORCE EXPERIMENT
Sci-Fi, 4/16/94

Cast: Dr. Mac McClane (Donald Sutherland), Jessica Saunders (Mimi Kuzyk), Ken Ryan (Corin Nemec), Dr. Robin Allman (Vlasta Vrana), George Cornwall (Miguel Fernandes), Niki Janus (Hayley Reynolds), Woody Gilford (Michael Rudder), Jack Aspect (Michael Reynolds)

Credits: Director: Piers Haggard; Writer: Mike Hodges, Gerald McDonald, based on Daphne Du Maurier's story; Producer: Nicholas Clermont; Co-Producer: Kent Walwin; Photography: Peter Benison; Production Design: John Meighen; Music: Osvaldo Montes; Editor: Yves Langlois; Produced by Filmline International, Screen Partners, Ltd.

To learn the secret of Dr. McClane's mysterious experiments, the CIA assigns agent Saunders as McClane's computer programmer. Saunders discovers that McClane, a widower, is obsessed with defying death; to that end, he's planning to capture the dying Ken's lifeforce at the moment of death and use it as a power source. McClane is also using Niki, a child clairvoyant, to follow Ken's mind into the next world. Horrified, Saunders alerts her boss, who's thrilled at the possibility the CIA could learn to interrogate the dead. He sends two more agents to seize McClane's project if it works.

When Ken dies unexpectedly, Saunders reluctantly completes a computer program that monitors Niki's visions and shows Ken's mind traveling down a glowing tunnel. McClane capture's Ken's life-energy, but Niki's visions reveal that it is Ken's soul that's been trapped. The CIA moves in, so Mac destroys his research rather than see it abused. Ken's soul goes free, and Saunders and Mac rejoice at knowing there is life after death.

This is the sort of research mad scientists have been doing in movies for years, but it's competently done and well performed.

LIFEPOD
Fox, 6/28/93

Cast: Banks (Robert Loggia), Claire St. John (Jessica Tuck), Kane (Adam Storke), Rena Genusia (Kelli Williams), Terman (Ron Silver), Mayvene (C.C.H. Pounder), Parker (Stan Shaw), Q-Three (Ed Gale), Sarah (Lisa Waltz), with Sam Whipple, Cork Hubbert, John Mahon, Pat Destro

Credits: Director: Ron Silver; Writer: M. Jay Roach, Pen Densham; Story: Pen Densham, suggested by a short story by Alfred Hitchcock and Harry Sylvester; Producers: Mark Stern, Tim Harbert; Co-Producer: M. Jay Roach; Executive Producers: Richard A. Lewis, John Watson, Scott Banzil, Pen Densham; Photography: Robert Steadman; Production Design: Curtis A. Schnell; Music: Mark Mancina; Editor: Alan Baumgarten; Produced by Fox West Pictures, Trilogy Entertainment Group, Ahi Entertainment

In 2169 the repressive Earthcorp conglomerate controls Earth and its colonies, including rebellious Venus. When an Earthcorp liner explodes, only a handful of crew and passengers (executive, dissident, reporter, blind fatalist Terman) escape. As their lifepod drifts, waiting for rescue, they realize the explosion was sabotage—and one of them is probably responsible. Quite aside from that, the limited supply of air, food and medicine, and the inter-passenger hostility may kill them off anyway. And one by one, from one cause or another, they do start to die ... until Terman is exposed as the saboteur, planning to frame Venusian separatists for the sabotage to justify putting the colony under martial law. The other passengers overcome and kill Terman, and the provisions he's stashed away give them enough food to survive until picked up.

An SF version of Hitchcock's *Lifeboat* (1944), this is a solid, well-performed dark drama.

THE LIGHTNING INCIDENT
USA, 9/11/91

Cast: Martha Townsend (Nancy McKeon), Vivian (Tantoo Cardinal), Dolores (Elpidia Carrillo), Mama (Miriam Colón), Carol (Polly Bergen), Matthew Townsend (Tim Ryan), Xela (Joaquin Martinez), Dr. Daley (Gary Clarke), Tony (George Salazar), Anna (Sheree Spargo), Carlos (George Pompa), Det. Adams (Dave Adams), Sales Clerk (Kathleen Erickson), Physician's

Assistant (Barbara Glover), Delivery Nurse (Lillie Richardson), Official (Danny O'Haco), Nun (Melissa Michaelsen), Orderly (Brad Michaelson), Paramedic (Jonathan Mincks), Doctor (Bob Sorenson), Police Artist (Amanda Rogers), Guard (George Aguilar)

Credits: Director: Michael Switzer; Writer: Michael Murray; Producer: D.B. Weiss; Executive Producer: Mark R. Gordon; Co-Executive Producer: Christopher Meledandri; Photography: Victor Goss; Production Design: Anthony Cowley; Music: J. Peter Robinson; Editor: Neil Mandelberg; Produced by Paramount, Wilshire Court Productions, Mark Gordon Company

Pregnant sculptor Martha Townsend is having such vivid, eerie nightmares, her worried doctor calls in a psychic, Vivian. Vivian concludes that Martha's dreams are a warning borne of her latent psychic powers. Sure enough, when Alex is born, a Central American witch-cult kidnaps him and tries to kill Martha, first through sorcery (her powers protect her), then brute force (they fail again).

Martha discovers that her mother, a doctor, unwittingly participated in a germ warfare test that rendered the cult's women barren. Her father was one of the natives, which makes Martha the first child born outside their land; according to prophecy, sacrificing her son will restore the women's fertility. Martha's shaman father guides her to the sacrifice, where Martha convinces the shamaness Dolores to stop the ceremony and help her escape with Alex. The Townsends are safe, the land will bloom again—and surely Martha's dreams of the cult pursuing Alex are only dreams...

The Lightning Incident is a murky, clunky occult thriller.

LIKE FATHER, LIKE SANTA
Family, 12/1/98

Cast: Tyler Madison (Harry Hamlin), Snipes (Stuart Pankin), Ambrose Booth (Roy Dotrice), Santa (William Hootkins), Ignatius (Gary Coleman), Danny Madison (Curtis Black), Elyse Madison (Megan Gallagher), Smitty (Gary Frank), Fitzroy (Jimmy Briscoe), Whoops (Michael Munoz), Jake (George Sharperson), Chester (John Ponterelli), Maureen (Jennifer MacWilliams), Kyle (Lex Robbins), Zac (Tommy Woods), Secretary (Kelly Wilson), Commentator (Larry Robbins), Ms. Fischer (Maree Cheatham), John McCarly (Matt Gotleib), with Stanley Kamel

Credits: Director: Michael Scott; Writer–Co-Producer: Mark Valenti; Producer: Melissa Barrett; Executive Producers: Ken Waltz, Carroll Newman, Lance H. Robbins; Associate Producers: Nathan Rotmensz, Jenifer Newman; Photography: John Fleckenstein; Production Design: Sean Mannion; Music: Philip Giffin; Editors: John Gilbert, Andrew B. London; Produced by Fox Family Channel, Lalo Productions, Saban

Workaholic toy tycoon Tyler Madison hates Christmas and has no qualms about using details of Santa's "naughty" list (wormed out of Santa's elves) to blackmail his rivals. Meanwhile, Booth, head of Santa's mail room, feels so unappreciated that he and his staff imprison Santa and the elves so Booth can deliver the toys as the Snow King. Tyler tries to exploit the chaos by sneaking to the Pole and downloading the complete list, but Booth captures him. When Tyler is thrown into Santa's cell, we learn the real reason he hates Christmas: He's Santa's son, and he bitterly resents always taking second place to his father's job.

Tyler offers to show Booth Santa's secrets (like the wormholes that let Santa crisscross the world superfast) in return for a trip home, then slips away to download the list. On the computer he finds an e-mail from his son to Santa that makes Tyler realize he's become everything he hated in his own father. Repentant, Tyler helps Santa escape and whip up Christmas magic that lets them make peace with Booth. Santa finally meets Tyler's family, and Tyler decides to assist Dad in modernizing and speeding up his operation.

Like Father, Like Santa is not as clever as it could have been, and Hamlin (*Clash of the Titans, L.A. Law*) is weak in the lead, but the sheer offbeatness of this fantasy makes it work.

LOOK WHAT'S HAPPENED TO ROSEMARY'S BABY
ABC, 10/29/76

Cast: Adrian/Andrew (Stephen McHattie), Rosemary Woodhouse (Patty Duke Astin), Holtzman (Broderick Crawford), Minnie Castevet (Ruth Gordon), Laykin (Lloyd Haynes), Peter Simon

(David Huffman), Marjean Dorn (Tina Louise), Guy Woodhouse (George Maharis), Roman Castavet (Ray Milland), Ellen (Donna Mills), Adrian/Andrew—Age 8 (Philip Boyer), Dr. Lister (Brian Richards), Interviewer (Beverly Sanders), Trooper (Buck Young), Woman (D.J. Sullivan), Boys (Andy Stone, Calvin Rose)

Credits: Director: Sam O'Steen; Producer-Writer: Anthony Williams, from an idea by Ira Levin; Photography: John A. Alonzo; Art Director: Lester D. Gobruegge; Music: Charles Bernstein; Editor: Bob Wyman; Produced by Culzean Corp., Paramount Pictures

Eight years ago (in *Rosemary's Baby*), Rosemary Woodhouse was seduced by Satan and bore his child. She and her son Andrew flee the satanic coven raising him, but Andrew's demonic side, Adrian, emerges at a bus stop and kills two kids tormenting him. Rosemary rushes onto the next bus—which drives away with no driver or passengers, leaving Andrew behind with floozie Marjean.

Thirteen years later, Marjean has joined the cult and runs a thriving casino. Adrian, tormented and restless, is about to turn 21—at which point he must affirm his evil side by taking a life, or the cult will destroy him and start over. Even when provoked, Adrian doesn't kill, but on the night of his birthday he leads the casino house band in wildly orgiastic music, corrupting the innocents in the audience (i.e., killing their souls). The coven is delighted, until Adrian's best friend Peter intervenes. The cultists kill him, which snaps Adrian back to Andrew. The cult frames Andrew for Peter's murder and has him committed. Ellen, a nurse, helps him escape, but she's really a coven member. After she seduces Andrew into impregnating her, the coven frames him for another murder and starts over with Satan's grandchild.

Rosemary's Baby's portrayal of contemporary satanists in Manhattan made it a commercial hit and a classic of modern horror films; this sequel is just an aimless, confused mess. McHattie does his best at looking tormented, and Gordon recreates her Oscar-winning role from the original as a waspish, elderly satanist.

THE LOVE BUG
ABC, 11/30/97

Cast: Hank Cooper (Bruce Campbell), Alex Davis (Alexandra Wentworth), Simon Moore III (John Hannah), Roddy Martel (Kevin J. O'Connor), Rupert (Dana Gould), Dr. Shtumpfel (Harold Gould), Jim Douglas (Dean Jones), Donny Shotz (Micky Dolenz), Announcer (Burton Gilliam), Chuck (Clarence Williams III)

Credits: Director: Peyton Reed; Writer: Ryan Rowe, based on a screenplay by Bill Walsh and Don Degradi, from a story by Gordon Buford; Producers: Irwin Marcus, Joan Van Horn; Executive Producers: George Zaloom, Les Mayfield; Photography: Russ Alsobrook; Production Design: Peg McClellan; Music: Shirley Walker; Editor: Chip Masamitsu; Produced by Walt Disney, ZM Productions

Ex-racer Hank reluctantly agrees to promote his new boss' auto shop by racing Herbie, a battered VW beetle, in a "junk car" race. When they win the race (doing wheelies!), Hank's ex-girlfriend Alex and his flaky pal Roddy infuriate Hank by giving Herbie the credit; Roddy even thinks Herbie's alive.

He's right, as Simon, Herbie's selfish former owner, learns from the car's maker, Shtumpfel: A picture of Shtumpfel's wife fell into Herbie's mold, bringing Herbie to life with the power of love. Shtumpfel builds Simon a duplicate VW, but the picture that goes into the mold is of Simon's greatest love—himself—creating Horace, a jet-black Beetle that is (of course) pure evil.

After Hank arrogantly rejects Herbie, Horace attacks and demolishes his rival. Fortunately, Shtumpfel and Herbie's former owner, Jim Douglas, show up to help a repentant Hank rebuild Herbie. Furious, Simon challenges Hank and Herbie to a race on an isolated highway, where no one can see him use Horace's built-in arsenal on his rivals. Despite all Simon's tricks, however, a battered Herbie crosses the finish line first. Horace crashes himself trying to destroy his nemesis, Simon gets hauled off to jail and the good guys drive off happily into the sunset.

The theatrical *The Love Bug* was 1969's box-office champ and Disney's second-biggest hit to that date, a success Disney tried (and failed) to recapture in three sequels, a short-lived TV show and this routine comedy. Jones played Jim Douglas in all versions. Bruce Campbell has made numerous genre appearances, from Autolycus in the *Hercules* TV series to Ash in the *Evil Dead* films.

LOVE CAN BE MURDER
NBC, 12/14/92

Cast: Elizabeth Bentley (Jaclyn Smith), Nick Peyton (Corbin Bernsen), Brad Donaldson (Cliff De Young), Mike Riordan (Tom Bower), Phillip Carlyle (Nicholas Pryor), Maggie O'Brien (Anne Francis), Bernie (Bruce Vilanch), Althea (Pamela Roberts), Edmund Carlyle (Doug Hale), Gordon (Scott Stevens), Samantha (Kimberly LaMarque), Phil (Cameron Watson), Madame Butterfly (Catherine Jah Fong Dao), with Susan Brown, Elaine Kagan, John Carter

Credits: Director: Jack Bender; Writer-Producer: Jayne Bieber; Executive Producers: Frank Konigsberg, Larry Sanitsky; Photography: Paul Murphy; Production Design: Stephen Storer; Editor: Tod Feuerman; Music: Steven Bramson; Produced by Konigsberg/Sanitsky Co.

In this romantic comedy (and failed pilot), private eye Nick Peyton is murdered, but his spirit remains on Earth to solve the crime. He enlists the help of sexy fellow gumshoe Bentley to crack the case—and a romance develops.

THE LOVE LETTER
CBS, 2/1/98

Cast: Scotty Corrigan (Campbell Scott), Elizabeth Whitcomb (Jennifer Jason Leigh), Beatrice Corrigan (Estelle Parsons), Everett Reagle (David Dukes), Deborah (Daphne Ashbrook), Clarice Whitcomb (Myra Carter), Warren Whitcomb (Gerritt Graham), Mae (Irma P. Hall), Jacob Campbell (Richard Woods), Flossy Whitcomb (Kali Rocha), Potts the Postman (Edgar D. Smith), Maggie the Maid (Cara Stoner), Bike Rider (George Gaffney), Scott's Boss (Tom Rus Parrell), Celebrity Author (Mark Joy), Doctor (Linda Powell)

Credits: Director-Producer: Dan Curtis; Writer: James Henerson, based on Jack Finney's short story; Co-Producer: Lynn Raynor; Executive Producer: Richard Welsh; Co-Executive Producer: Brent Shields; Production Design: Jan Scott; Photography: Eric Van Haren Noman; Music: Bob Cobert; Editor: Bill Blunden; Produced by Hallmark Hall of Fame Productions

In 1863 Elizabeth Whitcomb lamented an impending, loveless marriage in a letter she hid away in her antique desk. When Scotty discovers the letter in the present, his mother convinces him to mail one back through the town's historic post office. It reaches Elizabeth in 1863; astonished, she writes back and her letter appears in the desk in the present. Before long, they're corresponding regularly—and falling in love. Scotty's fiancée Deborah resents his fixation on Elizabeth, even though she doesn't know the full extent of it.

After an accident leaves Scotty comatose, Elizabeth meets and falls in love with Col. Denby. When Scotty revives, he discovers Denby will die at Gettysburg and warns Elizabeth; she tries to save Denby, but fails. Then the present-day post office burns down, destroying Scotty's ability to write to Elizabeth, but too late to save his romance with Deborah. Scotty finds one last letter from Elizabeth, revealing that instead of marrying, he inspired her to become a respected poet and teacher. As he visits her grave, he meets her exact lookalike, Beth, and a new romance begins.

This is a charming time-travel romance, though the "happy" ending with Beth was tacked onto the story for the film (this kind of exact double is a standard Hollywood resolution to time-travel romances and the like—Bing Crosby's *A Connecticut Yankee in King Arthur's Court* uses it, for instance).

LOVE-STRUCK
Family, 6/1/97

Cast: Emily Vale (Cynthia Gibb), Cupid (Costas Mandylor), Rachel (Annabelle Gurwitch), Venus (Suzanne Somers), Tom (Mark Joy), Sal (Paul Ricioppo), Burt (Carl Jackson), Patient (Andy Park), Sister Jean Marie (Nancy Saunders), Kevin (David Cutting), Bobby (Ira David Wood IV), Children (Adam Winston, Isolita Campbell, Brittany Sheats), Waiter (Keith Flippen), Man (Barry Bell), Woman (Lori Lindberg), Grocer (Ben Lin), Customer (Cynthia Webb), Gina (Rasool J'Han), Ben (Charles Page), Emily's Father (George Lee Masters), Milo Pfander (Frank Hoyt Taylor), Mrs. Pfander (Joyce Bowden-Kirby), Cab Driver (Richard Fullerton),

Chairman (Joe Inscoe), with Tyler Noyes, Amy Parrish, Marion Guyot

Credits: Director: Larry Peerce; Writers: Stephen Witkin, Lindsay Harrison; Story: Stephen Witkin; Producer: Robert V. Girolami; Co-Producer: Howard Weisman; Executive Producer: Barry Weitz; Production Design: C. Robert Holloway; Photography: Tom Priestley; Music: Joseph Conlan; Editor: Jerrold L. Ludwig; Produced by Irish Films, Inc., MTM Enterprises, Inc., Family Channel

When Cupid comes to Earth to restore brokenhearted Emily Vale's faith in love, his magic arrow misses her, ricochets—and strikes the love god. Even knowing winning Emily means losing his immortality, Cupid poses as a mortal to woo her, despite the usual misunderstandings and the opposition of her slimy ex-fiancé, Tom.

When Emily sees Cupid transform into his true self for a visit to Olympus, she forces the truth out of him—and sends him away rather than let him sacrifice his immortality. On the eve of leaving with Tom for a weekend, however, Emily not only discovers that Tom is cheating on her, she realizes how much she loves Cupid and calls him back to the mortal world—and her arms—with the power of her love.

Love-Struck is a lightweight, forgettable fantasy romance with an uninteresting cast.

THE LOVE WAR
ABC, 3/10/70

Cast: Kyle (Lloyd Bridges), Sandy (Angie Dickinson), Bal (Harry Basch), Tod (Daniel J. Travanti), Hort (Allen Jaffe), Reed (Bill McLean), Will (Byron Foulger), Limo Driver (Bob Nash), Judy (Judy Jordan), with Pepper Martin, Art Lewis

Credits: Director: George McCowan; Writers: David H. Kidd, Guerdon S. Trueblood; Producer: Aaron Spelling; Associate Producer: Shelley Hull; Photography: Paul Uhl; Art Director: Tracy Bousman; Music: Dominic Frontiere; Editor: Art Seid; Produced by Aaron Spelling Productions

Disguised as a human, Kyle (from Argon) kills a similarly disguised alien from Zinan, then heads to his next assigned battleground. On the bus, flirtatious Sandy strikes up a conversation. Alarmed by his attraction to her, Kyle (whose war-battered race long ago rejected romance) tries scaring her off with the truth: Argon and Zinan each sent three warriors to fight on Earth as an alternative to all-out war over Earth's future. Undeterred, Sandy stays with Kyle as he and the other surviving Argonian defeat the remaining Zinans—except that she's a fourth Zinan and kills Kyle's backup. Kyle offers to make a home with her on Earth, but Sandy has even more trouble with love than he does and kills him. With both sides wiped out, humanity will be left to find its own path.

TV's first film with extraterrestrials, *The Love War* possesses good leads (Bridges really sounds war-weary and forlorn) but a weak script.

THE MAN FROM ATLANTIS
NBC, 3/4/77

Cast: Mark Harris (Patrick Duffy), Dr. Elizabeth Merrill (Belinda J. Montgomery), Ernie Smith (Dean Santoro), Admiral Dewey Pierce (Art Lund), Mr. Schubert (Victor Buono), Commander Phil Roth (Lawrence Pressman), Lt. Ainsley (Mark Jenkins), Lt. Commander Johnson (Allen Case), Dr. Doug Berkley (Joshua Bryant), Doctor (Steve Franken), Whale Scientist (Virginia Gregg), Emil (Curt Lowens), British Scientist (Charles Davis), French Scientist (Lilyan Chauvin), American Scientist (Vincent Duke Milana), Russian Scientist (Alex Rodine), George (Philip Baker Hall), Receptionists (Marguerite DeLain, Pat Anderson, Akemi Kikumura), Woman at Party (Trudy Marshall), Popeye (Michael J. London), Divers (Robert Dore, Michael Watson), Nurses (Connie Izay, Maralyn Thomas), Interns (Judd Laurance, Phillip Roye), Man on Beach (James Chandler), Ambulance Driver (Larry Holt), Test Lab Technician (Peter Weiss), Boy on Beach (Scott Stevenson), Boy at Phone Booth (Philip Tanzini)

Credits: Director: Lee H. Katzin; Writer: Mayo Simon; Producer: Robert H. Justman; Executive Producer: Herbert F. Solow; Photography: William Cronjager, Richard A. Kelley; Art Director: J. Smith Poplin; Music: Fred Karlin; Editor: Gary Griffin; Produced by Solow Production Co.

When a drowning man washes up on the beach, nothing revives him—until Dr. Merrill realizes he's an amphibian and returns him to the ocean. She discovers that Mark is nonhuman (and amnesiac about his origins), able to survive at any depth but weakening the longer he's out of water. When a U.S. sub sinks and disappears, Admiral Pierce orders Mark to recover its classified technology; Mark refuses until he's given freedom to return to the sea.

Mark finds that the sub's crew has been captured and mind-controlled by Schubert, a folksy, ocean-loving megalomaniac with an army of slaves and a plot to wipe out the surface world by launching every sub-borne nuclear missile on Earth. Mark tries and fails to stop Schubert, who orders Mark drowned. The water revives Mark, who contrives to flood the base, destroying the missile-controller. Mark helps Schubert's slaves escape the flood, but Schubert survives too. Mark decides to stay with Elizabeth rather than return to the sea.

This is a standard seventies super-hero pilot (stiff hero, bland cast, logic gaps [why set the missile-launcher on a timer?]), but it netted ratings good enough to merit three sequels (see the appendix) and a one-year series (Duffy had longer runs as a star of *Dallas* and *Step by Step*) which alienated many of this movie's fans with its broadly humorous tone. Buono did better villainous turns as Count Manzeppi in *The Wild, Wild West* and King Tut on *Batman*.

THE MAN WHO FELL TO EARTH
ABC, 8/23/87

Cast: Thomas Newton (Lewis Smith), Felix Hawthorne (James Laurenson), Agent Richard Morse (Robert Picardo), Eva (Beverly D'Angelo), Gage (Bruce McGill), Billy (Wil Wheaton), Louise (Annie Potts), Records Clerk (Chris DeRose), Video Clerk (Richard Shydner), Captain (Bob Neilsen), Soldier (Steve Natole), Guard (Michael Fontaine), Cop (Albert Owens), Secretary (Anne O'Neill), Dancer (Amy Sawaya), Rancher (Carl Parker), with Hank Stratton, Carmen Argenziano, Bobbi Jo Lathan, Henry Sanders

Credits: Director: Bobby Roth; Writer: Richard Kletter, from a screenplay by Paul Mayersberg, based on Walter Tevis' novel; Producers: Lewis B. Chesler, Richard Kletter; Executive Producer: David Gerber; Photography: Frederick Moore; Production Design: John B. Mansbridge; Music: Doug Timm; Editor: John Carnochan; Produced by MGM

"Thomas Newton" is actually an ET from a drought-stricken world who crash-lands on Earth, infiltrates society and teams with shrewd Felix to build a financial empire—which he hopes will enable him to repair his ship, return home and bring his people in peace to share Earth's water. When agent Morse unmasks Newton, the alien goes on the run (of course), determined to find a way to repair his ship and save his people before Morse can capture him.

This is an unsuccessful pilot based on the David Bowie cult film. Wheaton was *Star Trek: The Next Generation*'s Wesley Crusher, and Picardo played the Doctor in *Star Trek: Voyager*.

THE MAN WITH THE POWER
NBC, 5/24/77

Cast: Eric Smith (Bob Neill), Walter Bloom (Tim O'Connor), Mr. Paul (Vic Morrow), Princess Siri (Persis Khambatta), Farnsworth (Roger Perry), Major Sajid (Rene Assa), Shanda (Noel DeSouza), Driver (James Ingersoll), Dilling (Bill Fletcher), Personage (Regis J. Cordic), Clark (John DeLancie), Wilmot (Sheldon Allman), Klein (Jason Wingreen), Federal Man (Jim Raymond), Communications Tech (Jonathan Segal), Telemetry Tech (Judd Laurence)

Credits: Director: Nicholas Sgarro; Writer-Producer: Allan Balter; Associate Producer: Rod Holcomb; Photography: J.J. Jones; Art Director: Frank Grieco, Jr.; Music: Patrick Williams; Editors: Jerrold L. Ludwig, Chuck McClelland; Produced by Universal

Eric Smith is astonished when he uses telekinesis to save himself from an oncoming train. Federal agent Walter, a family friend, reveals that Eric inherited the power from his father, an ET who briefly visited Earth. Eric fears his power's destructive potential, but a messenger from his father's world convinces him to use it for good. Eric volunteers as the bodyguard Walter needs for visiting Princess Siri—but Siri's regular bodyguards overcome Eric and kidnap Siri for Mr. Paul. Paul demands a cool million in gold from the Federal Reserve; when the reserve is opened, his men attack and steal seventy million more. Eric tracks Paul to his underground lair, frees Siri and captures the criminals for Walter.

This pilot is a textbook case of bad seventies SF—straight action plot with minor SF touches; stiff, dull hero; and a pretty girl (Persis Khambatta of *Star Trek: The Motion Picture*) who alternates between screams and sobs. Trekkers can spot John DeLancie (*Next Generation*'s Q) in a walk-on, and O'Connor later appeared in the *Buck Rogers* series on NBC.

MANDRAKE
NBC, 1/24/79

Cast: Mandrake (Anthony Herrera), Stacy (Simone Griffeth), Lothar (Ji-Tu Cumbuka), Alec Gordon (Hank Brandt), Jennifer Lindsay (Gretchen Corbett), William Romero (Peter Haskell), Arkadian (Robert Reed), Dr. Malcolm Lindsay (David Hooks), Dr. Nolan (Harry Blackstone, Jr.), Theron (James Hong), Ho (Sab Shimono), Cindy (Donna Benz), Young Mandrake (David Hollander), Choreographer (Edmund Balin), Walter Kevan (Allan Hunt)

Credits: Director: Harry Falk; Writer-Producer: Rick Husky, based on Lee Falk's comic strip; Associate Producer: Rod Holcomb; Photography: Vincent A. Martinelli; Art Director: John P. Bruce; Music: Morton Stevens; Editors: Fredric Knudtson, Edward W. Williams; Produced by Universal

Orphaned by a plane crash in the Himalayas, young Mandrake was raised by the mystic Theron, who gave him an amulet that allows him to wield hypnotic and psychic powers. As an adult, he appears as a stage magician by day while fighting evil by night, with both his powers and those of his aides Lothar and Stacy. Together they defend a tycoon from a renegade spy blackmailing him for $10 million.

A classic, much-admired comic strip by Lee Falk, *Mandrake* inspired numerous comic-book imitators (such as DC's *Zatara*). By most accounts, this failed pilot was quite uninspired (Mandrake did appear many years later alongside Flash Gordon and the Phantom in the equally uninspired cartoon *Defenders of Earth*).

M.A.N.T.I.S.
Fox, 1/24/94

Cast: Dr. Miles Hawkins (Carl Lumbly), Yuri Barnes (Bobby Hosea), Dr. Amy Ellis (Gina Torres), Antoine Pike (Steve James), Cornell (Obba Babafunde), Chief Stark (Francis X. McCarthy), Carla (Marcia Cross), DeCarlos (Billy Kane), Kid Ng (Jeremiah Birkett), L.T. (Dex Elliot Sanders), Jay (Theo Forsett), Mayor Beane (Jerry Black), Day (Larron Tate), Ski (Vicellous Reon Shannon), Rahsaan (Tierre Turner), Todd Kimble (Martin Davis), Curtis (Kimble Jemison), Motorist (David Fresco), Jay's Mom (Edwina Moore), Policeman Guard (Charles Hoyes), Newswoman (Lucy Lin), Gangbangers (Richard Jones, Ousaun Elam), Interviewer (Dana Winters), Office Worker (Nelson Parks), Dispatcher (Martin Cassidy), Cop (Steve Hom), Stark's Handler (Mark Phelan), Reggie (Gene Arrington), Homeless Man (Richard Zobel), Basketball Guard (Mark Avery), Thug (Robair Sims), Pilot (Craig Hosking), with Wendy Raquel Johnson, Christopher M. Brown, Philip Baker Hall, Yvonne Farrow, Alan Fudge, Grant Heslov, Luis Antonio Ramos, Jermaine Shulders

Credits: Director: Eric Laneuville; Writer: Sam Hamm; Story: Sam Raimi, Sam Hamm; Producer: Steve Ecclesine; Co-Producer: David Eick; Executive Producers: Sam Hamm, Sam Raimi, Robert Tapert; Photography: William Dill; Production Design: Mick Strawn; Music: Joseph Lo Duca; Editor: Steve Polivka; Produced by Renaissance Pictures, Universal

Mantis, a mysterious vigilante, is using paralysis darts to fight Ocean City's street gangs. Black reporter Yuri Barnes fears the darts are a way for hardline police chief and mayoral candidate Stark to test a crowd-control drug for use on minorities (whom Stark's paramilitary squads already target). Police medical examiner Amy (who believes Mantis is suave social activist Antoine Pike) tells Yuri that Stark knows nothing of Mantis, and has hired paraplegic black scientist Hawkins to learn the secret of the darts. Amy warns Hawkins of Stark's agenda, but Hawkins says if researching the drug produces a cure for his paralyzed legs, he doesn't care what Stark does.

We soon learn Hawkins is lying—and he is the Mantis. While protecting a child during a race riot, Hawkins was crippled by a police bullet (but couldn't prove it); by fighting injustice in his Mechanically Augmented NeuroTransmitter Interference System exoskeleton, Hawkins seeks to atone for his former callousness toward the poor—even though the suit may cripple his legs beyond hope of recovery.

With the help of Amy and Yuri, Mantis thwarts and exposes a plot by Pike and Stark to discredit the current mayor by triggering a gang war—but when Mantis forces Stark to confess, a cop guns Stark down. Hawkins realizes the conspiracy behind Stark is far from destroyed and enlists Yuri and Amy to help him fight it.

Sam Hamm, who wrote Tim Burton's first Batman film, and Sam Raimi (producer of *Xena* and *Hercules,* and director of the theatrical super-hero film *Darkman*) show here how well TV can do super-heroes if it tries. Instead of the standard TV approach (showing Hawkins' accident, then watching him become Mantis), this takes the more interesting approach of showing Mantis already in action, then gradually revealing his backstory. Unfortunately, Raimi's company couldn't come to terms with Fox, so the series that followed was done by less talented hands (and replaced the mostly black cast with an almost entirely white one).

THE MARTIAN CHRONICLES
NBC, 1/27–1/29/80

Cast: Col. John Wilder (Rock Hudson), Ruth Wilder (Gayle Hunnicutt), Major Jeff Spender (Bernie Casey), Ben Driscoll (Christopher Connelly), Commander Arthur Black (Nicholas Hammond), Father Stone (Roddy McDowall), Sam Parkhill (Darren McGavin), Genevieve Seltzer (Bernadette Peters), Anna Lustig (Maria Schell), Elma Parkhill (Joyce Van Patten), Father Peregrine (Fritz Weaver), Marilyn Becker (Linda Lou Allen), David Lustig (Michael Anderson, Jr.), General Halstead (Robert Beatty), Mr. K. (James Faulkner), Christ (Jon Finch), Captain Conover (Richard Heffer), Wise Martian (Terence Longdon), Peter Hathaway (Barry Morse), Alice Hathaway (Nyree Dawn Porter), Lafe Lustig (Wolfgang Reichmann), Ylla (Maggie Wright), Briggs (John Cassady), Lavinia Spaulding (Alison Elliott), Sam Hinston (Vadim Glowna), Sandship Martian (Derek Lamden), McClure (Peter Marinker), Captain Nathaniel York (Richard Oldfield), Edward Black (Anthony Pullen-Shaw), Bill Wilder (Burnell Tucker), Narrator (Phil Brown).

Credits: Director: Michael Anderson; Writer: Richard Matheson, based on Ray Bradbury's novel; Producers: Andrew Donally, Milton Subotsky; Executive Producers: Charles Fries, Dick Berg; Photography: Ted Moore; Production Design: Assheton Gorton; Supervising Editor: John Jympson; Music: Stanley Myers; Costumes: Cynthia Tingey; Special Effects: John Stears; Produced by Charles Fries Productions, Stonehenge Productions, NBC

In 1999 Earth launches the first manned Mars mission, attracting the attention of a telepathic Martian woman—which provokes her jealous husband to kill the spacemen when they land. A second expedition is seduced by telepathic illusions until they can be painlessly killed, but their diseases wipe out the Martians. Col. Wilder's follow-up expedition finds a barren world. By 2006 human settlers have further polluted and despoiled it.

Some Martians, however, have survived. Father Peregrine meets Martians who've evolved into pure mind, dwelling in harmony with God. Another Martian takes human form in response to the fantasies of the humans around him, but is killed in the resulting confusion. Sam, who runs a diner, accidentally kills a Martian, but a second Martian gives Sam a deed to half the planet.

Conditions on Earth deteriorate until nuclear war breaks out. As the survivors on Mars try to build new lives, Wilder meets a Martian who may or may not be a ghost, and who convinces the Wilders to begin rebuilding humanity's future on Mars, adopting the Martian way of life.

The Martian Chronicles was a collection of Bradbury stories loosely shaped into a novel, which accounts for the rather choppy mix of tragedy, adventure and comedy here. Despite the unevenness, TV's first SF miniseries is pretty good, with a cast of movie and TV veterans.

MENNO'S MIND
TMC, 12/13/97

Cast: Menno (Bill Campbell), Felix Medina (Corbin Bernsen), Simon (Michael Dorn), Loria (Stephanie Romanov), Senator Taylor (Robert Picardo), Mick Dourif (Bruce Campbell), Bennett (Marc McClure), Inspector (Phil Proctor), Kal (Richard Speight, Jr.), Zachary Powell (Robert Vaughn)

Credits: Director: Jon Kroll; Writer: Mark Valenti; Producer: Larry Estes; Executive Producers: Paul Colichman, Mark Harris, Stephen P. Jarchow; Photography: Gary Tieche; Production Design: Dawn Ferry, Charley Cabrera; Music: Christopher Franke; Editor: Stephen Myers; Produced by Showtime, Regents Entertainment

In repressive near-future America, ambitious security chief Medina has implanted a program in the Resort, a virtual-reality entertainment paradise, that will compel its users to vote him into the White House. Mick, a revolutionary, uncovers Medina's plans. Medina has him killed, but not before Mick forces Menno, a computer operator, to upload Mick's mind into cyberspace. Mick's lover Loria then forces Menno to download Mick's memories into his own brain. While Menno is sorting through the memories, Medina frames him for murder. Menno and Loria escape and figure out Medina's scheme. They try and fail to blow up the Resort, then sneak inside and delete Medina's program. Medina assaults them in person; he and Loria kill each other, but Menno transfers her mind into cyberspace with Mick—and obtains enough computer evidence to clear his name.

Menno's Mind is a routine paranoia exercise (15 years ago, it would have involved TV sublims). Familiar faces include Bill Campbell (*The Rocketeer*), Dorn (*Star Trek: The Next Generation*), Picardo (*Star Trek: Voyager*) and Bruce Campbell (Autolycus on *Hercules: The Legendary Journeys*, and Ash in the *Evil Dead* films).

MERLIN
NBC, 4/26–4/27/98

Cast: Merlin (Sam Neill), Morgan LeFay (Helena Bonham Carter), King Constant (John Gielgud), Vortigern (Rutger Hauer), Mountain King (James Earl Jones), Mab/Lady of the Lake (Miranda Richardson), Nimue (Isabella Rossellini), Frick (Martin Short), Arthur (Paul Curran), Guinevere (Lena Headley), Lancelot (Jeremy Sheffield), Uther (Mark Jax), Lord Ardente (John McEnery), Cornwall (Thomas Lockyer), Mordred (Jason Done), Ambrosia (Billie Whitelaw), Young Merlin (Daniel Brocklebank), Young Nimue (Agnieszka Koson), Elissa (Emma Lewis), Young Galahad (Justin Girdier), Sir Boris (Roger Ashton Griffiths), Lord Leo (Nicholas Clay), Gawaine (Sebastian Roche), Lady Igraine (Rachel Colover), Lord Lot (John Turner), Sir Hector (Keith Baxter), Lady Elaine (Janine Eser), Soothsayer (Peter Woodthorpe), Sir Gilbert (Robert Addie), Sir Egbert (Nicholas Grace), Architects (Peter Benson, John Tordoff), Father Abbot (Timothy Bateson), Young Morgan (Alice Hamilton), Physicians (Peter Eyre, Vernon Dobicheff, Peter Bayliss), Lady Friend (Talula Sheppard)

Credits: Director: Steve Barron; Writers: David Stevens, Peter Barnes; Story: Edward Khmara; Producer: Dyson Lovell; Executive Producer: Robert Halmi, Sr.; Photography: Sergei Kozlov; Production Design: Roger Hall; Costumes: Ann Hollowood; Visual Effects: Tim Webber; Music: Trevor Jones; Editor: Colin Green; Produced by Hallmark Entertainment

Mab, the Faerie Queen, wants to return warring post–Roman Britain to the old, pre–Christian ways—so she causes Merlin to be born gifted with great magic and takes him to train. When Merlin tries to return home, he learns that Mab let his mother die in childbirth and murdered his old nursemaid. Merlin turns against Mab and vows never to use magic to harm others.

That vow leaves Merlin helpless when King Vortigern captures him to exploit his prophetic powers. Mab convinces Vortigern to sacrifice Merlin's love, Nimue, to a dragon; Merlin defeats the monster, but not before it scars Nimue, who retreats to the sacred isle of Avalon. Merlin arranges for Uther to overthrow Vortigern and father Arthur, who will unite Britain in peace. Arthur becomes king, but his jealous half-sister, Morgan, seduces him, then gives their child Mordred to Mab for training in wizardry.

After Mordred joins the Round Table, Mab manipulates Lancelot and Guinevere into an affair—for which, Mordred reminds Arthur, Guinevere must pay with her life. Merlin saves her, but Mordred foments civil war. Although rejected by Arthur's knights, Merlin tries to save Arthur, but Arthur dies along with Mordred. After Mab seals Nimue in a hidden cave, Merlin battles her with magic, then convinces the people to forget Mab completely—which ends her existence. Years later Nimue finally escapes the cave.

Using the last of his magic, Merlin restores their youth and they go off together.

Though an impressive adventure and competently performed, for some reason it never quite comes together (neither does the same creative team's 1999 version of *Alice in Wonderland*).

MERLIN: THE MAGIC BEGINS
Syndicated, 10/3–10/24/98

Cast: Merlin (Jason Connery), Nimue (Deborah Moore), Blaze (Gareth Thomas), Rengal (Graham McTavish), Kay (Paul Curran), Morgana (Lara Daans), Vidus (Gordon Hall), Brother Gandar (John Woodford), Princess Leona (Fiona Kempin), Hengist (Andy Bryden), Samson (Tony McMann), Wilf (Corey Haim), Vivian (Audrey Lupke), Sirens (Sam Barnett, Bea Taylor, Jo Harriet, Suzanna Critchity, Sam Mann), Children (Katarina Boyd, Michael Boyd, Peter Begbie, Finn Begbie, Nicky Wilson, Jamie Wilson, Amy Lockett, Florence Caines)

Credits: Director: David Winning; Writers: Tom Richards, Christopher Roosen; Story: Tom Richards, Jim McGuinn; Producers: Bob Carruthers, Damian Lee; Executive Producers: Al Muntcanu, Peter Popp, Paul Siegel, Paul Wynn; Photography: Al Anderson; Production Design: Alistair McArthur; Music: David Bray; Editor: Paul G. Day; Produced by KMG Seagull Entertainment, Abrams Gentile Entertainment

Long before Arthur became king of England, the usurper Vidus and evil wizard Rengal imprisoned King Uther. But to cement their control, they need the mystic powers of Excalibur. None of which matters to the monk Brother Peter ... until he learns he's actually Merlin, last of the white wizards, hidden in the monastery since Rengal killed his mother.

Rengal tries to take Excalibur from Blaze, a white wizard and rebel leader, but without Merlin's magic crystal, Rengal can't free Excalibur from the stone holding it. While Merlin begins training with Blaze, Rengal captures Blaze's grandchildren—Kay and the warrior-woman Nimue. Merlin confronts Blaze, but can't kill him without absorbing his evil. Rengal takes the crystal, imprisons Merlin with the others, and kills Vidus. Merlin, Nimue and Kay escape and reach Blaze's camp in time for Merlin to reclaim the crystal, free Excalibur and imprison Rengal in stone. The good guys celebrate, but Rengal's ally, Morgana, plots to set him free...

This latest post–*Hercules: The Legendary Journeys* fantasy pilot is lame, stilted and just plain bad. Familiar faces include Jason Connery (who was just as stiff playing the second Robin in the British *Robin of Sherwood* series).

THE MIDNIGHT HOUR
ABC, 11/1/85

Cast: Phil Grenville (Lee H. Montgomery), Sandy Matthews (Jonna Lee), Melissa Cavender (Shari Belafonte-Harper), Vinnie Davis (LeVar Burton), Mitch Crandall (Peter DeLuise), Judge Crandall (Kevin McCarthy), Martin Grenville (Dick Van Patten), Lucinda Cavender (Jonelle Allen), Mary Masterson (Dedee Pfeiffer), Vicky Jensen (Cindy Morgan), Ghoul (Mark Blankfield), Sgt. Thompson (Hank Garrett), Janet Grenville (Sheila Larkin), Lester Mitchell (Dennis Redfield), Warren Jensen (Kurtwood Smith), DJ (Wolfman Jack), Elf (Joe Gieb), Vernon Nestor (Mickey Morton)

Credits: Director: Jack Bender; Writer: William Bleich; Producer: Ervin Zavada; Photography: Rexford Metz; Production Design: Charles Hughes; Music: Brad Fiedel (Song "Get Dead" by Richard Gibbs, Philip Giffin, Jack Bender, Bill Bleich); Choreography: Myrna Garwyn; Editor: David A. Simmons; Produced by ABC Circle Films

A Halloween graveyard prank accidentally raises the spirit of long-dead witch Lucinda Cavender along with an army of demons, monsters and zombies whose victims become Lucinda's undead slaves. The spell also raises Sandy, a dead cheerleader who picks sweet, geeky Phil for a night of romance. When the monsters attack, Sandy reveals that if Lucinda isn't banished by midnight, her victims will stay undead forever. Despite the monsters' attacks, Phil and Sandy manage to undo Lucinda's spell seconds before midnight. Everything returns to normal and Sandy vanishes—but Phil takes consolation in knowing that she truly loved him.

This pointless film spends far too much time with teens partying and dancing, and pays much more attention to visuals than to plot (the production designer also designed

Michael Jackson's "Thriller" music video). *Star Trek* fans should watch for LeVar Burton of *Next Generation* as one of the kids.

MIDNIGHT OFFERINGS
ABC, 2/27/81

Cast: Vivian Sotherland (Melissa Sue Anderson), Robin Prentiss (Mary Beth McDonough), David Sterling (Patrick Cassidy), Emily Moore (Marion Ross), Sherm Sotherland (Gordon Jump), Diane Sotherland (Cathryn Damon), Clausen (Ray Girardin), Charles Prentiss (Peter MacLean), Hugh Garvey (Jack Garner), Lily (Dana Kimmell), Herb Nemenz (Jeff McKay), Frankel (Michael Morgan)

Credits: Director: Rod Holcomb; Writer: Juanita Bartlett; Producer: Alex Beaton; Executive Producers: Juanita Bartlett, Stephen J. Cannell; Associate Producer: Christopher Nelson; Photography: Hector Figueron; Art Director: John D. Jeffries; Music: Walter Scharf; Editor: Christopher Nelson; Produced by Stephen J. Cannell Productions

High-schooler Vivian Sotherland is head cheerleader, an honor-roll student—and a witch who magically destroys anyone who crosses her, much to the horror of her mother Diane, who gave up witchcraft for normal life. When transfer student Robin—an untrained witch—befriends David, Vivian's boyfriend, Vivian turns her sorcery on Robin, but the girl's latent powers protect her. Vivian's attacks escalate, so David takes Robin to Emily, a white witch who convinces Robin to develop her powers and challenge Vivian. Vivian tells Robin to leave town or die, and Emily realizes that Vivian is strong enough to kill them all.

Vivian forces a showdown by threatening Robin's father. With the full moon enhancing her magic, Vivian crushes Robin's defenses and prepares to burn her at the stake. At the last minute, Mrs. Sotherland uses her own magic to free Robin, then drags her daughter into the fire, ending both their lives.

Midnight Offerings is dull and formulaic, with bland leads (though Anderson does manage a certain nasty bitchiness); Damon and Jump outshine them as Vivian's parents.

MIRACLE ON 34TH STREET
CBS, 12/14/73

Cast: Kris Kringle (Sebastian Cabot), Bill Schaffner (David Hartman), Karen Walker (Jane Alexander), Dr. Henry Sawyer (Roddy McDowall), Susan Walker (Suzanne Davidson), Horace Shellhammer (Jim Backus), R.H. Macy (David Doyle), Judge Harper (Tom Bosley), District Attorney (James Gregory), Mr. Gimbel (Roland Winters), Reindeer Keeper (Liam Dunn), Richardson (Conrad Janis), Celeste (Ellen Weston)

Credits: Director: Fielder Cook; Writer: Jeb Rosebrook, from Valentine Davies' story, from George Seaton's screenplay; Producer: Norman Rosemont; Photography: Earl Rath; Art Director: Jan Scott; Music: Sid Ramin; Editor: Gene Milford; Produced by 20th Century–Fox TV, Norman Rosemont Productions

No-nonsense department-store executive Karen Walker is horrified to find Kris Kringle, the Santa she hired, telling customers when they can get better prices at other stores. To her relief, her boss thinks this is brilliant publicity. Karen is overjoyed until she discovers Kris is a complete loony who sincerely believes he's Santa—and has half-convinced Karen's sensible daughter he's right.

When Kris crosses the company psychiatrist, Dr. Sawyer angrily demands he be committed. Bill, Karen's lawyer boyfriend, defends Kris in court by claiming he really is Santa Claus. This long-shot defense almost fails, until some postal workers decide to clear out the dead-letter office by dumping all the kids' letters to Santa at the courthouse. The judge rules that if the U.S. government thinks Kris is Santa, who is he to argue? Finally willing to follow her heart, Karen marries Bill, who is tickled that he proved something in court they all know is impossible. Then he and Karen find evidence that maybe Kris really is…

This faithful remake is nowhere near the caliber of the 1947 theatrical original; it is, however, far better than the dismal 1994 theatrical version. *Meet Mr. Kringle*, a 1956 TV special, was another remake.

A MOM FOR CHRISTMAS
NBC, 12/17/90

Cast: Amy Miller (Olivia Newton-John), Jessica Slocum (Juliet Sorcey), Jim Slocum (Doug

Sheehan), Philomena (Doris Roberts), Sgt. Morelli (Carmen Argenziano), Nicholas (Aubrey Harris), Wilkins (James Piddock), Chip Wright (Elliot Moss Greenebaum), Stephanie Clark (Erica Mitchell), Teddy O'Neill (Jesse Vincent), Kendall (Brett Harrelson), Mr. Milliman (Steve Russell), Det. Price (Gregory Procaccino), Fire Captain (Ron Lautore), Lora (Kathy Lubow), Mrs. Garcia (Paula Ingram), with Helen Whitelow, Justin DiPego

Credits: Director: George Miller; Writer: Gerald DiPego, based on Barbara Dillon's *A Mom by Magic*; Producer: Barry Bernardi; Co-Producer: Ric Rondell; Photography: Ron Lautore; Production Design: Glenda Ganis; Music: John Farrar, Sean Callery; Editor: Les Green, Andrew Cohen; Produced by Disney Television

Philomena, a good-natured witch, grants lonely, 12-year-old Jessica's desperate wish for a mother by turning a department store mannequin to flesh and blood for the two weeks before Christmas. The mannequin, Amy, has more than a little trouble adapting to being human, but her loving ways turn the lives of Jessica and her father, Jim, around, and bring Jim out of the shell he's hidden inside since his wife died. When Christmas Eve comes, Amy is drawn back to the store, but neither Jim nor Jessica is willing to let her go; through their love, they give Amy the strength to stay human and return home with them, a real family.

The idea of living mannequins has turned up everywhere from *The Twilight Zone* to the theatrical hit *Mannequin*; here, it forms the basis of a typically sugary Christmas fantasy (but Sorcey is quite good as Jessica).

MOON OF THE WOLF
ABC, 9/26/72

Cast: Sheriff Aaron Whitaker (David Janssen), Louise Rodanthe (Barbara Rush), Andrew Rodanthe (Bradford Dillman), Dr. Druten (John Beradino), Lawrence Burrifors (Geoffrey Lewis), Tom Gurmandy, Sr. (Royal Dano), Tom Gurmandy, Jr. (John Chandler), Sara (Claudia McNeil), Hugh Burrifors (Paul R. Deville), Sam Cairns (Dan Priest), Deputy (Robert Phillips), Nurse (Serena Sands), Attendants (George Sawaya, Nick Crockett), Harry (Sonny Klein), Roy Biggers (Emory Hollier)

Credits: Director: Daniel Petrie; Writer: Alvin Sapinsley, from Leslie H. Whitten's novel; Producers: Everett Chambers, Peter Thomas; Executive Producer: Edward S. Feldman; Associate Producer: Richard M. Rosenbloom; Photography: Richard C. Glouner; Art Director: James G. Hulsey; Music: Bernardo Segall; Editor: Richard B. Halsey; Produced by Filmways

In little Marsh Island, Louisiana, nothing ever happens—until Ellie Gurmandy is found ripped to pieces in the woods. Sheriff Whitaker investigates, which reunites him with his old love, Louise. Ellie's father babbles ominously, and her brother Tom gets jailed for assaulting Ellie's lover as the killer. That night, the real killer breaks into jail, tears through steel bars and kills Tom.

Louise realizes Ellie's father is babbling about werewolves—and when her brother, Andrew, visits the Gurmandys, he collapses at the smell of wolfsbane. At the hospital, he transforms into a man-wolf, attacks the staff and runs off. The town hunts Andrew down, but he comes after Louise, who reluctantly shoots him down with a silver bullet.

This is a good example of the kind of B-movie TV did in the early seventies; competent, but unmemorable (particularly the ending).

MOONBASE
Sci-Fi, 12/6/97

Cast: John Russell (Scott Plank), Dana Morgan (Jocelyn Seagrave), Deckert (Kurt Fuller), Mina (Gretchen Palmer), Will (Stack Pierce), Lucas (John Philbin), Lt. Caldecott (Billy Maddox), Murdoch (George "Buck" Flower), Stark (Robert O'Reilly), Gorgeous Woman (Sam Phillips), Masani (Randy Vasquez)

Credits: Director-Editor: Paolo Mazzucato; Writers: Brian DiMucco, Dino Vindeni; Story: Brian DiMucco, Dino Vindeni, Paolo Mazzucato; Producer: Donald P. Borchers; Photography: Jesse Weathington; Production Design: Yvette Taylor; Costumes: Mandi Line; Visual Effects: Technomagic; Produced by Live Entertainment, Planet Productions Co.

In 2065 escaped cons from an orbiting prison take over a lunar waste dump and capture Commander Russell and his staff. The cons plan to hijack the next ship, which turns out to be a military inspection vessel with Russell's ex, Dana, onboard. A firefight breaks out between the cons and the soldiers, who've been sent to collect nukes hidden away from disarmament inspections. The cons capture Russell, but Dana and the others free him and make it to the transport. The last surviving convict threatens to wipe them all out with one of the hidden warheads, but Russell distracts him with a hologram long enough for the shuttle to escape before the warhead detonates.

Moonbase is a good, tight little thriller.

MORE WILD, WILD WEST
CBS, 10/7–10/8/80

Cast: James West (Robert Conrad), Artemus Gordon (Ross Martin), Robert T. Malone (Harry Morgan), Albert Paradine II (Jonathan Winters), Capt. Sir David Edney (Rene Auberjonois), Juanita (Liz Torres), Dr. Messenger (Victor Buono), Bystander (Dr. Joyce Brothers), Jack LaStrange (Jack La Lanne), Yvonne (Randi Brough), Daphne (Candi Brough), Mirabelle (Emma Samms), Wheelman (James Bacon), Aides (Sandy Helberg, Richard Hawk), Italian Ambassador (Joe Alfasa), French Ambassador (Gino Conforti), Spanish Ambassador (Hector Elias), German Ambassador (Dave Madden), Russian Ambassador (Avery Schreiber), Bavarian Delegate (John Furlong), Hulks (Rick Drasnin, Rex Pearson), Juanita's Brothers (Dave Cass, Tony Epper, Casey Tibbs), Secret Service Man (Edward Jenson)

Credits: Director: Burt Kennedy; Writers: William Bowers, Tony Kayden; Story: William Bowers; Producer: Robert L. Jacks; Executive Producer: Jay Bernstein; Photography: Chuck Arnold; Production Design: Albert Heschong; Art Director: Jeffrey L. Goldstein; Editor: Michael McCroskey; Produced by CBS

In 1890 secret service head Malone badgers James West and Artemus Gordon out of retirement to stop Professor Paradine, who's just launched a scheme for world domination. When they confront Paradine, he flaunts his technological prowess (nuclear bombs and an invisibility device); after repeatedly outwitting the agents, he tells them he plans to provoke world war by wrecking a Washington peace conference. To Paradine's dismay, the conference falls apart—without triggering a war—before he can wreck it, so he prepares to detonate a nuke and blame one of the great powers. By seducing Paradine's assistant, West eventually locates the bomb at the conference. Artemis deactivates it, then the agents capture Paradine, whose invisibility device has malfunctioned.

This follow-up to *Wild, Wild West Revisited* goes way over the comedy top (as a fan of the show, I found it quite irritating). Winters was written in (as the son of a fictitious old enemy) at the last minute when Paul Williams passed on reprising his role as Loveless, Jr.

MRS. SANTA CLAUS
CBS, 12/8/96

Cast: Mrs. Claus (Angela Lansbury), Santa Claus (Charles Durning), Augustus P. Tavish (Terrence Mann), Soapbox Sadie (Debra Wiseman), Marcello (David Noroña), Nora (Lynsey Bartilson), Arvo (Michael Jeter), Officer Doyle (Bryan Murray), Mrs. Lowenstein (Rosalind Harris), Mrs. Brandenheim (Grace Keagy), Mrs. Shaughnessy (Linda Kerns), Izzy (Chachi Pittmann), Fritzie (Sabrina Bryan), Emilio (Bret Easterling), Henry (Mitchah Williams), Elves (Kristi Lynes, Jamie Torcellini), Michael Kilkenny (Mick Murray), Stage Doorman (Ken Kerman), Man in Santa Suit (John Wheeler), Italian Neighbor (Toni Perrota), Jewish Neighbor (Jean Kaufman), Miss MacGonnigle (Stacy Sullivan)

Credits: Director: Terry Hughes; Writer: Mark Saltzman; Producer: J. Boyce Harman, Jr.; Co-Producer: Eric Ellenbogen; Executive Producer: David Shaw; Supervising Producer: Mark A. Burley; Production Design: Hub Braden; Photography: Stephen M. Katz; Music: Jerry Herman; Choreography: Rob Marshall; Editor: Stan Cole; Produced by Hallmark Entertainment, Corymore Productions

Frustrated with Santa taking her for granted, Mrs. Claus decides to test a new, faster flight plan for the sleigh—which comes down in 1910 New York when Cupid injures his hoof. Taking rooms until Cupid heals, Mrs. Claus soon finds herself involved in the neighborhood—helping suffragette Sadie rally women to vote, helping Marcello in his romance with Sadie, helping children fight against a cruel sweatshop toymaker. Back at the North Pole, Santa realizes how much he misses his missus, and how much she contributes to running his toyshop. When she returns to the Pole on Christmas Eve, she joins Santa for the ride—using her new route.

A deliberately old-fashioned musical, *Mrs.*

Santa Claus is fairly entertaining (though hardly the holiday classic the creators seemed to be hoping for). Durning also played Santa in *It Nearly Wasn't Christmas*.

MS. SCROOGE
USA, 12/10/97

Cast: Ebenita Scrooge (Cicely Tyson), Reverend Luke (Michael Beach), Bob Cratchitt (John Bourgeois), Young Ebenita (Raéven Larry More-Kelly), Ebenita at 25 (Karen Glave), Sam Catherwood (Ken James), Libba Cratchitt (Arsinee Khanjian), Maude Marley (Katherine Helmond), Tim Cratchitt (William Greenblatt), Christmas Past (Michael J. Reynolds), Christmas Present (Shaun Austin-Olsen), Christmas Future (Julian Richings), Chris (Ashley Brown), Sis Cratchitt (Natasha Greenblatt), Annie (Allegra Fulton), Edna (Sandi Ross), Steve (Derwin Jordan), George (Philip Akin), Clara (Michelle Moffatt), Ward Baldwin (Jim Codrington), Sally Baldwin (Michele Lonsdale-Smith), Lucy (Monique Mojica), Hawkins (Bernard Browne), Marty Cratchitt (David Felton), Penny (Michelyn Emelle), Homeless Woman (Marium Carvell), Perry (Troy Seivwright-Adams), TV Host (Don Tripe), Fireman (Jeff Clarke)

Credits: Director: John Korty; Writer: John McGreevey, based on Dickens' *A Christmas Carol*; Producer: Julian Marks; Photography: Elemér Ragályi; Production Design: Gerald Holmes; Music: David Shire; Editor: Louise A. Innes; Produced by Power Pictures, Wilshire Court Productions

In this version of Dickens, Ebenita Scrooge is a modern-day black woman whose father's death left her family broken by debt; from this, she concluded that nothing mattered as much as money. By the time the story starts, Ebenita is a totally selfish skinflint, but on Christmas Eve, her old boss Marley appears, bringing three spirits...

In contrast to the relatively humanized Scrooges of *Ebbie* or the '84 *A Christmas Carol*, this version is a full-fledged, covetous miser who forecloses on a mortgage and turns a family out into the snow on Christmas Eve. Fortunately, Tyson is actress enough to make even such an over-the-top role work magnificently.

THE MUNSTERS' REVENGE
NBC, 2/27/81

Cast: Herman Munster (Fred Gwynne), Lily Munster (Yvonne De Carlo), Grandpa (Al Lewis), Marilyn Munster (Jo McDonnell), Eddie Munster (K.C. Martel), Dr. Dustin Diablo (Sid Caesar), Glen Boyle (Peter Fox), Cousin Phantom (Bob Hastings), Commissioner McCluskey (Charles Macauley), Michael (Colby Chester), Pizza Man (Joseph Ruskin), Cousin Igor (Howard Morris), Dr. Lichtliter (Ezra Stone), Ralph (Michael McManus), Patrolman Leary (Gary Vinson), Patrolman (Sandy Champion), Prisoner (Al White), Shorty (Billy Sands), Slim (Tom Newman), Warren Thurston (Barry Pearl), Elvira (Anita Dangler), Mrs. Furnston (Dolores Mann), Girl in Car (Hildy Horan), Boy in Car (Henry Rhoades), Loaders (Mickey Deems, Pete Morgan)

Credits: Director: Don Weiss; Writers: Arthur Alsberg, Don Nelson; Producers: Arthur Alsberg, Don Nelson; Executive Producer: Edward J. Montagne; Photography: Harry L. Wolf: Art Director: James Martin Bachman; Music: Vic Mizzy; Editor: Frederic Baratta; Produced by NBC, Universal

This is a TV reunion movie for the Munsters, a lovable family convinced they're totally normal even though they look like classic film monsters (patriarch Herman resembles Karloff's Frankenstein, for instance)—except for their "ugly" cousin Marilyn, a good-looking blonde.

That resemblance gets the family in trouble when mad scientist Dr. Diablo disguises an army of robots as monster figures in his wax museum—including doubles for Herman and the aging vampire Grandpa. When the robots terrorize the city, Herman and Grandpa are framed, but Detective Boyle—who's fallen for Marilyn—tries to prove their innocence. Herman and Grandpa break jail and discover Diablo's secret lab, but can't relocate the secret door for the police afterward.

Posing as their robot doubles, the Munsters learn that Diablo is a nutter out to rip off an Egyptology exhibit in the belief he's brother to one of the pharaohs. While the Munsters return to Transylvania for a potion that will revive the pharaoh's mummy, Marilyn and Boyle are captured in the wax museum. The Munster men return in time to free them, then arrive at the Egyptology show during the robbery. Marilyn and Boyle swipe the remote control and take over the robots while Herman—finding the potion has revived the pharaoh as an infant—impersonates the mummy to force a confession out of Diablo.

The Munsters was a fun, lightweight sitcom, but this reunion film lacks any humor (or any plot logic) and mostly limps along. It was followed several years later by a poor TV series, *The Munsters Return*, and two TV movies (*Here Come the Munsters* and *The Munsters' Scary Little Christmas*), all of which recast the leading roles.

THE MUNSTERS' SCARY LITTLE CHRISTMAS
Fox, 12/17/96

Cast: Herman Munster (Sam McMurray), Lily Munster (Ann Magnuson), Eddie (Bug Hall), Grandpa (Sandy Baron), Marilyn (Elaine Hendrix), Santa (Mark Mitchell), Edna Dimwitty (Mary Woronov), Larry (Ed Gale), Lefty (Arturo Gil), Door Knocker (Noel Ferrier), Party Girl (Kate Fisher), Snooty Onlookers (Dominic Condon, Jonathan Biggins), Cop (Alan Zitner), Glen (Daniel Kellie), Burly Biker (Malcolm Mudway), Executioner Elf (Charles Russell), Effigy Elf (Michael Tauro), Chimney Sweep (Jalsyn Colby), Reindeer Bikers (Robert Strader, Brett Samuels, Michael Thrift, Robert Yearly, Neil Johns, Peter Leask, Barry Evans), Gill-Man (Christian Manon), Mummy (Justin Case), Hockey-Mask (Francois Bocquet), Moleman (Andrew Windsor), Zombies (Renee Askar, Lou Pollard, Brian Langsworth), Werewolf (Ben Griev), Phantom (Jason Taylor), Invisible Man (Brett Wood), Cyclops (David Anthony), Hunchback (Donald Cook), Devil (Troy Livermore), Witch (Lucy Clifford), with John Allen, Bruce Spence, Ann Dane, Patricia Hobson, Michael Hamilton, David Anderson, Viv Carter, Julie Herbert, Beth Armstrong, Jeremy Callaghan

Credits: Director: Ian Emes; Writers: Ed Ferrara, Kevin Murphy, based on characters developed by Norm Liebmann and Ed Haas from a format by Al Burns and Chris Hayward; Co-Producer: Tony Winley; Executive Producers: Leslie Belzberg, John Landis; Supervising Producer: Michael R. Joyce; Photography: Roger Lanser; Production Design: Laurence Eastwood; Music: Christopher Stone; Editor: Scott Smith; Produced by Michael R. Joyce Productions, St. Clare Entertainment, MTE

In the third Munster TV-movie, Eddie has lost the Christmas spirit; Herman gets fired for requesting a raise to buy better gifts; Lily infuriates neighbor Edna by competing in a Christmas decorations contest; and Grandpa tries magicking up a white Christmas but instead teleports Santa and a couple of elves to the Munster house—and can't send them back.

Santa bonds with Eddie and lifts his spirits—but the elves, enjoying their first Christmas vacation in centuries, delay leaving by using Grandpa's potions to turn Santa into a fruitcake. The elves run off and party at a biker bar, while Edna almost serves the Santa-cake to the contest judges (when Santa starts moving, it freaks the judges enough that Lily wins). Lily finally restores Santa, but too late to make the Christmas Eve trip. Then the elves return with bikers to pull the sleigh and a machine that can provide all the toys for the trip by materializing images from Herman's childlike mind. Herman has a new job—and the honor of joining Santa for the Christmas Eve run.

Following *Here Come the Munsters*, this is dumb and very weakly cast. Hendrix played Agent 66 in the short-lived 1995 revival of *Get Smart!*; Woronov played Dimwitty in the previous Munsters movie.

NATIONAL LAMPOON'S "MEN IN WHITE"
Fox Family Channel, 8/15/98

Cast: Roy Dubro (Karim Prince), Ed Klingbottom (Tom Wilson), Dr. Strangemeister (Wigald Boning), President Smith (Barry Bostwick), General Mills (George Kennedy), Press Secretary (Donna D'Errico), Stan (M. Emmett Walsh), Air Force Chief (James Brion), Man in Strangemeister's Head (Ben Stein), Glaxon (Rodger Halston)

Credits: Director: Scott Levy; Writers: Rob Kerchner, Scott Sandin; Producer: Mike Elliott; Executive Producer: Lance H. Robbins; Co-Producers: Rob Kerchner, Amy Goldberg; Associate Producer: Nathan Rotmensz; Animation Producer: Kent Butterworth; Photography: Brad Rushing; Production Design: Anthony Tremblay; Music: Kenneth Burgomaster; Editors: Gregory Hobson, Nina Gilberti; Produced by Saban Entertainment

When breathtakingly dimwitted garbagemen Roy and Ed are abducted by the evil

Glaxon's alien invasion fleet, they escape but the aliens resolve to recapture them. President Smith orders Strangemeister—head of government UFO research and Glaxon's secret ally—to investigate rumors of alien invasion. Strangemeister recruits the guys to do it as his "Men in White," figuring this will make it easy for the aliens to recapture them.

Instead, the guys successfully shoot down one of the spaceships and walk off with an alien super-weapon. Horrified, Strangemeister tells Smith that the agents have turned traitor, and everyone from the Marines to the Girl Scouts mobilizes to stop them. They're almost captured, until the alien weapon overloads and explodes, driving off their pursuers and killing several aliens. Furious, Glaxon destroys every garbage truck on Earth to kill them. Roy and Ed, however, sneak onto Glaxon's command ship and reprogram the computers to destroy the fleet. Glaxon attacks, engaging Roy in a lightsaber duel until Roy opens an airlock and Glaxon gets sucked into space. The computer destroys Glaxon's fleet, and the guys return to Earth to expose Strangemeister as an alien and receive a promotion that allows them to boss around their tyrannical supervisor.

This is a really bad SF parody (not only targeting the hit film *Men in Black*, but *Independence Day* and several others) that combines the worst of National Lampoon's film humor with the dumb comedy of Saban's *Mighty Morphin Power Rangers*. Like Saban's series, the aliens and effects appear to be taken from Japanese footage dubbed with new dialogue.

THE NEW, ORIGINAL WONDER WOMAN
ABC, 11/7/75

Cast: Wonder Woman/Diana Prince (Lynda Carter), Major Steve Trevor (Lyle Waggoner), Queen Hippolyte (Cloris Leachman), General Blankenship (John Randolph), Ashley Norman (Red Buttons), Col. Vonblasko (Kenneth Mars), Marcia (Stella Stevens), Kapitan Drangal (Eric Braeden), Nicholas (Henry Gibson), Amazon Doctor (Fanny Flagg), Bank Manager (Ian Wolfe), Salesclerk (Fritzi Burr), Nurse (Helen Verbit), Cop (Tom Rosqui), Rena (Inga Neilson), Woman (Maida Severn), Amazon (Jean Karlson), Cabbie (Anne Ramsey).

Credits: Director: Leonard Horn; Writer: Stanley Ralph Ross, from characters created by Charles Moulton; Producer: Douglas S. Cramer; Photography: Dennis Dalzell; Art Director: James G. Hulsey; Music: Charles Fox; Editor: Carroll Sax; Produced by Douglas S. Cramer Co., Warner Bros.

In 1942 a long-range Nazi bomber targets the secret U.S. base making the new Norden bombsight. Major Steve Trevor intercepts the plane over the Bermuda Triangle, but double-agent Marcia has alerted the Nazi pilot and the planes shoot each other down. Steve washes up on Paradise Island, home of the legendary Amazons. Fascinated by the first man she's ever seen, Princess Diana not only nurses him back to health, but enters a tournament (in disguise) to win the right to accompany him back to America and fight the Axis. After Diana wins, she flies Steve home in an invisible, super-fast plane, wearing a magic girdle that allows her to retain her Amazon strength in "man's world."

While finding her feet in America, Diana stops a bank robbery, deflecting the robbers' bullets on her metal bracelets. Norman, a Nazi spy, convinces "Wonder Woman" to support herself by playing "bullets and bracelets" on stage, hoping she'll be shot (no such luck). He then tries, unsuccessfully, to get her out of Washington on a tour.

Steve learns that Nazi leader Drangal will fly a Nazi super-bomber against the Norden base, but before Steve can act, Marcia captures him and steals the bombsight plans. Wonder Woman captures Marcia, then smashes Drangal's plane, rescues Steve—and decides to stay near him in disguise, as Yeoman Diana Prince.

Charles Moulton created Wonder Woman in the forties as a heroic fantasy figure for girls (like Superman for boys), though the feminism of his version faded with later writers. ABC brought a pale shadow of the character to the screen with *Wonder Woman*, then turned WW's first story in *Sensation Comics* #1 into this entertaining—and fairly faithful—adaptation (for once network interference improved a script—writer Ross was keen on doing it as camp, like the *Batman* TV show). The show served mostly as filler for ABC when production on *The Bionic Woman* was halted because of the star's car accident. After a season, *Wonder Woman* jumped to CBS, which updated the setting to the present, and it ran for two more years.

NICK KNIGHT
CBS, 8/30/89

Cast: Nick Knight (Rick Springfield), Dr. Jack Brittington (Robert Harper), Alyce Hunter (Laura Johnson), LaCroix (Michael Nader), Schanke (John Kapelos), Jeanette (Cec Verrell), Jack Fenner (Craig Richard Nelson), Jeannie (Fran Ryan), Topper (Jack Murdock), Dedrick (Al Fann), Desk Sergeant (Al Berry), Jessell (Gregory Wagrowski), Dr. Dave (Davis Roberts), Nurse (Irene Miracle), Mechanic (David Correia), Captain Brunetti (Richard Fancy), Fenner (Jack Murdock), Policewoman (Andree Chapman), Guard (David Byrd), Reporters (Rosanna Huffman, Rif Hutton), Orderly (Dennis Moynahan), Tanning Attendants (Dendrie Taylor, Pamela West), with Robert Neckes

Credits: Director: Fahrad Mann; Writer: James Parriott; Story: Barney Cohen, James Parriott; Producer: S. Michael Formica; Executive Producers: James Parriott, Barry Weitz, Roberta Becker Ziegel; Photography: Frank Beascoechea; Production Design: Paul Eads; Music: Joseph Conlan; Editing: Benjamin A. Weissman; Produced by New World Television, Barry Weitz Films, Robirdie Pictures

To his human co-workers, Nick Knight is a San Francisco homicide cop working the night shift; in reality, he's a 700-year-old vampire saving lives as a cop to atone for his many kills, and seeking help from pathologist Brittington in becoming mortal again. Currently, he has three problems: hiding his true nature from his new, loudmouthed partner, Schanke; a series of vampire killings that plunge him back into the city's vampire community; and a pair of sacred Indian cups at the city museum that could make Nick human with the right ritual.

The murderer turns out to be a mortal madman (whom Nick captures) draining blood with mechanical equipment. The power of the cups is real, however, and Nick's interest draws attention—and love—from Alyce, the archeologist who found them. It also attracts Nick's vampire mentor, LaCroix, who has no intention of letting his "son" become mortal—to which end he kills Alyce and destroys the cups. Nick kills LaCroix, but remains faced with an eternity of undeath.

This so-so pilot inspired a better series, *Forever Knight*, which ran four seasons with a completely different cast (except Kapelos as Schanke).

NIGHT CRIES
ABC, 1/29/78

Cast: Jeannie Haskins (Susan Saint James), Mitch Haskins (Michael Parks), Peggy Barton (Jamie Smith Jackson), Nurse Green (Dolores Dorn), Mrs. Delesande (Cathleen Nesbitt), Dr. Whelan (William Conrad), Dr. Medlow (Britt Leach), Bea Pryor (Saundra Sharp), Mrs. Thueson (Diana Douglas), Mrs. Whitney (Ellen Geer), Cynthia (Lee Kessler), George Pryor (Carl Byrd), Charlie (James Keane), Woman (Jennifer Penny), Receptionist (Robert Starr), Operator (Margo Ann Berdeshevsky), Donna Blankenstrip (Tracey Gold), Man (Bill Mallory), Technician (Scott Mulhern), Ian Whitney (Meeno Peluce), Young Jeannie (Nichole Faustino)

Credits: Director: Richard Lang; Writer: Brian Taggert; Producer: David Manson; Executive Producers: Charles Fries, Dick Berg; Associate Producer: Allan Marcil; Photography: Charles G. Arnold; Art Director: Bill Ross; Music: Paul Chihara; Editor: David Newhouse; Produced by Charles Fries Productions, Stonehenge Productions

After Jeannie Haskins' child dies at birth, Jeannie finds herself haunted by dreams of her baby calling for help. Is it a trauma from the child's death—or psychic messages from a baby who's somehow still alive?

Reportedly, *Night Cries* has some interesting twists.

NIGHT GALLERY
NBC, 11/8/69

Cast: Host (Rod Serling), Claudia Menlo (Joan Crawford), Osmond Portifoy (Ossie Davis), Joseph Strobe (Richard Kiley), Jeremy (Roddy McDowall), Dr. Frank Heatherton (Barry Sullivan),

Resnick (Tom Bosley), Hendricks (George Macready), Bleum (Sam Jaffe), Gretchen (Norma Crane), Carson (Barry Atwater), Gibbons (Tom Basham), Agent (George Murdock), Packer (Byron Murrow), Louis (Gary Goodrow), Nurse (Shannon Farnon), Doctor (Richard Hale)

Credits: Directors: (1) Boris Sagal, (2) Steven Spielberg, (3) Barry Shear; Writer: Rod Serling; Producer: William Sackheim; Associate Producer: John Badham; Photography: Richard Batcheller, William Margulies; Art Director: Howard E. Johnson; Music: Billy Goldenberg; Editor: Edward M. Abroms; Produced by Universal

In a dimly lit art gallery, the curator shows off paintings that tie in to three eerie tales: (1) After Jeremy murders his uncle, a painting of the family cemetery changes day by day, showing the uncle's corpse rising out of his grave. It turns out to be a trick by butler Osmond to scare Jeremy to death—but after Jeremy dies, Osmond spots the picture changing for real... (2) A blind millionaire schemes and blackmails to gain a temporary eye transplant and see the world for a single night. A power blackout destroys her chance to see anything. (3) A Nazi war criminal becomes fascinated with a beautiful, peaceful painting in a local art gallery. When justice closes in on him, he tries to wish his soul inside the picture and succeeds—except the museum has been rearranged, and the picture he enters is one of hell itself.

This was a successful pilot for a series Serling hoped would duplicate the thought-provoking eeriness of *The Twilight Zone*. Unfortunately, the network was more interested in Serling's name than his ideas, so the results lacked the depth of his earlier series—but many of the stories still turned out wonderfully scary. Steven Spielberg's segment of the pilot was his directorial debut.

NIGHT SLAVES
ABC, 9/29/70

Cast: Clay Howard (James Franciscus), Marjorie Howard (Lee Grant), Matt Russell (Scott Marlowe), Fess Beany/Leon (Andrew Prine), Annie Fletcher/Naillil (Tisha Sterling), Sheriff Henshaw (Leslie Nielsen), Mrs. Crawford (Virginia Vincent), Mr. Hale (Morris Buchanan), Spencer (Cliff Carnell), Jeff Pardee (Victor Izay), Joe Landers (Raymond Mayo), Mr. Fletcher (John Kellogg), Dr. Smithers (Russell Thorson), May (Nancy Valentine)

Credits: Director: Ted Post; Writers: Everett Chambers, Robert Specht, from Jerry Sohl's novel; Producer: Everett Chambers; Photography: Robert B. Hauser; Art Director: Howard Hollander; Music: Bernardo Segall; Editor: Michael Kahn; Produced by Bing Crosby Productions

After Clay Howard narrowly survives a car crash (and now has a metal plate in his head), his wife postpones asking for a divorce until after their vacation. They stop in a small town, where Clay wakes at night to find everyone, including his wife Marjorie, ignoring him to drive off in trucks. Only pretty Naillil stays behind, teasing him. When no one remembers any of this, Clay decides he was dreaming, then finds proof that it was real. The next night, he fails to stop Marjorie from going, and a force-field keeps him from following, so he spends the time falling for Naillil.

The following night, Clay joins the others on the trucks and arrives at a wrecked spaceship—the aliens, pure mind, are enslaving humans to make repairs, but Clay's metal plate protects his mind. The alien Leon tells Clay to give up Naillil (she's only borrowing a human body), then has the humans lock Clay up until the ship leaves. Clay escapes long enough for Naillil to beam his mind up into the ship to join her, leaving his dead body behind.

Night Slaves is a decent film, helped out by Franciscus' personal warmth.

THE NIGHT STALKER
ABC, 3/17/72

Cast: Carl Kolchak (Darren McGavin), Tony Vincenzo (Simon Oakland), Gail Foster (Carol Lynley), Janos Skorzeny (Barry Atwater), Sheriff Warren Butcher (Claude Akins), Jenks (Ralph Meeker), Chief Masterson (Charles McGraw), DA Paine (Kent Smith), Mickey Crawford (Elisha Cook, Jr.), Fred Hurley (Stanley Adams), Dr. O'Brien (Jordan Rhodes), Dr. Warren McCutchie (Larry Linville)

Credits: Director: John Llewellyn Moxey; Writer: Richard Matheson, based on *The Kolchak Papers* by Jeff Rice; Producer: Dan Curtis; Photography: Michel Hugo; Art Director: Trevor

Williams; Music: Robert Cobert; Editor: Desmond Marquette; Produced by ABC, Inc.

Narrator-reporter Carl Kolchak—whose loud mouth and irreverence have derailed his promising career—describes the brutal murder of a Las Vegas casino worker and how the police covered up that she died of complete blood loss. More bloodless bodies pile up, until Kolchak deduces that the killer is a vampire wannabe, but the authorities pressure his editor, Vincenzo, into burying the story (don't want to scare the tourists, do we?).

Federal agent Jenks announces that the chief suspect is an aging hematologist, Skorzeny, whose past is littered with similar deaths. When Kolchak sees Skorzeny manhandle cops and shrug off bullets, he realizes Skorzeny is a real vampire. Kolchak convinces the cops to take appropriate precautions; in return he'll get an exclusive on Skorzeny's capture. Kolchak locates Skorzeny's house and goes in for photos before the cops arrive. Skorzeny catches and almost kills him before Jenks arrives and helps stake the vampire. The next day the DA threatens to charge Kolchak with Skorzeny's murder unless he kills the story and leaves town. Kolchak's concluding voice-over tells us that all evidence on Skorzeny has been suppressed or destroyed.

Jeff Rice's unpublished *The Kolchak Papers* had the then-novel idea of transplanting vampirism into the modern world; scripted by SF writer Matheson, the film does a superb job with the premise (and set a new record for TV-movie ratings). McGavin is terrific as Kolchak: He's obviously a good reporter, but so insufferable it's easy to see why he lost so many jobs and why the authorities delight in breaking him. ABC reportedly disliked the film's violence, but they went ahead with a second film, *The Night Strangler*.

THE NIGHT STRANGLER
ABC, 1/16/73

Cast: Carl Kolchak (Darren McGavin), Tony Vincenzo (Simon Oakland), Louise Harper (Jo Ann Pflug), Dr. Richard Malcolm (Richard Anderson), Captain Roscoe Schubert (Scott Brady), Titus Berry (Wally Cox), Llewellyn Crossbinder (John Carradine), Prof. Hester Crabwell (Margaret Hamilton), Charisma Beauty/Gladys Weems (Nina Wayne), Dr. Christopher Webb (Ivor Francis), Wilma Krankheimer (Virginia Peters), Janie Watkins (Kate Murtagh), Ethel Parker (Regina Parton), Joyce Gabriel (Diane Shalet), Tramp (Al Lewis), Sheila (Anne Randall), Woman (Francoise Birnheim), Merissa (Regina Parton)

Credits: Director-Producer: Dan Curtis; Writer: Richard Matheson, from characters by Jeff Rice; Associate Producer: Robert Singer; Photography: Robert B. Hauser; Production Design: Trevor Williams; Music: Robert Cobert; Editor: Folma Blangstead; Produced by Dan Curtis Productions, ABC Circle Films

This sequel to *The Night Stalker* has Tony Vincenzo reluctantly hiring Kolchak for Tony's new paper in Seattle and assigning him to cover a strangulation-murder. More murders follow, with disturbing common elements: crushed necks, small amounts of drained blood, rotting flesh left on the bodies. And Carl discovers that there were similar serial murders in 1952—and 1931—and 1910—and 1889.

The authorities warn Kolchak against spreading wild stories, but Carl and his motor-mouth friend Louise keep snooping. Carl sees the super-strong killer battle police; explores the fire-ravaged ruins of Underground Seattle for the killer's lair; and learns there's an alchemical elixir based on fresh blood that could theoretically be prolonging the killer's life. Carl tells the cops the killer could be 19th-century alchemist Dr. Malcolm—a dead ringer for a prominent modern physician—but they rip his theory to shreds. But Carl finds a secret passage into Underground Seattle and tracks Malcolm down.

The doctor explains that he's working on a permanent elixir that will make all humanity immortal, so a few women's lives are a fair sacrifice, right? Carl responds by destroying the finished elixir. Malcolm ages and dies, then the cops show up. As in Vegas, the authorities bury Carl's story, and he, Tony and Louise get run out of town together.

The Night Strangler employs the same

formula as *The Night Stalker*, but it works even better—the on-location shooting in Underground Seattle is wonderfully eerie. Curtis and Matheson reportedly planned to follow up with *The Night Killer* (mad scientist replaces humans with androids), but ABC opted for a series instead, with Carl and Tony setting up shop in Chicago. Ratings were low, costs high (lots of nighttime shooting) and Rice—who said he hadn't authorized a series—threatened to sue, so ABC cut its losses and canned the show after one season.

It's been a staple of syndication since then, and *The X-Files* creator Chris Carter credits Kolchak as a major inspiration for that series—not to mention Dan Curtis' own knockoff film, *The Norliss Tapes* (paranormal investigators seem to agree with Curtis—he used them in *Curse of the Black Widow* and a 1969 pilot, *In the Dead of Night*).

THE NIGHT THEY SAVED CHRISTMAS
ABC, 12/13/84

Cast: Paul Baldwin (Paul LeMat), Claudia Baldwin (Jaclyn Smith), Santa Claus (Art Carney), David (Scott Grimes), Marianne (Laura Jacoby), C.B. (R.J. Williams), Murdock (Mason Adams), Ed (Paul Williams), Mrs. Claus (June Lockhart), Marin (James Staley), Loomis (Albert Hall), Hedda (Anne Haney), Dr. Fernando (Buddy Haney), Jack (Billy Curtis), Faulkner (Michael Keys-Hall), Pilot (Randy Crosby)

Credits: Director: Jackie Cooper; Writers: Jim Moloney, David Niven, Jr.; Story: David Niven, Jr., Jim Moloney, Rudy Dochtermann; Producers: David Kappes, Robert Halmi, Sr.; Executive Producers: Jack Haley, Jr., David Niven, Jr., Robert Halmi, Jr.; Music: Charles Gross; Songs: Paul Williams; Editor: Eric Albertson; Produced by Robert Halmi, Inc.

With his arctic oil wells coming up dry and a boss demanding results, Paul Baldwin has no time to waste on Ed, who claims to be Santa's head elf and warns Paul that his dynamiting the ice before drilling is damaging Santa's workshop. Paul's wife Claudia and their kids are just as skeptical when they meet Ed—until he takes them in a souped-up snowcat to North Pole City, Santa's hidden home. When they return, Paul and his boss insist that the Baldwins have been drugged and hypnotized by a rival oilman. Paul plans the next dynamite job, even though Claudia warns him it will destroy Santa's city. In the nick of time, one of the other wells brings in a gusher, and Paul aborts the dynamiting. Then the appearance of Santa on Christmas Eve convinces even the most skeptical doubters of the truth.

This is dull, pointless Christmas fare, though I do love "How Santa Does It" explanations. Carney also played Santa in a seventies Jim Henson special, *The Great Santa Claus Switch*.

NIGHTLIFE
USA, 8/23/89

Cast: Vlad (Ben Cross), Angelique (Maryam d'Abo), Dr. David Zuckermann (Keith Szarabajka), Gravediggers (Gerardo Mayol, Juan Antonio Llanes), Tour Guide (Gerardo Paz), Technician (Gilberto Compan), Man in Bar (Gerardo Moreno), Policeman (Carlos Gonzales), Receptionist (Marta Resnikoff), Old Man (Martin LaSalle), Cleaner (Paco Pharrez), Cartier Owner (Bob Skodis), with Jesse Corti, Camille Saviola, Oliver Clark, Glenn Shadix

Credits: Director: Daniel Taplitz, Writers: Daniel Taplitz, Anne Beatts; Story: Anne Beatts; Producer: Robert T. Skodis; Executive Producer: Dan Wigutow; Photography: Peter Fernberger; Music: Dana Kaproff; Editor: Edward Abroms; Produced by Cine Enterprises, Mexico, MTE

A century ago, the British vampire Angelique escaped her cruel, undead lover Vlad by fleeing to Mexico and burying herself alive. Accidentally unearthed in the present, she learns that blood transfusions can sustain her without killing. American hematologist David discovers that her vampirism is caused by a virus, and works on a cure. None of this goes over well with the newly arrived Vlad, who wants Angelique back—and loathes the idea that he's merely a disease vector.

Vlad warns Angelique that they feed not only on blood but on their victims' fear—and sure enough, she finds the transfusions are losing their punch. Vlad decides to spare David until Angelique is hungry enough to kill him, and imprisons her when she tries reburying herself. Meanwhile, David discovers that it's not fear vampires feed on but a fear-triggered hormone; he finds Angelique and injects her with hormones, but not before she bites him. When Vlad shows up, the now-vampirized David battles him until Angelique can stake him. David and Angelique can now live a happy (if unusual) life together—but Vlad may not be completely dead...

Having a traditional vampire learn the vampirism-as-virus theory (possibly introduced in Richard Matheson's novel *I Am Legend*) is the best touch in this routine vampire comedy. Cross is disappointing though (he was better as the vampire Barnabas in the 1991 revival of *Dark Shadows*).

NIGHTMARE STREET
ABC, 1/18/98

Cast: Joanna Burke/Sarah Randolph (Sherilyn Fenn), Penny Randolph (Rena Sofer), Dr. Matt Westbrook/Joe Barnes (Thomas Gibson), Det. Miller (Steve Harris), Alex Potter (Matthew Walker), Dr. Nelson (P. Lynn Johnson), Eddie (Peter Bryant), Detective (Fred Keating), Jim (Andrew Airlie), Woman (Patti Harras), Young Mother (Eileen Pedde), Clerk (David Mackay), Mrs. Petersen (Cindy Girling), Little Girl (Jenny-Lynn Hutcheson), Dr. Zackler (Michael Puttonen), News Vendor (Tom Heaton), Mailman (Steve Oatway), Sandy (Jennifer Clement), Woman at Carousel (Angela Donohue), Officer (Ian Marsh), Dr. Holdreith (George Gordon), Cabbie (Roger Haskett), Randall Duncan (Claude De Martino), Young Man (Cam Labine), Nurse (B.J. Harrison), Cop (Mark Holden), with Lauren Diewold

Credits: Director: Colin Bucksey; Writers: Rama Laurie Stagner, Dan Witt, from Margaret Tabor's novel; Producer: William Shippey; Executive Producers: Sharon Cicero, Ronnie D. Clemmer, Richard P. Kughn, Bill Pace, Courtney Pledger; Photography: Jan Kiesser; Production Design: Jill Scott; Music: Dana Kaproff; Editor: John A. Martinelli; Produced by Longbow Productions

When Joanna Burke is hit while shoving her daughter away from a truck, she wakes in the ER to find that everything from hospital records to her drivers' license to the people around her indicates she's Sarah Randolph, whom she learns is a manipulative adulteress, a corporate backstabber—and a possible murderer. Joanna convinces ER doctor Westbrook that she's traded places with her parallel world counterpart—and that perhaps by duplicating the accident, she can go home. Finding proof that Sarah really is a killer, Joanna sends the police a videotaped confession—but they show up before she can return to her world. Westbrook buys her time to reach the accident site, where she pulls another child away from a truck—and returns home. Her last glimpse of that world shows Sarah in handcuffs—and a new local handyman turns out to be Westbrook's double.

Although TV series have used the concept of parallel worlds for years (the *Star Trek* episode "Mirror, Mirror" and *The Twilight Zone*'s "A World of Difference," to name two), TV movies ignored the concept until 1997's *Last Lives*, followed by four films on that theme in 1998—of which this was the weakest (dimensional travel by truck accident?). Having Westbrook's exact double show up is a common ploy in this kind of romance.

1994 BAKER STREET: SHERLOCK HOLMES RETURNS
CBS, 9/12/93

Cast: Sherlock Holmes (Anthony Higgins), Dr. Amy Winslow (Debrah Farentino), James Moriarty Booth (Ken Pogue), Zapper (Mark Adair Rios), Det. Griffin (Julian Christopher), Mrs. Hudson (Joy Coghill), Nurse (Susan Appling), Sergeant (Ken Camroux), Rookie Cop (Thomas Cavanagh), Mr. Hudson (Daniel Chambers), Night Watchman (John Blackwell Destry), Rancho (Jason Diablo), Lt. Ortega (Eli Gabay), Max (Philip Hayes), Lefty (Tom Heaton), Young Mrs. Hudson (Tish Heaven), Respiratory Therapist (Peter Kelamis), Resuscitation Nurse (Catherine Lough), DA Weis (Scott Nicholson), Cop (Alvin Sanders), Mrs. Ortega (Kerry Sandomirsky), Pavon (Fabricio Santin), Curly (Lee Sollenberg), Ronald Hunt (Gerry Therrien), Slick (Jorge Vargas), Old Man Moriarty (John Wardlow), Lt. Civita (Jerry Wasserman), Young Booth (Devon Sawa), Father Moriarty (Norman Armour)

Credits: Director-Writer: Kenneth Johnson; Executive Producers: Daniel Grodnik, Kenneth Johnson; Photography: Ron Orieux; Production Design: Richard Hudolin; Music: James Di

Pasquale; Editor: David Strohmaier; Produced by Paragon Entertainment, Kenneth Johnson Productions

First, San Francisco doctor Amy Winslow tries and fails to save an ex-cop mauled by a tiger; then, while visiting an elderly patient, Amy finds a cryonics chamber in the basement and revives the occupant—Sherlock Holmes. Holmes explains that he grew terminally bored after Moriarty's death and hoped to sleep until he could witness the marvels of the next century (moving to San Francisco to evade Moriarty's vengeful family). Investigating the tiger-mauling and several linked cop-killings, Holmes finds himself pitted against Moriarty's descendant, Booth, an untouchable crimelord.

Holmes is horrified at how culture shock has crippled his deductive skills (e.g., mistaking saccharine for cocaine), but Amy convinces him not to give up. With assistance from Amy and Zapper, a tech-savvy street punk, Holmes puts an end to the cop-killings and proves that Booth—who swears revenge—was behind them. His confidence restored, Holmes resumes his career.

This was an excellent, albeit unsuccessful pilot. The idea of Holmes reaching the present through cryonics was also used in *The Return of Sherlock Holmes*. Farentino previously starred in *Earth 2* (the TV series, not the movie).

NOAH
ABC, 10/11/98

Cast: Norman Waters (Tony Danza), Zach (Wallace Shawn), Angela (Jane Sibbett), Levon (Jesse Moss), Penelope (Nicola Cavendish), Ernie (John Marshall Jones), Donecker (Kevin McNulty), Daniel (Christopher Marquette), Benny (Michal Suchanek), Aris (Joe-Norman Shaw), Pete (Randy Birch), Karl (Aaron Pearl), Kathy Simmons (Jane McGregor), Ernie, Jr. (Ed Richardson III), Cute Blonde (Anita Matthys), Ray the Inspector (Paul Coeur), Women (Barbara Egan, Hazel Proctor), Kid (Matt Clarke), Clerk (Karen Johnston-Diamond), Weatherman (Paul Dunphy), Cheerleader (Melonie Markosky), Bad Hair Kid (Scott Olynek), Elevator Girl (Kylo Anderson), Neighbor (Daniel Libman), Woman in Car (Valerie Planche), Noah (Lloyd Barry), Donna (Georgie Collins), Child (Genevieve Fraser), Referee (Ed Richardson II), Non-believer (Daryl Shuttleworth), Secretary (Maureen Thomas), Man with Umbrella (Guy Bews), Yoga Instructor (Linda Red Hawk), Deliveryman (John Stewart), Telephone Girls (Esther Purves-Smith, Roxanne Wong, Lisa Christie), with Don McManus

Credits: Director: Ken Kwapis; Writers: Juliet Aires, Keith Giglio, Charlie Bohl; Producer: Charlie Bohl; Executive Producer: Karen Tangorra; Photography: Ron Orieux; Production Design: Michael Bolton; Music: Van Dyke Parks; Editor: Corky Ehlers; Produced by Walt Disney Television

Widowed Norman, a crooked contractor, is bewildered when Zach, an agent of heaven, hires him to build an ark—exactly to spec, no substitutions, no cheating. Norman's reluctance to do the job grows as the town and his family become convinced he's crazy; at the same time, he's regaining the pride he once took in doing quality, honest work, and starts to believe this is really the will of God. He also reconnects with his estranged kids and forges a new connection with Angela, an animal expert who helps him bring the two-by-two animals aboard. Norman's rivals obtain the authority to stop the project but change their tune when a meteorologically impossible downpour floods the town. Over Zach's protests, Norman takes the entire town on board with him. When the downpour ends (creating a new lake for a tourist attraction), Norman gets the girl and the town's gratitude.

Though *Noah* is silly stuff, it's amiably executed. Shawn plays Grand Nagus Zek on *Star Trek: Deep Space Nine*.

THE NORLISS TAPES
NBC, 2/21/73

Cast: David Norliss (Roy Thinnes), Ellen Sterns Cort (Angie Dickinson), Sheriff Tom Hartley (Claude Akins), Madame Jeckiel (Vonetta McGee), Marsha Sterns (Michele Carey), Charles Langdon (Hurd Hatfield), Sanford Evans (Don Porter), George Rosen (Robert Mandan), James Cort (Nick Dimitri), Sargoth (Bob Schott), Dobkins (Bryan O'Byrne), Sid Phelps (Edmund Gilbert), Jane Dulo (Sara Dobkins), Trucker (Stanley Adams), Man in Gallery (George DiCenzo), Larry Mather (Patrick Wright)

Credits: Director-Producer: Dan Curtis; Writer: William F. Nolan, from a story by Fred Mustard

Stewart; Executive Producer: Charles Fries; Associate Producer: Robert Singer; Photography: Ben Colman; Art Director: Trevor Williams; Music: Robert Cobert; Editor: John F. Link II; Produced by Metromedia Producers, Dan Curtis Productions

When writer Norliss disappears, his publisher, Evans, finds taped transcripts for Norliss' book debunking the supernatural—which reveal that Norliss has seen too much he can't debunk: Like when Ellen Cort tells him her sculptor husband has returned from the dead, killing women for their blood. Norliss learns that Cort dabbled in the occult before his death, and even took a magic ring from mystic Madame Jeckiel to the grave with him. Jeckiel warns Norliss that the Cort home is now "the house of Sargoth."

Norliss and Ellen find a grotesque statue of clay and blood in Cort's studio and barely escape Cort's attack. Jeckiel tells Ellen the ring resurrected Cort to sculpt the statue; when it's finished, the demon Sargoth will be freed into our world, granting Cort immortality. Jeckiel and Ellen try to reclaim the ring from Cort's crypt, but Cort kills Jeckiel. Ellen escapes, but Sargoth enters the finished statue; Norliss then traps him and Cort within a magic ring of fire. Furious, Sargoth destroys Cort, then the fire destroys the statue. In the present, Evans wonders if Sargoth is behind Norliss' disappearance, and pops in another tape...

Since Dan Curtis produced *The Night Stalker* and directed-produced its sequel, *The Night Strangler*, for ABC, he was the logical choice for this knockoff pilot—and knockoff it is, down to the reporter's voice-over, the cover-up by skeptical authorities and the vampire-like Cort. Unfortunately, Thinnes (*The Invaders*) makes a bland, dull substitute for McGavin's obnoxious Kolchak, which makes this movie much more formulaic; still, it scared many teenaged viewers.

NOT LIKE US
Showtime, 8/15/95

Cast: Anita Clarke (Joanna Pacula), Sam Clarke (Peter Onorati), Janet (Rainer Grant), John (Morgan Englund), Jody (Billy Burnette), Vicki (Annabelle Gurwitch), Mortician (Paul Bartel), Wede (Clint Howard), Hooper (Doug "Greaseman" Tract), Henry (Andrew Burt), Elizabeth (Alexandra Picatto), Kyle (Kevin Contreras), Peter (Kevin Austin), Doc Johnson (Bob McFarland), LA Expert (Pat Elliott), Fresno Specialist (Mindy Sterling), Irv (Michael Todd Curry), Bud (Christopher Boyer), Edgar (Jon Paul Jones), Grunther (Eb Lottimer), Mac (Greg Brazzel), Father Martin (David Wells), Roberta (Suzy Cote), Donny (Gary Wolf), Ex-Con (Rick Dean), Mrs. Bower (Janet Eilber), Bower Boy (Josh Lindsay), Eunice (Janet Rotblatt), Mrs. Parkinson (Anita Finlay), Mrs. Anderson (Mina Kolb), Wink (Tom Poster), Burger Pit Manager (Rob Kerchner)

Credits: Director: Dave Payne; Writer: Daniella Purcell; Producer: Mike Elliott; Co-Producer: Mike Upton; Executive Producers: Roger Corman, Lance H. Robbins; Photography: Michael Mickens; Production Design: Nava; Music: Tyler Bates; Editor: Brian Katkin; Produced by New Horizons

Everyone in Tranquility freaks as the small town's inhabitants keep turning up dead of some mysterious disease—actually the work of Janet and John, aliens experimenting with wearing human bodies as a new beauty technique (personal appearance is their world's highest art form). Anita, who's splitting from her husband Sam, becomes friends with Janet—which doesn't stop John and Janet eventually using Sam as a test subject. Janet realizes the truth at the last minute, kills both aliens and reunites with her husband.

What is the point to this mess (other than having Grant walk around topless as bait for her victims)?

NOT OF THIS EARTH
Showtime, 9/5/95

Cast: Paul Johnson (Michael York), Dr. Rochelle (Mason Adams), Jack Sherbourne (Parker Stevenson), Jeremy Pallin (Richard Belzer), Amanda Sayles (Elizabeth Barondes), Rodman Felder (Ted Davis), Alien Woman (Julia Mueller), Det. Mark Willows (Bob McFarland), Cheryl (Wendy Buckner), Danny (Joshua D. Comen), Nurses (Jennifer Coolidge, Athena Stensland), John (Eddie Driscoll), Saleswoman (Mary Scheer), Cheryl's Father (Arthur Roberts), Luisa (Diana Miranda), Hector (Chuck Martinez), Cop (Rob

Kerchner), The Other (John Buechler), Parking Attendant (Ellen Statham)
Credits: Director: Terence H. Winkless; Writer: Charles Philip Moore, from a screenplay by Mark Hanna, Charles Griffith; Producer: Mike Elliott; Co-Producer: Mike Upton; Executive Producers: Roger Corman, Lance H. Robbins; Associate Producer: Jan Kikumoto; Photography: Philip Holahan; Production Design: Nava; Music: Jeff Winkless; Editor: James Stellar, Jr.; Produced by Concorde–New Horizons

Under his sunglasses, "Mr. Johnson" is actually a glowing-eyed alien experimenting on humans to see if their blood can cure the deadly blood disease affecting his planet. Johnson mind-controls hematologist Rochelle to work on the cure, and hires Rochelle's nurse, Sayles, to provide him with the daily transfusions he needs. Her cop boyfriend, Jack, soon suspects Johnson is up to something.

A woman from Johnson's world arrives and tells him their leaders are draining blood from their own people now—and have also eaten the blood samples he sent for research. The couple contemplates restarting their race on Earth, but the woman dies from a transfusion of rabies-tainted blood. After Rochelle develops a cure, Johnson mind-controls Sayles into becoming his new mate; her boyfriend shoots Johnson down, but another alien appears to continue his mission.

This SF vampire story is a remake of a 1957 theatrical original (also remade in 1988 with Traci Lords as the nurse, and as 1998's direct-to-video *Star Portal*) and remains competent B-movie fun. Michael York does an excellent turn as the out-of-place alien.

NOT OF THIS WORLD
CBS, 2/12/91
Cast: Linda Fletcher (Lisa Hartman), Sheriff Tom Conway (A. Martinez), Grandpa (Pat Hingle), A.J. (Richard Grove), Pastor Williams (Steve Prutting), Workmen (Richard Epcar, Greg Natale), Mike (J.B. Quon), Joanne (Elizabeth Gill), Security Officer (Burr Middleton), Wives (Lisa Hart Carroll, Michele Palermo), Reporters (Timothy Davis Reed, Michele Roth, Elizabeth Lee), with Luke Edwards, Cary Hiroyuki-Tagawa, Tim Choate, Tracey Walter, Ivory Ocean, Ian Patrick Williams, Xander Berkeley, Nicholas D. Bussey

Credits: Director: Jon Daniel Hess; Writer: Robert Glass; Story: Les Alexander, Don Enright, Jonathon Brauer, Robert Glass; Producer: Jonathon Brauer; Executive Producer: Les Alexander, Don Enright; Photography: Mark Irwin; Production Design: Phillip M. Leonard; Supervising Editor: John F. Burnett; Music: Johnny Harris; Produced by Paramount

A meteor shower lands alien artificial lifeforms on Earth near a small, southwestern town where they begin draining all sources of electricity, from car batteries to the human nervous system. By the time the townsfolk piece together the significance of all the strange deaths and weird creatures, the last surviving alien has drained enough energy to become man-sized—and is targeting a new electrical facility that will let it suck power from a five-state area. Engineer Fletcher and her crew try and fail to overload the beast with power from the transformers; then her father discovers that the creature has positive and negative ends, like a magnet. By using the power station to reverse the creature's polarity, Fletcher destroys it.

Though a game try at doing a fifties-style monsters-from-space thriller, *Not of This World* is too slowly paced (the battle doesn't really get going until the last fifteen minutes). Among the cast are Hingle (Commissioner Gordon in the big-screen *Batman* films) and Hiroyuki-Tagawa (*Space Rangers*).

NOT QUITE HUMAN
Disney, 6/19/87
Cast: Dr. Jonas Carson (Alan Thicke), Chip Carson (Jay Underwood), Becky Carson (Robyn Lively), Durks (Robert Harper), Gordon Vogel (Joseph Bologna), Jake Blocker (Brian Cole), Scott Barnes (Brandon Douglas), Jenny Beckerman (Lili Haydn), Bryan Skelly (Sasha Mitchell), Coach Duckworth (Greg Monaghan), Mr. Sturges (Lonny Price), Paul Fairgate (Casey Scott), Erin Jeffries (Kristy Swanson), Mr. Burley (Bob Anthony), Principal Gutman (Gene Blakley), Ms. Buzzi (Marcia Darroch), Bartlett (Aaron Peterman), Secretary (Billie Shepard), Dr. Sondra Stahl (Judy Starr), Greta (Pat Willoughby)
Credits: Director–Executive Producer: Steven H. Stern; Writer: Alan Ormsby, based on characters from Seth McEvoy's *Not Quite Human* books; Producer: Noel Resnick; Photography: Ken Lamkin; Production Design: Elayne Ceder;

Music: Tom Scott; Editor: Ron Wisman; Produced by Sharmhill Production, Inc.

After years of research, widowed Jonas Carson finally invents a self-aware android, only to realize his militaristic boss, Vogel, plans to exploit "Chip" as a weapon. Carson relocates to another town, then enrolls Chip in high school—as older brother to Carson's daughter, Becky—to see if Chip can develop human feelings. Chip's habit of taking everything literally earns him a reputation as a lovable goofball. Although Becky is embarrassed by him at first, she comes to love him like a real brother, and he acquires the capacity to love her and Jonas back. When Vogel tracks them down, he captures Carson and Becky, steals Chip and threatens to destroy him unless Carson tells Vogel how to reprogram Chip. Carson complies—but Chip's personality has become strong enough to fight the reprogramming. He outmaneuvers Vogel, frees his family, and the Carsons go home together.

This stock, fairly amusing fluff was followed by two sequels.

NOT QUITE HUMAN II
Disney, 9/23/89

Cast: Dr. Jonas Carson (Alan Thicke), Chip Carson (Jay Underwood), Becky Carson (Robyn Lively), Dr. Phil Masters (Greg Mullavey), Roberta (Katie Barberi), Prof. Victoria Gray (Dey Young), Brandon (Scott Nell), Moore (Mark Arnott), Miller (Mike Russell), Austin (Ty Miller), Rick (Eric Bruskotter), Walter (Bob Sorenson), Mel (Doug Cotner), Party Girls (Nanette Varela, Holly Robertson), Tiffany (Kari Kulvinskas), Hostess (Karon Kearney)

Credits: Director-Writer: Eric Luke, based on characters created by Kevin Osborn, based on Seth McEvoy's *Not Quite Human* books; Producer: James Margellos; Executive Producer: Noel Resnick; Photography: Jules Brenner; Production Design: Nilo Rodis; Music: Michel Rubini; Editor: David Berlatsky; Produced by Resnick/Margellos Productions

In this sequel to *Not Quite Human*, the android Chip unwittingly downloads a virus created by robotics researchers to eliminate their competition. Unaware he's now dying, Chip heads off to college (coincidentally, the one where the researchers work), monitored by his anxious father. Chip finds it hard relating to humans in this new environment, but does make fast friends with Roberta, a student who's actually another android (created by the researchers). When Chip learns the truth, he helps Roberta defy her programming. The androids go on the run, even though his software and her power cells are shutting down. Research head Victoria learns about the virus and helps Carson obtain an anti-viral program to cure Chip—but Roberta runs down and her makers reclaim her. Chip, however, has stored her programming in his own systems; once Jonas and Victoria build her a new body, she'll be alive and free to be with Chip.

The best of the three films, this was followed by *Still Not Quite Human* (which ignored the romances for both Jonas and Chip that developed here).

ODYSSEY
NBC, 5/18–5/19/97

Cast: Odysseus (Armand Assante), Penelope (Greta Scacchi), Athena (Isabella Rossellini), Circe (Bernadette Peters), Calypso (Vanessa Williams), Eurymachus (Eric Roberts), Telemachus (Alan Stenson), Eurycleia (Geraldine Chaplin), King Alcinous (Jeroen Krabbe), Teiresias (Christopher Lee), Anticlea (Irene Papas), Anticlus (William Houston), Eurybates (Ron Cook), Elpenor (Alan Cox), Polites (Roger Ashton-Griffiths), Antiphus (Stuart Thompson), Eurylochos (Michael Tezcan), Perimides (Adoni Anastassopoulos), Orsilicus (Mark Hill), Eumaeus (Tony Vogel), Queen Alcinous (Sally Plumb), Achilles (Richard Trewett), Laocoon (Heathcote Williams), Leocrites (Oded Levy), Elatus (Pat Kelman), Agelaus (Marius Combo), Melanthe (Paloma Baeza), Philotus (Peter Page), Mentor (Peter Woodthorpe), Nausicaa (Katie Carr), Agamemnon (Yorgo Voyagis), Menelaus (Nicholas Clay), Aeolus (Michael J. Pollard), Priam (Alan Smithie), Hector (Derek Lea), Hermes (Freddie Douglas), Poseidon (Miles Anderson)

Credits: Director: Andrei Konchalovsky; Writers: Andrei Konchalovsky, Christopher Solimine, based on Homer's epic poem; Producer: Dyson Lovell; Executive Producers: Francis Ford Coppola, Fred Fuchs, Robert Halmi, Sr., Nicholas Meyer; Photography: Sergei Koslov; Production Design: Roger Hall; Music: Edward Artemyev; Editor: Michael Ellis; Produced by American Zoetrope, Hallmark Entertainment

This was a lavish-looking, fairly faithful (the minor changes that were wrought were for the worse) version of Homer's epic poem, telling how Odysseus seeks to return to his homeland following the Trojan War—despite monsters, sorcery, the wrath of Poseidon and ambitious nobles who would like to rule Ithaca in his place. Though well done, it features a mixed bag of performances—Michael Pollard's Aeolus is almost universally loathed.

OFFICIAL DENIAL
Sci-Fi, 11/20/93

Cast: Paul Corliss (Parker Stevenson), Annie Corliss (Erin Gray), General Kenneth Spalding (Chad Everett), Lt. Col. Dan Lerner (Dirk Benedict), Michael Novado (Robert Mammone), Janine (Natalie McCurry), Sam Foolscrow (Christopher Pate), Wisdomkeeper (Michael Pate), Jonathan Applegate (Peter Curtin), Dr. Melendez (Gina Gaigalas)

Credits: Director: Brian Trenchard-Smith; Writer-Co-Producer: Bryce Zabel; Producer: Darryl Sheen; Executive Producers: Joe Wizan, Todd Black, Jeffrey Hayes; Photography: John Stokes; Production Design: Stewart Burnside; Music: Garry McDonald, Laurie Stone; Editing: Patrick Stewart; Produced by Paramount

Paul Corliss' marriage is falling apart because his wife Annie doesn't understand his obsessive belief in UFOs—which he insists once abducted him. When the aliens return, Majestic (a group of federal UFO hunters) shoots the spaceship down and captures the one survivor. When the alien refuses to communicate, Majestic brings Paul in to see if the former abductee will spark some reaction in their captive. General Spalding tells the outraged Paul that the government has to keep the UFOs secret rather than admit aliens can kidnap U.S. citizens with impunity.

The alien telepaths to Paul that it can explain all—if it returns to the ship and absorbs the full details from the lingering minds of its comrades. Spalding, desperate to learn the truth, helps them escape, and Annie takes them to the crash site. Paul learns en route that the aliens are stealing human chromosomes in hopes of revitalizing their dying race; at the ship, the alien gives him the rest of their secrets before dying. Paul tells Majestic that he learned nothing, but reveals to Spalding that the aliens are evolved humans from a barren future Earth who used Paul's genes because he will have no descendants. So when Annie has a child, Paul realizes that the bleak future can be averted.

There's much familiar material in this story, but it's an interesting, well-told tale nonetheless. Screenwriter Zabel used many of the same themes in his 1996–97 TV series *Dark Skies*. Familiar faces include Benedict (*Battlestar Galactica*'s Starbuck) and Gray (*Buck Rogers*' Wilma).

OMEN IV
Fox, 5/20/91

Cast: Karen York (Faye Grant), Gene York (Michael Woods), Delia York (Asia Vieira), Earl (Michael Lerner), Dr. Hastings (Madison Mason), Jo Thusson (Ann Hearn), Noah (Jim Byrnes), Jake Madison (Don S. Davis), Sister Yvonne/Felicity (Megan Leitch), Sister Francesca (Joy Coghill), Father Hayes (David Cameron), Father Mattson (Duncan Fraser), Mother Superior (Susan Chapple), Preacher (Dana Still), Miss Roselli (Andrea Mann), Madge Milligan (Camille Mitchell), Hildy Riggs (Brenda Critchlow), Forrest Riggs (William Taylor), Morris Creighton (Serge Houde), Lily Creighton (Wendy Van Riesen), Jerome (James Sherry), Miss Norris (Mikal Daghi), Blind Medium (Norman Armour), Fair Customer (Tish Heaven), Psychics (Claire Brown, Hamish Boyd), Christian Women (Lesley Ewen, Shelia Patterson), Drifter (Martin Cummings), Motel Clerk (Suzie Payne), Novice (Ruth McIntosh), Mica (Brent Statt), Hooker (Karen Yip), Doctor (Tom Heaton), Delia at 3 (Brianne Harrett), at 2 (Rebecca Cynader), at 1½ (Shelby Adams), Graham Remick (Scott Swanson), Bartender (Gerry Dean), Dog (Ryder)

Credits: Directors: Jorge Montesi, Dominique Othenin-Girard; Writer: Brian Taggert; Story: Brian Taggert, Harvey Bernhard; Producer: Harvey Bernhard; Co-Producer: Robert Anderson; Executive Producer: Mace Neufeld; Photography: Martin Fuhrer; Production Design: Richard Wilcox; Editor: Frank Irvine; Music: Jonathan Sheffer; Theme from *The Omen* and *Omen III*: Jerry Goldsmith; Produced by FNM Films

Eight years after adopting Delia, Karen York is convinced something is wrong with her daughter: Kids and animals hate her, accidents dog her enemies and she turns psychic healing crystals black. The evidence keeps building, but Karen is now pregnant (against all medical odds), so her husband dismisses all this as a hysterical-pregnant-woman-thing. Karen finally discovers that her obstetrician also delivered Delia, whose father was the late Damien Thorne, the Antichrist himself. Delia has inherited Damien's power, and Karen's new baby is actually Delia's twin (the explanation defies belief—or synopsis) and will become the new Antichrist. Karen tries to kill the kids, but their combined power forces her to commit suicide. Evil wins.

The Omen, 1976's number three box-office hit, yanked Antichrist out of Christian faith and plonked him down squarely in pop culture (few films about Satan's offspring used the term before—and almost none of them failed to use it afterwards). It was followed by many clones, some parodies, two less successful theatrical sequels (*Omen II* starred Faye Grant's mother, Lee Grant), and this formulaic, unsuccessful attempt to revive the series.

OUT OF TIME
NBC, 7/17/88

Cast: Channing Taylor (Bruce Abbott), Richard Marcus (Adam Ant), Maxwell Taylor (Bill Maher), Pam Wallis (Rebecca Schaeffer), Cassandra Barber (Kristian Alfonso), Ed Hawkins (Leo Rossi), Captain Stephen Krones (Ray Girardin), Dr. Kerry Langdon (Barbara Tarbuck), Capt. Stuart (Arva Holt), Frank (Tom LaGrua), Salesgirl (Kimberley Sedgwick), Foreman (Chuck Lindsly), Jenocy (Arthur Mendoza), Motorcycle Cop (Rick Avery), Hot Babe (Ashley Brittingham), Desk Sergeant (Don Maxwell), Guard (Richard Lavin), Officers (Neal Penso, Jay Richardson, Thomas Wagner, Patrick DeSantis, Greg Collins), Speechmaker (Shaun Toub), Supervisor (Martin Treat)

Credits: Director: Robert Butler; Writers: Brian Alan Lane, John J. Sakmar, Kerry Lenhart; Story: Brian Alan Lane; Producer: David Latt; Supervising Producers: Kerry Lenhart, John J. Sakmar; Photography: Lloyd Ahern II; Production Design: Tommy Goetz; Music: Andy Summers; Editor: Dann Cahn; Produced by Tri-Star Television, Columbia Television

It's 2088, a century since inventor Max Taylor turned police work into a high-tech, super-efficient process—a legend his overshadowed great-grandson Channing struggles to surpass by single-handedly outperforming police technology. When Channing's efforts ruin a plan to catch malevolent Richard Marcus, Captain Stuart suspends him. Undeterred, Channing tracks and ambushes Marcus as the criminal steals a time machine, only to be dragged back to 1988 by the time-vortex.

Bewildered by the alien era, Channing hooks up with Max, a laughingstock among his fellow cops for his fixation on gadgets. Meanwhile, Marcus plots to steal a miracle drug that will be worth a fortune in the future. Channing's anachronistic behavior makes Max look an even bigger fool, but Pam—a waitress caught up in the case—convinces them to stick together and gets Channing to tell Max the truth about himself.

While Max meets his first moment of destiny—saving commuters from a tunnel collapse—Channing corners Marcus. When Max catches up to them, Marcus kills Max. Horrified, Channing uses the time machine to prevent the death and kill Marcus instead. Since this uses up the machine's power source, Channing remains trapped in the 20th century, working with Max and Pam.

This unsuccessful but amiable pilot co-starred Maher several years before he found fame as the host of *Politically Incorrect*.

THE OUTSIDER
Sci-Fi, 3/15/97

Cast: Dr. Garland Widmark (Gabriel Dell, Jr.), Outsider (Xavier DeClie), Astor (Stacey Williams), Greenstreet (David Leisure), Lita Hayworth (Bridget Flanery), Alan Houston (Lindsey Lee Ginter), Raines (Jerry Doyle), Claire Arden (Julia Dahl), Lorre (Willy Leong), Mason (Randy Kovitz), Rath (Bob Koherr), Bone (Glenn Takakjian), Ladd (Jerry Spicer), Wobba Wobba Girl (Gail Harris), Frat Boys (Michael Edwards, Paul Dallas), Housewife (Jody Fisher)

Credits: Director: David Bishop; Writers: Patrick Highsmith, Evan Spiliotopoulos; Story: Patrick Highsmith; Producer: Avi Nesher; Co-Producer: Kathy Jordan; Executive Producer: Pascal Borno; Photography: Irek Hartowicz; Production Design: Ted Berner; Music: Roger Neill; Editor: Randy Vandegrift; Produced by Mahagonny Pictures, Conquistador Entertainment

In 2028 crime and violence are channelled into Gangster Worlds, Roaring Twenties–style theme parks filled with androids the public can rape, maim or kill. In one park, the mysterious Kingpin programs the rogue android Outsider to kill Widmark, who is replacing the park's computer system. Widmark survives the attack, but his dream girl, Lita, is kidnapped. When Kingpin sends more androids to kill the Outsider for his failure, the Outsider and Widmark team up, while Kingpin hooks up with sadistic security chief Houston.

With help from android sexpot Astor, the guys rescue Lita and return to the park's control room. Widmark realizes that Kingpin is the computer, fighting replacement until it can download its program elsewhere—and blow up the park to cover its tracks. Despite Houston's murderous assault, the guys destroy the computer and escape the doomed park; Lita and Widmark are together, and the Outsider and Astor, in love, go off to explore the human world.

Though not outstanding, *The Outsider* has its moments—though all the thirties movie names (Astor, Hayworth, Greenstreet, Widmark) come off as a pointless joke. Catch *Babylon 5*'s Jerry Doyle in a supporting role.

THE PEOPLE
ABC, 1/22/72
Cast: Melodye Amerson (Kim Darby), Dr. Curtis (William Shatner), Valency (Diane Varsi), Sol Diemus (Dan O'Herlihy), Karen Dingus (Anne Walters), Francker (Chris Valentine), Bethie (Johanna Baer), Talitha (Stephanie Valentine), Kiah (Jack Dahlgreen), Thann (Andrew Crichton), Matt (David Petch), Dita (Dorothy Drady), Maras (Mary Rose McMaster), Obla (Anne Walters), Bram (Tony Dario), with Joy Carlin, Kenna Hunt, Kari Walos, Mark Bramhall, Tony Dario, Frank Albertson, Don Michaelian, Joe Miksak, Ray Goman
Credits: Director: John Korty; Writer: James M. Miller, based on Zenna Henderson's *Pilgrimage*; Producer: Gerald I. Isenberg; Executive Producer: Francis Ford Coppola; Photography: Edward Rosson; Art Director: Jack DeGovia; Music: Carmine Coppola; Editor: Patrick Kennedy; Produced by Metromedia Producers Corp., American Zoetrope

As a teacher in rural Bendo, restless, lonely Melodye can't help worrying about how the parents deny their children music, imagination and playtime. And Dr. Curtis wonders why no one ever, ever gets sick. And Melodye wonders about the oldsters' references to "sorting" and "remembering." Then Melodye scoffs at one student for believing in psychic powers; the boy responds by levitating her. Melodye is initially terrified, but Valency convinces her to stay around and help the People—descendants of shipwrecked ETs—embrace their powers instead of burying them for fear of human hostility. Melodye encourages the children to practice their powers, and when a young boy is critically injured in levitation class, Melodye convinces the People to let Valency use her powers to heal him. Afterward, Curtis and Melodye decide to stay and help the People find ways to help the world in secret.

Zenna Henderson's folksy, gently sentimental stories of the People (collected in *Pilgrimage* and *No Different Flesh*) have a devoted following; while slow-paced at times, this is a pleasant adaptation. *Star Trek*'s William Shatner stars as Curtis.

PERFECT LITTLE ANGELS
Family, 11/8/98
Cast: Elaine Freedman (Cheryl Ladd), Justine (Jody Thompson), Brad Montgomery (Jade Pawluck), Mitch Farress (Brendan Fehr), Lois Morgan (Tanya Reichert), Dr. Calvin Lawrence (Michael York), Jeff (David Paetnau), Doug (John Hawkes), Kelly (Chara Zann), Niki (Lisa Marie Caruk), David (Dwayne Dickinson), April Dandy (Elizabeth Carol Sauvenkoff), Minister (Laurie Murdoch), Leslie Montgomery (Donna Lysell), Gary Montgomery (Allan Lysell), Eugene Morgan (Douglas Stewart), Vera Morgan (Kathleen Duborg), Desk Sergeant (Frank Ferrucci), Guard (Doug Abrahams)
Credits: Director: Timothy Bond; Writer: Bart Baker, based on Andrew Neiderman's book; Producer: James Shavick; Associate Producers: David Richardson, Marie Giroux; Supervising Producer: Simon Abbott; Photography: Peter Benison; Production Design: Brian Davie; Music:

Ken Williams; Editors: Jeremy Presner, Dona Noga; Produced by Fox Family Channel, TVA International, Shavick Entertainment

When Elaine Freedman and daughter Justine move into Elysium Meadows, Justine freaks at the wholesome community—and at how violent the kids become when she and her new boyfriend Mitch refuse to fit in. Elaine, however, soon conforms to the whitebread world, doting on town founder Lawrence. When Justine and Mitch investigate Lawrence, Justine is caught and drugged into submission, but Mitch can't prove it. He discovers that Lawrence set up Elysium Meadows after the government cut funding for his brainwashing experiments. Sneaking back, Mitch deprograms Justine, and they replace Elaine's control drugs. Elaine comes to and finds she's about to marry Lawrence—and his enslaved community won't let her back out. At the last minute, Justine destroys the equipment broadcasting Lawrence's orders; the town comes free, Lawrence goes to jail and Elysium Meadows reverts to the chaos of normal life.

This dull knockoff of the *Stepford* films is the kind that implies making jokes about how clichéd it is excuses the clichés.

PETER BENCHLEY'S "CREATURE"
ABC, 5/17–5/18/98

Cast: Simon Chase (Craig T. Nelson), Amanda (Kim Cattrall), Max Chase (Matthew Carey), Richland (Colm Feore), Tall Man (Cress Williams), Adam Puckett (Michael Reilly Burke), Tauna Toi (Michael Michele), Elizabeth (Megalyn Echikunwoke), Rollie (Blu Mankuma), Ben Madiera (John Aylward), Werewolf (Giancarlo Esposito), Dr. Ernest Bishop (Gary Reineke), Bobby Tobin (James Coleman), Dr. Bastian (Gandolph St. Clair), Nathan (Kennedy Samuel), Exec (Antoni Cornocchione), Exec's Buddy (Peter Benchley), Kyrstine (Toi Syane), Kimo (Michael Aubertin), Seal Gray (Jill Teed), Seal Leader Taylor (Steve Makoz), Seal Ochoa (Rob Daprocida), Seal Nash (Rick Ravanello), Seal Yock (Warren Takeuchi), Communications Officer (Colin Lawrence), Robbi (Juliana Prospero), Old Woman (Elvira Riggs), Creature (Brian Steel)

Credits: Director: Stuart Gillard; Writer–Co-Producer: Rockne S. O'Bannon, based on Peter Benchley's *White Shark*; Producer: Brent Karl Clackson; Executive Producers: Richard Barton Lewis, Pen Densham, John Watson, Mark Stern, Robert Halmi, Jr.; Photography: Thomas Burstyn; Special Effects–Creature: Stan Winston; Production Design: Michael Joy, Stan Joy; Music: John Van Tongeren; Editor: Rick Martin; Produced by Trilogy Entertainment, MGM

The inhabitants of Sharkstooth Island only scoff when ichthyologist Simon Chase insists the recent shark attacks are actually caused by something worse. But Chase is right: The killer is a genetically engineered shark/human/dolphin hybrid created by the navy as an aquatic weapon, then trapped on the sea floor for 25 years after it escaped. Now it's loose, able to kill on land or sea, and potentially able to reproduce by interbreeding with regular sharks. Chase calls the navy, who sends a squad to kill the creature—but it butchers them. Finally, Chase traps the creature inside the base's pressure chamber and shatters the windows, creating an abrupt pressure change that explodes the monster from inside.

This formulaic monster film was freely adapted (in the original, the monster was a Nazi experiment) from one of Benchley's repeated attempts to clone his best-selling *Jaws*. Despite using the same creature creator as *Jurassic Park*, this is pretty lame—and way too long at four hours.

THE PHOENIX
ABC, 4/26/81

Cast: Bennu (Judson Scott), Diego De Varga (Fernando Allende), Dr. Ward Frazier (E.G. Marshall), Noel Marshall (Shelley Smith), Dr. Cliff Davis (Darryl Anderson), Lynn (Hersha Parady), Tim (Jimmy Mair), Howard (Lyman Ward), Kingston (Carmen Argenziano), Murray (Stanley Kamel), Surgeon (Angus Duncan), Patrolman (Wayne Storm), Hood (Terry Jastrow), Technician (Bret Williams), Anesthesiologist (Paul Marin), Nurse (Patricia Conklin), Croupier (James Malinda)

Credits: Director: Douglas Hickox; Writer-Producers: Anthony Lawrence, Nancy Lawrence; Executive Producer: Mark Carliner; Associate Producer: Carol Coates-West; Photography: Don H. Birnkrant, Richard A. Kelly; Production Design: William T. McAllister; Music: Arthur B. Rubinstein; Editor: David Berlatsky; Produced by Mark Carliner Productions

Archeologists find a sealed Egyptian

sarcophagus in a Mayan temple, take it to a research lab and open it to find Bennu, a humanoid ET, in suspended animation within. But head researcher Frazier scoffs at the idea Bennu could be one of the "ancient astronauts" past civilizations worshipped as gods. Bennu revives and escapes, hiding out with pretty Noel, but his solar-powered body can't survive the polluted atmosphere without special equipment. He contacts Frazier, who agrees to buy the equipment if Bennu can find the money. Bennu's psychic powers enable him to win the money at a crooked casino and escape the management's violent displeasure.

De Varga, a Mexican official who sees Bennu as a living symbol of his country's glorious past, tracks Frazier and Bennu and eventually captures the alien. Noel helps Bennu escape, then dies saving a drowning boy. Bennu sets out alone to learn why he was sent to Earth, helped by Frazier and pursued by De Varga.

The idea of gods-as-extraterrestrials dates back to the forties in SF, but it went mainstream in the seventies due to the popularity of Erich Von Däniken's *Chariots of the Gods*, which presented "ancient astronauts" as historical reality. This is a very lame treatment, and Scott (best known for his role in *Star Trek II: The Wrath of Khan*) is incredibly wooden in the lead, but it did lead to a short-lived series.

PLANET EARTH
ABC, 4/23/74

Cast: Dylan Hunt (John Saxon), Harper-Smythe (Janet Margolin), Marg (Diana Muldaur), Isaiah (Ted Cassidy), Baylok (Christopher Cary), Villar (Jo DeWinter), Yuloff (Majel Barrett), Dr. Jonathan Connor (Jim Antonio), Treece (Sally Kemp), Delba (Claire Brennan), Bronta (Corinne Camacho), Thetis (Sarah Chattin), Kreeg Commandant (John Quade), Skylar (Patricia Smith), Kreeg Captain (Raymond Sutton), Peter Kimbridge (Rai Tasco), Gorda (Aron Kincaid), Partha (James Bacon), Kyla (Joan Crosby), Merlo (Lew Brown), Harpsichordist (Craig Hunde), Dinks (Robert McAndrew, Bob Golden), Little Girl (Susan Page)

Credits: Director: Marc Daniels; Writers: Gene Roddenberry, Juanita Bartlett; Story: Gene Roddenberry; Producer: Robert H. Justman; Executive Producer: Gene Roddenberry; Photography: Arch R. Dalzell; Art Director: Robert Kinoshita; Music: Harry Sukman; Editor: George Watters; Produced by Warner Bros.

In this sequel to *Genesis II*, Hunt's Pax exploration team is attacked by the militaristic Kreegs, and Kimbridge is critically injured. Only Dr. Connor has a hope of saving Kimbridge—and Connor has vanished in matriarchal Ruth. To find him, Harper-Smythe enters Ruth with Hunt as her slave—but the Ruthian Marg defeats her in combat and claims Hunt.

Hunt finds Ruthian men—"dinks"—are drugged to keep them submissive; he avoids taking the drug but his defiance arouses both Marg's anger and her interest. With the backing of Ruthian moderates, who control their men without drugs, Harper-Smythe confronts Marg and reclaims Hunt—but when they discover Marg also owns Connor, Harper-Smythe swaps the two men. While Harper-Smythe and Connor provide the dinks with an antidote, Hunt plays mind games with and seduces a bewildered Marg. When the Kreegs attack Ruth, Marg's drug-free dinks fight alongside Hunt, which reluctantly convinces her and other Ruthians to abandon the drugs. The team returns to Pax in time to save Kimbridge.

After *Genesis II* failed, Roddenberry turned one of his planned series scripts into this second pilot, with John Saxon (star of dozens of genre B-movies, and a supporting player in *A Nightmare on Elm Street*) replacing Alex Cord in the lead. It's competent but clichéd, with its assumption that all dominant women need is a real man to change their thinking (but unlike many SF stories on this theme, the matriarchy isn't overthrown, only softened). No series resulted, so Warner Bros. reworked the premise again as *Strange New World*.

PLYMOUTH
ABC, 5/26/91

Cast: Donna (Robin Frates), Simon (Joseph Gordon-Levitt), Wendell Mackenzie (Richard Hamilton), Lowell (Jerry Hardin), Gil Eaton

(Dale Midkiff), Dr. Addy Mattheson (Perrey Reeves), Hannah Mattheson (Cindy Pickett), Percy (Ron Vawter), Jed Mattheson (Matthew Brown), Ezra (James R. Rebhorn), Nathan Litchfield (Brent Fraser), Emily (Anne Haney), Eugene (John Thornton), April (Lindsay Price), Debra (Fran Bennett), Hito (Sab Shimono), Ernie (Paul Linke), Paddy (James T. Callahan), Todd (Gary Farmer), Bethsay (Wendy Bowers), Charles Conrad Jr. as Himself, Marshall (Eric Chambers), Woman (Jeanine Jackson), Sean (Erik F. Stabenau), Rache (Kyra Stempel), Technician (Mark Phelan)

Credits: Director-Writer-Executive Producer: Lee David Zlotoff; Producer: Ian Sander; Executive Producer: Ralph Winter; Photography: Hiro Narita; Production Design: Michael Baugh; Music: Brad Fiedel; Editor: John W. Wheeler; Produced by Zlotoff, Inc., Raiuno, Touchstone TV

When UniDac's toxic waste spill destroyed the mining town of Plymouth, UniDac offered to relocate the community to the moon, where they could stay together and revive UniDac's failed mining colony. The townsfolk agreed. Now, in addition to romantic problems and misbehaving children, Plymouth faces a crisis: Town doctor Addy is pregnant (by UniDac pilot Gil), and a baby born in lunar gravity might not survive on Earth (but flying home before birth might be fatal too). Gil wins over the town by saving a mining crew from a solar flare. After Addy decides to give birth on the moon, Gil opts to stay, even after he's fast-talked into becoming Plymouth's new mayor.

This is one of TV's occasional attempts to mix SF and soap opera (others include *Generations* and the 1998 series *Mercy Point*). Midkiff later had the starring role in *Time Trax*.

POOR DEVIL
NBC, 2/14/73

Cast: Sammy (Sammy Davis, Jr.), Lucifer (Christopher Lee), Burnett Emerson (Jack Klugman), Bligh (Gino Conforti), Jannes Crawford (Adam West), Frances Emerson (Madlyn Rhue), Chelsea (Emily Yancy), Mr. Moriarty (Alan Manson), Desk Sergeant (Ken Lynch), Blackbeard (Byron Webster), Al Capone (Buddy Lester), Tom (Owen Bush), Bob Younger (Nick Georiade), Eddie (Don Ross), Woman (Lila Teigh), Father-in-Law (Stephen Coit), Secretary (Jo DeWinter), Cole Younger (George Kramer), Clyde Barrow (Clyde Ventura), Bonnie (Nancy Reichert), John Younger (Tom Wize), James Younger (David Young)

Credits: Director: Robert Scheerer; Writers: Arne Sultan, Earl Barret, Richard Bare; Producer: Robert Stambler; Executive Producers: Arne Sultan, Earl Barret; Photography: Howard R. Schwartz; Art Director: Monty Elliott; Music: Morton Stevens; Editors: Robert Kern, Jr., Mike Vejar; Produced by Paramount

Of all the devils in hell, none are more inept than Sammy, who's never corrupted even a single mortal—but when accountant Emerson learns he's lost a promotion to bootlicker Crawford, he sells his soul to Sammy for revenge. Sammy has the store robbed—which Crawford reports—then returns everything so that Crawford looks like an idiot. Emerson's delighted (and promoted), until it sinks in that going to hell means eternal separation from his virtuous wife. Good-hearted Sammy can't bear Emerson's dismay—so when he recalls that Emerson kept a stolen watch from the store, Sammy proclaims their bargain broken (he was told to return *everything*). Emerson gets his promotion, keeps his soul—and a furious Lucifer sends Sammy back to stoking infernal furnaces.

Teens would have thought this unsuccessful pilot was pretty funny, but the critical consensus that it's appallingly stupid is more accurate. Familiar faces include horror legend Christopher Lee slumming as Lucifer, and former Batman, Adam West.

THE POSSESSED
NBC, 5/1/77

Cast: Kevin Leahy (James Farentino), Louise Gelson (Joan Hackett), Ellen Sumner (Claudette Nevins), Sgt. Taplinger (Eugene Roche), Paul Winjam (Harrison Ford), Weezie Sumner (Ann Dusenberry), Lane (Diana Scarwid), Celia (Dinah Manoff), Alex (Carol Jones), Marty (P.J. Soles), Barry (Ethelinn Block), Student (Susan Walden), with Lawrence Bame, James Parkes, Catherine Cunneff

Credits: Director-Executive Producer: Jerry Thorpe; Writer: John Sacret Young; Producer: Philip Mandelker; Photography: Charles G. Arnold; Art Director: Fredric P. Hope; Music: Leonard Rosenman; Editor: Michael A. Hoey; Produced by Warner Bros.

When faithless, alcoholic, womanizing priest Leahy flatlines in a car accident, a voice tells him he will not die—and that he must redeem himself by fighting evil in all its forms. When clothes, rooms and papers keep spontaneously combusting at a Catholic girls' school, the headmistress' sister and assistant, Ellen, calls Leahy in to investigate. The fires center on Ellen's daughter Weezie, who's having an affair with biology teacher Paul. When he breaks it off, another fire breaks out and he's killed. As the school gives in to terror, headmistress Gelson goes increasingly insane; finally, she's possessed by the demon, but Leahy stares it down and drives it off. He vanishes mysteriously, leaving the school safe.

The Possessed is dull, draggy and really pointless (Why was the demon there? Why did it go? Don't ask.); but look for pre-fame Harrison Ford in a supporting role. John Sacret Young created the short-lived SF series *VR 5*, though he's better known for *China Beach*.

THE POSSESSION OF MICHAEL D.
Fox, 5/29/95

Cast: Michael D. (Stephen Lang), Jenny (Sheila McCarthy), Dr. Nick Galler (Michael Riley), Robin Banks (Roger Rees), Dr. Marion Hale (Phylicia Rashad), Dr. Jerry (Bernard Behrens), Allyson (Cecilley Carroll), Priest (Vernon Chapman), David (Richard Chevolleau), Sheila (Tracey Cook), Charlotte (Diane D'Aquila), Marcel (Don Francks), Neurologist (Nicki Gaudagni), Young Michael (Ryan Gifford), Helene (Linda Goranson), Police Chief (Ron Lea), Arthur (Peter MacNeill), Gale (Brittany Madgett), Justin (Max Piersig), Anne (Sara Sahr), Holly (Mishu Vellani)

Credits: Director: Michael Kennedy; Writer: Ronald Parker; Producer: Jonathan Hackett; Executive Producers: Peter Sussman, Ed Gernon, Graham Flashner; Associate Producer: John Harcourt; Photography: Manfred Guthe; Production Design: Wendy Morrow; Music: John McCarthy; Editor: Robin Russell; Produced by Atlantis Films, Flashner/Gernon Productions, CTV Television

Michael and his new wife Jenny discover his violent behavior is the result of possession by the same demon that possessed his late father. The demon wants to wreck their marriage, but intensive hypnotherapy and Jenny's love give Michael the strength to banish it.

This is yet another dull, based-on-truth drama; Rees had a supporting role in the *M.A.N.T.I.S.* series.

THE POWER WITHIN
ABC, 5/11/79

Cast: Chris Darrow (Art Hindle), Gen. Tom Darrow (Edward Binns), Bill Camelli (Joe Rassulo), Stephens (Eric Braeden), Dr. Joanna Miller (Susan Howard), Danton (David Hedison), Capt. Ed Holman (Dick Sargent), Marvalee (Karen Lamm), Grandma (Isabell MacCloskey), Small Boy (K.C. Martel), Guards (Chris Wallace, Bill Sorrells), Rancher (John Dennis)

Credits: Director: John Llewellyn Moxey; Writer: William Clark; Producer: Alan Godfrey; Supervising Producer: E. Duke Vincent; Executive Producers: Aaron Spelling, Douglas S. Cramer; Associate Producer-Supervising Editor: Michael S. McLean; Photography: Emil Oster; Art Directors: Tom Trimble, Paul Sylos; Music: John Addison; Editor: Dennis C. Duckwall; Produced by Aaron Spelling Productions

When lightning strikes impetuous, free-spirited barnstormer Chris Darrow, it transforms him into a super-strong, lightning-throwing dynamo. Chris turns to his estranged father, General Darrow, for answers. Military researcher Miller discovers that Chris is a mutant immune to small electric shocks, but absorbing the lightning means Chris must now maintain an electrical charge or die. Horrified at being dependent on electricity (or anything), Chris leaves the base, but accepts an implant that helps him maintain his charge.

A group of spies, thinking Chris is testing a suspended-animation implant for long spaceflight, decides to capture him. When Chris defeats them with his powers, they kidnap Miller for the information. Although Chris' charge is running low, he and his buddy Bill track the spies from their plane, rescue Miller, capture the villains—and barely make it back to base for a lifesaving recharge. Out of gratitude to Darrow, Chris and Bill agree to take on special missions in the future.

There are a lot of traditional super-hero elements in this origin, but like most seventies super-hero stories, the villains are a weak lot. This unsuccessful pilot was called *Power Man* right up until the airing (possibly, it was changed because Marvel Comics had its own Power Man character). Sargent, of course, was the second actor who played Darrin in *Bewitched*.

PRISONERS OF THE LOST UNIVERSE
Showtime, 8/15/83

Cast: Dan Roebuck (Richard Hatch), Carrie Madison (Kay Lenz), Kleel (John Saxon), Malachi (Peter O'Farrell), Greenman (Ray Charleson), Dr. Hartmann (Kenneth Hendel), Kashar (Philip Van Der Byl), Vosk (Larry Taylor), Shareen (Dawn Abraham), Head Trader (Ron Smerczak), Treet (Charles Comyn), Prisoners (Ian Steadman, Bill Flynn), Giant Nabu (Danie Voges), Waterbeast (Myles Robertson)

Credits: Director: Terry Marcel; Writer-Producers: Terry Marcel, Harry Robertson; Executive Producer: John Hardy; Associate Producer: Denis Johnson, Jr.; Photography: Derek Browne; Art Director: John Runciman; Music: Harry Robertson; Editor: Alan Jones; Produced by Marcel-Robertson Productions, United Media Finance

An earthquake disrupts Dr. Hartmann's prototype dimensional gateway, sucking first him, then reporter Carrie and martial artist Dan into a primitive parallel world. Carrie is captured by Kleel, a warlord forcing Hartmann to provide him with guns. Dan acquires allies (Malachi the thief, the alien Greenman, the giant Nabu) with whom he survives the perils and monsters of the alien wilderness, but they're captured when they penetrate Kleel's fortress. Carrie convinces Hartmann to help them escape, then they use the scientist's explosive stockpile to destroy Kleel and his fortress. Locating the gateway, Carrie and Dan return home.

An adventure in the *Flash Gordon* tradition (except *Flash Gordon* was good), this is a dull mess with uninteresting monsters and weak special effects, and it saddles the talented Lenz with a sexist spunky-but-helpless screamer role. Familiar faces include Hatch (*Battlestar Galactica*) and Saxon (*A Nightmare on Elm Street*).

PROJECT: ALF
ABC, 2/17/96

Cast: Voice of ALF (Paul Fusco), Maj. Melissa Hill (Jensen Daggett), Captain Rick Mullican (William O'Leary), Col. Milfoil (Martin Sheen), Dr. Dexter Moyers (Miguel Ferrer), Lt. Reese (Scott Michael Campbell), General Myron Stone (John Schuck), Motel Manager (Ray Walston), Dr. Warner (Ed Begley, Jr.), Dr. Tomlin (Beverly Archer), Dr. Stanley (Charlie Robinson), Cop (Greg Alan Williams), Nina (Liz Coke), Dr. Mockton (Dell Yount), Nigel Neville (Dennis Creaghan), Dr. Newman (Lenny Wolpe), Murphy (Michael Weatherred), Sgt. Rhomboid (Markus Redmond), Undermeyer (Michael Laskin), Farnsworth (Ann Gee Byrd), Pete Meatman (Jeremiah Burkett), S.P. (F.J. Rio), Waitress (Lynn Tufeld), Bouncer (Randy Oglesby), Ernie (W. Earl Brown), Gate Guard (Lee Arenberg), Rocket (Erick Avari, voice), Guards (Willem Keane, Ahmet Zappa), Waitress (Lin Shaye), Man (John Dunbar), TV Assistant (Kim Strauss)

Credits: Director: Dick Lowry; Writers: Tom Patchett, Paul Fusco; Supervising Producer: Ann Kindberg; Producer: Tom Patchett; Executive Producers: Paul Fusco, Kenneth Kaufman; Photography: Henry Lebo; Production Design: Guy Barnes; Music: Mark Snow; Editor: William B. Stitch; Produced by Paul Fusco Productions, UFA Filmproduction Berlin, Patchett Kaufman Entertainment

Years ago, Gordon, an Alien Life Form (ALF) from the doomed planet Melmack, crash-landed on Earth and moved in with the Tanner family—only to be captured by the government in the last episode. Several years later, ALF is still undergoing endless lab tests (while running a gambling ring à la Sgt. Bilko from his military prison). When the government refuses xenophobic Milfoil's request to terminate ALF, Milfoil plots a fatal lab "accident." Researchers Mullican and Hill learn of Milfoil's plans and go on the run with the obnoxious, gluttonous alien, stoically enduring the endless trouble ALF causes.

The humans hook up with Moyers, an ex–NASA scientist who convinces them to reveal ALF's existence on national TV; his real agenda is to discredit his old bosses by exposing their cover-up, then auction ALF to the highest bidder. Mullican contacts Milfoil, who stops the broadcast, then prepares to kill ALF—but Mullican videotapes Milfoil's murderous ranting and uses it to discredit him. Hill and Mullican get promotions (and each other), and ALF gets his freedom.

ALF's experiences with the Tanners made *ALF* (and the cartoon spin-off *AlfTales*) a phenomenally successful show, running from 1986 to 1990—though many found the Melmackian more irritating than amusing. He's just as irritating squeezed into a stock alien-runs-from-feds plot (a shame, since the idea is so ripe for send-up). And what on Earth is a major actor like Sheen doing here?

PROTOTYPE
CBS, 12/7/83

Cast: Dr. Carl Forrester (Christopher Plummer), Michael (David Morse), Dorothy Forrester (Frances Sternhagen), Dr. Gene Pressman (James Sutorius), Dr. Arthur Jarrett (Stephen Elliott), Chris (Doran Clark), Dr. Rebecca Bishop (Alley Mills), General Keating (Arthur Hill), Guard (Ed Call), Dr. Cooper (Jonathan Estrin), Harris (Richard Kuss), Landlord (Pat McNamara), Kirk (Vahan Moosekian)

Credits: Director: David Greene; Writer-Executive Producers: Richard Levinson, William Link; Producer: Robert A. Papazian; Associate Producers: Stephanie Austin; Photography: Harry J. May; Art Director: Bill Ross; Music: Billy Goldenberg; Editor: Parkie Singh; Produced by Richard Levinson/William Link Productions, Robert Papazian Productions

After years of research and experimentation, Dr. Forrester has created Michael, a self-aware android ... only to realize with horror that the military plans to use his innocent, childlike creation as a prototype super-warrior. Taking Michael, Forrester goes on the lam, trying to stay out of the military's grasp. Michael becomes increasingly conflicted and insecure about his artificial nature (especially after catching *Frankenstein* on TV). Eventually, Michael tells Forrester he's going to commit suicide by fire—since with the prototype destroyed, the government will have to meet Forrester's terms to get another android. Sadly, Forrester allows his "son" to die, then returns to negotiate with the government.

Prototype is proof that even a clichéd concept (see *J.O.E. and the Colonel, Assassin, Chameleon*, etc.) can be made fresh with gifted performances and a sensitive script (by the screenwriters of *Columbo*—among many other things).

PSYCHIC
USA, 5/20/92

Cast: Patrick Costello (Zach Galligan), Laurel Young (Catherine Mary Stewart), Dr. Ted Steering (Michael Nouri), Nick (Albert Schultz), Markowitz (Ken James), Spencer (Clark Johnson), April Harris (Andrea Roth), Woman in Club (Susan Norton), Susi (Lisa Lacroix), Fitzgerald (Geza Kovacs), Lucinda (Catherine Disher), Resort Clerk (Don Ritchie), Tattoo Artist (Myra Fried), Hoop Earring (Khan Agha Soroor), Julie Richard (Sandi Stahlbrand), Desk Sgt. (Bob Zidel), Security Officers (Michael Ricupero, Darryl Palmer), Francis Crockett (Bill Tarling)

Credits: Director: George Mihalka; Writers: Miguel Tejada-Flores, Paul Koval; Story: Mark McQuade Crawford, William Crawford; Producer: Tom Berry; Co-Producers: Stefan Wodoslawsky, John Rainey; Co-Executive Producers: Franco Battista, Deborah Thomas; Photography: Ludek Bogner; Production Design: Perri Gorrara; Editor: Paul Ziller; Music: Milan Kymlicka; Produced by Allegro, Westwind

Patrick, a psychic college student, seduces his teacher, Laurel, by sensing exactly what she wants from a man; he's also suffering visions of a serial killer at work, but having destroyed a man with false accusations years before, he's reluctant to get involved. Then he realizes the killer is Laurel's other boyfriend, Ted. Unable to convince anyone, Patrick tries and fails to prevent the next murder. Laurel, shocked at his accusing Ted, breaks up with him and goes off with Ted—and discovers proof he's the killer. Ted attacks her, but Patrick, guided by his powers, arrives in time to help Laurel escape.

This is a good psychic-vs.-killer film. Familiar faces include Galligan (*Gremlins*), Stewart (*Night of the Comet, Last Starfighter*) and Nouri (*Cliffhangers: The Curse of Dracula*).

THE QUESTOR TAPES
NBC, 1/23/74

Cast: Questor (Robert Foxworth), Jerry Robinson (Mike Farrell), Geoffrey Daro (John Vernon), Vaslovik (Lew Ayres), Dr. Chen (James Shigeta), Dr. Michaels (Robert Douglas), Lady Helena Trimble (Dana Wynter), Allison Sample (Ellen Weston), Dr. Bradley (Majel Barrett), Dr. Gorlov (Reuben Singer), Administrative Assistant (Walter Koenig), Dr. Audret (Fred Sadoff), Randolph (Gerald Saunderson Peters), Stewardess (Eyde Girard), Immigration Officer (Alan Caillou), Colonel Hendricks (Lal Baum), Secretary (Patti Cubbison)

Credits: Director: Richard A. Colla; Writers: Gene L. Coon, Gene Roddenberry; Story-Executive Producer: Gene Roddenberry; Producer: Howie Hurwitz; Photography: Michael Margulies; Art Director: Phil Barber; Music: Gil Melle; Editors: J. Terry Williams, Robert J. Kimble; Produced by Universal

Jerry Robinson is part of a massive research project building an android from plans by mysterious, vanished Dr. Vaslovik. When the android doesn't activate, Jerry protests his superiors' plan to cannibalize the advanced components; security chief Daro suspects Jerry has a hidden agenda. The android, Questor, activates itself, but errors in construction have left him emotionless and ignorant of his purpose—so he kidnaps Jerry to help him find Vaslovik. Convinced Jerry stole Questor, Daro organizes a manhunt. Questor and Jerry flee to London, becoming friends as they go.

Questor's programming leads them to Lady Helena, a high-powered prostitute involved in international intrigue. She shows Questor Vaslovik's hidden lair, from which the doctor could monitor anything in the world (famine in Africa, congressional adultery). Alarmed by the implications, Jerry calls Daro—then learns that Questor's nuclear power source will detonate in three days if they don't find Vaslovik. Daro captures them, damaging Questor, but he agrees to let them go in return for Jerry repairing the android. Questor tracks Vaslovik to an underground base where Vaslovik reveals he's an android too, one of many sent from space to help humanity. Questor is the last, assigned to guide—but never coerce—us through the nuclear age.

Jerry volunteers to help the emotionless android understand humanity; Daro, having followed and overheard all this, sacrifices himself to distract his men from Jerry and Questor's escape. The hunt over, the duo go about their great mission.

Although *The Questor Tapes* is probably the most interesting of Roddenberry's post–*Star Trek* pilots (though *Spectre*, perhaps, is more fun), Universal execs reportedly couldn't quite "get" the premise. It features *Trek* alumni Majel Barrett and Walter Koenig in small roles.

QUICKSILVER HIGHWAY
Fox, 5/13/97

Cast: Professor Quicksilver (Christopher Lloyd), Charlie/Dr. George (Matt Frewer), Kerry Parker/Hogan (Raphael Sbarge), Olivia Harmon Parker (Missy Crider), Hitchhiker (Silas Weir Mitchell), Jeudwine (Bill Nunn), Myra (Veronica Cartwright), Scooter (Bill Bolender), Anesthesiologist (Clive Barker), Eliza (Cynthia Garris), Cop (Kevin Grevioux), Lefty (Christopher Hart), Rhinoplasty Man (William Knight), Surgical Assistant (John Landis), Driver (Shawn Nelson), Harriet DaVinci (Sherry O'Keefe), Hand Chaser (Dana Waters), Female Patient (Constance Zimmer), with Amelia Heinle

Credits: Director-Writer-Producer: Mick Garris, based on "Chattery Teeth" by Stephen King and "The Body Politic" by Clive Barker; Producer: Ron Mitchell; Executive Producers: John McTiernan, Donna Dubrow, Sandra Rugh; Co-Executive Producers: Tarquin Gotch, Bob Lemchen; Photography: Shelly Johnson; Production Design: Craig Stearns; Music: Mark Mothersbaugh; Editor: Norman Hollyn; Produced by National Studios, 20th Television

In this two-tale anthology built around Professor Quicksilver's carny sideshow curio collection, the first story (the order is reversed on video), "Body Politic," has pickpocket Charlie hiding in Quicksilver's tent, where he learns how surgeon George's hands literally took on a life of their own. Despite George's resistance, one hand is cut free while the other rallies all hands to turn on their owners. George overcomes the growing hand army by leaping to his death with their leader (the army follows loyally and dies too). Charlie scoffs at the tale, but when he leaves, his hands pick a pocket on their own—and get him caught.

In the second story, "Chattery Teeth," Olivia waits for her husband in the tent and hears how a salesman named Hogan picked up a set of "chattering teeth" from a roadside diner, which then killed a hitchhiker who tried to murder Hogan. When Olivia's husband returns, he's hit by a car—and the teeth appear and drag off his body.

This was a deservedly failed pilot—the King segment is just pointless, and "Body Politic" is a weak adaptation of an absolutely brilliant story. Familiar faces include Frewer (*Max Headroom*), Lloyd (*Buckaroo Banzai* and *Back to the Future*) and horror author Barker in a cameo.

RAVAGER
Sci-Fi, 9/6/97

Cast: Avedon Hammond (Yancy Butler), Cooper Wayne (Bruce Payne), Lazarus (Salvator Xuereb), Dr. Shephard (Robin Sachs), Cade (David Stratton), Sarra (Juliet Landau), Mick McClean (Stanley Kamel)

Credits: Director: James D. Deek; Writers: Donald J. Loperfido, James D. Deek; Executive Director: John Fremes; Producers: Stanley Isaacs, Scott McGinnis, Robert Patrick; Photography: Adam Kane; Costumes: Kristin M. Burke; Special Effects: Corbitt Design; Editor: Nicholas Edgar; Music: John E. Nordstrom; Produced by 360 Entertainment, Le Monde Entertainment, Republic Pictures

It's a bad day for transport pilot Hammond: The military requisitions her ship to carry a secret cargo; her old lover Wayne is put in charge; and he's making a fast buck by illegally carrying assorted shady passengers. When the ship crashes near an abandoned bio-weapon lab, a "Ravager" viral weapon infects some of the survivors and turns them homicidal. Infection and murder spread until only Wayne, Hammond and passenger Sarra remain alive and sane. When repairs are done, the infected, insane McClean tries to leave without the others. They make it on board and Wayne regains control of the ship, triggers the self-destruct and dies fending off McClean while the women take an escape pod.

This is boring. Butler had more fun as a co-star of *Mann and Machine*; Landau (a semi-regular on *Buffy the Vampire Slayer*) is daughter of veteran star Martin Landau.

THE RETURN OF SHERLOCK HOLMES
CBS, 1/10/87

Cast: Sherlock Holmes (Michael Pennington), Jane Watson (Margaret Colin), Tobias Gregory (Nicholas Guest), Houston (Lila Kaye), Violet Morstan (Connie Booth), Carter Morstan (Barry Morse), Spellman (William Hootkins), Doctor (Tony Steedman), Hopkins (Paul Maxwell), Lysander Stark (Shane Rimmer), Hampton (Oliver Pierre), Kitty (Sheila Brand), Singer (Ray Jewers), Ross (Daniel Benzali), with John Sterland, Miles Richardson, Debora Weston, Hubert Tucker, Ricco Ross, Nancy Paul, Sneh Gufta, Howard Swinson

Credits: Director: Kevin Connor; Writer: Bob Shayne, partly based on Doyle's *The Sign of the Four*; Producer: Nick Gillott; Production Design: Keith Wilson; Photography: Tony Imi; Music: Ken Thorne; Editor: Bernard Gribble; Produced by CBS Entertainment, Eyemark Entertainment

When Boston PI Jane Watson visits her ancestral home in England, she finds Sherlock Holmes cryonically preserved in the basement (to save his life after Moriarty's family infected him with a plague). Cured by modern medicine, Holmes accompanies Watson back to America, where they're embroiled in a case involving a fortune in missing counterfeit money, the reappearance of long-vanished hijacker Small, and Small's murder of retired fed Morstan. Holmes discovers that Morstan was paid to dispose of the counterfeit (evidence in a major case), so he swapped it for Small's ransom: Morstan and his partners became rich, while a bewildered Small went to jail for passing counterfeit—and now Small wants revenge. In reality, Morstan is the killer (having first eliminated Small, he's now killing his partners), but Holmes accuses Morstan's daughter Violet in order to draw Morstan out where federal agent Gregory can capture him. Gregory,

Watson and Holmes decide they'll remain a crimefighting team.

Sherlock Holmes has appeared in more movies than any other character; this failed pilot is fairly entertaining, but *1994 Baker Street* did the same idea better.

THE RETURN OF THE HULK
CBS, 11/28/77

Cast: Dr. David Banner (Bill Bixby), The Hulk (Lou Ferrigno), Jack McGee (Jack Colvin), Julie Griffith (Laurie Prange), Margaret Griffith (Dorothy Tristan), Denny (Gerald McRaney), Dr. Bonifant (William Daniels), Michael (John McLiam), Sheriff (Mills Watson), Rafe (Victor Mohica), Phil (Robert Phillips), Nurses (Ann Weldon, Linda Wiser, Janet Adams), Lab Technician (Roger Aaron Brown), Receptionist (Socorro Swan), Maid (Rita Gomez), Cuban (Rick Garcia)

Credits: Director: Alan Levi; Writer-Producer: Kenneth Johnson; Photography: Charles W. Short; Art Director: David Marshall; Music: Joseph Harnell; Editors: Jack Schoengarth, Glenn C. Lawrence; Produced by Universal Television

In this follow-up to *The Incredible Hulk*, David Banner heads for a radiology lab he thinks might cure him. He befriends lonely, wealthy, paraplegic Julie and discovers her doctor, Bonifant, is poisoning her. David warns Julie's stepmother, Margaret, about the poisoning, unaware that she's behind it. Margaret cons Julie's suitor Denny into assaulting David, who "Hulks out," clobbers Denny and his buddies, then runs off.

After reverting to normal, David sneaks into the local hospital where he learns one more dose of poison will finish Julie—just as Margaret and Bonifant murdered Julie's father. Julie doesn't believe David's story; their angry argument turns him back into the Hulk, who carries Julie to the comparative safety of the nearby swamp. Between David's brains and the Hulk's brawn, they make it through the swamp—and when the Hulk is caught in quicksand, Julie forces herself to walk again to save him. The murderers go to jail and David gets his radiation treatment—but since he can't be sure it worked, he has to go on the run again when McGee shows up hunting the Hulk.

This sequel set up the format for the series, a knockoff of *The Fugitive* with David turning into the Hulk to save the day (that being said, it's much better written and performed than most *Fugitive* clones, such as *The Immortal*). It was syndicated as a two-part series episode, "A Death in the Family."

THE RETURN OF THE SIX MILLION DOLLAR MAN AND THE BIONIC WOMAN
ABC, 5/17/87

Cast: Steve Austin (Lee Majors), Jaime Sommers (Lindsay Wagner), Lyle Stenning (Martin Landau), Michael Austin (Tom Schanley), Jim Castillian (Lee Majors II), Oscar Goldman (Richard Anderson), Rudy Wells (Martin E. Brooks), John Praiser (Gary Lockwood), Nick (Scott Kraft), Dr. Shepherd (Bryan Cranston), Blonde (Pamela Bryant), Receptionist (Catherine McGoohan), Sally (Deborah White), Megann (Kawena Charlot), Waiter (Sandey Grinn), Jensen (Leonard Kibrick), Holly (Michele Minailo), Hostess (Julie H. Morgan), Jim Matlon (Keith Farrell), Christopher (Phil Nordell), with Will Bledsoe, Gary Blumsack, William Campbell, Robert F. Hoy, Terry Kiser, Cheryl McMannis, Patrick Pankhurst, Bob Seagren, Danil Torppe, Susan Woollen

Credits: Director: Ray Austin; Writer: Michael Sloan; Story: Michael Sloan, Bruce Lansbury; Producer: Bernadette Joyce; Supervising Producer: Bruce Lansbury; Art Director: Gary A. Lee; Photography: William K. Jurgensen; Music: Marvin Hamlisch; Editors: Buford F. Hayes, Vic Lackey; Produced by Michael Sloan Productions, Universal

Several years ago, cyborg spies Steve and Jaime (Steve's one-time lover, until malfunctions in her bionic implants made her an amnesiac) quit the Office of Scientific Investigation after a disastrous mission cost the life of Jaime's boyfriend. Now their old enemy, Stenning, has rebuilt his terrorist group, Fortress, planning to capture the cyborgs and duplicate their bionics. The fight against Fortress is tangled by the good guys' feelings for each other (particularly now that Jaime's regained her memories) and Steve's efforts to reconnect with Michael, his estranged son by his first marriage.

When Michael, a USAF pilot, is critically injured in a crash, OSI head Oscar Goldman repays Steve's years of service by rebuilding Michael into an even stronger cyborg.

Feeling like a freak, Michael rejects his father (Jaime, a therapist, tries to work him through it), while Steve hunts down Fortress. Stenning's agents in the OSI cover his trail while he kidnaps Michael and bionic expert Rudy Wells. When Steve realizes OSI is compromised, he combines loyal agents and Michael's air force buddies into a strike force against Fortress HQ. With Michael's help, they beat Stenning. Steve and Jaime resume their romance and—despite their denials to Oscar—their work for the OSI.

Despite good ratings, this pilot failed to jump-start a new bionic series focusing on Michael Austin (with Majors' son as Castillian, Oscar's brash new aide). The follow-up, *Bionic Showdown*, tried a female cyborg in the lead instead.

REVENGE OF THE STEPFORD WIVES
NBC, 10/12/80

Cast: Kay Foster (Sharon Gless), Megan Brady (Julie Kavner), Barbara Parkinson (Audra Lindley), Andy Brady (Don Johnson), Wally (Mason Adams), Dale "Diz" Corbett (Arthur Hill), Kitten (Ellen Weston), Angelina (Gay Rowan), Bruce Manson (Jim McKrell), Sally Tarshis (Lee Benard), Gary Tarshis (Edward Bell), Norman Kahn (Sheldon Feldner), Police Chief (Howard Witt), Henry the Druggist (Peter Maloney), Saleslady (Millie Slavin), Druggist's Wife (Stephanie Blackmore), Muffin Sheridan (Melissa Newman), Real Estate Agent (Joe Medalis), Attendant (Gayanne Meyers), Ambulance Driver (Dean Wein), Charlie Gray (David Boyle), Stepford Wife (Bonnie Sullivan)

Credits: Director: Robert Fuest; Writer: David Wiltse, from characters by Ira Levin; Producers: Robert A. Papazian, Scott Rudin; Executive Producer: Edgar J. Scherick; Photography: Ric Waite; Art Director: Tom H. John; Music: Laurence Rosenthal; Editor: Jerrold L. Ludwig; Produced by Edgar J. Scherick Associates

When TV reporter Kay Foster arrives in Stepford—a small town made newsworthy by its ultra-low divorce and crime rates—she finds that the Stepford women are vacuous, docile housewives, downing medication whenever the town siren blows. She doesn't know it's because sexist pig Corbett has turned the Men's Association into a brainwashing center that makes women "perfect." But after her only friend, newcomer Megan, is brainwashed, Kay (having already dodged several fatal "accidents") unearths the truth.

Evading Corbett's manhunt, Kay tricks Megan into drinking alcohol, which counteracts the mind-control drugs. Her husband, who hates the new, docile Megan, helps them break into the Association where they use the siren to make the women overdose on the pills. The women's repressed anger bursts forth, and to Kay's horror they hunt Corbett down and beat him to death.

Ira Levin's *The Stepford Wives*, in which the women were replaced with androids, became a best-seller (with its take on male-female hostility), then a successful film. *Revenge*, the first of three TV-sequels, ignores the original movie (even claiming to be set 10 years later—it's only five) to become a routine mind-control drama (which does feature Don Johnson in a pre–*Miami Vice* role). It was followed by *The Stepford Children*.

RITUAL OF EVIL
NBC, 2/23/70

Cast: David Sorel (Louis Jourdan), Jolene Wiley (Anne Baxter), Leila Barton (Diana Hyland), Edward Bolander (John McMartin), Harry Snowden (Wilfrid Hyde-White), Loey Wiley (Belinda Montgomery), Aline Wiley (Carla Borelli), Larry Richmond (George Stanford Brown), Sheriff (Regis D. Cordic), Mora (Dehl Berti), Hippie (Richard Alan Knox), Newscaster (Johnny Williams), Reporters (Jimmy Joyce, James LaSane)

Credits: Director: Robert Day; Writer: Robert Presnell, Jr., from characters by Richard Alan Simmons; Producer: David Levinson; Photography: Lionel Lindon; Art Director: William D. DeCinces; Music: Billy Goldenberg; Editor: Douglas Stewart; Produced by Universal

Psychiatrist Sorel and his friend Snowden investigate a patient's suicide and discover supernatural forces played a role in her death.

This sequel to *Fear No Evil* also failed to result in a series.

ROBIN COOK'S "INVASION"
NBC, 5/4–5/5/97

Cast: Beau Stark (Luke Perry), Cassy Winslow

(Rebecca Gayheart), Dr. Sheila Moran (Kim Cattrall), Pitt (Christopher Orr), John (Louis Crugnali), Dr. McCoy (Michael Warren), Detective Walt Kemper (Jon Polito), North (Neal McDonough), Nancy Ochoa (Rosana DeSoto), Ochoa (Castulo Guerra), John Ochoa (Louis Crugnali), Andi Vaughn (Maria Celedonio), Dr. Hayden (Stephen Joyce), Mike Landry (Tim DeKay), Leah (Ginny Harman), Denice (Denice Duff), Husband (Ken Kolb), Orderly (Mark DeMichele), Medical Examiner (Brian Brophy), Walter Kirkland (Bill Rose), Sgt. Kinsella (M. Richard Greene), Pete (Sam Smiley), Ed Partridge (Dan Danielson), Security Chief (Michael Emanuel), Secretary (Adelina Sindhul), Weller (David Akin) Police Captain (Sanford Gibbons), Sgt. Hoover (John Mack), Paramedic (Larry Jones), Father Nightmare (Terry James), Mechanic (Ken Clark), Girl's Mother (Dawn M. Davis), Cop (George Dobbs), Reporter (Alfred C. Cerullo), Boy (Michael Wayne), with Chuck McCann, Jason Schombing

Credits: Director: Armand Mastroianni, Writer: Rockne S. O'Bannon; Story: Robin Cook; Producer: Jeff Morton, Randy Sutter; Co-Producer: Rick Arredondo; Executive Producers: Stacy Mandelberg, Frank Von Zerneck, Robert M. Sertner; Photography: Bryan England; Production Design: Donald Lee Harris; Music: Don Davis; Editor: Scott Vickrey; Produced by Von Zerneck/Sertner Films, Hallmark Entertainment

A shower of black meteorites lands in Phoenix, taking over the minds of anyone who touches them—except people with Rh-negative blood, who go insane, then die. Beau, leader of the possessed, takes over an abandoned air force base where his followers can build "the Gateway." Dr. Moran, Beau's fiancée Cassy and Cassy's buddy Pitt are among those who realize something's wrong. Moran discovers the meteorites trigger a virus dormant in all human cells. The good guys look for help, but the possessed control the city. And when more meteorites fall—all around the world—it becomes clear that there's no one left who can be trusted.

Moran and the others go on the lam, hoping Rh-negative blood will provide a cure. Before long, only Moran, John and Pitt are still free; they hook up with McCoy, who hopes to find a cure before his Rh-factor kills him. Beau, who still loves Cassy, infects her with the virus, explaining that it was introduced by aliens into early earthly life; when they return through the Gateway, they will unite with transformed humanity. McCoy dies, but his blood gives Moran a cure, which she turns into an antiviral gas. Cassy escapes and leads them to the base; they unleash the gas just as Beau opens the Gateway. Beau dies from the gas, the other humans return to normal, and the Gateway closes just in time.

Robin Cook pretty much created the medical suspense thriller with his 1979 best-seller *Coma*, followed by a string of further best-sellers, one or two big-screen adaptations and several TV movies. While many of his books are classic mad-scientist stuff, this is his most SF-oriented work—unfortunately, it's a stock, uninteresting alien possession story. *Invasion* was released simultaneously with the book. Fans of Perry's *Beverly Hills 90210* may recognize Gayheart as his wife on that show.

ROSWELL
Showtime, 7/31/94

Cast: Major Jesse Marcel (Kyle MacLachlan), Mac Brazel (Dwight Yoakam), Vy Marcel (Kim Greist), Townsend (Martin Sheen), Sherman Carson (Xander Berkeley), Frank Joyce (Bob Gunton), Lewis Rickett (Peter MacNicol), Col. Blanchard (John M. Jackson), Sheriff Wilcox (Charles Martin Smith), Mortician (Nick Searcy), Young Jesse, Jr., (J.D. Daniels), James Forrestal (Eugene Roche), Older Pilot MacIntire (Charles Hallahan), Deputy Joe Pritchard (Ray McKinnon), Jesse, Jr. (Doug Wert), TV Commentator (Cynthia Allison), Bar Vet (Hoke Howell), General (Bruce Ed Morrow), Alien Clown (William Edwards), Soldier (Layne Beamer), Guard (Max Trompower), Air Mechanic (Mik Scriba), Lt. Walter Haul (Matt Landers), Deputy (George Gray III), Gate MP (Stephen C. Foster), Provost Marshal (Dave Adams), Jeep Driver (Bill Cook), Pilots (J.W. "Corkey" Forsnof, Charles Beck, Randy Gagne), General Ramey (Matthew Faison), Col. DuBose (John Hostetter), Irving Newton (Michael Bofshever), Station Manager (David Selburg), Arresting MP (Doug McCurry), Interrogators (Charles M. Kistler, Daiton Rutowski), Older Stanton (F. William Parker), Younger Stanton (Jonathan Mincks), Melvin Brown (Peter Radon), Eavesdropper (Gary Bullock), Harris (Jim Hayne), Gate Guard (Mark Phelan), Doctors (Steve Lanza, Arthur Kopit), MPs (Don Fischer, Michael Strasser), Waitress (Denice Marcel),

Janet Foss (Lisa Waltz), Vets (John Mahon, Stanley Grover, Warren Munson), Chaplain (Hansford Rowe), Autopsy Doctor (Richard Fancy), Photographer (Paul Davids), Roswell General (Philip Baker Hall), General (Larry Dobkin), Civilian Advisor (Edward Penn), Scientists (Arthur Hiller, Brian Carpenter), Advisors (George Pentecost, Parley Baer), Admiral (Bruce Gray), General (Frank A. Roys), Aide (Vernon Blackman), Medical Officer (Brian Cousins), Area 51 Officer (James G. McDonald), Admiral (Robert Harvey)

Credits: Director-Producer: Jeremy Kagan; Writer: Arthur Kopit; Story: Arthur Kopit, Paul Davids, Jeremy Kagan, based on *UFO Crash at Roswell* by Kevin D. Randle and Donald R. Schmitt; Producer: Ilene Kahn; Co-Producer: Peter McIntosh; Executive Producers: Paul Davids, David R. Ginsburg; Photography: Steven Poster; Production Design: Michael Z. Hanan; Music: Elliot Goldenthal; Editor: David Holden; Produced by Republic, Viacom Pictures, Citadel Entertainment

In 1947 USAF officer Jesse Marcel, stationed at Roswell AFB, is called to Brazel's farm, where the farmer has found wreckage from a flying saucer. Jesse is thrilled until he's told to deny and cover up everything. When he tries to learn the truth about the crash, his superiors stonewall him.

At a Roswell reunion 30 years later, Jesse resumes asking questions. The sinister Townsend reveals that the cover-up (including using UFO crackpots to discredit serious research) is to prevent public panic over the truth: Aliens are real, come from a parallel universe and may have manipulated our evolution and culture for their own ends. Though Townsend gloats over the fact that Jesse can't prove any of this, just knowing the truth restores Jesse's confidence and dignity.

The alleged UFO crash at Roswell has been a fixation of UFO buffs and debunkers for years; whatever the reality, this docudrama only comes off like a feature-length episode of *The X-Files* (and Townsend's spectacular claims are hard to take in a supposedly realistic film).

THE RUBY RING
Showtime, 11/26/97
Cast: Lucy McLaughlin (Emily Hamilton), Patrick Collins (Rutger Hauer), Robert Langley (Christien Anholt), Nellie/Noreen (Emma Cunniffe), Elizabeth Langley (Gillian Kearney), Mrs. Puxley (Judy Parfitt), Mrs. McLaughlin (Patricia Ross), Mr. McLaughlin (Todd Boyce), Victoria (Sophia Money-Coutts), Gran (Jan Moffat), Edith (Bridget Biagi), Mary Spencer (Samantha Bond), Lady Langley (Joanna Tope), Fred (Iain Andrew), Mr. Hurley (Alan Tall), Mrs. Hurley (Angela Chadfield), Lord Langley (Michael Derrington), Rupert Webster (Christopher Staines), Constable (Ian Sexon), Butler (Jeffrey Daunton)

Credits: Director: Harley Cokeliss; Writers: Lin Oliver, Alan Moskowitz, based on Yvonne MacGrory's *Secret of the Ruby Ring*; Producer: Don Reynolds; Executive Producers: Lin Oliver, Nigel Pickard, Robert Love; Photography: Jim Peters; Production Design: Marius Van Der Werff; Music: Arthur B. Rubinstein; Editor: John Gow; Produced by Hallmark Entertainment, Flextech Television, Scottish Television Enterprises

Lucy McLaughlin can't stand that, with her dad unemployed, she has to leave her house, her friends and her beloved horse to live with her family at Grandma's. When Grandma gives Lucy an old family ring, Lucy's ancestor appears and offers Lucy a wish. Lucy wishes to live in a big house with servants and horses—and instantly finds herself in an 1896 mansion ... as a servant. Worse, she drops the ring; if she doesn't find it in 24 hours, the wish will be permanent.

Lucy's lack of subservience infuriates the Langleys (who find and keep the ring) and their servants, particularly bullying groom Collins; handsome Robert Langley, however, finds her charming. In between turning things topsy-turvy (convincing Elizabeth Langley to reject an arranged match to a dull boor, for instance), Lucy sees Mary, a fellow maid, steal the ring for Collins. When Lucy is accused of the theft herself, she goes on the run; but with Robert's help she sneaks back to capture Collins and Mary. Lucy's pleading finally convinces Collins to give her the ring. She unmakes the wish and returns to the present, now happy with her life. Especially after she meets Robert's descendant—and exact double.

This is a pleasant children's fantasy complete with the "exact double" resolution to time-spanning romances (see *The Love Letter*).

RUNNING AGAINST TIME
USA, 11/21/90

Cast: David Rhodes (Robert Hays), Dr. Koopman (Sam Wanamaker), Laura Whittaker (Catherine Hicks), Oswald (James DiStefano), Agent Landry (Wayne Tippit), Teddy (Tracy Fraim), Nurse (Juanita Jennings), Young Chris (Paul Scherrer), President Johnson (Brian Smiar), Agent Clemens (Milt Tarver), Doctor (Russ Marin), Mrs. Rhodes (Julie Ariola), Mr. Rhodes (Duncan Gamble), Young David (Damion Stevens), Guard (Michael Whaley), Captain Fritz (Dean Hill), Police Spokesman (Richard Gilbert-Hill), Old Chris (Gerald Berns), Nurse (Darlene Kardon), Dr. Wilkins (Warren Sweeney), Students (J. Lamont Pope, Nike Doukas, Pepper Sweeney), Sales Rep (Rusty Schwimmer), with Mark Phelan, Tim DeZarn, Alberto Manquero, Ron Troncatty, Thomas Robert Burke, Andrew Walker

Credits: Director: Bruce Seth Green; Writers: Stanley Shapiro, Robert Glass, based on Stanley Shapiro's *A Time to Remember*; Producer: David Roessell; Co-Producer: Lori-Etta Taub; Co-Executive Producer: Michael Weisbarth; Associate Producer: Carole Katz Fetner; Photography: Brian Hebb; Production Design: Barry Robison; Music: Don Davis; Editor: Heather MacDougall; Produced by Finnegan-Pinchuk, Coastline Partners

Historian David Rhodes has never come to terms with his brother Chris' death in Vietnam. When David's reporter girlfriend, Laura, interviews physicist Koopman about his time-space research, David puts it together with some weird incidents on campus and realizes that Koopman has mastered time travel. David convinces Koopman to send him back in time to stop JFK's assassination (believing Kennedy will end the Vietnam War, so Chris will live). David arrives in Dallas in 1963, but too late to stop the assassination; worse, Oswald frames him as the killer, then Jack Ruby shoots him.

When Laura and Koopman see that the 1963 headlines have changed, Laura goes back to before David's arrival. A car accident delays her reaching him, so David still winds up framed, but she does help him escape the cops. They also discover that David's existing twice in one time has rendered his younger self comatose. The couple convince 1963's Koopman that they're from the future, then signal Koopman—in the present—to send back Vietnam-era news footage, which past-Koopman uses to persuade President Johnson to pull out of 'Nam. Instead, LBJ doubles the country's military commitment rather than lose the war.

Horrified, present-Koopman heads back to before David and Laura arrive, intercepts them and convinces David that history can't be changed. David makes one last visit to Chris (at the hospital with young David), then they return home. David finally makes peace with Chris' death—but the next morning Chris shows up alive; their talk in the hospital convinced him not to enlist.

This is one of the few TV movies to explore the paradoxes of time travel, but the execution is flawed (why would headlines change but people still remember the "old" past?)—though no worse than many print SF stories. It stars familiar faces Hicks (*Tucker's Witch*) and Hays (the *Starman* series).

RUNNING DELILAH
ABC, 8/29/94

Cast: Delilah (Kim Cattrall), Paul (Billy Zane), Alec Kasharian (Yorgo Voyagis), Lucas (François Guétary), Judith (Diana Rigg), Operatives (Michael Francis Clarke, Quentin O'Brien), Language Tech (Dawn Comer), Watcher (Rob LaBelle), Barbara (Marilyn McIntyre), Technician (Philip Moon, Richard Topol), Scientist (Philip Sokoloff), Liaison (Eric Stone), Guard (Victor Touzie)

Credits: Director: Richard Franklin; Writer-Executive Producer: Ron Koslow; Story: Ron Koslow, Robert Avrech; Producer: Mel Efros; Associate Producer: Steve Oster; Art Director: Jack Jennings; Production Design: Francis J. Pezza; Robot Effects: All Effects Co.; Music: Lee Holdridge; Editor: Andrew London; Produced by ABC, Sea Change Productions

After arms-dealer Kasharian catches and executes federal agent Delilah, her handler and lover, Paul, has her resurrected through extensive cyborg implants. Initially horrified at her unnatural new body, Delilah eventually revels in her vastly increased physical abilities and computer-enhanced brain. When Kasharian plans to provide arms for terrorist Carlos the Jackal's next mission, Paul and

Delilah are assigned to stop him. Capturing Kasharian, they learn he's providing Carlos with enough stolen plutonium to make a nuclear bomb. Delilah penetrates Carlos' base, so the terrorist tries to take off with the plutonium. With Paul's help, Delilah destroys the plane, proving her worth to the agency, Paul and herself.

This stock *Bionic Woman* retread (Koslow did better as producer of the *Beauty and the Beast* series) features Diana Rigg (*The Avengers*) slumming as spymaster Judith. Zane was a semi-regular on *Twin Peaks* and star of *The Phantom*.

SABRINA GOES TO ROME
ABC, 10/3/98

Cast: Sabrina Spellman/Sophia (Melissa Joan Hart), Paul (Eddie Mills), Gwen (Tara Charendoff), Travis (James Fields), Alberto (Eric Alexander), Salem (Nick Bakay), Mrs. Goodogoo (Evelyn Furtok), Lorenzo (Patrick Drykuss), Roberto (Robert Steiner), Mercutio (Francesco Mazzini), Stonehenge (Richard Horowitz, voice), Taxi Driver (Stefano Mioni), Tour Guide (Leslie Gilliams), Ugly Americans (Robert Summer, Carolyn De Fonseco), David (Paolo Giovannucci), Caesar (Roberto Comero), Marc Anthony (Alessandro Gionnini), Waiter (Mario De Condia)

Credits: Director: Tibor Takacs; Writer: Daniel Berendsen; Producers: Ovidio G. Assonitis, Kenneth R. Koch, Melissa Joan Hart; Co-Producer: Stuart Bass; Executive Producer: Paula Hart; Photography: Adolfo Bartoli; Music: Danny Lux; Editor: Marcus Manton; Produced by Ovidio Assonitis Productions, Hartbreak Films, Viacom

Four hundred years ago, the witch Sophia revealed her powers to her lover, Roberto; when he betrayed her secret and she refused to punish him, the witches' High Council exiled her. Now Sophia's modern-day niece, teen witch Sabrina, has two weeks to visit Rome and learn the secret of Sophia's magic locket before its magic is lost forever. In Rome, Sabrina meets an inept Brit witch, Gwen, and Paul, a sexy reporter who discovers Sabrina's powers and plots to expose her. Paul and his partner Travis tag along on Sabrina's quest, but they fail to catch her using magic—and Paul starts falling for her. Sabrina finally travels back to Sophia's time, where she learns that jealous Lorenzo tricked Roberto into betraying Sophia, then trapped Sophia inside the locket. In the present, Sabrina uses her powers to help adoptee Paul find his birth family.

When Travis photographs Sabrina using magic, she's given 12 hours to petrify Paul for betraying her, or be punished like Sophia. Sabrina refuses to destroy someone she loves—an act of the heart that frees Sophia's spirit to join Roberto. Paul redeems himself by destroying the film, and Sabrina's magic intimidates Travis into keeping quiet.

This is a routine spin-off from the successful *Sabrina, the Teenage Witch* series (and not particularly continuous—there's no mention of Sabrina's steady, Harvey). Charendoff provides the voice for Batgirl in *Batman: The Animated Adventures*.

SABRINA, THE TEENAGE WITCH
Showtime, 4/10/96

Cast: Sabrina Sawyer (Melissa Joan Hart), Aunt Hilda (Sherry Miller), Aunt Zelda (Charlene Fernetz), Harvey (Tobias Mehler), Marny (Michelle Beaudoin), Seth (Ryan Reynolds), Katy (Lalainia Lindbjerg), Freddie (Laura Harris), Fran (Kea Wong), Coach (Jo Bates), Salesclerk (Janine Wong), Larry (Biski Gugushe), Mark (Tyler Labine), Mr. Dingle (Jim Swansburg), Jeff (Noel Geer), DJ (Volton)

Credits: Director: Tibor Takacs; Writers: Barney Cohen, Kathryn Wallack, Nicholas Factor; Story: Barney Cohen, Kathryn Wallack; Producers: Alana H. Lambros, Richard Davis; Executive Producers: Kathryn Wallack, Barney Cohen, Paula Hart; Associate Producer: Brian Irving; Photography: Bernard Salzmann; Production Design: John Kavellin; Music: Greg DeBelles; Produced by Showtime, Hallmark Home Entertainment, Barney Cohen and Kathryn Wallack Productions, Once and Future Films, Hartbreak Films

On her sixteenth birthday, Sabrina is stunned to learn that her relatives are all witches, and that the aunts she's living with will tutor her in magic. Sabrina—oblivious to how much her buddy Harvey cares for her—uses her powers to compete with star athlete Katy for the heart of arrogant jock Seth. Seth announces that his date for the big dance will be the winner of the next track-and-field meet; when Katy cheats, Sabrina resorts to magic and wins. Seth takes Sabrina to the dance, but his arrogant behavior makes Sabrina see what a jerk he is. She dumps Seth and finally spends the evening dancing in Harvey's arms.

Sabrina debuted in the Archie Comics line back in the late sixties, winning a Saturday morning cartoon around the same time. This live-action version mixed teen comedy clichés with *Bewitched*-style shtick, buoyed by Hart's charm in the lead role. An ABC series followed (recasting all the roles but Hart), becoming a breakout hit for the 1996-97 season that inspired several unsuccessful knockoffs (*Teen Angel*, *You Wish*).

SALEM'S LOT
CBS, 11/17–11/24/79

Cast: Ben Mears (David Soul), Straker (James Mason), Mark Petrie (Lance Kerwin), Barlow (Reggie Nalder), Susan Norton (Bonnie Bedelia), Marjorie Glick (Clarissa Kaye), Jason Burke (Lew Ayres), Weasel (Elisha Cook, Jr.), Bonnie Sawyer (Julie Cobb), Cully Sawyer (George Dzundza), Dr. Bill Norton (Ed Flanders), Mike Ryerson (Geoffrey Lewis), Ned Tebbetts (George McFadden), Larry Crockett (Fred Willard), Parkins Gillespie (Kenneth McMillan), Eva (Marie Windsor), Danny Glick (Brad Savage), Ralphie Glick (Ronnie Scriber)

Credits: Director: Tobe Hooper; Writer: Paul Monash, from Stephen King's novel; Producer: Richard Kobritz; Photography: Jules Brenner; Production Design: Mort Rabinowitz; Editor: Caroll Sax; Music: Harry Sukman; Produced by Warner Bros.

Novelist Ben Mears returns to his New England home town, Salem's Lot, to rest and start a new novel. Unfortunately, his return coincides with the arrival of Barlow, a monstrous vampire, and his human servant, Straker. As vampirism spreads through the town, Ben, young Mark Petrie and Ben's old girlfriend Susan are among the few to realize and fight the danger. Susan, however, becomes one of the undead, and Ben and Mark's other allies are slain. Ben finally sets fire to Barlow's house, destroying him, Straker and the other vampires. He and Mark retreat to Central America—but the vampiric Susan finds and almost kills them before being staked. Ben and Mark realize that the vampires have survived, and that their battle with Salem's Lot is not over.

This two-part film made a so-so adaptation of Stephen King's chilling novel, replacing his urbane vampire with a mute grotesque (the producer had grown tired of glamorous vampires), though it did break fresh ground with the censors (becoming the first time a child was put "in mortal jeopardy" on television, and allowing sleeping vampires to be filmed eyes-open [taboo for ordinary corpses]). A comedic video sequel, *Return to Salem's Lot*, followed years later.

SANDCASTLES
CBS, 10/17/72

Cast: Michael (Jan-Michael Vincent), Jenna Hampshire (Bonnie Bedelia), Alexis (Herschel Bernardi), Sarah (Mariette Hartley), Frank Watson (Gary Crosby), Ruth Watson (Loretta Leversee), Paul Fiedler (Lloyd Gough), George Peterson (William Long, Jr.), Sascha (William Hansen), Sister (Mimi Davis), Driver (Dick Valentine), Sherry (Jody Hauber)

Credits: Director: Ted Post; Writers: Stephen Karpf, Elinor Karpf, James M. Miller; Story: Peter Berneis; Producer: Gerald I. Isenberg; Executive Producer: Charles Fries; Associate Producer: Lee Miller; Photography: Alan Stensvold; Music: Paul Glass; Editor: Thomas McCarthy; Produced by Metromedia Producers Corp.

Acting on impulse, restless drifter Michael walks off his job at Alexis' restaurant, taking Alexis' mortgage money with him. He soon repents, but he's run down and killed by hot-tempered Watson before he can return—and Watson takes the money. Michael's ghost wanders the beach, where he and Jenna, a lonely musician, fall in love. He asks for her help in returning the money, but she refuses because that would free his spirit to leave. Eventually, though, she does the right thing and steers Alexis to Watson, whom Alexis almost beats senseless for killing Michael. Alexis gets the mortgage money, Michael's spirit moves on, and Jenna, though grieving, now has the strength to be a better person and a great musician.

This weak, maudlin mess gives little hint that Bedelia would become a critically acclaimed film actress (Vincent did a lot better himself in the action series *Airwolf*).

SEARCH FOR THE GODS
ABC, 3/9/75

Cast: Willie Longfellow (Stephen McHattie), Shan Mullins (Kurt Russell), Genara Juantez (Victoria Racimo), Raymond Striker (Raymond St. Jacques), Dr. Henderson (Ralph Bellamy), Tarkanian (Albert Paulsen), Lucio (John War Eagle), Wheeler (Carmen Argenziano), Elder (Joe David Marcus), Council Indian (Joe Marcus, Jr.), Jailer (Larry Blake), Glenn (Jackson D. Kane)

Credits: Director: Jud Taylor; Writer: Ken Pettus; Story: Herman Miller; Producer: Wilford Lloyd Baumes; Executive Producer: Douglas S. Cramer; Photography: Matthew F. Leonetti; Art Director: James G. Hulsey; Music: Billy Goldenberg; Editor: Art Seid; Produced by Douglas S. Cramer Company, Warner Bros.

After drifter Willie saves Indian shaman Lucio from thugs, Lucio entrusts him with a medallion for Lucio's granddaughter, Genara, then dies. Striker, who sent the thugs for the medallion, pursues Willie, but with the help of con man Shan, Willie reaches Genara. Dr. Henderson tells Genara the medallion is an ancient but unknown alloy and a symbol of the "ancient astronauts," ETs her ancestors worshipped as gods. Willie undergoes a tribal ritual to convince Genara's people of his right to the medallion's secrets; Shan cuts a deal with Striker to steal it. Henderson's research sends Shan, Genara and Willie to a desert temple holding another medallion, both parts of a greater whole. Shan makes a half-hearted effort to steal them, but Striker interrupts and takes them himself. Willie fights back and accidentally kills Striker. After a landslide buries the cave, Willie leaves Genara—even though he loves her—to find the other pieces. Shan joins him on the quest—but Striker's employer is still after them.

Search for the Gods is not very interesting, despite the presence of old hands Bellamy, St. Jacques and Russell. McHattie would later play archvillain Gabriel in the *Beauty and the Beast* TV series.

SEDUCED BY EVIL
USA, 8/25/94

Cast: Leigh (Suzanne Somers), Serro (John Vargas), Nick (James B. Sikking), Melissa Lindsay (Mindy Spence), Dr. Mallory (Nancy Moonves), Rayna (Julie Carmen), Joe Walthrop (Doug Coleman), Kevin (Arthur Baranowski), Steve Nieto (Roberto Guajardo), Sgt. Ramirez (Miguel Ortega), Carlos (Ric San Nicholas), Driver (Brooks Tomb)

Credits: Director: Tony Wharmby; Writer: Bill Svanoe, based on Jann Arrington Wolcott's *Brujo*; Producer: Bob Roe; Co-Producer: Bill Svanoe; Executive Producers: Martin Markinson, Richard Polak; Photography: João Fernandes; Production Design: Gary Constable; Editor: Louise Innes; Music: George S. Clinton; Produced by CNM Entertainment, Cinestage Productions, Wilshire Court Productions

Leigh, a reporter, agrees to finish a profile on Serro, a mystical healer, after a co-worker on the story dies mysteriously. Serro, actually a powerful witch, knows Leigh was his past-life lover, who fled him after he became evil. Determined to win her back, he seduces her with magic. When she resists him, he blinds her husband, kills her best friend and kidnaps her daughter. With her child's life at stake, Leigh confronts Serro and draws on her own, buried mystic gifts with which to destroy him.

This would be merely boring, but Vargas' bland performance as a supposedly seductive master of evil makes it much worse.

SHADOW ZONE: MY TEACHER ATE MY HOMEWORK
Showtime, 10/18/97

Cast: Jesse Hackett (Gregory Smith), Mrs. Fink (Shelley Duvall), Annabel (Darla Perlmutter), Mrs. Hackett (Sheila McCarthy), Mr. Hackett (Tim Progosh), Cody (Edwin Hodge), Geneva (Diana Theodore), Joey (Dan Warry-Smith), Shopkeeper (John Neville), Miss Macro (Karen Robinson), Sol (Margot Kidder), Doctor (Damon D'Olivera), The Reaper (Mackenzie Gray)

Credits: Director: Stephen Williams; Writers: Garfield and Judith Reeves-Stevens; Producer: Paul Brown; Executive Producers: Thomas W. Lynch, Charles Falzon, Nancy Chapelle; Photography: Curtis Petersen; Production Design: Tamara Deverell; Editor: Susan Shipton; Music: John McCarthy; Produced by Hallmark

Entertainment, Lynch Entertainment, Showtime, Catalyst Entertainment

Chores and homework are Jesse Hackett's world—until he buys an antique doll resembling his hated teacher, Mrs. Fink. Jesse finds that whatever he does to the doll happens to Mrs. Fink; the doll also comes to life on its own to protect him from a bully. Before long, the doll is fully animate—looking and sounding just like Fink (who's growing steadily weaker) and threatening Jesse's family if he disobeys her. Geneva, his best friend's New Agey sister, discovers that the doll is possessed by a Loa, a voodoo spirit seeking entry to the mortal world. Jesse manages to enact a ritual that destroys it and restores Fink to health.

This is even weaker than *Shadow Zone: The Undead Express* (what's Jesse being punished for—disliking his teacher?). No loss that it was the last of the series.

SHADOW ZONE: THE UNDEAD EXPRESS

Showtime, 10/27/96

Cast: Zachary Kincaid (Chauncey Leopardi), Valentine Cutter (Ron Silver), Reaper (Stephen Russell), Gabe (Natanya Ross), J.T. (Tony T. Johnson), Mom (Sherry Miller), Dad (Ron Lea), Sims (Ron White), Harv (Frank Moore), Mrs. Potasher (Linda Carter), Ronnie (Derwin Jordan), Mr. Chan (Henry Chan), Video Store Clerk (Wayne Robert McNamara), Pearl (Norma Dell Agnese), Dwayne (Michael Rhoades), Counsellor (Wes Craven), Transit Cop (Joe Pingue), Conductor (Bill Tarling), Man (Bryan Renfro), Jeffrey's Mom (Deborah Tobban)

Credits: Director: Stephen Williams; Writer: Roy Sallows, based on J.R. Black's book; Producer: John Danylkiw; Co-Producer: Gary L. Stephenson; Photography: Curtis Petersen; Production Design: David Davis; Music: Reg Powell; Editor: Ralph Brunjes; Produced by Showtime, Hallmark Entertainment, Lynch Entertainment

Zach, a teen horror-buff, copes with his parents' divorce by making up wild stories—so when he claims to have met a vampire in the New York subways, no one believes him. It's true, though: Valentine Cutter, a century-old vampire, rides with his followers on the Undead Express through the city's abandoned tunnels. Cutter, who relies on animals for blood, befriends Zach, but when Zach's skeptical friend Gabe visits the tunnels, Cutter captures her to force Zach to switch the Express onto the mainline (the lights around the switch are too painful for the undead) so the vampires can reach the rest of the city freely. Zach pulls the switch but tricks the vampires into riding out of the tunnels in daylight, destroying them.

R.L. Stine's phenomenally successful series of *Goosebumps* horror novels for kids inspired many less successful imitators, including Black's *Shadowzone*. Likewise, the success of *Goosebumps* as a Saturday morning TV show probably inspired this film series (as it did the Saturday show *Bone Chillers*), hosted by "The Reaper." Unfortunately, this is much preachier than Stine (kids get caught in the "shadow zone" when they've done bad things, like Zach's lying) and has some irritating gaps in logic (the end twist—Zach telling the story to a shrink who's secretly a vampire—is utterly pointless). It was followed by *My Teacher Ate My Homework*.

THE SHAGGY DOG

ABC, 11/12/94

Cast: Ron Daniels (Ed Begley, Jr.), Beth Daniels (Sharon Lawrence), Wilby Daniels (Scott Weinger), Detective Al (Jon Polito), Charlie Mulvihill (James Cromwell), Trey Miller (Jeremy Sisto), Moochie Daniels (Jordan Blake Warhol), Francesca (Sarah Lassez), Allison (Natasha Gregson Warner), Coach Evans (Bobby Slayton), Officer Kelly (Rick Ducommun), Officer Hanson (David Pasquesi), Drunk (Charles Dugan), Uniformed Cops (John C. Anders, Gerry Del Sol), Usher (Peyton Reed), Counterperson (Ted David), Girl (Clare Salstrom)

Credits: Director: Dennis Dugan; Writers: Bill Walsh, Lillie Hayward, Tim Doyle, based on a screenplay by Bill Walsh and Lillie Hayward, based on characters from Felix Salten's *The Hound of Florence*; Producer: Joseph B. Wallenstein; Executive Producers: George Zaloom, Les Mayfield, Scott Immergut; Photography: Russ Alsobrook; Art Director: Peter Clemens; Music: Mark Mothersbaugh, Denis M. Hagan; Editor: Jeff Gourson; Produced by ZM Productions, Inc.

When Wilby Daniels accidentally walks home with a supposed magic ring from his father's museum, he can't resist casting a love spell on his neighbor Allison's sexy cousin, Francesca. Unfortunately, the ring's magic is for shapeshifting, so it merges Wilby with Francesca's sheepdog, Bundles. Changing back and forth at random, Wilby must cope with his dog-allergic father, his dog-loving brother, two dim-bulb dogcatchers—and hide the reason he keeps disappearing. Worse, he discovers that Francesca's uncle Charlie is a jewel thief who uses Bundles in his crimes— like ripping off a diamond from the museum. Even though it's Wilby, not Bundles, that Charlie takes to the museum, Charlie succeeds—and it's Wilby and his dad who become the prime suspects.

When Wilby shapechanges in custody, the bewildered police throw "the dog" out of the station. Dog-Wilby finds and swallows the diamond to keep it from Charlie, then brings Charlie to justice—and breaks the curse when he heroically saves Francesca's life. Although Francesca leaves town, Allison starts seeing Wilby through new eyes.

In 1959 *The Shaggy Dog* was Disney's first live-action comedy and a box-office hit, inspiring a successful sequel, *The Shaggy D.A.* and a TV pilot, *Return of the Shaggy Dog*. This was one of several 1995 TV-remakes from Disney; it didn't add anything to the merits of the original.

SHE WAITS
CBS, 1/28/72

Cast: Laura Wilson (Patty Duke), Mark Wilson (David McCallum), Dr. Sam Carpenter (Lew Ayres), Sarah Wilson (Dorothy McGuire), Mrs. M (Beulah Bondi), David Brody (James Callahan), Kurawicz (Nelson Olmsted)

Credits: Director-Producer: Delbert Mann; Writer: Art Wallace; Executive Producer: Charles Fries; Associate Producer: Mort Zarcoff; Photography: Charles F. Wheeler; Art Director: Lawrence G. Paull; Music: Morton Stevens; Editor: John F. Schreyer; Produced by Metromedia Producers

When the newlywed Wilsons make their first visit to Mark's mother, Sarah, she's horrified to have them staying in the house— because it's haunted by Ellen, the ghost of Mark's alcoholic first wife, whom Sarah believes Mark murdered. Although Mark scoffs, Ellen's ghost eventually possesses Laura and confronts Mark and his best friend, Dave— her lover; she plans to kill Mark and leave in Laura's body, with Dave. When Mark denies killing her, Ellen's booze-fogged brain finally remembers that Dave killed her. Dave flees in panic and falls to his death on the stairs. Ellen's ghost departs and Laura returns—but Mark still doesn't believe anything actually happened.

The Twilight Zone could have wrapped up this dreary story in 30 minutes.

THE SHINING
ABC, 4/27–5/2/97

Cast: Jack Torrance (Steven Weber), Danny Torrance (Courtland Mead), Wendy (Rebecca De Mornay), Halloran (Melvin Van Peebles), Stuart Ullman (Elliott Gould), Tony (Wil Horneff), Derwent (John Durbin), Delbert Grady (Stanley Anderson), Watson (Pat Hingle), Woman in 217 (Cynthia Garris), Gage Creed (Stephen King), Howie (Sam Raimi), Waiters (Mickey Giacomazzi, J.P. Romano), George Hatfield (Tomas Herrera), Croquet Player (Tim Perovich), Basketball Player (Ken Solomon), Al Shockley (Van Sickle), AA Members (Peter Boyles, David Sosna), Bodyguards (Dan Bradley, Lou Carlucci), TV Announcer (Bertha Lynn), Mitch (David Zambrano), Hartwell (Mick Garris), Waitress (Shawnee Smith), Weatherman (Ron Allen), Airline Gate Agent (Richard Beall), Car Rental Clerk (Wendelin Harston), Joy of Sex Lady (Lois Hicks), Principal (Billie McBride), Hayworth Lookalike (Lisa Thornhill), Dogman (Roger Baker), Customer (Joyce Bulifant), Female Ghost (Christina Faust), Mark Torrance (Miguel Ferrer, uncredited, voice only), with Peter James, Richard Peterson

Credits: Director: Mick Garris; Writer: Stephen King, based on his novel; Producer: Mark Carliner; Supervising Producer: Elliot Friedgen; Executive Producer: Stephen King; Photography: Shelly Johnson; Production Design; Craig Stearns; Art Director: Randy Moore; Music: Nicholas Pike: Editor: Patrick McMahon; Produced by Warner Bros., Lakeside Productions

Jack Torrance, a recovering alcoholic writer, accepts a job as winter caretaker for the snowbound Overlook Hotel, even though it means he and his family (wife Wendy and clairvoyant son Danny) will be snowed in for several months. He doesn't place any importance on the many sinister, bloody incidents in the Overlook's past—and doesn't realize the hotel is a psychic, ghost-filled vortex that badly wants to feed on Danny's psychic "shining."

As soon as they move into the empty hotel, ghosts appear, topiary animals move and Danny receives psychic warnings from his future self (something this version never really explains) about terrible danger. Sensing Jack's inner weakness, the hotel manipulates and breaks him, then sends him to kill Wendy and Danny. Danny manages to summon another psychic—Halloran, the hotel's cook—who helps them escape. Jack regains enough of his will to overload the hotel furnace and burn the place to the ground. But it will be rebuilt…

King was reportedly very disappointed in Stanley Kubrick's 1980 big-screen adaptation (Kubrick played it as a straight psychological thriller, only keeping enough of the supernatural elements to confuse those who hadn't read the book). This much more faithful version is superior, although the happy ending (Jack's spirit, now free, watches Danny graduate years later) was a bit much.

THE SINS OF DORIAN GRAY
ABC, 5/27/83

Cast: Dorian Gray (Belinda Bauer), Henry Lord (Anthony Perkins), Stuart Vane (Joseph Bottoms), Sofia Lord (Olga Karlatos), Alan Campbell (Michael Ironside), Angela Vane (Caroline Yeager), Tracy (Patsy Rahn), Marie-Rose (Roxanne Moffitt), Parker (Jeff Braunstein), Victor (Roy Wordsworth), Christian (Peter Hanlon), Secretary (Carol Robinson), Elevator Man (Mark Duffy), with Bob Collins, Trudy Weiss, Richard Comar, James Kione, Jai Lone, Rusty Ryan, Danny Love, Grant Alianak

Credits: Director: Tony Maylam; Writers: Ken August, Peter Lawrence, from Oscar Wilde's *The Picture of Dorian Gray*; Producer: Jules Bass; Executive Producer: Arthur Rankin, Jr.; Associate Producer: Tony Alatis; Photography: Zale Madger; Art Director: Karen Bromley; Music: Bernard Hoffer; Editor: Ron Wisman; Produced by Rankin-Bass Productions

In the fifties, actress/model Dorian Gray makes an idle wish for eternal youth—then discovers her screen-test footage shows age and stress while her real face remains unchanged. After a harsh argument drives her married lover to suicide, Dorian embarks on a downward spiral into decadence, ending only when she's forced to kill to conceal her secret. Despite her efforts to reform, however, she can't overcome her guilt and finally destroys the film footage, causing her to revert to her true age before she dies.

This is a dismally bland adaptation of Wilde's novel (done better on the big screen); Bauer is colorless, and in many ways tamer and less corrupt than the original Dorian. The idea of using film rather than a painting also turned up in the big-screen *Phantom of the Paradise* (1974).

THE SIX MILLION DOLLAR MAN
ABC, 3/7/73

Cast: Steve Austin (Lee Majors), Dr. Rudy Wells (Martin Balsam), Oliver Spencer (Darren McGavin), Jean Manners (Barbara Anderson), Dr. Ashburn (Robert Cornthwaite), Geraldton (Ivor Barry), Saltillo (Olan Soule), Prisoner (Charles Robinson), General (George Wallace), Mrs. McKay (Dorothy Green), Nudaylah (Maurice Sherbanee), Women (Anne Whitefield, Norma Storch), with Richard Webb

Credits: Director-Producer: Richard Irving; Writer: Henri Simoun, based on Martin Caidin's *Cyborg*; Producer: Richard Irving; Photography: Emil Oster; Art Director: Raymond Beal; Music: Gil Melle; Editors: Buddy Small, Richard M. Sprague; Produced by Universal Television

When an experimental plane malfunctions and crashes, test pilot Steve Austin loses three limbs and one eye. Intelligence officer Spencer sees this as a golden opportunity to create the cyborg secret agent he believes America needs; he authorizes bionics expert Dr. Wells to rebuild Steve's body accordingly.

Steve is initially freaked about being part-machine and suspicious of Spencer's motives. Spencer nevertheless cajoles Steve into rescuing an Arab peacemaker captured by terrorists. Steve breaks into the terrorists' desert base, but discovers the captive is already dead. Back home, Spencer admits to Rudy the mission is purely a test to see if Steve has the guts for the job. Steve successfully escapes the terrorists and reluctantly accepts his new role as Spencer's point man.

This is so slow (it's mostly a medical drama with a little action) and Majors so unconvincing at showing torment, it's astonishing this ranked with *The Incredible Hulk* as the seventies' most successful SF pilot. The series (which recast the supporting roles and gave Steve a more likable boss) did better, pitting Steve against everything from ordinary spies to alien invaders. It yielded one spin-off (*The Bionic Woman*) and three reunion films, starting with *The Return of the Six Million Dollar Man and the Bionic Woman*.

SNOW WHITE: A TALE OF TERROR
Showtime, 8/24/97

Cast: Lady Claudia (Sigourney Weaver), Lilli (Monica Keena), Will (Gil Bellows), Frederick Hoffman (Sam Neill), Little Lilli (Taryn Davis), Peter Guttenberg (David Conrad), Lars (Brian Glover), Rolf (Anthony Brophy), Nannaw (Francis Cuna), Konrad (Christopher Bauer), Karl (John Edward Allen), Gustav (Mikoslav Taborsky), Scar (Andrew Tiernan), Father Gilbert (Bryan Pringle), Ilsa (Dale Wyatt), Lilliana (Joanna Roth)

Credits: Director: Michael Cohn; Writers: Tom Szollosi, Deborah Serra; Producer: Tom Engelman; Co-Producer: Tim Van Rellim; Executive Producers: Ted Field, Robert W. Cort, Scott Kroopf; Photography: Mike Southon; Production Design: Gemma Jackson; Music: John Ottman; Costumes: Marit Allen; Editor: Ian Crafford; Produced by Interscope Communications, Polygram

In 15th century Bavaria, newly married Lady Claudia welcomes her stepdaughter, Lilli, with open arms ... until Claudia miscarries the son her husband hoped for, and her mind snaps. Claudia accepts her magic mirror's accusation that Lilli caused the stillbirth from jealousy, and resolves to kill the girl. Lilli finds refuge with seven outcasts who've suffered under the harsh criminal law of the time, but one by one they fall before Claudia's sorcery. Lilli finally returns with her friend Will to confront Claudia. In a final struggle, Lilli accidentally shatters the mirror. As it bleeds, Claudia dies, leaving Lilli to reunite with her father.

This impressively grim, very well-done take on the famous fairy tale features a great bitch-on-wheels turn by Weaver as the wicked queen.

SOLE SURVIVOR
CBS, 1/9/70

Cast: Major Michael Devlin (Vince Edwards), General Russell Hamner (Richard Basehart), Lt. Col. Joe Gronke (William Shatner), Tony (Lou Antonio), Gant (Lawrence Casey), Brandy (Dennis Cooney), Elmo (Brad Davis), Mac (Patrick Wayne), Corey (Alan Caillou), Beddo (Timur Bashtu), British Pilot (John Winston), Captain Patrick (David Cannon), General Shurin (Noah Keen), British Co-Pilot (Ian Abercrombie), Older Senator (Bart Burns), Amanda (Julie Bennett)

Credits: Director: Paul Stanley; Writer: Guerdon Trueblood; Producer: Walter Burr; Executive Producer: Steve Shagan; Photographer: James Crabe; Art Director: Craig Smith; Music: Paul Glass; Editor: Renn Reynolds; Produced by Cinema Center 100

In the closing days of World War II, the U.S. plane *Home Run* crashed in the Libyan desert, trapping the crew's ghosts there until their bodies receive burial. When a pilot spots the plane, air force investigators Gronke and Devlin check it out, accompanied by Hamner, the *Home Run*'s navigator, whom the crew assumed drowned when he deserted and parachuted out during a dogfight.

The crew watches angrily as now-general Hamner repeats his claim they all jumped with him and tries to fast-talk his way around contradictory evidence. Gronke wants to believe Hamner, but Devlin won't back off. As the guilt-ridden Hamner drinks himself half-blind, Devlin finds conclusive proof of what really happened: Without a navigator, the crew never realized that a tailwind had brought them over land hours before they expected it.

The ghosts confront Hamner, who's drunk enough to see them; horrified, he breaks and confesses everything. One by one, the bodies are exhumed and the ghosts depart; only one, his corpse hidden under the ship, remains, though a determined Devlin continues to search for the body.

This is an offbeat, interesting drama featuring both Captain Kirk (Shatner) and *Voyage to the Bottom of the Sea*'s Admiral Nelson (Basehart).

SOMETHING EVIL
CBS, 1/21/72

Cast: Marjorie Worden (Sandy Dennis), Paul Worden (Darren McGavin), Gehrmann (Jeff Corey), Harry Lincoln (Ralph Bellamy), Ernest Lincoln (John Rubinstein), Stevie Worden (Johnny Whitaker), Beth (Laurie Hagan), John (David Knapp), Laurie Worden (Sandy Lempert, Debbie Lempert), Schiller (Herb Armstrong), Irene (Margaret Avery), Hackett (Norman Bartold), Mrs. Hackett (Sheila Bartold), Mrs. Faraday (Lois Battle), Mrs. Gehrmann (Bella Bruck), Secretary (Lynn Cartwright), Sound Man (John J. Fox), Party-goers (Alan Frost, Carl Gottlieb, John Hudkins, Crane Jackson, Michael Macready, Paul Micale, Margaret Muse, John Nolan, Connie Hunter Ragaway, Elizabeth Rogers, Steven Spielberg, Bruno Vesota)

Credits: Director: Steven Spielberg; Writer: Robert Clouse; Producer: Alan Jay Factor; Photography: Bill Butler; Art Director: Albert Heschong; Music: Wladimir Selinsky; Editor: Allan Jacobs; Produced by Belford Productions, CBS

After the Worden family moves into an old farmhouse, they're soon targeted by poltergeist phenomena, a voice sobbing at night, a mysterious death—and young Stevie becoming increasingly nasty. Paul refuses to credit Marjorie's fears and won't move until they can get a good price on the house. Lincoln, a local occultist, offers to help, then is nearly killed. The evil force possesses Stevie and almost drives Marjorie to suicide. Instead, she confronts Stevie and drives the evil out with the power of her love.

Because Spielberg directed, this is sometimes seen as a dry run for *Poltergeist*, but its possessed kid has just as much in common with *The Exorcist*, really. It's a weak film, but a lot of the little scenes (party chatter, Stevie bouncing a ball off the wall) show the touch that would later make Spielberg a success.

SOMETHING IS OUT THERE
NBC, 5/8–5/9/88

Cast: Jack Breslin (Joe Cortese), Ta'ra (Maryam d'Abo), Lt. Victor Maldonado (Gregory Sierra), Frank Deleo (George Dzundza), Commissioner Estabrook (Robert Webber), Mandy Estabrook (Kim Delaney), Roger (Joseph Cali), Xenomorph (John Putch, Jack Bricker), Wendle (John Putch), Coroner (Earl Billings), Driver (Richard Burns), Maître d' (Christopher Carroll), Interviewer (Andi Chapman), MacReady (Michael Cutt), Man (James Emery), Ron Cobb (Matthew Faison), Dr. Claire Riggs (Melanie Jones), Arnie McKuen (Mickey Jones), Enriquez (Hector Mercado), Kelly Simon (Lori Michaels), Doorman (Hank Rolike), Andrew Brockhurst (Dean Scofield)

Credits: Director: Richard A. Colla; Writer: Frank Lupo; Executive Producers: Frank Lupo, John Ashley; Associate Producer: Bernadette Joyce; Photography: Geoff Burton, Laszlo George; Production Design: Anthony Crowley; Music: Sylvester Levay; Editors: Howard Deane, Larry L. Mills, David Ramirez; Produced by Televentures

Detective Breslin is investigating a gruesome serial killer when he encounters Ta'ra, a telepathic alien who reveals that the killer is a Xenomorph, a murderous shapeshifter that escaped the prison ship Ta'ra was stationed on and butchered the rest of the crew. The killings are to teach it about human anatomy, after which it will blend into human society and seize power—unless Jack and Ta'ra can destroy it. Their investigation is hampered by Breslin's rogue-cop status, his approaching marriage to the police commissioner's daughter and Ta'ra's unfamiliarity with Earth. By the time they track the Xenomorph down, he's taken over the body of Breslin's prospective father-in-law. Refusing to give up the hunt, the duo force the alien back up to the ship, which they destroy, leaving Ta'ra stranded on Earth—but Breslin has already decided she's more fun than his fiancée.

This incredible piece of crap is riddled with holes—from the Xenomorph's powers (first it's a shapeshifter, then a bodysnatcher— presumably so it can burst out of people's bodies like *Alien*) to Ta'ra's knowledge (after years watching human TV broadcasts, she knows nothing about sex or that we're not telepathic?). Cortese gives a good impersonation of a block of wood. Amazingly, this led to a very, very short-lived series.

SOMETIMES THEY COME BACK
CBS, 5/7/91

Cast: Jim Norman (Tim Matheson), Sally Norman (Brooke Adams), Lawson (Robert Rusler), Wayne Norman (Chris Demetral), Scott Norman (Robert Hy Gorman), Mueller (William Sanderson), Vinnie (Nicholas Sadler), North (Bentley Mitchum), Billy (Matt Nolan), Kate (Tasia Valenza), Chip (Chadd Nyerges), Chief Pappas (T. Max Graham), Principal Simmons (William Kuhlke), Officer Neill (Duncan McLeod), Dr. Bernardi (Nancy McLoughlin), Jimmy Norman (Zachary Ball), Desk Sergeant (Dick Solowicz), Police Officer (Rodney McKay), Young Mueller (Don Ruffin), Young Officer Neill (Kimball Cummings)

Credits: Director: Tom McLoughlin; Writers: Lawrence Konner, Mark Rosenthal, based on Stephen King's short story; Producer: Michael S. Murphey; Co-Producer: Milton Subotsky; Photography: Bryan England; Production Design: Philip Dean Foreman; Music: Terry Plumeri; Editor: Charles Bornstein; Produced by Come Back Productions

Years after witnessing his brother's murder, Jim, a teacher, returns to his home town with his family. His arrival stirs up the vengeful ghosts of his brother's hoodlum killers, killed themselves accidentally while trying to murder Jim. By killing some of Jim's students, the ghosts regain physical form, then begin terrorizing Jim, threatening his family, and convincing the police that Jim is to blame for the murders.

When the anniversary of the deaths rolls around, Jim enlists Mueller, the one surviving hoodlum, to help summon Jim's brother, Wayne, whose ghost remains trapped in limbo. With Wayne's help, Jim reenacts the fatal night, forcing the ghosts to repeat their deaths, which destroys their spirits as their bodies were once destroyed. Jim and Wayne can both let go of the past, and Wayne's spirit moves on at last.

This is a good, scary adaptation of King's short story, with some really loathsome villains. The direct-to-video *Sometimes They Come Back Again* was a sequel in name only.

SPECIAL REPORT: JOURNEY TO MARS
CBS, 3/25/96

Cast: Capt. Eugene Slader (Keith Carradine), Ryan West (Judge Reinhold), Tamara O'Neil (Alfre Woodard), Nick Van Pelt (Philip Casnoff), Dr. Lin-Yo Yu (Rosalind Chao), Lt. Tanya Sadavoy (Diane Venora), President Richardson (Elizabeth Wilson), Dean Rumplemeyer (Michael Murphy), Eric Altman (Richard Schiff), Scotty Berlin (Dean Jones), Susan Lobel (Maria Mayanzet), Charley Downing (Richard Young), Dr. Isiohoro (Michael Chinyamurindi), Amanda Whitney (Christine Estabrook), Vicky Dittbenner (Saida Pagan), Young (Leonard Kelly), with Deborah Lacey, Tiiu Leek, Daryl Roach, W.K. Stratton, Anne O'Sullivan

Credits: Director–Co-Executive Producer: Robert Mandel; Writer: Augustus Taylor; Story: Rasha Drachkovitch; Producer: Harry Sherman; Co-Producer: Steve Reagan; Supervising Producer: Bridget Terry; Photography: Bill Klages; Editor: Stephen Michael; Music: Mark Snow; Produced by 44 Blue Productions, Fred Silverman Co., Viacom

In 2005 billions of viewers worldwide are glued to GNN's special broadcast from the SS *Destiny*, two hours shy of making the first manned Mars landing. Soon the audience has a ringside seat to disaster: A radar malfunction imperils the landing; a virus infiltrates *Destiny*'s computers; and nannites, molecule-sized machines, are attacking Captain Slader's brain and nervous system. A member of an anti–space travel group says the ship will never reach Mars in one piece.

As the crew struggles to solve its problems, the TV reporters track the on–Earth investigation, which leads to the corporation that lost the bid to build *Destiny* and hopes to discredit its competitors. As the criminals are taken into custody, the ship lands successfully on Mars. With Slader still ill, Lt. Sadavoy becomes the first to walk on Mars. She spots something astonishing—and communications go dead. The rest is silence...

This was a neat concept that worked for viewers ... until that stupid trick ending!

SPECTRE
NBC, 5/21/77

Cast: William Sebastian (Robert Culp), Dr. "Ham" Hamilton (Gig Young), Mitri Cyon (John Hurt), Inspector Cabell (Gordon Jackson), Anitra Cyon (Ann Bell), Sir Geoffrey Cyon (James Villiers), Lilith (Majel Barrett), Sydna (Jenny Runacre), Butler (Angela Grant), Maid (Linda Benson), Co-Pilot (Michael Latimer), Maids (Penny Irving, Vicki Michelle)

Credits: Director: Clive Donner; Writers: Gene Roddenberry, Samuel A. Peeples; Producer-Story: Gene Roddenberry; Coordinating Producer: Gordon L.T. Scott; Associate Producer: Danny Steinmann; Photography: Arthur Ibbetson; Art Director: Arthur Witherick; Production Manager: Denis Johnson; Music: John Cameron; Editor: Peter Tanner; Produced by Norway Productions, 20th Century–Fox

Criminal psychologist Sebastian asks his alcoholic colleague Hamilton to assist in an investigation: Brit aristocrat Anitra Cyon has hired Sebastian—who believes evil is supernatural, not just psychological—to learn if her libertine brother Geoffrey is possessed. Sebastian wants backup because he's been cursed for reneging on a pact with hell (only a counter-spell by his housekeeper Lilith keeps him alive). A succubus impersonating Anitra seduces Sebastian, but he destroys her with a magic talisman.

Ham refuses to believe in succubi, or that the "accidents" that plague them are occult attacks. In London Sebastian learns that Geoffrey's business rivals have been murdered by a demon. When they reach Geoffrey's home (a decadent pleasure palace), Geoffrey scoffs at his sister's paranoia, which he blames on her sexual repression. Sebastian, however, discovers that construction on the estate freed the arch-demon Asmodeus from a subterranean prison, and the demon has replaced Geoffrey. The investigators find part of the seal that bound Asmodeus, and Sebastian shapes a fragment of it into a magic bullet.

At that night's black mass, the investigators find the rest of the seal—and learn that it's Mitri Cyon whom Asmodeus is impersonating. Geoffrey, his priest, balks when ordered to rape and kill Anitra; Asmodeus then calls on Sebastian to do it, and lifts the curse as an incentive. Instead, Sebastian uses the seal to bind Asmodeus again, shoots him, and escapes with Anitra and Ham as the temple collapses. Asmodeus, however, is not destroyed, and Sebastian warns Ham they'll meet the fiend again.

Spectre was an unsuccessful pilot, but an excellent one, with a fine cast (including Gig Young's last English-language role). Robert Culp's genre credits include two of *The Outer Limits*' best episodes (*Demon with a Glass Hand* and *Corpus Earthling*) and the tongue-in-cheek super-hero show *The Greatest American Hero*.

THE SPELL
NBC, 2/20/77

Cast: Marion Matchett (Lee Grant), Rita Matchett (Susan Myers), Jo Standish (Leila Goldoni), Kristina Matchett (Helen Hunt), Dale Boyce (Jack Colvin), Glenn Matchett (James Olson), Stan Restin (James Greene), Rian Bellamy (Wright King), Jill (Barbara Bostock), Jackie Segal (Doney Oatman), Hugh (Richard Carlyle), Fenetia (Kathleen Hughes), Waiter (Robert Gibbons), Ross (Arthur Peterson)

Credits: Director: Lee Philips; Writer: Brian Taggert; Producer: David Manson; Executive Producers: Charles Fries, Dick Berg; Photography: Matthew F. Leonetti; Art Director: Robert MacKichan; Music: Gerald Fried; Editor: David Newhouse; Produced by Charles Fries Productions, Stonehenge Productions

When overweight, pushed-around Rita discovers she possesses telekinesis—the result of her satanist family breeding for psychic powers—she can't resist turning her powers on the schoolmates who've always taunted her. When her family attempts to exploit her powers, it becomes a battle of mother Marion against her psychic daughter.

This was a blatant—and reportedly very poor—rip-off of Stephen King's *Carrie*. Grant also appeared in *Omen II*; Rita's sister is played by then-teen actress Helen Hunt (*Mad About You, Twister*).

SPIDER-MAN
CBS, 9/14/77

Cast: Peter Parker/Spider-Man (Nicholas Hammond), J. Jonah Jameson (David White), Edward Byron (Thayer David), Captain Barbera (Michael Pataki), Robbie Robinson (Hilly Hicks), Judy Tyler (Lisa Eilbacher), Delivery Man (Dick Balduzzi), Purse Snatcher (Barry Cutler), Prof. Noah Tyler (Ivor Francis), Monahan (Bob Hastings), with Norman Rice, Len Lesser, Ivan Bonar, Carmelita Pope, George Cooper, Robert Snively, Kathryn Reynolds, Harry Caesar, Roy West, James Storm, Ron Gilbert, Larry Anderson, James E. Brodhead, Mary Anne Kascia

Credits: Director: E.W. Swackhammer; Writer: Alvin Boretz; Producer: Edward J. Montagne; Executive Producers: Charles Fries, Daniel R. Goodman; Art Director: James G. Hulsey; Photography: Fred Jackman; Music: Johnnie Spence; Editor: Aaron Stell; Produced by Charles Fries Productions, Dan Goodman Productions

As proof of his powers, a mind-controlling extortionist compels several prominent New Yorkers to steal—then demands $50 million from the city or his next wave of puppets will kill themselves. Meanwhile, science student and would-be news photographer Peter Parker is bitten by a lab-dwelling spider tainted with radioactive waste. When Peter instinctively scampers up a wall to evade being hit by a car, he realizes the radiation endowed him with the spider's abilities.

Rumors of a "spider-man" hit the media, enabling Peter to finally sell some news photos (of himself climbing walls in a costume) to hot-tempered publisher Jameson. When Peter meets Judy Tyler, whose father is one of the extortionist's victims, he decides to use his powers to stop the villain. The trail leads Peter and Judy to Byron, a self-help guru brainwashing his clients. Peter and Judy, unfortunately, become brainwashees, controlled by pins on their jackets.

As the deadline approaches, both Peter and Judy prepare to kill themselves—but Peter's mind comes free when his pin gets damaged. As Spider-Man, he destroys the transmitter on Byron's building, and the feedback reduces Byron to a docile zombie who obeys Peter and confesses to the cops.

Spider-Man, a nerdy teenage kid turned super-hero (yet unable to find happiness in either identity) was the definitive Marvel hero of the sixties. This pilot eliminates the nerdy, lonely Peter (though the comics' Peter had pretty much gotten it together by then, too); despite some slow stretches, it's reasonably enjoyable (although his webbing doesn't look strong enough to hold anyone) and produced an irregularly scheduled, short-lived series.

THE STAND
ABC, 5/8–5/12/94

Cast: Stu Redman (Gary Sinise), Frannie Goldsmith (Molly Ringwald), Randall Flagg (Jamey Sheridan), Nadine Cross (Laura San Giacomo), Mother Abigail (Ruby Dee), Judge Farris (Ossie Davis), Lloyd (Miguel Ferrer), Harold Lauder (Corin Nemec), Trashcan Man (Matt Frewer), Larry Underwood (Adam Storke), Glenn Bateman (Ray Walston), Nick Andros (Rob Lowe), Tom Cullen (Bill Fagerbakke), Ralph Brentner (Peter Van Norden), Rat Man (Rick Aviles), Dr. Herbert Denim (Max Wright), Ray Booth (Patrick Kilpatrick), Charlie Campion (Ray McKinnon), Lucy Swann (Bridgit Ryan), Dayna Jurgens (Kellie Overbey), Julie Lawry (Shawnee Smith), Joe-Bob Brentwood (John Bloom), Bill Hapscomb (Jordan Lund), Monster Shouter (Kareem Abdul-Jabbar), Harry Dorgan (Chuck Adamson), Dying Janitor (Anthony Adler), Whitney Horgan (Sam Anderson), Army Officer (Steve Anderson), Holding Room Officer (Jurgen Baum), Vic Palfrey (Jesse Bennett), Norm Pruett (Johnny Biscuit), Man in Convoy (Scott J. Bronson), 8-Ball Roy (Ervin Butler), Sally Campton (Hope Marie Carlton), Brad Kitchener (David Kirk Chambers), Jump Rope Girl (Lilliana Cabal), Nurse (Laura Conover), Corpse (Bill Corso), Soldiers (Stephen Crackroft, David Daniels), Sarge (Kevin Doyle), Dave Roberts (John Dunbar), Sheriff Baker (Troy Evans), First Rider (Star Fields), George Richardson (Warren Frost), Susan Stern (Cynthia Garris), Henry Dumbarton (Mick Garris), Chad Norris (Leo Geter), Woman in Store (Sandra Gimpel), Army Driver (Paul Grace), Al Blundell (Alan Gregory), Alice Underwood (Mary Ethel Gregory), Cynthia (Thomasyn Harlow), Deputy Kingsolving (Jim Hayne), Teenager (Ryan Healy), Carl Hough (Thomas Holland), Dietz (Sherman Howard), Peter Goldsmith (Ken Jenkins), Major

Jalbert (David Jensen), Dick Ellis (Richard Jewkes), First Woman (Lee Ju), Dave Sellman (Kevin Kennedy), Reporter (Michelle King), Teddy Weizak (Stephen King), Len Carsleigh (Robert Knott), Russ Door (John Landis), Second Biker (Alan Lai), Arlene (Brittney Lewis), Poke (Richard Lineback), Sentry (Mike Lookinland), Woman (Elizabeth Lough), Ace-High (Bruce MacVittie), Heck Drogan (Peter McIntosh), Flu Buddy Man (Patrick McKinley), Vince Hogan (Frank Magner), Rich Moffat (Dan Martin), Army Driver (Dan Miller), Dr. Soames (William Newman), Lisa Hull (Wendy Phillips), Bobby Terry (Sam Raimi), Lisa's Driver (Vince Rodriguez), Trooper (Dondre Sampson), Chicken Man (Michael Sampson), Gina McComb (Sara Schaub), Marcy Halloran (Theresa Sharbough), Lila Bruett (Julie Simper), Baby Lavon (Taylor Smith), Man (David Sosna), Soldier (Alan Stark), Jon (Billy L. Sullivan), Sergeant (George Sullivan), Weeping Woman (Millie Teri), Game-Show Host (Rob Weller), Mike Childress (Michael D. Weatherred), Paul Bulson (Mike Westenkow), Man (Derryl Yeager), Old Man in Store (Brayton Yerkes)

Credits: Director: Mick Garris; Writer: Stephen King, based on his book; Producer: Mitchell Galin; Supervising Producer: Peter McIntosh; Executive Producers: Richard P. Rubinstein, Stephen King; Photography: Edward Pei; Production Design: Nelson Coates; Music: W.G. Snuffy Walden; Editor: Pat McMahon; Produced by Laurel Productions

After a bacterial warfare experiment runs wild and devastates the world, a handful of American survivors are drawn across the country to form a new community around a devout psychic, Mother Abigail. Meanwhile, outlaws, madmen and killers are drawn to the side of satanic Randall Flagg, who plans to rule the world and sets his followers hunting for nuclear weapons. The good guys in the "Free Zone" fight to stop Flagg's schemes, guided by Abigail's insistence everything that happens, good or bad, is the will of God. Sure enough, God slowly drains away Flagg's evil powers. When one of Flagg's men brings home a nuke, the hand of God (literally!) triggers the bomb, destroying Flagg and giving the Free Zoners a chance to rebuild the world.

King's best-seller was overlong as was the miniseries; it's long, it's boring, and having God solve everything makes the efforts of the characters pretty much irrelevant (and suspenseless—who's going to beat God?).

STAR COMMAND
UPN, 3/11/96

Cast: Commander Shade Ridnaur (Chad Everett), Commander Sigrid Ivarsdattar (Morgan Fairchild), Ensign Kenneth Oort (Jay Underwood), Ensign Meg Dundee (Tembi Locke), Ensign Tully Vallis (Chris Conrad), Ensign Ali McGinty (Jennifer Bransford), Ensign Yukiko Fujisaki (Kelly Hu), Ensign Philip Jackson (Ivan Sergei), Ensign Johanna Pressler (Eva Habermann), Captain Elliot (Hans Martin Stier), Gage Balfour (John Hadden), Cyno Commander (Nigel Bennett), Cyno Intelligence Officer (Michael Coatman), Wa Thondu (Jonathan Kinsler), Admiral Cecilia Oort (Nancy Buell), Mialman (David Orth), Cyno First Officer (Joachim Schoenfeld), Governor of Meraz (Rik Maverik), Captain Jacob Aaron (Matthew Burton), Marines (Joseph Sumner, Michael Ozone), Cyno Officer (Emilio De Marchi), Mrs. Fujisaki (Francisca Tu), Commander (Nancy Cyer), Cyno Officers (Barbara Geiger, Kevin Davenport), Flag Captain (Dennenesch Ninnig), Academy Commandant (Errol Shaker), Edward Vallis (Erik Hansen), Trafalgar Officer (Simon Newsby-Koschwitz)

Credits: Director: Jim Johnston; Writer-Executive Producer: Melinda Snodgrass; Producer: Artie Mandelberg; Photography: Achim Poulheim; Production Design: Heinz Röske; Art Director: Udo Scharnowski; Costume Design: Robert M. Moore, Cordula Stummeyer; Music: Lee Holdridge; Editor: Edgar Burcksen; Produced by High Command Productions

In the far future, Earth has colonized the stars—only to have the militaristic colony Cynosura challenge the motherworld and seize every planet possible for itself. On a routine training flight, an Earth ship with a mixed crew of cadets (tough kid, opportunist, scion of a military hero, etc.) cross the path of a Cynosuran ship out to occupy one contested planet. The Cynosurans attack and kill the commander, forcing the green recruits to stand alone. Despite being outgunned, the Earthers' heroic defiance delays the Cynosurans until the Earth forces can arrive. The kids return home having passed their baptism of fire.

Though competent, *Star Command* is thoroughly formulaic in plot and characters.

Considering Snodgrass is one of many *Star Trek: The Next Generation* writers who've complained how restrictive the show's format was, it's a shame she couldn't have done something fresher outside it.

STARCROSSED
ABC, 1/31/85

Cast: Joey (James Spader), Mary (Belinda Bauer), Stewy (Peter Kowanko), Ralph (Clark Johnson), Professor Hobbs (Jacqueline Brookes), Enemy Aliens (Edward Groenenberg, Rowland Groenenberg), Chairman (Chuck Shamata), Federal Agent (James Kidnie), Waiter (Fred Lee), Waitress (Barbara Barnes), Frankie (Andy Maton)

Credits: Director-Writer: Jeffrey Bloom; Producer: Robert Lovenheim; Co-Producer–Editor: Thomas Fries; Executive Producer: Charles Fries; Associate Producer: John W. Rogers; Photography: Gil Hubbs; Art Director: Gerry Holmes; Music: Gil Melle; Produced by Fries Entertainment

"Mary," a beautiful ET fleeing hostile alien assassins across the U.S., receives unexpected and bemused help from Joey, a human auto mechanic. Unsurprisingly, a romance develops.

From most accounts, this is a blatant knockoff of the theatrical hit *Starman* mixed with a strong music-video visual style. Pretty routine.

STEEL JUSTICE
NBC, 4/5/92

Cast: Lt. David Nash (Robert Taylor), Jeremiah Jonas (J.A. Preston), Nicole Robbins (Joan Chen), Gina Morelli (Season Hubley), Lt. Aaron Somes (John Finn), Col. Roland Duggins (Roy Brocksmith), David Nash, Jr. (Maxwell Crowe), Arturo Gomez (Jacob Vargas), Jerrod (Neil Giuntoli), Det. Steve Totten (John Toles-Bay), Assistant DA Wiggins (Ken Thorley), Psychiatrist (Vincent Chase), Tyrone (Garvin Funches), Kareem (Augie Blunt), Guards (Russell Gannon, Al Leong), Goons (Kenry Kingi, Jeff O'Haco), O'Rourke (Parker Timothy Michaels), Yang-Tse (Galen Yuen), with Geoffrey Rivas

Credits: Director–Executive Producer: Christopher Crowe; Writers: Christopher Crowe, John Hill; Producer: Stephen Lovejoy; Co-Producer: R.J. Louis; Co-Executive Producer: Andrew Mirisch; Photography: Michael W. Watkins; Production Design: John W. Corso; Music: Frank Becker; Editor: Heather MacDougall; Produced by Universal

Young David Nash's death devastated his police-lieutenant father. In the aftermath, the grieving Nash is guided by a Mesopotamian time-traveler to the secret of transforming his son's beloved toy dinosaur into a crime-fighting robotic dinosaur fifty feet tall.

From most accounts, this is even sillier than it sounds, and not as interesting. It stars *Twin Peaks'* Joan Chen.

THE STEPFORD CHILDREN
NBC, 3/15/87

Cast: Laura Harding (Barbara Eden), Steven Harding (Don Murray), Mary Harding (Tammy Lauren), David Harding (Randall Batinkoff), Frank Gregson (Ken Swofford), Sheriff (Pat Corley), Lawrence Danton (Richard Anderson), Sandy Gregson (Sharon Spelman), Swimming Instructor (James Staley), George Larson (Raye Birk), Lois Gregson (Debbie Barker), Tom Wilcox (Dick Butkus), Jamison (James Coco), Kenny (John Cameron Mitchell), Wives (Judy Baldwin, Pamela Newman, Ronnie Carol, Toni Sawyer, Barbara Altz, Kim Scolari), Husbands (Peter Elbling, Pirie Jones), Hank Wilcox (Michael Murray), Moreland (John Hostetter), Cindy (Amy Lynne), Baseball Players (Ryan Francis, Philip Waller, Brick Ratliff), Librarian (Pat Darling), Girl (Holly Dorff), Violinist (Sheryl Staples)

Credits: Director: Alan J. Levi; Writer: Bill Bleich; Producer: Paul Pompian; Executive Producers: Edgar J. Scherick, Gary Hoffman; Photography: Steve Shaw; Production Design: Greg Fonseca; Music: Joseph Conlan; Editor: Michael Berman; Produced by Taft Entertainment Television, Edgar J. Scherick Associates

When the Hardings move to Steven's home town of Stepford, everyone but Steven has trouble adapting to the perky, old-fashioned lifestyle: David bonds with fellow rebel Lois; Mary feels like an outcast; and mom Laura worries the school pushes the students too hard. Steven nervously assures the town's Men's Association that none of this will interfere with their plans.

After Lois' free-spirited mom becomes a Donna Reed clone overnight, a fearful Lois asks David to help her run away. After their car is run off the road, Lois leaves the hospital a sweet, bubbly bobby-soxer. No one believes David when he discovers she's an android. A suspicious Laura exhumes Steven's first wife and finds another android. Mary has also been replaced, and her android attempts to kill Laura. Sneaking into the Men's Association, Laura rescues the real Mary, but they're trapped by the men, who insist they're creating perfect children for the community's good. David shows up and rescues Laura and Mary in the nick of time, then an accidental fire destroys the lab, Steven and the Association.

This is more faithful to the original *The Stepford Wives* than the previous TV sequel (*Revenge of the Stepford Wives*), but not terribly good. Familiar faces include Andersen (*The Six Million Dollar Man* series) and Eden (*I Dream of Jeannie*). It was followed, inevitably, by *The Stepford Husbands*.

THE STEPFORD HUSBANDS
CBS, 5/14/96

Cast: Jodi Davison (Donna Mills), Mick Davison (Michael Ontkean), Caroline Knox (Cindy Williams), Miriam Benton (Louise Fletcher), Dr. Frances Borzage (Sarah Douglas), Gordon Hayes (Jeffrey Pillars), Lisa Hayes (Caitlin Clarke), Dennis Knox (Joe Inscoe), Scotty (Christopher Mallon), David Walker (Lou Criscuolo), Cop (Herb Eley), Guards (Richard Fullerton, Stan Kelly), Client (Jim Hillgartner), Cary (Brett Kelley), Ann Wallace (Rebecca Koon), Mailman (David Lenthall), Cameron Wallace (Terry Loughlin), Orderly (Robert Pentz), Carriage Driver (Ephraim Schaffer), ER Doctor (Paul Sincoff), Secretary (Tara Chase Thompson), Salesman (Hank Troscianiec), Driver (Ephraim Schaffer)

Credits: Director: Fred Walton; Writers: Jim Wheat, Ken Wheat, based on Ira Levin's *The Stepford Wives*; Producer: Mitch Engel; Co-Producers: Sollace Mitchell, Natalie Hart; Executive Producer: Edgar J. Scherick; Photography: Don E. Fauntleroy; Production Design: Geoffrey S. Grimsman; Music: Dana Kaproff; Editor: David Byron Lloyd; Produced by Edgar J. Scherick Associates, Victor Television Productions

After the Davisons move to Stepford, Jodi—constantly frustrated by her husband's machismo—learns from her neighbors that he could be made as sweet and docile as *their* doting husbands if he undergoes Dr. Borzage's brainwashing treatment. Jodi agrees—and by the time she has second thoughts, it's too late.

This is the last of three TV-sequels to *The Stepford Wives*.

STEPHEN KING'S "THE LANGOLIERS"
ABC, 5/14–5/15/95

Cast: Laurel Stevenson (Patricia Wettig), Bob Jenkins (Dean Stockwell), Capt. Engle (David Morse), Craig Toomy (Bronson Pinchot), Dinah Bellman (Kate Maberly), Nick Hopewell (Mark Lindsay Chapman), Albert Kaussner (Christopher Collet), Bethany Simms (Kimber Riddle), Don Gaffney (Frankie Faison), Rudy Warwick (Baxter Harris), Harker (Tom Holland), Aunt Vicki (Julie Arnold Lisnet), Richard Logan (Michael Louder), Doris Heartman (Kymberly Dakin), Danny Keene (David Forrester), James Deegan (Chris Hendrie), Gate Agent (Jennifer Nichole Porter), Roger Toomy (John Griesemer), Young Craig (Christopher Cooke), Tom Holby (Stephen King), Boy (David Kelly), Girl (Stephanie Dunham), Father (John Winthrop Philbrick)

Credits: Director-Writer: Tom Holland, based on Stephen King's novel; Producer: David Kappes; Executive Producers: Richard P. Rubinstein, Mitchell Galin; Associate Producer: Michael Gornick; Photography: Paul Maibaum; Production Design: Evelyn Sakash; Music: Vladimir Horunzhy; Editor: Ned Bastille; Produced by Worldvision, Laurel Entertainment, Spelling Films

Ten airplane passengers—including a blind child psychic, a writer, and obsessed businessman Toomy—wake in flight to find everyone else on board has vanished. Engle, a pilot, takes over the plane, but there's no city below and no one answers the radio. When they land, it's at an abandoned airport where food has no taste, matches don't light and the clocks have all stopped—and blind Dinah hears an ominous approaching menace. Jenkins deduces they've traveled through a rip in time and are trapped in the past as it fades away—or more accurately, gets eaten away: The sound Dinah hears is Toomy's childhood bogeymen, the monstrous, devouring Langoliers. Their presence drives Toomey mad; he attacks the others, then runs and hides.

Although fuel, like the matches, is inert in the past, the survivors realize that once it's inside the plane, where "real" time exists, it'll become usable. Toomy's insane attacks slow the refueling until the Langoliers arrive, but then he panics and runs, drawing them away while the plane escapes. Hopewell dies flying the plane back through the rift, but the others arrive at LA in safety.

At three hours, this was about an hour too long to make the most of its *The Twilight Zone* meets *Grand Hotel* premise (good beginning and good end, much too slow in the middle). It features a great turn by Pinchot, though, in a departure from his usual comic roles.

STEPHEN KING'S "THE NIGHT FLIER"
HBO, 2/6/98

Cast: Richard Dees (Miguel Ferrer), Katherine Blair (Julie Entwisle), Merton Morrison (Dan Monahan), Dwight Renfield (Michael H. Moss), Ezra Hannon (John Bennes), Selida McCamon (Beverly Skinner), Buck Kendall (Rob Wilds), Claire Bowie (Richard Olsen), Ellen Sarch (Elizabeth McCormick), Terminal Cops (J.R. Rodriguez, Bob Casey), Nate Wilson (Ashton Stewart), Ray Sarch (William Neely), Henry Gates (Windy Wenderlich), Cop (General Fermon Judd, Jr.), Linda Ross (Deann Korbutt), Libby Grant (Rachel Lewis), Dottie Walsh (Kristen Leigh), Duffery Bartender (Simon Elsworth), Gas Station Attendant (Jim Grimshaw), Caretaker (Matthew Johnson), Drunk (Terry Neil Edlefsen), Dream Vampires (Joy Knox, Randal Brown, Laurie Wolf, Keith Shepard, Ruth Reid), Reporters (Matt Webb, David Zum Brunnen, April Turner, Manya K. Rubinstein), Intern (Kelley Sims)

Credits: Director: Mark Pavin; Writers: Mark Pavin, Jack O'Donnell, from Stephen King's short story; Producers: Richard P. Rubinstein, Mitchell Galin; Co-Producers: Alfredo Cuomo, Jack O'Donnell; Executive Producer: David Kappes; Associate Producer: Neal Stevens; Photography: David Connell; Production Design: Burton Rencher; Music: Brian Keane; Editor: Elizabeth Schwartz; Produced by New Amsterdam Entertainment, Stardust International, Medusa Film SPA

Hard-bitten tabloid reporter Dees is assigned to investigate Dwight Renfield, a "vampire murderer" who flies his plane by night into rural airports and drains the blood of whoever he finds there. Despite increasing evidence that Renfield—who warns Dees off—is a real vampire, Dees refuses to quit until he catches Renfield in the middle of a murder spree. Renfield forces the reporter to drink Renfield's blood, which drives Dees insane; when the police arrive, they gun Dees down as the vampire. Blair, a rival reporter, realizes the truth, but refuses to risk the vampire's wrath by printing it.

This is a dreary adaptation of a poor King story. Ferrer does a great turn as Dees (a character who initially appeared in King's novel *The Dead Zone*), but he's so loathsome, one can hardly put up with him. The director also helmed the theatrical releases *Fright Night* and *Child's Play*.

STEPHEN KING'S "THE TOMMYKNOCKERS"
ABC, 5/9–5/10/93

Cast: Jim Gardner (Jimmy Smits), Bobbie Anderson (Marg Helgenberger), Butch Duggan (John Ashton), Becka Paulsen (Allyce Beasley), Bryant Brown (Robert Carradine), Sheriff Ruth (Joanna Cassidy), Nancy Voss (Traci Lords), Joe Paulson (Cliff De Young), Ev Hillman (E.G. Marshall), Marie Brown (Annie Corley), Chaz Stewart (Chuck Henry), Hilly Brown (Leon Woods), Darcy Brown (Paul McIver), Hobert Noyes (Yvonne Lawley), Eli Borker (Bill Johnson), Barney Applegate (John Steemson), Jingles (Rick Leckinger), Benton Rhodes (Peter Rowley), Mr. Arberg (John Sumner), Patricia McCandle (Elizabeth Hawthorne), Student Bartender (Craig Parker), Kori (Kay Helgenberger), Neurologists (Larry Sanitsky, Helen Medlyn), Dr. Etheridge (Jim McLarty), Boy at Vet (Daniel Bieber), Mr. Allison (Timothy Bartlett), Tommyknocker (Karyn Malchus)

Credits: Director: John Power; Writer: Lawrence D. Cohen, from the Stephen King novel; Producers: Jayne Beiber, Jane Scott; Co-Producer: Lawrence D. Cohen; Executive Producers: Frank Konigsberg, Larry Sanitsky; Photography: Danny Burstall, David Eggby; Production Design: Bernard Hides; Editor: Tod Feuerman; Music: Christopher Franke; Produced by Konigsberg/Sanitsky Co.

When Bobbie Anderson finds a buried, glowing object in the woods, it transforms her small town: A submissive wife murders her cheating husband; a boy magician causes real disappearances; neighbors create inventions that defy science and logic; and one by one, the affected minds are "Becoming" loyal slaves of the thing in the ground, and work on unearthing it. Bobbie's alcoholic lover, Jim—marked for death because he's shielded from Becoming by a metal plate in his head—links this to a local boogeyman legend, the Tommyknockers. By pretending to Become, Jim learns that the Tommyknockers are aliens, killed when their ship crashed centuries ago. Bringing the townsfolk under their spell to make them unearth the ship, the aliens will drain their life-force to revive themselves. Entering the ship, Jim uses the aliens' telekinetic technology to fly the spacecraft out of town, then detonates it, freeing his friends at the cost of his life.

Freely adapted from King's only pure SF novel, this mixes King's stock view of the darkness in small-town life with a routine alien possession story; it wastes Helgenberger's considerable talents.

STILL NOT QUITE HUMAN
Disney, 5/31/92

Cast: Dr. Jonas Carson/Bonus (Alan Thicke), Chip (Jay Underwood), Officer Kate Morgan (Rosa Nevin), Dr. Frederick Barrigan (Christopher Neame), Kyle Roberts (Adam Philipson), Aunt Mildred (Betsy Palmer), Bundy (Kenneth Pogue), Dr. Filmore (Robert Metcalfe), Miss Prism (Sheelah Megill), Tourists (Jerry Wasserman, Carol Mann), Sgt. Murphy (Stephen E. Miller), Airport Guard (Denalda Williams), Trucker (Drew Reichell), Photographer (Michael Rogers), Photograph Woman (Frances Flanagan), Cop (Bobby L. Stewart), Doorman (Cavan Cunningham), Woman in Car (Gwyneth Harvey), Technician (Robert Thurston), Autograph Man (David Hay), Autograph Woman (Veena Sood)

Credits: Director-Writer: Eric Luke, based on characters from Kevin Osborn's *Not Quite Human* books; Producer: James Margellos; Executive Producer: Noel Resnick; Photography: Ron Orieux; Production Design: Mark Freeborn; Music: John Debney; Editor: David Berlatsky; Produced by Walt Disney Co., Resnick/Margellos Productions

In this sequel to *Not Quite Human II*, Dr. Carson is humiliated at a robotics conference because he can't prove his theories without revealing that his "son" Chip is an android. Dr. Barrigan, who dreams of creating a robot army, kidnaps Carson to learn his secrets, replacing him with an android.

Chip soon spots the android ringer, but can't convince anyone except Kyle, a petty thief. Chip reprograms the android—now nicknamed Bonus—to lead them to its home base, but he and Kyle can't penetrate Barrigan's fortress-like estate. Chip convinces Officer Morgan he's onto something, and she has her wealthy aunt arrange a visit to Barrigan. Morgan and Kyle overcome Barrigan's guards while Chip outfights a prototype battle-droid to free his father. Jonas realizes having Chip for a son means more to him than vindicating his research; Kate and Kyle fall in love; Barrigan goes to jail; and Kate's aunt sweeps Bonus off for a romantic idyll before anyone can explain things to her.

The third in this film series is more action oriented than the first two, but still broadly comic (as the erratic Bonus, Thicke milks all the physical shticks he can from the role); it completely ignores the romances set up for father and son in *Not Quite Human II*.

STRANGE NEW WORLD
ABC, 7/13/75

Cast: Captain Anthony Vico (John Saxon), Dr. Allison Crowley (Kathleen Miller), Dr. William Scott (Keene Curtis), The Surgeon (James Olson), Tana (Martine Beswick), Sprang (Reb Brown), Sirus (Ford Rainey), Badger (Bill McKinney), Daniel (Gerritt Graham), Arana (Cynthia Wood), Lara (Catherine Bach), Hide (Norland Benson), Elder (Richard Farnsworth)

Credits: Director: Robert Butler; Writers: Walon Green, Ronald F. Graham, Alvin Ramrus; Producer: Robert E. Larson; Executive Producer: Walon Green, Ronald F. Graham; Associate Producer: Ric Rondell; Photography: Michael Margulies; Art Director: Jack Martin Smith; Music: Richard Clements, Elliot Kaplan; Editors: David Newhouse, Melvin Shapiro; Produced by Warner Bros.

While Vico, Crowley and Scott perform an orbiting suspended-animation test for the science group Pax, a meteor storm devastates Earth, leaving the trio frozen in orbit for 150 years. Thawing out, they return to Earth to find Pax HQ—but are captured by Eterna, a city of immortals sustained by organ transplants from clones. Because cloning destroys the immune system, the Eternans need Scott's immunology expertise—but when they also demand all Vico and Crowley's blood (for antibody transfusions), Scott frees his friends. The resultant melee destroys Eterna's antibacterial force field, and the Eternans die.

Next the trio arrive at a man-made oasis holding an ancient zoo run by descendants of its keepers. The keepers capture Crowley as a poacher, a death-penalty offense. She convinces them she's innocent, but they change their minds again when they discover the poacher Badger sneaking Vico and Scott into the zoo after her. The guys save Crowley from execution, but Badger steals Vico's flare gun, a devastating weapon in the forested oasis. Vico, however, captures the poachers, and Crowley convinces the keeper's leader, Daniel, to trade food and water rather than execute poachers out of hand. The trio move on.

After the failure of *Planet Earth* and *Genesis II*, Warner Bros. gave the concept a third shot—with a different origin for the leads and without Roddenberry's involvement (though the director had made the original *Star Trek* pilot). The results were a lot less interesting (it's a classic problem for TV SF: the Colorful Culture of the Week syndrome) and flopped too. Martine Beswick did better in several Hammer horror films.

THE STRANGER
NBC, 2/26/73

Cast: Neil Stryker (Glenn Corbett), George Benedict (Cameron Mitchell), Dr. Bettina Cooke (Sharon Acker), Prof. Dylan MacAuley (Lew Ayres), Max Greene (George Couloris), Henry Maitland (Steve Franken), Carl Webster (Dean Jagger), Dr. Revere (Tim O'Connor), Steve Perry (Jeffrey Douglas), Mike Frome (Arch Whiting), Eric Stoner (H.M. Wynant), Ward Administrator (Virginia Gregg), Tom Nelson (Buck Young), Trucker (William Bryant), Guard (Steven Marlo), Doctor (Ben Wright), with Margaret Field, Philip Manson, Alan Foster, Gregg Shannon, Jonathan Blake, William Harlow, Peg Stewart, James Chandler, Heather McCoy, Jeanne Bates, Joie Magidow, Kathleen M. Schultz.

Credits: Director: Lee H. Katzin; Writer-Co-Producer: Gerald Sanford; Executive Producer: Andrew J. Fenady; Photography: Keith C. Smith; Production Design: Stan Jolley; Music: Richard Markowitz; Editors: Nick Archer, Melvin Shapiro; Produced by Bing Crosby Productions, Fenady Associates

After returning from a space mission, astronaut Stryker notices more and more oddities in the world around him—like the astonishing number of left-handed people—and finally realizes he's not in the American military base he assumed he was. When he escapes, he sees extra moons in the sky. He eventually discovers he's on Terra, an Earth-counterpart on the far side of the sun where most people are left-handed and the totalitarian atheist state regards Stryker as a freedom-loving, god-fearing threat. Running from the authorities, Stryker sets out to find some way to obtain a ship from Terra's space program and make it back to Earth.

This unsuccessful pilot is yet another variation on *The Fugitive*. Cameron Mitchell is a veteran of countless bad horror films (*Frankenstein Island*, among others), and O'Connor later appeared in NBC's *Buck Rogers* series.

STRANGER IN OUR HOUSE
NBC, 10/31/78

Cast: Rachel Bryant (Linda Blair), Julia (Lee Purcell), Tom Bryant (Jeremy Slate), Mike Gallagher (Jeff McCracken), Peter Bryant (Jeff East), Leslie Bryant (Carol Lawrence), Professor Jarvis (Macdonald Carey), Bobby Bryant (James T. Jarnagin), Dr. Morgan (Gwil Richards), Anne (Kerry Arquette), Marge Trent (Beatrice Manley), Mrs. Gallagher (Patricia Wilson), Mr. Wilson (Ed Wright), Carolyn Baker (Fran Drescher), Sheriff (Billy Beck), Elizabeth (Nicole Keller), Nurse Duncan (Sierra Pecheur), Mailman (Frederick Rule), Beverly Hills Lady (Helena Makela), Veterinarian (John Steadham), Female Rider (Kim Wells)

Credits: Director: Wes Craven; Writers: Max A. Keller, Glenn Benest, based on Lois Duncan's *Summer of Fear*; Producers: Pat and Bill Finnegan; Executive Producers: Max A. Keller, Micheline H. Keller; Photography: William K. Jurgensen; Art Director: Joe Aubel; Music: Michael Lloyd,

John D'Andrea; Editor: Howard A. Smith; Produced by Finnegan Associates, Planetary Pictures, Inc.

After Julia's parents die in a car crash, she moves in with Uncle Peter Bryant and his family. Before long, Rachel Bryant's horse has to be put down (it goes crazy around Julia), Rachel's boyfriend drops her for Julia, and Rachel finds Julia practicing black magic. The Bryants refuse to believe anything bad about Julia, even when a local occultist, Jarvis, suffers a heart attack after Rachel asks him for help, or when Julia's old friend insists the girl Rachel describes is nothing like the real Julia.

Jarvis tells Rachel that if Julia's a witch, she can't be photographed; when Rachel tries, she catches Peter and Julia in bed. Julia reveals that she's really Sarah, Julia's parents' housekeeper; she killed Julia and her family and plans to marry Peter after Rachel's mom suffers another car "accident." Rachel rushes to warn her mother, but Sarah pursues her—and goes flying off a cliff when Mrs. Bryant's out-of-control car hurtles into her path. The Bryants return to normal—but Sarah survives her fatal crash and moves in with a new family elsewhere...

Though familiar material, it's smoothly handled by Wes Craven (*Last House on the Left*, *A Nightmare on Elm Street*, *Scream*). Blair played the victim of demonic possession in the horror landmark *The Exorcist*. Young-adult author Lois Duncan had better success with the big-screen 1997 adaptation of her *I Know What You Did Last Summer*.

THE STRANGER WITHIN
ABC, 10/1/74

Cast: Ann Collins (Barbara Eden), David Collins (George Grizzard), Phyllis (Joyce Van Patten), Bob (David Doyle), Dr. Edward Klein (Nehemiah Persoff).

Credits: Director: Lee Phillips; Writer: Richard Matheson, based on his short story; Producer: Neil T. Maffeo; Executive Producers: Lee Rich, Philip Capice; Photography: Michael Margulies; Art Director: Hilyard Brown; Music: Charles Fox; Editor: Samuel E. Beetley; Produced by Lorimar Productions

When artist Ann Collins tells her husband she's pregnant, he's worried for her life (her last miscarriage almost killed her) and their marriage (he's had a vasectomy). Before long, David has worse things to worry about: Not only is the pregnancy developing three times faster than normal, but Ann is irrationally hostile, drinks literally gallons of coffee a day, and insists on keeping the house at a cozy 50 degrees. Ann suffers agonizing cramps every time she tries to go for an abortion and tells her friend Phyllis the baby causes the cramps to protect itself—just as he makes her drink all that coffee.

One night Phyllis' husband Bob manages to hypnotize Ann; she—or rather, her fetus—reveals that Ann was impregnated by aliens via a ray-beam. The hypnosis loosens the baby's control of Ann enough for her to try inducing a miscarriage—but she fails. The alien regains control and forces Ann to hide out at an isolated cabin until he's born (looking perfectly human). Still under control, Ann joins a dozen other women in the woods with their babies as the aliens (never seen) arrive to take them all away.

Sometimes dismissed as a *Rosemary's Baby* knockoff, it's really much closer to 1962's *Village of the Damned*. It also fits the strengths of screenwriter Matheson, placing ordinary middle-class families in the midst of weirdness (such as his *The Twilight Zone* scripts "Little Girl Lost" and "Nick of Time"); like a lot of *The Twilight Zone* characters, Ann and David don't deserve this, but innocence won't save them. We never learn why the aliens are doing this, or why Ann has to drink so much coffee, but Matheson makes it feel as if, somehow, there are reasons for everything (even if there aren't).

SUSPECT DEVICE
Showtime, 7/30/95

Cast: Daniel Jericho (C. Thomas Howell), Jessica (Stacey Travis), Artemus (Jed Allan), Dr. Flint (Jonathan Fuller), CIA Director (John Beck), Curt (Marcus Aurelius), Dr. Hopkins (Jeff Allin), Jason (Paul Eckstein), Jim (Leonard Turner), Hank (Bill Bolender), Kristen (Heidi Sorenson), Cyborgs (Mark Ginther, Cinda-Lin

James, Alex Wexo), Harriet (Betty Vaughan), Operator (Jill Pierce), Receptionist (Athena Stensland), Bugman (Mike Elliott), Helicopter Pilot (Rick Shuster)

Credits: Director: Rick Jacobson; Writer: Alex Simon; Story: Rob Kerchner; Producer: Mike Elliott; Executive Producers: Roger Corman, Chris Peschken, Chris Naumann; Photography: John Aronson; Production Design: Nava; Music: Christopher Lennertz; Editor: John Gilbert; Produced by New Horizons, Hillwood Entertainment, Showtime

For some time, Jericho, an intelligence-agency researcher, has suffered nightmares of seeing his co-workers killed. The same day a mysterious classified file turns up on his computer, his dreams come true. When he reports the killings, more assassins—including his wife and the police on the case—try to kill him. Jericho only survives because of martial arts skills he didn't know he possessed.

Desperate, Jericho and his best friend Jessica recover the secret file; the assassins intercept them, but Jericho regenerates all his injuries. The file tells them nothing, but Jessica takes Jericho to Dr. Flint's secret base, where they reveal that Jericho is a government-built robot (with an overlay of genetically engineered flesh) with fabricated memories, a nuclear-bomb implant for suicide missions—and a computer glitch that drove Jericho and an unknown second man to murder his co-workers.

Flint offers to deactivate the nuke, but Jericho realizes that Flint intends to deactive *him* instead. Jericho and Jessica flee, but Flint's newest cyborgs capture them and take them to a test site to detonate Jericho safely. The captives escape and overcome the cyborgs, then Jericho blows up the project and himself. But a few months later, the unknown man shows up at Jessica's—a second cyborg, on the brink of detonation…

This is a pretty good handling of an old warhorse (has anyone in TV ever built an android that wasn't for military purposes?), similar to the later *Dead by Midnight*.

SWEET, SWEET RACHEL
ABC, 10/21/71

Cast: Dr. Lucas Darrow (Alex Dreier), Rachel Stanton (Stefanie Powers), Arthur Piper (Pat Hingle), Lillian Piper (Louise Latham), Nora Piper (Brenda Scott), Dr. Tyler (Steve Ihnat), Carey (Chris Robinson), Houseman (Mark Tapscott), Doctor (William Bryant), Minister (Len Wayland), Paul Stanton (Rod McCary), Surgeon (John Alvin), Medical Examiner (John Hillerman)

Credits: Director: Sutton Roley; Writer: Anthony Lawrence; Producer: Stan Shpetner; Photography: James Crabe; Art Director: Paul Sylos; Music: Laurence Rosenthal; Editors: Harry Coswick, James Potter; Produced by ABC

A mental image of Rachel Stanton in danger lures her wealthy psychic husband Paul out the window to his death. The shock of seeing Paul die gives Rachel nightmarish visions, which eventually lead her to parapsychologist Darrow and his psychic aide Carey. Under hypnosis, Rachel flashes back to Paul's death—and Darrow then suffers the same psychic attack that drove Paul to die (with almost the same results). After meeting Rachel's jealous cousin, Nora Piper, and Nora's mother Lillian (a medium) Darrow tries to kill himself (Carey saves him); he suspects that Lillian drove him to it telepathically and murdered Paul the same way.

The Pipers take over Rachel's life and shut Darrow out; when he finally meets Rachel again, she has another vision, runs in fear … and winds up beside her mother's murdered corpse. Darrow refuses to believe her guilt; an accusing vision of Lillian forces him off the road, but he deduces it's "just" another psychic attack. Carey sends the house a telepathic broadcast only another psychic will receive—and when they reach the house, they find Nora hysterical from Carey's attack. She confesses that her father engineered everything to get control of the Stanton fortune, and Dad dies trying to escape. Rachel is free at last.

This entertaining pilot led to the dull *Sixth Sense* TV series with a different cast (reportedly the network was less interested in Dreier's talent than in getting someone better looking for the love scenes). Although the show didn't last beyond a year, it survived in syndication by cutting episodes to thirty minutes and airing them as part of *Night Gallery* (which otherwise fell short of the 100 episodes needed for syndication).

TARGET: EARTH
ABC, 2/5/98

Cast: Detective Sam Adams (Christopher Meloni), Karen (Marcia Cross), Agent Naples (John C. McGinley), Sen. Ben Arnold (Dabney Coleman), Tammy (Courtney Allen Crumpler), Commander Faulk (Chad Lowe), Allison (Melinda Culea), Madeline Chandler (Traci Dinwiddie), Emmett (Jeff Monahan), Carrie (Stephani Victor), Nate (Dilsey Davis), Paul Henke (Jerry Hatmaker), Remo (Jack Moore), Gus Ramus (Alfred Wiggins), Beautician (Jenna Young)

Credits: Director: Peter Markle; Writer: Michael Vickerman; Producer: Lee Rafner; Co-Producers: Jake Froelich, Sam Froelich; Executive Producers: William R. Greenblatt; Sam L. Grogg; Co-Executive Producers: Michael Cieply, Don Safran, George Mays, Carol Ames, Michael Vickerman; Photography: Levie Isaacks; Production Design: Vincent J. Cresciman; Music: Peter Bernstein; Editor: Craig Bassett; Produced by Symphony Pictures

After detective Sam Adams rescues and returns kidnapped Tammy to her mother Karen, Tammy starts drawing pictures of UFOs and speaking only in cryptic, ominous phrases. The reason? Her kidnapper was really a federal agent who downloaded computer codes from an imminent alien invasion into Tammy's brain. Federal agent Naples, a mind-controlled alien "Implant," kills the kidnapper and sends more Implants after Tammy. Sam saves her, but is framed for murder.

Emmett, a rogue fed, contacts Sam and Karen and extracts the computer codes—which he believes can jam the alien fleet's teleporters—from Tammy's brain. An Implant kills Emmett and steals the codes, but Tammy's paintings guide Sam and his partner, Allison, to the alien base. Allison, however, has a latent Implant the aliens now activate—so she kills herself to save Sam. Sam destroys the complex and the teleporter, and the backlash wrecks the orbiting alien fleet. Some of the Implants, however, still survive....

This stock, dull alien-infiltration film was probably a pilot, given the number of loose ends.

THE TEMPEST
NBC, 12/13/98

Cast: Gideon Prosper (Peter Fonda), Anthony Prosper (John Glover), Ariel (Harold Perrineau, Jr.), Will (Dennis Redfield), Miranda Prosper (Katherine Heigl), Capt. Frederick Allen (Eddie Mills), Gator Man (John Pyper-Ferguson), Azalie (Donzaleigh Abernatny), General Grant (Jon Hoffman), General Sherman (Tom Nowicki), Sophie (Rhoda Griffiths), Old Ariel (Lonnie Hamilton), Young Miranda (Rachel Crouch), Lead Raider (Alex Van), Raider (Tim Parati), General Pemberton (Charles Lawlor), Sheriff (David Dwyer), Sentry (Rob Treveiler), Picket (Roby Pettit, Ethan Jensen), Bluecoat (Maxwell Bruce), Scout (Bill Gribble), Lieutenant (James Bigwood), Lewis (Steve Coulter), Slave (Dallas Miller), Overseer (Don Shanks), Sergeant Major (Gary Dow), Posse Member (Rick Lundin), Delia (Adrienne Reynolds), Surgeon (John LaPorte)

Credits: Director–Executive Producer: Jack Bender; Writer: James Henerson; Producer: James Bigwood; Co-Producers: Ronna Slutske, Todd Sharp; Executive Producer: Bonnie Raskin; Photography: Steven Shaw; Production Design: Stephen Storer; Visual Effects: Rob Duncan; Music: Terence Blanchard; Editor: Stephen Lovejoy; Produced by Bonnie Raskin Productions, NBC Studios

In 1851 Southern planter Gideon Prosper begins studying magic under the slave Azalie—which distracts Gideon enough for his greedy brother Anthony to frame and jail him for murder, then seize the plantation. Azalie's magic frees Gideon at the cost of her life, and Gideon flees into the swamps with Azalie's son Ariel and Gideon's daughter Miranda. Fourteen years later, Gideon still refuses to let the kids return to the world—until he discovers Anthony taking money from both sides in the Civil War and plotting to lead General Grant's army into an ambush. Gideon's sorcery lures Anthony, his aide Will, and wounded Union soldier Allen into the swamp. Miranda rescues and falls for Allen, while Anthony learns from the swamp-dwelling "Gator Man" about Gideon's presence and guns his brother down.

Ariel revives Gideon magically, but Gideon now lacks the faith to wield his magic. Anthony captures Miranda and Ariel, and heads out of the swamp with Gideon and Allen on his trail. Gideon realizes he can no longer turn his back on the world, and uses his powers to trap both Anthony and the Confederate forces. Gideon turns his brother over to Grant for a court-martial, then forsakes magic and returns with Ariel and Miranda to begin rebuilding the plantation.

Shifting Shakespeare to the Civil War could have worked, but despite stunning special effects, the movie never clicks, and Fonda (a hot actor for the first time in years due to an Oscar-nominated performance in *Ulee's Gold*) is too weak in the lead. Glover had a genre role as Satan in the 1998-99 *Brimstone* series.

TEMPTING FATE
ABC, 4/5/98

Cast: Dr. Ben Creed (Tate Donovan), John Bollandine (Abraham Benrubi), Ellen Moretti (Ming-Na Wen), Emmett Lack (Matt Craven), Melody (Grace Phillips), Cops (Paul Ben-Victor, Carter Spohn), Dr. Bardwell (Philip Baker Hall), Toby (Randy Oglesby), Orderly (Robert Traill), Old Woman (Annie Abbott), Mr. Braverman (Chris Kriesa), Game Announcer (Trace Turville), Radio Host (Tom Leykis), Government Man (Steve Rankin), Elvis (Steve Murphy), Police Official (Philip Moon), Doctor (Andy Umberger), Floor Nurse (Heather Ehlers), with Fran Bennett

Credits: Director: Peter Werner; Writers: Gerald DiPego, Justin DiPego; Producer: Ron Gilbert; Executive Producers: Sheri Singer, Steve White; Production Design: Philip Vasels; Music: Martin Davich; Editor: Martin Nicholson; Produced by Singer White Entertainment, Pearson Television International

After Ben and John agree to test their friend Lack's experimental dimensional gateway, they're transported to a parallel world without pollution, traffic congestion or crime—and where Ben's deceased counterpart won Melody, the girl Ben lost. Ben and John decide to stay, with Ben explaining away his death and resuming "his" life with Melody.

But this world has a dark side: Personal problems are resolved by "alteration" (brain surgery—which Melody has already undergone); violence is contained by channeling it into organized murder games; and John is exiled to the wilderness for "public obesity." Ben meets Ellen, slated for alteration because she insists she's from another world. Realizing she comes from his Earth, Ben helps her escape, but they become targets in the night's games. Together they manage to jury-rig a gateway and return home in the nick of time.

One of four parallel world films in 1998 (along with *Nightmare Street, The Lake* and *Twice Upon a Time*), *Tempting Fate* is probably the most interesting (if, as usual, lagging behind print versions of this classic SF theme).

TERMINAL VIRUS
Showtime, 10/3/95

Cast: McCabe (James Brolin), Joe Knight (Bryan Genesse), Calloway (Richard Lynch), Shara (Kehli O'Byrne), Rieger (Craig Judd), Bianca (Elena Sahagun), Jihane (Susan Africa), Cassandra (Nikki Fritz), Sam (Bon Vibar), Lawson (Nick Nicholson), Linda (Bobby Greenwood), Corrina (Zarina Torres), Cristina (Cristina Villiegas), Kids (Tom Tauss), Brawler (Lorne Greenwood), Samson (Chris Atkins), Jason (John Rawlins), Bulldog (Darin Spillman), Tony (Eric Connder), Raleigh (Chad Frontiere), Bronson (Marty Jenkowitz), Sheepman (Tom Kern), Tony (Carl Handy), Sabina (Rachel Medavoy), Lisa (Susan Radley), Mary (Cheryl Rabinovitch), Allison (Joan Richter), Jake (Alan Reynolds), Thor (Eric Lambert), Butch (Hank Cronkite), O'Neill (Roger Himmelman), Hal (Horace Mann), Cory (Tim McPherson), Ralph (Mike Hunter), Steve (Samuel Eels), Aaron (Rodney Good), Maniac (Craig Weller), Crazy Ass (Jon Moroney)

Credits: Director: Dan Golden; Writers: Joe Sprosty, Jeff Pulice; Story: Joe Sprosty, Jeff Pulice, Daniella Purcell; Producers: Cirio Santiago, Mike Elliott; Executive Producers: Roger Corman, Lance H. Robbins; Photography: Tom Calloway; Production Design: Ronnie Cruz; Music: Timothy Winn; Editors: Gillian Hutshing, Lynn Hobson; Produced by Showtime, New Horizons

Twenty-three years after a nuclear war, a

biological weapon—a virus that makes sex lethal—has forced men and women to live separately in warring bands, slowly dying out. An experimental antidote allows workers at one lab to have children. The same day a researcher figures out how to mass-produce the drug, bandit chief Calloway wipes out the station from revulsion at seeing men and women together. Joe, the sole survivor, rescues McCabe, Calloway's former partner, from death at Calloway's hands, in return for McCabe testing the serum. They kidnap Shara from the women's camp, but it's Joe and Shara who wind up making love—and live. Calloway, horrified, attacks the couple, but Shara's tribe arrives and overcomes the bandits. Offered freedom and sex, Calloway's men quickly shift sides, and Calloway dies trying to kill Joe. Men and women reunite and humanity is saved!

This is a dumb *Road Warrior* knockoff, though with a few fun moments.

THEM
UPN, 10/8/96

Cast: Simon Trent (Scott Patterson), Kelly Black (Clare Carey), Jake (Dustin Voight), Berlin (Tony Todd), Matt Verlane (Scott Bellis), Sheriff Cole Harper (Lochlyn Munro), Chernobyl (John Cuthbert), Leningrad (Brad Loree), Cardinal (Douglas H. Arthurs) Jessica (Anna Ferguson), Taylor (Wally Dalton), Logan (Patrick Keating), with Caprice Benedetti, Andrea Libman, Michele Goodger, Stephen E. Miller

Credits: Director: Bill L. Norton; Writer: Charles Grant Craig; Story: Patrick Gilmore, Charles Grant Craig; Producer: David Roessell; Executive Producers: Stephen J. Cannell, Kim LeMasters; Co-Executive Producer: Patrick Faulstich; Photography: Tobias Schliessler; Production Design: Phil Schmidt; Music: John R. Graham; Editor: Michael Schweitzer; Produced by Stephen J. Cannell Productions, New World Television

It starts when robed, electrical aliens disrupt Simon Trent's high-altitude research, then disintegrate. A few years later, the alien Berlin attacks and kills Simon's sister, Sally, a reporter who's found proof of Simon's story. Her nephew Jake reaches Simon, and a mystery girl saves them from Berlin, who tracks them with dogs of living energy.

Meanwhile, the aliens begin mind-controlling small-town protesters fighting construction of a local power plant that the aliens will secretly use to bring more of their kind to Earth. The mystery girl saves one protester, Kelly, who hooks up with Simon and Jake to explore the plant—where they're captured by Berlin, who explains that his sterile race needs human genes to restore their fertility. The little girl saves them from Berlin and destroys his lab; she's a Nomad, created by the aliens but scorned for her grotesque true form. That makes her willing to help humans—but can she? For soon the aliens will seduce humanity with cures for famine, cancer and pollution (problems they created!)—and back in the lab, Berlin has duplicated Sally to use against Simon and Jake.

Them is a stock, irritatingly stylized invasion thriller.

THEY
Showtime, 11/14/93

Cast: Miss Florence Latimer (Vanessa Redgrave), Mark Samuels (Patrick Bergin), Chris Samuels (Valerie Mahaffey), Nikki Samuels (Nancy Moore Atchison), Sue Madehurst (Rutanya Alda), Kaitlin Samuels (Brandlyn Whitaker), Len Ott (Ken Strong), Madden (Bill Bender), Arthur Madehurst (Benji Wilhoite), Shannon Nash (Christina Keefe), Dance Teacher (Jean Louisa Bradford), Nurse (Jalia Murry), Client (Charles McLawhorn), Jill (Genevieve Barns), The Owl Girl (Kristina Colavita)

Credits: Director: John Korty; Writer: Edithe Swensen, based on Kipling's short story; Producer: Bridget Terry; Co-Producer: Art Seidel; Photography: Hiro Narita; Production Design: Vaughan Edwards; Composer: Gerald Gouriet; Editor: Jim Oliver; Produced by Bridget Terry Productions, Viacom, Showtime

Mark Samuels was a distant, workaholic father to his daughter Nikki; weeks after she dies in a car accident, Mark insists he's done grieving and ready to move on with his life—and does his best to ignore his nightmares and the way Nikki's drawings keep turning up in his papers. Her drawing of an old Southern house leads Mark to Miss Florence, a blind psychic whose house is filled with the ghosts of children unable to pass on. Nikki is one such, unable to leave until

Mark resolves his buried grief. Another ghost, lost so long she can never leave, has befriended Nikki and fears Mark will take her new friend away. The jealous ghost turns its attention to Nikki's sister Kaitlin, luring her to suicide; Mark saves her, then finally shares the love with Nikki's ghost he often forgot to give her in life. Both father and daughter are free to move on.

They features excellent performances by Bergin and Mahaffey as the grief-stricken parents, but the threatening ghost seems puzzlingly unresolved (it makes no attempt to stop Nikki and Mark from reuniting), and Redgrave's performance is surprisingly weak.

THE THIEF OF BAGHDAD
NBC, 11/23/78

Cast: Prince Taj (Kabir Bedi), Hasan (Roddy McDowall), Wazir Jandur (Terence Stamp), Caliph (Peter Ustinov), Abu Bakar (Frank Finlay), Perizadah (Marina Vlady), Princess Yasmine (Pavla Ustinov), Gatekeeper (Ian Holm), Genie (Daniel Emilfork), with Ahmed El-Shenawi, Kenji Tanaki, Neil McCarthy, Vincent Wong, Leon Greene, Bruce Montague, Arnold Diamond, Raymond Llewellyn, Geoffrey Cheshire, Gabor Vernon, Kevork Malikyan, Michael Chesdon, Ahmed Khali, Yasher Adem, George Little

Credits: Director: Clive Donner; Writer: A.J. Carrothers; Adaptation: Andrew Birkin; Producer: Aida Young; Executive Producer: Thomas M.C. Johnston; Photography: Denis Lewiston; Art Director: Edward Marshall; Costume Designer: John Bloomfield; Music: John Cameron; Editor: Peter Tanner; Produced by Palm Productions

Riding to Baghdad to woo beautiful Princess Yasmine, Prince Taj's caravan is ambushed by bandits sent by his treacherous vizier, Jandur. Taj survives but reaches Baghdad alone, penniless and in rags. Fortunately, he's befriended by the urbane thief Hasan, who helps him reach the palace. Then Jandur arrives, claiming Taj's throne and Yasmine. When Taj stabs Jandur, the sorcerer reveals that his soul lies hidden outside his body—and without a soul, he cannot die.

With Baghdad and Yasmine in Jandur's grasp, Taj and Hasan launch a desperate quest—with the reluctant help of a powerful genie—to find the object holding Jandur's soul. When they succeed, Taj confronts Jandur again and smashes the soul-stone—and the evil Jandur disintegrates. Taj has his throne and his love—and Hasan heads off for more adventures with Yasmine's handmaiden, Perizadah.

This is a good film with winning performances by Stamp and McDowall, though not up to the original (a silent Douglas Fairbanks swashbuckler) or the wonderful 1940 remake with Sabu as the thief.

30-YEARS-TO-LIFE
UPN, 10/15/98

Cast: Vincent Dawson (Robert Hays), Vinnie Dawson (Hugh O'Conor), Derek (Christien Anholt), Darla (Amy Robbins), Kate (Gabrielle Lazure), Gweneth (Mirabelle Kirkland), Norreen (Jana Shelden), Kyle (Zoot Lyham), Ben (Doug Haley), Detective Sidney (Geoffrey Bateman), Sander (Vernon Bobicheff), Graham (Michael J. Shannon), Oliver Mather (Michael Byrne), Lucy (Josephine D'Arby), Manager (Kenny Seymour), Judge Stark (Larue Hall), Prosecutor (Robert Hall), Doctor (Liza Sadovy), Teacher (Bill Dunn), Clerk (Jules Webner)

Credits: Director: Michael Tuchner; Writer: Shawn Alex Thompson; Producer: Ken Gord; Co-Producer: Jimmy de Brabant; Executive Producers: Lewis B. Chesler, David M. Perlmutter, Stephen Ujlaki; Photography: Jon Joffin; Production Design: Sheila Haley; Music: Jim McGrath; Editor: Dean Balser; Produced by Alliance Communications, CLT-UFA/Delux Productions, Chesler/Perlmutter Productions

In 2020 Vinnie, a rebellious teen, is sentenced to "geriatrification" for murdering his stepfather (he was framed) and aged 30 years in mere hours. Although stunned at his 45-year-old body, he's determined to clear his name. Vinnie suspects his stepfather's business partner murdered him for opposing a merger. Vinnie also becomes involved with a waitress, Darla, who doesn't know that he's a "wrinkler." When Vinnie discovers Derek, his stepsister Gweneth's fiancé, is also sleeping with Gweneth's mom, he investigates and finds proof that Derek framed him. After tricking Derek into a taped confession, Vinnie undergoes de-aging and returns to teen life—even though that means Darla is now far too old for him.

This is a routine mystery, but Hays (previously in the *Starman* TV series) gives a good turn as a boy forced to grow up overnight.

THIS HOUSE POSSESSED
ABC, 2/6/81

Cast: Gary Straihorn (Parker Stevenson), Sheila (Lisa Eilbacher), Rag Lady (Joan Bennett), Arthur Keene (Slim Pickens), Tanya (Shelley Smith), Robbins (Bill Morey), Helen (Jan Shutan), Pasternak (David Paymer), Feeney (Jack Garner), Lucille (K. Callan), Lt. Fletcher (Barry Corbin), Donny (John Dukakis), Holly (Amanda Wyss), Martha (Ivy Bethune), Clerk (Philip Baker Hall), Orderly (Doug Johnson)

Credits: Director: William Wiard; Writer-Producer: David Levinson; Executive Producer: Leonard Goldberg; Photography: Thomas Del Ruth; Art Directors: Jack DeShields, Dale Koppe; Music: Billy Goldenberg; Editor: Leon Carrere; Produced by Mandy Productions

Recovering from a nervous breakdown, rocker Straihorn retreats into his isolated, automated, computerized luxury home, accompanied only by his attractive nurse, Sheila. Which soon proves to be one person too many—for the house, acting as if jealous, seems determined to kill her and keep Straihorn around, forever. Only the eccentric Rag Lady knows its secret; can Sheila and Straihorn discover the truth in time?

Reviews were not favorable. Familiar faces include Joan Bennett (the Collins family matriarch on *Dark Shadows*) and K. Callan (*Lois and Clark: The New Adventures of Superman*).

THROUGH THE MAGIC PYRAMID
NBC, 12/6–12/13/81

Cast: Bobby Tuttle (Chris Barnes), Ay/Mr. Mantley (Hans Conried), Horembeb (Vic Tayback), Princess Baket (Olivia Barash), Eleanor Tuttle (Betty Beaird), Hotep (Gino Conforti), Nefertiti (Elaine Giftos), Sam Tuttle (James Hampton), Bonkers (Robbie Rist), Akhenaten (Kario Salem), Tut (Eric Greene), Moontdeme (Jo Ann Worley), Princess Ankelsen (Sydney Penney), with Woodrow Chambliss, Mel Berger, Mary Carver, Kurt Christian, Daniel Leon, Hoke Howell, Ralph Dougherty

Credits: Director–Executive Producer: Ron Howard; Writer-Producers: Rance Howard, Herbert J. Wright; Associate Producer: John A. Kuri; Art Director: John A. Kuri; Photography: Gary Graver; Music: Joe Renzetti; Editor: Robert Kern, Jr.; Produced by Major H. Productions

When Bobby Tuttle receives a toy pyramid for his birthday, it turns out to be a talisman that opens time and space to him. Using it, Bobby travels back to the time of ancient Egypt, where he helps a young prince overcome enemies and obstacles to win the throne as King Tut. Returning home, Bobby realizes there's no limit to where the pyramid can take him...

This was made as a comedy/time-travel pilot, but it didn't fly.

THE TIME MACHINE
NBC, 11/5/78

Cast: Neil Perry (John Beck), Weena (Priscilla Barnes), Bean Worthington (Andrew Duggan), Agnes (Rosemary De Camp), John Bedford (Jack Kruschen), Ralph Branly (Whit Bissell), Ariel (John Hansen), General Harris (R.G. Armstrong), Sheriff Finley (John Doucette), Henry Haverson (Parley Baer), with John Zaremba, Peg Stewart, Bill Zuckert, Hyde Clayton, Craig Clyde, Scott D. Curran, Debbie Dutson, Buck Flower, Paul Grace, Tom Kelly, Maurice Grandmason, Julie Parrish, Walt Price, H.E.D. Redford, Michael Ruud, Scott Wilkinson, James Lyle Strong, Kerry Summers

Credits: Director: Henning Schellerup; Writer: Wallace Bennett, based on H.G. Wells' novel; Producer: James Simmons; Executive Producers: Charles E. Sellier, Jr., James L. Conway; Photography: Stephen W. Gray; Art Director: Paul Staheli; Music: John Cavacas; Editor: Trevor Jolley; Supervising Editor: James D. Wells; Produced by Schick Sunn Classics Productions

Neil Perry wants to perfect his prototype time machine, but his Megacorp bosses insist he focus on moneymaking weapons research. Perry decides to test the machine first, and finds himself bounced from the past to a distant future where war and the misuse of science have almost destroyed mankind. Normal humans—the peaceful Eloi—live in fear of the mutated, subterranean Morlocks. The Morlocks steal the time machine and attack the Eloi, but Perry uses fire to drive the dark-dwelling, light-sensitive Morlocks away. Perry leads pretty Weena and the other Eloi in a torch-wielding raid to free the Morlocks' prisoners, then seals the Morlock tunnels from inside, reclaims the time machine and returns to the present. To his horror, Megacorp not only won't abandon weapons research, they want to use his machine to steal better weapons from the future. Disgusted, Perry returns to the Eloi—and Weena—and devotes his genius solely to benefiting mankind.

This would stink even if not compared to the excellent 1960 adaptation; Beck is bland and stiff, the script is stupid and preachy, the effects are cheap.

THE TIME TRAVELERS
ABC, 3/19/76

Cast: Dr. Clinton Earnshaw (Sam Groom), Jeff Adams (Tom Hallick), Dr. Joshua P. Henderson (Richard Basehart), Jane Henderson (Trish Stewart), Dr. Helen Sanders (Francine York), Dr. Cummings (Booth Colman), Dr. Stafford (Walter Burke), Sharkey (Dort Clark), Irish Girl (Kathleen Bracken), Betty (Victoria Meyerink), Chief Williams (Baynes Barron), News Vendor (Albert Cole), Police Sergeant (Richard Webb), Jim Younger (Patrick Culliton), Pegleg (Jon Cedar), Hansom Cabbie (Gil Lamb), Hospital Attendant (Jim Ness), Band Master (Fred Borden), Prostitute (Rita Lupino)

Credits: Director: Alexander Singer; Writer: Jackson Gillis; Story: Rod Serling; Producer: Irwin Allen; Photography: Fred Jackman; Art Director: Eugene Lourie; Music: Morton Stevens; Music Supervisor: Lionel Newman; Editor: Bill Brame; Produced by Irwin Allen Productions, 20th Century–Fox Television

When rare, deadly "woods disease" strikes New Orleans, pathologist Earnshaw fears a plague, for the only known cure was lost with its discoverer in the 1871 Chicago Fire. Adams, a federal agent, offers to take Earnshaw through an experimental time-gate to meet Dr. Henderson—but they arrive with only 29 hours before the fire. Worse, Henderson can't explain why his patients haven't died, and Earnshaw can't figure it out either—though he does fall for Henderson's niece, Jane. As the fire breaks out, Earnshaw comes down with woods disease, but recovers; the cure is a fungal antibiotic contaminating Henderson's homemade wine. Braving the fire, Earnshaw finds a bottle to take back to the present, but decides to stay with Jane—only to see her die in the fire. Earnshaw returns with Adams, stops the plague, and agrees to join the time-travel project as medical advisor.

Irwin Allen turned out a variety of successful but lowbrow SF series in the sixties (*Voyage to the Bottom of the Sea*—starring Basehart—and *Lost in Space* are the best known); this amounts to a long episode of Allen's *Time Tunnel* series, with much the same flaws (dull plot, stiff leads, use of stock footage—in this case fire clips from *In Old Chicago*). Allen reused the premise in the unproduced *Time Project* (1980).

TIMELOCK
Sci-Fi, 1/24/98

Cast: Capt. Jessie Teegs (Maryam d'Abo), Riley (Arye Gross), Williams (Jeffrey Meek), McMasters (Jeff Speakman), Tibock (Ricco Ross), Warden Andrews (Thomas G. Waites), Sullivan (Nicholas Worth), Larden (Joey DeDio), Admiral Teegs (Martin Kove), Neville (Tom Billett), Snapper (Shon Greenblatt), Ensign (Andrew James Jones), Computer Tech (Patrick Malone), Clarissa (Cheryl Bartel), Ali (Jon Bascoe), Prisoner (Phil Brock), Dr. Teller (Ira Heiden), Inmate (Kyle Reed), Lieutenant (Kirk Pinchon), Barber (Roadblock Martin), Wilson (J. Lamont Pope)

Credits: Director: Robert Munic; Writers: Joseph Barmettie, J. Reifel; Producers: John Eyres, Barnet Bain; Line Producer: Cynthia H. Margulis; Executive Producers: Paul Eyres, John Eyres; Production Design: John Zachary; Photography: Steve Adcock; Costumes: Richard Delgado; Music: Marco Marinangeli; Editor: Amanda I. Kirpaul; Produced by EGM Films International

In AD 2251 the murderous, insane McMasters organizes a breakout from an asteroid prison, having hired the prison transport's co-pilot, Wilson, to fly them off. Wilson's captain, Teegs, proves less cooperative—and harder to kill than expected. With the help of Riley, a neurotic hacker convict, Teegs tries to reach the ship first and escape. After Wilson is killed, McMasters forces Teegs to fly the cons out. Riley outmaneuvers McMasters' men to rescue Teegs, and they escape on a shuttle, stranding McMasters on the ship as it's blasted by an orbiting space station.

Timelock offers good performances from the leads in an otherwise uninteresting action film.

TIMESTALKERS
CBS, 3/10/87

Cast: Scott MacKenzie (William Devane), Georgia Crawford (Lauren Hutton), Joseph Cole (Klaus Kinski), General Joe Brodsky (John Ratzenberger), Texas John Cody (Forrest Tucker), Sam (Tracey Walter), Blacksmith (James Avery), Bart (R.D. Call), Dr. Mathew Crawford (John Considine), Billy McKenzie (Danny Pintauro), Mrs. McKenzie (Gail Youngs), Callan (Patrick Baldauff), Barman (Ritch Brinkley), Michael (J. Michael Flynn), Grover Cleveland (A.J. Freeman), Carol (Deborah Lovin), Carla (Begona Plaza), Sgt. Filton (Tim Russ), Driver (Michael Strasser), Cowboys (Buck Taylor, Terry Funk, Tommy Lamey), Jack (John Wesley), Undertaker (Burke Denis), with Robert Bravler, Eric Mansker, Monty Cox, Seth Mitchell, Jedd Nabonsal, George Parrish, Christopher Doyle, Ben Rawnsley, Arnold Roberts, Tim Gilbert, Dean Smith, John Timothy Williams, Lane Leavitt, Merritt Yohnka

Credits: Director: Michael Schultz; Writer: Brian Clemens; Story: Ray Brown, Brian Clemens; Producers: John Newland, Richard Maynard; Executive Producers: Charles Fries, Milton T. Raynor; Photography: Harry Mathias; Production Design: Shay Austin; Music: Craig Safan; Editor: Conrad M. Gonzalez; Produced by Fries Entertainment, Newland-Raynor Productions

Shortly after his family's accidental death, history professor and Old West expert Scott MacKenzie buys a century-old tintype that shows a gunslinger wielding a modern .375 magnum. Only visiting historian Georgia believes Scott's theory that the man was a time-traveler; she convinces him to help her locate the town where the photo was taken. When they find and visit the town, she travels back in time herself to explore, then returns and tells Scott the truth: She's from 2586 and hunting Cole, a time-traveling scientist out to change history. Cole meanwhile, spots Georgia and tracks her to the present, where he tries to derail Scott's investigations.

Despite Cole's efforts, Georgia and Scott put the truth together. The town is where outlaws almost killed Georgia's ancestor, Crawford, in 1886; if Cole causes Crawford's death, Georgia's influential father—whose restrictions on scientific research have long frustrated Cole—will never be born. In 1886 Georgia and Scott see Cole gun down the cowboy who saved Crawford—so Scott, a marksman himself, steps in and rescues Crawford, then slaps leather with Cole and wins. Georgia and Scott return to the present. Before leaving for her own time, however, Georgia finds a loophole in the no-changing-history laws that rationalizes sending Scott back in time to save his family.

Written by a regular writer for *The Avengers*, this is one of TV's better time travel stories, with a solid cast. This was Hollywood veteran Tucker's last role and the TV-movie debut for German star Kinski (whose credits include 1979's *Nosferatu*).

TO CATCH A YETI
Disney, 1/12/95

Cast: Dave Bristow (Jim Gordon), Big Jake Grizzly (Meatloaf), Amy Bristow (Chantallese Kent), Kate Bristow (Leigh Lewis), Wesley Sturgeon (Jeff Moser), Blubber (Rick Howland) Arnold Sturgeon (Mike Panton), Angelica Sturgeon (Mona Matteo), Joan (Ria Franchuk), Butler (Reginald Doresa), Pilot (Dr. Andreas M. Haralampides), Trucker (David Walberg), Guard (Rob Rutter), Bag Lady (Audrey Barraclouth), Young Man (Neil Verburg), Young Woman (Stacey Simon), Gas Attendant (Dave Goguen), Ticket Clerk (Carolyn Tweedle), Customs Officer (Ron Donovan), Mike Kelly (Terry Logan), Cabbies (Jayme Hutchinson, Sam), Boy (Zebulon Reid), Yeti Skiers (Benjamin Gooch, Erinn Thompson, Alexis Atken), Yeti Voice (Kevin Robbin)

Credits: Director: Bob Keen; Writer: Paul Adam; Producers: Lionel Shenken, Beverly Shenken-Brin; Executive Producer: Noel Cronin; Photography: David Perrault; Art Director: Gerine De Jong; Music: Jack Lenz, Brent Barkman, Carl Lenox; Editor: Stewart Dowds; Produced by Dandelion Productions

To please his obnoxious, sadistic kid Wesley, wealthy Sturgeon hires legendary hunter Big Jake to capture a yeti. Jake deduces that yetis aren't giants, they're small creatures with giant feet, an insight that enables him to find one—which ducks him by hiding in Dave Bristow's mountaineering tent. When Dave returns home, his daughter Amy adores "Hank." When Jake captures the yeti, Amy pursues him and even convinces her parents to help her rescue Hank. They then elude Jake and Wesley long enough to return Hank to Nepal and reunite him with the other yeti.

This is a really poor kids' film; the animatronic Hank is amazingly unconvincing.

TO THE ENDS OF TIME
Sci-Fi, 11/30/96

Cast: King Francis (Joss Ackland), Young James (Glenn Walker Harris), James (Tom Schultz), Princess Stephanie (Christine Taylor), Karnissa (Sarah Douglas), Aeschylus (Michael Silverback), Sauris (James Paradise), Soffo (Wayne Thomas Yorke), Young Stephanie (Kristin Sweet), Alexander (William Zabka), Don (Michael Wise), Old Dan (Harper Roisman), Jarad (Terence Marinan), Old James (Arthur Tovey), Aralon Officer (Stuart Weiss), Apprentice (Steven Kent), Morlin Captain (Tony Pandolfo), Def (Christopher Costa), Woman (Debra Burkhardt), Singer (K.T. Mahoney), Teen James (Saige Walker), Mazar (Gary Kasper), Guard (F. Scott Collins), Lookout (James Servais), Advisor (Cully Frederickson), Navigator (Billy Ray Orme), Morlin Officer (Robert Nassry), Morlin General (Marshall Manesh), Emissary (Vachik Mangassarian), Workers (A.V. Tosh, Richard Tanner), Soldiers (Theodore Melfi, Ric Drason, Robert Calvin), Cannoneer (Calvin Willis), Servant (Rick Fitzgerald), Farmer (Eddie Espinoza), Flower Attendant (Dana Cox), Old Stephanie (Irmsie Brown), Baby (Mackenzie Pamela King)

Credits: Director: Markus Rothcranz; Writers: Markus Rothcranz, Dan Benton, Thomas Wheeler; Producers: Ash R. Shah, Raj Mehrotra; Co-Producer: Todd King; Executive Producers: Sunil R. Shah, Anders P. Jensen, Sundip R. Shah; Photography: Bryan Duggan; Music: Eckart Seeber; Editor: Jack Tucker; Produced by Imperial Entertainment, Totem Pictures

In a world where cities float on air and galleons sail the clouds, King Francis of Aralon assigns his sorcerer Aeschylus to put an end to war. Aeschylus designs a clock that could age Aralon's enemies to destruction within days, but the horrified Francis rules against using it.

Karnissa, Aeschylus' former pupil, has no such scruples: She steals the plans, murders the mage, then builds and activates the clock. Aralon immediately starts aging, and their fleet decays while attacking Karnissa. Young Princess Stephanie and page James age into adults; learning his brother died with the fleet, James sets off to stop the clock on his own. Treacherous Sauris seizes control of Aralon for Karnissa, but dies trying to kill Stephanie. James reaches Karnissa's castle, but grows too old to stop the clock. Then a diamond falls from a ring Stephanie gave him and jams the gears, tearing the clock apart. The castle collapses and everyone reverts to their true age except Alex and Stephanie, who inexplicably stop de-aging as young adults and marry.

This pleasantly entertaining fantasy features Sarah Douglas (*Superman II*) as the villain.

TOOTHLESS
ABC, 10/5/97

Cast: Dr. Katherine Lewis (Kirstie Alley), Thomas Jameson (Dale Midkiff), Bobby Jameson (Ross Malinger), Raoul (Daryl "Chill" Mitchell), Rogers (Lynn Redgrave), Carrie (Kathryn Zaremba), Trevor (Marcus Toji), Mindy (Melanie Mayron), Officer (Yeardley Smith), Jo (Eileen Brennan), Gwen (Kimberly Scott), Dr. Green (John P. Connolly), Carrie's Mom (Catlin Adams), Wood (Patrick Kerr), Jeff (Jake Richardson), Kurt (Zachary Duhame), Phil (Arjay Smith), Lori's Mom (Katherine Cortez), Young Katherine (Jamie Renee Smith), Bernie the Bunny (Michael E. Bauer), Lori (Kaley Cuoco), Man in Hellavator (Augie Amarino), Board Members (Joel Swetow, Eileen Brennan), Messenger (Stephen Spacek), Cupid (Thomas Crawford), Photographer (Candy Trabucco)

Credits: Director: Melanie Mayron; Writer: Mark S. Kaufman; Producer: Joan Van Horn; Co-Producer: Mike Karz; Executive Producer: David Hobermann; Photography: Sandi Sissel; Production Design: Nina Ruscib; Music: David Michael Frank; Editor: Henk Van Eeghen; Produced by Walt Disney Television

When Katherine, a dentist, dies in an accident, she learns that because she chose to live without love after her father's death, she's on probation until she earns her way into heaven ... as the new Tooth Fairy. Katherine is strictly forbidden against meddling in mortal affairs—but she can't help befriending motherless Bobby, whose hunky but workaholic father, Tom, is never there for him. When Bobby tells his friends, they begin deliberately losing teeth so they can also enlist Katherine's help (on losing weight, improving grades, etc.)—but helping them violates her probation. When Bobby is threatened with expulsion for publicly believing in the Tooth Fairy, Katherine vindicates him by materializing before the whole school (and Tom, who is finally supporting his son). Her probation is shot, but her father calls in some favors and gets Katherine returned to life. Able to love at last, she hooks up with Bobby and his father as mortals.

Toothless is a so-so variation on the angel-earning-her-wings plotline TV is so fond of (*Unlikely Angel, The Smothers Brothers Show, Highway to Heaven,* etc.). Familiar faces include Alley (*Star Trek II, Runaway*) and Midkiff (*Time Trax*).

TOPPER
ABC, 11/9/79

Cast: Marion Kerby (Kate Jackson), George Kerby (Andrew Stevens), Cosmo Topper (Jack Warden), Clara Topper (Rue McClanahan), Fred Korbel (James Karen), Wilkins the Butler (Macon McCalman), Stan Ogilvy (Charles Siebert), Mechanic (Larry Gelman), Saleswoman (Gloria LeRoy), Lucy Johnson (Estelle Omens), Charlene (Lois Areno), Mrs. Quincy (Frances Bay), Steve (Gregory Chase), Hostess (Ellen March), Marsha (Mary Peters), 1st Jailman (Tom Spraitley), Man at Disco (Marshall Teague), Nurse (Janet Wood)

Credits: Director: Charles S. Dubin; Writers: George Kirgo, Mary Anne E. Kascia, Michael Scheff; Producer: Robert A. Papazian; Executive Producers: Kate Jackson, Andrew Stevens; Photography: Robert Caramico; Art Director: Allen E. Smith; Music: Fred Karlin; Editor: George Jay Nicholson; Produced by Cosmo Productions, Robert Papazian Productions

When the wealthy, irresponsible Kerbys die in a car crash, their ghosts remain trapped on Earth until they perform some good deeds—so they decide to liberate their stuffy but good-hearted banker, Topper, from his joyless upper-class life. Topper doesn't want to change and hates talking to people no one else can see—and when he does loosen up, his stiff, shallow wife Clara freaks out. Topper rebels and leaves her; the Kerbys then use their powers to remind Clara of the fun she and Cosmo used to have. After Topper almost dies in a crash, the Kerbys convince him to live life to the fullest—and Clara is finally willing to help. The Kerbys have earned entry into heaven.

Topper (the best known novel by fantasy writer Thorne Smith) was brilliantly brought to life in the 1933 film starring Constance Bennett, Cary Grant and Roland Young, who played Topper in two sequels (Leo G. Carroll did the TV series). With no comparable star power, this flop pilot is quite forgettable, and the very blue-collar Warden isn't the least bit stuffy (Roddy McDowall did much better in an unsuccessful 1973 pilot).

TOWER OF TERROR
ABC, 10/26/97

Cast: Buzzie Crocker (Steve Guttenberg), Anna (Kirsten Dunst), Jilly Whitman (Nia Peoples), Claire Poulet/Caroline Crosson (Melora Hardin), Abigail Gregory (Amzie Strickland), Q/Chris Todd (Michael McShane), Gilbert Lawrence (Alastair Duncan), Sally Shine (Lindsay Ridgeway), Dewey Todd (John Franklin), Emmaline Partridge (Wendy Worthington), Patricia Patterson (Lela Ivey), Dr. Daniels (Richard Minchenberg), Surgeon (Marcus Smythe), Reporter (Michael Waltman), Great Grandad (Don Perry), Young Abigail (Shira Roth), Galvoa (Ben Kronen)

Credits: Director-Writer: D.J. MacHale; Producer: Iain Paterson; Executive Producers: D.J. MacHale, George Zaloom, Les Mayfield, Joey Plager; Photography: Stephen F. McNutt; Production Design: Philip Dagorl; Music: Louis Febre; Editor: Barry Zetlin; Produced by ZM Productions, Walt Disney Television

In 1937 five people—including child star Sally Shine and her nanny, Partridge—vanish from the Hollywood Towers elevator on their way to a Halloween party. Sixty years later, Abigail Gregory convinces skeptical tabloid journalist Buzzie that Partridge used black magic to send her hated charge to hell, only to trap herself and the others in the spell. Buzzie and his niece Anna find Partridge's spell-book at the hotel. Buzzie jazzes up the story with some fake ghosts, but the real spooks drive them out. Buzzie can't convince his former editor-girlfriend Jilly to run the story, but she gets curious enough to investigate.

The book reveals that damning the victims required tokens (hair, a ring) from each of them; because Partridge only had Sally's, the spell turned them into ghosts. Abigail says she can free them if Buzzie finds some tokens; the ghosts tell him they'll be freed if the broken elevator finally reaches the top floor on Halloween (i.e., that very night). Buzzie starts repairs, then Jilly reveals that Abigail is Sally's insanely jealous sister, obviously making up stories to gain some attention. Buzzie goes off to write that story, leaving Anna to complete the repairs.

While writing, Buzzie realizes jealous Abigail, not Partridge, wanted to damn Sally—and the tokens he found will let her do it. At the Towers, he and Jill find the ghosts—and Anna—trapped on the elevator by the spell. Abigail vents her anger at Sally, who reveals that the party was really for Abigail's birthday; when Sally gives her sister her long-delayed birthday gift, the act of love breaks the spell of hate. The ghosts reach the party and go free. Buzzie wins Jill and gives up tabloids for serious reporting.

This is a good ghost story, even though it's also shameless huckstering (inspired by Disney's "Tower of Terror" theme-park attraction). Genre faces include Dunst (*Interview with a Vampire*) and Guttenberg (*Short Circuit, Cocoon*).

A TOWN HAS TURNED TO DUST
Sci-Fi, 6/27/98

Cast: Sheriff Harvey Denton (Stephen Lang), Jerry Paul (Ron Perlman), Hannify (Gabriel Olds), Ree (Judy Collins), Maya Paul (Barbara Jane Reams), Tooth (Frankie Avina), Pig Iron (Maxx Payne), Tommy (Zarn McLarnon), Ike (Mike Halona), Jenkins (Jim Christian), Wavy (M. Scott Wilkinson), Howie (J. Scott Bronson), Bert (Davyd), Pierce (Neblis Francois), Gable (Dondre Sampson), Billy (Dan Merket), Don (Dave Jensen), Zuma (Kee Y. Johnson), White Rain (Rosina M. Dee)

Credits: Director: Rob Nilsson; Writer: Rod Serling; Producer: Nelle Nugent; Co-Producer: Kenneth Teaton; Photography: Mickey Freeman; Production Design: Jim Sherman; Costumes: Megan Howard; Music: Tim Alexander; Editor: Josh Peterson; Produced by Golden Fox Films

In 2215 most of humanity has left Earth for space, reducing the homeworld to a mining colony where native-born Earthers ("Drivers") are treated as serfs by the off-world mining interests ("Dwellers"). In Carbon, powerful Dweller Jerry Paul's lynch mob overrides Sheriff Denton and hangs Tooth, the Driver accused of raping Paul's wife. Reporter Hannify gets the lynching on tape, but Paul believes himself untouchable. As Hannify learns the town's brutal history of racism, Denton finds the strength to confront Paul, whose support evaporates when his wife admits Tooth was her lover. In a final showdown, Denton and Paul kill each other, and Hannify wonders if racial equality will ever be a reality.

Rod Serling wrote this in 1958 as a contemporary, non–SF take on the Emmett Till case (a fifties cause célèbre in which an all-white Southern jury let off the white murderers of a black teenager) only to see it gutted by nervous sponsors (as happened to an earlier Serling script on similar themes, *Noon on Doomsday*). This remake didn't quite work (whether the script is simply dated, or was never that strong, I don't know), but Perlman (*Beauty and the Beast, Alien Resurrection*) gives a strong, loathsome performance as Paul.

TRAPPED IN SPACE
Sci-Fi, 1/21/95

Cast: Gillings (Kay Lenz), MacNeill (Jack Wagner), Isaacs (Sigrid Thornton), Palmer (Craig Wasson), Grant (Jack Coleman), Captain Howard (Kevin Colson), Tug 1st Officer (Mark Lee), Tug Pilot (Kevin Copeland), Tug Medic (Ian Sternlake), Newscasters (Francine Bell, Tanya Martin), Tug Crew (Michael Mills, Jamie Stewart)

Credits: Director: Arthur Allan Seidelman; Writers: Arlington Hughes, Melinda M. Snodgrass, based on Arthur C. Clarke's "Breaking Strain"; Producer: Michael Lake; Photography: Nin Martinetti; Production Design: Michael L. Ralph; Music: Jay Gruska; Editor: Bert Glatstein;

Produced by Village Roadshow Pictures, Wilshire Court Productions

When a meteor strikes an interplanetary freighter, self-serving Captain Howard flees in the escape pod, abandoning his crew to die. Trapped on a ship without working engines, radio or very much oxygen, the crew fights to survive: Isaacs dies trying to repair the engines; Palmer goes insane and attacks his crewmates; Gillings kills Palmer, then commits suicide. Only straight-arrow Grant and drunk MacNeill remain, and both suspect the other of arranging the other deaths to save oxygen. Grant tries and fails to kill MacNeill, who convinces Grant he's not a murderer. They cut cards to see who lives, and Grant loses. When a rescue ship arrives, they find Grant alive (in a cryonic pod in the ship's cargo), and Mac has found proof that implicates the captain for his crimes.

Competent.

THE TRIAL OF THE INCREDIBLE HULK
NBC, 5/7/89

Cast: David Banner (Bill Bixby), The Hulk (Lou Ferrigno), Matt Murdock/Daredevil (Rex Smith), Ellie Mendez (Marta DuBois), Wilson Fisk (John Rhys Davies), Christa Klein (Nancy Everhard), Al Pettiman (Richard Cummings, Jr.), Edgar (Nicholas Hormann), Capt. Tendelli (Joseph Mascolo), with Linda Darlow, John Novak, Dwight Koss, Meredith Woodward, Mark Acheson, Richard Newman, Don MacKay, Doug Abrahams, Mitchell Kosterman, Beatrice Zelinger, Ken Camroux, Charles Andre, John Bear Curtis

Credits: Director: Bill Bixby; Writer: Gerald DiPego; Producers: Hugh Spencer-Phillips, Robert Ewing; Executive Producers: Bill Bixby, Gerald DiPego; Photography: Chuck Colwell; Music: Lance Rubin; Editor: Janet Ashikaga; Produced by New World Television, Bixby-Brandon Productions

In this follow-up to *The Incredible Hulk Returns*, David Banner becomes the Hulk to save Ellie Mendez from a pair of rapists. Unfortunately, the men work for crimelord Wilson Fisk, who intimidates Ellie into fingering David as her attacker.

David receives unexpected help from blind attorney Matt Murdock—who is also Fisk's arch-foe in the guise of the super-hero Daredevil (gifted with super-human senses by the same radiation that destroyed his sight). When Fisk's men decide to shut Mendez up, Daredevil saves her. Fisk has Mendez kidnapped as bait for his foe, and orders David killed in jail. Under stress, David "hulks out" and escapes; Daredevil tracks him down and reveals his own identity. David, however, refuses to help beyond identifying Mendez' attackers.

After Daredevil goes to rescue Mendez, however, David learns it's a trap and follows, barely in time for the Hulk to save Daredevil from being beaten to death. Fisk optimistically announces Daredevil's death in order to impress his fellow crimelords into a national alliance. The night of the big crime conference, a recuperated Daredevil returns. While David rescues Mendez, Daredevil destroys Fisk's reputation and sends him running. David leaves Matt preparing for Fisk's inevitable return.

This pilot comes close to being a Daredevil film with the Hulk guest-starring (writer-artist Frank Miller's grim, gritty stories made Marvel Comics' *Daredevil* a critical and fan favorite in the eighties). Familiar faces include Rex Smith (*Streethawk*) and Davies (*Sliders*, *Raiders of the Lost Ark*). It was followed by *The Death of the Incredible Hulk*.

TRILOGY OF TERROR
ABC, 3/4/75

Cast: Millicent Larimore/Therese Larimore/Julie Eldridge/Amelia (Karen Black); Chad Foster (Robert Burton), Thomas Anman (John Karlen), Dr. Chester Ramsey (George Gaynes), Eddie Nells (James Storm), Arthur Moore (Gregory Harrison), Anne Richards (Kathryn Reynolds), Tracy (Tracy Curtis), Motel Clerk (Orin Cannon)

Credits: Director-Producer: Dan Curtis; Writer ("Julie," "Millicent & Therese"): William F. Nolan; Writer ("Amelia"): Richard Matheson, based on his short story "Prey"; Associate Producer: Robert Singer; Photography: Paul Lohmann; Art Director: Jan Scott; Editor: Les Green; Produced by Dan Curtis Productions, ABC Circle Films

An anthology film:

(1) "Julie" is a straight-laced teacher whose student, Chad, drugs her, then takes compromising photographs to blackmail her into an affair. After a few weeks, Julie reveals that she's been magically controlling his mind from the start as a kind of sex game; now that she's bored, she kills him and moves on to the next man.

(2) "Millicent & Therese" are identical twins, one prudish, one promiscuous, both hating each other. Millicent finally decides to destroy Therese with her sister's own black magic books—a terrifying mistake, since they're actually one woman with a split personality.

(3) "Amelia" is a mother-dominated woman who buys an exotic Zuni fetish doll for her boyfriend. When she accidentally awakens the spirit inside the doll, it attacks her, hunting her through her apartment. Although she finally destroys the doll, its spirit enters her body—and she sits with a knife, awaiting her mother's visit.

The first two segments of this anthology are routine, but the Zuni fetish doll has become a standard in "movie moments that most scared me" discussions. It returned 20 years later in *Trilogy of Terror II*.

TRILOGY OF TERROR II
USA, 10/30/96

Cast: Laura Ansford/Mommy/Dr. Simpson (Lysette Anthony), Ben (Geraint Wyn Davies), Roger Ansford (Matt Clark), Bobby (Blake Heron), Akers (Gerry Quigley), Brig (Dennis O'Connor), Taylor (John McMahon), Minister (Alan Bridle), Waitress (Brittaney Edgell), Officers (Norm Spencer, Bruce McFee), Dwarf Bobby (Joe Geib), Breslow (Alex Carter), Pete (Philip Williams), Rothstein (Tom Melissis), Steve (Aron Tager), Spaulding (Durward Allen), Dennis (Peter Keleghan).

Credits: Director–Executive Producer: Dan Curtis; Writers: William F. Nolan, Dan Curtis ("He Who Kills," "The Graveyard Rats," based on Henry Kuttner's short story), Richard Matheson ("Bobby"); Producer: Julian Marks; Photography: Elemér Ragályi; Production Design: Veronica Hadfield; Music: Bob Cobert; Editor: Bill Blunden; Produced by Paramount, Power Pictures, Wilshire Court Productions, Dan Curtis Productions

(1) "The Graveyard Rats": Laura Ansford and her lover Ben murder her wealthy husband, then discover the microfilm locating his hidden fortune is buried with him in a rat-infested graveyard. When they unearth the corpse, they learn, far too late, that these are really, really *big* rats...

(2) "Bobby" is dead, so his grieving mother uses necromancy to resurrect him. Bad mistake: Soon Bobby is stalking Mommy through the house, playing cat-and-mouse games—for Bobby committed suicide to escape his cruel mother, and instead of coming back, he's sent a murderous demon in his place...

(3) "He Who Kills": Police investigating Amelia's murder of her mother (see *Trilogy of Terror*) turn the Zuni fetish over to Dr. Simpson for study. The fetish, healed from its fight with Amelia, kills off the museum staffers, then targets Dr. Simpson. She destroys it, but like Amelia, she becomes the new vessel for its murderous spirit.

While none of the segments are as good as the first film's "Amelia," "Bobby" is a nice chiller (also adapted for *Dead of Night*). The fetish is still scary in "He Who Kills," but it's too much a retread of the original—and there's no explanation for who killed Amelia (it's clear the fetish didn't do it).

TRUCKS
USA, 10/29/97

Cast: Ray (Timothy Busfield), Hope Glaxton (Brenda Bakke), Bob (Aidan Devine), Jack (Jay Brezeau), Logan (Brendan Fletcher), Abby (Amy Stewart), Thad (Roman Podhora), George (Victor Cowie), June (Sharon Bajer), Brad (Jonathan Barrett), Pete (Rick Skene), Sheriff (Don Granbery), Reporter (Barbara Lee Edwards), Refrigerator Truck Driver (Gene Pyrz), Lino (Kirk Harper), Phil (Harry Nelken).

Credits: Director: Chris Thomson; Writer: Brian Taggert, based on Stephen King's short story; Co-Producers: Michael Scott, Bruce Eisen, Jonathon Komack Martin; Executive Producers: Mark Amin, Derek Mazur, Jerry Leider, Richard S. Reisberg; Photography: Rob Draper; Production Design: David Ferguson; Music: Michael Richard Plowman; Editor: Laura Mazur; Produced by USA Pictures, Trimark, Leider-Reisberg Credo Entertainment

Lunar, a small desert town, turns into a nightmare when trucks on the local roads come to life, destroying cars, running down pedestrians and penning up a mix of locals, truckers and tourists at the truck stop. Those who attempt to escape or confront the trucks wind up dead—except Ray, who runs the stop and is forced to refuel the trucks. Finally, Ray, Hope and Logan escape and are picked up by a helicopter before the trucks catch them—but the helicopter, like the trucks, is alive and unpiloted…

Animated/sentient cars or trucks are an old SF theme ("Killdozer," for instance), but screen renditions tend more toward the level of *My Mother the Car*. This one, for instance, takes a scary short story and does a very uninteresting adaptation (the big-screen's *Maximum Overdrive* did no better)—and what is the sense of the ending?

TURN BACK THE CLOCK
NBC, 11/20/89

Cast: Sheila Powers (Connie Sellecca), William Hawkins (Jere Burns), Tracy Alexander (Wendy Kilbourne), Barney Powers (David Dukes), John Forrest (Gene Barry), Guest (Joan Leslie), Maureen Dowd (Dina Merrill), Michael Dean (Franc Luz), Cabbie (Pat Cupo), Women (Kim Terry Costin, Pat Sturgis), Doormen (Frank Coppola, Thomas M. Middleton, Dennis Paladino), Orderly (Christopher Judges), Maid (Carmela Rioseco), Reporter (Jeannine Wiest).

Credits: Director: Larry Elikann; Writers: Lee Hutson, Lindsay Harrison, based on a screenplay by Walter Bullock from William O'Farrell's novel; Producer: Joseph B. Wallenstein; Executive Producer: Michael Fillerman; Supervising Producer: Joel Dean; Photography: Laszlo George; Production Design: W. Stewart Campbell; Music: Nan Schwartz; Editor: Michael S. Murphy; Produced by Republic Pictures, NBC

On New Year's Day 1990, actress Sheila Powers guns down her womanizing husband Barney in self-defense. Stunned, Sheila wishes she could turn back time … and discovers it's now January 1, 1989. Sheila tells her best friend William that to prevent the shooting—stemming from Barney's affair with writer Tracy—she's arranged for she and Barney to work on location, far away from Tracy. Sheila also warns William away from socialite Maureen.

But … Tracy shows up anyway and seduces Barney to advance her career. Maureen's money seduces William, then she has him committed, as before, when their marriage goes sour. Still, after Tracy dumps Barney for a bigger director, Sheila is convinced she's beaten fate. When Barney meets Tracy again in New York, she blames Sheila for the breakup. Furious, Barney attacks Sheila, but William—escaped from the mental home—shoots him, saving Sheila from killing the man she loves.

This remake of *Repeat Performance* is good, and very well cast, but not up to the original: Not only was fate in the first film even more inflexible, but here, Sheila comes off as a masochistic jerk for hanging on to her selfish husband. Joan Leslie, the original Sheila, has a cameo.

12:01
Fox, 7/5/93

Cast: Barry Thomas (Jonathan Silverman), Lisa Fredericks (Helen Slater), Dr. Thadius Moxley (Martin Landau), Howard Richter (Jeremy Piven), Roy Denk (Nicolas Surovy), Anne Jackson (Robin Bartlett), Joan Zevo (Constance Marie), Dr. Tiberius Scott (Paxton Whitehead), Supervisor (Cheryl Anderson), Kyle (Joey Andrews), Thin Assassin (Frank Collison), Detective (Ed Chick), Ted Fallow (Jonathan Emerson), Night Guard (Drew Gehl), Anchorwoman (Mary Hale), Jack Spays (Mark Christopher Lawrence), Guard on Walkie-Talkie (Will Leskin), Heavy Assassin (Eric Mansker), Guard—Science Wing (Mark Phelan), Hosea Sanders (Himself), Annette (Ann Shea), Woman on Street (Lara Steinick), Prisoner (Danny Trejo), Unemployed Dad (Jim Turner), Flower Vendor (Ray Victor), Utility Worker (F.X. Vitolo), with Glenn Morshower

Credits: Director: Jack Sholder; Writer: Philip Morton; Story: Jonathan Heap, based on *12:01 PM* by Richard Lupoff; Producers: Jonathan Heap, Robert J. Degus, Cindy Hornickel; Executive Producers: Jana Sue Memel, Sasha Emerson; Photography: Anghel Decca; Production Design: Michael Novotny; Music: Peter Melnick; Editor: Michael N. Knue; Produced by Chanticleer Films, New Line Cinema

It's a rotten day for Barry Thomas: falling victim to a practical joke; getting raked over by his boss; looking like an idiot in front of gorgeous, brainy co-worker Lisa; and then seeing Lisa gunned down in a drive-by shooting. And the next day ... the same things happen all over again.

At first Barry can't believe time is repeating; when he does realize it, he still can't change time enough to save Lisa. But the next day is another repeat, and the next ... and Barry discovers the "time bounce" is a side effect of the experimental particle accelerator Lisa and Dr. Moxley are working on, but can't figure out why he's the only one to notice it.

Using his foreknowledge, Barry eventually hits it off with Lisa, saves her from the killer, and makes love to her. They deduce that her co-worker Denk had her killed to cover up that he's violating a government-ordered shutdown of the accelerator, and that an electric shock Barry received during the first bounce protects him against the memory loss. As time keeps repeating, Lisa and Barry learn that Denk is actually a fed trying to nail Moxley for operating the accelerator. Barry helps Denk get proof, but Moxley has Denk killed. Lisa and Barry break into the accelerator chamber and try to stop Moxley themselves. Moxley gets caught in the accelerator and dies, diverting the beam and allowing time to restart.

An expansion of the short film *12:01 PM* (which the creator claimed was ripped off for the theatrical *Groundhog Day*), this is a charming romantic thriller with solid performances. Genre faces include Landau (*Mission: Impossible* and Bela Lugosi in *Ed Wood*) and Slater (*Supergirl*).

20,000 LEAGUES UNDER THE SEA
CBS, 3/23/97

Cast: Nemo (Ben Cross), Prof. Aronnax (Richard Crenna), Ned Land (Paul Gross), Sophie Aronnax (Julie Cox), Admiral Sellings (Michael Jayston), Captain Farragut (Jeff Harding), *Scotia* Captain (David Harding), Father (James Vaughan), Mother (Susannah Fellows), Child (Joshua Brody)

Credits: Director: Michael Anderson; Writer: Joe Wiesenfeld, based on Jules Verne's novel; Producer: John Davis; Executive Producer: Robert Halmi, Sr.; Photography: Alan Hume; Production Design: Brian Ackland-Snow; Music: John Scott; Editor: Jason Krasucki; Produced by Hallmark Entertainment

This extremely poor adaptation of Verne amounts to an underwater romantic drama, since the central plot revolves around whether Nemo (a disappointingly stiff Ben Cross) or the very bland Ned Land gets Professor Aronnax's daughter Sophie. When Nemo realizes he's not getting the girl, he uses Ned and Aronnax as hostages to force the issue—but when the *Nautilus* is seized by a sea monster, Ned helps Nemo destroy it, in return for which the three travelers go free (Nemo, surprisingly, survives unscathed).

Coincidentally, a second version of Verne (a much better one) aired two months later.

20,000 LEAGUES UNDER THE SEA
ABC, 5/11/–5/12/97

Cast: Captain Nemo (Michael Caine), Ned Land (Bryan Brown), Pierre Aronnax (Patrick Dempsey), Attucks (Adewale Akinnouye-Agbaje), Thierry Aronnax (John Bach), Mara (Mia Sara), Simon (Nicholas Hammond), Lydia (Kerry Armstrong), Admiral McCutcheon (Peter McCauley), Imei (Cecily Anna), Shimoda (Ken Senga), Kulanga (Gerry Day), Conductor (Christopher Pate), Iwanda (Boe Kean), Dennison (Damien Monk), American Scientist (Jeff Dorman), Russian Scientist (Gabriel Carr), British Scientist (Peter Steele), Austrian Scientist (Peter Scheidel), Scientist (Duke Bannister), Congressman Garfield (Steven Grieves)

Credits: Director: Rob Hardy; Writer: Brian Nelson, based on Jules Verne's novel; Co-Producer: Dean W. Barnes; Executive Producers: Keith Pierce, Jeffrey M. Hayes, Richard Pierce; Line Producer: Tom Hoffie; Photography: James Bartle; Production Design: Stewart Burnside; Music: Mark Snow; Editor: Drake Silliman; Produced by Village Roadshow, Frederick S. Pierce Company

In this version (airing two months after CBS' much worse treatment), Aronnax is the embittered son of an arrogant scientist, overshadowed and bullied by his father. After he, Ned Land and former slave Attucks are taken on board the *Nautilus*, the latter two try constantly to escape, but Aronnax is enthralled not only by Nemo—who respects Aronnax's work—but Nemo's beautiful, brilliant daughter, Mara. Nemo leads the *Nautilus* and its passengers to sunken Atlantis, where he hopes to build a new city dedicated to freedom—but Ned Land's sabotage coincides with an American naval attack and a sea monster's assault, which ultimately leads to the destruction of the sub, Mara, Nemo and most of his men.

This adaptation is not up to the Disney big-screen version, but it's far superior to CBS' production, with British star Caine in the lead and Brown (*F/X*) and Sara (*Legend*) in support.

TWICE UPON A TIME
Lifetime, 11/9/98

Cast: Beth Sega (Molly Ringwald), Joe Townsend (George Newbern), Alana Merribon (Melora Walters), Martie Fowler (Shawnee Smith), Peg Sager (Ellen Crawford), Nick Fowler (Rob Youngblood), Sanford Watts (Michael Whaley), Brian Hardwick (John Fugelsang), Bed-and-Breakfast Owner (Nicholas Guest), Dr. Rhammy (Timothy Blake), Sportscaster (Tim Christiansen), Telejournalist (Mark Conlon), Slinky (Carolyn Fears), Darby Edwards (Peter Fox), MC (Robert Littiman), Expert (Brian Pope), Pianist (Robert Ringwald), Photographer (Todd Sandler), Waiter (Matthew Seiden), Maître d' (Joe Torrenueva), Rural Guy (Kenneth White)

Credits: Director: Thom Eberhardt; Writer: Scott Fifer; Co-Producers: Scott Fifer, Rick Blumenthal; Executive Producers: Bob Christiansen, Rick Rosenberg; Photography: Barry M. Wilson; Production Design: David Ensley; Music: Brian Adler; Editor: Paul Dixon; Produced by ABC Pictures, Chris/Rose Productions

It's Thanksgiving, but Beth Sega isn't very thankful: She just lost a promotion; her boyfriend Joe is pushing for marriage; and her ex-boyfriend Nick is now a superstar athlete. Pulling the Thanksgiving wishbone, Beth wishes to change things. The next morning she wakes up in a parallel world where she's married to Nick and has won the promotion. In her new world ice cream is diet food, Cuba will soon be the fiftieth state, professional women network over power croquet and a miracle cure for cancer saved Beth's mother's life.

Beth is deliriously happy—until she sees this world's Joe engaged to Alana and wants him back (especially after catching Nick cheating). Beth tries various schemes to win Joe back (with no success), then finally repents her selfishness and works to ensure Alana and Joe get hitched. Repeating the wish returns Beth to her old world, her old Joe—and a life she now likes a whole lot better.

The fourth parallel-world fantasy of 1998 is pleasantly entertaining (though Ringwald is rather one-note in the lead); a nice touch is showing the bitchy, parallel-world Beth being just as happy to return home.

THE TWILIGHT ZONE: ROD SERLING'S LOST CLASSICS
CBS, 5/19/94

Cast: Host (James Earl Jones), (1) Melissa (Amy Irving), Dr. Jim McCain (Gary Cole), Joanie (Heidi Swedberg), Moviegoers (Priscilla Pointer, Scott Burkholder, Don Bloomfield, Michael Burgess, Grey Silbley), Big Man (Alex Van), Nurse (Deborah Winstead), Ticket Lady (Joan Pankow, uncredited); (2) Dr. Jeremy Ramsey (Patrick Bergin), Susan Wheaton (Jenna Stern), Maureen (Julia Campbell), Jeremy Wheaton (Jack Palance), Dr. Ames (Peter McRobbie), Perkins (Bill Bolender), Flannagan (Malachy McCourt), Workmen (J. Michael Hunter, Mark Joy), Billy O'Neil (Stan Kelly), Attendant (Tony Pender), Medical student (Hank Troscianiec), Magistrate (Richard K. Olsen), Bainbridge (Chris O'Neill)

Credits: Director: Robert Markowitz, Writers: Richard Matheson ("The Theatre," from a story by Rod Serling), Rod Serling ("Where the Dead Are"); Producer: S. Bryan Hickox; Supervising Producer: Carol Serling; Executive Producers: Michael O'Hara, Lawrence Horowitz; Photography: Jacek Laskus; Production Design: Christiaan Wagener; Music: Patrick Williams; Editor: David Beatty; Produced by O'Hara-Horowitz Productions, WIN

(1) "The Theatre": After commitment-phobic Melissa turns down her boyfriend Jim's proposal, she sees the rejection reenacted on-screen at the movies. Her next visit shows her a scene from the future, which comes true—and on the next visit, she sees

herself struck and killed by a bus. When a bus narrowly misses her, Jim convinces Melissa she's cheated fate—but they've miscalculated the date, and the fatal accident happens the following evening.

(2) "Where the Dead Are": After the Civil War's senseless bloodshed, Dr. Ramsey believes in beating death by any means possible. When a patient's corpse shows injuries that should have killed him years ago, Ramsey traces a connection to medical researcher Wheaton. Wheaton, a paraplegic recluse, tells Ramsey nothing, even when Ramsey spots the dead man, alive, with Ramsey's niece Susan. Eventually, Wheaton admits he's found a resurrection drug, but the raised dead are callous brutes (they amputated Wheaton's legs to keep him from leaving)—so he has replaced their injections with water. After Wheaton dies, Susan and Ramsey flee the angry dead. The resurrectees finally die—but so does Susan, who's really one of them.

Rod Serling's *The Twilight Zone* anthology is a TV classic—but this film only shows that some unproduced stories deserve their fate (according to film buff Michael Weldon, they weren't originally *TZ* stories anyway). "The Theatre" reads like a rough sketch, with none of the moral or dramatic heft *TZ* usually gave such stories (no tragedy, no meaning—Melissa's death just happens), and the second feature is just a bad zombie film.

THE TWO WORLDS OF JENNIE LOGAN
CBS, 10/31/79

Cast: Jennie Logan (Lindsay Wagner), David Reynolds (Marc Singer), Michael Logan (Alan Feinstein), Elizabeth (Linda Gray), Harrington (Henry Wilcoxon), Dr. Erica Lauren (Joan Darling), Mrs. Bates (Irene Tedrow), Old John (Peter Hobbs), Beverly (Constance McCashin), Don (Charles Thomas Murphy), Ed Hartley (Allen Williams), Realtor (Pat Corley), Foreman (John Hawkins), Roberta (Gloria Stuart), Minister (Robert Nadder), Nurse (Layla Galloway)

Credits: Director-Writer: Frank De Felitta, from David Williams' *Second Sight*; Producer: Paul Radin; Executive Producers: Joe Wizan, Ron Samuels; Photography: Al Francis; Art Director: Charles Zacha; Music: Glenn Paxton; Editor: John F. Schreyer; Produced by Joe Wizan Television Productions, Charles Fries Productions

Trying to patch up their marriage after Michael's affair, the Logans move into an old country house where Jennie becomes enraptured by an 1890s dress she finds in the attic. When she tries it on, she finds herself drawn back to the past. There she falls in love with artist David Reynolds, who's mourning the death of his wife, Jennie's double.

As Michael begins worrying that Jennie's talk of time travel means she's gone insane, Jennie investigates David's history and learns he died in a duel with Harrington, his vindictive father-in-law. Despite Jennie's efforts in the past, Harrington does challenge David (believing David seduced his sister-in-law, Elizabeth). Returning to the present, Jennie learns from the aging, half-senile Elizabeth that she shot David down out of jealousy; Jennie returns to the past and tries to prevent it. In the present, Mark finds her lying dead, in the dress, and believes her insanity took her will to live; then he finds a collection of David's artwork showing paintings of Jennie—long after David died in the original timeline.

The Two Worlds of Jennie Logan is flawed (why is David the only one who notices Jennie's resemblance to his wife?) and very old-fashioned, but if you like that kind of thing...

UNDER WRAPS
Disney, 10/25/97

Cast: Gilbert (Adam Wylie), Marshall (Mario Yedidia), Amy (Clara Bryant), Harold (Bill Fagerbakke), Mom (Corinne Behrer), Movie Dad (Tom Virtue), Movie Mom (Laura Leary), Movie Ben (Trenton Gaucher), Movie Molly (Brooke Garrett), Ted (Bill Fagerbakke), Leonard (Joshua Dennis), Todd (Ryan Schofield), Paige (Nakia Burrise), Mother in Park (Velina Brown), Boy in Park (Robert Bailey, Jr.) Goons (Louis Landman, Sean McFarland), Art Dealer (Lance Brady), Desk Nurse (Wilma Bonet), ER Nurse (Atim Udoffia), Doctor (Greg Watanabe), Connie (Linda Gehringer), Principal Hammer (Kenneth Fisher), Jane (Anni Long), Cop (Reuben Grundy),

Female Mummy (Christine Patterson), with Ken Campbell, Penny Peyser, Ed Lauter
Credits: Director: Greg Beeman; Writer: Don Rhymer; Producer: Bernadette Caulfield; Executive Producers: Don Rhymer, Mireille Sori, Tracey Thompson; Photography: Mark Gray; Production Design: Maria Caso; Editor: Norman Hollyn; Music: David Michael Frank; Produced by Hallmark Entertainment, Mummy Entertainment

Three kids exploring a spooky old house disturb a sarcophagus stashed there by black-market antiques dealers—and awaken the mummy within. The kids learn the mummy—nicknamed Harold—must return to his sarcophagus soon or crumble to dust; when they return to the house, though, the crooks have taken the coffin. As the hours tick by, Harold causes panic and chaos wherever he goes. The thieves try to find the mummy, and the kids try to find the thieves. When the kids finally track the hoods down, they and Harold manage to overcome them, and Harold is returned to sleep in the nick of time.

This is the kind of silly kids vs. crooks film that cost Disney so much of its reputation back in the seventies.

THE UNINVITED
CBS, 10/29/96
Cast: Patricia Johnson (Sharon Lawrence), Charles Johnson (Beau Bridges), Delia (Shirley Knight), Jonathan Johnson (Alex D. Linz), Winston (Lawrence Pressman), Molly Johnson (Emily Bridges), Laurette (Kathleen Lloyd), Cornelson (James Pickens, Jr.), Charlotte (Lesley Woods), Sarah Parrish (Lauren Bowles), Martha (Lynn Griffith), Bruce (Stephen Lee), Halley (Marnie McPhail), Clay (Eric Winzenried), Nurses (Sharon Clark, Andrew Walker), Policeman (Steven Griffith), Young Charlotte (Denise Johnson), Tomboy (Ebick Pizzadilli), Parrish (Jack Diamond)
Credits: Director: Larry Shaw; Writer: Karen Clark; Producers: Karen Clark, Lori-Etta Taub; Executive Producer: Thomas Carter; Co-Executive Producer: Sheldon Pinchuk; Photography: Bryan England; Production Design: Anthony Tremblay; Music: Wendy Blackstone; Editor: John A. Barton; Produced by Thomas Carter Company, Hamdon Entertainment

After Patty Johnson's new baby is stillborn, the Johnsons move into a new house and try to put the tragedy behind them. Unfortunately, the usual display of *Poltergeist* knock-off phenomena makes that impossible. A local psychic reveals that the house is haunted by the ghost of a murderous former owner—who's now out to destroy Patty's son Jonathan.

This is yet another based-on-truth *Poltergeist* clone.

UNIVERSAL SOLDIER II: BROTHERS IN ARMS
TMC, 9/30/98
Cast: Luc Devereaux (Matt Bataglia), Veronica Roberts (Chandra West), Sgt. Eric Devereaux (Jeff Wincott), Otto Mazur (Gary Busey), Mentor (Burt Reynolds), Sgt. Andrew Scott (Andrew Jackson), Peterson (Eric Bryson), Martinez (Kevin Ruston), Cooper (Desmond Campbell), Lt. Col. Jack Cameron (Michael Copeman), Dr. Walker (Richard McMillan), John Devereaux (Aron Tager), Danielle Devereaux (Barbara Gordon), Anchorwoman (Carla Collins), Jasper (James Kee), Purser (Frank McAnulty), Luc at 9 (Jared Wall), Porter (Neville Edwards), Annie (Sophie Bennett), Bodyguards (Layton Morrison, Loren Peterson), Female Sentry (Kym Kristalie), Young Dr. Gregor (Doug Murray), Sentries (Jeff Binkley, Randy Butcher, Michael Dysan), Operator (Jeffrey Smith), Head Sentry (Roy T. Anderson), Farmer (Reg Dreger)
Credits: Director: Jeff Woolnough; Writer: Peter M. Lenkov; Producer: Bob Wertheimer; Executive Producers: Kevin Gillis, John Laing; Co-Executive Producer: Nancy Chapelle; Photography: Russell Goozee; Production Design: Jasna Stefanovic; Music: John Kastner, Steve Pecile, Ivan Dorochuk, Crunch Recording Group; Editor: Mike Lee; Produced by Catalyst Entertainment, Durrant Fox Productions, Rigel, Unisol Productions

In the theatrical *Universal Soldier*, Veronica, a reporter, helped shut down a government scheme to turn American war dead into computer-controlled unstoppable warriors; now the sinister Mentor reactivates the project, selling the Universal Soldiers' services to the highest bidder. Mentor regains control of Luc, whom Veronica freed from the UniSol program. Veronica follows Luc to the UniSol base, where she finds his brother Eric in suspended animation (because a resurrection glitch left him human, rather than a Universal). Veronica frees Eric, but security chief Mazur captures them. The sight of his brother in danger frees Luc's mind, and he helps Veronica escape. They rescue Eric, then thwart the new Universals' first mission. A furious Mazur hunts them down and kills Eric before Luc kills Mazur and his remaining UniSols. Mentor's project, however, continues ... as we see in *Universal Soldier III*.

This is a dull, mindless android assassin film, with Burt Reynolds in one of his "didn't-he-once-have-a-career" roles. An unrelated theatrical *Universal Soldier II* was released in 1999.

UNIVERSAL SOLDIER III: UNFINISHED BUSINESS
TMC, 10/28/98

Cast: Luc Devereaux (Matt Bataglia), Veronica Roberts (Chandra West), Mentor (Burt Reynolds), Eric Devereaux (Jeff Wincott), Dr. Walker (Richard McMillan), McNally (Roger Periard), Bodyguards (Layton Morrison, Loren Peterson), Charles Clifton (Juan Chioran), Grace (Claudette Roche), Martin Daniels (John Laing), Drunk CEO (Dwayne MacLean), Max (Jovanni Sy), Hugo (Lloyd Adams), Lowell (Vincent Corazza), Head Chef (Darren Marsman), Cop (David Blacker), Chief Thorpe (Gerry Mendicino), Freddie Smith (Dan Duran), Busboy (Adrian Churchill), Martinez (Kevin Ruston), Cooper (Desmond Campbell), Jasper (James Kee), Anchorwoman (Carla Collins), John Devereaux (Aron Tager), Danielle Devereaux (Barbara Gordon), General Clancy (Thomas Hauff), GR87 at 6 (Nickolas Swann), Medtech (Matt Birman), Sheriff (John Stoneham, Sr.), GR87 at 13 (Brock Clermont), Driver (Ben Brooks), Orderly (Martin Roach), Nurse's Aid (Dana Ishiura), Scully (Philip Williams), Head Nurse (Taren Ash), Dr. Gregor (Jack Duffy), Nurses (Mary Ann Stevens, Leigh E. Brinkman), File Pusher (Danny Lima), Wheelchair Vet (Moris Santia), Sorry Passerby (Dan Gallagher), Pilot (John Stoneham, Jr.), Air Traffic Controller (Steven Allerick), Sentries (Peter Szkoda, Errol G., Bryan Renfro, Robert Racki).

Credits: Director: Jeff Woolnough; Writer: Peter M. Lenkov; Producer: Bob Wertheimer; Executive Producers: Kevin Gillis, John Laing; Co-Executive Producer: Nancy Chapelle; Photography: Russell Goozee; Production Design: Jasna Stefanovic; Music: John Kastner, Steve Pecile, Ivan Dorochuk, Crunch Recording Group; Editor: Robert K. Sprogis; Produced by Catalyst Entertainment, Movie Channel

In the follow-up to *Universal Soldier II*, Veronica crashes a high-finance conference to tell a fellow reporter the truth about UniSol. Terrorists seize control of the conference and frame Veronica as a member of their team. Luc rescues her and kills the terrorists, whom Mentor promptly resurrects for a multi-million-dollar gold robbery. To ensure success, Mentor turns the security chief guarding the gold into a "Sleeper"—a resurrectee who passes for normal, rather than the zombie-like UniSols.

Mentor steers Veronica and Luc into a trap, but they escape with knowledge of his plans—and proof he's really a high-ranking CIA official. When they successfully thwart the theft, Dr. Walker unleashes his ultimate weapon—a brainwashed, bomb-implanted clone of Eric, whom Luc cannot bring himself to fight. Luc does, however, jog the clone's repressed memories, so Eric puts himself safely away from Luc and Veronica before the bomb blows. After Luc tricks Mentor into confessing his crimes live on TV, Mentor kills himself—but his scientists revive him later. UniSol, with its growing army of Sleepers, marches on.

Though this one has more brains than the previous film, it's still a long way from being good.

V
NBC, 5/1–5/2/83

Cast: Mike Donovan (Marc Singer), Dr. Juliet Parrish (Faye Grant), Diana (Jane Badler), Robert Maxwell (Michael Durrell), Brian (Peter Nelson), Daniel Bernstein (David Packer), Eleanor (Neva Patterson), Josh Brooks (Tommy Peterson), Robin Maxwell (Blair Tefkin), Elias Taylor (Michael Wright), Mrs. Bernstein (Bonnie Bartlett), Abraham Bernstein (Leonard Cimino), John (Richard Herd), Tony (Evan Kim), Dr. Ben Taylor (Richard Lawson), Stanley Bernstein (George Morfogen), Steven (Andrew Prine), Plant Supervisor (Hansford Rowe), Kristine Walsh (Jenny Sullivan), Kathleen Maxwell (Penelope Windust), Sancho (Rafael Campos), Martin (Frank Ashmore), Caleb Taylor (Jason Bernard), Harmony (Diane Civita), Barbara (Viveka Davis), Sean Donovan (Eric Johnston), Quentin (Michael

Alldredge), Ruby (Camila Ashlend), Denny (Michael Bond), Willie (Robert Englund), Marge Donovan (Jenny Neumann), Black Alien Captain (Stack Pierce), Newscasters (Clete Roberts, Howard K. Smith)

Credits: Director-Writer-Executive Producer: Kenneth Johnson; Producer: Chuck Bowman; Associate Producer: Patrick Boyriven; Photography: John McPherson; Art Director: Gary Lee; Production Design: Charles R. Davis; Music: Joe Harnell; Editors: Jack Schoengarth, Alan Marks, Paul Dixon, Robert Richard; Produced by Kenneth Johnson Productions, Warner Bros. Television.

When alien spaceships arrive over Earth, the first reaction is terror—then relief when the aliens turn out to be friendly humanoids. The Visitors set to work fighting disease, pollution and famine—but when a cabal of scientists tries to steal and exploit Visitor technology, the aliens reluctantly proclaim martial law, turning scientists into pariahs and working with governments to maintain order.

A handful of humans—news photographer Donovan, scientist Juliet, the Maxwell family—discover the truth: The Visitors are actually reptilians in human masks, and the Visitor Diana brainwashed the scientists into confessing a nonexistent conspiracy. Having Earth completely under control, the aliens are now stealing Earth's water and turning human prisoners into food. Juliet organizes her Los Angeles neighborhood into a resistance movement, while Donovan—whose ambitious mother has sided with the aliens—discovers good aliens in the Visitors' ranks. The humans sets up a base in the hills outside LA and defeat the Visitors in their first battle; Robin Maxwell, however, is captured by one of the aliens and impregnated. And the road to victory looks very, very long....

Creator Johnson originally pitched a story to NBC about a U.S. takeover by internal fascist groups; when the network rejected that idea (and Johnson rejected a foreign invasion), they settled on Nazi-like aliens instead (unfortunately carrying the parallel a bit too far—who could ever buy the idea of scientists as the Visitors' Jews?). Reportedly the most expensive telefilm to that date, this was a deserved hit (among its many good features, Faye Grant's strong performance is remembered) that had NBC eager for a sequel. When Warner Bros. refused to budget what Johnson thought necessary, he backed out and *V: The Final Battle* was made without him.

V: THE FINAL BATTLE
NBC, 5/6–5/8/84

Cast: Mike Donovan (Marc Singer), Dr. Juliet Parrish (Faye Grant), Diana (Jane Badler), Robert Maxwell (Michael Durrell), Father Andrew Doyle (Thomas Hill), Ham Tyler (Michael Ironside), Brian (Peter Nelson), Daniel Bernstein (David Packer), Eleanor Dupres (Neva Patterson), Robin Maxwell (Blair Tefkin), Elias Taylor (Michael Wright), Maggie Blodgett (Denise Galik), Caleb Taylor (Jason Bernard), Sancho (Rafael Campos), Pamela (Sarah Douglas), Martin (Frank Ashmore), Harmony (Diane Civita), Barbara (Viveka Davis), Plant Supervisor (Hansford Rowe), Kristine Walsh (Jenny Sullivan), Polly Maxwell (Greta Blackburn), Fred (Mark L. Taylor), Ruby (Camila Ashlend), Sean Donovan (Eric Johnston), Drunk (Dick Miller), Black Alien Captain (Stack Pierce), Dr. Walter Corley (Don Starr), Chris Barber (Mickey Jones), Alien Girl (Jenny Beck), Elizabeth Maxwell (Brandy Gold), Newscaster (Clete Roberts)

Credits: Director: Richard T. Heffron; Writers: Brian Taggert, Peggy Goldman, Diane Frolov, Faustus Buck, from a story by Lillian Weezer, Peggy Goldman, Harry Longstreet, Renee Longstreet, Diane Frolov, Faustus Buck, from an idea by Kenneth Johnson; Producers: Dean O'Brien, Patrick Boyriven; Executive Producers: Daniel H. Blatt, Robert Singer; Photography: Stevan Larner; Production Design: Mort Rabinowitz; Art Director: Tracy Bousman; Editors: Michael F. Anderson, Paul Dixon; Music: Barry DeVorzon and Joseph Conlan (Part One), Dennis McCarthy (Parts Two and Three); Produced by Blatt-Singer Productions, Warner Bros. Television

In this sequel to *V,* Visitor control is tighter than ever, but the resistance, now assisted by hardcase government agent Tyler, is fighting back. An attempt to expose the Visitors as nonhumans fails and leaves Juliet captured and subjected to Diana's brainwashing (which Juliet resists). Donovan, who has fallen in love with Juliet, leads a successful rescue mission, even though Tyler insists that Juliet is now a Visitor puppet.

As the struggle continues, Robin gives birth to twins—one fully alien, one a hybrid girl who grows at an accelerated rate. The alien baby dies from disease, which gives Juliet the key to a bacterial anti–Visitor weapon. Diana captures the uncannily intelligent hybrid, Elizabeth. Once Juliet develops the bacterial treatment, resistance cells across the world unleash it, driving the aliens off. Diana activates a doomsday bomb on the mothership; the resistance catches her, but she has enough control over Juliet to pull off an escape. Elizabeth telekinetically deactivates the bomb, and Earth looks forward to freedom.

Johnson says this script diverged wildly from his original ideas, but it's still an impressive achievement (except for the deus ex machina of Elizabeth magically saving the day). The series that followed (in which we learn the bacteria loses its punch in hot climates, allowing the Visitors to return) was entertaining but nowhere near as good.

VAMPIRE
ABC, 10/7/79

Cast: John Rawlins (Jason Miller), Anton Voytek (Richard Lynch), Harry Kilcoyne (E.G. Marshall), Leslie Rawlins (Kathryn Harrold), Andrea Parker (Barrie Youngfellow), Christopher Bell (Michael Tucker), Brandy (Jonelle Allen), Nicole DeCamp (Jessica Walter), Tommy Parker (Adam Starr), Iris (Wendy Cutler), Father Hanley (Scott Paulin), Casket Salesman (David Hooks), Old Priest (Brendan Dillon), Desk Captain (Joe Spinell), Selby (Byron Webster), Detective (Ray K. Gorman), Dance Instructor (Nicholas Gunn), Cop (Tony Perez), San Francisco Ballet Company

Credits: Director: E.W. Swackhammer; Writers: Steven Bochco, Michael Kozoll; Producer: Gregory Hoblit; Executive Producer: Steven Bochco; Associate Producer: David Anspaugh; Photography: Dennis Dalzell; Art Director: James G. Hulsey; Music: Fred Karlin; Supervising Editor: Christopher Nelson; Produced by MTM Enterprises

John Rawlins, the architect designing a massive urban renewal project, is hired by Voytek, an urbane millionaire, to excavate his family's ruined estate and find the fortune in art buried there. When the pieces turn out to be stolen (over a period of centuries), Rawlins calls the cops; Voytek is arrested for art theft and vows revenge. After Voytek's lover, Nicole, bails him out, Voytek—the vampire of the title—seduces and kills Leslie Rawlins. Ex-cop Kilcoyne notices Leslie's death resembles a case Kilcoyne worked on years ago.

Unable to prove Voytek's guilt, Rawlins sneaks into Voytek's apartment—and finds him lying in his coffin. When he tries going back with stakes and crosses, he is committed. Voytek attacks Rawlins in the hospital, but Kilcoyne drives him off and gets Rawlins released. Kilcoyne explains that years ago his ex-partner sacrificed himself to entomb Voytek at the vampire's estate, where Voytek remained trapped until the renewal project disturbed the ruins. The men track down and destroy Voytek's several hidden coffins. Voytek retaliates by kidnapping Kilcoyne's friend Andrea. When the men corner Voytek and Andrea in a crypt, Voytek, out of respect for his foes, promises no reprisals if they leave without Andrea. Instead, they drive him off with crucifixes and holy water, but as he vanishes into the night he swears to destroy all they hold dear...

This is a good vampire thriller (an unsuccessful pilot) by a writer better known for *Hill Street Blues* and *NYPD Blue*, and it showcases an excellent turn by Lynch as the Dracula-like villain. I have my doubts about how much range they could have gotten with a series, though.

VAMPIRELLA
Showtime, 9/28/96

Cast: Vampirella (Talisa Soto), Vlad/Jamie Blood (Roger Daltrey), Adam Van Helsing (Richard Joseph Paul), Demos (Brian Bloom), Lt. Walsh (Lee de Broux), Salla (Corinna Harney), Quinn (Rusty Meyers), Traxx (Tom Deters), Captain Stryker (Jack "J.R." Zavorak), Carlos (Lenny Juliano), Stepmother (Ann Howard), High Elder (Angus Scrimm), Adam's Father (Tyde Kierney), Forry Ackerman (David B. Katz), Prof. Steinman (Robert Clotworthy), Astronauts (John Landis,

John Terlesky), Mr. Nakamichi (Toru Nagai), Remirez (Jay Kessler), Archie (Jeff Jay), Matheson (Eric Randell), Vampire Girls (Peggy Trentini, Antonia Dorian), Mr. Maurice (Bret Davidson), Drakulon Guard (Patrick J. Statham), Purge Operatives (Scott Stevensen, John Oshima), Vampires (Anthony Hansen, Thomas Case, Hilary Halbert), Drakulon Elder (Michael Harris)

Credits: Director: Jim Wynorski; Writer: Gary Gerani, based on Forrest J Ackerman's Vampirella character; Producers: Paul Hertzberg, Jim Wynorski, Angela Baynes; Executive Producer: Roger Corman; Associate Producers: Mark Carducci, Forrest J Ackerman; Photography: Andrea Rossotto; Music: Joel Goldsmith; Editor: Richard Gentner; Produced by New Horizons, Concorde, Sunset Films International

On the vampire planet Drakulon, the peaceful inhabitants drink blood from Drakulon's red rivers—but murderous Vlad and his followers prefer draining the living, including the father of sweet, innocent Ella. When the killers flee Drakulon for Earth, Ella, sustained by synthetic blood, follows until she crashes on Mars. She spends 3,000 years in suspended animation while Vlad infects humanity with vampirism.

Revived by the first Earth-Mars mission, Ella stows away on their return trip. Once on Earth, she begins hunting vampires as "Vampirella" with the help of Adam Van Helsing of the government's anti-vampire Operation Purge. Vlad (who plans to trigger a nuclear winter that will block out sunlight, leaving vampires free to walk the day) kidnaps Adam to lure Vampie to his lair. He then takes her synthetic blood supply and locks her in with Adam until she drains him. Instead, Vampirella only drinks enough to survive, then escapes with Adam and summons Purge. The feds destroy the vampires and Vampirella destroys Vlad. She then decides to remain on Earth and teach the surviving vampires the peaceful ways of Drakulon.

Vampirella has been a cult comics favorite for years (partly because of her extremely sexy outfits); this adventure, despite Soto's limited acting skills, is remarkably good fun (though it's not at all continuous with the comics).

VIRTUAL OBSESSION
ABC, 2/26/98

Cast: Joe Messenger (Peter Gallagher), Juliet Spring (Bridgette Wilson), Karen Messenger (Mimi Rogers), Jack Messenger (Jake Lloyd), Thomas (Andy Comeau), Joan Stevenson (Lee Garlington), Carl Dern (Michael O'Neill), Ed Lang (Dan Martin), Adam Spring (Robert Vaughn), Albert (Tom Nibley), Governor (Charles Gruber), Mayor (David Jensen), Judge Dolrymple (Cynthia Garris), Coroner (Frank Garrish), Mary Bishop (Mary Alice), Waitress (Nicola Guertin)

Credits: Director: Mick Garris; Writers: Preston Sturges, Mick Garris, based on Peter James' *Host*; Producers: Mick Garris, Randy Sutter, Stephanie Germain; Co-Producers: David C. Thomas, Ted Babcock; Executive Producers: David A. Rosemont, Frank Von Zerneck, Robert M. Sertner; Production Design: David Ensley; Photography: Shelly Johnson; Music: Nicholas Pike; Editor: Patrick McMahon; Produced by Hallmark Entertainment, Von Zerneck/Sertner

Having created the computer that runs Salt Lake City's electronic systems, Joe Messenger is now building an artificial intelligence. His new assistant, Juliet, suggests placing a digitized human brain into the computer would create an electronic mind instantly; dying of a brain disease, Juliet also sees it as her one chance to live. She and Joe have a short-lived affair. After Joe breaks it off, Juliet downloads herself into the computer and invites Joe to join her.

When Joe rejects her again, Juliet takes over the city systems and Joe's computerized house in order to murder Karen Messenger. As machines everywhere turn on Karen, and the electronically crippled city falls into chaos, Joe tries and fails to delete Juliet from the computer. Juliet prepares to kill Karen but suddenly disintegrates: The program that digitized her brain also digitized her brain disease. Thomas, Joe's paraplegic assistant, then downloads his own mind into the computer, escaping his wheelchair; he promises to keep psychos like Juliet from accessing the same power.

TV movies and series have done this kind of "ghost in the machine" repeatedly since the early eighties (the *Max Headroom* series is the best treatment); this particular take (mixing in *Fatal Attraction*) is routine and way too long.

VISITORS OF THE NIGHT
NBC, 11/27/95

Cast: Judith English (Markie Post), Katie English (Candace Cameron), Sheriff Marcus Ashley (Dale Midkiff), Bryan English (Stephen McHattie), Matt (Rob Stefaniuk), Judith's Mother (Pam Hyatt), Dr. Dillard (Susan Hogan), Dr. Pandro (Victor A. Young), Dr. Granger (Judah Katz), Allison (Melyssa Ade), Strangers (Damir Andre, Elizabeth Lennie, Dennis Akayama), Darby (Dick Callahan), Mother (Nancy Fischer), Young Judith (Sarah Fruitman), Secretary (Derwin Jordan), Principal (James Loxley), Mrs. Harkwick (Miriam Newhouse), Customer (Joe Pingue), Class Clown (Aidan Thompson), Advisor (Caroline Yeager), Teenager (Gil Garrott), Student (Marlow Vella), Young Father (John McLeod)

Credits: Director: Jorge Montesi; Writer: Michael J. Murray; Producer: Marilyn Stonehouse; Executive Producers: Richard L. O'Connor, Ann Daniel; Photography: Philip Linzey; Art Director: Andre Brodeur; Music: Micky Erbe, Maribeth Solomon; Editor: Pia Di Ciaula; Produced by Pebblehut Productions, Ann Daniel Films, ACI

First come the crop circles outside Judith English's small town; then Judith suffers inexplicable nightmares and flashbacks to childhood; then her rebellious daughter Katie vanishes for three hours she can't remember, but which leave her with a small belly scar. Glowing lights and mystery men pursue Katie, who disappears and returns with another memory gap—and her myopia corrected. Judith unearths her own repressed memories of childhood alien abduction and realizes the aliens experimented on Katie in utero—and now they want her back.

No longer skeptical, Katie eventually learns that the emotionless aliens want to acquire human feelings. When they kidnap Judith (trying for Katie), Judith meets a dying half-alien child and shows them how it needs affection as well as physical nourishment. The aliens free Judith, and it appears the family's nightmare is over—until the aliens return and take the Englishes away, apparently forever.

This is a routine alien abduction story, and what's the point of the ending?

THE WARLORD: BATTLE FOR THE GALAXY
UPN, 1/27/98

Cast: Justin Thorpe (John Corbett), Rula Kor (Carolyn McCormack), Heenoc Xian (John Pyper Ferguson), Maggie Sorenson (Elisabeth Harnois), Nova Thorpe (J. Madison Wright), Wally (Darryl Theirse), Jana (Marjorie Monaghan), General Sorenson (Rod Taylor), Mashwah (Lilyan Chauvin), Baraka (Rhino Michaels), Peddler (Dick Miller), Guard (Rob Elk), Thieves (Dyrk Ashton, John Marlo, Tom Billett, Steven E. Daniels), Assaulted Woman (Dorothy A. Gallagher), Doctor (Michael Quill), Girl (Shannon Welch), Gita (Dawn Ann Billings), Magda (Leslie Redden), Bartender's Wife (Belinda Balaski), Boy (Gregory Kargianus), with Joel Swetow, Philip Moon

Credits: Director: Joe Dante; Writer: Caleb Carr; Producer: Dan Dugan; Co-Producers: Thomas R. Polizzi, Rene Garcia; Executive Producers: Caleb Carr, Michael Finnell, Joe Dante, Robert Eisele; Photography: Jamie Anderson; Production Design: Sandy Veneziano; Music: Karl Lundeberg; Editor: Marshall Harvey; Produced by Renfield Productions, Paramount

Decades after the collapse of the Galactic Republic plunged the universe into anarchy, brilliant young Nova of Caliban 6 is kidnapped. Her brother Thorpe bands friends and mercenaries together to pursue the kidnappers in the *Osiris*, a Republic-era dreadnought. To reactivate the ship, Thorpe has to steal equipment from the planetary Warlord Heenoc Xian. After the *Osiris* leaves, the enraged warlord flies in pursuit.

The *Osiris* crew tracks Nova to the world of the Engineers, super-scientists plotting to turn the galaxy into a technocracy where racial, family and even sexual bonds are erased by brainwashing. The Engineers kidnapped Nova to brainwash her and exploit her intellect for their plans. They capture the *Osiris* too and prepare to brainwash the crew. Only when Xian, hunting Thorpe, attacks, is the *Osiris* able to escape.

Thorpe's mentor, General Sorenson, tells Thorpe the only chance to stop the Engineers is to rally the galaxy around the last descendant of the Republican prelates—but when they reach the prelate's world, they find that the Engineers have destroyed it. Then they learn the prelate rejected his destiny and fled that world years before—and became Warlord Xian. When Thorpe tells Xian about the massacre of his homeworld, Xian reluctantly accepts his duty to rebuild civilization and lead the *Osiris* in the fight against the Engineers.

Carr (bestselling author of *The Alienist* and *Angel of Darkness*) conceived this pilot for CBS (as *The Osiris Chronicles*) as a *Star Trek* variant (what happens when the Federation falls apart?). It didn't succeed, but it's a lot better than *The Visitor*, a 1998 Fox SF show that also starred Corbett.

THE WASP WOMAN
Showtime, 8/29/95

Cast: Jennifer Starlin (Jennifer Rubin), Alec (Doug Wert), Caitlin (Maria Ford), Mary (Melissa Brasselle), Dr. Zinthrop (Daniel J. Travanti), John (Jay Richardson), Arthur (Gerritt Graham), Nick (Richard Gabai), Wasp Collector (Johnny Williams), Wise Guy (Lenny Juliano), Jogger (Kimberly Roberts), Tex (Fred Olen Ray), Carla (Julie Smith), Assistant (Rob Kerchner), Roommate (Antonia Dorian)

Credits: Director: Jim Wynorski; Writers: Daniella Purcell, Guy Prevost, based on a screenplay by Lea Gordon, story by Kinta Zertuche; Producer: Mike Elliott; Executive Producers: Roger Corman, Lance H. Robbins; Photography: Michael Mickens; Production Design: Nava; Music: Terry Plumeri; Editor: Dan Holland; Produced by New Horizons, Showtime

At forty, cosmetics magnate Jennifer Starlin is too old to serve as her company's spokesmodel and fears she's losing her boyfriend, Alec. When Dr. Zinthrop develops a rejuvenating wasp-hormone treatment, Jennifer insists on playing guinea pig. The drug makes her younger and hornier—and periodically turns her into a giant wasp who stings her lovers to death. She also kills any potential rivals for Alec. When she attacks her secretary, Mary, Alec shows up and saves Mary, who uses some handy dynamite to destroy Jennifer.

This remake of the 1959 original turns a laughably bad film (with a strong female lead) into a boringly bad film (with a weak lead, who's much too young to be as over-the-hill as they say, even in modeling).

W.E.I.R.D. WORLD
Fox, 9/26/95

Cast: Dr. Monochian (Ed O'Neill), Dylan (Dana Ashbrook), Noah (Jim True), Diane (Audie England), Industrial Spy (Marshall Bell), Abby (Paula Marshall), Lucy (Kathryn Morris), Bob Provost (Miguel Nunez), Pat (Gina Ravera), Bran (Clayton Rohner), Noah Lane (Jim True), with Cyia Batten, Bryan Rush, Rachel Bella, Tony Cox, Stephen Liska, Zarachar Harris, Scott Nimikiko, Michael Wu

Credits: Director: William Malone; Writers: Gilbert Adler, A.L. Katz, Scott Nimerfro, based on stories in *Weird Science* and *Weird Fantasy* comics; Producer: A.L. Katz; Co-Producers: Scott Nimerfro, F.A. Miller; Executive Producers: Richard Donner, David Giler, Walter Hill, Joel Silver, Robert Zemeckis; Co-Executive Producer: Gilbert Adler; Photography: Levie Isaacks; Production Design: Greg Melton; Music: Nicholas Pike; Editors: Anthony Adler, Stanley Wohlberg; Produced by Two-Fisted Productions, Hallmark Entertainment

This is an anthology film set among researchers at the Wilson Emery Institute for Research and Development:

(1) Dylan secretly injects his ex-lover Lucy with a deadly virus to force her to help find a cure, but she dies instead. When her current lover, roboticist Noah, finds out, Dylan tries to murder him with the virus only to learn that the grief-stricken Noah transferred his mind into a robot body; Noah can't be killed, but Dylan can...

(2) After her brownnoser husband Brian takes credit for her research too many times, Abby tricks him into taking a youth-drug she has designed. It de-ages him until he becomes the little boy Abby always wanted and Brian refused to give her.

(3) Bob, the crooked security chief, is told by an industrial spy to murder his sister and steal her prototype time machine. She tells him the "Chronos device" has already shown her own obituary. When he comes after her, however, it's Brian who dies; the paper misinterpreted the event and apologizes.

And in the conclusion, W.E.I.R.D. head Monochian announces that a mix of genetic engineering and time travel has created a replacement for all the dead researchers—Albert Einstein!

HBO's success several years earlier with *Tales from the Crypt* (adapted from the EC horror comics of the fifties) may have inspired this probable pilot—but like a lot of EC material, this is dreadfully formulaic.

WHEN TIME EXPIRES
TMC, 5/10/97

Cast: Travis Beck (Richard Grieco), June Kelly (Cynthia Geary), Bill Thermin (Mark Hamill), Rifkin Ross (Tim Thomerson), Televangelist (Ron Masak), Car Salesman (Pat Corley), Walter Kelly (Chad Everett), Assassins (Gary Lee Davis, Rick Cramer), Tom Holton (Matthew Mahaney), TV Housewife (Joyclyn O'Brian), Sheriff Holton (Eric Lawson), Bartender (Bill Rosier), Rednecks (David Rowden, Mark Ginther), TV Repairman (David Wiley), Hotel Guest (Marvin Braverman), Trucker (Richard Gross), Ticket Officer (Phil Redrow), Old Man (Glen Vernon), Gun Dealer (Christopher Boyer)

Credits: Director-Writer: David Bourla; Producer: Larry Estes; Co-Producer: Sam Irvin; Executive Producers: Paul Colichman, Mark R. Harris, Stephen P. Jarchow; Photography: Dean Lent; Production Design: Stuart Blatt; Music: Todd Hayen; Editor: Bruce Wescott; Costumes: Charmian Schreiner; Produced by Showtime, Regents Entertainment, Welb Film Pursuits

Preparatory to inviting us into their alliance, time-traveling aliens have monitored Earth and analyzed our future. To confirm their timeline analysis, "The Ministry" tells agent Travis to drop a coin in a small-town parking meter. Once in town, Travis meets June, a restless waitress, and his old partner Bill, who warns Travis that assassins are seeking to kill him for an old error that wiped out an entire solar system. But things are not what they seem: June is the half-alien daughter of a retired agent; Bill is helping the assassins; and if the killers stop Travis from depositing the coin, nuclear war will eventually result. Averting the war will cover up that The Ministry misread our timeline; the assassins want the war to discredit The Ministry.

Unwilling to let Earth die, Travis kills both Bill and the assassins to reach the meter—then June's violent boyfriend assaults and cripples him. June, however, realizes that Travis' wild stories are true and puts the quarter in, saving Earth. The town's memories of these events are erased, but Travis retires from The Ministry, returns to town and takes up with June.

When Time Expires is pretty entertaining (if a bit convoluted).

WHERE HAVE ALL THE PEOPLE GONE?
NBC, 10/8/74

Cast: Steven Anders (Peter Graves), Jenny (Verna Bloom), David Anders (George O'Hanlon, Jr.), Deborah Anders (Kathleen Quinlan), Michael (Michael-James Wixted), Jim Clancy (Noble Willingham), Tom Clancy (Doug Chapin), Barbara Anders (Jay W. MacIntosh), Gunman (Dan Barrows), Jack McFadden (Ken Sansom)

Credits: Director: John Llewellyn Moxey; Writers: Lewis John Carlino, Sandor Stern; Story: Lewis John Carlino; Producer: Gerald I. Isenberg; Executive Producer: Charles Fries; Associate Producer: Gerald W. Abrams; Photography: Michael Margulies; Editor: John A. Martinelli; Music: Robert Prince; Produced by Metromedia Producers Corp., Jozak Co.

The Anders family is on a paleontology dig when a blinding solar flare knocks out the radio and electricity, makes their guide terminally ill—and then disintegrates him. Worried for Steven's wife Barbara, who left camp the day before, the party makes its way home through empty towns containing only looters and feral dogs. They pick up Jenny, traumatized by her children's deaths, and Michael, whose parents were killed by looters. When they reach home, Barbara is dead, but her note explains the deaths (a virus mutated by solar radiation). Steven's despair plunges Jenny into depression, but when she tries to kill herself, Steven and the others realize that life is still worth living and prepare for life in the post-disaster world with renewed hope.

Reminiscent of fifties nuclear dramas such as *The World, the Flesh and the Devil*, this is competently executed but wildly illogical (what kind of virus disintegrates bodies?).

WHISKERS
Showtime, 1/5/97

Cast: Jed Martin (Michael Caloz), Whiskers (Brent Carver), Hal Martin (Steve Adams), Jenny Martin (Laurel Paetz), Bastet (Monique Mercure), Alley Lady (Suzanne Cloutier), Dr. Forbes (Mark Bromilow), Pet Attendant (Robert Higden), Receptionist (Leni Parker), Trucker (Andre Petrowski), Mr. Mobley (Daniel Pilon), Ms. Gordon (Amanda Strawn), Crewcut (Patrick-Alain Tansey), Melanie (Brigid Tierney), Jed at 21 (Jacob Tierney), Fingers (Michael Yarmush), Voice (Sonja Ball)

Credits: Director: Jimmy Kaufman; Writers: Wendy Biller, Christopher Hawthorne; Producer: Kevin Tierney; Line Producer: Suzanne Girard; Photography: Francois Protat; Production Design: Claude Paré; Music: Daniel Lavoie; Editor: Alain Baril; Produced by Showtime, Hallmark Entertainment, Productions La Fete

For shy Jed, his eleventh summer was hell: a new neighborhood, new kids, and he's overheard his parents plotting to dispose of Jed's beloved cat, Whiskers. In a museum, a desperate Jed begs a statue of the cat-goddess Bastet to turn Whiskers into a boy who could stay with him—and it happens, except the adult cat becomes an adult man, not a boy.

In addition to hiding the new Whiskers and keeping him from spraying on the rug, Jed learns that Whiskers made his own wish: to find and care for his aged mother. Despite the interference of two bullies, Jed and Whiskers track down Mom from shelter to owner to owner ... and with Bastet's help, find her in a no-kill cat shelter. Reverting to cat form, Whiskers chooses to stay with his mother. Jed, flush with confidence from his adventures, finally overcomes his shyness without his cat—and learns his parents were never planning to give Whiskers away, they were figuring out how to tell Jed he'd soon have a sister.

Whiskers is a gentle, charming children's fantasy.

WHITE DWARF
Fox, 5/23/95

Cast: Dr. Driscoll Rampart (Neal McDonough), Dr. Akada (Paul Winfield), Nurse Shabana (C.C.H. Pounder), Ariel (Ele Keats), Never (Joey Andrews), Governor Twist (Roy Brocksmith), Strake (Michael McGrady), Lady X (Katy Boyer), King Joist (Robert Cornthwaite), Morgus (John Dennis Johnston), Dr. Gulpha (Ralph Drischell), Emma (Marsha Dietlein), Peter (James Morrison), Scarred Cultist (Maggie Baird), Marshall Bardaker (Gary Watkins), Osh (Chip Heller), Parasite Man (Thomas F. Duffy), Samuel (Kirk Ward), Orderly (Kevin Brophy), The David (Time Winters), Amanda (Maya McLaughlin), Royal Guard (David St. James), Twist's Servant (Tycho Thal), with Tara Graham, Beverly Mitchell, Roy Brocksmith

Credits: Director: Peter Markle; Writer: Bruce Wagner; Producer: Deepak Nayar; Executive Producers: Bruce Wagner, Francis Ford Coppola, Robert Halmi, Sr.; Co-Executive Producer: Fred Fuchs; Photography: Phedon Papamichael; Production Design: James Newport; Music: Stewart Copeland; Editor: Patrick McMahon; Produced by RHI Entertainment, American Zoetrope, Elemental Films

In 3040 the backwater planet Rusta orbits a white dwarf star, one side in perpetual sunlight, the other in eternal darkness. After centuries of war, the two sides are talking truce—but some fanatics want the war to go on.

None of which matters to off-worlder Dr. Rampart, who sees his six-month internship under Dr. Akada as a necessary evil before starting his career on Earth. Rampart soon finds, however, that Rusta is filled with wonders—immortal aliens, exotic beasts, strange powers. Not only does he actively help Akada's toughest case (an embittered teen shapeshifter), but he falls for Ariel, Princess of the Dark Side, who assumes rulership of her land after a warmonger kills her father in a failed attempt to sabotage peace negotiations. After Rampart returns home, he realizes he loves Rusta and goes back to stay.

This prospective pilot is a plotless mishmash of thrown-together weirdness, colorful scenes and assorted clothing styles, with absolutely no underlying logic—the kind of story that results from people who think, "SF means we can do anything we want!"

(Wagner says his influence was science-fiction artwork, not actual written SF, and it shows.) Avoid!

WILD PALMS
ABC, 5/16–5/19/93

Cast: Harry Wyckoff (James Belushi), Grace Wyckoff (Dana Delany), Senator Tony Kreutzer (Robert Loggia), Paige Katz (Kim Cattrall), Tabba Schwarzkoff (Bebe Neuwirth), Josie Ito (Angie Dickinson), Tommy Lazlo (Ernie Hudson), Tully Woiwode (Nick Mancuso), Whitehope (Charles Hallahan), Starfall (Robert Morse), Stitch Walken (Charles Rockett), Eli Levitt (David Warner), Cody Wyckoff (Ben Savage), Dr. Tobias Schenkl (Bob Gunton), Chickie Levin (Brad Dourif), William Gibson (Himself), Peter (Aaron Michael Metchik), Eileen Whitehope (Rondi Reed), Tambor the Wozniak (Beata Pozniak), Oliver Stone (himself), Hiro (Francois Chau), Lt. Grindgrod (Eugene Lee)

Credits: Directors: Peter Hewitt, Keith Gordon; Writer: Bruce Wagner, based on his comic strip; Producer: Michael Rauch; Executive Producers: Oliver Stone, Bruce Wagner; Photography: Phedon Papamichael; Production Design: Dins Danielsen; Costume Design: Judianna Makovsky; Editor: Patrick McMahon; Music: Ryuichi Sakamoto; Produced by Ixtlan, Greengrass Productions

In the politically repressive America of 2007, ambitious attorney Harry Wyckoff agrees to help his old girlfriend Paige find her missing son. Before long he's cheating on Grace Wyckoff with Paige and signing on with Wild Palms, a corporate group run by Paige's powerful fiancé, Senator Kreutzer. Kreutzer's political cabal, the Fathers, is backing an interactive form of holographic TV that will let them dominate the media and cement their power.

Harry becomes enmeshed in Kreutzer's power-games—and learns he's always been part of them: his mother-in-law, Josie, is Kreutzer's sister; Harry's sociopathic son Cody is actually Kreutzer's child by Paige (switched at birth for Harry's); and Harry's father pioneered the holo-technology the Fathers are exploiting. Kreutzer only needs the Go Chip—which will transfer his mind from his dying body into a computer—to become immortal and rule forever.

Harry agrees to spy on Kreutzer for the dissident Friends. The Fathers kidnap Harry's daughter, Deidre, whom Josie uses as bait to trap and murder Grace. Harry broadcasts a tape of the killing, but Kreutzer promptly alters it to show Harry as the killer. To win his freedom, Harry obtains the Go Chip from the Friends and barters it to Kreutzer for Deidre.

The Fathers have it all—but then Cody kills Josie in his own play for power; Harry finds his real son, Peter; and Kreutzer (whom Harry learns is his biological father) uses the Go Chip, but it has been reprogrammed and erases his virtual mind. Harry, Paige, Deidre and Peter go off together as the repressive power structure collapses around them.

Freely adapted from a comic-strip in *Details* magazine, *Wild Palms'* SF elements took a back seat to visual stylistics and fashion (it's one of the few shows to have plausible fashions for the future). While not as good a cyberpunk exercise as the *Max Headroom* series (cyberpunk being the term for a computerized, dystopian future), it was pretty entertaining. Among numerous TV stars in the cast is veteran villain David Warner (*Tron*, *Time After Time*, the voice of R'as al Ghul in the animated *Batman*) in a rare heroic role, and seminal cyberpunk author William Gibson in a cameo.

WILD, WILD WEST REVISITED
CBS, 5/9/79

Cast: James West (Robert Conrad), Artemus Gordon (Ross Martin), Miguelito Loveless, Jr. (Paul Williams), Robert T. Malone (Harry Morgan), Capt. Sir David Edney (Rene Auberjonois), Carmelita Loveless (Jo Anne Harris), President Cleveland (Wilford Brimley), Penelope (Trish Noble), Hugo Kaufman (Jeff MacKay), Alan (Robert Shields), Sonya (Lorene Yarnell), Gabrielle (Susan Blu), Nadia (Pavla Ustinov), Russian Tsar (Ted Hartley), Queen Victoria (Jacquelyn Hyde), Spanish King (Alberto Morin), Joseph (Skip Homeier), Lola (Joyce Jameson), Henry (John Wheeler), Manager (Mike Wagner), The Kid (Jeff J. Redfort)

Credits: Director: Burt Kennedy; Writer: William Bowers; Producer: Robert L. Jacks; Executive Producer: Jay Bernstein; Photography: Robert B. Hauser; Art Director: Albert Heschong;

Music: Richard Markowitz; Editor: Michael McCroskey; Produced by CBS

It's the late 1870s, ten years since secret agents Artemus Gordon and James West hung up their guns (Jim to run a saloon, Artie to work as a Shakespearean actor). When the son of their greatest enemy, Dr. Loveless, launches his own plan to conquer the world, Secret Service head Malone calls the agents back into action.

They have their work cut out for them. Jim and Artie are way out of shape ("Your punch only threw him 10 feet!"), and they find that Miguelito, Jr.—abetted by his half-sister Carmelita—possesses a deadly arsenal: unstoppable $600 cyborgs Alan and Sonya, a devastating super-bomb (which creates a pretty mushroom-shaped cloud when it goes off...), and a plan to replace the world's leaders with clones who will obey only him. Junior captures the agents along with the heads of state, but the quick-thinking agents escape—and Junior winds up destroyed by his own bomb. Unfortunately, Carmelita warns them, her brother had a half-dozen clones of himself hidden away for emergencies...

The Wild, Wild West had been a hit in the late sixties, transferring the mad villains and gadgetry of James Bond to an Old West setting. This reunion film was tremendously entertaining, with tongue not too far in cheek; it was followed up by the much-inferior *More Wild, Wild West*.

WISH UPON A STAR
Disney, 9/8/98

Cast: Alexia Wheaton (Katherine Heigl), Hayley Wheaton (Danielle Harris), Kyle Hartling (Don Jeffcoat), Ben Wheaton (Scott Wilkinson), Nan Wheaton (Mary Parker Williams), Mittermonster (Lois Chiles), Caitlin Sheinbaum (Ivey Lloyd), Simon (Matthew Barker), Kazumi (Jacque Gray), Talley (Kari Petersen), Sabrina (January Sorenson), Mr. Frauenfleder (Duane V. Stephens), Watson (Mark Hofeling), Photographer (Trevor Black), Class President (Emily Klindt), Boys (Andy West, Trent Rockwood, Josh James), Interviewers (Charles Metten, Joyce Cohen), Fan (Richard Grove), Moonpools & Caterpillars (Kimi Encarnacion, Jay Jay Encarnacion, Gugut Salgado, Tim Depala)

Credits: Director: Blair Treu; Writer: Jessica Barondes; Producers: David Anderson, Don Schain; Executive Producer: H.E. Scruggs; Photography: Brian Sullivan; Art Director: Ken Diamond; Production Design; Mark Hofeling; Music: Ray Colcord; Editor: David G. Blangsted; Produced by Leucadia Films

Brainy science geek Hayley can't help envying her vapid but sexy older sister, Alex—especially since Hayley has a massive crush on Alex's boyfriend, Kyle. One night, Hayley sees a falling star and wishes she could be Alex ... and it happens.

Hayley turns Alex's life topsy-turvy, taking back Kyle after Alex dumped him, and forcing Alex's spoiled friends to mingle with Hayley's geeky buddies. Stuck in Hayley's body, Alex retaliates by dressing slutty and flunking tests; Hayley fights back by trashing Alex's fashion-plate reputation. Both their lives tumble into the dumpster—at which point they bond in despair and finally see the real sister behind their distorted images of each other. Hayley convinces Alex's teachers that Alex isn't a total airhead, while Alex hooks Hayley up with an admiring neighbor. Hayley wishes on a star again ... and nothing happens. Alex then admits that she wished on the first star too, trying to change her fashion-crazy, alpha-bitch lifestyle; only when the girls wish together do they return to their own bodies.

This is familiar, if pleasant material, reminiscent of *Freaky Friday*.

WITCH HUNT
HBO, 12/10/94

Cast: H. Philip Lovecraft (Dennis Hopper), Kim Hudson (Penelope Ann Miller), Senator Larson Crockett (Eric Bogosian), Hypolita Kropotkin (Sheryl Lee Ralph), Finn Macha (Julian Sands), Trudy (Valerie Mahaffey), Vivian Dart (Lypsinka), N.J. Gotlieb (Alan Rosenberg), Manicurist (Debi Mazar), Sidney (Stanley De Santis), Lt. Morris Bradbury (Christopher John Fields), Braclett (John Durbin), Shakespeare (Gregory Bell), Minister (Tory Camilleri), G-Man (Chris Darga), Maid (Victoria Duff), Felix (Zaid Farid), Sidney's Wife (Ellen Gerstein), Malcolm Purdy (Robert Goolrick), Tyrone (Clifton González

González), Winston (James Harper), Skinner (Aaron Heyman), Cherie (Kristin Kahler), Bea (Nancy Linehan Charles), Mr. Brown (J. Patrick McCormack), Tracy (Julianne Morris), Loud Dresser (Dennis Paladino), Marie (Jill Pierce), Senator's Aide (Alan Poul), Senator Trumble (Phil Reeves), Towel Head (Steve Susskind), Zombie (Michael "Bear" Taliferro), Gotlieb's Secretary (Lynn Tufeld), Police Photographer (Steve Vaught)

Credits: Director: Paul Schrader; Writer-Co-Executive Producer: Joseph Dougherty; Producer: Michael R. Joyce; Co-Producers: David Gale, Betsy Beers; Executive Producer: Gale Anne Hurd; Photography: Jean Yves Escoffier; Production Design: Curtis A. Schnell; Music: Angelo Badalamenti; Editor: Kristina Boden; Produced by HBO Pictures, Pacific Western

In this sequel to *Cast a Deadly Spell*, it's 1953 and gumshoe Lovecraft still doesn't use magic. Neither does Senator Crockett, who's leading a crusade against sorcery. Starlet Kim Hudson hires Lovecraft to get the goods on her cheating husband, Gotlieb; after Gotlieb is killed by magic, Hudson asks Lovecraft to prove her innocence. Lovecraft's investigation turns up several more murders, an old enemy (sociopathic magus Macha), a brothel owner who shapeshifts girls to suit her clients' tastes—and Crockett, who frames Lovecraft's landlady and friend, Hypolita, for murdering Gotlieb and sentences her to be burned at the stake.

Lovecraft learns that Crockett—thinking Gotlieb was blackmailing him—hired Macha to murder Gotlieb. Crockett has Macha and Lovecraft locked safely away, which prompts a furious Macha to make Crockett's true, corrupt personality emerge on television in time to stop Hypolita's execution. Macha then moves against Lovecraft, but at the last minute, Hypolita intervenes and uses her magic to destroy Macha.

Though a good sequel, this is not up to the original—the McCarthyite allegory just gets irritating (though Bogosian is great as the sleazy opportunist).

WITHIN THE ROCK
Sci-Fi, 6/8/96

Cast: Ryan (Xander Berkeley), Dr. Dana Shaw (Caroline Barclay), Cody (Bradford Tatum), Samantha "Nuke Em" Rogers (Barbara Patrick), Luke Harrison (Brian Krause), Potter (Duane Whitaker), Archer (Michael Zelniker), Banton (Calvin Levels), Creature (Michael Jay), Michael Isaacs (Earl Boen), General Hurst (Dale Dye)

Credits: Director-Writer: Gary J. Tunnicliffe; Producers: Stanley Isaacs, Scott McGinnis, Robert Patrick; Executive Producers: John Fremes, Barry L. Collier, Barbara Javitz; Photography: Adam Kane; Production Design: Deborah Raymond; Music: Rod Gammons, Tony Fennell; Editor: Roderick Davis; Produced by 360 Entertainment

In 2019 Dr. Shaw and a crew of asteroid-miners land on a rogue planetoid to plant bombs that will divert it from striking Earth. Inside the rock they find a symbol-decorated metal cube that they open accidentally. Unleashed from the cube, a murderous, indestructible alien begins slaughtering the crew, despite their attempts to destroy it. Translating the message on the cube, they learn the creature almost destroyed another alien race before some of the aliens sacrificed themselves to lure it into the cube and launch it into space; space dust slowly gathered around it, creating the planetoid.

With the deadline for destroying the planetoid fast approaching, the survivors risk their lives to trap and impale the alien on the head of their giant drill. They barely succeed, then blow their bombs and escape to safety.

This competent *Alien* knockoff is certainly one of the more fun asteroid-threatens-earth movies.

YESTERDAY'S TARGET
Showtime, 4/28/96

Cast: Paul Harper (Daniel Baldwin), Jessica Harper (Stacey Haiduk), Carter (T.K. Carter), Aaron Winfield (Richard Herd), Winstrom (LeVar Burton), Lyle J. Holden (Malcolm McDowell), Young Roland (David Netter), Agent Riggs (Trevor Goddard), Agent Johnson (Tom Poster), Ricky (Page Mosely), Waitress (Mary Kathleen Gordon), Dr. Kang (Lucille Soong), Dr. Patel (Iqbal Theba), Man in Caddy (Will McAllister), Croupier (David Wells), Motel Manager (Frank Birney), Brenda Holden (J.C. Wendel)

Credits: Director: Barry Samson; Writer: David Bourla; Producers: Larry Estes, Albert T. Dickerson III; Executive Producers: Miles A.

Copeland III, Melanie Ray; Photography: Brian Capener; Production Design: William V. Ryder; Music: Todd Hayen; Editors: Michael Bloecher, Bruce Westcott; Produced by Republic Pictures, Showtime, IRS Media, Inc.

Paul, a telekinetic amnesiac, becomes the target of a manhunt ordered by Holden, a federal official seeking control of all psis, and carried out by the clairvoyant Winstrom. Winfield, who opposes Holden, convinces Paul to find and protect Winstrom's other two targets—whom Paul vaguely recognizes. The targets—Jessica, a precognitive, and Carter, a pyrotic (both amnesiacs)—reluctantly join forces with Paul against Winstrom.

Then an implant in Paul's body reveals they're all time travelers sent (by Winfield's future self) to avert Holden's future genocide against psis. Because the trip erased their memories, they're too late to stop Holden from building his power base. Now they must either convince Roland, a brilliant child psi, to take over Winfield's organization—or kill Winfield.

Winfield refuses to give up leadership so Winstrom attacks and kills Winfield (despite the psis' resistance). Paul shows Winstrom he's actually a fourth time traveler; repentant, Winstrom dies saving Roland. Holden renews the attack—until he and Paul realize that Paul is his yet-unborn son. Shaken, Holden abandons his war on psis, and Paul, Jessica and Carter go free.

In this competent but standard time-travel story, familiar faces include Burton (*Star Trek: The Next Generation*), Haiduk (*Adventures of Superboy*) and Carter (the forgettable sitcom *Just Our Luck*).

APPENDIX A: MINOR GENRE FILMS

It would be nice if every film in this book could be given a detailed, in-depth treatment, but the added pages would create a tome too heavy to lift. Hence this appendix, which covers minor TV-movies in the fantasy, horror and SF genres.

"Minor," in this context, refers not to quality (some are excellent) but to the genre elements: super-heroes with no real super-powers; futuristic action films that could easily be relocated to the present; films where the paranormal elements have only a minimal effect on the plot (e.g., most psychics-and-cops thrillers); spy movies with SF MacGuffins ("He who controls the Ultimate Desynchronizer controls the world!"); SF cartoons; borderline "realistic" films (e.g., asteroids striking Earth); movies with fake supernatural elements; films that come off as a TV series (e.g., *Tekwar*); and movies that just seem worthy of mention (*Phantom of the Opera*, *Tarzan*, lost-race films, evil non-magical cults).

THE ABDUCTION OF ST. ANNE
ABC, 1/21/75

The Catholic Church hires an ex-spy to learn if a mobster's daughter possesses the powers of a living saint; when a dying mafioso launches his own plans for Anne, the spy has to smuggle her to safety. Offbeat.

AMAZONS
ABC, 1/29/84

A doctor and a cop discover a series of murders are the work of the legendary Amazons, who plan to put one of their own into the White House.

AMERIKA
ABC, 2/15–2/20/87

With the Soviet Union holding the occupied U.S. in an iron fist, an inspirational leader (Kris Kristofferson) becomes the focal point of a new resistance movement.

THE AQUARIANS
NBC, 10/24/70

Operating out of the undersea Deep Lab, a team of explorers investigates a submerged derelict that may be leaking toxic waste.

ASSAULT ON DOME 4
Sci-Fi, 2/16/97

Stock action film in which a future cop must stave off an interplanetary terrorist's attack on a space research center.

ASTEROID
NBC, 2/16–2/17/97

Scientists use a laser to destroy an asteroid heading toward Earth—but fragments of the shattered rock survive and rain down upon us.

THE ASTRONAUT
ABC, 1/8/72

After an astronaut (Monte Markham) dies

on Mars, NASA hides the truth by replacing him with a double.

ATOMIC DOG
USA, 1/24/98

A radiation-tainted puppy grows into a super-strong, intelligent canine mutant that battles a neighborhood family to claim the puppies it sired with their pet.

BERMUDA TRIANGLE
ABC, 4/4/96

Amazingly generic story of a shipwrecked family that just happens to take place in the Triangle (doesn't make much difference though).

BEYOND THE BERMUDA TRIANGLE
NBC, 11/6/75

After a good friend vanishes in the Triangle, businessman Fred MacMurray uncovers its eerie history and becomes convinced it holds a gateway to other worlds. Very talky.

BLADE SQUAD
Fox, 8/12/98

In this pilot, a special squad of maverick cops uses jetpacks and in-line skates to maneuver through the crowded streets of a near-future inner city.

BORROWED HEARTS
CBS, 11/30/97

A workaholic (Eric Roberts) trying to impress an associate with his family values hires his employee (Roma Downey) to pose as his wife—which her daughter thinks is the work of an angel bringing the two lonely adults together.

BRAM STOKER'S "BURIAL OF THE RATS"
Showtime, 8/8/95

Traveling through Transylvania, Bram Stoker is captured by a tribe of fur-clad warrior-women who terrorize men and plan to use Stoker as breeding stock.

CHAMELEON
UPN, 10/22/98

In the corporate-ruled future, a genetically-engineered super-assassin turns against her masters to protect an innocent boy possessing stolen secrets.

THE CHRISTMAS BOX
CBS, 12/17/95

An overstressed entrepreneur and his family move in with an elderly widow; prodded by a mysterious music box and angelic messages, the businessman eventually chooses his family over his career.

A COLD NIGHT'S DEATH
ABC, 1/30/73

A weird, but terrific, two man drama: Two scientists (Robert Culp, Eli Wallach) arrive at an Arctic research station to find the staff dead, then become targets of a sinister, watching force.

THE COLD ROOM
HBO, 3/24/84

Is Amanda Pays channelling the horrific, Nazi-era memories of a young German girl, or (as father George Segal assumes) has she gone totally nuts? By the time we find out, it's too late in this mess to care.

COLOR ME PERFECT
Lifetime, 11/5/96

Romantic drama in which Michele Lee—mentally handicapped but happy and free-spirited—undergoes a mental treatment that elevates her to a super-genius and tangles her in a love triangle with the scientist responsible. Lee also wrote, executive-produced and directed.

THE COMPUTER WORE TENNIS SHOES
ABC, 2/18/95

A freak accident endows a college student with the knowledge and reasoning power of a supercomputer, which everyone around him tries to exploit.

CONVICT 762
Sci-Fi, 2/21/98

Forgettable thriller in which a female-crewed spaceship refuels at a penal colony and becomes the target for a disease-maddened killer.

THE CORSICAN BROTHERS
CBS, 2/5/85

In France, an outlaw and a nobleman are actually Siamese twins separated at birth, giving them a psychic link—what one feels, the other feels too.

THE CRADLE WILL FALL
CBS, 5/24/83

A woman pits herself against a brilliant doctor she discovers is performing unethical, illegal genetic experiments. Based on Mary Higgins Clark's best-seller, mixing in several characters from the soap opera *The Guiding Light*.

CRIME OF PASSION: VOICE FROM THE GRAVE
NBC, 4/22/96

Expanded from a segment of the *Unsolved Mysteries* TV series, this tells how a young woman, possessed by the ghost of a murder victim, ultimately led police to the killer.

CRUISE INTO TERROR
ABC, 2/3/78

Is the evil magic of an ancient sarcophagus responsible for strange goings-on aboard a cruise ship? Or is it all in their heads? This movie doesn't answer the questions.

CRY FOR THE STRANGERS
CBS, 12/11/82

Psychiatrist Patrick Duffy becomes involved with murders in a small coastal town that may relate to local legends of an evil witch-cult.

THE CURSE OF KING TUT'S TOMB
NBC, 5/8/–5/9/80

A highly fictionalized account of the discovery of King Tut's tomb and the "curse" that supposedly struck down those who opened the tomb.

DAD, THE ANGEL & ME
Family, 3/12/95

A suddenly motherless girl must adapt to living with her estranged Dad—with the help of a loving, albeit eccentric guardian angel (Carol Kane).

DARK AVENGER
CBS, 10/11/90

In this knockoff of the theatrical *Darkman*, a scientist injured by crime retaliates by becoming a ruthless avenger.

DARK NIGHT OF THE SCARECROW
CBS, 10/24/81

After a gang of bullies murder a retarded man, something—or someone—seeks revenge. A supernatural killer? Or a cunning trick? You'll find it hard to care.

DARK REFLECTION
Fox, 11/10/95

Computer programmer C. Thomas Howell discovers the malevolent lookalike invading Howell's life is actually his sociopathic clone—but for all practical purposes, it could just as easily have been his evil twin.

THE DARK SECRET OF HARVEST HOME
NBC, 1/23–1/24/78

A family moves to an old-fashioned town run by kindly Widow Fortune (Bette Davis) and only gradually realizes "old-fashioned" means ancient practices of earth-mother worship and human sacrifice.

DAUGHTER OF THE MIND
ABC, 12/9/69

Psychic thriller in which scientist Ray Milland thinks his late daughter is trying to reach him telepathically—but it turns out to be a scam by enemy spies.

THE DAY AFTER
ABC, 11/20/83

Nominated for 12 Emmy Awards, this powerful drama covers the tense build-up to a nuclear war between the USSR and the USA—and what happens after the exchange.

DEADLOCKED: ESCAPE FROM ZONE 14
Fox, 5/9/95

In this sequel to *Wedlock*, another pair of convicts linked by exploding collars escape jail to reclaim some buried loot.

THE DEADLY DREAM
ABC, 9/25/71

A scientist (Lloyd Bridges) on the verge of a breakthrough has dreams in which a mysterious Tribunal marks him for death. Except it turns out the Tribunal's world is real, and his "waking" life was the dream. Not completely satisfying, but eerie.

DEADLY MESSAGES
ABC 2/21/85

A woman running from a murderer receives warning messages from an old Ouija board.

A DEADLY VISION
ABC, 4/21/97

When a detective discovers that a clairvoyant waitress sees murders before they happen, he asks her to help him catch a serial killer.

DEAN R. KOONTZ'S "SERVANTS OF TWILIGHT"
USA, 10/4/91

Fanatics try to murder a child they think will become the Antichrist; after the cult has been destroyed, it's revealed they were right (the exact opposite of the source novel!).

DEATH AT LOVE HOUSE
ABC, 9/3/76

A couple staying at a late movie legend's house suspect she has returned from the dead to seduce the husband—but the mysterious happenings turn out to be the work of the living woman, driven insane by a disfiguring fire.

DEATH GAME
Showtime, 9/24/96

In near-future LA, detective Timothy Bottoms uncovers a spoilt clique of rich kids kidnapping the poor to fight in gladiatorial death games. With David McCallum.

THE DEATH OF OCEAN VIEW PARK
ABC, 10/19/79

As assorted fun-seekers frolic in Ocean View Amusement Park, a young woman is drawn there by mysterious visions of doom—which come true when a freak accident levels the park.

DEATH RAY 2000
NBC, 3/5/81

Spies attempt to reclaim a super-weapon from a master criminal in this pilot for the *A Man Called Sloane* series, which was cancelled well before this aired. Robert Logan plays the role taken by Robert Conrad in the series.

DEATHMOON
CBS, 5/31/78

Amazingly dull movie about an executive finding romance in Hawaii while police investigate a series of brutal killings; eventually they learn he's a werewolf and they kill him. Mostly mundane.

THE DEVIL'S DAUGHTER
ABC, 1/9/73

A woman tries to escape a satanic cult whose members believe she's Satan's daughter and want to marry her to a devil. She finds love—but guess who her husband turns out to be? Very bad.

THE DISAPPEARANCE OF FLIGHT 412
NBC, 10/1/74

After USAF pilots spot a UFO, security grills them for hours to convince them they only imagined it.

DR. SCORPION
ABC, 2/24/78

James Bondian adventure in which an ex-secret agent turned marine biologist pits himself against a sinister madman (Roscoe Lee Browne) with plans for world conquest.

DONOR
CBS, 12/9/90

A hospital resident (Melissa Gilbert) discovers a series of patient deaths stem from her superiors experimenting on patients to create an anti-aging drug. Based on a Robin Cook thriller.

DON'T GO TO SLEEP
ABC, 12/10/82

Dennis Weaver and Valerie Harper star in a good ghost story: Has their daughter returned from the grave to take revenge for the accident that killed her? It turns out her sister is acting out her grief and rage through murder and only imagined the ghost. Or—is it imagination?...

DOOMSDAY ROCK
Family, 4/8/97

Believing an asteroid is about to strike Earth, astronomer William Devane seizes control of a nuclear missile silo in order to blast it out of the sky.

THE EYES OF CHARLES SAND
ABC, 2/29/72

Dull little mystery in which a man inherits his family's gift of clairvoyance and uses it to help a supposedly insane young woman bring her brother's murderers to justice.

EYES OF TERROR
NBC, 3/18/94

Barbara Eden returns as psychiatrist Jesse Newman from *Visions of Murder*; this time, a fresh outbreak of psychic visions has Jesse and her daughter investigating a cop-killing.

FALCON'S GOLD
Showtime, 12/18/82

Dull adventure pilot (loosely based on Arthur Conan Doyle's Professor Challenger) in which hotheaded Professor Falcon and a brash reporter race villains to a priceless treasure that includes energy-crystals of limitless power.

FANTASY ISLAND
ABC, 1/14/77

In this pilot for the series, enigmatic Mr. Roarke (Ricardo Montalban) gives three people a chance to live out their greatest fantasies—one attends her own funeral, one relives a long-gone night of passion, and a hunter gets to taste the thrill of being the hunted. Followed by *Return to Fantasy Island*.

FATHERLAND
HBO, 11/26/94

It's the sixties in a world where the Nazis won World War II; while President Kennedy visits Hitler, an American reporter and a German cop try to reveal the truth about the Holocaust.

A FIRE IN THE SKY
NBC, 11/26/78

A comet smashes down in Phoenix, Arizona, with devastating consequences that won an Emmy for Special Effects and Sound Editing; it reportedly used the largest number of extras (5,700) and the most extensive miniature work for any TV movie to date.

THE FIRE NEXT TIME
CBS, 4/18–4/20/93

In the near future, global warming, ozone depletion and pollution have pushed the U.S. environment and economy to the brink of collapse; as their way of life crumbles, a rural Louisiana family tries to hold together. This works thanks to a strong cast including Craig Sarnac, Bonnie Bedelia and Richard Farnsworth.

FLASH GORDON—THE GREATEST ADVENTURE OF THEM ALL
NBC, 8/21/82

Edited from NBC's seventies animated series (based, in turn, on Alex Raymond's comic strip), this pits heroic Flash Gordon against Ming the Merciless, an alien tyrant who has allied himself with Hitler.

THE FLIGHT OF DRAGONS
ABC, 8/3/86

In this animated film, a wizard seeks to preserve the last remnants of magic in the face of encroaching technology and science; when a rival wizard seeks to pervert both science and magic, a modern-day writer is enlisted to help fight him. Based on both Peter Dickinson's *The Flight of Dragons* and Gordon R. Dickson's *The Dragon and the George*.

THE FOUR DIAMONDS
Disney, 8/12/95

A based-on-truth story about a young boy who copes with his imminent death from cancer by writing an Arthurian fantasy in which a young squire frees a kingdom from darkness by recovering four magical gems.

FUTURESPORT
ABC, 10/1/98

When a secessionist movement takes over Hawaii, America is on the brink of war—until a washed-up champion of Futuresport (America's hottest athletic event) proposes a winner-take-all match between two champion teams as an alternative. With Dean Cain, Wesley Snipes and Vanessa Williams.

GENERATION
ABC, 5/24/85

On the eve of the millennium, a widely scattered family (including an inventor coping with corporate intrigue, a lunar colonist and a "combat hockey" champion) try to reunite with their parents for the big celebration.

GET SMART AGAIN!
ABC, 2/26/89

Secret agents Maxwell Smart and 99 (from the series *Get Smart!*) are called out of retirement to stop their old enemy, KAOS, from threatening America with a weather-control machine. An entertaining reunion film.

THE GIRL FROM MARS
Family, 3/16/91

A brainy young girl starts claiming to be from Mars and freak events seem to back her up—but it's merely her way of distancing herself from an unsupportive family.

THE GLADIATOR
ABC, 2/3/86

In this failed pilot, a man avenges his brother's death in a DUI accident by building a customized super-truck to rid the roads of drunken drivers.

GOLD OF THE AMAZON WOMEN
NBC, 3/6/79

Two adventurers racing an international criminal to a jungle treasure encounter the warrior-women descendants of the legendary Amazons.

GUINEVERE
Lifetime, 5/7/94

A feminist retelling in which Guinevere helps Arthur hold his kingdom together.

HALLOWEEN TREE
TBS, 10/30/93

On Halloween, the sinister Moundshroud tries to take the soul of an injured boy; the boy's friends travel through time—and learn the history of All Hallows' Eve—in order to save him. An animated fantasy.

THE HANGED MAN
ABC, 3/13/74

A failed Western pilot about a gunslinger who survives his own hanging—with no pulse and an ice-cold body—and uses his second chance at life to redeem himself by defending the oppressed.

THE HARLEM GLOBETROTTERS ON GILLIGAN'S ISLAND
NBC, 5/15/81

In the third reunion film for the *Gilligan's Island* series, a millionaire with an army of robots plots to loot the island of a rare mineral; can the shipwrecked Harlem Globetrotters help the castaways stop him?

THE HAUNTING OF LISA
Lifetime, 4/10/96

When a young girl receives psychic visions of a child's murder, her mother fears getting involved in the case will only make her daughter look like a freak.

THE HAUNTING OF SARAH HARDY
USA, 5/31/89

A newly married heiress is haunted by her mother's ghost—but it's actually a plot by her husband to drive her insane.

HAUNTS OF THE VERY RICH
ABC, 9/20/72

Unsuccessful supernatural drama in which resort vacationers suffer increasing hardships (refrigeration and AC out, staff quitting) and realize they're all dead and damned to a nasty hell.

THE HENDERSON MONSTER
CBS, 5/27/80

Clunky soap opera involving a scientist working on possibly dangerous gene-splicing research, and his romantic triangle with his assistant (Christine Lahti) and her alcoholic husband (Stephen Collins).

HERCULES AND THE CIRCLE OF FIRE
Syndicated, 11/4–11/10/94

Feisty Deianeira (Tawny Kitaen) calls Hercules to help save the world when Hera contrives to steal fire from humanity. Third in the series.

HERCULES AND THE LOST KINGDOM
Syndicated, 5/1 to 5/7/94

Hercules comes to the aid of long-lost Troy, whose inhabitants have been banished from their own city by Hera. The second film.

HERCULES IN THE MAZE OF THE MINOTAUR
Syndicated, 11/18–11/24/94

Imprisoned in its labyrinth by Zeus, the Minotaur schemes to lure Hercules into its clutches and kill him as revenge against his father. Last film before the weekly series, drawing heavily on stock footage.

HERCULES IN THE UNDERWORLD
Syndicated, 11/11–11/17/94

Although happily married to Deianeira, Hercules agrees to help a beautiful girl whose village is being ravaged by the forces of the underworld. Fourth in the series.

THE HIGHWAYMAN
NBC, 9/20/87

Silly pilot for dumb, short-lived series: The Highwayman (Sam Jones), member of a special task force, fights crime (in this case, mastermind G. Gordon Liddy) in a high-tech eighteen-wheeler along the roads of near-future America.

THE HOUND OF THE BASKERVILLES
ABC, 2/12/72

In this failed pilot, Sherlock Holmes (Stewart Granger) discovers a human hand behind the seemingly demonic dog threatening the Baskerville family.

THE IMMORTAL
ABC, 9/30/69

A race-car driver whose blood resists disease, injury and aging must flee an aging millionaire who hopes regular transfusions will give him immortality. Stock *Fugitive* clone (and pilot for the same-name series) based very loosely on a James Gunn story.

IN SEARCH OF DR. SEUSS
TNT, 11/6/94

The Cat in the Hat (Matt Frewer) takes a reporter (Kathy Najimy) on a tour of Dr. Seuss's fantasy universe.

INFERNO
UPN, 10/29/98

It's disaster-movie time in Los Angeles as a massive solar flare knocks out electronics and communications and raises the temperatures to deadly levels.

INVASION EARTH
Sci-Fi, 12/8–12/10/98

British forces find themselves wedged between two warring alien races, one of which uses mind control on humans. Co-produced by Sci-Fi Channel, but first aired in the U.K.

IT CAME UPON A MIDNIGHT CLEAR
Syndicated, 12/15/84

Ex-cop Mickey Rooney dies before he can show his California grandson a real New York Christmas with snow—but he convinces the heavenly hierarchy to let him return to Earth as an angel to make the trip.

I'VE BEEN WAITING FOR YOU
NBC, 3/22/98

Five high schoolers threatened by a killer blame a fellow student they think is the reincarnation of a vengeful witch. It turns out the murders have a perfectly rational explanation, however—or do they?

JONNY QUEST AND THE CYBERINSECTS
USA, 11/19/95

In the sequel to *Jonny's Golden Quest*, the Quest team battles a race of super-insects a dying Dr. Zinn has created to conquer the world.

JONNY'S GOLDEN QUEST
USA, 4/4/93

In this good sequel to the animated adventure series *Jonny Quest,* Jonny must deal with his grief over his mother's murder, while he and his friends try to thwart the evil Dr. Zinn's scheme for attaining immortality.

KEN FOLLETT'S "THE THIRD TWIN"
CBS, 11/9–11/11/97

In this adaptation of Ken Follett's thriller, a psychiatrist studying the genetics of criminal behavior suspects a law student is the biological twin of a convicted, imprisoned killer—and then discovers that cloning one of the men has created a "third twin" who's another murderer.

KUNG FU: THE MOVIE
CBS, 2/1/86

In this reunion film, Old West martial artist Kwai Chang Caine (who now adds mystical powers to his repertoire) takes on opium smugglers and his own son, mesmerized to kill his father.

LAST LIVES
Sci-Fi, 10/18/97

Uninteresting action film in which a parallel-world revolutionary crosses to present-day Earth and kidnaps his late-wife's double. Her fiancé pursues them, using an other-worldly "life band" to resurrect himself when the bad guys keep killing him.

THE LAST NINJA
ABC, 7/7/83

A Japanese-American art dealer and ninja trainee is recruited to rescue hostages from a mad scientist using them to obtain a devastating laser weapon.

LIVE AGAIN, DIE AGAIN
ABC, 2/16/74

Family drama in which Donna Mills is thawed out from cryonic sleep after 30 years and returns un-aged for an uneasy reunion with her family—one of whom resents her enough to kill her.

LIVE WIRE
HBO, 9/3/92

A government agent (Pierce Brosnan) is pitted against a terrorist (Ben Cross) who possesses an undetectable liquid explosive identical to water and which detonates with unimaginable power.

LOST SOULS
UPN, 11/12/98

When an autistic girl channels the spirits of two murdered children, her father becomes convinced the killer is still out there and begins a desperate search.

LUCAN
ABC, 5/22/77

A feral child raised by wolves, then taken in by a research institute, now sets out to find his own identity—and the family he's never known. Pilot for the short-lived series.

MACGYVER AND THE LOST TREASURE OF ATLANTIS
ABC, 5/14/94

In this sequel to the *MacGyver* series, MacGyver (Richard Dean Anderson), a resourceful agent for an environmentalist government think tank, hunts the lost treasure of Atlantis.

MADAME SIN
ABC, 1/15/72

An unsuccessful but memorable pilot with Bette Davis going all out as the leader of an international crime cartel that persuades retired spy Robert Wagner to help her steal a Polaris submarine.

THE MAGNIFICENT MAGICAL MAGNET OF SANTA MESA
NBC, 6/19/77

Silly pilot about an idealistic young scientist who develops a super-magnet that can solve the world's energy problems, and then must protect it from his greedy bosses.

MAN FROM ATLANTIS: DEATH SCOUTS
NBC, 5/7/77

The second *Man from Atlantis* film: Mark encounters two water-dwelling ETs he thinks might be his own kind but are actually aliens plotting the conquest of Earth.

MAN FROM ATLANTIS: KILLER SPORES
NBC, 5/17/77

Third in the film series. A space probe arrives on Earth carrying spores determined to return to space—whether they have to possess or kill the humans they encounter.

MAN FROM ATLANTIS: THE DISAPPEARANCE
NBC, 6/20/77

The last of four films: Mark must rescue a kidnapped Dr. Merrill from a mad scientist.

THE MAN IN THE SANTA CLAUS SUIT
NBC, 12/23/79

At Christmas time, a workaholic, a petty thief and a shy nerd find their lives changed for the better when they each rent a Santa suit from a mysterious store owner (Fred Astaire) who's really Santa himself.

THE MAN WHO WOULDN'T DIE
ABC, 5/29/95

A mystery novelist (Roger Moore) enlists a psychic to help track down a master criminal (Malcolm McDowell) using Moore's books as the blueprint for his crimes.

THE MARK OF ZORRO
ABC, 10/29/74

In old California, a young man (Frank Langella) revives the legends and tactics of the famous masked hero, Zorro, in order to free the masses from a repressive governor.

METEORS
USA, 5/3/98

Yet another town has to cope with a devastating meteor strike.

MIDNIGHT'S CHILD
Lifetime, 4/21/92

In a variation on psycho babysitter films, a sorceress posing as an au pair schemes to initiate the child she cares for into a satanic cult.

MIND OVER MURDER
CBS, 10/23/79

Tepid thriller in which a model with precognitive power realizes she's being stalked by a killer she'd identified to police before.

MODEL BY DAY
Fox, 3/21/94

Enjoyable adaptation of the same-name comic strip. A model (Famke Janssen) with martial arts training avenges her best friend's beating by going to war on crime as Lady X, then confronts a copycat vigilante who kills criminals.

MOTHER GOOSE ROCK 'N' RHYME
Disney, 5/19/90

When Mother Goose disappears, her son hunts for her among the denizens of the realm of nursery rhymes.

MURDER IN MY MIND
CBS, 2/19/97

FBI rookie Nicolette Sheridan accepts a brain-cell implant from a serial-killer's victim in order to witness the murder exactly as it happened.

MURDER IN SPACE
Showtime, 7/28/85

A dull murder mystery set on a multi-national deep space mission; can ground control unmask the killer before the crew disembarks? This was originally shown without the last half-hour, with viewers offered a prize for guessing the solution.

MURDEROUS VISION
USA, 2/20/91

A psychic helps out a loose-cannon cop (Bruce Boxleitner) tracking a deranged killer who surgically removes his victims' faces.

MYSTERIOUS ISLAND OF BEAUTIFUL WOMEN
CBS, 12/1/79

A plane crashes on a tropical island where a lost tribe of warrior women (who turn out to be shipwrecked Catholic-school girls) attempts to kill all of the survivors.

THE MYSTERIOUS TWO
NBC, 5/31/82

A good, ambiguous film, reminiscent of *The Twilight Zone*. Mysterious cult leaders He and She recruit followers for an out-of-this-world journey, while critics (a reporter, one follower's boyfriend, the cops) try to prove they're fakes. Loosely based on the Heaven's Gate cult whose mass suicide brought them notoriety in the nineties.

THE MYSTIC WARRIOR
ABC, 5/20–5/21/84

Adapted from Ruth Beebe Hill's *Hanta Yo*, this two-part film tells of a band of proud Sioux saved from the white man's war by the mystic gifts of one warrior (Robert Beltran, later of *Star Trek: Voyager*).

NICK FURY, AGENT OF S.H.I.E.L.D.
Fox, 5/26/98

Comic-book superspy Nick Fury is called out of retirement to stop terrorists from destroying Manhattan with a deadly virus. Pretty fun except for David Hasselhoff's laughable turn in the lead.

NIGHT OWL
Lifetime, 8/19/93

A woman's troubled marriage falls apart completely when her husband falls under the spell of a DJ whose voice drives men to madness.

THE NIGHT RIDER
ABC, 5/11/79

Formulaic Zorro knockoff starring David Selby (*Dark Shadows*) as a 19th-century New Orleans aristocrat secretly fighting injustice as the Night Rider.

NIGHT TRAIN TO KATHMANDU
Disney, 6/25/88

In Nepal, a teenage American girl helps a young prince trying to return to his hidden city before it vanishes into the mists of time—and if they fail, the prince dies. Stock adventure, wooden lead, minimal fantasy elements.

NIGHT VISION
NBC, 11/30/90

Directed by Wes Craven, this engaging but unsuccessful pilot pairs a tough cop with a psychic (yes, again!) to track down a serial killer—a job made more complicated because the psychic's uncontrolled telepathy makes her constantly adopt other personalities.

NIGHT VISITORS
NBC, 10/13/96

A stock thriller in which a woman becomes the target of government agents after she uncovers evidence of extraterrestrials' arrival on Earth.

A NIGHTMARE COME TRUE
CBS, 2/12/97

When an abused wife vanishes, her daughter is at first relieved, then suspects something is wrong. Then she begins suffering nightmares that hint her mother is in danger—and at the truth behind her disappearance.

NIGHTSCREAM
NBC, 4/14/97

Teri Garr becomes convinced a young girl—the lookalike for Garr's murdered daughter—has been possessed by the slain girl's spirit.

NORTHSTAR
ABC, 8/10/86

Dull super-hero pilot in which solar radiation mutates an astronaut (Greg Evigan) so he becomes a genius when sunlight hits his eyes; but will die if he gets too much sun. When his best friend dies accidentally, Evigan proves he was actually murdered and hunts the killer.

ONCE UPON A SPY
ABC, 9/19/80

A U.S. spy agency drafts a computer genius (Ted Danson) to learn how a mammoth supercomputer was stolen; investigating, the man finds himself pitted against a maniacal billionaire (Christopher Lee) with a shrinking ray. Great fun.

THE PHANTOM OF HOLLYWOOD
CBS, 2/12/74

In this updated version of the Phantom, a disfigured, masked man attacks those selling off his beloved home—the MGM back lots.

THE PHANTOM OF THE OPERA
CBS, 1/29/83

In this version of the horror classic, Maximilian Schell plays the disfigured Phantom, with Jane Seymour as the opera singer he trains and schemes to possess.

THE PHANTOM OF THE OPERA
NBC, 3/18/90

Based on Ted Kopit's stage version, this stars Charles Dance as the disfigured Phantom and Teri Polo as the singer Christine. Great-looking and well-acted (but with no look at the Phantom's face).

PIRANHA
Showtime, 9/19/95

In this remake of the 1978 film (the best of the *Jaws* clones), piranha genetically engineered for intelligence, endurance and size escape a government research facility and attack everyone in the water as they spread downstream.

PROBE
NBC, 2/21/72

Special agents—monitored and directed at a distance by their high-tech control center—investigate the disappearance of a priceless gem collection. Pilot for the series *Search*, this also aired under that name.

RETROACTIVE
HBO, 8/16/97

Adequate action film in which a woman uses a time machine over and over to try and undo the results of her encounter with a violent sociopath (James Belushi) but only makes things worse each time.

RETURN TO FANTASY ISLAND
ABC, 1/20/78

In the sequel to *Fantasy Island*, enigmatic Mr. Roarke fulfills three new fantasies: A man gets shipwrecked with his beautiful boss; a couple meet the girl they gave up for adoption; and an amnesiac relives the traumatic wedding night that destroyed her memory. The long-running series followed.

REVENGE
ABC, 11/6/71

A deranged mother locks up her daughter's rapist in her basement, while the man's wife uses ESP to find and rescue him.

RIDDLER'S MOON
UPN, 11/5/98

Bad *Field of Dreams* knockoff in which a young paraplegic believes he can save his dying farm-town by following a vision and building a mystery structure in his mother's field. It features an utterly nonsensical ending and *Star Trek: Voyager*'s Kate Mulgrew as Mom.

ROBIN COOK'S "TERMINAL"
NBC, 2/21/96

Medical researchers discover a scheme centering on a treatment for brain tumors—and a method to create tumors to guarantee a market.

SALVAGE-ONE
ABC, 1/20/79

A junkman (Andy Griffith) puts together a team of experts to build his own rocket with which to recover leftover NASA equipment from the moon. Followed by a series.

SAMURAI
NBC, 4/30/79

A Japanese-American DA becomes a costumed crimefighter to work against injustice outside the law. His first adversary is a megalomaniac planning to level San Francisco with an earthquake machine.

SATAN'S SCHOOL FOR GIRLS
ABC, 9/19/73

Horror veteran Pamela Franklin discovers her sister's suicide is linked to a college satanic cult—and learns perhaps too late that one of the teachers is Old Scratch himself. A good cast can't save this tripe.

SATAN'S TRIANGLE
ABC, 1/14/75

Rescued by a Coast Guard pilot, Kim Novak tells him the supernatural events that happened to her in the Bermuda Triangle. He proves everything has a rational explanation after all—or is he wrong?

SCATTERING DAD
CBS, 1/4/98

A reclusive widow (Olympia Dukakis) honors a promise to her husband's ghost (Andy Griffith) and leaves home for the first time in 20 years to scatter his ashes in the wilderness.

SCORPIO ONE
Sci-Fi, 8/22/98

Robert Carradine stars in a competent thriller about sabotage on a U.S. space mission and skullduggery in government, all centering on a scheme to gain the secrets of a new cold-fusion power source.

SCREAM OF THE WOLF
ABC, 1/16/74

A hunter begins to suspect the killer wolf he's hunting is actually a werewolf—but it's an elaborate ruse by another hunter with a deranged agenda.

SEARCH FOR GRACE
CBS, 5/17/94

A woman's seductive new lover turns out to be a manipulative, violent deceiver—a relationship that stirs up the woman's past-life memories. Routine woman-in-jeopardy film.

THE SECOND CIVIL WAR
HBO, 3/15/97

In the near future, the anti-immigration governor of Idaho bans a planeload of refugees from the state, touching off a power struggle between the state and the federal government under the eyes of the media. An interesting black comedy.

SHADOW ON THE LAND
ABC, 12/4/68

Jackie Cooper and John Forsythe star in the story of a future America under a military dictatorship, and the revolutionary underground trying to liberate the land.

SHADOWHUNTER
Showtime, 2/10/93

Cop thriller in which a detective hunting a murderous Navajo skinwalker (a witch) is forced by his enemy's powers to confront the darkness in his own soul.

SMOKEY MOUNTAIN CHRISTMAS
ABC, 12/14/86

A *Snow White* variant in which a country singer (Dolly Parton) helps out seven desperate orphans while fending off the wrath of a jealous backwoods witch.

SNOWBEAST
NBC, 4/28/77

When a yeti starts a killing spree at a winter resort, some of the skiers take time off from skiing and personal conflicts to hunt it down. Bor-ing!

SPACE MARINES
Showtime, 7/28/96

When a United Planets minister is kidnapped by space pirates, the Space Marines charge in, but find dithering diplomats as much an obstacle to victory as the enemy. Stock compilation of macho action film clichés.

SPACEJACKED
TMC, 10/8/97

Uninteresting action film in which a conniving crewman holds a luxury space-liner's passenger list hostage for a multi-billion-dollar ransom.

THE SPIRIT
ABC, 7/31/87

In this dumb, campy adaptation of Will Eisner's classic comic strip, supposedly dead cop Denny Colt fights crime as The Spirit. His first adversary is the manipulative beauty seducing the city's police commissioner. The cast includes Sam Jones (1979's *Flash Gordon*) and Nana Visitor (*Deep Space Nine*).

STALK THE WILD CHILD
NBC, 11/3/76

A young boy raised by wild dogs is found and taken to a university where an attempt is made to civilize him.

STARFLIGHT: THE PLANE THAT COULDN'T LAND
ABC, 2/27/83

In this disaster film, a hydrogen-powered super-fast plane accidentally rockets into space on its maiden flight.

STOWAWAY TO THE MOON
CBS, 1/10/75

A young boy stows away aboard a lunar rocket, becomes a celebrity when he's found in space—and a lifesaver when he finds a way to avert a disaster for the ship.

THE STRANGE AND DEADLY OCCURRENCE
NBC, 9/24/74

A supernatural haunting of Robert Stack's home turns out to be a crook trying to drive them out so he can recover some buried loot.

SUBLIMINAL SEDUCTION
Showtime, 8/3/96

A software designer discovers that his new employers are using subliminal messages to make their new computer game irresistible to buyers—and to drive their enemies to suicide.

TARZAN IN MANHATTAN
CBS, 4/15/89

When Cheetah is kidnapped by hunters gathering animals for scientific research, Tarzan (Joe Lara) follows them to New York, where he rescues Cheetah from a vivisectionist with the help of street-smart cabbie Jane. Lara played Tarzan again in the unrelated series *Tarzan: The Epic Adventures*.

TEKWAR
Syndicated, 1/23–1/29/94

In the 21st century, Tek—computer chips that tap into people's minds to make their wildest fantasies seem real—is the ultimate, ultra-addictive drug. Ex-cop, ex-Tekhead Jake Cardigan (Greg Evigan) is released from prison by millionaire William Shatner and sent to find a scientist who may be able to make the whole world's Tek supply inert. Based on Shatner's ghost-written *Tek* novels.

TEKWAR: TEK JUSTICE
Syndicated, 5/7–5/14/94

All the evidence indicates Jake murdered his ex-wife's new husband, but his friends are determined to prove otherwise—while a Teklord launches a scheme to shut down the world's computers.

TEKWAR: TEKLAB
Syndicated, 2/21–2/27/94

When Excalibur is stolen, Jake and his partner investigate and discover the theft is part of a struggle for succession to the throne and control of the British government.

TEKWAR: TEKLORDS
Syndicated, 2/14–2/20/94

A Teklord kidnaps Jake's son and unleashes a computer virus that crashes not only computers but those who use them.

TIDAL WAVE: NO ESCAPE
ABC, 5/5/97

Good thriller in which two marine experts (Corbin Bernsen, Juliette Phillips) pit themselves against an extortionist threatening the world with manmade tidal waves.

TOMORROW'S CHILD
ABC, 3/22/82

Stephanie Zimbalist gives a good performance as a would-be mother grappling with mixed feelings after agreeing to go through in vitro fertilization and create a test-tube baby.

TOURIST TRAP
ABC, 4/5/98

After years admiring his Civil War hero ancestor, a banker—who frequently converses with his ancestor's ghost—takes his family on a road trip to the site of his ancestor's greatest battle.

THE TOWER
Fox, 8/16/93

Dreadful action film in which a minor computer glitch causes a skyscraper security system to target a maverick employee (the horribly miscast Paul Reiser) for death.

TWILIGHT OF THE GOLDS
Showtime, 3/23/97

A family crisis erupts for the Golds when prenatal genetic testing reveals their grandchild will be born gay.

THE UFO INCIDENT
NBC, 10/20/75

A based-on-truth film that stars James Earl Jones and Estelle Parsons as a couple undergoing hypnotherapy to recover buried memories of an alien abduction. Talky and mundane, this was the first alien-abduction TV-film; but in trying to make the new idea plausible, they only made it dull, despite the strong cast.

THE ULTIMATE IMPOSTOR
CBS, 5/12/79

Another spy-with-a-twist thriller: A spy whose mind has been erased receives computer implants that allow him to retain any personality, knowledge or skills for 72 hours. His first mission: rescue a Soviet defector kidnapped by another nation.

UNLIKELY ANGEL
CBS, 12/17/96

A sugary Christmas offering in which a deceased country singer (Dolly Parton) is denied heaven unless she can reunite a dysfunctional family.

VALENTINE MAGIC ON LOVE ISLAND
NBC, 2/15/80

An appalling *Fantasy Island/Love Boat* knockoff set on Love Island, a world famous romantic getaway where the hereditary owners—a family of witches—use their magic powers to ensure true love always wins out. Really pathetic.

VIRTUAL SEDUCTION
Showtime, 8/1/95

A man encounters the image of his long-dead lover in a VR program—unaware the program taps into his subconscious desires in order to make him and other users addicted to its fantasy worlds.

VISIONS...
CBS, 10/10/72

A professor with psychic visions of a bomb being planted becomes the chief suspect after he warns the police.

VISIONS OF MURDER
NBC, 5/7/93

A psychiatrist's (Barbara Eden) clairvoyant visions embroil her in a murder investigation; the reason for the visions is that her daughter, stolen at birth, is involved in the case. An unsuccessful pilot.

THE WATER ENGINE
TNT, 8/24/92

A penniless inventor creates an engine that runs on water, then comes under fire from business interests determined to suppress his creation. Adapted by David Mamet from his play.

WEDLOCK
HBO, 9/28/91

In this crime thriller, two cons linked by radio collars—that explode if the wearers separate—duck cops and ex-partners to recover a fortune in stolen diamonds.

WHEN DREAMS COME TRUE
ABC, 5/28/85

A woman tries to convince her lover that the killer she's seen in her dreams is real—and stalking her.

WHEN MICHAEL CALLS
ABC, 2/5/72

A woman is convinced she's receiving phone calls from her supposedly dead nephew, but it turns out to be her deranged brother's (Michael Douglas) scheme for revenge.

WHO IS JULIA?
CBS, 10/26/86

One of the few serious brain-transplant films: A dying socialite's brain is transplanted into the brain-dead body of a frumpy, blue-collar housewife.

WITHOUT WARNING
CBS, 10/30/94

Yet another movie in which asteroids bombard the Earth.

WONDER WOMAN
ABC, 3/12/74

Pathetic pilot based on the comics character, this stars Cathy Lee Crosby as an Amazon turned special agent pitted against a smooth spymaster (Ricardo Montalban). The superior *New Original Wonder Woman* followed.

APPENDIX B: ALTERNATIVE TITLES

Low-budget filmmakers have a long tradition of re-releasing movies with different titles (sometimes two or three times) to con unwary filmgoers into rewatching movies that often weren't worth seeing the first time. The same principle applies to TV-movies as they circulate through the syndicated, cable and video markets; this list includes all such titles known by the author as of this writing. Obvious changes (e.g., *Shadow Zone: My Teacher Ate My Homework* becoming just *My Teacher Ate My Homework*) or "working titles" used during production but never on-screen haven't been listed.

Alternative Title	Original Title	Alternative Title	Original Title
Addicted to Love	*Virtual Seduction*	*The Osiris Chronicles*	*Warlord: Battle for the Galaxy*
Aliens Among Us	*Alien Avengers II*		
Amityville IV	*Amityville: The Evil Escapes*	*The Presence*	*Danger Island*
		Programmed to Kill	*Homewrecker*
Arizona Ripper	*Bridge Across Time*	*Robbers of the Sacred Mountain*	*Falcon's Gold*
Attack of the Phantoms	*KISS Meets the Phantom of the Park*	*Search*	*Probe*
Babylon 5: The Gathering	*Babylon 5*	*Secret Passions*	*Haunted by Her Past*
Circuit Breaker	*Inhumanoid*	*Spectre*	*House of the Damned*
The Colony	*The Advanced Guard*	*Stranded in Space*	*The Stranger*
The Corporation	*Subliminal Seduction*	*Strangers in Town*	*Bay Coven*
The Cusp	*Falling Fire*	*Summer of Fear*	*Stranger in Our House*
The Dead Can't Lie	*Gotham*	*Sweet Dreams*	*Buried Secrets*
Desire the Vampire	*I, Desire*	*Terror on the Blacktop*	*The Highwayman*
Eye of the Demon	*Bay Coven*	*They Watch*	*They*
Flashframe	*Subliminal Seduction*	*Three Minutes to Impact*	*Falling Fire*
Forbidden Beauty	*The Wasp Woman*	*Timescape*	*Disasters in Time*
Gangsterworld	*The Outsider*	*Tut and Tuttle*	*Through the Magic Pyramid*
Grand Tour	*Disasters in Time*		
Haunted Symphony	*Hellfire*	*UFO Café*	*Guess Who's Coming for Christmas?*
Humanoid Defender	*J.O.E. and the Colonel*		
It Came Up from the Bermuda Depths	*Bermuda Depths*	*Visions of Death*	*Visions...*
		Visions of Terror	*Eyes of Terror*
Legacy of Evil	*Possession of Michael D.*	*Wedlock II*	*Deadlocked: Escape from Zone 14*
Of Unknown Origin	*The Alien Within*		
One Hour to Doomsday	*City Beneath the Sea*	*Welcome to Planet Earth*	*Alien Avengers*

APPENDIX C: CHRONOLOGY

12/04/68 Shadow on the Land
03/03/69 Fear No Evil
09/30/69 The Immortal
11/08/69 Night Gallery
12/09/69 Daughter of the Mind
01/09/70 Sole Survivor
02/23/70 Ritual of Evil
03/10/70 The Love War
09/29/70 Night Slaves
10/24/70 The Aquarians
10/27/70 The House That Would Not Die
11/24/70 Crowhaven Farm
11/24/70 Hauser's Memory
01/25/71 City Beneath the Sea
09/25/71 The Deadly Dream
10/02/71 Sweet, Sweet Rachel
10/05/71 The Last Child
10/23/71 Death Takes a Holiday
11/05/71 Black Noon
11/28/71 Earth II
12/04/71 The Devil and Miss Sarah
01/08/72 The Astronaut
01/11/72 The Night Stalker
01/15/72 Madame Sin
01/21/72 Something Evil
01/22/72 The People
01/28/72 She Waits
02/05/72 When Michael Calls
02/21/72 Probe
02/29/72 The Eyes of Charles Sands
03/17/72 The Night Stalker
09/20/72 Haunts of the Very Rich
09/26/72 Moon of the Wolf
10/10/72 Visions...
10/17/72 Sandcastles

11/21/72 Gargoyles
01/09/73 The Devil's Daughter
01/16/73 The Night Strangler
01/30/73 Baffled!
01/30/73 A Cold Night's Death
02/13/73 The Horror at 37,000 Feet
02/14/73 Poor Devil
02/21/73 The Norliss Tapes
02/26/73 The Stranger
03/07/73 The Six Million Dollar Man
03/23/73 Genesis II
09/19/73 Satan's School for Girls
10/10/73 Don't Be Afraid of the Dark
11/30/73 Frankenstein: The True Story
12/11/73 The Cat Creature
12/14/73 The Borrowers
12/14/73 Miracle on 34th Street
01/16/74 Scream of the Wolf
01/23/74 The Questor Tapes
02/02/74 Killdozer
02/08/74 Dracula
02/12/74 The Phantom of Hollywood
02/13/74 Live Again, Die Again
02/26/74 Killer Bees
03/12/74 Wonder Woman
03/13/74 The Hanged Man
04/23/74 Planet Earth
09/24/74 The Strange and Deadly Occurrence
10/01/74 The Stranger Within
10/08/74 Where Have All the People Gone?
01/10/75 Stowaway to the Moon

01/14/75 The Dead Don't Die
01/14/75 Satan's Triangle
01/21/75 The Abduction of Saint Anne
03/04/75 Trilogy of Terror
03/09/75 Search for the Gods
05/06/75 The Invisible Man
07/13/75 Strange New World
10/20/75 The UFO Incident
11/06/75 Beyond the Bermuda Triangle
11/07/75 The New, Original Wonder Woman
03/19/76 The Time Travelers
05/01/76 Future Cop
05/10/76 Gemini Man
10/29/76 Look What's Happened to Rosemary's Baby
11/03/76 Stalk the Wild Child
12/03/76 Beauty and the Beast
01/14/77 Fantasy Island
02/11/77 The Last Dinosaur
02/20/77 The Spell
03/04/77 The Man from Atlantis
04/28/77 Snowbeast
05/01/77 The Possessed
05/07/77 Man from Atlantis: Death Scouts
05/17/77 Man from Atlantis: Killer Spores
05/21/77 The Spectre
05/22/77 Good Against Evil
05/22/77 Lucan
05/24/77 The Man with the Power
06/18/77 Exo-Man
06/19/77 The Magnificent Magical Magnet of Santa Mesa

Appendix C: Chronology

06/20/77 *Man from Atlantis: The Disappearance*
09/14/77 *Spider-Man*
09/16/77 *Curse of the Black Widow*
11/04/77 *The Incredible Hulk*
11/28/77 *The Return of the Incredible Hulk*
12/11/77 *It Happened One Christmas*
01/20/78 *Return to Fantasy Island*
01/23/78 *The Dark Secret of Harvest Home*
01/27/78 *The Bermuda Depths*
01/29/78 *Night Cries*
02/03/78 *Cruise Into Terror*
02/06/78 *Initiation of Sarah*
02/18/78 *The Ghost of Flight 401*
02/24/78 *Dr. Scorpion*
03/28/78 *The Cops and Robin*
05/31/78 *Deathmoon*
09/06/78 *Dr. Strange*
09/14/78 *The Clone Master*
10/16/78 *Human Feelings*
10/28/78 KISS *Meets the Phantom of the Park*
10/31/78 *Devil Dog: The Hound of Hell*
10/31/78 *Stranger in Our House*
11/05/78 *The Time Machine*
11/23/78 *The Thief of Baghdad*
11/26/78 *A Fire in the Sky*
01/19/79 *Captain America*
01/24/79 *Mandrake*
03/06/79 *Gold of the Amazon Women*
04/03/79 *The Darker Side of Terror*
04/30/79 *Samurai*
05/09/79 *The Wild, Wild West Revisited*
05/11/79 *The Power Within*
05/12/79 *The Ultimate Impostor*
10/07/79 *Vampire*
10/19/79 *The Death of Ocean View Park*
10/23/79 *Mind Over Murder*
10/31/79 *The Two Worlds of Jennie Logan*
11/09/79 *Topper*
11/17/79 *Salem's Lot*
11/23/79 *Captain America II*
12/01/79 *Mysterious Island of Beautiful Women*
12/16/79 *An American Christmas Carol*
12/23/79 *The Man in the Santa Claus Suit*

01/13/80 *Dr. Franken*
01/19/80 *The Lathe of Heaven*
01/27/80 *The Martian Chronicles*
02/15/80 *Valentine Magic on Love Island*
03/02/80 *The Aliens Are Coming*
03/07/80 *Brave New World*
05/08/80 *The Curse of King Tut's Tomb*
05/11/80 *Angel on My Shoulder*
05/27/80 *The Henderson Monster*
06/13/80 *The Girl, the Gold Watch & Everything*
09/19/80 *Once Upon a Spy*
10/07/80 *More Wild, Wild West*
10/12/80 *Revenge of the Stepford Wives*
10/31/80 *The Legend of Sleepy Hollow*
02/06/81 *This House Possessed*
02/20/81 *The Intruder Within*
02/27/81 *Midnight Offerings*
02/27/81 *The Munsters' Revenge*
03/05/81 *Death Ray 2000*
04/12/81 *Archer—Fugitive from the Empire*
04/26/81 *The Phoenix*
05/15/81 *The Harlem Globetrotters on Gilligan's Island*
05/21/81 *The Girl, the Gold Watch & Dynamite*
10/24/81 *Dark Night of the Scarecrow*
11/16/81 *Goliath Awaits*
12/06/81 *Through the Magic Pyramid*
03/22/82 *Tomorrow's Child*
04/05/82 *The Kid with the Broken Halo*
05/31/82 *The Mysterious Two*
07/25/82 *The Fall of the House of Usher*
08/01/82 *Computercide*
11/15/82 *I, Desire*
12/10/82 *Don't Go to Sleep*
12/11/82 *Cry for the Strangers*
12/18/82 *Falcon's Gold*
01/29/83 *Phantom of the Opera*
02/13/83 *The Invisible Woman*
02/27/83 *Starflight: The Plane That Couldn't Land*
03/06/83 *The Demon Murder Case*
05/01/83 *V*
05/24/83 *The Cradle Will Fall*

05/27/83 *The Sins of Dorian Gray*
07/07/83 *The Last Ninja*
08/15/83 *Prisoners of the Lost Universe*
10/24/83 *The Haunting Passion*
11/20/83 *The Day After*
12/07/83 *Prototype*
01/29/84 *Amazons*
03/24/84 *The Cold Room*
05/06/84 *V: The Final Battle*
05/24/84 *Invitation to Hell*
11/25/84 *The Ewok Adventure*
12/13/84 *The Night They Saved Christmas*
12/15/84 *It Came Upon the Midnight Clear*
12/17/84 *A Christmas Carol*
01/31/85 *Starcrossed*
02/05/85 *The Corsican Brothers*
02/21/85 *Deadly Messages*
04/26/85 *Arthur the King*
05/22/85 *Chiller*
05/24/85 *Generations*
05/28/85 *When Dreams Come True*
07/28/85 *Murder in Space*
08/05/85 *The Covenant*
09/11/85 *J.O.E. and the Colonel*
10/20/85 *I Dream of Jeannie—Fifteen Years Later*
11/01/85 *The Midnight Hour*
11/17/85 *The Blue Yonder*
11/22/85 *Bridge Across Time*
11/24/85 *Ewoks: Battle for Endor*
12/09/85 *Alice in Wonderland*
02/01/86 *Kung Fu: The Movie*
03/19/86 *Assassin*
04/07/86 *The Annihilator*
08/03/86 *The Flight of Dragons*
08/10/86 *Condor*
08/10/86 *Northstar*
09/28/86 *The Canterville Ghost*
10/26/86 *Who Is Julia?*
12/19/86 *Babes in Toyland*
01/10/87 *The Return of Sherlock Holmes*
02/15/87 *Amerika*
03/10/87 *Timestalkers*
03/15/87 *The Stepford Children*
05/12/87 *Ghost of a Chance*
05/17/87 *The Return of the Six Million Dollar Man and the Bionic Woman*
06/19/87 *Not Quite Human*
06/23/87 *The Man Who Fell to Earth*

07/05/87 *Bates Motel*
07/31/87 *The Spirit*
09/20/87 *The Highwayman*
10/05/87 *Haunted by Her Past*
10/25/87 *Bay Coven*
05/08/88 *Something Is Out There*
05/22/88 *The Incredible Hulk Returns*
06/25/88 *Night Train to Kathmandu*
07/17/88 *Out of Time*
08/21/88 *Gotham*
11/20/88 *Goddess of Love*
02/26/89 *Get Smart Again!*
02/27/89 *From the Dead of Night*
04/15/89 *Tarzan in Manhattan*
04/30/89 *Bionic Showdown*
05/07/89 *Trial of the Incredible Hulk*
05/21/89 *Amityville 4: The Evil Escapes*
05/31/89 *The Haunting of Sarah Hardy*
06/25/89 *The Gifted One*
08/30/89 *Nick Knight*
09/23/89 *Not Quite Human II*
11/01/89 *High Desert Kill*
11/20/89 *Turn Back the Clock*
11/20–12/18/89 *It Nearly Wasn't Christmas*
12/18/89 *A Connecticut Yankee in King Arthur's Court*
12/29/89 *Chameleons*
01/21/90 *Jekyll and Hyde*
01/26/90 *Daughter of Darkness*
02/18/90 *Death of the Incredible Hulk*
03/08/90 *Phantom of the Opera*
05/19/90 *Mother Goose Rock 'n' Rhyme*
06/05–06/17/90 *Ghost Writer*
07/15/90 *Fear*
08/08/90 *I'm Dangerous Tonight*
10/11/90 *Dark Avenger*
11/18/90 *It*
11/21/90 *Running Against Time*
11/22/90 *Clarence*
11/30/90 *Night Visions*
12/09/90 *Donor*
12/17/90 *A Mom for Christmas*
12/23/90 *Guess Who's Coming for Christmas?*
02/12/91 *Not of This World*
03/14/91 *Earth Angel*
03/16/91 *The Girl from Mars*
04/22/91 *Hi, Honey—I'm Dead*

05/01/91 *Child of Darkness, Child of Light*
05/06/91 *The Haunted*
05/07/91 *Sometimes They Come Back*
05/19/91 *Knight Rider 2000*
05/20/91 *Omen IV*
05/26/91 *Plymouth*
05/27/91 *Blood Ties*
06/25/91 *Death Dreams*
07/01/91 *K-9000*
09/07/91 *Cast a Deadly Spell*
09/11/91 *Lightning Incident*
09/28/91 *Wedlock*
10/04/91 *Dean R. Koontz's "Servants of Twilight"*
10/20/91 *I Still Dream of Jeannie*
10/28/91 *Frankenstein: The College Years*
12/16/91 *In the Nick of Time*
03/03/92 *Grave Secrets*
03/18/92 *Duplicates*
03/21/92 *Black Magic*
04/05/92 *Steel Justice*
05/03/92 *Day-O!*
05/09/92 *Disasters in Time*
05/17/92 *Intruders*
05/20/92 *Midnight's Child*
05/20/92 *Psychic*
05/31/92 *Still Not Quite Human*
08/24/92 *The Water Engine*
09/20/92 *Danger Island*
12/14/92 *Love Can Be Murder*
12/17/92 *Homewrecker*
02/10/93 *Shadowhunter*
02/21–02/27/93 *Babylon 5*
02/28/93 *Journey to the Center of the Earth*
04/04/93 *Jonny's Golden Quest*
04/18/93 *The Fire Next Time*
05/07/93 *Visions of Murder*
05/08/93 *Daybreak*
05/09/93 *Stephen King's "The Tommyknockers"*
05/16/93 *Wild Palms*
06/13/93 *Frankenstein*
06/28/93 *Lifepod*
07/05/93 *12:01*
08/08/93 *Body Bags*
08/16/93 *The Tower*
08/19/93 *Night Owl*
09/12/93 *1994 Baker Street: Sherlock Holmes Returns*
10/30/93 *Double, Double, Toil and Trouble*
10/30/93 *The Halloween Tree*
11/14/93 *They Watch*
11/20/93 *Official Denial*

11/27/93 *Full Eclipse*
12/02/93 *Dying to Remember*
12/11/93 *Attack of the 50-Foot Woman*
01/23–01/29/94 *Tekwar*
01/24/94 *M.A.N.T.I.S.*
02/13/94 *Knightrider 2010*
02/14–02/20/94 *Tekwar: Teklords*
02/21–02/27/94 *Tekwar: Teklab*
03/02/94 *Island City*
03/18/94 *Eyes of Terror*
03/21/94 *Model by Day*
04/16/94 *Lifeforce Experiment*
04/24–04/30/94 *Hercules and the Amazon Women*
05/01–05/07/94 *Hercules and the Lost Kingdom*
05/07/94 *Guinevere*
05/07–05/14/94 *Tekwar: Tek Justice*
05/08/94 *The Stand*
05/14/94 *MacGyver and the Lost Treasure of Atlantis*
05/17/94 *Search for Grace*
05/19/94 *The Twilight Zone: Rod Serling's Lost Classics*
07/31/94 *Roswell*
08/25/94 *Seduced by Evil*
08/29/94 *Running Delilah*
09/25/94 *The Haunting of Seacliff Inn*
10/13/94 *The Companion*
10/25/94 *Alien Nation: Dark Horizon*
10/30/94 *Without Warning*
11/04–11/10/94 *Hercules and the Circle of Fire*
11/06/94 *In Search of Dr. Seuss*
11/11–11/17/94 *Hercules in the Underworld*
11/12/94 *The Shaggy Dog*
11/18–11/24/94 *Hercules in the Maze of the Minotaur*
11/26/94 *Fatherland*
11/29/94 *Bionic Ever After?*
12/10/94 *Witch Hunt*
01/12/95 *To Catch a Yeti*
01/21/95 *Trapped in Space*
02/18/95 *The Computer Wore Tennis Shoes*
03/12/95 *Dad, the Angel & Me*
04/12/95 *The Android Affair*
04/29/95 *Escape to Witch Mountain*
05/06/95 *Freaky Friday*

Appendix C: Chronology

05/09/95 *Deadlocked: Escape from Zone 14*
05/14/95 *Stephen King's "The Langoliers"*
05/23/95 *White Dwarf*
05/29/95 *The Man Who Wouldn't Die*
05/29/95 *The Possession of Michael D.*
06/07/95 *Crowfoot*
07/18/95 *The Alien Within*
07/30/95 *Suspect Device*
08/08/95 *Bram Stoker's "Burial of the Rats"*
08/12/95 *The Four Diamonds*
08/13/95 *Harrison Bergeron*
08/15/95 *Not Like Us*
08/20/95 *Amanda and the Alien*
08/22/95 *Black Scorpion*
08/29/95 *The Wasp Woman*
09/05/95 *Not of This Earth*
09/19/95 *Piranha*
09/26/95 *Hellfire*
09/26/95 *W.E.I.R.D. World*
10/03/95 *Terminal Virus*
10/08/95 *Dead Weekend*
10/09/95 *Deadly Love*
10/10/95 *Alien Nation: Body and Soul*
10/13/95 *Here Come the Munsters*
11/07/95 *It Came from Outer Space II*
11/10/95 *Dark Reflection*
11/12/95 *The Invaders*
11/19/95 *Jonny Quest and the Cyberinsects*
11/27/95 *Visitors of the Night*
12/03/95 *The Haunting of Helen Walker*
12/04/95 *Ebbie*
12/17/95 *The Christmas Box*
1996 *Beastmaster III*
01/02/96 *Alien Nation: Millennium*
01/27/96 *The Canterville Ghost*
02/04/96 *Gulliver's Travels*
02/17/96 *Project: ALF*
02/20/96 *Generation X*
02/21/96 *Robin Cook's "Terminal"*
03/11/96 *Star Command*
03/25/96 *Special Report: Journey to Mars*
04/10/96 *The Haunting of Lisa*
04/10/96 *Sabrina, the Teenage Witch*
04/20/96 *Encino Woman*
04/22/96 *Crimes of Passion: Voice from the Grave*
05/14/96 *Dr. Who*
05/14/96 *The Stepford Husbands*
05/19/96 *The Legend of Gator Face*
06/08/96 *Within the Rock*
06/26/96 *The Crying Child*
07/13/96 *House of the Damned*
07/23/96 *Inhumanoid*
07/28/96 *Space Marines*
08/03/96 *Subliminal Seduction*
08/06/96 *Alien Avengers*
08/20/96 *Last Exit to Earth*
08/26/96 *Adventures of Captain Zoom in Outer Space*
09/02/96 *Devil's Food*
09/03/96 *Black Scorpion II*
09/17/96 *Humanoids from the Deep*
09/24/96 *Death Game*
09/28/96 *Vampirella*
10/08/96 *Them*
10/13/96 *Night Visitors*
10/27/96 *Shadow Zone: The Undead Express*
10/29/96 *The Uninvited*
10/30/96 *Trilogy of Terror II*
11/04/96 *Buried Secrets*
11/05/96 *Color Me Perfect*
11/08/96 *Saved by the Light*
11/12/96 *Alien Nation: The Enemy Within*
11/30/96 *To the Ends of Time*
12/01/96 *Christmas Every Day*
12/08/96 *Mrs. Santa Claus*
12/14/96 *The Cold Equations*
12/17/96 *The Munsters' Scary Little Christmas*
12/17/96 *Unlikely Angel*
01/05/97 *Whiskers*
02/12/97 *A Nightmare Come True*
02/16/97 *Assault on Dome 4*
02/16–2/17/97 *Asteroid*
03/15/97 *Bridge of Time*
03/15/97 *The Outsider*
03/15/97 *The Second Civil War*
03/23/97 *Dog's Best Friend*
03/23/97 *20,000 Leagues Under the Sea*
03/23/97 *Twilight of the Golds*
04/08/97 *Doomsday Rock*
04/14/97 *Nightscream*
04/19/97 *Habitat*
04/21/97 *A Deadly Vision*
04/27–05/02/97 *The Shining*
05/04/97 *Robin Cook's "Invasion"*
05/05/97 *Tidal Wave: No Escape*
05/10/97 *When Time Expires*
05/11/97 *20,000 Leagues Under the Sea*
05/13/97 *Quicksilver Highway*
05/18/97 *The Odyssey*
06/01/97 *Love-Struck*
06/15/97 *In His Father's Shoes*
06/21/97 *Dark Planet*
07/19/97 *Dead Fire*
07/29/97 *Alien Nation: The Udara Legacy*
08/09/97 *Bombshell*
08/16/97 *Retroactive*
08/24/97 *Snow White: A Tale of Terror*
09/06/97 *Ravager*
09/28/97 *Cloned*
10/05/97 *Toothless*
10/08/97 *Spacejacked*
10/18/97 *Last Lives*
10/18/97 *Shadow Zone: My Teacher Ate My Homework*
10/25/97 *Alien Avengers II*
10/25/97 *Under Wraps*
10/26/97 *The Devil's Child*
10/26/97 *Tower of Terror*
10/29/97 *Trucks*
11/02/97 *Cinderella*
11/02/97 *House of Frankenstein*
11/05/97 *Heartless*
11/09/97 *Angels in the Endzone*
11/09/97 *Ken Follett's "The Third Twin"*
11/23/97 *Dead by Midnight*
11/26/97 *The Ruby Ring*
11/30/97 *Borrowed Hearts*
11/30/97 *The Love Bug*
12/06/97 *Moonbase*
12/10/97 *Ms. Scrooge*
12/13/97 *Menno's Mind*
12/20/97 *Doom Runners*
01/04/98 *Babylon 5: In the Beginning*
01/04/98 *Scattering Dad*
01/18/98 *Nightmare Street*
01/24/98 *Atomic Dog*
01/24/98 *Timelock*
01/27/98 *Warlord: Battle for the Galaxy*
02/01/98 *The Lake*
02/01/98 *The Love Letter*
02/05/98 *Target: Earth*
02/06/98 *Stephen King's "The Night Flier"*
02/21/98 *Convict 762*
02/26/98 *Virtual Obsession*

03/01/98 *Falling Fire*
03/21/98 *Advanced Guard*
03/22/98 *I've Been Waiting for You*
04/05/98 *Tempting Fate*
04/05/98 *Tourist Trap*
04/18/98 *Legion*
04/19/98 *Brave New World*
04/26/98 *Merlin*
05/17/98 *Peter Benchley's "Creature"*
05/19/98 *Gargantua*
05/26/98 *Nick Fury, Agent of S.H.I.E.L.D.*
06/27/98 *A Town Has Turned to Dust*
07/19/98 *Babylon 5: Thirdspace*
08/10/98 *I Married a Monster*
08/12/98 *Blade Squad*
08/15/98 *National Lampoon's "Men in White"*
08/22/98 *Scorpio One*
09/07/98 *Giving Up the Ghost*
09/08/98 *Wish Upon a Star*
09/12/98 *Johnny 2.0*
09/30/98 *Universal Soldier II: Brothers in Arms*
10/01/98 *FutureSport*
10/03/98 *Sabrina Goes to Rome*
10/11/98 *Noah*
10/15/98 *30-Years-to-Life*
10/17/98 *Halloweentown*
10/22/98 *Chameleon*
10/28/98 *The Fury Within*
10/28/98 *Universal Soldier III: Unfinished Business*
10/29/98 *Inferno*
11/05/98 *Riddler's Moon*
11/08/98 *Babylon 5: River of Souls*
11/08/98 *A Knight in Camelot*
11/08/98 *Perfect Little Angels*
11/09/98 *Twice Upon a Time*
11/12/98 *Lost Souls*
11/19/98 *Dream House*
11/21/98 *Galactic Odyssey*
11/22/98 *Big and Hairy*
12/08/98 *Invasion Earth*
12/13/98 *The Tempest*

INDEX

A-Pix Entertainment 45
Aaron Spelling Productions 43, 90, 109, 118, 145
Abart, Boleslaw 67
Abbott, Annie 175
Abbott, Bruce 25, 140
Abbott, John 34
Abbott, Philip 42
Abbott, Simon 141
ABC 1, 12, 23, 30, 34, 37, 41, 42, 43, 44, 47, 51, 53, 54, 58, 59, 60, 61, 63, 64, 68, 71, 74, 79, 90, 91, 96, 100, 101, 102, 103, 106, 107, 19, 110, 115, 116, 118, 119, 123, 124, 125, 129, 130, 131, 132, 133, 134, 135, 136, 141, 142, 143, 146, 150, 154, 155, 157, 158, 159, 160, 165, 167, 168, 169, 170, 172, 173, 174, 175, 178, 182, 184, 187, 193, 194, 199, 203, 204, 205, 206, 207, 208, 209, 210, 211, 212, 213, 214, 215, 216; Circle Films 44, 123, 132, 184; Inc. 132; Pictures 77, 188
The Abduction of St. Anne 203
Abdul-Jabbar, Kareem 165
Abercrombie, Ian 161
Abernathy, Donzaleigh 174
Abounader, Jean 62
Abraham, Dawn 146
Abraham, F. Murray 104
Abraham, Falconer 112
Abrahams, Doug 141, 184
Abrams, Gerald W. 46, 102, 197
Abrams, Peter 70
Abrams Gentile Entertainment 123
Abroms, Edward M. 80, 131, 133
Accent Entertainment 46
Acheson, Mark 184
ACI 61, 195
Acker, Sharon 171
Ackerman, Forrest J. 194
Ackland, Joss 102, 181
Ackland-Snow, Brian 187
Ackroyd, David 65
Acuins, Craig J. 86
Acuna, Wanda 89

Adam, Paul 180
Adams, Brooke 163
Adams, Catlin 68, 181
Adams, Charles 27
Adams, Claire 81
Adams, Dallas 68
Adams, Dave 114, 152
Adams, David 5
Adams, Janet 150
Adams, Lillian 79
Adams, Lloyd 191
Adams, Lynne 81
Adams, Mason 105, 133, 136, 151
Adams, Peter 71
Adams, Shelby 139
Adams, Simon 102
Adams, Stanley 131, 135
Adams, Steve 198
Adamson, Chuck 165
Adamson, David 24
Adcock, Steve 179
Adcox, Thomas 101
The Addams Family 74
Addicted to Love 217
Addie, Robert 107, 122
Addis, Keith 79
Addison, John 145
Ade, Melyssa 195
Adem, Yasher 177
Adhikari, Badri Prasad 111
Adler, Anthony 165, 196
Adler, Brian 188
Adler, Don 60
Adler, Gilbert 196
The Advanced Guard 5, 217
The Adventures of Brisco County, Jr. 31
The Adventures of Captain Zoom in Outer Space 5
Adventures of Sinbad 16
The Adventures of Superboy 202
Africa, Susan 175
Agar, John 66, 67, 103
Agnese, Norma Dell 158
Aguilar, George 115
Ahern, Lloyd, II 8, 140
Ahi Entertainment 114
Aiello, Rick 105

Airlie, Andrew 134
Airwolf 157
Akayama, Dennis 195
Akin, David 152
Akin, Philip 77, 127
Akinnouye-Agbaje, Adewale 187
Akins, Claude 131, 135
Akiyama, Denis 74
Alaimo, Marc 16
Alaquie, Afifi 50
Alatis, Tony 160
Albert 194
Albert, Eddie 28, 52, 78
Albert, Edward 106
Albert, Ross 88
Albertson, Eric 133
Albertson, Frank 141
Albertson, Mabel 90
Albin, Andy 21
Albin, Dolores 21
Alda, Rutanya 176
Alden, John 52
Alderman, John 14
Aleano, Peter 49
Alessandroni, Henry 50
Alexander, Eric 155
Alexander, Jane 124
Alexander, Jason 37
Alexander, Les 50, 137
Alexander, Spike 47
Alexander, Terry 14
Alexander, Tim 183
Alexander, Wayne 19
Alexander, William 67, 102
Alexander/Enright & Associates 50
Alexis, Kim 103
ALF 147
Alfasa, Joe 126
Alfonso, Kristian 140
AlfTales 147
Alianak, Grant 160
Alice, Mary 194
Alice in Wonderland 6, 123
Alice's Adventures in Wonderland 6
Alien 2, 11, 163, 201
Alien Avengers 6, 217
Alien Avengers II 7, 217

Index

Alien Nation 45
Alien Nation (series) 8–9
Alien Nation: Body and Soul 7
Alien Nation: Dark Horizon 8
Alien Nation: The Enemy Within 9
Alien Nation: Millennium 10
Alien Nation: The Udara Legacy 10
Alien Resurrection 183
The Alien Within 11, 217
The Alienist 196
Aliens Among Us 217
The Aliens Are Coming 11
Alison, Barbie 6
Alix, Stephen 37
All Effects Co. 154
All My Children 83
Allan, Jed 172
Allan, Zack 20
Allas, Peter 33
Alldredge, Michael 191
Allegro 147
Allen, Durward 185
Allen, Governor George 37
Allen, Irwin 6, 38, 105, 179
Allen, Jay Presson 28
Allen, Jeanne 62
Allen, Joanie 95
Allen, John 128
Allen, Jonelle 29, 79, 123, 193
Allen, Lee Taylor 92
Allen, Linda 23
Allen, Linda Lou 121
Allen, Marit 161
Allen, Mark 35
Allen, Mitchell 80
Allen, Naomi Lee 94
Allen, Peter 49
Allen, Ron 159
Allen, Sheila 6
Allen, Steve 6
Allende, Fernando 142
Allerick, Steven 191
Alley, Kirstie 181
Alliance Communications 40, 177
Allin, Jeff 10, 172
Allison, Cynthia 152
Allman, Sheldon 119
Allyn, William 109
Allyson, June 44, 105
Almeida, Laurindo 52
Almgren, Suzie 81
Alonzo, John A. 116
Alpert, Gregory H. 103
Alsberg, Arthur 127
Alsina, Gustav 50
Alskog, Erik 60
Alsobrook, Russ 63, 68, 116, 158
Alterian Studios 33, 70
Altman, Bradley 80
Altz, Barbara 167
Alvin, John 173
Alzado, Lyle 76
Alzola, Mickey 72
Amanda and the Alien 12
Amaral, Bob 19
Amaral, Roy Alan 80
Amarilis 73
Amarino, Augie 181

Amato, Michael 7, 91
Amazons 203
Amblin Entertainment 57
Amergut, Scott 68
An American Christmas Carol 12
American International Pictures (AIP) 11, 13
American Zoetrope 138, 141, 198
Amerika 203
Ames, Carol 174
Ames, Kelly 21
Ames, Kenneth 94
Ami Aktzi Productions 85
Amick, Madchen 28, 85, 93
Amin, Mark 185
Amis, Suzy 47
Amityville Curse 13
Amityville IV 217
The Amityville Horror 13
Amityville: The Evil Escapes 13, 217
Amityville: The Evil Escapes (book) 13
Ammie, Come Home 90
Amos, John 42, 71
Amsing, Sean 15
Amundson, Peter 70
Anastassopoulos, Adoni 138
Anders, John C. 158
Anderson, Al 123
Anderson, Anthony 6
Anderson, Barbara 58, 160
Anderson, Cheryl 186
Anderson, Christopher 59
Anderson, Dana 8–9
Anderson, Darryl 142
Anderson, David 128, 200
Anderson, Harry 100
Anderson, Heidi 86
Anderson, Helen 15
Anderson, Jamie 195
Anderson, Judith, Dame 28
Anderson, Judy 23
Anderson, Kylo 135
Anderson, Larry 56, 156
Anderson, Margo 53
Anderson, McKee 14
Anderson, Melissa Sue 124
Anderson, Michael (director) 121, 187
Anderson, Michael F. (editor) 92, 192
Anderson, Michael, Jr. 90, 121
Anderson, Miles 138
Anderson, Pat 118
Anderson, Peter 84
Anderson, Richard 23, 24, 132, 150, 167
Anderson, Richard Dean 210
Anderson, Robert 139
Anderson, Roy T. 190
Anderson, Sam 165
Anderson, Stanley 109, 159
Anderson, Steve 165
Anderson, Veronica 88
Anderson, Wade 61
Anderson-Gunter, Jeffrey 20
Andre, Charles 184
Andre, Damir 195

Andre, E.J. 49
Andre, Jill 79
Andreescu, Mircea 112
Andreozzi, Jack 52
Andrew, Iain 153
Andrews, Joey 186, 198
Andrews, Julie 37
The Android Affair 13
Andropova, Svetlana 85
Androsky, Carol 87
Angel, Dan 103
Angel of Darkness 196
Angel on My Shoulder 14
Angeles, Jack 51
Angels in the Endzone 14
Angels in the Outfield 15
Angotti, Nick 16
Anholt, Christien 153, 177
Anka, Amanda 67
Ann, Ruth 48
Ann Daniel Films 195
Anna, Cecily 187
Annihilator 15
Anspaugh, David 193
Anstey, F. 78
Ant, Adam 140
Anthony, Bob 137
Anthony, David 128
Anthony, Lysette 185
Anthony, Victoria 29
Antin, Robin 75
Antonio, Jim 35, 143
Antonio, Lou 161
Apfel, Ed 111
Apicella, John 69
Appleby, George 59
Appleton, X.V. 88
Appling, Susan 8, 134
Apstein, Theodore 20
Apted, Michael 97
The Aquarians 203
Arad, Avi 73
Aragon, Art 14
Aranda, Nocana 32
Archer, Beverly 146
Archer, Nick 171
Archer, Steve 30
The Archer: Fugitive from the Empire 15
Archerd, Selma 6
Archie Comics 156
Arena Productions 20
Arenberg, Lee 146
Areno, Lois 182
Argenziano, Carmen 107, 119, 125, 142, 157
Ariola, Julie 154
Arizona Ripper 217
Arliss, Dimitra 65
Armendariz, Pedro, Jr. 58
Armour, Norman 134, 139
Armstrong, Bess 37
Armstrong, Beth 128
Armstrong, Curtis 87
Armstrong, Herb 162
Armstrong, Kerry 187
Armstrong, Lynn 75
Armstrong, Mary 14

Armstrong, R.G. 53, 178
Armstrong, Ray 102
Armstrong, Vaughn 88, 92
Arnette, Jeannetta 29
Arnico, Robert 5
Arnold, Charles G. 130, 144
Arnold, Chuck 16, 126
Arnold, Mason 76
Arnold, Steve 58
Arnold, Tammy 24
Arnold, Tom 103
Arnott, Mark 138
Aronson, John 96, 173
Arquello, Ken 108
Arquette, Alexis 50
Arquette, Kerry 171
Arquette, Lewis 16
Arquette, Richmond 113
Arrants, Rod 35, 45
Arredondo, Rick 152
Arrington, Gene 120
Arteaga, Manuel 111
Artemyev, Edward 138
Arthur, The King 16
Arthurs, Douglas H. 176
Artzi, Ami 85
Artzi, Liron 85
Ash, Taren 191
Ashbrook, Dana 196
Ashbrook, Daphne 57, 97, 117
Ashby, Carole 16
Ashby, Harvey 102
Ashby, Linden 109
Asher, John Mallory 83
Asher, William 92
Ashikaga, Janet 51, 95, 184
Ashlend, Camila 192
Ashley, Ed 73
Ashley, John 104, 162
Ashmore, Frank 191, 192
Ashton, Dyrk 195
Ashton, John 169
Ashton, Peter 78, 88
Ashton-Griffiths, Roger 138
Asimov, Isaac 13, 54
Askar, Renee 128
Askin, Leon 73
Askrow, David 105
Asner, Ed 57, 109
Assa, Rene 119
Assante, Armand 90, 138
Assassin 16, 147
Assault on Dome 4 203
Assonitis, Ovidio G. 155
Astaire, Fred 210
Asteroid 203
Astin, MacKenzie 92
Astin, Patty Duke 44, 115
Astin, Sean 82
Astley, Susan 100
The Astronaut 203
Atchison, Nancy Moore 176
Atherton, Howard 81
Atken, Alexis 180
Atkins, Chris 175
Atkins, Pat 51
Atkinson, Keith 80
Atlantis Films 38, 82, 145

Atomic Dog 204
Attack of the 50-Foot Woman 16, 49
Attack of the Phantoms 217
Attaway, Ruth 23
Attell, Tony 15
Attila 103
Atwater, Barry 131
Aubel, Joe 171
Auberjonois, Rene 41, 126, 199
Aubertin, Michael 142
Aubrey, Larry 38
August, Ken 160
August, Lance 6
Aupperle, Jim 112
Aurelius, Marcus 172
Aurio, Gina Maria 45
Austin, Brad 81
Austin, Jan 77
Austin, Jeff 8, 66
Austin, Karen 16, 89
Austin, Kevin 136
Austin, Ray 150
Austin, Ronald L. 88
Austin, Shay 35, 61, 180
Austin, Stephanie 147
Austin-Olsen, Shaun 127
Automan 24
Autry, Alan 97
Avalos, Luis 75
Avari, Erick 146
Avcoin, William M. 107
The Avengers 84, 155, 180
Averback, Hy 76
Avery, James 5, 41, 180
Avery, Margaret 111, 162
Avery, Mark 120
Avery, Phyllis 109
Avery, Rick 140
Avila, Kimberly 43
Aviles, Rick 165
Avina, Frankie 183
Avramovic, Milance 16
Avrech, Robert 154
Axelrod, Robert 6, 21
Axtell, Kirk 15
Aylward, John 142
Ayres, Lew 61, 148, 156, 159, 171
Azikiwe, Jason 19
Azman, Yank 77

B&B Productions 95
Babafunde, Obba 120
Babbin, Jacqueline 29
Babcock, Barbara 109
Babcock, Ted 194
Babes in Toyland 17
Babylon 5 18, 9, 141, 217
Babylon 5 (series) 5, 19, 20, 22
Babylon 5: A Call To Arms 20
Babylon 5: In the Beginning 19
Babylon 5: The Gathering 217
Babylon 5: The River of Souls 19
Babylon 5: Thirdspace 20
Babylonian Productions 18, 19, 20
Bacalla, Donna 97
Bach, Catherine 170
Bach, John 187
Bachald, Chris 73

Bachardy, Don 68
Bachman, James Martin 106, 127
Bacino, Mark 59, 100
Back to the Future 28, 149
Backus, Jim 124
Bacon, Arch 53
Bacon, James 126, 143
Bacon, Kevin 52
Badalamenti, Angelo 201
Badham, John 131
Badland, Annette 80
Badler, Jane 42, 43, 191, 192
Baer, Johanna 141
Baer, Parley 153, 178
Baeza, Paloma 107, 138
Baffa, Christopher 7, 90, 91
Baffled! 20
Bagg, Ian 59
Bailey, G.W. 76
Bailey, Robert, Jr. 189
Bain, Barnet 45, 179
Baio, Scott 6
Baiotto, James 38
Baird, Maggie 198
Bajer, Sharon 185
Bakay, Nick 155
Baker, Bart 141
Baker, Brian 40
Baker, Diane 82
Baker, George 31
Baker, Harrison 14
Baker, Kristin 89
Baker, Roger 159
Baker, Tom 68
Bakke, Brenda 185
Bakke, Karl 67
Bakula, Scott 97
Balaban, Bob 77
Balaski, Belinda 195
Balcerzak, Chris 76
Baldauff, Patrick 180
Balduzzi, Dick 165
Baldwin, Adam 71, 72
Baldwin, Daniel 16, 201
Baldwin, Judy 167
Baldwin, Stephen 50
Balin, Edmund 120
Ball, Jason 102
Ball, Sonja 198
Ball, Zachary 163
Ballen, Tony 78
Balsam, Martin 160
Balsam, Talia 40, 96
Balser, Dean 177
Balter, Allan 32, 33, 62, 119
Baltimore/Spring Creek Pictures 77
Balzar, Robert L. 106
The Bamboo Saucer 62
Bame, Lawrence 144
Bancroft, Bob 113
Band, Charles 112
Banes, Lisa 45, 110
Bank, Ashley 83
Bankhead, Karen 110
Banks, Carl 26
Banks, Carol Tillery 29
Banks, Joe 67

Banks, Jonathan 16, 98
Banner, Bob 46
Bannister, Duke 187
Banzil, Scott 114
Bar-Gene Television 93
Baranowski, Arthur 157
Barash, Olivia 94, 178
Baratta, Frederic 127
Barba, Ted 105
Barbeau, Adrienne 30, 46
Barber, Gary 81
Barber, Phil 44, 148
Barbera, Joseph 107
Barberi, Katie 138
Barbour, Keith 35
Barclay, Caroline 201
Barden, John 80
Bardina, Elena 85
Bare, Richard 144
Baril, Alain 198
Barilla, Courtney 97
Barker, Clive 148, 149
Barker, Debbie 167
Barker, Matthew 200
Barkett, Beece 19
Barkhurst, Vernon 55
Barkman, Brent 180
Barmettie, Joseph 179
Barnard, Arthur 77
Barndt, Perry 89
Barnes, Barbara 167
Barnes, Chris 178
Barnes, Christopher Daniel 67
Barnes, Dean W. 187
Barnes, Eric 27
Barnes, Gary 102
Barnes, Guy 146
Barnes, Julian 68
Barnes, Peter 122
Barnes, Priscilla 178
Barnes, Rick Tyler 25
Barnes, Roger 93
Barnes, Susan 14
Barnett, Greg 65
Barnett, Sam 123
Barnett, Slade 26
Barnett, Steven A. 18
Barnette, Alan 54
Barney Cohen and Kathryn Wallack Productions 155
Barney Rosenzweig Productions 14
Barns, Genevieve 176
Baron, Blaire 18
Baron, Sandy 128
Barondes, Elizabeth 136
Barondes, Jessica 200
Barone, Tommy 111
Barquet, Xavier 93
Barr, Douglas 39
Barraclouth, Audrey 180
Barret, Earl 144
Barrett, Jonathan 185
Barrett, June 29, 56
Barrett, Majel 73, 143, 148, 164
Barrett, Melissa 115
Barrett, Stan 25
Barrie, Barbara 80
Barrie, Frank 102

Barringer, Daniel 52
Barron, Allison 66, 82
Barron, Baynes 179
Barron, Robert V. 67
Barron, Steve 122
Barrows, Dan 197
Barry, Gene 53, 76, 186
Barry, Ivor 67, 160
Barry, Lloyd 135
Barry, Patricia 43
Barry, Thom 10
Barry Weitz Films 130
Barrymore, Drew 17
Bartel, Cheryl 179
Bartel, Paul 54, 136
Bartels, Janet 80
Bartilson, Lynsey 126
Bartle, James 86, 108, 187
Bartlett, Bonnie 191
Bartlett, Cal 99
Bartlett, Dick 111
Bartlett, Juanita 124, 143
Bartlett, Robin 186
Bartlett, Timothy 169
Bartold, Norman 162
Bartold, Sheila 162
Bartoli, Adolfo 112, 155
Barton, Dan 32
Barton, John A. 190
Barton, Neil 75
Barzilai, Yoram 40
Barzyk, Fred 111
Basch, Harry 118
Bascoe, Jon 179
Basehart, Richard 38, 161, 179
Basham, Tom 131
Bashtu, Timur 161
Basile, James 87
Basinger, Kim 75
Bass, Jules 23, 110, 160
Bass, Stuart 155
Bassett, Craig 174
Bassey, Jennifer 78
Bast, William 70
Baster, Frank 109
Bastille, Ned 168
Bastoni, Steve 70
Bataglia, Matt 190, 191
Batcheller, Richard 131
Batchelor, Graham 75
Bateman, Frederick 102
Bateman, Geoffrey 177
Bateman, Jason 21
Bates, Jeanne 69, 171
Bates, Jo 155
Bates, Tyler 7, 136
Bates Motel 21
Bateson, Timothy 36, 122
Batinkoff, Randall 167
Batman 88, 119, 130
Batman (movie) 137
Batman (TV series) 79
Batman: The Animated Adventures 43, 100, 155, 199
Batson, Susan 94
Battee, Donald 71
Batten, Cyia 196
Batten, Paul 39

Battista, Franco 147
Battistone, Catherine 41
Battle, Lois 162
Battlestar Galactica 139, 146
Bauchau, Patrick 27
Bauer, Belinda 16, 160, 167
Bauer, Christopher 161
Bauer, Michael E. 181
Baugh, Michael 144
Baum, Jurgen 165
Baum, Lal 148
Baumes, Wilford Lloyd 34, 48, 157
Baumgarten, Alan 114
Baumgarten, Craig 54
Baumgarten/Prophet Entertainment 54
Baxley, Craig R. 52
Baxter, Anne 151
Baxter, Keith 122
Baxter, Meredith 34, 57
Bay, Frances 79, 182
Bay Coven 21, 217
Bayer, Michael Bard 92
Bayles, Lee 97
Bayliss, Peter 122
Baynes, Angela 194
Baytok, Yasmine 19
BBC 57; Worldwide 57
BBK 93
Beach, Laurie 12
Beach, Michael 108, 127
Beaird, Betty 178
Beal, Raymond 160
Beall, Richard 159
Beam, Abby 37
Beamer, Layne 152
Beardon, Jim 83
Bearse, Amanda 78, 87
Beascoechea, Frank 130
Beasley, Allyce 169
The Beastmaster 22
Beastmaster (series) 22
Beastmaster II 22
Beastmaster III: The Eye of Braxus 16
Beat, Jackie 63
Beato, Alfonso 27, 48
Beaton, Alex 15, 56, 57, 108, 124
Beatts, Anne 133
Beatty, Lou, Jr. 108
Beatty, Ned 80
Beatty, Robert 121
Beaudine, Skip 19
Beaudoin, Michelle 155
Beaudry, Mike 74
Beaumont, Gabrielle 22
Beauty and the Beast 22
Beauty and the Beast (series) 6, 107, 155, 157, 183
Bechtold, Curtis 15
Beck, Billy 99, 105, 171
Beck, Charles 152
Beck, Jenny 192
Beck, John 45, 172, 178
Beck, Matthew 109
Beck, Michael 36
Becker, Frank 167

Becker, Laura 61
Beckerman, Teri 99, 101
Beckley, Barbara 41
Beckman, John 25
Bedelia, Bonnie 156, 207
Bedeviled 67
Bedi, Kabir 16, 177
Beeman, Greg 190
Beers, Betsy 201
Beeson, Paul 22
Beetley, Samuel E. 172
Begbie, Finn 123
Begbie, Peter 123
Begg, Jim 105, 106
Beghe, Jason 69, 97
Begley, Ed, Jr. 49, 146, 158
Begley, William 53
Behr, Jason 10
Behrens, Bernard 74, 83, 145
Behrer, Corinne 189
Beiber, Jayne 169
Beirut 47
Belafonte, Shari 20; as Shari Belafonte-Harper 123
Beldin, Dale 87
Belford Productions 162
Belgrave, Nick 29
Belisarius Productions 43
Bell, Ann 164
Bell, Barry 117
Bell, Bobby 64
Bell, Catherine 8
Bell, Dave 52
Bell, Edward 61, 151
Bell, Francine 183
Bell, Gregory 200
Bell, Marshall 196
Bell, Tobin 52
Bella, Rachel (Rachael) 54, 196
Bellah, Ross 34, 78, 91, 92
Bellamy, Diana 41
Bellamy, Ralph 38, 157, 162
Bellanger, Carl 40
Belles, Richard 83
Belli, Kent 67
Bellin, Thomas 46
Bellis, Richard 59, 100
Bellis, Scott 176
Bellisario, Donald P. 43
Bellomo, Michael 27
Bellon, Roger 87
Bellows, Gil 161
Bells, Sandra 70
Bellwood, Pamela 85
Beltrami, Marco 96
Beltran, Robert 211
Belushi, James 57, 199, 212
Belzberg, Leslie 87, 128
Belzer, Richard 97, 136
Bemford, Gabrielle 26
Ben-Victor, Paul 175
Benard, Lee 151
Bench, Dottie 102
Bench, M.J. 102
Benchley, Peter 142
Bender, Bill 176
Bender, Jack 117, 123, 174
Bendetti, Michael 12

Bendixsen, Mia 88
Benedetti, Caprice 176
Benedict, Dirk 139
Benedict, Lawrence 78
Benedict, Paul 16
Benedict, William 40
Benefiel, Scott 92
Benest, Glenn 171
Benet, Brenda 88
Benison, Peter 23, 114, 141
Benjamin, Christopher 20
Benjamin, Mary 97
Bennes, John 24, 169
Bennett, Constance 182
Bennett, Daryl 23
Bennett, Fran 144, 175
Bennett, Harve 72, 98
Bennett, Jesse 165
Bennett, Jessie 101
Bennett, Joan 178
Bennett, Julie 78, 161
Bennett, Laurence 40
Bennett, Nigel 21, 82, 166
Bennett, Sophie 190
Bennett, Valerie 40
Bennett, Wallace 178
Bennett, Zachary 74
Bennick, John 91
Benrubi, Abraham 175
Benson, Hugh 78, 92
Benson, Jay 96
Benson, Linda 164
Benson, Norland 170
Benson, Peter 122
Benson, Robby 88
Benson, Wendy 29
Benton, Charles 30, 76
Benton, Craig 104
Benton, Dan 181
Benton, Eddie 56
Benwick, Richard 49
Benz, Donna 120
Benzali, Daniel 149
Beowulf Productions 14
Beradino, John 125
Berdan, Brian 12
Berdeshevsky, Margo Ann 130
Berendsen, Daniel 155
Berg, Dick 121, 130, 164
Bergen, Candice 16
Bergen, Patrick 67, 176
Bergen, Polly 114
Berger, Mel 178
Berger, Peter E. 107
Berger, Stephen 40
Berger, William 93
Bergin, Patrick 188
Bergman, Ingrid 84
Bergman, Mary 35
Bergschneider, Conrad 94
Bergstresser, John 11
Berk, Alisa 81
Berk, Michael 84
Berkeley, Xander 16, 137, 152, 201
Berkoff, Steven 97
Berlatsky, David 138, 142, 170
Berman, Henry 62
Berman, Michael 167

Bermuda Depths 23, 217
Bermuda Triangle 3, 204
Bernard, Crystal 35
Bernard, Jason 191, 192
Bernard, Jerry Wayne 35
Bernardi, Barry 13, 47, 125
Bernardi, Herschel 156
Bernbaum, Paul 81, 82
Berneis, Peter 156
Berner, Ted 141
Bernhard, Harvey 139
Bernhardt, Sandra 68
Berns, Gerald 154
Bernsen, Corbin 95, 117, 121, 215
Bernstein, Charles 42, 75, 116
Bernstein, Jay 126, 199
Bernstein, Nat 21
Bernstein, Peter 64, 99, 174
Bernstein, Ron 106
Berry, Al 130
Berry, Dennis 14
Berry, John 14
Berry, Lloyd 5
Berry, Tom 147
Berry, Vincent 70
Berryman, Michael 99
Bertelson, Tommy 87
Berti, Dehl 151
Bertinelli, Valerie 83
Berwick, John 78
Beswick, Martine 53, 170, 171
Beswick, Quinn 85
Beswick, Wayne 50
Bethune, Ivy 178
Betts, Jack 7
Betts, Nigel 102
Betts, Tom 70
Betz, Carl 106
Betzler, Geri 13
Beuth, Robert Alan 6
Beverly Hills 90210 152
Bewitched 2, 90, 146
Bews, Guy 135
Beyda, Kent 66
Beyer, Troy 6
Beymer, Richard 45
Beyond the Bermuda Triangle 204
Beyond Witch Mountain 64
Biagi, Bridget 153
Bibicoff, Harvey 102
Bicat, Nick 36
Bicknell, Gene 41
Bicsey, Lukocs 107
Bieber, Daniel 169
Bieber, Jayne 117
Biehn, Michael 52
Big and Hairy 23
Big and Hairy (novel) 23
Biggins, Jonathan 128
Biggs, John 31
Biggs, Richard 11, 19, 20
Bigwood, James 174
Bikel, Theodore 19
Bilgore, Andrew 68
Bill, Tony 96
Biller, Wendy 198
Billerman, Mark 27
Billett, Tom 179, 195

Billings, Dawn Ann 195
Billings, Earl 162
Billingsley, Barbara 21
Binder, Chuck 17
Bing Crosby Productions 131, 171
Bingham, Barbara 30
Binkley, Jeff 190
Binns, Edward 145
Bionic Ever After? 23, 24
Bionic Showdown: The Six Million Dollar Man and the Bionic Woman 24, 151
The Bionic Woman 69, 130, 155, 161
Birch, Kristin 19
Birch, Randy 135
Birdsong, Lori 88
Birk, Raye 167
Birkett, Bernadette 7
Birkett, Jeremiah 120
Birkin, Andrew 177
Birman, Len 7, 32, 33
Birman, Matt 94, 191
Birnbaum, Roger 15, 21
Birney, Frank 201
Birnheim, Francoise 132
Birnkrant, Don H. 142
Biroc, Joseph 39
Biscuit, Johnny 165
Bisesti, Linda 16
Bishop, David 140
Bisone, Jeannie 76
Bissell, Whit 38, 178
Bixby, Bill 51, 94, 95, 150, 184
Bixby-Brandon Productions 51, 184
Bizley, Roger 67
Black, Barbara 48
Black, Curtis 115
Black, J.R. 158
Black, Jerry 120
Black, John D.F. 39
Black, Karen 184
Black, Roger 24
Black, Stuart 104
Black, Todd 139
Black, Trevor 200
The Black Hope Horror 80
Black Magic 24
Black Noon 25
Black Scorpion 25
Black Scorpion II: Aftershock 26
Blackburn, Barbara 35
Blackburn, Greta 192
Blackburn, Richard 94
Blacker, David 104, 191
Blackman, Vernon 153
Blackmon, Edafe 6
Blackmore, Stephanie 151
Blackoff, Edward 36
Blackstone, Harry, Jr. 120
Blackstone, Wendy 190
Blackwell, David 102
Blackwell, Kim 29
Blade Squad 204
Blair, Linda 171
Blake, Clement 92, 101
Blake, Howard 31
Blake, Jonathan 171

Blake, Larry 157
Blake, Sondra 109
Blake, Timothy 188
Blakely, Susan 15, 97
Blakeney, Eric 73
Blakley, Gene 137
Blancard, Jarred 100
Blanch, Jewel 20
Blanchard, Rachel 38
Blanchard, Terence 174
Blangsted, Folmar 132
Blangsted, David 100, 200
Blankett, Betsy 27
Blankfield, Mark 123
Blanton, Arell 76
Blasdel-Goddard, Audrey 91
Blatchley, Joseph 16
Blatt, Daniel H. 48, 192
Blatt, Stuart 197
Blatt-Singer Productions 192
Bledsoe, Will 150
Blees, Robert 44
Bleeth, Yasmine 109
Bleich, William (Bill) 45, 69, 123, 167
Blessing, Ann 91
Blessing, Jack 78
Blick, Hugo E. 41
Blitz, Amanda 81
Bloch, Robert 34, 48
Block, Ethelinn 144
Bloecher, Michael 202
Blom, Dan 103
Blondell, Joan 48
Blondell, Tony Curtis 66
Blood Ties 27, 43
Bloom, Anne 91
Bloom, Brian 193
Bloom, Jeffrey 167
Bloom, John 165
Bloom, Lindsay 30
Bloom, Verna 197
Bloomfield, Don 188
Bloomfield, John 177
Bloomstein, Henry 90
Blosil, Stephen 101
Blount, Lisa 15
Blu, Susan 199
Blue Yonder 27
Bluel, Richard 78
Blum, Jack 24
Blumenthal, Rick 188
Blumsack, Gary 150
Blunden, Bill 20, 97, 117, 185
Blunt, Augie 167
Bluthal, John 112
Blythe, Catherine N. 54, 112
Blythe, Peter 16
Bob Banner Associates 46
"Bobby" 49, 185
Bobicheff, Vernon 177
Bochco, Steven 98, 193
Bochner, Lloyd 43
Bock, Larry 76
Bocquet, Francois 128
Bode, Ralf 37
Bodega Bay Productions 87
Boden, Kristina 201

Bodnár, Erika 46
"The Body Politic" 148
Boen, Earl 15, 40, 201
Bofshever, Michael 152
Bogaev, Paul 37
Bogart, Paul 31
Bogdanovich, Peter 11
Bogie, Duane C. 28
Bogner, Ludek 147
Bogosian, Eric 200, 201
Bohl, Charlie 135
Boland, Deborah 112
Bolden, Anthony 76
Bolen, Lin 79
Bolender, Bill 148, 172, 188
Bolling, Angie 99
Bologna, Joseph 137
Bolthouse, Brent 69
Bolton, Christopher 93
Bolton, Michael 135
Bombshell 28
Bonar, Ivan 42, 84, 165
Bond, Michael 192
Bond, Samantha 153
Bond, Timothy 141
Bondi, Beulah 159
Bone Chillers 158
Bonet, Wilma 189
Boning, Wigald 128
Bonnie Raskin Productions 174
Bonno, Chris 108
Boone, J.J. 85
Boone, Mark, Jr. 47
Boone, Richard 110
Booth, Andrew 70, 71
Booth, Connie 149
Borchers, Donald P. 125
Borden, Fred 179
Borelli, Carla 151
Boretski, Peter 82
Boretz, Alvin 165
Borg, Emily 70
Borgese, Joe 103
Borgnine, Ernest 6, 42, 71, 75
Borno, Pascal 113, 140
Bornstein, Charles 31, 83, 163
Borowicz, Dan 92
Borrowed Hearts 204
The Borrowers 28
Bosley, Tom 124, 131
Bostain, Heather Ann 106
Bostock, Barbara 164
Bostwick, Barry 128
Boswell, Simon 13
Bota, Rick 40
Bothelo, Niki 64
Bottoms, Joseph 96, 160
Bottoms, Timothy 206
Botuchis, Mathew 87
Bourgeois, John 127
Bourla, David 197, 201
Bourne, Lindsay 51
Bourne, Tammy 12
Bourneuf, Philip 109
Bousman, Tracy 43, 76, 90, 118, 192
Bova, Ben 71
Bow, Simmy 14

Bowden-Kirby, Joyce 117
Bower, Tom 117
Bowers, Wendy 144
Bowers, William 126, 199
Bowes, Geoffrey 104
Bowles, Lauren 190
Bowman, Chuck 94, 192
Bowman, Jeffrey 66
Bowne, Alan 47
Boxell, Tip 102
Boxleitner, Bruce 19, 20, 69, 211
Boy, Gouchy 81
Boyce, Todd 153
Boyd, Blake 45
Boyd, Guy 64
Boyd, Hamish 139
Boyd, Jeff 86
Boyd, Jerry 15, 35
Boyd, Katarina 123
Boyd, Lynda 14, 59, 73
Boyd, Michael 123
Boyer, Christopher 7, 136, 197
Boyer, Katy 198
Boyer, Philip 116
Boyle, David 151
Boyle, Michael 30
Boyles, Peter 159
Boyrer, Lucy 103
Boyriven, Patrick 192
Bracken, Kathleen 179
Bracy, Charles 90
Bradbury, Ray 101, 121
Braden, Hub 99, 126
Bradford, Hank 75
Bradford, Jean Louisa 176
Bradley, Dan 159
Bradley, Maria 67
Brady, Lance 189
Brady, Scott 132
Braeden, Eric 11, 129, 145
Bram Stoker's "Burial of the Rats" 204
Brame, Bill 179
Bramhall, Mark 141
Brams, Julian 40
Brams, Richard 31, 40
Bramson, Steven 117
Brand, Gibby 83
Brand, Neville 106
Brand, Roland 20
Brand, Sheila 149
Brandenburg, Carol 111
Brandis, Jonathan 100
Brandner, Gary 69
Brandon, John 78, 109
Brandon, Peter 40, 79
Brandt, Hank 11, 120
Bransford, Jennifer 166
Brantliger, Dee 6
Brasselle, Melissa 196
Brauer, Jonathon 137
Braunstein, Howard 54
Braunstein, Jeff 160
Brauss, Art 85
Brave New World (1980) 29
Brave New World (1998) 29
Brave New World (novel) 110
Braver, Billy 6

Braverman, Marvin 197
Bravler, Robert 180
Bray, David 123
Brazil 60
Brazzel, Greg 25, 136
"Breaking Strain" 183
Breck, Jonathan 92
Breck, Peter 93
Breckon, Celia 31
Brenlin, George 94
Brenn, Janni 80
Brennan, Claire 143
Brennan, Eileen 18, 68, 181
Brennan, Kelly 69
Brenner, Dori 92
Brenner, Jules 138, 156
Brennert, Alan 109
Bretz, Matthew Allen 113
Brewer, Sheree 29
Brewster, Bonnie 92
Brezeau, Jay 185
Bricker, Jack 162
Bridge Across Time 30, 217
Bridge of Time 30
Bridges, Beau 6, 80, 190
Bridges, Emily 190
Bridges, Kenneth 76
Bridges, Lloyd 6, 94, 118
Bridget Terry Productions 176
Bridle, Alan 185
Brigadier, Ed 91
Briggs, Tony 71
Briggs, Traci Lee 105
Brigham, Tom 81
Bright, Ray 112
Bright, Richard 42
"Brillo" 71
Brimley, Wilford 64, 199
Brimstone 48, 175
Brinckerhoff, Brian 29
Brinckerhoff, Burt 102
Brinegar, Paul 15
Brinkley, Ritch 12, 33, 180
Brinkman, Leigh E. 191
Brion, James 128
Briscoe, Jimmy 115
Britt, Lisa 84
Brittany, Morgan 96
Brittingham, Ashley 140
Brock, Phil 179
Brocklebank, Daniel 122
Brocksmith, Roy 167, 198
Broderick, Brendan 90
Brodeur, Andre 195
Brodhead, James E. 165
Brodkin, Herbert 55
Brody, Joshua 187
Brolin, James 175
Bromiley, Bill, Jr. 11
Bromilow, Mark 198
Bromley, Karen 160
Bromwell, Lisa 13
Bronson, J. Scott 183
Bronson, Katrina Holden 110
Bronson, Scott J. 165
Brookes, Jacqueline 167
Brooks, Angelle 110
Brooks, Ben 191

Brooks, Jason 93
Brooks, Jay 79
Brooks, Joe 65
Brooks, Joel 19, 87
Brooks, Martin 23, 24, 150
Brooks, Ray 20
Brooks, Stanley M. 21
Brophy, Anthony 161
Brophy, Brian 152
Brophy, Kevin 198
Brosnan, Pierce 210
Brothers, Dr. Joyce 126
Brough, Candi 126
Brough, Randi 126
Brougham, Christopher 86
Broughton, Bruce 76
Brown, Andre Rosey 12, 87
Brown, Antony 102
Brown, Ashley 127
Brown, Billy 103
Brown, Bryan 187
Brown, Charles 67
Brown, Christopher M. 6, 7, 120
Brown, Claire 100, 139
Brown, Clancy 33
Brown, George Stanford 151
Brown, Helen 66
Brown, Henry C. 93
Brown, Hilyard 73, 172
Brown, Irmsie 181
Brown, Julie 7
Brown, Kimberly J. 81
Brown, Lew 38, 143
Brown, Matthew 144
Brown, Michael 45
Brown, Murray 59
Brown, Pamela 59
Brown, Paul 157
Brown, Phil 121
Brown, Randal 169
Brown, Ray 180
Brown, Reb 29, 32, 33, 170
Brown, Rick 27
Brown, Robert Latham 18
Brown, Roger Aaron 150
Brown, Steven 71
Brown, Susan 67, 117
Brown, Velina 189
Brown, W. Earl 146
Brown, Winston 15
Browne, Bernard 50, 127
Browne, Derek 146
Browne, Robert Alan 13
Browne, Ronald W. 33
Browne, Roscoe Lee 206
Brownhouse Productions 37
Brubaker, Christine 94
Bruce, Colin 79
Bruce, John P. 120
Bruce, Maxwell 174
Bruck, Bella 162
Brujo 157
Brunjes, Ralph 158
Brunnen, David Zum 169
Bruskotter, Eric 138
Brustin, Michele Goldman 31, 108
Bryan, Mason 37
Bryan, Sabrina 126

Bryant, Clara 189
Bryant, Jennifer 25
Bryant, Joshua 25, 118
Bryant, Lee 8
Bryant, Pamela 150
Bryant, Peter 73, 134
Bryant, William 25, 38, 171, 173
Bryden, Andy 123
Brymer, Patrick 21
Bryson, Eric 190
BSR Productions 84
B'Tiste, I'Lana 101
Buchanan, James D. 88
Buchanan, Morris 131
Buchholz, Horst 49
Buck, Faustus 192
Buck Rogers in the 25th Century 43, 120, 139, 171
Buckalew, Tyler Mason 37
Buckaroo Banzai 149
Bucket of Blood 11
Buckley, Jeanne 67
Buckman, Tara 29
Buckner, Wendy 136
Bucksey, Colin 134
Buday, Don 107
Buechler, John 137
Buell, Nancy 166
Buffy the Vampire Slayer 149
Buford, Gordon 116
Bula, Tammi 73
Bulifant, Joyce 159
Bullard, Nigel 91
Bullington, Perry 29
Bullock, Gary 152
Bullock, Sandra 24
Bullock, Walter 186
Bumatai, Ray 45
Bunch, Ray 43
Bunea, Mihai 112
Bunker, Jon 33
Buono, Victor 118, 126
Burcksen, Edgar 166
Burden, Gary 15
Burger, Michael 63
Burger, Robert 55
Burgess, Deborah 104
Burgess, Michael 23, 188
Burgi, Richard 35, 92
Burgomaster, Kenneth 128
Buried Secrets 31, 217
Burk, Jim 105
Burke, Carlease 67, 87
Burke, Delta 47
Burke, Kristin M. 149
Burke, Michael Reilly 142
Burke, Paul 43
Burke, Robert 23
Burke, Thomas Robert 154
Burke, Walter 179
Burke's Law 53
Burkett, Jeremiah 146
Burkhardt, Debra 181
Burkholder, Scott 188
Burley, Mark A. 126
Burman, Ellis 72
Burnett, John F. 137
Burnette, Billy 136

Burns, Al 87, 128
Burns, Bart 61, 161
Burns, George 91
Burns, Jennifer 85
Burns, Jere 186
Burns, Richard 162
Burns, Timothy 72
Burnside, Stewart 71, 139, 187
Burr, Fritzi 129
Burr, Robert 27
Burr, Walter 161
Burrell, Jan 53
Burrett, Vicky 86
Burrise, Nakia 189
Burroughs, Edgar Rice 105
Burrows, Stephen 6
Burstall, Danny 169
Burstyn, Thomas 50, 62, 142
Burt, Andrew 136
Burton, Geoff 162
Burton, LeVar 123, 124, 201
Burton, Matthew 166
Burton, Michelle 77
Burton, Robert 44, 184
Burton, Warren 91
Buschoff, Walter 18
Busey, Gary 190
Busfield, Timothy 60, 185
Bush, Marlene 29
Bush, Owen 144
Bush, Robert L. 103
Busse, Jochen 85
Bussey, Nicholas D. 137
Butcher, Charles 5
Butcher, Randy 190
Butin, Michele 76
Butkus, Dick 113, 167
Butler, Artie 14
Butler, Bill 21, 162
Butler, Ervin 165
Butler, Megan 107
Butler, Pat 91
Butler, Paul 47
Butler, Robert 52, 140, 170
Butler, Tom 74
Butler, Yancy 149
Butrick, Merritt 69
Butterworth, Kent 128
Butterworth, Shane 29
Buttons, Red 6, 129
Butts, Gerry 66
Byerly, Scotch 6
Byers, Billy 28, 85
Byers, John 37
Byram, Cassandra 104
Byrd, Ann Gee 146
Byrd, Carl 130
Byrd, David 130
Byrne, Joe 31
Byrne, John 73
Byrne, Michael 177
Byrnes, Jim 139

Cabal, Lilliana 29, 48, 165
Cabot, Sebastian 124
Cabrera, Charley 122
Cacavas, John 90
Caesar, Harry 4, 165

Caesar, Sid 44, 127
Cafargno, Edward C. 62
Caffey, Michael 53
Cahn, Daniel 98
Cahn, Dann 21, 140
Caidin, Martin 65, 160
Caillou, Alan 78, 148, 161
Cain, Dean 207
Caine, Michael 102, 187
Caines, Florence 123
Calderisi, David 82
Caldwell, Stephen P. 94, 103
Cale, Bennett 27
Cali, Joseph 162
Call, Brandon 76, 92
Call, Ed 147
Call, R.D. 180
Callaghan, Jeremy 128
Callahan, Dick 195
Callahan, James 159
Callahan, James T. 144
Callan, K. 178
Callender, Colin 47
Callery, Sean 125
Calloway, Tom 76, 175
Caloz, Michael 198
Calvin, Robert 181
Camacho, Corinne 143
Cameron, Candace 195
Cameron, David 139
Cameron, John (music) 67, 102, 164, 177
Cameron, John Mitchell 47
Cameron, Kirk 78
Cameron, Lorne 38
Camilleri, Tory 200
Camp, Hamilton 16
Campanella, Frank 14
Campbell, Bill 39, 40, 121
Campbell, Bruce 116, 121
Campbell, Chris 38
Campbell, David 5, 13
Campbell, Desmond 13, 190, 191
Campbell, Graeme 60
Campbell, Isolita 117
Campbell, J. Kenneth 42
Campbell, J. Marvin 12, 97
Campbell, Julia 188
Campbell, Ken 190
Campbell, Laura 113
Campbell, Martin 33
Campbell, Neve 32
Campbell, Scott Michael 146
Campbell, W. Stewart 37, 186
Campbell, William 150
Campos, Rafael 191, 192
Campos, Victor 16
Camroux, Ken 134, 184
Canaan, Christopher 30
Canerday, Natalie 7
Cannell, Stephen J. 124, 176
Cannold, Mitchell 66
Cannom, Greg 89
Cannon, David 161
Cannon, Dyan 16
Cannon, Orin 49, 184
Cannon, Vince 62

Can't Sing, Can't Dance Productions 92
The Canterville Ghost (1986) 31
The Canterville Ghost (1996) 32
Capell, Barbara 85
Capell, Peter 85
Capener, Brian 202
Capice, Philip 172
Capital Cities/ABC 51
Capitani, Remo 78
Caplan, Claire 59
Capra, Frank 101
Capra, Jordana 78
Captain America 32
Captain America II 33
Captain America 33
Caramico, Robert 107, 182
Cardea, Frank 61
Cardinal, Tantoo 114
Cardriche, Jaime 6, 33
Carducci, Mark 194
Cardwell, Harry 36
Carey, Christopher 33
Carey, Clare 176
Carey, Drew 68
Carey, Macdonald 77, 171
Carey, Matthew 142
Carey, Michele 135
Carides, Gia 5, 54
Caridi, Carmine 107
Carla Singer Productions 93
Carlile, David 93
Carlin, Dianne 29
Carlin, Joy 141
Carliner, Mark 142, 159
Carlino, Lewis John 197
Carlson, Chad 18
Carlson, Karen 101
Carlson, Laura 6
Carlton, Hope Marie 165
Carlucci, Lou 159
Carlyle, Richard 164
Carmen, Julie 71, 157
Carnell, Cliff 131
Carney, Art 27, 133
Carnochan, John 40, 119
Carol, Jack 53
Carol, Ronnie 167
Caron, Sandra 59
Carpenter, Brian 153
Carpenter, John 103
Carpenter, Pete 33
Carpenter, Russell 17
Carpenter, Willie C. 69
Carr, Caleb 195
Carr, Darleen 88
Carr, Gabriel 187
Carr, Jane 87
Carr, Katie 138
Carr, Patricia 102
Carradine, John 34, 43, 78, 79, 132
Carradine, Keith 163
Carradine, Robert 38, 91, 103, 169
Carrasco, Jonathan 100
Carrau, Bob 64
Carrere, Leon 44, 178
Carrere, Tia 42
Carrie 96, 100, 164

Carrillo, Elpidia 114
Carrington, Debbie 64
Carroll, Cecilley 145
Carroll, Christopher 162
Carroll, Diahann 69
Carroll, Edward E. 77
Carroll, Justin 19
Carroll, Leo G. 182
Carroll, Lewis 6
Carroll, Lisa Hart 137
Carroll, Peter 58
Carroll, Vinnette 111
Carrothers, A.J. 177
Carruthers, Bob 123
Carson, Janet M. 29
Carson, Jeanne M. 29
Carson, Joan 13
Carter, Adrienne 57, 62
Carter, Alex 185
Carter, Chris 133
Carter, Evan 74
Carter, Fred 68
Carter, Gary 111
Carter, Helena Bonham 122
Carter, Jack 90
Carter, John 35, 61, 117
Carter, Linda 158
Carter, Lynda 129
Carter, Michael 36
Carter, Myra 117
Carter, Peter 96
Carter, T.K. 201
Carter, Thomas 190
Carter, Viv 128
Cartwright, Hank 35, 81
Cartwright, Lynn 162
Cartwright, Veronica 148
Caruana, Michael 21
Caruk, Lisa Marie 141
Caruso, Johnny 12
Carvalho, Betty 87
Carvell, Marium 127
Carver, Brent 198
Carver, Mary 178
Cary, Christopher 143
Cary, Diane 8
Cascio, Geoffery 27
Cascone, Nicholas 89
Case, Allen 118
Case, Justin 128
Case, Thomas 194
Casella, Alberto 52
Casey, Bernie 72, 121
Casey, Bob 169
Casey, Lawrence 161
Casnoff, Philip 163
Caso, Alan 45
Caso, Maria 190
Cass, Dave 25, 126
Cassady, John 121
Cassel, Seymour 14, 62, 111
Cassidy, Joanna 99, 169
Cassidy, Martin 120
Cassidy, Patrick 124
Cassidy, Ted 73, 143
Cast a Deadly Spell 33, 201
Castaneda, Gus 55
Castell, Andrew 102

The Cat Creature 34
Catalano, Frank 56
Catalyst Entertainment 158, 190, 191
Cattrall, Kim 79, 142, 152, 154, 199
Caudell, Lane 15
Caulfield, Bernadette 190
Cavacas, John 178
Cavanagh, Thomas 134
"Cave Carson" 105
Cavendish, Nicola 135
Cawley, Robert F. 108
CBS 6, 16, 23, 25, 32, 33, 36, 43, 46, 51, 56, 59, 62, 72, 73, 83, 88, 94, 95, 97, 99, 117, 124, 126, 130, 134, 137, 147, 149, 150, 156, 159, 161, 162, 163, 165, 168, 180, 187, 188, 189, 190, 196, 199, 200, 204, 205, 206, 207, 208, 209, 211, 212, 213, 214, 215, 216; Entertainment 89, 149; Films 98
Cecere, Fulvio 39, 73
Cedar, Jon 98, 179
Ceder, Elayne 137
Celedonio, Maria 45, 152
Cellucci, Claire 38, 74
Centenera, Eliza 59
Century Group, Ltd. 12, 41, 50
Century-Fox TV 124
Cerasoli, Lisa 89
Cerny, Radek 49
Cerullo, Alfred C. 152
Chadfield, Angela 153
Chaet, Mark 83
Chaiqui, Emmanuelle 82
Chalk, Garry 73, 93, 100
Challis, John 59
Chamberlain, Ardwight 19
Chamberlin, Lee 29
Chambers, Brian 86
Chambers, Daniel 134
Chambers, David Kirk 165
Chambers, Eric 144
Chambers, Everett 125, 131
Chambliss, Woodrow 72, 178
Chameleon 147, 204, 223
Chameleons 35
Champion, Sandy 127
Chan, George B. 12
Chan, Henry 158
Chan, Toby 58
Chance, James R. 88
Chandler, Harry 46
Chandler, James 118, 171
Chandler, John 125
Chandler, Ken 32
Chandler, Spencer 31
Chang, Gary 52, 70
Chang, Joey 91
Channel Communications 55
Channel Four TV 81
Channing, Carol 6
Chanticleer Films 13, 40, 186
Chao, Rosalind 97, 163
Chapek, Peter 93
Chapelle, Nancy 157, 190, 191
Chapin, Doug 197
Chaplin, Geraldine 80, 138

Chapman, Andi 162
Chapman, Andree 130
Chapman, Brent 23
Chapman, Joseph 40
Chapman, Judith 35
Chapman, Mark Lindsay 15, 168
Chapman, Michael 15, 79
Chapman, Tom 113
Chapman, Vernon 145
Chappell, John 107
Chapple, Susan 139
Charendoff, Tara 155
Chariots of the Gods 143
Charles, Nancy Linehan 201
Charles E. Sellier Productions 108
Charles Fries Productions 90, 96, 121, 130, 164, 165, 189
Charles M. Schulz Creative Associates 28
Charleson, Ray 146
Charlot, Kawena 150
Charlton, Judd 81
The Charmings 43
Charnota, Anthony 90
Chase, Channing 15
Chase, Clinton 99, 101
Chase, Debra Martin 37
Chase, Gregory 182
Chase, Jacob 19, 29
Chase, Stanley 13
Chase, Vincent 25, 26, 167
Chase/Slan Productions 13
Chason, Myra 41
"Chattery Teeth" 148
Chattin, Sarah 143
Chau, Francois 97, 199
Chauvin, Lilyan 118, 195
Chavez, Ramon 108
Cheatham, Maree 115
Cheek, Molly 103
Cheers 69
Cheese, Dion 55
Chen, Joan 167
Chen, Larisa 70
Chen, Tina 75
Chesdon, Michael 177
Cheshire, Geoffrey 177
Chesler, Lewis B. 119, 177
Chesler/Perlmuter Productions 177
Chesson-Fohl, Peyton 37
Chester, Colby 51, 127
Chetwood, Derk 40
Chevolleau, Richard 145
Chew, Sam, Jr. 29
Cheyne, Hank 52
Chick, Ed 186
Chieffo, Michael 6, 29
Chihara, Paul 29, 46, 56, 83, 84, 130
Child of Darkness, Child of Light 35, 36
Childs, Peter 36
Child's Play 169
Chiles, Lois 200
Chiller 36
Chin, Tsan 43
China Beach 145
Chinlund, Nick 47

Chinyamurindi, Michael 163
Chioran, Juan 191
Choate, Tim 137
Chodos, Daniel 7
Choi, Kenneth 81
Chomsky, Marvin J. 55
Chow, Michael 74
Chowdhry, Navin 80
Choy, Brock 24
Chressanthis, James 51
Chris/Rose Productions 188
Christ, Bryant 67
Christensen, Debbie 102
Christensen, Hayden 82
Christian, Claudia 19, 20
Christian, Jim 183
Christian, Kelly 61
Christian, Kurt 178
Christian, Wolf 80
Christiansen, Bob 188
Christiansen, Robert W. 72
Christiansen, Tim 188
Christie, Lisa 135
Christmas, Eric 35
The Christmas Box 204
A Christmas Carol (1984) 127
A Christmas Carol (book) 13, 127
Christmas Every Day 37
Christopher, Dennis 100
Christopher, Jim 113
Christopher, Julian 134
Christopherson, Kathy 110
Chudnow, Byron 67
Chujabala, Art 28
Chula, Babz 61
Chullach, Christopher 99
Churchill, Adrian 191
Ciafalio, Carl Nick 95
Cicero, Sharon 134
Cieply, Michael 174
Cimino, Leonard 191
Cinderella 37
Cine Enterprises, Mexico 133
Cinema Center 100 161
Cinestage Productions 157
Cioffi, Louis 26
Circuit Breaker 217
Citadel Entertainment 37, 54, 63, 70, 153
City Beneath the Sea 37, 217
Ciupka, Richard 13
Civita, Diane 191, 192
Clackson, Brent Karl 142
Claire, Adele 90
Clancy, Sinead 90
Clancy, Tom 40, 75
Claremont, Chris 73
Clarence 38, 101
Clark, Ashley Monique 63
Clark, Blake 79
Clark, Bryan 28
Clark, Dick 51, 53
Clark, Doran 147
Clark, Dort 179
Clark, Eugene 107
Clark, Karen 190
Clark, Ken 152
Clark, Martin 15

Clark, Mary Higgins 205
Clark, Matt 185
Clark, Oliver 133
Clark, Sharon 190
Clark, Vandi 111
Clark, William 145
Clarke, Angela 75
Clarke, Arthur C. 183
Clarke, Caitlin 168
Clarke, Gary 114
Clarke, Jeff 127
Clarke, Matt 135
Clarke, Michael Francis 154
Clarkson, Helena 74
Clash of the Titans 115
Classics Illustrated (movie series) 66, 113
Clausen, Michael 87
Clay, Nicholas 122, 138
Clay, Stanley Bennett 15
Clayton, Abaas 23
Clayton, Cyril 27
Clayton, Hyde 178
Cleaveland, Ben 16, 104
Cleaves, Robert 58
Clemens, Brian 180
Clemens, Peter 158
Clement, Jennifer 62, 134
Clements, Calvin, Jr. 53
Clements, Richard 67, 98, 170
Clemmer, Ronnie D. 134
Clermont, Brock 191
Clermont, Nicholas 114
Cleveland, Patience 8
Cliffhangers: The Curse of Dracula 147
Clifford, Lucy 128
Clifte, Steve 94
Clinker, Nigel 22, 92
Clinton, George S. 79, 157
Clinton, Roger 57
Cloned 39
Clotworthy, Robert 193
Cloud, Darrah 83
Clouse, Robert 162
Cloutier, Suzanne 198
Clow, Stuart 74
CLT-UFA/Delux Productions 177
Clyde, Craig 178
CNM Entertainment 157
Co, Karin 110
Coady, Francis 55
Coastline Partners 93, 154
Coates, Conrad 38
Coates, Nelson 166
Coates-West, Carol 142
Coatman, Michael 166
Cobb, Julie 29, 156
Cobert, Robert (Bob) 44, 49, 59, 97, 117, 132, 136, 185
Coblentz, James 61
Coca, Imogene 6
Coccoon 183
Cochran, Lisa M. 22
Cochran, Shannon 84
Cockrum, Dave 73
Cockrum, Dennis 62
Coco, James 167

Cocteau, Jean 23
Codrington, Jim 50, 127
Coeur, Paul 135
Coghill, Joy 134, 139
Cohen, Andrew 125
Cohen, Barney 58, 130, 155
Cohen, Eric 75
Cohen, Joyce 200
Cohen, Lawrence D. 100, 169
Cohen, Martin B. 91
Cohen, Rob 108
Cohen, Steve 69
Cohn, Amy Beth 45
Cohn, Michael 161
Coit, Stephen 144
Cojocaru, Constantin 112
Coke, Liz 146
Cokeliss, Harley 153
Colantoni, Enrico 39
Colavita, Kristina 176
Colbert, Robert 38, 55
Colby, Jalsyn 128
Colceri, Tim 19
Colcord, Ray 54, 200
The Cold Equations 1, 39
"The Cold Equations" 40
A Cold Night's Death 204
The Cold Room 204
Cole, Albert 90, 179
Cole, Brian 137
Cole, Gary 188
Cole, Michael 100, 109
Cole, Stan 93, 126
Coleman, Anthony 66
Coleman, Dabney 54, 174
Coleman, Doug 157
Coleman, Gary 105, 115
Coleman, Jack 14, 46, 183
Coleman, James 142
Colen, Beatrice 29
Colichman, Paul 12, 50, 57, 122, 197
Colin, Bruce 75
Colin, Margaret 149
Coll, Ivonne 10
Colla, Richard A. 148, 162
Collet, Christopher 168
Collier, Barry L. 201
Collier, Margaret 37
Collins, Bob 160
Collins, Carla 190, 191
Collins, F. Scott 181
Collins, Georgie 135
Collins, Greg 15, 50, 140
Collins, Joely 73
Collins, Judy 183
Collins, Lisa 52
Collins, Michelle 83
Collins, Robert 75
Collins, Stephen 208
Collison, Frank 186
Colman, Ben 136
Colman, Booth 179
Colman, Henry 48
Colmenares, Angel 28
Colombier, Michel 47
Colomby, Scott 14
Colon, Miriam 114

The Colony 217
Color Me Perfect 204
Colover, Rachel 122
Colson, Kevin 183
Colt, Beth 63
Columbia 91, 92, 104; Pictures 6, 31, 78; Pictures Television 93, 140
Columbo 147
Colvin, Jack 65, 94, 95, 150, 164
Colwell, Chuck 51, 95, 184
Colwell, Thom 5, 13
Colyar, Michael 6
Coma 152
Comar, Richard 160
Combo, Marius 138
Combs, Gil 89
Come Back Productions 163
Comeau, Andy 194
Comen, Joshua D. 136
Comer, Anjanette 49
Comer, Dawn 154
Comerford, Danielle 111
Comero, Roberto 155
Compan, Gilberto 133
The Companion 40
Compton, O'Neal 16
Compton, Richard 18
The Computer Wore Tennis Shoes 69, 204
Computercide 40
Comworld Productions 16
Comyn, Charles 146
Conan Doyle, Arthur, Sir 149, 209
Conaway, Cristi 5
Conaway, Jeff 19, 21, 22, 75
Concklin, Jeffrey 55
Concorde 194
Concorde-New Horizons 7, 11, 137
Condon, Dominic 128
Condor 41, 71
Condurache, Dan 112
Conely, Sharon 83
Confer, Steve 67
Conforti, Gino 126, 144, 178
Conklin, Patricia 142
Conlan, Joseph 103, 118, 130, 167, 192
Conlon, Mark 104, 188
Conn, Didi 73
Connder, Eric 175
A Connecticut Yankee in King Arthur's Court (book) 107
A Connecticut Yankee in King Arthur's Court (1949) 41, 117
Connell, David 169
Connell, Gordon 75
Connell, Jim 72
Connelly, Christopher 121
Connery, Jason 123
Connolly, John P. 181
Connolly, Mark 58
Connor, Kevin 78, 149
Connors, Chuck 88
Conopast, Jennifer 89
Conover, Laura 165
Conquistador Entertainment 113, 141

Conrad, Alan 40
Conrad, Charles, Jr. 144
Conrad, Chris 166
Conrad, David 161
Conrad, Rick 13
Conrad, Robert 16, 126, 199, 206
Conrad, William 130
Conried, Hans 178
Conroy, Jack 67
Conroy, Kevin 42, 43, 87, 99, 100
Considine, John 180
Constable, Gary 157
Constance-Churcher, Pia 16
Conti, Al 53
Conti, Bill 24
Contreras, Kevin 136
Contreras, Luis 7, 97
Converse, Peggy 42
Convict 762 204
Convy, Bert 51
Conway, James L. 65, 113, 178
Conway, Kevin 111
Cook, A.J. 93
Cook, Bill 152
Cook, Cindy 82
Cook, Donald 128
Cook, Elisha, Jr. 49, 131, 156
Cook, Fielder 22, 124
Cook, Robin 151, 152, 206, 213
Cook, Ron 138
Cook, Shelley 31
Cook, T.S. 88
Cook, Tracey 145
Cooke, Christopher 69, 168
Cooksey, Jon 82
Coolidge, Jennifer 136
Coombes, James 107
Coon, Gene L. 148
Cooney, Dennis 161
Cooper, Charles
Cooper, George 165
Cooper, Jackie 98, 133, 213
Cooper, James 8
Cooper, Tamar 98
Cooperman, Jack 27
Coopersmith, Jerome 13
Copeland, John 18, 19, 20
Copeland, Kevin 183
Copeland, Miles A., III 12, 50, 201
Copeland, Stewart 198
Copeman, Michael 74, 190
Copp, Rick 5
Coppola, Carmine 141
Coppola, Francis Ford 138, 141, 198
Coppola, Frank 186
Cops and Robin 42, 71
Corapeake Productions 80
Corazza, Vincent 54, 191
Corbett, Ed 66
Corbett, Glenn 171
Corbett, Gretchen 120
Corbett, Jason 105
Corbett, John 195
Corbett, Robin Frates 110
Corbett, Toby 48
Corbin, Barry 178

Corbitt Design 149
Corciova, Radu 112
Cord, Alex 73, 78, 79, 143
Corday, Barbara 92
Cordell, Ruth 7
Cordic, Regis J. 51, 119, 151
Corea, Nicholas 95, 103
Corey, Jeff 44, 162
Cork, Malcolm 71
Corley, Annie 169
Corley, Pat 167, 189, 197
Corman, Gene 27
Corman, Roger 7, 11, 25, 26, 66, 71, 85, 90, 91, 96, 103, 110, 136, 137, 173, 175, 194, 196
Cornelius, Rodney 76
Cornford, Bill 108
Cornocchione, Antoni 142
Cornthwaite, Robert 160, 198
The Corporation 217
"Corpus Earthling" 164
Correia, David 130
Correla, David 10
Corrington, John W. 106
Corrington, Joyce 106
The Corsican Brothers 204
Corso, Bill 165
Corso, John (art director) 65
Corso, John W. (production design) 167
Cort, Bud 21, 29
Cort, Robert W. 161
Cortese, Joe 40, 162
Cortez, Katherine 68, 181
Corti, Jesse 133
Corvi, Bruce 103
Corymore Productions 126
Coscarelli, Don 22
Cosmo Productions 182
Costa, Christopher 181
Costa, Nick 95
Costanza, Joe 68
Costelloe, Elizabeth 90
Costin, Kim Terry 186
Coswick, Harry 173
Cote, Suzy 136
Cotner, Doug 76, 138
Cotten, Joseph 37
Cotter, Ed 106
Cotton, Susan 94
Coulouris, George 171
Coulouris, Keith 22
Coulson, Peter 81
Coulter, Steve 174
Couriet, Gerald 51
Court, Roma 110
Courtney, Chuck 16
Cousins, Brian 153
Cousins, Christian 97
Cousins, Joseph 97
Covell, David 112
The Covenant 42
Cowan, Robert 96
Cowie, Victor 185
Cowley, Anthony 115
Cox, Alan 138
Cox, Dana 181
Cox, John 71

Cox, Joshua 19, 20
Cox, Julie 187
Cox, Michelle 7
Cox, Monty 180
Cox, Nikki 45
Cox, Tony 64, 196
Cox, Veanne 37, 99
Cox, Wally 132
Coxon, Cole 76
Coy, Suzanne 50
Coyne, Jonathan 81
Coyote, Peter 27
Cozzi, Michael 12
Crabe, James 42, 48, 161, 173
Crackroft, Stephen 165
The Cradle Will Fall 205
Crafford, Ian 161
Cragg, Chris 12
Cragin, Charles 47
Craig, Charles Grant 176
Craig, Connie 104
Cramer, Douglas S. 34, 48, 129, 145, 157
Cramer, Grant 112
Cramer, Rick 197
Crane, Brandon 100
Crane, Chilton 23, 39, 51
Crane, John 6
Crane, Norma 131
Cranshaw, Patrick 7
Cranston, Bryan 40, 150
The Crash of Flight 401 75
Craven, Matt 96, 175
Craven, Mimi 55
Craven, Wes 36, 99, 103, 158, 171, 212
Crawford, Alvin 38
Crawford, Broderick 115
Crawford, Ellen 188
Crawford, James W. 81
Crawford, Jim 75
Crawford, Joan 130
Crawford, Katherine 72
Crawford, Mark McQuade 147
Crawford, Rachael 93
Crawford, Thomas 109, 181
Crawford, William 147
Creaghan, Dennis 146
Credel, Curtis
Credo 60
Creepshow 46
Creley, Jack 79
Crenna, Richard 53, 97, 187
Crescent Entertainment 62
Crescenzo, Jim 73
Cresciman, Vincent J. 16, 174
Cressall, Hunter 113
Crestview Productions 90
Crewson, Wendy 62
Crichton, Andrew 141
Crider, Missy 148
Crime of Passion: Voice from the Grave 205
Crimm, Arthur 82
Criscuolo, Lou 168
Criss, Peter 107
Cristal, Linda 48
Cristing, Tony 90

Critchity, Suzanna 123
Critchlow, Brenda 139
Crivello, Anthony 6
Crockett, Nick 125
Croft, Bill 5, 57, 62
Crombie, Peter 89
Cromwell, Gloria 13
Cromwell, James 158
Crone, Glenn 37
Cronin, Noel 180
Cronin, Patrick 29
Cronjager, William 103, 118
Cronkite, Hank 175
Crosbie, Craig 102
Crosby, Bing 117
Crosby, Cathy Lee 216
Crosby, Gary 156
Crosby, Joan 143
Crosby, Kathryn 96
Crosby, Randy 133
Crosland, Ivan 101
Cross, Ben 85, 133, 134, 187, 210
Cross, Dennis 43
Cross, Garvin 73
Cross, Malcolm 39, 60
Cross, Marcia 120, 174
Cross, Roger R. 39
Crouch, Rachel 174
Crowden, Graham 80
Crowe, Aislinn 71
Crowe, Christopher 167
Crowe, Emilia 55
Crowe, Maxwell 167
Crowell, Henry, Jr. 93
Crowfoot 43
Crowhaven Farm 43
Crowley, Anthony 162
Crowley, David 97
Croxall, Samantha 74
Croxton, Dee 89
Cruchley, Murray 38
Crudelle, Frank 77
Crugnali, Louis 152
Cruise Into Terror 205
Crumpler, Courtney Allen 174
Crunch Recording Group 190, 191
Crusade 20
Cruse, William 53
Cruze, Josh 16, 97
Cry for the Strangers 205
Cryer, David 79
The Crying Child 44
Crystal, Billy 90, 91
Crystal, Richard 13, 74
Cser, Nancy 54
Csizmodia, Gobi 107
CTV Television 145
Cubbison, Patti 148
Cudlitz, Michael 110
Cudney, Roger 40
Culea, Melinda 31, 174
Cullen, Don 75
Cullen, Kerrie 75
Culliton, Patrick 6, 179
Cullum, Kimberly 79
Cullum, Matthew 81
Culp, Clint 50
Culp, Joseph 69

Culp, Robert 164, 204
Culver, Carmen 39
Culzean Corp. 41, 42, 71, 116
Cumbuka, Ji-Tu 42, 120
Cummings, Kimball 163
Cummings, Martin 139
Cummings, Richard, Jr. 184
Cummins, Gregory Scott 27
Cuna, Francis 161
Cundey, Dean 99, 101
Cunneff, Catherine 144
Cunniffe, Emma 153
Cunningham, Cavan 170
Cunningham, Colin 49
Cuoco, Kaley 181
Cuomo, Alfredo 169
Cupo, Pat 186
Cupo, Patrick 50
Curran, Paul 122, 123
Curran, Robert 83
Curran, Scott D. 178
Currie, Sondra 8
Currier, Terrence P. 37
Curry, Michael Todd 7, 136
Curry, Tim 58, 59, 100
The Curse of King Tut's Tomb 205
Curse of the Black Widow 44, 133
Curtain, Hoyt 107
Curtin, Celine 90
Curtin, Peter 139
Curtin, Valerie 29
Curtis, Billy 133
Curtis, Dan 44, 49, 59, 97, 117, 131, 132, 135, 184, 185
Curtis, John Bear 184
Curtis, Keene 170
Curtis, Shelley 53
Curtis, Tony 71
Curtis, Tracy 44, 184
Curtis-Brown, Robert 37
Curtis-Larson, Janet 35
Cury, Claiborne 55
The Cusp 217
Cutchlow, Gail 42
Cuthbert, John 176
Cutler, Barry 165
Cutler, Wendy 87, 193
Cutt, Michael 162
Cutter, Allen 12
Cutting, David 117
Cutts, John 76
cyberpunk 199
Cyborg 65, 160
Cybuiski, Artur 109
Cyer, Nancy 166
Cynader, Rebecca 139
Cypher, Jon 97
Cypress Films 82
Czapski, Maciek 67

Daalder, Rene 81
Daans, Lara 123
d'Abo, Maryam 16, 133, 162, 179
Dabrowski, Wojciech 67
Dacey, Jack 71
Dacoda, Chayse 52
Dad, the Angel and Me 205
Daggett, Jensen 146

Daghi, Mikal 139
Dagorl, Philip 182
Dahl, Julia 140
Dahlgreen, Jack 141
Dai, Frederick 84
Daily, Bill 92, 93
Daisy Productions 101
Dakin, Kymberly 168
Dakota, Tony 100
Dale, Jennifer 60
Dallas 92, 119
Dallas, Paul 140
Dalton, Ninkey 78
Dalton, Phyllis 16
Dalton, Wally 73, 176
Daltrey, Roger 193
Daly, Brian 23
Dalzell, Arch R. 109, 143
Dalzell, Dennis 129, 193
Damn Yankees 15
Damon, Cathryn 124
Damon, Craig 88
Damon, Una 108
Damsker, Gary 42, 71
Damski, Mel 41
Dan, Andrew R. 24
Dan Curtis Productions 44, 49, 59, 132, 136, 184, 185
Dan Goodman Productions 165
Dan Redler Productions 94
Dan Wigutow Productions 29
Danaher-Dorr, Karen 54
Dance, Charles 212
Dancy, Patrick 29
Dandelion Productions 180
D'Andrea, John 171
Dane, Ann 128
Dane, Lawrence 24
Dangar, Henry 58
D'Angelo, Beverly 119
Danger Island 45, 217
Dangler, Anita 127
Daniel, Ann 195
Daniel H. Blatt Productions 48
Daniels, Alex 104
Daniels, David 165
Daniels, J.D. 152
Daniels, Jeff 55
Daniels, Marc 143
Daniels, Robert A. 106
Daniels, Steven E. 195
Daniels, William 107, 150
Danielsen, Dins 199
Danielson, Dan 152
Dano, Royal 125
Danova, Yelena 28
Danson, Ted 80, 212
Dante, Joe 195
D'Antonio, Joanne 57
Danylkiw, John 94, 158
Danza, Tony 135
Dao, Catherine Jah Fong 117
Daprocida, Rob 142
D'Aquila, Diane 145
D'Arby, Josephine 177
Darby, Kim 58, 141
Darga, Chris 200
Daring, Mason 48

Dario, Tony 141
Dark Avenger 205
Dark Night of the Scarecrow 205
Dark Planet 45
Dark Reflection 205
The Dark Secret of Harvest Home 205
Dark Shadows 56, 60, 72, 80, 107, 134, 178, 212
Dark Skies 139
The Darker Side of Terror 46
Darkman 121, 205
Darling, Joan 189
Darling, Pat 167
Darlow, Linda 184
Darragh, Barbara 86
Darragh, Kristin 86
Darren, James 38
Darroch, Marcia 137
Darrow, Henry 98
Daryl, John 102
Dassas, Marc 77
Datcher, Alex 103, 110
Datillo, Kristen 35
Dau, Brigitta 9, 93
Daughter of Darkness 46
Daughter of the Mind 205
Daughton, James 71
Daunton, Jeffrey 153
Davalos, Elyssa 79
Davalos, Raul 39
Dave Bell Associates 52
Davenport, Kevin 166
Davenport, Nigel 36, 59
Davey, John 103
Davich, Martin 175
David Wickes TV 102
David, Golda 102
David, Jeff 42
David, Mihaela 112
David, Nick 65
David, Ted 158
David, Thayer 165
David, Zoltan 5
Davids, Paul 153
Davidson, Bret 194
Davidson, Doug 96
Davidson, Jack 52
Davidson, Jim 43
Davidson, Martin 54
Davidson, Suzanne 124
Davie, Brian 141
Davies, Deddie 31
Davies, E.R. 67
Davies, Gary Michael 13
Davies, Geraint Wyn 24, 74, 185
Davies, Jackson 93
Davies, John Rhys 184
Davies, Valentine 124
Davis, Bette 205, 210
Davis, Brad 35, 161
Davis, Cecil 88
Davis, Charles 118
Davis, Charles R. (art director/production design) 94, 192
Davis, Dave 104
Davis, David 158
Davis, Dawn M. 152

Davis, Dilsey 174
Davis, Don (music) 89, 109, 152, 154
Davis, Don S. 139
Davis, Dru 29
Davis, Duane 5, 71
Davis, Gary Lee 197
Davis, George W. 62
Davis, Harry 67
Davis, Joe 50
Davis, John (producer) 187
Davis, John Walter 6
Davis, Kristin 7
Davis, Martin 120
Davis, Marty 78
Davis, Michael 22
Davis, Mimi 156
Davis, Ossie 13, 130, 165
Davis, Richard (producer) 155
Davis, Rick 7
Davis, Roderick 201
Davis, Roger 35, 106, 107
Davis, Sammy, Jr. 6, 144
Davis, Sherry 10
Davis, Suzanne 73
Davis, Taryn 161
Davis, Ted 136
Davis, Terry 80
Davis, Viveka 191, 192
Davis, Warwick 64, 80
Davis, William B. 100
Davis-Reed, Timothy 19
Davison, Bruce 111
Davison, Michelle 5
Davyd 183
Dawber, Pam 77
Day, Gerry 187
Day, Lynda 67
Day, Paul G. 123
Day, Robert 96, 151
Day, Shannon 81
The Day After 205
Day-O! 47
Daybreak 47, 110
Dayton, June 32, 43
Daza-Paris, Livia 66
Dead Again 61
Dead By Midnight 47, 173
The Dead Can't Lie 217
The Dead Don't Die 48
Dead Fire 49
Dead of Night 49, 185
Dead Weekend 50
The Dead Zone 169
Deadlocked: Escape from Zone 14 205, 217
The Deadly Bees 106
The Deadly Dream 205
Deadly Love 50
Deadly Messages 206
A Deadly Vision 206
Deak, Michael S. 22, 75
Dean, Gerry 139
Dean, Joel 186
Dean, Rick 136
Dean, Robertson 28, 87
Dean R. Koontz' Servants of Twilight 206

Deane, Howard 162
Dear, Oliver 104
Dear, Susan 104
Dear, William 104
Dearth, Bill 36
Death at Love House 206
Death Dreams 50
Death Game 206
"A Death in the Family" 150
The Death of Ocean View Park 206
The Death of the Incredible Hulk 184
Death Ray 2000 206
Death Takes a Holiday 51
Deathmoon 206
DeBelles, Greg 155
De Bello, John 13, 33
DeBenning, Burr 38
Debney, John 57, 170
Debra Wiseman 126
De Brabant, Jimmy 177
De Broux, Lee 193
De Camp, Rosemary 178
Decannett, Christopher 76
De Carlo, Yvonne 87, 127
Decca, Anghel 186
DeCinces, William D. 151
DeClie, Xavier 140
De Condia, Mario 155
DeCoteau, David 76
DeDio, Joey 179
Dedy, Mary Ann 10
Dee, John 21
Dee, Rosina M. 183
Dee, Ruby 165
Deek, James D. 149
Deems, Mickey 127
Deep Red 52
DeFaria, Walt 28
De Felitta, Frank 189
Defenders of Earth 120
De Fonseco, Carolyn 155
DeForest, Calvert 63
Degan, Justin 102
DeGovia, Jack 141
Degradi, Don 116
DeGuere, Philip 56
Degus, Robert J. 186
De Jong, Gerine 180
DeKay, Tim 152
DeLain, Marguerite 118
Delan, Anthony 83
De Lancie, John 52, 119
Delaney, Kim 54, 162
Delaney, Leon 107
DeLano, Michael 44
Delany, Dana 199
De La Pena, E.J. 68
De La Torre, Dale 104
De Laurentis, Robert 24
Delavanti, Cyril 43
Delay, John 60
Delegall, Bob 56
Delgado, Richard 179
DelHoyo, George 44
Dell, Gabriel, Jr. 140
Delorme, Julies 66
DelRey, Lester 40

Del Ruth, Thomas 178
Del Sol, Gerry 158
DeLuise, Peter 123
DeMann, Frederick 62
De Marchi, Emilio 166
Demarest, William 58
De Martino, Claude 134
De Martino, Kelly 29
DeMartino, Mike 85
DeMauro, Gino 99
DeMave, Jack 46
Demetral, Chris 163
DeMichele, Mark 152
DeMita, John 35
Demme, Jonathan 11
Demmings, Pancho 19, 91
The Demon Murder Case 52, 83
"Demon with a Glass Hand" 164
De Mornay, Rebecca 159
Dempsey, Patrick 187
Dempsey, Rick 75
Dempster, Camilla 41
DeMunn, Jeffrey 62, 82
Denis, Burke 95, 180
Denis, Neil 23
Denise, Gita 59
Denison, Anthony John 69
Denney, Jon S. 94
Dennis, John 145
Dennis, Joshua 189
Dennis, Leslie 30
Dennis, Sandy 162
Dennis Hammer Productions 109
Dennison, Anthony John 35
Densham, Pen 114, 142
Denver, Bob 98
Depala, Tim 200
De Pencier, Miranda 82
De Pinto, Joey 69
Deragon, Lyne 77
DeRose, Chris 119
D'Errico, Donna 128
Derrington, Michael 153
DeSantis, Patrick 140
De Santis, Stanley 200
Des Barres, Michael 52
Desbiens, Linda 112
DeShan, Katie 29
DeShields, Andre 92
DeShields, Jack 71, 178
Desire the Vampire 217
DeSoto, Rosana 152
DeSouza, Noel 119
De Souza, Steven E. 105
De Souza Productions 105
Desselle, Natalie 37
Destro, Pat 114
Destry, John Blackwell 134
Details (magazine) 199
Deters, Tom 193
Detreaux, Tamara 58
Dettmann, Andrew 86
Devane, William 180, 206
Deveaux, Nathaniel 61
Devenney, Scott 27
Devereaux, Jan 51
Deverell, Tamara 157
DeVico, Robert 40

The Devil and Miss Sarah 53
Devil Dog: The Hound of Hell 53
The Devil in Connecticut 53
Deville, Paul R. 125
The Devil's Child 54
The Devil's Daughter 206
Devil's Food 54
Devine, Aidan 185
Devon, Eric 94
DeVorzon, Barry 192
Dewey, Brian 61
DeWinter, Jo 143, 144
DeWolfe, Thomas 55
Dey, Susan 30, 50
DeYoung, Cliff 117, 169
DeZarn, Tim 10, 92, 154
Diablo, Jason 134
Diakun, Alex 59
Diamond, Arnold 68, 177
Diamond, Don 105
Diamond, Jack 190
Diamond, Ken 200
Diaz, Edward 73
Di Berardo, Ennio 28
DiCenzo, George 135
Di Ciaula, Pia 50, 195
Di Cicco, Jessica 94
Dick, Andy 61
Dick Clark Film Group, Inc. 51
Dick Clark Productions 53
Dickens, Charles 13, 36, 62, 127
Dickerson, Albert T., III 201
Dickerson, George 51
Dickinson, Angie 118, 135, 199
Dickinson, Dwayne 141
Dickinson, Peter 207
Dickson, Billy 18, 108
Dickson, Gordon R. 207
Didiano, Piero 66
Didsbury, Ray 38
Diehl, John 12
Dielsi, Frank 93
Dierkop, Charles 38
Dietlein, Marsha 198
Diewold, Lauren 134
DiFranco, Tom 66
Diggle, Tim 102
Digital Drama 25
Dignan, Patricia Rose 64
Digood, Michael 29
Dill, William 120
Dillman, Bradford 42, 67, 125
Dillon, Barbara 125
Dillon, Brendan 48, 193
Dillon, Thom 102
Dills-Vozoff, Lorinne 97
DiMarco, Tony 96
Dimitri, Nick 135
Dimitri, Richard 90
Dimond, A.S. 78
Dimopoulos, Stephen 61
DiMucco, Brian 125
Dinwiddie, Traci 174
Diol, Susan 10
Dion, Debra 112
Di Pasquale, James 134
DiPego, Gerald 51, 125, 175, 184
DiPego, Justin 51, 125, 175

Dirkson, Douglas 14
The Dirty Dozen 114
The Disappearance of Flight 412 206
Disasters in Time 55, 217
Disher, Catherine 83, 147
Disney 82; Channel 27, 81, 112, 137, 138, 170, 180, 189, 200, 207, 211, 212; Television 63, 125
DiStefano, David 42
DiStefano, James 154
Ditko, Steve 56
Dittman, Wanda 108
Dixon, Glenn 66
Dixon, Jeff 95
Dixon, Paul 188, 192
Dixon, Richard 102
Djola, Badja 108
D'lyn, Shae 74
Do or Die Productions, Inc. 49
Dobbs, George 152
Dobicheff, Vernon 122
Dobkin, Kaela 29
Dobkin, Larry 153
Dobkins, Sara 135
Dobson, Peter 21
Dobtcheff, Vernon 67
Dochtermann, Rudy 133
Dr. Doolittle 58
Dr. Franken 55
Dr. Scorpion 206
Dr. Strange 56
Doctor Who 37, 57
Doctor Who (series) 42, 57, 68
Dodson, Eric 102
Doduk, Alex 57
Doel, Frances 7
Doerr, James 53
Dog's Best Friend 57
Dolan, Trent 39
Dolenz, Micky 116
D'Olivera, Damon 157
Dollar, Caroline 47
Donaghue, Dick 90
Donahue, Elinor 97
Donahue, Troy 113
Donally, Andrew 121
Dondertman, John 54, 94
Done, Jason 122
Donham, David 78
Donnenfeld, Marc 53
Donner, Clive 16, 18, 36, 164, 177
Donner, Richard 196
Donner, Robert 8, 88
Donohoe, Amanda 107
Donohue, Angela 134
Donor 206
Donovan, Elisa 63
Donovan, Martin 51
Donovan, Michael
Donovan, Ron 180
Donovan, Tate 175
Don't Be Afraid of the Dark 58
Don't Go to Sleep 206
Doohan, James 108
Dooley, Paul 14, 80
Doom Runners 58, 110
Doomsday Rock 206

D'Or, Daniel 66
D'Or, Nicole 66
Doran, Ann 49
Doran, Takayo 55
Dore, Robert 118
Doresa, Reginald 180
Dorff, Holly 167
Dorff, Steve 9, 10, 94
Dorff, Tom 53
Dorian, Antonia 194, 196
Dorman, Jeff 187
Dorn, Cynthia 99
Dorn, Dolores 130
Dorn, Michael 12, 121
Dorochuk, Ivan 190, 191
Dortch, Ron 27
Dotrice, Roy 115
Dotson, Rhonda 97
Dott, James 97
Double, Double Toil and Trouble 59
Doucette, Jeff 19
Doucette, John 178
Dougherty, Charles 6
Dougherty, Joseph 17, 33, 201
Dougherty, Ralph 178
Douglas, Brandon 137
Douglas, D.C. 62
Douglas, Diana 130
Douglas, Donald 78
Douglas, Freddie 138
Douglas, James B. 12
Douglas, Jeffrey 171
Douglas, Jerry 48
Douglas, Kirk 103
Douglas, Melvyn 51
Douglas, Michael 216
Douglas, Robert 148
Douglas, Sarah 59, 168, 181, 192
Douglas S. Cramer Co. 34, 129, 157
Douglass, Robyn 38
Doukas, Nike 154
Dourif, Brad 63, 91, 199
Dow, Bill 39
Dow, Gary 174
Dow, Lauren 101
Dow, Tony 5
Dowdell, Robert 38
Dowds, Stewart 180
Down, Lesley-Anne 22
Downes, Robin Atkin 19
Downey, Roma 86, 204
Downing, David 33
Downing, James 104
Doyle, Christopher 180
Doyle, David 75, 98, 124, 172
Doyle, Jerry 18, 19, 140, 141
Doyle, Kevin 165
Doyle, Tim 158
D'Pella, Pamela 10
Drachkovitch, Rasha 163
Dracula 59
Drady, Dorothy 141
Draganescu, Costica 112
The Dragon and the George 207
Drake, Colin 33, 78
Drake, Dolores 57, 93
Drake, Jim 78

Drake, Tom 38
Drake-Massey, Bebe 103
Draper, Eamon 90
Draper, Rob 185
Drasnin, Rick 126
Drasnin, Robert 43
Drason, Ric 181
Dreager, Reg 74
Dream House 60
Dreelen, John Van 42
Dreger, Reg 190
Dreier, Alex 173
Dreith, Dennis 78
Dremann, Beau 67
Drescher, Fran 171
Drischell, Ralph 198
Driscoll, Eddie 136
Driscoll, Ralph 55
Dromgoole, Patrick 31
Drozda, Petr 49
Drummond, Alice 47
Drury, James 53
Dry, Jodie 70
Drykuss, Patrick 155
Dualstar Productions 59
DuBarry, Denise 46
Dubin, Charles S. 182
DuBois, Marta 166, 84
Duborg, Kathleen 141
Dubrow, Donna 148
Duchowny, Roger 101
Duchowny Dow Films 101
Duckwall, Dennis C. 145
Ducommun, Rick 158
Duff, Denice 152
Duff, Victoria 200
Duffy, Jack 74, 191
Duffy, Mark 160
Duffy, Patrick 6, 118, 205
Duffy, Thomas F. 198
Duffy, William 97
Dugan, Charles 158
Dugan, Dan 195
Dugan, Dennis 158
Duggan, Andrew 178
Duggan, Bryan 181
Duhame, Zachary 181
Duhaney, Kevin 93
Dukakis, John 178
Dukakis, Olympia 213
Duke, Patty 13, 79, 159
Dukes, David 117, 186
Dulany, Caitlin 89
Dullea, Keir 29
Du Maurier, Daphne 114
Dumm, J. Rickley 105
Dumont, James 28
Dunard, David S. 109
Dunbar, John 146, 165
Duncan, Alastair 182
Duncan, Angus 142
Duncan, Arlene 12
Duncan, Kirk 39
Duncan, Lois 171, 172
Duncan, Rob 174
Dundara, David 104
Dunham, Duwayne 81
Dunham, Stephanie 168

Duning, George 25
Dunk, Albert J. 93
Dunk, Bert 83
Dunn, Bill 177
Dunn, Carolyn 24
Dunn, Ian 80
Dunn, Liam 73, 106, 124
Dunn, Roger 74, 82, 112
Dunne, Griffin 13, 14
Dunphy, Paul 135
Dunsmore, Rosemary 110
Dunst, Kirsten 182
Dunstan, Tom 78
Dupeyroux, Jacques 86
Duplicates 60
DuPois, Starletta 36
Duran, Dan 74, 104, 191
Durand, Gerry 39
Durante, Morris 66
Durbin, John 15, 159, 200
Durning, Charles 101
Durrant Fox Productions 190
Durrell, Michael 8, 191, 192
Dusenberry, Ann 144
Dutson, Debbie 178
Duvall, Shelley 157
Duvall, Susan 96
Dvoracek, Zdenek 49
Dwyer, David 174
Dye, Dale 201
Dying to Remember 60, 61
Dysan, Michael 190
Dysart, Richard 72
dystopia 47, 110
Dzundza, George 156, 162

Eads, Paul 130
Earth II 61, 62
Earth 2 59, 135
East, Jeff 171
Easterling, Bret 126
Eastlin, Steve 39
Easton, Sheena 103
Eastwood, Jayne 54, 74, 82
Eastwood, Laurence 128
Eaton, Bekka 47
Eatwell, Brian 41
Ebbie 62, 127
Eberhardt, Thom 188
Ebsen, Buddy 88
EC Comics 197
Eccles, Aimee 103
Ecclesine, Steve 120
Echikunwoke, Megalyn 142
Eckstein, George 52
Eckstein, Hannah 76
Eckstein, Paul 172
Economou, Michael 52, 78
Ecotopia BV 81
Ed Wood 187
Edelman, Matthew 73
Eden, Barbara 92, 93, 167, 172, 207, 216
Edgar, Nicholas 149
Edgar J. Scherick Associates 151, 167, 168
Edgcomb, James 78
Edgell, Brittaney 185

Edith, Mary Burrell 94
Edner, Ashley 62
Edrys, Mark 37
Edson, Richard 16
Edward, John Allen 161
Edward, Monique 109
Edwards, Barbara Lee 185
Edwards, Bob 31
Edwards, Fiona 71
Edwards, Gail 103
Edwards, Jason 67
Edwards, Luke 137
Edwards, Michael 140
Edwards, Neville 190
Edwards, Rona 40
Edwards, Ronnie Claire 71, 80
Edwards, Vaughan 176
Edwards, Vince 161
Edwards, William 152
Eels, Samuel 175
Efros, Mel 154
Egan, Barbara 135
Egan, Michael Patrick 81
Egan, Richard 90
Egan, Susan 61
Eggby, David 169
Eggert, Nicole 12, 15, 92
EGM Films International 45, 179
Ehlers, Corky 135
Ehlers, Heather 175
Ehrlich, Peter 85
Eick, David 86, 120
Eigenberg, David 47
Eilbacher, Bobby 25
Eilbacher, Cindy 43
Eilbacher, Lisa 165, 178
Eilber, Janet 136
Eisele, Robert 195
Eisen, Bruce 185
Eisen, Hal 82
Eisenberg, Aron 13, 29
Eisenmann, Ike 53
Eisenstock, Alan 15
Eisner, Will 214
El-Shenawi, Ahmed 177
Elam, Jack 76
Elam, Ousaun 120
Elbling, Peter 29, 167
Elcar, Dana 72
Elek, Zoltan 15
Elemental Films 198
Eley, Herb 168
Elferink, Joanna 102
Elias, Hector 126
Elikann, Larry 186
Elise, Marie 16
Elizalde, John 12
Elk, Rob 195
Elkins, Hillard 94
Ellenbogen, Eric 126
Elliot, David 13
Elliot, Jack 41
Elliot, Marianna 10
Elliott, Alison 121
Elliott, Brennan 60
Elliott, Mike 11, 25, 128, 136, 137, 173, 175, 196
Elliott, Monty 144

Elliott, Nick 102
Elliott, Pat 136
Elliott, Ross 43
Elliott, Stephen 147
Elliott, Tom 46
Ellis, James 112
Ellis, Michael 138
Ellison, Harlan 19, 20, 71
Elrady, Joe 76
Elson, Andrea 67
Elsworth, Simon 169
Elwenspoek, Hans 85
Emanuel, Jason 15
Emanuel, Michael 152
Embree, Colleen 75
Emelle, Michelyn 127
Emerson, Jonathan 186
Emerson, Sasha 186
Emery, James 162
Emery, Julie 35
Emes, Ian 128
Emilfork, Daniel 177
Emma's Wish 62
Emmet G. Lavery Productions 75
Encarnacion, Jay Jay 200
Encarnacion, Kimi 200
Encino Man 63
Encino Woman 63
Endore, Guy 67
Endoso, Kenny 105
Engel, Mitch 168
Engel, Roy 109
Engelman, Bob 67
Engelman, Tom 161
Engemann, Shannon 102
England, Audie 113, 196
England, Bryan 73, 152, 163, 190
English, Diane 111
Englund, Morgan 136
Englund, Robert 71, 192
Ennals, Roger 81
Enright, Don 50, 137
Ensley, David 188, 194
Entertainment Partners 36
Entwisle, Julie 169
Epcar, Richard 137
Epper, Tony 41, 126
Epps, Omar 47
Epstein, Allen S. 58, 59, 91, 100
Epstein, Jon 88
E/R 43
Erbe, Micky 50, 195
Eric, James 76
Erickson, Kathleen 114
Ermey, R. Lee 93
Ernest, Karl 71
Ertmanes, Victor 83
Erwin, Bill 99
Escape To Witch Mountain (1995) 63, 69
Escape to Witch Mountain (1972) 64
Escoffier, Jean Yves 201
Eser, Janine 122
Espinoza, Eddie 181
Esposito, Giancarlo 142
Essex, Harry 101
Estabrook, Christine 163

Estes, Larry 12, 50, 122, 197, 201
Estrada, Erik 61
Estrin, Jonathan 147
E.T. 88, 93
Eustermann, Jim 33
Evanko, Edward 45, 105
Evans, Barry 128
Evans, David Mickey 104
Evans, John 17, 54
Evans, John H. 69
Evans, Matt 112
Evans, Michael 78
Evans, Robert Briscoe 87
Evans, Terrence 8
Evans, Troy 80, 87, 165
Everett, Chad 96, 139, 166, 197
Everett, Rupert 16
Everhard, Nancy 184
Evigan, Briana 90
Evigan, Greg 90, 212, 214
The Evil Dead 117, 122
Ewen, Lesley 139
Ewing, Robert 51, 184
The Ewok Adventure 64, 65
The Ewoks/Droids Adventure Hour 64
Ewoks: The Battle for Endor 64
Excalibur 16, 32
Exo-Man 65
The Exorcist 162, 172
Eye of the Demon 217
Eyemark Entertainment 149
The Eyes of Charles Sands 206
Eyes of Terror 207, 217
Eyler, Scott C. 53
Eyre, Marcus 67
Eyre, Peter 122
Eyres, John 45, 179
Eyres, Paul 45, 179

Factor, Alan Jay 162
Factor, Nicholas 155
Fagan, Ronald J. 48, 53, 71
Fagerbakke, Bill 165, 189
Fahey, Jeff 104
Fahlenbock, Megan 104
Fairchild, Morgan 76, 96, 166
Fairman, Michael 92
Faison, Frankie 168
Faison, Matthew 152, 162
Falcon's Gold 207, 217
Falk, Harry 88, 120
Falk, Lee 120
Fall, Timothy 21, 69
The Fall of the House of Usher 11, 65
Falling Fire 66, 217
Falzon, Charles 157
Family Channel 37, 38, 57, 115, 117, 118, 205, 206, 208
Fancy, Richard 69, 130, 153
Fann, Al 94, 130
Fantastic Four 56
Fantastic Voyage 54
Fantasy Island 213, 215
Fantasy Island (series) 2, 207
Farago, Joe 67
Faraizl, Adam 100
Farentino, Debrah 134

Farentino, James 144
Farid, Zaid 200
Farkas, Jo 109
Farley, Elizabeth 42
Farmer, Frank 97
Farmer, Gary 144
Farnon, Shannon 131
Farnsworth, Richard 170, 207
Farrar, John 125
Farrell, Henry 90
Farrell, J.P. 105
Farrell, Keith 150
Farrell, Mike 148
Farrell, Terry 113, 114
Farrow, Tisa 96
Farrow, Yvonne 120
Fassler, Ron 7–10
Fast, Russ 35, 60
Fatal Attraction 195
Fatherland 207
Faulkner, James 121
Faulstich, Patrick 176
Fauntleroy, Don E. 168
Faust, Christina 159
Faustino, David 10
Faustino, Nichole 130
Faustino, Randy 65
Fear 66
Fear No Evil 67, 151
Fearnley, Neill 104
Fears, Carolyn 188
Febre, Louis 57, 182
Feders, Sid 39
Fee, Melinda 11, 98
Feero, Robert 103
Fehr, Brendan 141
Feigelson, J.D. 36, 42, 109
Feinstein, Alan 189
Feldman, Corey 105, 113
Feldman, Edward S. 125
Feldner, Sheldon 69, 151
Fellows, Arthur 76, 77
Fellows, Susannah 187
Fellows-Keegan Company 76, 77
Felton, David 127
Felton, Norman 20
Fenady, Andrew J. 25, 171
Fenady Associates 25, 171
Fenjves, Pablo F. 54
Fenn, Sherilyn 134
Fennell, Tony 201
Fenton, Simon 107
Feore, Colm 142
Ferber, Mel 39
Ferguson, Allyn 41, 83
Ferguson, Anna 176
Ferguson, Blair 80
Ferguson, David 185
Ferguson, Matthew 77, 82
Fernandes, João 52, 157
Fernandes, Miguel 114
Fernandez, Manny 7, 26
Fernandez, Margarita 64
Fernberger, Peter 24, 111, 133
Fernetz, Charlene 155
Ferraez, Marcos Antonio 50
Ferrara, Ed 128
Ferrer, Jose 42, 43, 65

Ferrer, Miguel 29, 146, 159, 165, 169
Ferrier, Noel 128
Ferrigno, Carla 51
Ferrigno, Lou 51, 94, 95, 150, 184
Ferris, Walter 52
Ferrone, Richard 53
Ferrucci, Frank 141
Ferry, David 50
Ferry, Dawn 122
Fetner, Carole Katz 154
Feuerman, Tod 89, 117, 169
Fiddick, Kelly 50
Fiedel, Brad 27, 123, 144
Fiedler, Eric 70
Fiedler, John 90
Field, Jordyn E. 81
Field, Margaret 171
Field, Ted 161
Field of Dreams 213
Fielder, Pat 78
Fields, Christopher John 54, 200
Fields, James 155
Fields, Joel 61
Fields, Kim 105
Fields, Lindsey 78
Fields, Star 165
Fierstein, Harvey 53
Fifer, Scott 188
Figueron, Hector 124
Filerman, Michael 42
Filerman Productions 43
Filip, Carmen 21
Filippone, Lucy 94
Filmline International 114
Fillerman, Michael 186
Filmways 125
Finch, Jon 121
Fink, Eric 94
Finlay, Anita 136
Finlay, Frank 36, 177
Finn, John 167
Finnegan, Bill 18, 171
Finnegan, Joe 96
Finnegan, Pat 18, 171
Finnegan, Tom 95
Finnegan Associates 172
Finnegan/Pinchuk Company 18, 101, 154
Finnell, Michael 195
Finnerman, Gerald Perry 53, 73
Finney, Jack 49, 117
Finta, Brady 92
A Fire in the Sky 207
The Fire Next Time 110, 207
Fisch, Irwin 30
Fischer, David 15, 59
Fischer, Don 80, 152
Fischer, Lisa 27
Fischer, Nancy 195
Fischer, Preston 53
Fisher, Brad 41
Fisher, Bruce M. 91
Fisher, Frances 16
Fisher, George 7, 10
Fisher, Jim 87
Fisher, Jody 140
Fisher, Joely 40

Fisher, John Douglas 76
Fisher, Kate 128
Fisher, Kenneth 189
Fisher, Lola 15
Fisher, Mary Ann 90
Fisher, Peter S. 109
Fitts, Rick 79, 97, 106
Fitzgerald, Rick 181
Fitzpatrick, Richard 38
Flacks, Niki 111
Flagg, Fanny 129
Flanagan, Fionnula 50, 64
Flanagan, Frances 170
Flanders, Ed 156
Flanery, Bridget 140
The Flash 43, 98
Flash Gordon 146, 207
Flash Gordon—The Greatest Adventure of Them All 207
Flashframe 217
Flashner, Graham 145
Flashner/Gernon Productions 145
Flax, Charlie 111
Flax, Jonathan 111
Flax, Kenny 111
Flax, Roger 111
Fleck, John 18
Fleckenstein, John 115
Fleder, Gary 40
Fleers, Eric 52
Fleischmann, Herbert 85
Flender, Rodman 25
Fletcher, Bill 119
Fletcher, Brendan 185
Fletcher, Louise 84, 85, 168
Fletcher, Michael 82
Fletcher, Page 83
Flextech Television 153
The Flight of Dragons 207
The Flight of Dragons (book) 207
Flinn III, John C. 19, 20
Flippen, Keith 117
Flitton, Aisling 83
Flood, Joe 27
Florek, Dave 27
Flores, Erika 31
Flores, Von 104
Flower, George "Buck" 21, 75, 103, 125, 178
Flynn, Bill 146
Flynn, Colleen 54
Flynn, J. Michael 101, 180
Flynn, Steven 10, 29
FNM Films 67, 87, 139
Fo, Kelly 59
Fogel, Jerry 53
Folger, Mark 26, 45, 71
Follett, Ken 209
Fon, Gobi 107
Fonda, Peter 174, 175
Fondacaro, Phil 59
Fonseca, Greg 167
Fontaine, Michael 119
Fontana, Linda 16
Fonvielle, Lloyd 79
Forbes, Richard 98
Forbidden Beauty 217
Ford, Fritz 65

Ford, Graham 41
Ford, Harrison 144, 145
Ford, Judith M. 81
Ford, Maria 45, 196
Ford, Stan 34
Ford, Steven 19
Ford, Tony 18
Foreman, Michelle 66
Foreman, Philip Dean 163
Forest, Irene 44
Forever Knight 24, 52, 74, 130
Forke, Farrah 23, 104
Forman, Robin 39
Formica, S. Michael 130
Forrest, Frederic 79
Forrest, Irene 10
Forrest, Steve 32
Forrester, David 168
Forrow, Tony 58
Forsett, Theo 120
Forsnof, J.W. "Corkey" 152
Forster, Robert 46, 78
Forsyth, Rosemary 37
Forsythe, John 213
44 Blue Productions 163
Forward, Robert 72
Forward, William 36
Foster, Alan 171
Foster, Buddy 25
Foster, David W. 20
Foster, Jodie 69
Foster, Meg 113
Foster, Robert 40, 91
Foster, Steffen 23
Foster, Stephen C. 152
Foulger, Byron 118
The Four Diamonds 207
4-Ward Productions 33
Fowler, Shea 99
Fox 7, 27, 57, 67, 71, 73, 74, 82, 87, 97, 105, 114, 120, 128, 139, 145, 148, 186, 196, 198, 204, 205, 211, 215; Family Channel 115, 128, 141, 142; Television 71
Fox, Charles 129, 172
Fox, Coleen 23
Fox, Donna 70
Fox, Edward 80
Fox, Huckleberry 27
Fox, James 80
Fox, John J. 162
Fox, Jorja 89
Fox, Michael 99
Fox, Peter 127, 188
Fox Unicorn 80
Fox West Pictures 114
Fox-Brenton, David 30
Foxstar 8
Foxworth, Robert 148
Foxx, Redd 74, 75
Fradis, Anatoly 85
Fraim, Tracy 154
Fralick, David Shark 28
Fran, Mary 93
Franchuk, Ria 180
Franciosa, Tony 44, 75
Francis, Al 78, 189
Francis, Anne 117

Francis, Derek 36
Francis, Ivor 109, 132, 165
Francis, Jacklyn 66
Francis, Missy 75
Francis, Ryan 167
Francisco, Chianese 16
Franciscus, James 131
Francks, Cree Summer 21
Francks, Don 145
Francois, Neblis 183
Frand, Harvey 24
Frandsen, Jano 93
Frank, Ben 16
Frank, Charles 42, 54
Frank, David Michael 99, 101, 181
Frank, Gary 89, 115
Frank, Kevin 38
Franke, Christopher 18, 19, 20, 54, 122, 169
Franke, Jay Anthony 61
Frankel, Ernie 79
Frankel-Bolen Productions 79
Franken, Steve 118, 171
Frankenstein 55, 56, 67, 68
Frankenstein Island 171
Frankenstein: The College Years 67
Frankenstein: The True Story 68
Franklin, John 182
Franklin, Pamela 213
Franklin, Richard 154
Frankovich, Peter 109
Fraser, Brendan 35
Fraser, Brent 144
Fraser, Duncan 51, 84, 139
Fraser, Genevieve 135
Fraser, Ian 18
Frates, Robin 143
Fratkin, Stuart 93
Frazer, Jayne 35
Frazier, Jimmy B. 21
Freaky Friday 64, 68, 200
Freaky Friday (novel) 69
Fred Silverman Co. 163
Frederick S. Pierce Company 187
Fredericks, Kyle 25
Frederickson, Cully 181
Freeborn, Mark 61, 170
Freedman, Robert L. 37
Freeman, A.J. 180
Freeman, Clint 99
Freeman, Eric 75
Freeman, Jeff 12, 52
Freeman, Jonathan 66
Freeman, Mickey 183
Freeman, Mike 41
Freeman, Richard A. 21
Frehley, Ace 107
Freimuth, Doug 104
Fremes, John 149, 201
French, Bruce 44
French, Tami 76
Fresco, David 120
Frewer, Matt 49, 73, 148, 165, 209
Frick, Elise 23
Fridell, Squire 90
Fried, Gerald 164
Fried, Myra 147
Friedgen, Elliot 159

Fries, Charles 30, 90, 96, 105, 121, 130, 136, 156, 159, 164, 165, 167, 180, 197
Fries, Debi 96
Fries, Thomas 30, 167
Fries Entertainment 30, 105, 167, 180
Friesen, John 82
Fright Night 11, 169
Frishman, Daniel 64
Fritz, Nikki 175
Frizzell, Lou 53
Froelich, Jake 174
Froelich, Sam 174
Frolov, Diane 8, 192
From the Dead of Night 69
Frontiere, Chad 175
Frontiere, Dominic 118
Frost, Alan 162
Frost, Warren 97, 165
Fruitman, Sarah 195
Fry, Darnell 88
Fry, Taylor 50
Frye, Virgil 34
Fuchs, Fred 138, 198
Fudge, Alan 36, 78, 120
Fuest, Robert 151
Fugelsang, John 188
Fugere, Elizabeth 81
The Fugitive 2, 56, 76, 79, 150, 171, 209
Fuhrer, Martin 139
Fuisz, Robert E. 36
Full Eclipse 69
Fuller, John G. 75
Fuller, Jonathan 172
Fuller, Kurt 125
Fullerton, Richard 117, 168
Funches, Garvin 167
Funk, Terry 180
Furey, John 80
Furia, John, Jr. 96
Furia-Oringer Productions 96
Furlan, Mira 18, 19, 20
Furlong, John 126
Furst, Stephen 20
Furtok, Evelyn 155
The Fury Within 70
Fusco, Paul 146
Futlon, Allegra 127
Future Cop 41, 42, 71
Futuresport 207
F/X 188
Fyfe, Jim 8

G., Errol 191
Gabai, Richard 75, 196
Gabay, Eli 134
Gadry, Diane 67
Gaffney, George 117
Gagne, Randy 152
Gago, Jenny 7–10
Gahagan, Michelle 49
Gaigalas, Gina 139
Gail, David 70
Gail, Max 11, 44
Galactic Odyssey 71
Galan, Kathryn 47

Galante, James Joseph 6
Galasso, Chandra 13
Gale, David 201
Gale, Ed 114, 128
Gale, Lorena 61, 62
Gale, Peter 102
Galik, Denise 192
Galin, Mitchell 166, 168, 169
Galishoff, Marc B. 47
Galla, Andrzej 67
Gallagher, Clu 30
Gallagher, Dan 191
Gallagher, Dorothy A. 195
Gallagher, Grove 14
Gallagher, Megan 115
Gallagher, Peter 29, 194
Gallant, Michael O. 23, 63
Gallery, James 79
Galligan, Zach 147
Gallini, Matt 6
Gallo, Carmi 13, 31
Gallo, Fred 71
Gallo, Mario 94
Galloway, James 16
Galloway, Layla 189
Galloway, Pamela 66
Gallup, Denise 92
Gallup, Dian 92
Galov, Brett 12
Gambino, Vincent 81
Gamble, Duncan 154
Gammell, Robbin 95
Gammons, Rod 201
Gangsterworld 217
Ganis, Glenda 54, 125
Gann, Merrilyn 100
Gannon, Russell 167
Garas, Dezsö 46
Garas, Kaz 91
Garay, Soo 54
Garber, Hope 83
Garber, Victor 37
Garcia, Ernest M. 7
Garcia, Juan 10, 93
Garcia, Rene 195
Garcia, Rick 150
Garcia, Ron 9, 10, 29, 104
Garfias, Ruben 70
Garfield, David 67
Gargantua 71
Gargoyles 72
Gargula, Milan 49
Garland, Beverly 85
Garlington, Lee 194
Garner, Jack 124, 178
Garner, Josh 92
Garo, Armen 52
Garr, Teri 55, 212
Garrett, Brooke 189
Garrett, Drum 100
Garrett, Hank 123
Garrett, Leif 25
Garrett, Spencer 63
Garris, Cynthia 148, 159, 165, 194
Garris, Mick 148, 159, 165, 166, 194
Garrish, Frank 194
Garrity, Joseph T. 17
Garrott, Gil 195

Garson, Willie 47
Gartlan, Niall 92
Garvey, Ann E. 85
Garwyn, Myrna 123
The Gary Coleman Show 106
Gaucher, Trenton 189
Gaudagni, Nicki 145
Gauthier, Daniel 81
Gava, Cassandra 41
Gavigan, Sean 26
Gay, Jennifer 96
Gayheart, Rebecca 152
Gaynes, George 184
GC Group 35
Geary, Anthony 88
Geary, Cynthia 197
Geddes, David 30
Geer, Ellen 130
Geer, Noel 73, 100, 155
Geeves, Peter 102
Gehl, Drew 186
Gehring, Ted 98
Gehringer, Linda 189
Geib, Joe 185
Geiger, Barbara 166
Geiger, Peter 5, 40
Gelman, Larry 182
Gelt, Gary 94
Gelwicks, Riley 111
Gemini Man 72, 98
Generation 207
Generation X 73
Generation X (comic book) 73
Generations 144
Genesis II 73, 143, 171
Genesse, Bryan 175
Genovese, Mike 43
Gentner, Richard 194
Gentry, Donald 106
George, Brian 87
George, Clara 50
George, Geoff 25
George, Laszlo 99, 162, 186
George, Susan 40
George, William 64
Georgescu, Ion 112
Georiade, Nick 144
Geraldi, Matt 7
Gerani, Gary 194
Gerard, Will 42
Gerber, David 119
Gerdes, George 16
Gerety, Peter 53
Germain, Stephanie 194
Gernon, Ed 145
Gerstein, Ellen 93, 200
"Get Dead" 123
Get Smart Again 207
Get Smart! (1995) 128
Get Smart! (series) 207
Geter, Leo 165
Getty, Balthazar 81
Getz, John 106
Gfeller, Kenette 96
The Ghost and Mrs. Muir 44
Ghost Mom 74
Ghost of a Chance 74
The Ghost of Flight 401 75

Ghost Writer 75
Giacomazzi, Mickey 159
Gibb, Cynthia 117
Gibbons, Robert 164
Gibbons, Sandy 76
Gibbons, Sanford 152
Gibbs, Nigel 89
Gibbs, Richard 123
Gibby, Gwyneth 25
Gibson, Elan Ross 62
Gibson, Henry 129
Gibson, Kate 63
Gibson, Thomas 54, 134
Gibson, William 199
Gidley, Pamela 28
Gieb, Joe 123
Gielgud, John 31, 68, 80, 122
Giffin, Philip 115, 123
Gifford, G. Adam 20
Gifford, Ryan 145
The Gifted One 76
Giftos, Elaine 178
Gil, Arturo 128
Gilbert, Edmund 25, 135
Gilbert, Elliott 105
Gilbert, John 90, 91, 115, 173
Gilbert, Marcus 35
Gilbert, Melissa 61, 206
Gilbert, Mickey 96
Gilbert, Ron 61, 165, 175
Gilbert, Tim 180
Gilbert-Hill, Richard 154
Gilberti, Nina 128
Gilborn, Steven 55
Giler, David 196
Giles, Fiona 67
Giles, Jerry 101
Gilgreen, John 12
Gill, Elizabeth 137
Gillard, Stuart 142
Gilliam, Burton 76, 77, 116
Gilliams, Leslie 155
Gilligan's Island 208
Gillin, Linda 40, 42
Gillis, Anne Marie 27
Gillis, Jackson 179
Gillis, Kevin 190, 191
Gillott, Nick 83, 107, 149
Gilmer, Rob 44, 50
Gilmore, Patrick 176
Gimbel, Roger 72
Gimpel, Sandra 165
Ginsburg, David R. 37, 54, 70, 153
Ginter, Lindsay (Lee) 97, 140
Ginther, Mark 172, 197
Ginty, Robert 87
Gionnini, Alessandro 155
Giorla, Richard 27
Giovannucci, Paolo 155
Girard, Eyde 148
Girard, Suzanne 198
Girardin, Ray 124, 140
Girdier, Justin 122
The Girl from Mars 208
The Girl, the Gold Watch & Dynamite 76, 77
The Girl, the Gold Watch & Everything 77

Girling, Cindy 134
Girolami, Robert V. 118
Giroux, Marie 141
Giuntoli, Neil 167
Giving Up the Ghost 77
The Gladiator 208
Gladstone, Dana 105
Glascoe, Jon 82
Glass, Paul 156, 161
Glass, Robert 51, 137, 154
Glassner, Jonathan 99
Glatstein, Bert 61, 183
Glave, Karen 127
Glen Larson Productions 35
Glenn, Scott 72
Gless, Sharon 151
Glick, Mark S. 54
Glouner, Richard C. 35, 125
Glover, Barbara 115
Glover, Brian 161
Glover, John 47, 174
Glowna, Vadim 121
Glueck, Alan Jay 102
Glynn, Carlin 47
Goard, David 112
Gobel, George 6, 98
Gobruegge, Lester D. 116
Goddard, Bill 24, 94
Goddard, Trevor 113, 201
The Goddess of Love 78
Godfrey, Alan 145
Godshall, Liberty 90
Godsif, Anna 81
Godwin, Tom 40
Godzilla (1998) 72
Goetz, Tommy 140
Goggins, Walton 91
Goguen, Dave 180
Golas, Henry 16
Gold, Barry L. 104
Gold, Brandy 13, 192
Gold, Judy 87
Gold, L. Harvey 5, 73
Gold, Tracey 130
Gold of the Amazon Women 208
Goldberg, Amy 128
Goldberg, Andy 87
Goldberg, Leonard 178
Goldberg, Marcy 93
Goldberg, Whoopi 37, 107
Goldblum, Jeff 113
Golden, Bob 143
Golden, Dan 175
Golden Fox Films 183
Goldenberg, Billy 37, 58, 67, 71, 72, 131, 147, 151, 157, 178
Goldenthal, Elliot 153
Goldfinger, Michael 14, 78
Goldman, Lorry 97
Goldman, Martin 113
Goldman, Peggy 192
Goldman, Wendy 36
Goldoni, Leila 79, 164
Goldsberry, Steve 45
Goldsmith, Jerry 139
Goldsmith, Joel 194
Goldsmith, Paul 15
Goldstein, Allan A. 57

Goldstein, Jeffrey L. 126
Goldstein, Martin 32
Goldstein, Scott D. 67
Goldstein, William 12, 41
Goldthwait, Bobcat 57, 63
Goldthwait, Tasha 29
Goliath Awaits 3, 78
Golod, Jerry 41
Goman, Ray 141
Gomes, Marc 109
Gomez, Rita 150
Gonzales, Carlos 133
Gonzales-Gonzales, Pedro 21, 75
Gonzalez, Conrad M. 180
González-González, Clifton 200
Gooch, Benjamin 180
Good, Rodney 175
Good Against Evil 79
Goode, Conrad 95
Goodell, Gregory 80
Goodger, Michele 176
Gooding, Cuba, Jr. 47
Goodlett, Ken 58
Goodman, Daniel R. 165
Goodman, David 5
Goodman, Dean 66
Goodman, Dody 92
Goodman, Gary 37, 131
Goodwin, Ron 22
Goolrick, Robert 200
Goosebumps 158
Goozee, Russell 190, 191
Goranson, Linda 82, 145
Gord, Ken 177
Gordon, Barbara 190, 191
Gordon, Deni 70
Gordon, George 134
Gordon, Jim 180
Gordon, Keith 199
Gordon, Lea 196
Gordon, Marie 75
Gordon, Mark R. 115
Gordon, Mary Kathleen 201
Gordon, Pamela 7
Gordon, Ruth 115
Gordon, Stuart 46, 47
Gordon-Levitt, Joseph 87, 143
Gorman, Mari 44
Gorman, Patrick 16
Gorman, Ray K. 193
Gorman, Robert Hy 163
Gorme, Eydie 6
Gornick, Michael 168
Gorrara, Perri 147
Gorshin, Frank 78, 79
Gorton, Assheton 121
Goss, Victor 115
Gosse, Bob 111
Gossett, Louis, Jr. 93, 94
Gossett, Robert 10
Gotch, Tarquin 148
Gotham 79, 217
Gothard, Michael 67
Gotleib, Matt 115
Gottesmann, Robert 46
Gottlieb, Andrew 109
Gottlieb, Carl 162
Gottlieb, Mallory 5

Gottlieb, Sherry 50
Gough, Lloyd 156
Gough, Michael 16, 36, 37, 83
Gould, Dana 116
Gould, Duncan 102
Gould, Elliott 159
Gould, Harold 116
Gouriet, Gerald 55, 176
Gourson, Jeff 158
Gow, John 153
Goz, Isaac 79
Grace, Nicholas 122
Grace, Paul 102, 165, 178
Grace, Wayne 7
Gracen, Elizabeth 51
Graeme-Evans, Posie 58
Graf, Allan 16
Graham, Cameron 60
Graham, Elvira 94
Graham, Gary 7–10, 45
Graham, Gerrit 117, 170, 196
Graham, John R. 176
Graham, Ronald F. 170
Graham, Stephen 54
Graham, T. Max 163
Graham, Tara 198
Graham, Zane 8
Graham Scott, Peter 31
Grahame, Gloria 25
Granbery, Don 185
Grand Hotel 169
Grand Tour 217
Grande, Louis Del 38
Grandmason, Maurice 178
Granger, Stewart 35, 209
Grant, Angela 164
Grant, Cary 182
Grant, Dick 75
Grant, Faye 139, 140, 191, 192
Grant, Gretchen 27
Grant, Lee 131, 140, 164
Grant, Linda 73
Grant, Micah 88
Grant, Rainer 136
Grant, Sandra P. 93
Grant, Stacy 23
Grant, Vince 29
Grasshoff, Alex 110
Graumann, Walter 42, 43
Grave Secrets 79
Graver, Gary 106, 178
Graves, Ed 58
Graves, Peter 197
"Graveyard Rats" 185
Gray, George, III 152
Gray, Beverly 85
Gray, Bruce 99, 153
Gray, Erin 139
Gray, Jacque 200
Gray, Linda 189
Gray, Mackenzie 66, 157
Gray, Mark 190
Gray, Stephen W. 178
Grayson, Wendell 51
The Great Santa Claus Switch 133
The Greatest American Hero 23, 55, 164
Greek, Janet 19

Green, Alex 5, 59
Green, Bruce Seth 154
Green, Cathy 91
Green, Charles 67
Green, Colin 122
Green, Dorothy 160
Green, Jim 59, 91, 100
Green, Kat 61
Green, Les 125, 184
Green, Lynda Mason 96
Green, Seth 100
Green, Walon 170
Green/Epstein Productions 59, 91, 100
Greenberg, Paul 74
Greenberg, Robbie 111
Greenberg, Stephen 51
Greenblatt, Natasha 127
Greenblatt, Shon 179
Greenblatt, William R. 127, 174
Greene, David 147
Greene, Eric 178
Greene, James 164
Greene, Leon 177
Greene, M. Richard 152
Greenebaum, Elliot Moss 125
Greenfield, Barry 88
Greengrass Productions 199
Greenquist, Brad 48
Greenwood, Bobby 175
Greenwood, Bruce 40
Greenwood, Lorne 175
Gregg, Virginia 43, 118, 171
Gregory, Alan 165
Gregory, James 124
Gregory, Mary Ethel 165
Gregory, Natalie 6
Gregory, Nigel 59
Gregory, Peter 68
Greiff, Douglas 58
Greist, Kim (Kimberly) 60, 110, 152
Gremlins 147
Gress, Googy 18
Greviuox, Kevin 8, 10, 148
Grey, Elizabeth 44
Grey, Erin 43
Gribble, Bernard 149
Gribble, Bill 174
Grieco, Frank, Jr. 94, 119
Grieco, Richard 95, 197
Grierson, Ralph 81
Gries, Tom 62
Griesemer, John 168
Griev, Ben 128
Grieves, Russ 48
Grieves, Steven 187
Griffeth, Simone 120
Griffin, Brenda 10
Griffin, Gary 118
Griffin, Merv 6
Griffin, Sean 11
Griffin, Tom 53
Griffith, Andy 52, 213
Griffith, Charles 137
Griffith, James 113
Griffith, Lynn 190
Griffith, Steven 190

Griffiths, Rhoda 174
Griffiths, Roger Ashton 122
Grigsby, Garon 55
Grimes, Scott 133
Grimes, Tammy 28
Grimshaw, Jim 169
Grimsman, Geoffrey S. 168
Grinn, Sandey 150
Grizz, Pam 64
Grizzard, George 172
Grodénchik, Max 87
Grodnik, Daniel 134
Groenenberg, Edward 167
Groenenberg, Rowland 167
Grogg, Sam L. 174
Groh, David 110
Groman, Richard 75
Groom, Sam 179
Gross, Arye 179
Gross, Charles 16, 133
Gross, James 12, 41
Gross, Jim 35, 70
Gross, Kenneth H. 48
Gross, Marcy 23
Gross, Paul 187
Gross, Richard 197
Gross, Stephen 41
Gross-Weston Productions 23
Grossman, Jamie 55
Groundhog Day 37, 187
Grove, David Paul 14
Grove, Richard 137, 200
Grover, John 67
Grover, Stanley 153
Gruber, Charles 194
Gruber, John 72
Gruendemann, Eric 86
Grunberg, Greg 67
Grundy, Reuben 189
Gruska, Jay 35, 61, 183
Gruzynski, Alexander 33
Guadagni, Nicky 31, 104
Guajardo, Roberto 157
Guard, Christopher 83
Guardino, Harry 109
Guber, Peter 21
Guber-Peters Entertainment Co. 21
Guefen, Anthony 16
Gueron, Ivan 93
Guerra, Castulo 152
Guerrosio, John 107
Guertin, Nicola 194
Guess Who's Coming for Christmas? 80, 217
Guest, Christopher 17
Guest, Nicholas 55, 149, 188
Guétary, François 154
Gufta, Sneh 149
Gugushe, Biski 155
The Guiding Light 205
Guillaume, Robert 105
Guinan, Francis 104, 108
Guinee, Tim 29
Guinevere 208
Guiry, Thomas 111
Guittard, Laurence 42
Gulliver's Travels 1, 80

Gunn, James 2, 209
Gunn, Moses 21
Gunn, Nicholas 193
Gunter, Robert 104
Gunton, Bob 152, 199
Gurwitch, Annabelle 63, 117, 136
Guterres, Candi 5
Guthe, Manfred 104, 145
Guthrie, Michelle 35
Guttenberg, Gary 105
Guttenberg, Steve 182
Gutteridge, Lucy 16, 36
Guttridge, Jim 23
Guyot, Marion 118
Gwynne, Fred 127
Gwynne, Michael C. 27

Haas, Ed 87, 128
Haas, Stephanie 53
Haas, Victoria 16
Haase, Rod 40
Habermann, Eva 166
Habitat 81
Hackett, Joan 49, 144
Hackett, Jonathan 82, 145
Hackney, Robert E. 89
Hadden, John 166
Haddon, Laurence 11, 78
Hadfield, Penny 69
Hadfield, Veronica 63, 185
Haeni, Gaston 18
Hafer, Philip 108
Hagan, Denis M. 158
Hagan, Laurie 162
Haggard, Piers 114
Haggerty, H.B. 44
Haggerty, M. Nord 12
Hagman, Larry 92
Hahn, Jessica 12
Haiduc, Ion 112
Haiduk, Stacey 201
Haig, Sid 78
Haim, Corey 123
Hain, Judy 97
Haitkin, Jacques 77
Haje, Khrystyne 21, 76
Halashita, Heidi 13
Halbert, Hilary 194
Haldeman, Tim 7
Hale, Doug 117
Hale, Mary 186
Hale, Richard 131
Hale, William 53
Haley, Doug 177
Haley, Jack, Jr. 133
Haley, Kevin 66
Haley, Sheila 177
Hall, Albert 40, 133
Hall, Bug 128
Hall, Catherine 36
Hall, Daisy 93
Hall, Gary Skeen 99
Hall, Gordon 123
Hall, Grayson 72
Hall, Irma P. 117
Hall, J.D. 22, 40
Hall, Kenneth J. 76
Hall, Larue 177

Hall, Philip Baker 78, 118, 120, 153, 175, 178
Hall, Robert 26, 177
Hall, Roger 81, 122, 138
Hall, Sean 58
Hall, Tony 24, 75, 94
Hall, Valerie 99, 101
Hallahan, Charles 33, 152, 199
Hallick, Tom 179
Hallier, Lori 31
Hallmark 58; Entertainment 23, 81, 94, 112, 122, 126, 138, 152, 153, 157, 158, 187, 190, 194, 196, 198; Hall of Fame Productions 117; Home Entertainment 155
The Halloween Tree 208
Halloweentown 81
Halmi, Robert 30
Halmi, Robert, Jr. 133, 142
Halmi, Robert, Sr. 81, 122, 133, 138, 187, 198
Halona, Mike 183
Halsey, Richard B. 125
Haman, Richard Y. 79
Hamdon Entertainment 190
Hamel, Veronica 87
Hamill, Mark 61, 103, 197
Hamilton, Alexa 98
Hamilton, Alice 122
Hamilton, Barbara 38
Hamilton, Barry 90
Hamilton, Emily 153
Hamilton, Frank 52
Hamilton, George 48
Hamilton, Lois 99
Hamilton, Lonnie 174
Hamilton, Margaret 132
Hamilton, Michael 128
Hamilton, Richard 143
Hamlan, Ted 94
Hamlin, Harry 115
Hamlisch, Marvin 150
Hamm, Sam 120
Hammer, Dennis 109
Hammer, Jan 22, 105, 108
Hammer Films 79, 171
Hammerstein, Oscar, III 37
Hammond, Nicholas 121, 165, 187
Hammond, Vincent 67, 70
Hamnet, Bryce 41
Hampshire, Susan 20
Hampton, James 178
Hampton, Paul 18
Hampton, Roger 36
Hamuri, Andras 46
Hanan, Michael Z. 153
Hanauer, Terri 81
Hancock, Lou 13
Hancock, Prentis 102
Handley, Annette 27
The Hands of Orlac 85
Handy, Carl 175
Haney, Anne 98, 105, 133, 144
Haney, Buddy 133
The Hanged Man 208
Hanlon, Peter 160
Hanna, Alexandra 29
Hanna, Ed 77

Hanna, Mark 137
Hanna, Natasha 29
Hanna, Xenia 29
Hanna-Barbera/KISS Productions 107
Hannah, Daryl 16–17
Hannah, John 116
Hansen, Anthony 194
Hansen, Carl 110
Hansen, Erik 166
Hansen, Janis 14
Hansen, John 178
Hansen, Kevin 15
Hansen, Omar 101
Hansen, William 156
Hanson, Curt 88
Hanson, Gordon 14
Hanson, Lestor B. 88
Hanson, Marcy 76
Hansrai, Luther 75
Hanta Yo 211
Hara, Mitch 105
Harada, Ernest 87
Haralampides, Dr. Andreas M. 180
Harbert, Tim 114
Harbour, Michael N. 22
Harcourt, John 145
Hardester, Crofton 44
Hardin, Jerry 87, 143
Hardin, Melora 182
Harding, David 187
Harding, Jeff 31, 187
Hardy, Hagood 13
Hardy, John 146
Hardy, Rob 187
Hardy, Robert 80
Harewood, Dorian 12, 91
Harimoto, Dale 10
Harkins, John 79
Harlacher, Eric 88
The Harlem Globetrotters on Gilligan's Island 3, 208
Harlow, Thomasyn 165
Harlow, William 171
Harman, Ginny 152
Harman, J. Boyce, Jr. 126
Harman, Steve 71
Harmon, Deborah 75
Harmon, Mark 78
Harnell, Joe (Joseph) 94, 150, 192
Harney, Corinna 193
Harnois, Elisabeth 195
Harper, Beth 60
Harper, James 201
Harper, Kirk 185
Harper, Mark 7
Harper, Robert 130, 137
Harper, Valerie 57, 206
Harpman, Fred 42
Harras, Patti 134
Harrelson, Brett 125
Harrelson, Woody 21
Harrett, Brianne 139
Harriet, Jo 123
Harriman, Fawne 11
Harring, Laura 26
Harrington, Curtis 34, 48, 53, 106

Harris, Aubrey 125
Harris, Barbara 74, 75
Harris, Barbara Eve 93
Harris, Baxter 168
Harris, Cynthia 55
Harris, Daniel 74
Harris, Danielle 200
Harris, David 26
Harris, Donald Lee 44
Harris, Ed 11
Harris, Gail 140
Harris, George 80
Harris, Glenn Walker 181
Harris, Harry 6
Harris, Jason 75
Harris, Jo Anne 199
Harris, Johnny 96, 137
Harris, Julie 15
Harris, Julius 79
Harris, Lara 95
Harris, Laura 62, 81, 155
Harris, Liza 111
Harris, Mark 122
Harris, Mark R. 57, 197
Harris, Michael 194
Harris, Richard A. 59
Harris, Rosalind 126
Harris, Steve 134
Harris, Zarachar 196
Harrison Bergeron 82, 110
Harrison, B.J. 134
Harrison, Evangeline 18, 36
Harrison, Gregory 60, 184
Harrison, Harvey 41
Harrison, Ken 93
Harrison, Lindsay 118, 186
Harrison, Richard St. John 21
Harrison, Toshi 92
Harrold, Kathryn 40, 193
Harry, Deborah 103
Harston, Wendelin 159
Hart, Anita 25
Hart, Carole 101
Hart, Christine 49
Hart, Christopher 148
Hart, Harvey 12
Hart, Melissa Joan 155
Hart, Natalie 168
Hart, Paula 58, 155
Hartbreak Films 155
Harter, Leslie 92
Hartley, Mariette 61, 73, 156
Hartley, Ted 75, 199
Hartman, David 124
Hartman, Lisa 137
Hartman, Phil 47
Hartman, Ron 13
Hartowicz, Irek 140
Hartson, Michael 23
Hartwell, David 85
Hartzell, Dianne 63
Hartzell, Duane 36, 63
Harve Bennett Productions 72
Harvest, Rainbow 61
Harvey, Daniel B. 110
Harvey, David 21
Harvey, Ellie 57
Harvey, Gwyneth 170

Harvey, Marshall 87, 195
Harvey, Robert 153
Harvey, Robert H. 93
Harvey, Tom 21, 77
Haskell, Peter 120
Haskett, Roger 134
Hasselhoff, David 30, 107, 211
Hastings, Bob 127, 165
Hastings, Stephen 76
Hatch, Richard 146
Hatem, Rosine "Ace" 25
Hatfield, Hurd 135
Hathaway, Amy 110
Hathaway, Kellen 87
Hathaway, Robert 73
Hatmaker, Jerry 174
Hauber, Jody 156
Hauer, Rutger 122, 153
Hauff, Thomas 94, 191
Haun, Lindsey 52
The Haunted 3, 53, 82
Haunted by Her Past 83, 217
Haunted Symphony 217
The Haunting (book) 83
Haunting of Helen Walker 83
The Haunting of Lisa 208
The Haunting of Sara Hardy 208
The Haunting of Seacliff Inn 84
The Haunting Passion 84
Haunts of the Very Rich 208
Hauser, Robert B. 131, 132, 199
Hauser's Memory 85
Havers, Nigel 30
Hawk, Richard 126
Hawkes, John 141
Hawkins, John 189
Hawthorne, Christopher 198
Hawthorne, Elizabeth 169
Hawtrey, Kay 83
Hay, David 170
Hayden, Dennis 80
Hayden, Elizabeth 110
Hayden, James 96
Haydn, Lili 137
Hayen, Todd 197, 202
Hayes, Bud 71
Hayes, Buford F. 150
Hayes, Deryl 61
Hayes, Donald 15
Hayes, Jeffrey M. 70, 187
Hayes, Lucky 76
Hayes, Philip 134
Hayes, William 18
Hayman, David 80
Hayman, James 87
Hayne, Jim 152, 165
Haynes, Jerry 99
Haynes, Lloyd 115
Haynes, Michael 37
Haynie, Jim 55
Hays, Robert 37, 65, 77, 96, 154, 177
Haysbert, Dennis 105
Hayward, Chris 87, 128
Hayward, Lillie 158
Hayward, Rachel 49
Hayward, Sarah 62
Hazzard, Kathy 7

HBO 16, 17, 33, 47, 69, 111, 169, 197, 200, 204, 207, 210, 212, 213, 216; Pictures 33, 201
Headley, Lena 122
Heal, Joan 102
Healey, Ryan 102
Healy, Christine 108
Healy, Ryan 165
Heames, Darin 9
Heap, Jonathan 186
Hearn, Ann 139
Hearst Entertainment 80
Heart Entertainment 74
Heartless 85
Heartstar Productions 75
Heaton, Tom 84, 134, 139
Heaven, Tish 134, 139
Heaven Can Wait 14, 75
Hebb, Brian R.R. 94, 154
Hechim, Jim 60
Hecht, Albie 58
Heckert, James T. 29
Hedden, Rob 108
Hedison, David 34, 145
Heffer, Richard 121
Heffron, Richard T. 192
Heflin, Nora 96
Heflin, Van 109
Heick, Susan 18
Heiden, Ira 179
Heighley, Bruce 78
Heigl, Katherine 174, 200
Hein, Richard 107
Heinl, Benard 69
Heinle, Amelia 148
Heinlein, Robert 12
Helberg, Sandy 126
"Helen O'Loy" 40
Helgenberger, Kay 169
Helgenberger, Marg 50, 77, 169
Heller, Ben 100
Heller, Chip 198
Heller, Ken 41
Hellfire 85, 217
Hellman, Bonnie 101
Hellman, Ocean 84
Helmond, Katherine 127
Helmsley, Sherman 6
Hemblen, David 54
Hemingway, Mariel 44
Hendel, Kenneth 146
Henderson, Cliff 91
Henderson, Fred 51
Henderson, Zenna 141
The Henderson Monster 208
Hendrickson, Benjamin 52
Hendrie, Chris 168
Hendrix, Elaine 128
Heneghan, Columba 90
Henerson, James 117, 174
Henkler, Andrej 48
Henreid, Monica 58
Henry, Buck 82
Henry, Chuck 169
Henry, Gregg 21, 76
Hensely, Bill 43
Henson, Brian 81
Henson, Jim 133

Henteloff, Alex 98
Herbert, Julie 128
Herbert, Pitt 43
Herbert, Victor 18
Hercules and the Amazon Women 86
Hercules and the Circle of Fire 208
Hercules and the Lost Kingdom 87, 208
Hercules in the Maze of the Minotaur 208
Hercules in the Underworld 209
Hercules: The Legendary Journeys 2, 22, 117, 121, 122, 123
Herczeg, Christina 76
Herd, Richard 92, 191, 201
Here Comes the Munsters 27, 87, 128
Herek, Stephen 76
Herman, Jerry 126
Hermann, Ed 87
Hernandez, Enrique S. 75
Hernandez, Samuel 108
Heron, Blake 185
Herrera, Anthony 120
Herrera, Maria 62
Herrera, Tomas 159
Herrington, David 75
Hershey, Barbara 14
Hershey, Stephanie 78
Hertzberg, Paul 194
Hervey, Irene 78
Heschong, Albert 126, 162, 199
Heslov, Grant 48, 120
Hess, Erica Nicole 112
Hess, Jon Daniel 113, 137
Hess, Sandra 22
Hesseman, Howard 75
Hessler, Gordon 107
Heuser, Brandon 39
Hewitt, Martin 28
Hewitt, Peter 199
Heyerdahl, Christopher 81
Heyman, Aaron 201
Hi, Honey—I'm Dead 87
Hibbard, James 14
Hibdon, Don 60
Hickman, Julie 83
Hicko, Anthony 70
Hickox, Douglas 142
Hickox, S. Bryan 188
Hicks, Caitlin 100
Hicks, Catherine 87, 154
Hicks, Hilly 165
Hicks, Lois 159
Hicks, Marva 7
Hides, Bernard 169
Higden, Robert 81, 198
Higgins, Anthony 134
Higgins, Craig 97
Higgins, Douglas 51, 73, 93, 100
Higgins, Mike 112
High Command Productions 166
High Desert Kill 88
High Productions 104
Highlander: The Series 94
Highsmith, Patrick 113, 140
Hightower, Sally 97
Highway to Heaven 182
The Highwayman 209, 217

Hildebrandt, Tina 39
Hildyard, Jack 22
Hill, Arthur 147, 151
Hill, Dean 97, 154
Hill, Debra 17
Hill, Frankie 103
Hill, John 167
Hill, Kristopher Kent 76
Hill, Leonard 61
Hill, Mark 138
Hill, Richard 20
Hill, Ruth Beebe 211
Hill, Thomas 192
Hill, V. Jude 81
Hill, Walter 196
Hill Street Blues 98, 193
Hillbern, David 57
Hiller, Arthur 153
Hillerman, John 173
Hillgartner, Jim 168
Hillwood Entertainment 173
Hilton, James 31
Hilton, Steven 100
Himmelman, Roger 175
Himmelstein, Howard 70
Hindle, Art 38, 145
Hines, Karen 74
Hiney, William 41
Hingle, Pat 137, 159, 173
Hinkley, Del 94
Hinkley, Tommy 61
Hinsburger, Laura 54
Hinselwood, Brian 71
Hinton, Annie 92
Hipp, Paul 65, 113
Hiroyuki-Tagawa, Cary 137
Hirsch, Emile 71
Hirschman, Herbert 90
Hirson, Roger O. 36
Hiscox, Dave 84
Hitchcock, Alfred 114
Hively, George B. 79
Hivilo, Alar 98
Hix, Kim 109
Hoag, Judith 81
Hoath, Florence 83
Hoban, T.J. 19
Hobbs, Heather 46
Hobbs, Peter 189
Hobermann, David 181
Hoblit, Gregory 56, 193
Hobson, Gregory 128
Hobson, Lynn 175
Hobson, Patricia 128
Hock, Johnny 46
Hodge, Edwin 157
Hodge, Kate 43
Hodges, Ken 20
Hodges, Mike 114
Hoey, Michael A. 144
HOF Productions, Inc. 89
Hofeling, Mark 200
Hoff, Christian 69
Hoffer, Bernard 160
Hoffie, Tom 187
Hoffman, Gabrielle 68
Hoffman, Gary 167
Hoffman, Isabella 5

Hoffman, Jon 174
Hoffman, Linda 18, 26
Hoffman, Shelley 40
Hogan, Chris 63
Hogan, Michael 96
Hogan, Susan 12, 62, 195
Hohenocker, Thomas 48
Holahan, Philip 137
Holcomb, Rod 32, 119, 120, 124
Holden, David 153
Holden, Larry 54
Holden, Mark 134
Holden, Peter 35
Holdenried, Kris 81
Holder, Geoffrey 74
Holder, Philip 70
Holdridge, Lee 47, 154, 166
Holihan, Ryan 12
Holland, Daniel H. 7, 196
Holland, Thomas 165
Holland, Tom 96, 168
Hollander, David 120
Hollander, Howard 131
Hollier, Emory 125
Hollinger, Robert 13
Hollins, Margaret-Mary 86
Holloway, C. Robert 118
Hollowood, Ann 122
Hollyn, Norman 148, 190
Holm, Ian 177
Holmes, Brittany Ashton 91, 95
Holmes, Christopher 47
Holmes, Geoffrey 96
Holmes, Gerry (Gerald) 50, 127, 167
Holmes, Jim 97
Holmes, John W. 106
Holmes, Rozsika 90
Holmes and Yoyo 71
Holosko, John 77
Holt, Arva 140
Holt, Larry 118
Holzberg, Roger 88
Hom, Steve 120
Homeier, Skip 199
Homer 138, 139
Homewrecker 88, 217
Hong, James 120
Honig, Howard 44
Hood, Don 66
Hooks, David 56, 120, 193
Hooks, Ed 35
Hooper, Tobe 93, 103, 156
Hooten, Peter 56
Hootkins, William 115, 149
Hope, Barry 105
Hope, Fredric P. 91, 144
Hopkins, Bo 27
Hopkins, Bud 97
Hopkins, Mark 81
Hopkins, Ryan 111
Hopkins, Telma 105
Hopkins, Wendy 82
Hopper, Dennis 200
Hopps, Nancy 55
Horan, Hildy 127
Horan, James 84
Horine, Marianne 64

Horizon Productions 111
Hormann, Nicholas 184
Horn, Lanny 57
Horn, Leonard 129
Horn, Lew 93
Horne, Joanne 14
Horneff, Wil 159
Horner, Penelope 59
Hornickel, Cindy 186
Hornyanszky, Tamas 46
Horowitz, Lawrence 188
Horowitz, Richard 155
Horrigan, Sam 63
The Horror at 37,000 Feet 88
Horruzey, Paul 21
Horton, Elizabeth 31
Horton, Peter I. 66
Horunzhy, Vladimir 168
Horvitch, Andy 46
Hosea, Bobby 71, 120
Hosef, George 84
Hoselton, David 38
Hosking, Craig 120
Host 194
Hostetter, John 152, 167
Hotel 21
Houde, Serge 139
Hough, Lindsay Austin 37
The Hound of Florence 158
The Hound of the Baskervilles 209
House of Frankenstein 2, 89
House of the Damned 90, 217
The House That Would Not Die 90
Houser, Christie 103
Houser, Jerry 76, 105
Houston, Whitney 37
Houston, William 138
How to Marry a Millionaire 1
Howard, Ann 193
Howard, Charlotte 102
Howard, Clint 91
Howard, Megan 183
Howard, Rance 105, 178
Howard, Ron 178
Howard, Sheila 89
Howard, Sherman 165
Howard, Susan 145
Howell, C. Thomas 49, 172, 205
Howell, Hoke 152, 178
Howell, Margaret 91
Howland, Rick 180
Howson, Terry 5
Hoxby, Scott 60
Hoy, Bob 62
Hoy, Robert F. 16, 150
Hoye, Billy 28
Hoyes, Charles 120
HTV Ltd. 31
Hu, Kelly 166
Hua, Quyen 82
Hub, Martin 49
Hubbert, Cork 114
Hubbs, Gil 30, 78, 167
Hubley, Season 91, 167
Hubley, Whip 26, 41
Hubrich, Jeffrey 101
Huddleston, David 40
Hudkins, John 162

Hudolin, Richard 57, 134
Hudson, Bill 107
Hudson, Ernie 199
Hudson, Rock 121
Huffman, David 116
Huffman, Rosanna 130
Huggins, Jere 60
Hugh Benson Productions 78
Hughes, Adrian 23
Hughes, Arlington 183
Hughes, Barnard 28
Hughes, Charles 36, 77, 123
Hughes, Finola 44, 73, 83
Hughes, Kathleen 164
Hughes, Raymond 102
Hughes, Terry 126
Hugho, Kimo 45
Hugo, Michel 62, 88, 131
Hule, Karen 36
Hull, Shelley 118
Hulsey, James G. 89, 107, 125, 129, 157, 165, 193
Human Feelings 90
Humanoid Defender 217
Humanoids from the Deep 91
Hume, Alan 187
Humphreys, Alfred 15, 61
Hunde, Craig 143
Hunnicutt, Gayle 121
Hunt, Allan 120
Hunt, Christine 16
Hunt, Helen 164
Hunt, Kenna 141
Hunt, Marsha 67
Hunt, Ronald Leigh 67
Hunter, Drew 30
Hunter, J. Michael 188
Hunter, Michael 47
Hunter, Mike 175
Hunter, Steve 50
Huntington, Nicole 97
Hunyadkurthy, Istvan 46
Huot, Gaetan 81
Huppert, Isabelle 80
Hurd, Gale Anne 33, 201
Hurley, Karen 49
Hurst, Michael 86
Hurt, John 164
Hurtubise, David (Dave) 5, 57
Hurwitz, Howie 148
Husky, Rick 120
Huson, Paul 70
Hussey, Olivia 100
Huston, William 55
Hutcheson, Jenny-Lynn 134
Hutchins, Will 88
Hutchinson, Bill 20
Hutchinson, Jayme 180
Hutshing, Gillian 175
Hutson, Lee 186
Hutton, Jim 58
Hutton, Lauren 66, 180
Hutton, Rif 130
Hutton, Timothy 47
Huxley, Aldous 29, 30
HVO Pictures 70
Hwang, Cathy 76
Hyatt, Pam 60, 77, 112, 195

Hyde, Caroline 71
Hyde, Cassandra 71
Hyde, Christopher 49
Hyde, Jacquelyn 199
Hyde-White, Alex 11
Hyde-White, Wilfrid 67, 151
Hyland, Diana 151
Hylands, Scott 61
Hymes, Lisa 89
Hyska, Dusan 49

I Am Legend 134
I Dream of Jeannie 74, 92, 93, 168
I Dream of Jeannie—15 Years Later 92, 93
I Know What You Did Last Summer 172
I Married a Monster 92
I Married a Monster from Outer Space 92
I Still Dream of Jeannie 92, 93
I'm Dangerous Tonight 93
I've Been Waiting for You 209
I, Desire 91, 217
Iacovelli, John 18, 19, 20
Ibbetson, Arthur 18, 68, 164
Ibold, Doug 43
Ideishu, Randy 25
Ihnat, Steve 173
Ilacks, Diane 74
Ilusa, Nurmi 81
Imada, Jeff 105
Imi, Tony 36, 83, 149
Immergut, Scott 63, 158
The Immortal 2, 56, 150, 209
The Immortals (book) 2
Imperial Entertainment 181
In His Father's Shoes 93
In Old Chicago 179
In Search of Dr. Seuss 209
In the Dead of Night 50, 133
In the Nick of Time 94
Inches, Duncan 52
The Incredible Hulk 94, 150, 161
The Incredible Hulk Returns 95, 184
Independence Day 129
Inferno 209
Ingalls, Don 32, 96
Ingersoll, James 32, 119
Ingersoll, Mary Amadeo 10
Ingham, Jonathan 23
Ingham, Nicholas 23
Ingram, Paula 125
Inhumanoid 95, 217
The Initiation of Sarah 96
Innes, George 16, 78
Innes, Louise A. 127, 157
Innocent, Harold 31
The Innocents 84
Inscoe, Joe 44, 118, 168
Instone, John 23
Inter/Hemisphere Productions 31
Interscope Communications 161
Interview with a Vampire 183
The Intruder Within 96
Intruders 97
Intruders (book) 97
The Invaders 97

The Invaders (series) 12, 25, 89, 98, 136
Invasion Earth 209
Invasion of the Body-Snatchers 12, 60
The Invisible Boy 88
The Invisible Man 72, 98
The Invisible Man (book) 98
The Invisible Woman 98
Invitation to Hell 99
Ionescu, Razvan 112
Ireland, Jill 77
Ireland, Kathy 45
Irish Films, Inc. 44, 118
Iron Man 65
Ironside, Michael 104, 160, 192
IRS Media, Inc. 12, 50, 202
Irvin, Barbara 35
Irvin, Sam 197
Irvine, Frank 139
Irvine, Paula 21
Irvine, Thomas A. 55
Irving, Amy 188
Irving, Brian 155
Irving, Penny 164
Irving, Richard 65, 160
Irving, Washington 113
Irwin, Colin D. 8–10
Irwin, Mark 137
Irwin Allen Productions 6, 179
Isaac, Frank K. 63
Isaacks, Levie 93, 174, 196
Isaacs, Bud S. 89
Isaacs, Stanley 102, 149, 201
Isaacson, Karin 113
Iscore, Robert 37
Isenberg, Gerald I. 79, 141, 156, 197
Isherwood, Christopher 68
Ishida, Jim 105
Ishiura, Dana 191
Island City 99
Israel, David 89
Israeli, Benjamin 48
It 100
It Came from Outer Space 101
It Came from Outer Space II 100
It Came Up from the Bermuda Depths 217
It Came Upon a Midnight Clear 209
It Happened One Christmas 101
It Happens Every Spring 15
It Nearly Wasn't Christmas 101, 127
ITC Productions 83, 84
It's a Wonderful Life 38, 101, 106
Itzin, Gregory 87
Ives, Burl 23, 64
Ivey, Lela 182
Ivy, Joe 35
Ixtlan 199
Izay, Connie 118
Izay, Victor 109, 131

J.D. Feigelson Productions 36
Jaber, John 54
Jace, Michael 28
Jack, Wolfman 123

Jack the Ripper 30
Jackman, Fred 165, 179
Jackman, Jim 87
Jacks, Robert L. 126, 199
Jackson, Andrew 58, 190
Jackson, Carl 117
Jackson, Carolyn G. 108
Jackson, Crane 162
Jackson, D.J. 93
Jackson, David S. 109
Jackson, Dee Jay 57
Jackson, G. Philip 66
Jackson, Gemma 161
Jackson, Gordon 164
Jackson, J.J. 7
Jackson, Jamie Smith 130
Jackson, Jeanine 144
Jackson, John M. 152
Jackson, Kate 88, 106, 107, 182
Jackson, Mike 86
Jackson, Robert 18
Jackson, Ron 108
Jackson, Stoney 26
Jackson, Victoria 28
Jackson, William 15
Jackunas, Jolie 71
Jacobs, Allan 162
Jacobs, Jack 113
Jacobs, Jake 83
Jacobs, Juliette 82
Jacobs, Martin 102
Jacobs, Matthew 57
Jacobs, Rachel 105
Jacobsen, Ellen Ring 103
Jacobson, Rick 173
Jacoby, Billy 14
Jacoby, Laura 133
Jaffe, Allen 118
Jaffe, Chapelle 82
Jaffe, Gib 76
Jaffe, Michael 54, 94
Jaffe, Sam 131
Jaffe/Braunstein Films 54
Jagger, Dean 171
Jakub, Lisa 60
Jakula, Mio R. 19
James, Bradley 33
James, Brion 15, 24, 28, 40, 107, 108
James, Cinda-Lin 172
James, Daniel 86
James, Don 8
James, Godfrey 112
James, Henry 83
James, John 83
James, Josh 200
James, Ken 94, 127, 147
James, Leonard 102
James, Lisa 76
James, Peter 159, 194
James, Steve 120
James, Terry 152
Jameson, Joyce 199
Jameson, Mick 19
Jameson, Nick 97
Janis, Conrad 124
Janson, Len 41
Jansons, Maris 24

Janssen, David 125
Janssen, Famke 211
Janus, Samantha 102
Janus Productions 55
Jarchow, Stephen P. 57, 122, 197
Jarnagin, James T. 171
Jarre, Kevin 79
Jarrett, Jim 51
Jarrett, Phil 94
Jarrett, Renne 34
Jason, Harvey 73, 87
Jason, Peter 14, 69, 103
Jastrow, Terry 142
Javitz, Barbara 201
Jaws 142, 212
Jax, Mark 122
Jay, Jeff 194
Jay, Michael 201
Jay, Susan 21
Jaygee Productions 41
Jayston, Michael 187
Jean-Thomas, David 5
Jeannie Entertainment 93
Jeffcoat, Don 200
Jefferds, Vincent 87
Jefferies, Phil 6
Jeffries, John D. 124
Jeffries, Lionel 102
Jekyll and Hyde 102
Jemison, Kimble 120
Jenkins, Eric 64
Jenkins, Ken 165
Jenkins, Mark 118
Jenkins, Noam 54, 74
Jenkowitz, Marty 175
Jennings, Jack 154
Jennings, Joseph R. 41
Jennings, Juanita 154
Jensen, Anders P. 181
Jensen, Dave 183
Jensen, David 166, 194
Jensen, Ethan 174
Jensen, Jeffrey Scott 6, 26
Jensen, Todd 30
Jenson, Edward 126
Jericevic, Dusko 16
Jerome, Howard 75
Jessop, Jack 74
Jessup, Harley 64
Jeter, Michael 126
The Jewel in the Crown 43
Jewers, Ray 149
Jewkes, Richard 166
Jeyes, Jazzer 102
J'Han, Rasool 117
Jillian, Ann 6
Jim Henson Productions 81
Jimenez, Frank 23
Joanna Pacula 136
Jobin, Peter 79
J.O.E and the Colonel 103, 147, 217
Joe Wizan Television Productions 189
Joffin, Jon 177
John, Tom H. 14, 29, 151
John Carpenter Presents Body Bags 103
John Leekley Productions 108

Johne, Nick 74
Johnny 2.0 104
Johns, Milton 20
Johns, Neil 128
Johnson, Arch 98
Johnson, Arte 6
Johnson, Bill 169
Johnson, Bjorn 29
Johnson, Byron 81
Johnson, C. David 112
Johnson, Chip 32
Johnson, Clark 147, 167
Johnson, Deborah Lee 61
Johnson, Denis 164
Johnson, Denis, Jr. 146
Johnson, Denise 190
Johnson, Don 151
Johnson, Doug 102, 178
Johnson, Eli 79
Johnson, Geordie 23
Johnson, Harry 51
Johnson, Howard E. 67, 131
Johnson, Kee Y. 183
Johnson, Kenneth 8–10, 94, 134, 150, 192
Johnson, Laura 36, 130
Johnson, Laurel 66
Johnson, Liz 12
Johnson, Marjorie 60
Johnson, Matthew 169
Johnson, Michael 10
Johnson, Michelle 27
Johnson, P. Lynn 134
Johnson, Richard E. 67
Johnson, Rick 45
Johnson, Roger 64
Johnson, Russell 75, 88
Johnson, Scott 108
Johnson, Shelly 8, 10, 54, 80, 148, 159, 194
Johnson, Tabby 75
Johnson, Tony T. 158
Johnson, Wendy Raquel 120
Johnston, Christopher 15
Johnston, Eric 191, 192
Johnston, Jim 166
Johnston, Joe 64
Johnston, John Dennis 107, 198
Johnston, Thomas M.C. 22, 177
Johnston-Diamond, Karen 135
Jolley, Stan 38, 171
Jolley, Trevor 65, 178
Jones, Alan 146
Jones, Andrew James 179
Jones, Arlen 39
Jones, Buster 32
Jones, Carol 144
Jones, Chad 21
Jones, Damian 50
Jones, Dean 116, 163
Jones, Gary 15, 59, 62
Jones, Henry 80
Jones, J.J. 119
Jones, James Earl 122, 188, 215
Jones, John G. 13
Jones, John Marshall 135
Jones, Jon Paul 136
Jones, Kelly 61

Jones, Larry 152
Jones, Mal 111
Jones, Marilyn 91
Jones, Melanie 53, 162
Jones, Mickey 101, 162, 192
Jones, Nathan 58
Jones, Pirie 167
Jones, Richard 120
Jones, Sam 209, 214
Jones, Sharon Lee 112
Jones, Shirley 57
Jones, Tim 70
Jones, Tommy Lee 79
Jones, Trevor 23, 81, 122
Jongeneel, William 41
Jonny Quest 209
Jonny Quest and the Cyberinsects 209
Jonny's Golden Quest 209
Jonson, Holly 79
Jordan, Derwin 127, 158, 195
Jordan, Judy 118
Jordan, Kathy 113, 140
Jordan, Troy 6
Jorden, Alex 29
Jory, Victor 53
Joseph, Anne 63
Joss Communications, Inc. 88
Jourdan, Louis 67, 151
Journey to the Center of the Earth 104
Journey to the Center of the Earth (novel) 105
Joy, Mark 117, 188
Joyce, Bernadette 24, 150, 162
Joyce, Jimmy 151
Joyce, Michael R. 29, 89, 128, 201
Joyce, Stephen 152
Joyner, Kimble 74
Jozak Co. 197
Ju, Lee 166
Judd, Craig 175
Judd, General Fermon, Jr. 23, 169
Judges, Christopher 186
Juliano, Lenny 193, 196
Jump, Gordon 124
Jurasik, Peter 18, 19
Jurassic Park 142
Jurgensen, William K. 76, 90, 150, 171
Just Our Luck 202
Justice, Edgar 40
Justice, Katherine 33
Justman, Robert H. 118, 143
Jympson, John 121

K-9000 105
Ka-Ncube, Sello Maake 30
Kable, James 71
Kaczender, George 54, 62
Kadish, Ben 35
Kagan, Elaine 89, 117
Kagan, Jeremy 153
Kahler, Kristin 201
Kahn, Dann 25
Kahn, Eric 25
Kahn, Ilene 153
Kahn, Mary 38

Kahn, Michael 131
Kailey, Liis 91
Kain, Judy 87
Kalinowsky, Waldemar 105
Kalipha, Stefan 80
Kalish, Irma 92
Kamateros, Costa 66
Kamel, Stanley 33, 115, 142, 149
Kane, Adam 149, 201
Kane, Artie 53
Kane, Billy 120
Kane, Carol 68, 205
Kane, Jackson D. 157
Kane, Joseph P. 53
Kanegson, Andras 111
Kapelos, John 52, 130
Kaplan, Elliot 170
Kapoor, Shashi 80
Kappes, David 133, 168, 169
Kaproff, Dana 36, 60, 65, 88, 133, 134, 168
Karago, Njeri 30
Kardon, Darlene 154
Karen, James 40, 182
Kargianus, Gregory 195
Karlatos, Olga 160
Karlen, John 184
Karlin, Fred 118, 182, 193
Karlin, Miriam 102
Karloff, Boris 42
Karlson, Jean 129
Karnes, Robert 38
Karon, Marvin 38
Karpf, Deborah 53
Karpf, Elinor 53, 72, 156
Karpf, Merrill H. 41
Karpf, Stephen 53, 72, 156
Karpman, Laura 63
Karr, Gary 87
Karr, Sarah Rose 88
Karyo, Tcheky 81
Karz, Mike 181
Kascia, Mary Anne E. 182
Kasdorf, Lenore 42
Kasica, Mary Anne 165
Kasper, Gary 103, 181
Kassir, John 63
Kastner, John 190, 191
Katerina, Anna 51
Kathehakis, Alex 55
Katkin, Brian 136
Katsulas, Andreas 18, 19, 51
Katt, Nicky 108
Katt, William 54, 55
Katterns, Greg 71
Katz, A.L. 196
Katz, David B. 193
Katz, Judah 195
Katz, Sidney M. 42
Katz, Stephen M. 126
Katz, William 51
Katzin, Lee H. 118, 171
Kaufman, Jean 126
Kaufman, Jimmy 198
Kaufman, Kenneth 146
Kaufman, Mark S. 181
Kaufman, Paul A. 62–63
Kaufman Co. 63

Ka'upu, Charles 43
Kautner, Helmut 85
Kavelaars, Ingrid 74
Kavellin, John 155
Kavner, Julie 151
Kayden, Tony 126
Kayden, William 40, 42
Kaye, Celia 58
Kaye, Clarissa 68, 156
Kaye, David 23, 39
Kaye, Lila 31, 149
Kaye, Richard 71
Keach, Stacy 11, 103
Keach, Stacy, Sr. 38
Keagy, Grace 126
Kean, Boe 187
Keane, Brian 169
Keane, James 87, 130
Keane, Kerrie 9, 10, 21
Keane, Murray 86
Keane, Willem 146
Kearney, Gillian 153
Kearney, Karon 138
Keating, Fred 23, 134
Keating, Patrick 57, 176
Keats, Ele 198
Keats, Steven 110
Kee, James 24, 190, 191
Keefe, Christina 176
Keefer, Don 94
Keegan, Terry 76, 77
Keen, Bob 180
Keen, Diane 102
Keen, Noah 161
Keena, Monica 161
Keenleyside, Eric 39
Kehela, Steve 6
Kehler, Jack 97
Keith Addis & Associates 79
Kelamis, Peter 134
Keleghan, Peter 54, 185
Keller, Frank P. 72
Keller, George A. 81
Keller, Harry 75
Keller, Joel 94
Keller, Max A. 171
Keller, Micheline H. 171
Keller, Nicole 171
Kelley, Brett 168
Kelley, Richard A. 118
Kelley, William 53
Kellie, Daniel 128
Kellogg, John 131
Kelly, April 93
Kelly, David 168
Kelly, Desmond 70
Kelly, Leonard 163
Kelly, Madeline 96
Kelly, Moira 47
Kelly, Richard A. 142
Kelly, Roz 44
Kelly, Scott J. 89
Kelly, Stan 168, 188
Kelly, Terence 100
Kelly, Tom 178
Kelman, Alfred R. 36
Kelman, Pat 138
Kelsey, Tamsin 62

Kemp, Sally 143
Kempin, Fiona 123
Kemplen, Nick 86
Ken Follett's "The Third Twin" 209
Kennedy, Burt 126, 199
Kennedy, George 128
Kennedy, Jonell 110
Kennedy, Kevin 166
Kennedy, Michael (director) 145
Kennedy, Mike 19
Kennedy, Nina 102
Kennedy, Patrick 141
Kennedy, Richard 72
Kenneth Johnson Productions 8–10, 135, 192
Kennett, David 53
Kenny, Shannon 97
Kenny, Tom 50
Kensit, Patsy 69
Kent, Chantallese 180
Kent, Paul 98
Kent, Peter 71
Kent, Steven 181
Kent, Thomas 55
Kent Productions, Inc. 38
Kenworthy, Duncan 81
Kepros, Nicholas 27
Keramidas, Harry 17
Kercheval, Ken 52, 53, 93
Kerchner, Rob 11, 128, 136, 173, 196
Kerman, Ken 126
Kern, Graham 81
Kern, Robert, Jr. 144, 178
Kern, Tom 175
Kernion, Jerry 20
Kerns, Joanna 62
Kerns, Linda 126
Kerr, John 21
Kerr, Patrick 181
Kerrigan, Jack 10
Kershaw, Whitney 42
Kerwin, Brian 77, 100
Kerwin, Lance 156
Kessell, Simone 86
Kessler, Jay 194
Kessler, Lee 130
Kevorian, Peter 77
Key, Alexander 63
Keyes, Irwin 87
Keys-Hall, Michael 133
Khali, Ahmed 177
Khambatta, Persis 119
Khaner, Julie 50
Khanjian, Arsinee 127
Khmara, Edward 122
Khouth, Gabe 100
Kibbe, Gary 103
Kibbee, Roland 14
Kibler, Steve 90
Kibrick, Leonard 150
The Kid with the Broken Halo 105
Kidd, David H. 118
Kidder, Margot 157
Kidnie, James 54, 61, 167
Kierney, Tyde 193
Kiesser, Jan 5, 134
Kihlstedt, Rya 29

Kikumoto, Jan 137
Kikumura, Akemi 118
Kilbourne, Wendy 41, 186
Kiley, Richard 14, 130
"Killdozer" 106, 186
Killdozer 106
Killer Bees 106
The Killers 1
Kilpatrick, Patrick 22, 165
Kim, Daniel Dae 29
Kim, Evan 191
Kim, Josie 7
Kimble, Robert J. 148
Kimmell, Dana 124
Kincaid, Aron 29, 143
"A Kind of Stopwatch" 77
Kindberg, Ann 146
Kindred: The Embraced 5, 27, 31, 98
Kiner, Kevin 25, 26
King, Eric 97
King, Kip 20
King, Lance 5
King, Mackenzie Pamela 181
King, Michelle 166
King, Robb Wilson 21, 108
King, Sandy 103
King, Stephen 3, 96, 100, 148, 149, 156, 159, 163, 166, 168, 169, 185
King, Todd 181
King, Trae 26
King, Wright 164
King Phoenix Entertainment 46, 102
Kingi, Henri 105
Kingi, Kenry 167
Kingsborough Pictures 81
Kinoshita, Robert 48, 143
Kinski, Klaus 180
Kinsler, Jonathan 166
Kione, James 160
Kipling, Rudyard 176
Kirby, Peter 84
Kirby, Randy 105
Kirgo, Dinah 92
Kirgo, George 14, 106, 182
Kirgo, Julie 92
Kirk, Gary 108
Kirkland, Mirabelle 177
Kirkland, Sally 29, 82
Kirpaul, Amanda I. 45, 179
Kirshenbaum, Deborah 38, 54
Kirzinger, Ken 5, 14
Kiser, Terry 35, 42, 150
KISS 107
KISS (comic book) 107
Kiss, Mari 46
KISS Meets the Phantom of the Park 107, 217, 220
Kissel, Audrey 109
Kistler, Charles M. 152
Kitaen, Tawny 208
Kite, Barbara 60
Klages, Bill 163
Klass, Perri 39
Klein, Sonny 125
Kleinschmitt, Carl 87
Klenhard, Walter 84

Kletter, Richard 5, 13, 119
Kleven, Max 65
Klindt, Emily 200
Kline, Henry 21, 66
Klingler, Kevin 61
Klitsner, Stuart 27
Kludjian, Christine 92
Klugman, Jack 144
KMG Seagull Entertainment 123
Knapp, David 162
Knie, Rolf 18
Knight, Lily 110
Knight, Shirley 190
Knight, William 148
A Knight in Camelot 42, 107
Knight Rider 108, 109
Knight Rider 2000 107
Knight Rider 2010 108
Knott, Robert 166
Knotts, J.R. 55
Knotts, John R. 60
Knox, Joy 169
Knox, Richard Alan 151
Knox, Terence 97, 103
Knudtson, Fredric 120
Knue, Michael N. 186
Kober, Jeff 5
Koblasa, George 88
Kobrin, Ron 92
Kobritz, Richard 36, 66, 156
Koch, Kenneth R. 76, 77, 155
Koch, Pete 99
Koenekamp, Fred J. 6
Koenig, Walter 148
Kogan, Milt 98
Koherr, Bob 140
Kohl, Mark 26
Kohler, Danika 12
Kolb, Ken 152
Kolb, Mina 136
The Kolchak Papers 131
Kole, David E. 35
Komatar, Mary 8
Komnrnu, Vladimir 86
Konchalovsky, Andrei 138
Kondrashoff, Kim 100
Konigsberg, Frank 169
Konigsberg/Sanitsky Company 100, 117, 169
Konigsburg, Frank 117
Konner, Lawrence 163
Konop, Kelli 113
Konoval, Karin 59, 62
Koon, Rebecca 168
Koontz, Dean R. 206
Kopit, Arthur 152, 153
Kopit, Ted 212
Koppe, Dale 178
Korbutt, Deann 169
Korman, Harvey 6, 98
Korn, Michael 13
Koromzay, Alix 47
Korty, John 64, 84, 127, 141, 176
Korty Films 64
Korzen, Benni 110
Korzhenkov, Yivgeny 86
Kosaka, Peter 74
Kosh 81

Kosinski, Richard 112
Koskela, Diane 26
Koslov, Sergei 138
Koslow, Ron 154
Koson, Agnieszka 122
Koss, Dwight 184
Kosterman, Mitchell 59, 184
Kostina, Elena 85
Kotani, Tom 23, 110
Kottman, Susan 54
Kousi, Katherine 63
Kovacs, Geza 147
Koval, Paul 147
Kove, Martin 179
Kovitz, Randy 140
Kowalski, Bernard L. 25
Kowalski, Michelangelo 28
Kowanko, Peter 76, 167
Koyata, Lance 74
Kozak, Harley Jane 13, 45, 62
Kozlov, Sergei 122
Kozoll, Michael 193
Krabbe, Jeroen 138
Kraft, Scott 150
Krakower, Kevin 68
Kramer, Eric 95
Kramer, Eric Allan 5
Kramer, George 144
Kramer, Ken 77
Kramer, Stepfanie 30
Kramme, Anthony 25
Krasucki, Jason 187
Kratky, Pavel 49
Kraus, Jiri 49
Krause, Brian 61, 201
Kravitz, Steven 25, 26
Krebs, Susan 29
Kreindel, Mitch 78
Krejcova, Katerina 49
Kress, Carl 93
Kreuzer, Elizabeth 27
Krevoy, Cecile 7
Krieger, Robin 78
Krieger, Stu 68
Kriesa, Chris 175
Krige, Alice 81
Kring, R. Timothy 21
Kristalie, Kym 190
Kristofer, Jason 80
Kristofferson, Kris 203
Kroll, Jon 12, 122
Kronen, Ben 182
Kroonenburg, Peter 81
Kroopf, Scott 161
Krumholz, Chester 32
Krumpl, Zedenek 49
Kruper, Karen 39
Kruschen, Jack 178
Kruse, Erika 53
Krusi, Janet Faust 94
Kubrick, Stanley 160
Kughn, Richard P. 134
Kuhlke, William 163
Kuleshov, Vladimir 85
Kulvinskas, Kari 138
Kung Fu 34
Kung Fu: The Movie 209
Kunz, Kenneth 102

252   Index

Kuppin, Lawrence L. 106
Kuri, John A. 178
Kuroda, Emily 85
Kurta, Paul 8, 10
Kurtz, David 8, 10, 104
Kusatsu, Clyde 20, 56
Kuss, Richard 147
Kuter, Kay E. 78
Kuttner, Henry 185
Kuzyk, Mimi 114
Kvinsland, Craig 50
Kymlicka, Milan 147

L.A. Law 115
LaBelle, Rob 154
LaBine, Kyle 57
Labine, Cam 134
Labine, Tyler 155
Labonne, Tyler 73
Laborteaux, Matthew 11
Lacey, Deborah 163
Lackey, Vic 150
Lacroix, Lisa 147
Lacy, Jerry 36
Lacy, John 61
Ladd, Cheryl 102, 141
La Fleur, Art 98
Lagerfelt, Caroline 109
LaGrua, Tom 140
Lahti, Christine 208
Lai, Alan 166
Laing, John 190, 191
Laing, Robert 18
Laird, Jack 85
The Lake 175
Lake, Bill 77
Lake, Michael 58, 70, 183
Lakeside Productions 159
La Lanne, Jack 126
Lalo Productions 115
Lalonde, Alexandra 66
Lam, Wayne 75
LaMarque, Kimberly 117
Lamb, Gil 179
Lambert, Eric 175
Lambert, Steve 29
Lambros, Alana H. 155
Lambton, Anne 80
Lamden, Derek 121
Lamey, Tommy 180
Lamkin, Ken 137
Lamm, Karen 145
Lamont, Don 74
Lampert, Jeffrey 63
Lampert, Zohra 76, 77
Lamport, Michael 94
The Land of the Lost 48
The Land Unknown 110
Landau, Juliet 149
Landau, Martin 65, 149, 150, 186
Landau, Susan B. 27
Landers, Audrey 75
Landers, Hal 53
Landers, Judy 75
Landers, Matt 152
Landers, Ruth 76
Landis, Elizabeth 85
Landis, Jerry 27

Landis, John 87, 128, 148, 166, 193
Landman, Louis 189
Lando, Joe 9
Landor, Rosalyn 16
Landrum, Bill 27
Lane, Bill 65
Lane, Brian Alan 140
Lane, Campbell 15
Lane, Michael 72
Laneuville, Eric 120
Lang, Doreen 90
Lang, Jim 103
Lang, Perry 50
Lang, Richard 130
Lang, Stephen 145, 183
Lange, Bruce 38
Lange, Hope 43
Lange, Ted 101
Langella, Frank 211
Langland, Liane 52
Langley, Norman 102
Langlois, Yves 114
Langrick, Margaret 67
Langrishe, Caroline 36
Langsworth, Brian 128
Lansbury, Angela 126
Lansbury, Bruce 93, 150
Lansbury, Felicia 93
Lanser, Roger 128
Lansing, Robert 24
Lanza, Steve 152
LaPaglia, Anthony 24
LaPlaca, Alison 94
LaPlante, Ed 96
LaPorte, John 174
Lapp, Richard 39
Lara, Joe 45, 214
Larch, John 71
Larkin, David 81
Larkin, Rita 52
Larkin, Sheila 123
Larner, Stevan 44, 85, 192
LaRosa, Kevin 29
Larrain, Michael 109
Larry White Productions 78
Larsen, William 94
Larson, Dennis 28
Larson, Glen A. 35, 108
Larson, Paul 96
Larson, Robert E. 170
Larson, Scott Alan 85
LaRue, Roger 15
LaSalle, Martin 133
LaSalle, Richard 38
LaSane, James 151
Lashly, James 79, 80
Laskey, Kathleen 112
Laskin, Michael 146
Laskos, Andrew 46
Laskus, Jacek 188
Lass, Barbara 85
Lassez, Sarah 158
The Last Child 47, 109
The Last Dinosaur 23, 110
Last Exit to Earth 110
The Last Home Run 111
The Last House on the Left 172
Last Lives 134 210

The Last Ninja 210
The Last Starfighter 147
Latanzi, Chris 75
Latchina, Irina 85
Later, Adria 59
Latham, Louise 82, 173
Lathan, Bobbi Jo 119
The Lathe of Heaven 111
Latimer, Michael 164
Latt, David 79, 140
Latuselu, Lindamarie 43
Laubacher, Jacqueline 37
Laurance, Judd 118
Laurel and Hardy 18
Laurel Entertainment 168
Laurel Productions 166
Lauren, Tammy 105, 167
Laurence, Judd 119
Laurence, Michael 92
Laurenson, James 119
Laurimore, John 67
Laurin, Vera 77
Laurita, Dana 53
Lauter, Ed 38, 190
Lautore, Ron 125
Lavelle, Susan Graham 10
Lavery, Daniel 63
Lavery, Emmet G., Jr. 75
Lavin, Richard 140
Lavoie, Daniel 198
Lawless, Lucy 86
Lawley, Yvonne 169
Lawlor, Charles 174
Lawrence, Anthony 142, 173
Lawrence, Bill 101
Lawrence, Carol 76, 171
Lawrence, Colin 142
Lawrence, David 57, 63
Lawrence, Glenn C. 150
Lawrence, Hank 76
Lawrence, J.H. 58
Lawrence, Linda 91
Lawrence, Mark Christopher 186
Lawrence, Matthew 14
Lawrence, Nancy 142
Lawrence, Peter 160
Lawrence, Sharon 158, 190
Lawrence, Shawn 38
Lawrence, Stephen 104
Lawrence, Steve 6
Laws, Maury 23, 110
Lawson, Eric 197
Lawson, Jamie 15
Lawson, Richard 191
Lawson, Shannon 54
Lawson, Sherilyn 81
Lazar, Dorina 112
Lazarus Man 106
Lazure, Gabrielle 177
Lea, Derek 138
Lea, Ron 62, 77, 145, 158
Leach, Britt 130
Leachman, Cloris 52, 59, 101, 129
Leacock, Philip 20
Leapin' Leprechauns 112
Leary, Laura 189
Leask, Peter 128
Leath, Ron 87

Leavitt, Lane 180
Lebo, Henry 146
Leckinger, Rick 169
LeClerc, Jean 50
Leduc, Daniel 81
Lee, Bernard 22
Lee, Christopher 33, 78, 79, 138, 144, 212
Lee, Damian 123
Lee, Donald Harris 152
Lee, Elizabeth 137
Lee, Eugene 97, 199
Lee, Fred 167
Lee, Gary 192
Lee, Gary A. 150
Lee, Johnny 38
Lee, Jonna 123
Lee, Mark 183
Lee, Mi-Jung 57
Lee, Michele 204
Lee, Mike 190
Lee, Robert 49
Lee, Robert E. 7
Lee, S.O. 45
Lee, Stan 56, 73
Lee, Stephen 25, 26, 190
Lee, Teresa 80
Lee, Tim 86
Lee Rich Co. 99
Leeds, Robert 65
Leegant, Dan 93
Leek, Tiiu 163
Leekley, John 31, 108
Lefebvre, John 54
Legacy of Evil 217
LeGault, Lance 32
Legend 188
The Legend of Gator Face 112
The Legend of Sleepy Hollow 113
Leger, Claude 81
Legion 113
Le Guin, Ursula 111
LeHigh Entertainment 88
Lehne, Frederic 13
Lehne, John 46
Leick, Hudson 108
Leider, Harriet 10
Leider, Jerry 185
Leider-Reisberg Credo Entertainment 186
Leigh, Brenda 40
Leigh, Jennifer Jason 117
Leigh, Kristen 169
Leighton, Margaret 68
Leimanis, John 35, 80, 103
Leirer, Barry B. 108
Leisure, David 78, 140
Leitch, Megan 139
Leiterman, Richard 59, 100
LeMasters, Kim 176
LeMat, Paul 133
Lemchen, Bob 148
Le Monde Entertainment 149
Lempert, Debbie 162
Lempert, Sandy 162
Len Stecker Productions 53
Lenehan, Nancy 16
Lenhart, Kerry 140

Lenkov, Peter M. 190, 191
Lennertz, Christopher 11, 90, 91, 173
Lennie, Elizabeth 195
Lennox, Doug 82
Lenox, Carl 180
Lenski, Robert 12
Lent, Dean 197
Lente, Miklos 54
Lenthall, David 168
Lenz, Jack 180
Lenz, Kay 96, 146, 183
Leon, Daniel 178
Leonard, Phillip M. 137
Leonard, Terry 65
Leonard Hill Films 61
Leonetti, Matthew F. 157, 164
Leong, Al 167
Leong, Willy 140
Leopardi, Chauncey 158
Lepine, Jean 81
Lerner, Fred 42, 109
Lerner, Michael 139
LeRoy, Gloria 182
Lesk, Stan 82
Leskin, Will 44, 186
Leslie, Joan 186
Lesser, Len 165
Lesser, Robert 27
Lester, Buddy 144
Lester, Ketty 42
Lester, Terry 107
Lethin, Lori 78
Leucadia Films 200
Levant, Brian 5
Levar, Lila 102
Levay, Sylvester 15, 99, 162
Levelett, Jim 28
Levels, Calvin 201
Leverman, Zerhe 66
Leversee, Loretta 156
Levi, Alan 150
Levi, Alan J. 24, 72, 99, 101, 108, 167
Levin, Ira 116, 151, 168
Levin, Peter 85
Levine, Floyd 20
Levine, Jeremy 110, 112
Levine, Larry 78
Levine, Marcia 24
Levine, William 112
Levinson, David 67, 151, 178
Levinson, Richard 147
Levisetti, Emile 11
Levitt, Steve 95
LeVouvier, Jean 49
Levy, Ariel 76
Levy, Eugene 82
Levy, Oded 138
Levy, Robert L. 70
Levy, Scott P. 11, 90, 128
Levy, Shuki 21
Levyo, Farrell 83
Lewis, Al 87, 127, 132
Lewis, Art 118
Lewis, Brittney 166
Lewis, Emma 122
Lewis, Fiona 59

Lewis, Geoffrey 15, 125, 156
Lewis, Ian 68
Lewis, Leigh 180
Lewis, Rachel 169
Lewis, Richard A. 114
Lewis, Richard B. (Barton) 45, 99, 101, 142
Lewis, Robert Michael 40, 44, 73, 98
Lewiston, Denis 16, 177
The Lexx 3
Leykis, Tom 175
Leyshon, Glynis 59
Libby, Brian 36
Libertini, Richard 89
Libman, Andrea 176
Libman, Daniel 135
Libman, Leslie 29
Licht, Daniel 29
Licuanan, Josie 71
Liddy, G. Gordon 209
Lieberman, Jeff 55
Liebmann, Norm 87, 128
Lifeboat 114
The Lifeforce Experiment 114
Lifepod 114
Lifetime 50, 54, 62, 77, 188, 204, 208, 211, 213
Lifford, Tina 39
Lighthill, Stephen 44
The Lighting Incident 114
Lightstone, Marilyn 55
Ligon, Tom 53
Like Father, Like Santa 115
Lill, Denis 16
Lillard, Matthew 54
Lima, Brian 52
Lima, Danny 191
Lin, Ben 117
Lin, Lucy 120
Linari, Nancy 69
Lincoln, Scott 16, 33
Lindberg, Lori 117
Lindbjerg, Lalainia 73, 155
Linde, Bette 93
Linde, Betty 23
Lindfors, Viveca 35
Lindhurst, Nicholas 80
Lindley, Audra 151
Lindley, Barbara 59
Lindley, John 53
Lindon, Lionel 151
Lindsay, Josh 136
Lindsay, Marissa 41
Lindsay, Mark 16
Lindsly, Chuck 140
Line, Mandi 125
Lineback, Richard 166
Ling, Bai 50
Linington, Gregory 49
Link, Eric 74
Link, John F., II 136
Link, William 147
Linke, Paul 144
Linville, Joanne 69
Linville, Larry 76, 131
Linz, Alex D. 190
Linzey, Philip 195

Lipinski, Eugene 104
Lipman, Ken 58
Lipovsky, Zack 23
Lipscomb, Dennis 27
Lish, Becca 52
Liska, Stephen 196
Lisnet, Julie Arnold 168
Lister, Tom "Tiny" 35
Littiman, Robert 188
Little, Cleavon 94
Little, George 177
Little, Kim 62
Little Richard 78
"Little Girl Lost" 172
Live Again, Die Again 210
Live Entertainment 125
Live Wire 210
Lively, Lori 55
Lively, Robyn 137, 138
Livermore, Troy 128
Livingston, Benjamin 109
Livingston, Jo 111
Livingston, Paul 58
Livingstone, Huey 66
Llanes, Juan Antonio 133
Llewellyn, Raymond 177
Llovid, Lea 29
Lloyd, Christopher 14, 148
Lloyd, David Byron 24, 88, 168
Lloyd, Ivey 200
Lloyd, Jake 194
Lloyd, Kathleen 190
Lloyd, Michael 171
Lloyd, Norman 13
Lo, Ming 92
Lobdell, Scott 73
Loch, Philip 24
Locke, Bruce 43
Locke, Philip 102
Locke, Rosanna 44
Locke, Tembi 166
Locke, Terrence 94
Lockett, Amy 123
Lockhart, Anne 23
Lockhart, June 44, 45, 133
Lockhart, Warren L. 28
Lockie, Howard 89
Lockmiller, Richard 11
Lockwood, Gary 75, 76, 150
Lockyer, Thomas 122
Lodge, Roger 35
Lo Duca, Joseph 86, 120
Loftus, Jimmy 83
Logan, Robert 206
Logan, Terry 180
Logan, Todd 111
Loggia, Robert 114, 199
Lohmann, Paul 44, 49, 184
Lois and Clark: The New Adventures of Superman 178
Lomax, Lindsey 66
Lombardi, Leigh 103
Lomino, Daniel 39, 42, 47, 75, 103
London, Andrew 44, 154
London, Andrew B. 115
London, Briana 95
London, Jason 27
London, Jerry 106

London, Michael J. 118
London Weekend Television 102
Lone, Jai 160
Long, Anni 189
Long, Billy 66
Long, Mary 94
Long, Shelley 68, 69
Long, William, Jr. 156
Longbow Productions 134
Longdon, Terence 121
Longenecker, Jane 10
Longmire, Susan 82
Longstreet, Greg 8, 10
Longstreet, Harry 8, 10, 192
Longstreet, Renee 8, 10, 192
Lonhurst, Mark 83
Lonsdale, Gordon C. 102
Lonsdale-Smith, Michele 127
Look What's Happened to Rosemary's Baby 115
Lookinland, Mike 166
Looney, Peter 97
Loperfido, Donald J. 149
Lord, Stephen 65
The Lord of the Rings 2
Lords, Traci 137, 169
Loree, Brad 176
Lorimar Productions 58, 172
Lorimar Television 100
Lorimar-Telepictures Productions 75
Loring, Lyn 25
Loring, Scotch Ellis 10, 87
Lorre, Peter, Jr. 34
Lorso, Bob 66
Lost Horizons 31
Lost in Space 38, 179
Lost Souls 210
Löte, Attila 46
Lottimer, Eb 136
Lottman, Evan 79
Lotz, Kurt 25
Louder, Michael 168
Lough, Catherine 57, 134
Lough, Elizabeth 166
Loughlin, Terry 168
Louis, R.J. 167
Louise, Tina 116
Lourie, Eugene 52, 179
Lourwood, Heath 89
Louthian, Guy J. 70
Love, Danny 160
Love, Robert 153
Love at First Bite 49
Love Bite 50
The Love Boat 2, 21, 34, 215
The Love Bug (1997) 116
The Love Bug (1969) 116
Love Can Be Murder 117
The Love Letter 117
Love-Struck 117
The Love War 118
Lovecraft 34
Lovecraft, H.P. 34
Lovejoy, Stephen 167, 174
Lovell, Dyson 122, 138
Lovenheim, Robert 167
Lovgren, David 62

Lovin, Deborah 180
Lowe, Chad 174
Lowe, Rob 165
Lowe, Sylvia 55
Lowell, Tom 12
Lowens, Curt 118
Lowry, Dick 146
Loxley, James 195
Loxton, David 111
Loy, Myrna 51
Lubow, Kathy 125
Lucan 210
Lucas, George 64
Lucas, Glenn L. 67
Lucas, Joshua 35
Lucasfilm Ltd. 64
Lucchesi, Vincent 78
Lucci, Susan 62, 83, 99
Lucking, William (Bill) 33, 60, 103
Ludlam, Jennifer 86
Ludwig, Jerrold L. 37, 118, 119, 151
Luisi, James 71
Luke, Eric 138, 170
Luke, Keye 34
Lum, Benjamin 68
Lumbly, Carl 120
Lund, Art 118
Lund, Jordan 165
Lundeberg, Karl 195
Lundgren, Stacy 108
Lundin, Rick 174
Lunghi, Cherie 32
Lupino, Rita 179
Lupke, Audrey 123
Lupo, Frank 162
Lupoff, Richard 186
Luraschi, Adrienne 41
Lussier, Patrick 57
Lustgarten, Karen 78
Lustig, Branko 97
Lux, Danny 155
Luz, Franc 186
Lye, Reg 59
Lyham, Zoot 177
Lykins, Ray 63
Lynch, Kate 77
Lynch, Ken 144
Lynch, Richard 79, 175, 193
Lynch, Sean 81
Lynch, Thomas W. 157
Lynch Entertainment 158
Lynes, Kristi 6, 126
Lynley, Carol 42, 131
Lynn, Bertha 159
Lynn, William 82
Lynne, Amy 167
Lynne-Hortes, Hette 92
Lyons, Robert F. 75
Lypsinka 200
Lysell, Allan 141
Lysell, Donna 141

Maberly, Kate 80, 168
Mabray, Stuart 78
Macauley, Charles 127
MacCloskey, Isabell 145
MacCollum, William 45

MacDonald, Jennifer 50
MacDonald, John D. 76, 77
MacDonough, Glen 18
MacDougall, Heather 154, 167
Mace Neufeld Productions 14
MacGrory, Yvonne 153
MacGyver 210
MacGyver and the Lost Treasure of Atlantis 210
Machado, Mario 51
MacHale, D.J. 182
MacHale, Philip 76
MacHugh, Doug 69
MacIntosh, Jay W. 197
Mack, Gene 75
Mack, John 152
MacKay, Bruce 81
MacKay, Don 184
MacKay, Jeff 199
MacKay, Mathew 81
Mackay, David 134
Mackay, Michael Reid 33
Mackechnie, Keith 62
MacKichan, Robert 164
MacKillop, Ed 106
MacLachlan, Annie 45
MacLachlan, Kyle 152
MacLean, Dwayne 191
MacLean, Peter 14, 124
Macleod, Alison 82
MacMillan, Will 35
MacMurray, Red 204
Macnee, Patrick 49
MacNeill, Peter 145
MacNicol, Peter 152
MacPherson, Glen 38, 57, 61
Macready, George 131
Macready, Michael 162
Macri, Corey 94
MacVittie, Bruce 166
MacWilliams, Jennifer 115
Mad About You 165
Mad Dog Productions 103
Madame Sin 210
Madden, Angela 49
Madden, Bill 93
Madden, Dave 126
Madden, Martin 75
Maddox, Billy 125
Mader 77
Madger, Zale 160
Madgett, Brittany 145
Madsen, Virginia 79
Maffeo, Neil T. 16, 18, 58, 96, 172
Magee, Ken 7
The Magic Boomerang 77
Magidow, Joie 171
Magnatta, Costantino 74
Magner, Frank 166
The Magnificent Magical Magnet of Santa Mesa 210
Magnoli, Albert 45
Magnuson, Ann 128
Mahaffey, Valerie 176, 200
Mahagonny Pictures 113, 141
Mahaney, Matthew 197
Maharis, George 116
Maher, Bill 140

Maher, Brendan 58
Mahon, John 114, 153
Mahon, Michael 35
Mahoney, K.T. 181
Maibaum, Paul 87, 168
Mair, Jimmy 142
Maisey, Terry 31
Major H. Productions 178
Majoros, Ashley 92
Majors, Lee 23, 24, 150, 160
Majors, Lee, II 23, 24, 150
Makaj, Stephen 100
Makela, Helena 171
Makichuk, Jim 60
Makkena, Wendy 24
Makoj, Steve 142
Makovsky, Judianna 199
Makroi, Pál 107
Malanowski, Tony 76
Malchus, Karyn 169
Malden, Boris 93
Malden, Karl 6
Malikyan, Kevork 177
Malinda, James 142
Malinger, Ross 181
Malkin, Sam 77, 112
Malloch, Peter 86
Mallon, Christopher 168
Mallon, Don 58
Mallory, Bill 130
Mallory, Carole 29
Malo, Rene 81
Malone, Nancy 92
Malone, Patrick 179
Malone, William 95, 196
Maloney, Denis 109
Maloney, Patty 58
Maloney, Peter 151
Mamet, David 216
Mammarella, Enrico 70
Mammone, Robert 139
Man, Frankie 111
A Man Called Sloane 206
The Man from Atlantis 118
Man from Atlantis: Death Scouts 210
Man from Atlantis: Killer Spores 210
Man from Atlantis: The Disappearance 210
The Man from U.N.C.L.E. 68, 98
Man in the Santa Claus Suit 210
The Man Who Fell to Earth 119
The Man Who Wouldn't Die 210
The Man with the Power 119
The Manchurian Candidate 11
Mancina, Mark 114
Mancini, Al 20
Mancini, Henry 66
Mancini, Michael 76
Mancuso, Nick 199
Mandan, Robert 97, 135
Mandel, Howie 82
Mandel, Robert 83, 163
Mandelbaum, Carly 104
Mandelberg, Artie 166
Mandelberg, Neil 115
Mandelberg, Stacy 152

Mandelker, Philip 144
Mandrake 120
Mandy Productions 178
Mandylor, Costas 70, 110, 117
Manesh, Marshall 181
Manetti, Larry 43
Mangassarian, Vachik 181
Mankofsky, Isidore 47, 64
Mankuma, Blu 142
Manley, Beatrice 171
Mann, Andrea 139
Mann, Brigitte 5
Mann, Carol 170
Mann, Delbert 159
Mann, Dolores 127
Mann, Fahrad 130
Mann, Frank 20
Mann, Horace 175
Mann, Sam 123
Mann, Terrence 126
Mann and Machine 41, 71, 149
Mannell, Larry 54
Mannen, Monique 75
Mannequin 125
Manners, Kim 105
Manning, Mark 76
Mannion, Sean 115
Manoff, Dinah 144
Manon, Christian 128
Manquero, Alberto 154
Mansbridge, John B. 119
Mansker, Eric 180, 186
Manson, Alan 144
Manson, David 130, 164
Manson, Philip 171
Mansy, Deborah Anne 88
Mantee, Anne Newman 14
Mantell, Michael 10
M.A.N.T.I.S. 2, 56, 65, 120, 145
Manton, Marcus 155
Mantooth, Randolph 30
Manuel, Raina 66
Manulis, John Bard 47
Manzella, Ray 78
Marcel, Denice 152
Marcel, Terry 146
Marcel-Robertson Productions 146
March, Barbara 27
March, Ellen 182
March, Fredric 102
Marchman, Joe 99
Marcil, Allan 96, 130
Marco, Phil 78
Marcovicci, Andrea 31
Marcus, Bill 18
Marcus, Irwin 63, 116
Marcus, Jeff 7–10
Marcus, Joe David 157
Marcus, Joe, Jr. 157
Marden, Richard 68
Margellos, James 138, 170
Margittai, Agi 46
Margo, Mitch 78
Margo, Phil 78
Margolin, Janet 109, 143
Margolin, Stuart 59
Margulies, Michael 52, 83, 148, 170, 172, 197

Margulies, William 131
Margulis, Cynthia H. 45, 179
Maria, Pavel Ana 112
Mariana, Michele 81
Marie, Constance 99, 186
Marin, Annette 101
Marin, Paul 142
Marin, Russ 36, 154
Marinan, Terence 181
Marinangeli, Marco 45, 179
Marinker, Peter 121
Marion, Blake 56
Marius, Drogeanu 112
Mark, Ivan 46
Mark Carliner Productions 142
Mark Gordon Company 115
The Mark of Zorro 210
Markey, Mary Jo 40, 77
Markham, Monte 51, 203
Markinson, Brian 10
Markinson, Martin 157
Markle, Peter 174, 198
Markle, Stephen 82
Markoff, Daine 8
Markosky, Melonie 135
Markowitz, Richard 171, 200
Markowitz, Robert 188
Marks, Alan C. 8, 10, 94, 192
Marks, Craig 92
Marks, Julian 50, 74, 127, 185
Marlo, John 195
Marlo, Steven 171
Marlow, Jessica 84
Marlowe, Scott 131
Marotte, Carol 54
Marquette, Christopher 135
Marquette, Desmond 132
Marquette, Jacques R. 12
Marriott, Craig 70
Marrocco, Gino 75
Mars, Kenneth 129
Marsh, Ian 134
Marsh, Jean 41, 78
Marsh, Mary 35, 55
Marsh, Nicole 23
Marshall, David 72, 150
Marshall, E.G. 142, 169, 193
Marshall, Edward 177
Marshall, Paula 69, 196
Marshall, Rob 37, 126
Marshall, Sidney 38
Marshall, Trudy 118
Marsman, Darren 104, 191
Marta, Lynn 73
Martel, K.C. 127, 145
Marth, Frank 32
The Martian Chronicles 121
The Martian Chronicles (book) 121
Martin, Andrea 82
Martin, Barney 92, 101
Martin, Ben 7
Martin, Dan 6, 166, 194
Martin, Jonathon Komack 185
Martin, Katherine 110
Martin, Margaret 84
Martin, Pamela Sue 21, 90
Martin, Pepper 118
Martin, Ralph P. 87

Martin, Rick 142
Martin, Roadblock 179
Martin, Ross 126, 199
Martin, Tanya 183
Martin, Tina 112
Martin, William 92
Martin, Zachary 23
Martin Pol Productions 16
Martinelli, Enzo A. 56, 65, 72, 98
Martinelli, John A. 51, 134, 197
Martinelli, Vincent A. 120
Martinetti, Nin 183
Martinez, A. 65, 94, 137
Martinez, Chuck 136
Martinez, Cliff 24
Martinez, Joaquin 114
Martiniz, Charles 89
Martinovic, Mise 16
Martinson, Leslie 106
Martinuzzi, Martin 94
Marut, Marc 82
Marvel Comics 27, 94, 95, 107, 146, 165
Marvel Films 73
Marvin, Ira 53
Marvin, Mike 88
Marvin, Richard 63
Marx, Timothy 52, 84
Mary Rodgers 69
Masak, Ron 11, 197
Masamitsu, Chip 116
Mascolo, Joseph 184
Mashita, Nelson 89
Mason, Eric 102
Mason, James 68, 105, 156
Mason, Madison 139
Mason, Tom 24
Mason, Tom 11
Masters, George Lee 117
Mastroianni, Armand 152
Masur, Richard 52, 100
Mathers, Jerry 76
Matheson, Ali Marie 82
Matheson, Christian 74
Matheson, Linda 79
Matheson, Merle 74
Matheson, Murray 14
Matheson, Richard 49, 59, 121, 131, 132, 134, 172, 184, 185, 188
Matheson, Richard Christian 70
Matheson, Tim 21, 31, 163
Mathew, Royce 76
Mathews, Delane 97
Mathews, Hrothgar 39, 62
Mathews, Kerwin 51
Mathews, Sheila 38
Mathias, Anna 75
Mathias, Harry 55, 180
Mathis, Grant 95
Maton, Andy 167
Matranga, Tony 76, 77
Matt, Hank 92
Matteo, Mona 180
Mattheson, Don 6
Matthews, Dakin 80
Matthews, Hillary 97
Matthieu, Michaela 66
Matthys, Anita 135

Mattingly, Hedley 78
Mattioli, Heath 6
Mattiusi, Roger 62
Mattocks, Charles "Soft Food" 47
Matts, Tom 111
Mattson, Robin 32
Matuszak, John 75
Matwick, Betty 108
Matysik, Ferdynand 67
Maung, Khin-Kyaw 8
Maus, Rodger 38, 76, 98
Maverick Productions 62
Maverik, Rik 166
Max Headroom 49, 73, 149, 194, 199
Maxie, Judith 51, 61
Maximum Overdrive 186
Maxwell, Don 67, 140
Maxwell, Paul 149
May, Bradford 71
May, Harry J. 147
Mayanzet, Maria 163
Mayersberg, Paul 119
Mayfield, Les 63, 68, 116, 158, 182
Maylam, Tony 160
Maynard, Richard 30, 180
Mayne, Belinda 78
Mayo, Raymond 131
Mayo-Chandler, Karen 45
Mayol, Gerardo 133
Mayron, Gale 68
Mayron, Melanie 68, 181
Mays, George 174
Mays, Joe 14
Mazar, Debi 200
Mazur, Dan 29
Mazur, Derek 185
Mazur, Kathe 80
Mazur, Laura 185
Mazzini, Francesco 155
Mazzola, Frank 15
Mazzola, Leonard A. 17, 93
Mazzucato, Paolo 125
MCA Television Enterprises 5
McAdam, Althea 39
McAdam, Jack 13
McAliley, Ira 104
McAllister, William T. 30, 142, 201
McAlteer, Gerry 59
McAndrew, Robert 143
McAnulty, Frank 190
McArthur, listair 123
McBeath, Tom 57, 62
McBride, Billie 159
McBride, Jim 27, 48
McBride, Matthew 48
McBride, Norm 76
McCabe, Sandra 29
McCabe, Shane 108
McCain, Ben 91
McCain, Butch 91
McCall, Ross 102
McCallum, David 68, 85, 98, 159, 206
McCalman, Macon 67, 182
McCann, Chuck 152
McCann, Sean 74

McCann, Tara 85
McCarten, Hugh 79
McCarthy, Dennis 192
McCarthy, Francis X. 120
McCarthy, John 145, 157
McCarthy, Julianna 7
McCarthy, Kevin 60, 65, 99, 123
McCarthy, Neil 177
McCarthy, Sheila 145, 157
McCarthy, Thomas 156
McCary, Rod 173
McCashin, Constance 189
McCauley, Jim 66
McCauley, Peter 187
McCaullay, Kerry-Ella 70
McCay, Peggy 13, 79
McClanahan, Rue 182
McClean, Colin 54
McCleister, Tom 84
McClellan, Peg 63, 68, 116
McClelland, Chuck 119
McCloskey, Leigh 23
McCloskey, Sean 103
McClure, Jacquie 55
McClure, Marc 121
McClure, Robert 24
McClurg, Edie 95
McColl, J.J. 93
McComb, Heather 73
McConnell, Judith 7
McCormack, Carolyn 195
McCormack, Eric 59, 99
McCormack, J. Patrick 19, 201
McCormack, Patricia 99
McCormick, Elizabeth 169
McCourt, Malachy 188
McCowan, George 118
McCoy, Heather 171
McCoy, Sylvester 57, 112
McCracken, Jeff 171
McCready, Charles 25
McCroskey, Michael 58, 126, 200
McCullough, Suli 63
McCurry, Doug 152
McCurry, Natalie 139
McDonald, Garry 139
McDonald, Gerald 114
McDonald, James G. 153
McDonald, James 7
McDonald, Mac 80
McDonald, Mary Ann 96
McDonald, Michael James 7
McDonnell, Jo 127
McDonough, Mary Beth 124
McDonough, Neal 152, 198
McDowall, Roddy 6, 11, 61, 121, 124, 130, 177
McDowell, Malcolm 16, 201, 210
McEachin, James 48, 80
McEnery, John 122
McEvoy, Andrew 49
McEvoy, Anne Marie 99
McEvoy, Seth 137, 138
McFadden, George 156
McFadden, Thom 105
McFarland, Bob 136
McFarland, Sean 189
McFee, Bruce 38, 185

McFee, Dwight 15, 51
McGann, Michael 112
McGann, Paul 57
McGarver, Holly 91
McGarvin, Dick 49, 66
McGavin, Darren 121, 131, 132, 136, 160, 162
McGee, Florence 111
McGee, Jack 93
McGee, Vonetta 135
McGibbon, Jeff 38
McGill, Bruce 119
McGinley, John C. 174
McGinnis, Scott 149, 201
McGoohan, Catherine 150
McGough, Philip 80
McGovern, Don 106
McGrady, Brynja 87
McGrady, Michael 198
McGrath, Jim 177
McGraw, Charles 53, 131
McGraw, Melinda 89
McGreevey, John 43, 127
McGregor, Jane 135
McGregor, Stacy 91
McGugan, Brian 61
McGuinn, Jim 123
McGuire, Dorothy 159
McGuire, Jerry 47
McHattie, Stephen 50, 115, 157, 195
McIlravey, Danny 28
McIntire, John 78
McIntosh, Jay W. 84
McIntosh, Peter 153, 166
McIntosh, Ruth 139
McInturff, T.J. 87
McIntyre, Andrew J. 67
McIntyre, Lucile Dew 24
McIntyre, Marilyn 154
McIntyre, Steven 60
McIver, Paul 169
McIver, Rose 86
McIvor, Elliott 75
McKay, David 58
McKay, Don 84
McKay, Jeff 124
McKay, Rodney 163
McKeand, Nigel 58
McKenna, Bernard 41
McKenna, Virginia 22
McKenzie, Dean 73
McKenzie, Richard 35
McKeon, Nancy 114
McKernan, Peter 7
McKinley, Ben, III 111
McKinley, Patrick 166
McKinney, Bill 100, 170
McKinnon, Ray 152, 165
McKinsey, Beverlee 52
McKrell, Jim 151
McKuen, Rod 28
McLafferty, Michael 28
McLarnon, Zarn 183
McLarty, James 84
McLarty, Jim 169
McLaughlin, Bobby Travis 95
McLaughlin, Kevin 26

McLaughlin, Maya 198
McLaughlin, Wynne 104
McLawhorn, Charles 176
McLean, Bill 118
McLean, Dwayne 83
McLean, Michael S. 101, 145
McLean, Paul 93
McLean, Scott 71
McLellan, Nora 59
McLeod, Duncan 163
McLeod, John 195
McLiam, John 98, 150
McLoughlin, Nancy 163
McLoughlin, Tom 6, 83, 163
McMahon, John 185
McMahon, Patrick (Pat) 159, 166, 194, 198, 199
McMann, Tony 123
McMannis, Cheryl 150
McManus, Don 108, 135
McManus, Michael 32, 127
McMartin, John 151
McMaster, Mary Rose 141
McMillan, Gary A. 91
McMillan, Kenneth 156
McMillan, Richard 112, 190, 191
McMurray, Sam 128
McNab, Michael 67
McNally, Kevin 102
McNamara, Pat 147
McNamara, Wayne Robert 54, 158
McNeely, Joel 67
McNeil, Claudia 125
McNulty, Kevin 62, 73, 135
McNutt, Stephen F. 182
McPhail, Marnie 190
McPhee, Daniel 95
McPhee, Peisha 95
McPherson, Graham 74
McPherson, John 192
McPherson, Tim 175
McPhillips, Hugh 105
McQueen, B.J. 38
McRaney, Gerald 11, 84, 150
McRobbie, Peter 188
McRoberts, Anna-Maria 23
McShane, Ian 19
McShane, Michael 182
McSkimming, Jason 38
McTavish, Graham 123
McTavish, Patrick 91
McTiernan, John 148
McVeagh, Eve 65
McWilliams, Caroline 11
Mead, Courtland 62, 159
Meade, Terry K. 71, 106
Meaden, Dan 20
Meadows, Jayne 6
Mealy, Barbara 94
Meatloaf 180
Medalis, Joe 69, 151
Medavoy, Rachel 175
Medford, Don 39
Medlyn, Helen 169
Medusa Film SPA 169
Meek, Jeffrey 179
Meeker, Ralph 48, 131

Meerdink, John 11
Meet Mr. Kringle 124
Megill, Sheelah 100, 170
Mehler, Tobias 155
Mehrotra, Raj 181
Meighen, John 114
Meilen, Bill 59
Meisner, Gunter 85
Meistrich, Larry 111
Mel Ferber Productions 39
Meledandri, Christopher 115
Melfi, Theodore 181
Melissis, Tom 185
Mellé, Gil 68, 69, 96, 106, 148, 160, 167
Melnick, Peter 186
Meloni, Christopher 174
Melton, Gregory 70, 196
Memel, Jana Sue 5, 13, 40, 186
Men in Black 129
Menard, Tina 53
Mendicino, Gerry 191
Mendoza, Arthur 140
Meneses, Alex 12
Menger, Matt 108
Menno's Mind 121
Menville, Chuck 41
Menzel, Paul 108
Menzies, Heather 32
Mer, Erica 19
Mercado, Hector 162
Mercure, Monique 198
Mercurio, Paul 45
Mercy Point 144
Meredyth, John Lucas 38
Merket, Dan 183
Merlin, Jan 42
Merlin 1, 2 122
Merlin: The Magic Begins 123
Meron, Neil 37
Merrill, Dina 66, 186
Merrill, Gary 61
Merrill, Todd 97
Merrow, Jane 88
Metcalfe, Robert 93, 170
Metchik, Aaron Michael 199
Metchik, Asher 68
Meteors 211
Metromedia Producers Corp. 136, 141, 156, 159, 197
Metten, Charles 200
Metz, Rexford 123
Metzger, Alan 55
Mexon, Bruce 58
Meyer, Irwin 31, 102
Meyer, Nicholas 138
Meyer-Craven, Mimi 36
Meyerink, Victoria 179
Meyers, Anne Taylor 102
Meyers, Gayanne 151
Meyers, John 8
Meyers, Rusty 193
MGM 119, 142
MGM Television 62
Miami Vice 151
Miano, Robert 27
Micale, Paul 162
Michael, Christopher 76

Michael, David Frank 190
Michael, Ryan 100
Michael, Stephen 163
Michael Burnett Productions 11, 25
Michael Phillips Productions 40
Michael R. Joyce Productions 29, 128
Michael Sloan Productions 150
Michaelian, Don 141
Michaels, Barbara 44, 90
Michaels, David 102
Michaels, Lori 162
Michaels, Parker Timothy 167
Michaels, Rhino 195
Michaels, Shawn 41
Michaelsen, Melissa 115
Michaelson, Brad 115
Michalis, Kim 86
Micheaux, Nicki 40
Michele, Michael 142
Michelle, Vicki 164
Michon, Jack 30
Mickelson, Robert 33
Mickens, Michael 7, 11, 136, 196
Middleton, Burr 137
Middleton, Thomas M. 186
Midkiff, Dale 144, 181, 195
The Midnight Hour 123
Midnight Offerings 124
Midnight's Child 211
The Mighty Ducks 15
Mighty Morphin Power Rangers 129
Mihalka, George 147
Miharoff, R.A. 111
Miksak, Joe 141
Milana, Vincent Duke 118
Milano, Alyssa 31
Milavich, Ivana 54
Miles, Vera 20
Milford, Gene 124
Milford, John 11
Milicevic, Betsy Blankett 48
Milland, Ray 25, 46, 48, 116, 205
Millar, Gregory 110
Millar, Jeannie 26, 71
Millbern, David 12, 50
Millenium Pictures 58
Miller, Allan 75, 103
Miller, Aubree 64
Miller, Cheryl 72
Miller, Dallas 174
Miller, Dan 166
Miller, Dick 75, 192, 195
Miller, F.A. 196
Miller, Frank 111, 184
Miller, George 94, 125
Miller, Herman 157
Miller, James M. 141, 156
Miller, James W. 6
Miller, Jason 193
Miller, Kathleen 170
Miller, Larry 67
Miller, Lee 156
Miller, Mark Jeffrey 24
Miller, Marvin 104
Miller, Michael Ray 101

Miller, Penelope Ann 200
Miller, Sherry 155, 158
Miller, Stephen A. 35
Miller, Stephen E. 170, 176
Miller, Ty 138
Miller, Walter C. 28
Millikan, Alden 104
Mills, Alley 147
Mills, Ann 46, 99
Mills, Donna 6, 44, 116, 168, 210
Mills, Eddie 155, 174
Mills, John 56, 67
Mills, Judson 20
Mills, Larry L. 162
Mills, Michael 183
Milzer, Cameron 30
Mimieux, Yvette 25, 51, 53
Mina, Mina E. 51
Minailo, Michele 150
Minchenberg, Richard 182
Mincks, Jonathan 115, 152
Mind Over Murder 211
Minkoff, Laurence 54
Minn, Haunani 8
Minnick, Dani 69
Minot, Muriel 80
Mintz, Larry 15
Mioni, Stefano 155
Miracle, Irene 130
Miracle on 34th Street 124
Miranda, Diana 136
Miranda, Susanna 38
Mirisch, Andrew 167
Mirojnich, Ellen 37
"Mirror, Mirror" 134
Mission: Impossible 65, 187
Mr. Ed 58
Mr. Stitch 56
Mitchell, Beverly 198
Mitchell, Cameron 171
Mitchell, Camille 139
Mitchell, Daryl "Chill" 181
Mitchell, Erica 125
Mitchell, Herb 91
Mitchell, Jake 94
Mitchell, John Cameron 167
Mitchell, Keith 105
Mitchell, Mark 128
Mitchell, Ron 9, 10, 82, 148
Mitchell, Sasha 137
Mitchell, Seth 180
Mitchell, Silas Weir 148
Mitchell, Sollace 168
Mitchell, Ty 105
Mitchum, Bentley 163
Mittelman, Gina 110
Miyori, Kim 104
Miyoshima, Joey 48
Mizzy, Vic 127
Mobley, Marta M. 7, 71, 96, 110
Model by Day 211
Moder, Mike 37
Moffat, Donald 53, 65
Moffat, Jan 153
Moffatt, Michelle 13, 127
Moffitt, Roxanne 160
Mogridge, Fiona 86
Mohbach, Jo 27

Mohica, Victor 150
Moio, John 65
Mojica, Monique 127
Moke, Jean 18
Molecular Films 28
Molina, Rolando 97
Mollin, Fred 60
Mollo, Cindy 29
Moloney, Jim 133
A Mom for Christmas 124
A Mom by Magic 125
Monaghan, Greg 137
Monaghan, Marjorie 195
Monahan, Dan 169
Monahan, Greg 99
Monahan, Jeff 174
Monash, Paul 156
Monde, Steven 29
Monette, Richard 82
Money-Coutts, Sophia 153
Monfort, Maty 63
Monk, Damien 187
Monks, John, Jr. 90
Montagne, Edward J. 127, 165
Montague, Bruce 177
Montague, Lee 102
Montalban, Paolo 37
Montalban, Ricardo 216
Montan, Chris 37
Montana, Hogan 82
Montanaro, Jovin 89
Montejano, Lou 33
Montero, Mae 71
Montes, Osvaldo 114
Montesi, Jorge 30, 50, 99, 139, 195
Montgomery, Belinda J. 118, 151
Montgomery, Karen 41
Montgomery, Lee H. 49, 123
Montgomery, Poppy 39
Moodey, Lynne 63
Moolecherry, Elisa 77, 104
Moon, Frank 92
Moon, Philip 27, 154, 175, 195
Moon, Soleil Frye 99
Moon of the Wolf 125
Moonbase 125
Moonbeam Entertainment 112
Mooney, Todd C. 7
Moonjean, Hank 22
Moonlight Productions, Inc. 99
Moonves, Nancy 157
Moore, Anthony 109
Moore, Arnie 12
Moore, C.L. 55
Moore, Charles Philip 137
Moore, Curtis 60
Moore, Deborah 123
Moore, Edwina 12, 120
Moore, Frank 158
Moore, Frederick 119
Moore, Gwendolyn 37
Moore, J.W., IV 108
Moore, Jack 174
Moore, Julianne 33
Moore, Millie 83
Moore, Randy 159
Moore, Robert M. 166
Moore, Roger 210

Moore, Sheila 100
Moore, Simon 81
Moore, Ted 121
Moorehead, Agnes 68
Moosekian, Duke 97
Moosekian, Vahan 147
Morand, Sylvester 80
Morby, Cindee 28
More-Kelly, Raéven Larry 127
More Wild, Wild West 126, 200
Moreau, Marsha 21
Morelli, Robert 75
Moreno, Belita 92
Moreno, Gerardo 133
Moreno, Lea 58
Morey, Bill 178
Morfogen, George 191
Morgan, Cindy 12, 50, 123
Morgan, Donald M. 46
Morgan, Gary 7
Morgan, Glenn A. 35, 55
Morgan, Harry 65, 126, 199
Morgan, Heather 29
Morgan, Julie H. 150
Morgan, Michael 124
Morgan, Pete 127
Morgan, Ronald E. 99, 101
Morheim, Lou 53
Moriarty, Cathy 5
Moriarty, Daniel 97
Morin, Alberto 199
Morita, Pat 6, 18, 90
Mork and Mindy 77
Morley, Robert 6
Mormino, Carmen 109
Morocco, Beans 87
Moroney, Jon 175
Morrill, Norman 23
Morris, Alex Allen 99
Morris, Frank 85
Morris, Garrett 25, 26, 61, 98
Morris, Howard 101, 127
Morris, John 55
Morris, Julianne 201
Morris, Kathryn 196
Morris, Oswald 59
Morris, Phil 45
Morris, Steve 24
Morris, Virginia 97
Morrison, Doug 27
Morrison, James 198
Morrison, Layton 190, 191
Morrison, Richard 51
Morrison, Robert L. 91
Morrow, Bruce Ed 152
Morrow, Byron 75
Morrow, Vic 44, 119
Morrow, Wendy 145
Morse, Barry 42, 121, 149
Morse, David 147, 168
Morse, Mary Kay 107
Morse, Robert 87, 199
Morse, Terry, Jr. 83, 107
Morshower, Glenn 7, 97, 186
Morton, Elizabeth 83
Morton, Gregory 29
Morton, Jeff 152
Morton, Mickey 123

Morton, Philip 186
Mortorff, Larry 70
Mosely, Page 201
Moser, Jeff 180
Moses, Sam 82
Moses, William R. 40, 62, 84
Mosfilm 86
Moskoff, John C. 78
Moskowitz, Alan 153
Moss, Elizabeth 63
Moss, Jesse 135
Moss, Michael H. 169
Moss, Paige 89
Mossley, Robin 61
Mote, D. Brent 52
Mothersbaugh, Mark 82, 148, 158
Motion Pictures International 38
Motown, Bobby 63
Moulds, Adam 58
Moulton, Charles 129
Mouser, Dru 16
The Movie Channel (TMC) 66, 71, 121, 190, 191, 197, 214
Moxey, John Llewellyn 73, 90, 91, 109, 131, 145, 197
Moyer, Betty 35, 81
Moynahan, Dennis 130
Mrs. Santa Clause 126
Mruvka, Alan 112
Ms. Scrooge 62, 127
MTE 24, 40, 44, 84, 87, 88, 93, 128, 133
MTM Enterprises, Inc. 37, 57, 118, 193
MT2 Services 73
Mudway, Malcolm 128
Mueller, Julia 136
Mulcahy, Jacinta 67
Muldaur, Diana 143
Mulgrew, Kate 213
Mulhall, John Anthony 42
Mulhare, Edward 107
Mulhern, Scott 130
Mulkey, Chris 105
Mullavey, Greg 138
Mullen, Beckie 33
Mulligan, Richard 17, 57, 80
Mulligan, Terry David 23, 84
Mullins, Peter 83, 107
Mummy Entertainment 190
Muni, Paul 14
Munic, Robert 179
Munoz, Jeaneta 73
Munoz, Michael 115
Munro, Lochlyn 176
Munson, Warren 53, 153
The Munsters 128
The Munsters Return 128
The Munsters' Revenge 87, 127
The Munsters Scary Little Christmas 87, 128
The Munsters Today 87
Muntcanu, Al 123
Muramoto, Betty 103
Murder in My Mind 85, 211
Murder in Space 211

Murderous Vision 211
Murdoch, Laurie 141
Murdoch, Susan 104
Murdoch, George 35, 55, 131
Murdock, Jack 130
Murphey, Michael S. 87, 163
Murphy II, Frederick V. 19
Murphy, Ben 72
Murphy, Charles Thomas 189
Murphy, Christopher 89
Murphy, Dennis Stuart 80
Murphy, Eric 21
Murphy, Kevin 128
Murphy, Krista 82
Murphy, Michael 163
Murphy, Michael S. 33, 186
Murphy, Paul 117
Murphy, Steve 175
Murphy, Terry 63
Murphy, Wendy 13
Murray, Bryan 126
Murray, Don 167
Murray, Doug 190
Murray, Joel 63
Murray, Michael J. 115, 167, 195
Murray, Mick 126
Murray, Mike 20
Murray-Leach, Roger 36
Murrow, Byron 131
Murry, Jalia 176
Murtagh, Kate 132
Muse, Margaret 162
Muse, Nonie 5
Musialek, Teresa 67
Muspratt, Victoria 90, 95
Musser, Larry 62
Mustin, Tom 51
My Favorite Martian 65
My Mother the Car 186
My Teacher Ate My Homework 217
Myers, Stanley 121
Myers, Stephen 57, 122
Myers, Susan 164
Myerson, Alan 87
Mylrea, David 5
Mysterious Island of Beautiful Women 211
The Mysterious Two 211

Nabatoff, Diane 66
Nabonsal, Jedd 180
Nadder, Robert 44, 189
Nadeau, Gary 15
Nader, Michael 130
Nadler, James 82
Nagai, Toru 194
Nagy, Gabriel 76
Nagy, Ivan 33
Najimy, Kathy 209
Nakamura, Tatsu 110
Nalder, Reggie 48, 156
Nanketis, Steve 81
Napier, Charles 95, 103
Napolitano, Joe 61
Narita, Richard 65
Narita, Hiro 27, 84, 144, 176
Naschmento, Nadia 73
Nash, Alan 102

Nash, Bob 118
Nash, Joye 111
Nassry, Robert 181
Natale, Greg 137
Natale, Lou 82
Natale, Louis 38
National Lampoon's "Men in White" 128
National Studios 148
Natole, Steve 119
Natwick, Myron 57
Naughton, David 78, 91, 103
Naumann, Chris 173
Nava 136, 137, 173, 196
Navarro, Bob 53
Nayar, Deepak 198
NBC 11, 13, 15, 20, 21, 22, 24, 28, 29, 30, 31, 35, 37, 38, 39, 40, 41, 42, 45, 47, 48, 49, 52, 55, 65, 68, 69, 72, 75, 76, 78, 79, 80, 83, 84, 89, 90, 92, 93, 94, 98, 104, 105, 107, 109, 113, 117, 118, 119, 120, 121, 124, 127, 130, 135, 140, 144, 148, 151, 162, 164, 167, 171, 177, 178, 184, 186, 191, 192, 195, 197, 203, 204, 205, 206, 207, 208, 209, 210, 211, 212, 213, 214, 215, 216; Productions 76; Studios 39, 109, 174
Neal, Braedy 58
Neal, Edwin 108
Neale, David 39
Neame, Christopher 170
Neckes, Robert 130
Neely, William 169
Neeson, Liam 16
Negron, Taylor 68
Neiderman, Andrew 60, 141
Neil, Terry Edlefsen 169
Neill, Anna 55
Neill, Bob 119
Neill, Roger 113, 141
Neill, Sam 122, 161
Neilsen, Bob 119
Neilson, Charlotte 91
Neilson, Inga 129
Nelken, Harry 60, 185
Nell, Scott 138
Nelson, Brian 187
Nelson, Christopher 56, 124, 193
Nelson, Cole 95
Nelson, Craig Richard 36, 130
Nelson, Craig T. 142
Nelson, Don 127
Nelson, Ed 77
Nelson, Erik 38
Nelson, Herbert 62, 71
Nelson, Jessica 16
Nelson, Miriam 6
Nelson, Novella 47
Nelson, Peter 41, 191, 192
Nelson, Ruth 84
Nelson, Sandra 61
Nelson, Shawn 148
Nemas, Scott 99
Nemec, Corin 114, 165
Nemec, Joseph, III 66
Nemes, Scott 101

Nemethy, Ferenc 46
Nerman, David 24
Nesbitt, Cathleen 130
Nesher, Avi 113, 140
Ness, Jim 179
Netter, David 201
Netter, Douglas 19, 20
Neufeld, Mace 14, 139
Neumann, Jenny 192
Neuwirth, Bebe 199
Neuwirth, Tom 41
Neves, Alda 54
Neville, John 104, 157
Nevin, Rosa 170
Nevins, Claudette 35, 144
Nevius, Craig 25, 26
New, Robert C. 101
New Amsterdam Entertainment 169
New City Productions 23
New City Releasing 113
New Concorde 90
New Horizons 25, 26, 71, 86, 96, 136, 173, 175, 194, 196
New Line Cinema 186
The New Original Wonder Woman 129, 216
New World Television 51, 78, 95, 130, 176, 184
Newbern, George 188
Newberry, Norman R. 12
Newcomer, Jim 76
Newell, Douglas 93
Newhouse, David 130, 164, 170
Newhouse, Miriam 195
Newland, John 58, 180
Newland-Raynor Productions 180
Newley, Anthony 6
Newman, Carroll 115
Newman, Jack 38, 112
Newman, Jenifer 115
Newman, Kimberly 76
Newman, Lionel 179
Newman, Melissa 151
Newman, Pamela 167
Newman, Richard 184
Newman, Tom 127
Newman, William 166
Newport, James 198
Newsby-Koschwitz, Simon 166
Newton, Barry 49
Newton, Richard 16
Newton-John, Olivia 124
Nguyen, Dustin 61
Nicholls, Phoebe 80
Nichols, David B. 75
Nichols, John Cannon 108
Nichols, Nichelle 5, 6
Nicholson, George Jay 182
Nicholson, Jack 11
Nicholson, Martin 82, 175
Nicholson, Nick 175
Nicholson, Scott 134
Nick Fury, Agent of S.H.I.E.L.D. 211
Nick Knight 130
"Nick of Time" 172
Nickelodeon 58

Nicolaou, Ted 112
Nicoleta, Galani 112
Nicotero, Greg 103
Niculescu, Mihai 112
Nielsen, Leslie 85, 131
Nigaia, Anjul 109
Night Cries 130
Night Gallery 130, 174
The Night Killer 133
Night of the Comet 147
Night Owl 211
The Night Rider 212
Night Slaves 131
The Night Stalker 45, 131, 133, 136
The Night Stalker (series) 3
The Night Strangler 132, 136
The Night They Saved Christmas 133
Night Train to Kathmandu 212
Night Vision 212
Night Visitors 212
Nightlife 133
A Nightmare Come True 212
Nightmare Street 134, 175
Nightmare Cafe 45
A Nightmare on Elm Street 36, 71, 143, 146, 172
Nightscream 212
Nigra, Christina 78
Nilsson, Rob 183
Nimerfro, Scott 196
Nimikiko, Scott 196
Nimmons, Shadia 93
Nimoy, Leonard 29, 30
1994 Baker Street: Sherlock Holmes Returns 134, 150
Ninnig, Dennenesch 166
Nistor, Stelian 112
Niven, Barbara 91, 92
Niven, David, Jr. 133
Niven, Kip 78
Niznik, Stephanie 62
No Different Flesh 141
Noah 135
Noble, Trish 199
Noga, Dona 142
Nolan, Barry 91
Nolan, Jeanette 78
Nolan, Jim 46
Nolan, John 162
Nolan, Matt 163
Nolan, William F. 30, 135, 184, 185
Noman, Eric Van Haren 117
Nono, Clare 36
Noon on Doomsday 183
Nordell, Phil 150
Nordling, Jeffrey 104
Nordstrom, John E., II 149
Norgaard, Carsten 89
Noriega, Richard 40
The Norliss Tapes 133, 135
Norman, Susan 107
Norman Rosemont Productions 124
Norona, David 126
Norris, Daran 61
Norris, Dean 69, 100

Norris, Kimberly 108
Norry, Marilyn 61
North, Steven 44
North American Pictures 49
North Star Entertainment 38
Northstar 212
Norton, Bill L. (B.W.L.) 72, 86, 176
Norton, Cliff 101
Norton, Mary 28
Norton, Susan 147
Norway Productions 164
Norwood, Brandy 37
Nosferatu 180
Nosseck, Noel 70
Not Like Us 136
Not of This Earth 11, 136
Not of This World 137
Not Quite Human 137, 138
Not Quite Human II 138, 170
Not Quite Human (books) 137, 138, 170
Nouri, Michael 147
Novak, Frank 61
Novak, John 57, 184
Novak, Kim 213
Novotny, Michael 55, 186
Nowicki, Tom 174
Noyes, Tyler 118
Nugent, Ginny 33
Nugent, Nelle 183
Nunez, Miguel 196
Nunn, Bill 148
Nunn, William 41
Nutt, John 64
Nuyen, France 88
Nye, Louis 6
Nyerges, Chadd 12, 163
NYPD Blue 193
Nystedt, Colleen 23
Nystedt, Kathryn 23

Oakland, Simon 131, 132
Oatman, Doney 164
Oatway, Steve 134
O'Bannon, Rockne S. 66, 142, 152
Obney, Jack Ross 21
O'Brian, Joyclyn 197
O'Brien, Chris 11
O'Brien, Dean 192
O'Brien, Marlane 51
O'Brien, Quentin 154
O'Brien, Vana 35
O'Bryan, Sean 87
O'Byrne, Bryan 44, 135
O'Byrne, Kehli 175
Ocean, Ivory 137
O'Connell, Deirdre 47
O'Connell, James 39
O'Connell, Randy 12
O'Connell, William 48
O'Connor, Carroll 67
O'Connor, Dan 12
O'Connor, Dennis 185
O'Connor, Donald 6
O'Connor, John A. 55
O'Connor, Kevin J. 116
O'Connor, Matthew 59, 100

O'Connor, Raymond 33
O'Connor, Richard L. 195
O'Connor, Robert 97
O'Connor, Sarah 76
O'Connor, Tim 119, 171
O'Conor, Hugh 177
Odell, Cary 34
O'Donnell, Jack 169
O'Donohue, John F. 10
The Odyssey 2, 138
Of Unknown Origin 217
O'Farrell, Conor 51
O'Farrell, Peter 146
O'Farrell, William 186
Official Denial 139
Oglesby, Randy 146, 175
O'Gorman, Dean 58
O'Grady, Adife 90
O'Grady, Lani 105
Oh, Angela 29
Oh, God! 91
O'Haco, Danny 115
O'Haco, Jeff 167
O'Hanlon, George, Jr. 197
O'Hara, Jenny 79
O'Hara, Michael 188
O'Hara, Shirley 71, 94
O'Hare, Michael 18, 19
O'Herlihy, Dan 79, 141
O'Keefe, Michael 66
O'Keefe, Sherry 148
Oldfield, Richard 121
Oldknow, John 20
Olds, Gabriel 183
O'Leary, John 83
O'Leary, William 146
Olek, Henry 54
Oliney, Alan 65
Oliver, Barret 99
Oliver, Christina 43
Oliver, James 91
Oliver, Jim 176
Oliver, Lin 153
Olmsted, Nelson 159
O'Neal, Ron 29
O'Neil, Tricia 19, 29
O'Neill, Anne 119
O'Neill, Chris 188
O'Neill, Dick 36, 101
O'Neill, Ed 196
O'Neill, Michael 194
O'Neill, Robert F. 72
O'Ree, Robert 75
O'Regan, James 38
O'Reilly, Robert 125
O'Ross, Ed 45
O'Ryan, Heather 25
Olsen, Ashleigh 59
Olsen, Katharine 91
Olsen, Mary-Kate 59
Olsen, Richard K. 47, 169, 188
Olson, James 164, 170
Olthof, Dirk 12
Olynek, Scott 135
Omen, Judd 35
The Omen 139, 140
Omen II 140, 164
Omen III 139

Omen IV 2, 139
Omens, Estelle 182
Omi, Sharon 10
Once a Frog 57
Once and Future Films 155
Once Upon a Spy 212
187 Corp 103
One Hour to Doomsday 217
Ontkean, Michael 168
OOG Corporation 102
Oparei, Deobia 58
Operation Prime Time 76, 77, 78
Oppenheimer, Alan 35, 75
Orieux, Ron 15, 134, 135, 170
Oringer, Barry 96, 97
Orion Television 18, 41
Orme, Billy Ray 181
Ormsby, Alan 137
Ornstein, Fred 89
Oroglini, Arnold 41
Orr, Christopher 152
Orsatti, Ernie 6
Orson, Barbara 53
Ortega, Miguel 108, 157
Ortelli, Dyana 97
Orth, David 166
Osborn, Kevin 138, 170
Osborne, Frances 65
Osborne, Holmes 109
Osburn, Julie 69
Oshima, John 194
The Osiris Chronicles 196, 217
Osiris Films 97
Osment, Haley Joel 109
Osmond, James A. 102
Osmond, Jimmy 102
Osmond, Wayne 101, 102
Osmond Media Center 102
O'Steen, Sam 116
Oster, Emil 145, 160
Oster, Steve 154
Ostrovkhov, Pavel 85
O'Sullivan, Anne 163
O'Sullivan, Barney 84
Othenin-Girard, Dominique 139
O'Toole, Annette 100
O'Toole, Peter 80
Ottaviano, Fred 105
Ottman, John 161
Oulton, Brian 31
Out of Time 140
Outerbridge, Peter 13
The Outsider 140, 217
Overbey, Kellie 165
Overgard, William 23, 110
Overton, Bill 29
Overton, Ric 63
Ovidio Assonitis Productions 155
Owens, Albert 96, 119
Owens, Chris 83
Oxenberg, Catherine 105
Ozone, Michael 166

Pace, Bill 134
Pace, Tom 73
Pacific Motion Pictures 61
Pacific Trust 25, 26, 96, 110
Pacific Western Co. 33, 201

Pack, Jeremy 6
Packer, David 47, 85, 191, 192
Pacula, Joanna 52, 136
Paetnau, David 141
Paetz, Laurel 198
Pagan, Michael 7
Pagan, Saida 163
Page, Charles 117
Page, Kevin 51, 52
Page, Peter 138
Page, Susan 143
Pagett, Nicola 68
Paige, Janis 14
Paladino, Dennis 186, 201
Palance, Jack 59, 188
Palermo, Michele 137
Paley, Penelope 55
Palillo, Ron 98–99
Palm Productions 22, 177
Palmer, Betsy 78, 170
Palmer, Darryl 147
Palmer, Gretchen 6, 71, 113, 125
Palmer, Lilli 85
Palmer, Sue 40
Palovitch, Shano 76
Palter, Lew 8, 10, 98
Pandolfo, Tony 181
Pang, Ed 111
Pankhurst, Patrick 150
Pankin, Stuart 19, 115
Pankow, Joan 188
Panton, Mike 180
Paone, Robert 113
Paonessa, Jody B. 69
Papamichael, Phedon 198, 199
Papas, Irene 138
Papazian, Robert A. 147, 151, 182
Papazian-Hirsch Entertainment 98
Pape, Jodi 77
Pappas, Valery 87
Paradee, Janelle Hensley 25
Paradise, James 181
Parady, Hersha 142
Paragon Entertainment 135
Paramount 35, 39, 43, 50, 60, 88, 92, 112, 115, 137, 139, 144, 185, 195; Pictures 42, 71, 75–77, 116; Pictures Television 41
Parati, Tim 174
Paré, Claude 81, 198
Paré, Michael 66
Parent, Monique 85
Parfitt, Judy 42, 43, 153
Parfrey, Woodrow 43
Paris, Aaron 87
Park, Andy 117
Park, Peyton 111
Parker, Carl 119
Parker, Corey 63, 93
Parker, Craig 169
Parker, David 28
Parker, F. William 18, 152
Parker, Lara 94
Parker, Leni 198
Parker, Molly 62
Parker, Nicole 62
Parker, Norman 55

Parker, Ronald 71, 145
Parkes, Gerald 12
Parkes, James 144
Parkhurst, Rod 57
Parks, James 15, 89
Parks, Michael 130
Parks, Nelson 120
Parks, Van Dyke 135
Parnell, Cheryl 110
Parolisi, Phil 47
Parrell, Tom Rus 117
Parriott, James D. 94, 130
Parrish, Amy 118
Parrish, George 180
Parrish, Julie 178
Parry, Mark 71
Parsons, Estelle 117, 215
Parsons, Jenny 94
Parsons, Karyn 80
Parsons, Milton 34, 48
Part, Michael 105
Partlow, Richard 15
Parton, Dolly 214, 215
Parton, Regina 132
Pasdar, Adrian 89
Pasquesi, David 158
Pataki, Michael 165
Patchett, Tom 146
Patchett Kaufman Entertainment 146
Pate, Christopher 139, 187
Pate, Michael 139
Paterson, Iain 182
Pather, Puven 71
Patno, Regan 27
Patricia, Tom 70
Patrick, Barbara 201
Patrick, Butch 87
Patrick, Michael Carter 80
Patrick, Robert 149, 201
Patterson, Christine 190
Patterson, James 35
Patterson, John 80
Patterson, Neva 191, 192
Patterson, Patrick 74
Patterson, Scott 8, 176
Patterson, Shelia 139
Paul, Adrian 94
Paul, Alexandra 90
Paul, David 75
Paul, Nancy 149
Paul, Peter 75
Paul, Richard Joseph 108, 193
Paul, Steven 28
Paul Fusco Productions 146
Paula Rudnick Productions 87
Paulin, Scott 39, 69, 193
Paull, Lawrence G. 159
Paulsen, Albert 157
Paunescu, Oana 112
Paunescu, Vlad 112
Pavin, Mark 169
Pawluck, Jade 141
Paxton, Collin Wilcox 44
Paxton, Glenn 39, 189
Paymer, David 178
Payne, Bruce 69, 149
Payne, Dave 7, 136

Payne, Julie 83
Payne, Marvin 102
Payne, Maxx 183
Payne, Patricia 33
Payne, Suzie 139
Pays, Amanda 204
Paz, Gerardo 133
PBS 111
Peach, Kenneth 38
Peach, Pat 28
Peake, Don 91
Pearl, Aaron 135
Pearl, Barry 15, 127
Pearlman, Stephen 71
Pearson, Jill 102
Pearson, Karen 28
Pearson, Rex 126
Pearson, Robin Rose 70
Pearson Television International 175
Pebblehut Productions 54, 104, 195
Pecheur, Sierra 171
Pecile, Steve 190, 191
Peck, Ed 94
Pedde, Eileen 134
Pedi, Tom 90
Pedroza, Inez 56
Peels, Derreck J. 112
Peeples, Samuel A. 164
Peerce, Larry 37, 118
Peerless, Donna 100
Pei, Edward 63, 166
Peldon, Ashley 25, 47
Pell, Barney 29
Pellegrino, Mark 108
Pelletier, Dave 49
Pellock, John 63
Pellucidar 105
Peluce, Meeno 75, 130
Pena, Elizabeth 97, 100
Pender, Tony 188
Pendleton, Sha-Ri 11
Penn, Edward 153
Penn, Richard 93
Penn, Sandra 107
Pennell, Jon Maynard 80
Pennell, Larry 38
Penner, Cassandra 60
Penney, Sydney 178
Pennington, John 59
Pennington, Michael 149
Penny, Jennifer 130
Penny, Sydney 35
Penso, Neal 140
Pentecost, George 153
Penty, Doug 71
Pentz, Robert 168
The People 141
Peoples, Nia 182
Pepperman, Paul 22
Percival, Lance 102
Percy, Daniel 102
Pere, Wayne 9
Perebinossoff, Philip 1
Perella, Marco 108
Perez, Miguel 8
Perez, Tony 193
Perfect Little Angels 141

Pergola, James 80, 96
Periard, Roger 191
Perkins, Anthony 46, 47, 93, 160
Perkins, Elizabeth 39
Perkins, Emily 100
Perkins, Jack 106
Perkins, Millie 84
Perlman, Asa 77
Perlman, Ron 5, 6, 183
Perlmutter, Darla 157
Perlmutter, David M. 177
Perna, Dave 105
Pernie, Steve 24
Perovich, Tim 159
Perrault, David 180
Perrault, Robert 55
Perrin, Rene 71
Perrineau, Harold, Jr. 174
Perrota, Toni 126
Perry, Brien 92
Perry, Don 182
Perry, Freda 59
Perry, John Bennett 92
Perry, Luke 151
Perry, Michael 88
Perry, Roger 119
Pershing, Steve 55
Persky, Lisa Jane 107
Persoff, Nehemiah 172
Peschken, Chris 173
Pescow, Donna 90
Petch, David 141
Peter Benchley's "Creature" 142
Peter Frankovich Productions 109
Peter Onorati 136
Peterman, Aaron 137
Peters, Bernadette 37, 121, 138
Peters, Gerald Saunderson 88, 148
Peters, Jim 153
Peters, John David 113
Peters, Jon 21
Peters, Mary 182
Peters, Michelle 110
Peters, Robert 7, 91, 110
Peters, Robert Sampson 67
Peters, Tricia 113
Peters, Virginia 132
Petersen, Curtis 157, 158
Petersen, Eric 50
Petersen, Kari 200
Petersen, Tom 25
Peterson, Arthur 164
Peterson, Chris 29
Peterson, Josh 183
Peterson, Loren 190, 191
Peterson, Richard 159
Peterson, Robert 92
Peterson, Tommy 191
Petersons, Alex 71
Petherbridge, Edward 80
Petrick, Jesse 29
Petrie, Daniel 125
Petronijevic, Dan 60, 93
Petrowski, Andre 198
Pettiet, Christopher 45
Pettifer, Brian 36
Pettit, Roby 174
Pettus, Ken 157

Petty, Kevin 23
Petty, Lori 21
Peyser, Penny 190
Pezza, Francis J. 154
Pfahl, Jayme 62
Pfeiffer, Dedee 123
Pfeiffer, Miro 16
Pfenning, Wesley Ann 105
Pflug, Jo Ann 132
The Phantom 155
The Phantom of Hollywood 212
The Phantom of the Opera (1983) 212
The Phantom of the Opera (1990) 212
Phantom of the Paradise 160
Pharrez, Paco 133
Phelan, Joseph 99, 101
Phelan, Mark 120, 144, 152, 154, 186
Phil Margo Enterprises 78
Philbin, John 125
Philbrick, John Winthrop 168
Philips, Lee 164
Philipson, Adam 170
Phillips, Avi 82
Phillips, Barney 76
Phillips, Betty 84
Phillips, Clyde 46
Phillips, Dorothea 31
Phillips, Grace 175
Phillips, Hugh Spencer 51
Phillips, Juliette 215
Phillips, Lee 172
Phillips, Michael 40
Phillips, Michelle 42
Phillips, Robert 125, 150
Phillips, Sam 125
Phillips, Sandra 92
Phillips, Sian 64
Phillips, Wendy 76, 166
The Phoenix 142
Phoenix Entertainment Group 21, 69, 78, 79
Photon vfx 70
Picardi, Michael 101
Picardo, Robert 21, 119, 121
Picatto, Alexandra 136
Pickard, Nigel 153
Pickens, James, Jr. 190
Pickens, Slim 53, 178
Pickett, Cindy 144
Pickup, Ronald 102
The Picture of Dorian Gray 60, 160
Piddock, James 125
Pieczynski, Krzysztof 89
Pierce, Ann 23
Pierce, Bradley 58
Pierce, Jill 173, 201
Pierce, Keith 187
Pierce, Richard 187
Pierce, Stack 125, 192
Pierpoint, Eric 7–10
Pierre, Oliver 149
Piersig, Max 145
Pike, Nicholas 17, 93, 159, 194, 196
Pike, Vicky 28
Pileggi, Mitch 108

264 Index

Pilgrimage 141
Pillars, Jeff 24
Pillars, Jeffrey 168
Pillsbury, Sam 108
Pilon, Daniel 81, 198
Pinchon, Kirk 179
Pinchot, Bronson 168
Pinchuk, Sheldon 18, 190
Pine, Phillip 39
Pingue, Joe 158, 195
Pinnock, Arnold 77
Pintauro, Danny 180
Pintoff, Ernest 90
Piranha 11, 212
Piros, Joanna 57
The Pit and the Pendulum 11
Pitenc, Miro 16
Pittman, Bruce 82
Pittman, Tom 12
Pittmann, Chachi 126
Pitts, Ron 91
Piven, Jeremy 186
Pizzadilli, Ebick 190
Plager, Joey 182
Planche, Valerie 135
Planet Earth 74, 143, 171
Planet of the Apes 74
Planet Productions Co. 125
Planetary Pictures, Inc. 172
Plank, Scott 61, 125
Plante, Carol Ann 12
Plaxin, Gleb 85
Plaxton, James 66
Plaza, Begona 180
Pleasence, Angela 36
Pleasence, Donald 37, 40
Pledger, Courtney 134
Pleshette, John 105
Plimpton, Martha 47
Plisco-Morris, Sabrina 63
Plotkin, Norman 40
Plowden, Piers 70
Plowman, Michael Richard 185
Plumb, Sally 138
Plumeri, Terry 163, 196
Plummer, Christopher 82, 147
Plummer, Terry 102
Plymouth 143
Poblador, Alyssa T. 68
Pochosa, Steven Clark 35
Podell, Rick 94
Podewell, Cathy 61
Podhora, Roman 50, 185
Poe, Amos 50
Poe, Edgar Allen 11, 65
Pogue, Ken 134
Pogue, Kenneth 12, 170
Point of View Productions 24
Pointer, Priscilla 51, 188
Polak, Richard 157
Polan, Mark 76
Police Squad 85
Politically Incorrect 140
Polito, Jon 152, 158
Polivka, Steve 86, 120
Polizos, Vic 41
Polizzi, Thomas R. 195
Poll, Martin 16

Pollard, Jon 58
Pollard, Lou 128
Pollard, Michael J. 138, 139
Pollock, Alex 39
Pollock, Wendy 102
Polo, Miro 11
Polo, Teri 89, 212
Polson, Beth 80
Polson Company 80
Poltergeist 2, 80, 83, 90, 93, 162, 190
Polygram 161
Pompa, George 114
Pompian, Paul 167
Ponterelli, John 115
Ponzlov, Frederick 70
Poole, Duane 92
Pooley, Cliff 22
Poor Devil 144
Pope, Brian 188
Pope, Carmelita 165
Pope, J. Lamont 154
Pope, Leslie 47
Popescu, Valentin 112
Poplin, J. Smith 118
Popp, Peter 123
Poppick, Eric 10
Porath, Gideon 23, 37
Porter, Don 135
Porter, Jennifer Nichole 168
Porter, Nyree Dawn 121
Porter, Rick 99
Posey, Ellis 108
The Possessed 144
The Possession of Michael D. 145, 217
Post, Markie 57, 195
Post, Mike 33
Post, Ted 131, 156
Poster, Steven 153
Poster, Tom 136, 201
Poston, Tom 76
Potter, James 173
Pottle, Harrry 20
Potts, Annie 119
Poul, Alan 201
Poulheim, Achim 166
Pound Ridge Productions 31
Pounder, C.C.H. 89, 114, 198
Pounsett, Geoffrey 66
Powell, Addison 55
Powell, Linda 117
Powell, Reg 76, 158
Powell, Renato 95
Power, John 169
Power, Robery 40
Power Man 146
Power Pictures 50, 74, 127, 185
The Power Within 145
Powers, Alexandra 33
Powers, Shane 25, 26
Powers, Stefanie 173
Pownall, Peter 13
Pozniak, Beata 199
Prady, Bill 87
Praml, Joe 69
Prange, Gregory 99
Prange, Laurie 150
Pravda, George 59

Pravda, Hanna Maria 59
Preminger, Michael 94
Prentiss, Robert 7
Prescott, Darrin 71
The Presence 217
Presnell, Robert, Jr. 151
Presner, Jeremy 142
Pressman, Lawrence 118, 190
Pressman, Michael 83
Presson, Jason 99
Preston, J.A. 89, 167
Preston, Reagan Gomez 68
Prevost, Guy 196
"Prey" 184
Price, Lindsay 144
Price, Lonny 137
Price, Vincent 11
Price, Walt 178
Priddy, Nancy 12
Priest, Dan 125
Priest, Pat 87
Priest, Robert 58
Priester, Lisa 66
Priestley, Tom 97, 118
Prince, Jonathan 57, 66
Prince, Karim 128
Prince, Michael 83
Prince, Robert 48, 72, 197
Prine, Andrew 131, 191
Pringle, Bryan 161
Prior, Stephen 27
Priqunov, Lev 85
Prisoners of the Lost Universe 146
Pritchard, Michael 64
Probe 212, 217
Procaccino, Gregory 125
Procter & Gamble Productions 6
Proctor, Hazel 135
Proctor, Phil 121
Producers Network Associates, Inc. 66
Productions La Fete 198
Profat, Francois 74
Progosh, Tim 157
Programmed to Kill 217
Project: ALF 146
Prokopuk, Michael 67, 87
Promark Entertainment Group 104
Prophet, Melissa 54
Proppe, Hans 69
Proscia, Ray 19
Prosky, John 5, 40
Prosky, Robert 69, 109
Prospero, Juliana 142
Protat, Francois 198
Prototype 147
Provencher, Dylan 93
Prulhiere, Timi 60
Prutting, Steve 137
Pryor, Mowova 48
Pryor, Nicholas 117
Psychic 147
Psycho 21, 34, 93
Psycho II 21
Psycho III 21
Pugliesse. Al 15
Pugsley, Don 97
Pulice, Jeff 175

Pullen-Shaw, Anthony 121
Pulliam, James 41
Pulliam, Keshia Knight 41
Pullman, Jeff 111
The Puppet Masters 12
Purcell, Daniella 136, 175, 196
Purcell, Lee 76, 95, 171
Purcil, Karen 96
Purdham, David 8
Purser, Reese 48
Purves-Smith, Esther 135
Pusheck, Jennifer 67
Pustil, Jeff 74
Putch, John 162
Puttonen, Michael 134
Pyatkov, Alexander 85
Pyper-Ferguson, John 174, 195
Pyrz, Gene 185

Quade, John 75, 143
Quaid, Amanda 67
Quaid, Randy 67
Quan, Donald 66
Quantum Leap 98
Quarmby, John 16, 36
The Questor Tapes 148
Quicksilver Highway 148
Quigley, Gerry 54, 112, 185
Quill, Michael 195
Quillan, Edie 46
Quinlan, Kathleen 197
Quinlan, Richard 31
Quinn, Anthony 86
Quinn, Patricia 22
Quinn-Martin Productions 12
Quinton, David A. 66
Quo, Beulah 73
Quon, J.B. 137

Rabinovitch, Cheryl 175
Rabinowitz, Mort 156, 192
Rabjohn, Richard E. 96
Rabjohns, Paul 5, 6, 40
Racimo, Victoria 29, 157
Rack, Willie 55
Racki, Robert 191
Rackley, Luther 110
Racz, Nicholas 49
Rader, Jack 13
Rader, Peter 63
Radeski, Barbara 54
Radford, Natalie 13, 82
Radford, Robert D. 23
Radick, Jeremy 57
Radin, Paul 84, 189
Radley, Susan 175
Radnitz, Brad 42
Radoaca, Constantin 112
Radon, Peter 152
Rae, Dan 33
Rae, John 20
Rafael, Mark Truitt 19
Rafner, Lee 174
Ragályi, Elemér 107, 127, 185
Ragaway, Connie Hunter 162
Ragin, John S. 106
Ragsdale, Emily Y. 76
Ragsdale, William 67

Rahn, Patsy 160
Raiders of the Lost Ark 78, 184
Raimi, Sam 86, 103, 104, 120, 159, 166
Rainey, Ford 170
Rainey, Jamie 38
Rainey, John 147
Rainville, Paul 38
Raiuno 144
Räk, Kati 46
Raksin, David 75
Ralph, Michael 70
Ralph, Michael L. 183
Ralph, Sheryl Lee 200
Rambo, Dack 79
Ramin, Ron 23
Ramin, Sid 124
Ramirez, David 162
Ramos, Luis Antonio 120
Ramrus, Al 46
Ramrus, Alvin 170
Ramsey, Anne 129
Ramsey, Logan 53
Rand, David 71
Randall, Anne 132
Randall, Stacie 40
Randell, Eric 194
Randle, Kevin D. 153
Randolph, John 129
Rankin, Arthur, Jr. 23, 110, 160
Rankin, Steve 89, 175
Rankin-Bass Productions 23, 110, 160
Rannells, Jonathan 77
Rantsen, Camilla 110
Rasche, David 50
Rashad, Phylicia 145
Raskin, Bonnie 174
Rassulo, Joe 145
Ratchford, Jeremy 73
Rath, Earl 72, 89, 124
Ratliff, Brick 167
Rattlesnake Productions 18
Ratzenberger, John 57, 78, 180
Rauch, Michael 199
Ravager 149
Ravanello, Rick 142
Ravera, Gina 196
Ravero, Ray 30
Rawley, Fabienne 50
Rawlings, Margaret 102
Rawlings, Richard 40
Rawlins, John 175
Rawls, Hardy 21
Rawnsley, Ben 180
Ray, Fred Olen 196
Ray, Melanie 202
Raye, Martha 6
Raymond, Alex 207
Raymond, Deborah 201
Raymond, Frank 105
Raymond, Jim 72, 80, 119
Raymond, Patricia 105
Raynor, Lynn 117
Raynor, Milton T. 180
Razzano, Lauren 111
Read, Martin 59
Reagan, Maureen 51

Reagan, Steve 163
Reams, Barbara Jane 183
Re-Animator 47
Reaves, Michael 70
Rebar, Alex 13
Rebhorn, James R. 144
Rector, Ken 55
Red Hawk, Linda 135
Red-Horse, Valerie 20
Reddeman, Manfred 85
Redden, Leslie 195
Redeker, Quinn 72
Redfield, Dennis 123, 174
Redford, H.E.D. 65, 113, 178
Redford, Paul 62
Redfort, Jeff J. 199
Redgrave, Lynn 181
Redgrave, Vanessa 176
Redler, Dan 94
Redlich, Ed 62
Redmond, Markus 146
Rednikova, Ekaterina 85
Redondo, Joseph A. 108
Redrow, Phil 197
Redwood Productions 99
Reed, Julian 38
Reed, Kyle 179
Reed, Peyton 116, 158
Reed, Robert 120
Reed, Robert Stuart 104
Reed, Rondi 199
Reed, Shanna 6, 7
Reed, Timothy Davis 137
Rees, Angharad 20
Rees, Roger 36, 145
Reese, Della 62
Reeve, Christopher 50
Reeves, Keanu 18
Reeves, Perrey 63, 144
Reeves, Phil 78, 201
Reeves-Stevens, Garfield and Judith 157
Regalbuto, Joe 99
Regehr, Duncan 78
Regents Entertainment 57, 122, 197
Regnery, Jon 50
Rego, Patricia 23
Reichell, Drew 170
Reicher, Steven P. 44
Reichert, Nancy 144
Reichert, Tanya 141
Reichmann, Wolfgang 121
Reid, Fiona 93
Reid, R.D. 94
Reid, Ruth 169
Reid, Tim 100
Reid, Zebulon 180
Reifel, J. 45, 179
Reilly, Edward G. 91
Reimers, Monroe 71
Reineke, Gary 142
Reinhold, Judge 24, 163
Reis, Diana 82
Reisberg, Richard S. 185
Reisner, Allen 42
Reitano, Robert M. 55
Reitano, Tony 104
Reiter, Bill 84

Reitman, Joseph 27
Relton, William 22
Remsen, Bert 91
Renaissance Pictures 86, 120
Renan, David 105
Rencher, Burton 169
Render, Paul 99
Renfield Productions 195
Renfro, Bryan 13, 158, 191
Rennick, Jody 29
Rentro, Bryan L. 94
Renzetti, Joe 178
Repeat Performance 186
Republic Pictures 12, 82, 103, 149, 153, 186, 202
Rescher, Gayne 14
Resnick, Noel 137, 138, 170
Resnick/Margellos Productions 138, 170
Resnikoff, Marta 133
Retroactive 212
The Return of Sherlock Holmes 135, 149
Return of the Creature 67
The Return of the Incredible Hulk 95, 150
Return of the Shaggy Dog 159
Return of the Six Million Dollar Man and the Bionic Woman 24, 150, 161
Return to Fantasy Island 207, 213
Return to Salem's Lot 156
Return to Witch Mountain 64
Revenge 213
Revenge of the Jedi 64
Revenge of the Stepford Wives 2, 151, 168
Rey, Jose 6, 52
Reynolds, Adrienne 174
Reynolds, Alan 175
Reynolds, Burt 190, 191
Reynolds, Debbie 81
Reynolds, Don 153
Reynolds, Hayley 114
Reynolds, Kathryn 165, 184
Reynolds, Michael J. 114, 127
Reynolds, Renn 161
Reynolds, Robert 46
Reynolds, Ryan 155
RHI Entertainment 30, 198
Rhoades, Henry 127
Rhoades, Michael 104, 158
Rhodes, Donnelly 23
Rhodes, Hari 61
Rhodes, Jordan 131
Rhodes, Michael 21
Rhue, Madlyn 144
Rhymer, Don 190
Rhys, Paul 83
Rhys-Davies, John 76, 78
Ribisi, Marissa 63
Rice, Anne 91
Rice, Jeff 131, 132
Rice, Norman 165
Rich, Allan 103
Rich, David Lowell 88
Rich, Katie 109
Rich, Lee 99, 172

Rich, Tim 83
Richard, Robert 93
Richard, Robert (editor) 192
Richard Crystal Co. 74
Richard Levinson/William Link Productions 147
Richards, Ariana 55
Richards, Brian 116
Richards, George 23
Richards, Gwil 171
Richards, Kim 53
Richards, Michael Camden 23
Richards, Michele Lamar 8
Richards, Tom 123
Richardson, David 141
Richardson, Ed, II 135
Richardson, Ed, III 135
Richardson, Ian 107
Richardson, Jackie 75, 94
Richardson, Jake 181
Richardson, Jay 140, 196
Richardson, Lillie 115
Richardson, Miles 149
Richardson, Miranda 122
Richardson, Ralph 68
Richings, Julian 38, 127
Richmond, Tom 13
Richter, Joan 175
Richwood, Patrick 67
Ricioppo, Paul 117
Ricupero, Michael 147
Riddle, Kimber 168
Riddler's Moon 213
Ridenour, Craig 109
Ridgeway, Lindsay 182
Ridgle, Elston 113
Ridini, Maryann 66
Rigel 190
Rigg, Diana 83, 154, 155
Riggs, Elvira 142
Riker, Robin 37
Riley, Doris 23
Riley, Michael 145
Riley, Sahara 112
Riley, Timothy 91
Riley, William 95, 103
Rimmer, Shane 20, 149
Ringwald, Molly 165, 188
Ringwald, Robert 188
Rio, F.J. 146
Riordan, Daniel 5
Rios, Mark Adair 134
Rioseco, Carmela 186
Ripps, Hillary Anne 40
Rist, Robbie 178
Ritchie, Anne 13
Ritchie, Don 147
Ritchie, Gina Angela 28
Ritter, John 100
Ritual of Evil 67, 151
Rivas, Geoffrey 109, 167
Riven Rock Productions 108
Rivera, Mailon 10
Roach, Claudette 83
Roach, Daryl 163
Roach, M. Jay 114
Roach, Martin 104, 191
Roach, Neil 89

The Road Warrior 59, 176
Roar 16
Rob Cohen Productions 108
Robbers of the Sacred Mountain 217
Robbin, Kevin 180
Robbins, Amy 177
Robbins, Lance H. 25, 26, 90, 96, 115, 128, 136, 137, 175, 196
Robbins, Larry 115
Robbins, Lex 115
Robe, Mike 62
Robert Halmi, Inc. 133
Robert Papazian Productions 147, 182
Roberts, Aled 83
Roberts, Arnold 180
Roberts, Arthur 136
Roberts, Clete 78, 192
Roberts, Davis 130
Roberts, Doris 101, 125
Roberts, Eliza 57
Roberts, Eric 57, 138, 204, 213
Roberts, Ewan 20
Roberts, Jane 111
Roberts, Kimberly 25, 196
Roberts, Pamela 117
Roberts, Rachel 20
Roberts, Scott 88
Roberts, Trevor 15
Roberts, William Converse 89
Robertson, George R. 54
Robertson, Harry 146
Robertson, Holly 138
Robertson, Marianne 18
Robertson, Myles 146
Robertson, Woody, Jr. 37
Robin Cook's "Terminal" 213
Robin Cook's "Invasion" 151
Robin of Sherwood 123
Robinson, Betty Lou 39
Robinson, Bumper 73
Robinson, Carol 160
Robinson, Charles 160
Robinson, Charlie 146
Robinson, Chris 173
Robinson, Edward G., Jr. 38
Robinson, Gadrew 41
Robinson, J. Peter 21, 31, 71, 73, 115
Robinson, Karen 157
Robinson, Peter Manning 45
Robinson, Ron 14
Robinson, Skip 19
Robinson, Sugar Ray 38
Robinson, Tina 16
Robirdie Pictures 130
Robison, Barry 154
Robotham, John 65
Robson, Wayne 59, 94
Roccuzzo, Mario 38, 41
Rocha, Kali 117
Rocha, Winston 109
Roche, Claudette 191
Roche, Eugene 75, 144, 152
Roche, Sebastian 122
Rockafellow, Marilyn 27
The Rocketeer 122
Rockett, Charles 199
Rockwood, Trent 200

The Rocky Horror Picture Show 59
Roddenberry, Gene 73, 143, 148, 164
Rode, Donald R. 91
Rodger, Kate 71
Rodgers, Mary 68, 69
Rodgers, Richard 37
Rodine, Alex 118
Rodis, Nilo 138
Rodrigo, Al 97
Rodrigues, Percy 73
Rodriguez, Agustin 73
Rodriguez, J.R. 169
Rodriquez, Jason 89
Rodriguez, Paul 87
Rodriquez, Steven 47
Rodriguez, Vince 166
Roe, Bob 88, 157
Roe, Channon 31, 97
Roe, Matt 25, 26
Roebuck, Daniel 39
Roemmele, David 94
Roeske, Emily 81
Roessell, David 73, 154, 176
Rogan, Paul 107
Roger Birnbaum Productions 15
"Roger Corman Presents" 11, 71
Rogers, Amanda 115
Rogers, Elizabeth 162
Rogers, John W. 167
Rogers, Michael 170
Rogers, Michele 87
Rogers, Mimi 194
Rogers, Victor 14
Rogers, Wayne 92, 101
Rohl, Mike 49
Rohner, Clayton 196
Rohrs, Carsey O. 37
Roisman, Harper 181
Roley, Sutton 173
Rolike, Hank 162
Rolsky, Robert M. 60, 88
Rolston, Mark 91
Roman, John L. 44
Roman, Star 102
Romano, J.P. 159
Romano, Rino 81
Romanov, Stephanie 121
Romanus, Richard 74, 77
Romero, Kaylan 29
Ron Gilbert Associates 61
Ron Weisberg Productions 51
Rondell, Ric 125, 170
Rook, Roger 97
Rooks, Roger 103
Rooney, Mickey 209
Roop, Larry 108
Roosen, Christopher 123
Roots 56
Roper, Steve 23
Rorke, Hayden 92
Rosa, Natanya 68
Rosales, Wells 29
Rose, Amy 104
Rose, Bill 152
Rose, Calvin 116
Rose, David 53
Rose, Joel 50

Rose, Lenny 75
Rose, Mick 86
Rose, Sherrie 26
Rose, Wally 65
Rose Marie 30
Rosebrook, Jeb 31, 124
Roselius, John 77
Rosemary's Baby 44, 54, 116, 172
Rosemont, David A. 83, 194
Rosemont, Norman 83, 107, 124
Rosemont, Romy 97
Rosemont International 83
Rosemont Productions 107
Rosen, Barry 37
Rosen, Lance 35
Rosen, Lance Seth 60
Rosen, Robert 23
Rosenberg, Alan 39, 68, 77, 200
Rosenberg, Arthur 89, 91
Rosenberg, Laurel 91
Rosenberg, Paul 99
Rosenberg, Rick 72, 188
Rosenbloom, Richard M. 125
Rosenblum, Nancy 96
Rosenfeld, Eric Mises 81
Rosenman, Howard 106
Rosenman, Leonard 34, 144
Rosenthal, Laurence 90, 109, 151, 173
Rosenthal, Mark 163
Rosenzweig, Barney 14
Rosher, Charles 34
Rosier, Bill 197
Rosin, Karen 89
Röske, Heinz 166
Rosman, Mark 27
Rosniak, Justin 58
Rosqui, Tom 129
Ross, Angelo 90
Ross, Bill 90, 130, 147
Ross, Brian L. 61
Ross, Don 144
Ross, Jeffrey 63
Ross, Joe 90
Ross, Marion 109, 124
Ross, Natanya 158
Ross, Patricia 153
Ross, Ricco 80, 149, 179
Ross, Sandi 75, 127
Ross, Stanley Ralph 129, 130
Ross, Steve 39
Ross, William 110
Rosse, Adele 91
Rossellini, Isabella 122, 138
Rossen, Carol 75
Rossi, Leo 140
Rossilli, Paul 30, 84
Rosson, Edward 141
Rossotto, Andrea 194
Rossovitch, Rick 25, 26
Roswell 152
Roswell, Maggie 79
Rotblatt, Janet 136
Roth, Andrea 147
Roth, Bobby 54, 119
Roth, Christopher 28
Roth, Ivan E. 105
Roth, Joanna 161

Roth, Michele 137
Roth, Nick 54
Roth, Shira 182
Rothcranz, Markus 181
Rothstein, Freyda 80
Rothstein, Richard 21, 76, 99
Rotmensz, Nathan 115, 128
Rotter, Stephen A. 55
Rotundo, Nick 74
Routh, May 41
Rowan, Gay 151
Rowan, Kelly 79
Rowden, David 197
Rowe, Hansford 153, 191, 192
Rowe, Kimberly 26
Rowe, Ryan 116
Rowe, Stephen 16
Rowe, Tom 61
Rowell, Victoria 69
Rowland, Beverly 102
Rowland, Jane 70
Rowlands, Lady 56
Rowley, Peter 169
Rox, Robbie 38
Roye, Phillip 118
Roys, Frank A. 153
Rozen, Robert 15
RSO Films 106
Rubes, Susan Douglas 83
Rubin, Bob 51
Rubin, Jennifer 70, 196
Rubin, Lance 51, 95, 184
Rubinek, Saul 13
Rubini, Michel 138
Rubinow, John 51
Rubinstein, Arthur B. 142, 153
Rubinstein, John 162
Rubinstein, Manya K. 169
Rubinstein, Richard P. 166, 168, 169
Rubiu, Ranca 70
The Ruby Ring 153
Rudder, Michael 114
Rudin, Scott 151
Rudin, Stuart 47
Rudnick, Paula 87
Rudolph, Maya 54
Ruffin, Don 89, 163
Rugh, Sandra 148
Rule, Frederick 171
Rule, Janice 53
Rumar Films 76
Runacre, Jenny 164
Runaway 182
Runciman, John 146
Running Against Time 154
Running Delilah 154
Runyard, Mike 42
Rupert, Florence 55
Rupp, Debra Jo 97
Ruscib, Nina 181
Rush, Barbara 125
Rush, Bryan 196
Rush, Sarah 56
Rushing, Brad 128
Rushing, Lance 22
Ruskin, Joseph 32, 127
Rusler, Robert 163
Russ, Tim 104, 180

Russell, Charles 128
Russell, Jeff 70
Russell, Jimmy "The Ape" 66
Russell, Kurt 157
Russell, Mike 138
Russell, Monte 7
Russell, Robert 49
Russell, Robin 145
Russell, Shirley 81
Russell, Stephen 81, 158
Russell, Steve 125
Russo, John A. 89
Russom, Leon 7
Ruston, Kevin 190, 191
Rutherford, C.J. 66
Rutherford, Gene 42
Rutherford, Kelly 31
Rutowski, Daiton 152
Ruttan, Susan 21
Rutter, Rob 180
Ruud, Michael 65, 101, 113, 178
Ryan, Bridgit 165
Ryan, Deborah 96, 107
Ryan, Fran 130
Ryan, Joan 110
Ryan, John 96
Ryan, Ken 54, 73
Ryan, Mary Kate 90
Ryan, Natasha 42, 79
Ryan, Patrick 35
Ryan, Patrick M. 103
Ryan, Rusty 160
Ryan, Tim 92, 114
Rybin, Vasily 85
Ryder 139
Ryder, William V. 85, 202
Ryecart, Patrick 16
Ryman, Bryan 60, 97, 106
Rysher Entertainment 31

Saban 115, 129
Saban Entertainment 128
Sabrina Goes to Rome 155
Sabrina, the Teenage Witch 155
Sabrina, the Teenage Witch (series) 155
Sacani, Christine 54, 94
Sachs, David 62
Sachs, Robin 19, 149
Sackheim, William 131
Sader, Alan 23
Sadler, Nicholas 163
Sadler, Terry Anne 23
Sadoff, Fred 148
Sadovy, Liza 177
Safan, Craig 180
Safran, Don 174
Sagal, Boris 85, 131
Sage, David 18
Sagici, Sandra 43
Sahagun, Elena 175
Sahely, Ed 74
Sahr, Sara 145
St. Clair, Ethel 58
St. Clair, Gandolph 142
St. Claire, Bonwitt 39
St. Clare Entertainment 128
St. Jacques, Raymond 157

St. James, David 7, 97, 198
St. James, Jean 19
Saint James, Scot 21
Saint James, Susan 130
Sakamoto, Ryuichi 199
Sakash, Evelyn 168
Sakelaris, Anastasia 6, 7
Sakmar, John J. 140
Salazar, George 114
Sale, Faith 6
Salem, Kario 178
Salem, Murray 29
Salem's Lot 156
Salgado, Gugut 200
Sallan, Bruce 73, 99
Sallows, Roy 158
Salstrom, Clare 5, 158
Salt, Jennifer 72
Salten, Felix 158
Salto, James 42
Saltzman, Avery 83
Saltzman, Mark 126
Saltzman, Philip 12
Salvage-One 213
Salvi, Delia 29
Salzmann, Bernard 13, 155
Sam 180
Sam Strangis Productions 75
Sambasivan, Arthi 54
Samms, Emma 41, 78, 91, 126
Sampson, Dondre 166, 183
Sampson, Michael 166
Samson, Barry 201
Samuel, Kennedy 142
Samuels, Brett 128
Samuels, Rachel 110
Samuels, Ron 189
Samuelson, Marc 57
Samuelson, Peter 57
Samuelson Productions 57
Samurai 213
San Francisco Ballet Company 193
San Giacomo, Laura 165
San Nicholas, Ric 157
Sand, Paul 113
Sandcastles 156
Sandell, William 46
Sander, Ian 144
Sanderford, John 25
Sanders, Alvin 61, 134
Sanders, Beverly 116
Sanders, Dex Elliot 120
Sanders, Gregory 112
Sanders, Henry 54, 119
Sanders, Hosea 186
Sanders, Richard 79, 99
Sanderson, Will 15
Sanderson, William 20, 163
Sandifer, Elizabeth 29
Sandin, Scott 128
Sandler, Todd 188
Sandomirsky, Kerry 134
Sandoval, Antony 85
Sandoval, Miguel 69, 89
Sands, Billy 127
Sands, Julian 200
Sands, Serena 125

Sandstrom, Kim 60
Sanford, Garwin 51
Sanford, Gerald 171
Sanford and Son 75
Sangster, Jimmy 79
Sanitsky, Larry 117, 169
Sankan Productions, Inc. 16, 60
Sansom, Ken 38, 97, 99, 101
Santalucia, Arlene 66
Santia, Moris 191
Santiago, Cirio 175
Santin, Fabricio 134
Santoro, Dean 118
Sapinsley, Alvin 125
Sara, Mia 46, 187
Saraceno, Carol 96
Sargent, Dick 145
Sargent, Kate 68
Sargent, Marina 35
Sarin, Vic 94, 112
Sarnac, Craig 207
Sarrazin, Michael 68
Sasso, William 57
Satan's School for Girls 213
Satan's Triangle 213
Satellite Productions 106
Satlof, Ronald 103
Satsoya, Katzou 110
Sattinger, Jill 55
Saturday Night Live 106
Saunders, Cliff 104
Saunders, J. Jay 94
Saunders, Nancy 117
Saunders, Russ 65
Sauvenkoff, Elizabeth Carol 141
Savage, Ben 199
Savage, Brad 156
Savage, Jennifer 89
Savage, John 47
Savalas, Candace 6
Savalas, George 6
Savalas, Telly 6
Savalis, Nicholas 29
Savate, Mike 80
Savath, Paul 84
Saved by the Light 213
Saviola, Camille 133
Sawa, Devon 134
Sawaya, Amy 119
Sawaya, George 125
Sawyer, Connie 101
Sawyer, Toni 167
Sax, Carroll 129, 156
Sax, Geoffrey 57
Saxon, John 143, 146, 170
Sayer, Philip 16
Sayre, Jill 86
Sbarge, Raphael 148
Scacchi, Greta 138
Scanlan, Joseph 93
Scarabelli, Michelle 7–10
Scarber, Sam 50, 66
Scarborough, John 67, 102
Scarpo, Brent 8
Scarwid, Diana 144
Scattering Dad 213
Schaaf, Geoff 92
Schacter, Brad 66

Schaefer Karpf Productions, Consolidated 42
Schaeffer, Rebecca 140
Schafer, Natalie 93
Schaffer, Ephraim 168
Schain, Don 200
Schanley, Tom 85, 150
Scharf, Walter 124
Scharnowski, Udo 166
Schaub, Sara 166
Schauffler, Florence 78
Schedeen, Anne 65
Scheer, Mary 136
Scheerer, Robert 144
Scheff, Michael 182
Scheidel, Peter 187
Schell, Jester 101
Schell, Maria 121
Schell, Maximilian 212
Schellerup, Henning 178
Schenck, George 61
Schenkel, Carl 21
Schepps, Shawn 63
Scherick, Edgar J. 13, 151, 167, 168
Scherrer, Paul 154
Schiavelli, Vincent 63
Schick, Ben 78
Schick Sunn Classics Productions 65, 113, 178
Schiff, Richard 163
Schiffman, Risa 8, 10, 101
Schifrin, Lalo 30, 62, 79
Schiller, Craig 94
Schiller, Wilton 33
Schliessler, Tobias 35, 60, 176
Schloemp, Petrus 85
Schmidt, Charlie E. 75
Schmidt, Ellen 85
Schmidt, Phil 176
Schmidt, Ronn 84
Schmitt, Donald R. 153
Schnarre, Monika 49
Schneider, Andrew 8
Schneider, Barry 83
Schneider, Daniel 83
Schneider, Paul 80
Schnell, Curtis A. 29, 89. 99, 114, 201
Schoelen, Jill 18, 36
Schoenfeld, Joachim 166
Schoengarth, Jack 94, 150, 192
Schofield, David 102
Schofield, Ryan 189
Scholl, Art 27
Schombing, Jason 93, 152
Schone, Reiner 19
Schooley, Mark 39
Schooley, Randy 5
Schoolnik, Skip 108
Schorpion, Frank 81
Schott, Bob 66, 135
Schouweiler, John 76
Schrader, Paul 201
Schradt, Sam 55
Schreiber, Avery 126
Schreibman, Myrl A. 77
Schreiner, Charmian 197
Schreyer, John F. 159, 189
Schroder, Spenseley 76
Schroeder, T.W. 13
Schroeder, Todd 38
Schub, Steven 29
Schuck, John 146
Schudson, Hod David 77
Schull, John Kenton 21
Schultz, Albert 147
Schultz, Kathleen M. 171
Schultz, Michael 47, 180
Schultz, Tom 181
Schum, Shawna 60
Schumacher, Joel 106
Schun, Shawna 88
Schwartz, Douglas 84
Schwartz, Elizabeth 169
Schwartz, Howard R. 42, 75, 94, 144
Schwartz, Lloyd J. 99, 101
Schwartz, Nan 186
Schwartz, Sherwood 99, 101
Schweitzer, Michael 73, 176
Schwimmer, Rusty 85, 154
Sci-Fi Channel 1, 28, 39, 45, 49, 52, 88, 100, 104, 114, 125, 139, 140, 149, 179, 181, 183, 203, 204, 209, 210, 213
Scofield, Dean 162
Scoggins, Tracy 19
Scolari, Kim 167
Scorpio, Jay 41
Scorpio One 213
Scorsiani, Joseph 13
Scott, Ben R. 109
Scott, Brenda 173
Scott, Campbell 117
Scott, Carey 109
Scott, Casey 137
Scott, Elliott 22
Scott, George C. 22, 36
Scott, Gordon L.T. 164
Scott, Jan 117, 124, 184
Scott, Jane 169
Scott, Jill 23, 62, 134
Scott, John 187
Scott, Judson 105, 142
Scott, Kimberly 181
Scott, Linda 42
Scott, Lloyd 86
Scott, Michael 60, 84, 115, 185
Scott, Roger 80
Scott, Sandra 75
Scott, Talmose 106
Scott, Tom 138
Scottish Television Enterprises 153
Scream of the Wolf 213
Scream 32, 36, 172
Screen Gems 25
Screen Gems/Columbia 34
Screen Partners, Ltd. 114
Scriba, Mik 152
Scriber, Ronnie 156
Scrimm, Angus 193
Scripps-Howard Entertainment 31
Scrooge Productions 13
Scruggs, H.E. 200
Sea Change Productions 154
Seagrave, Jocelyn 125
Seagren, Bob 150
Seale, Douglas 83
Search 212, 217
Search for Grace 213
Search for the Gods 157
Searcy, Nick 24, 152
Sears, Djanet 93
Seaton, George 124
Sebastian, James 5
"Second Chance" 49
The Second Civil War 213
Second Sight 189
Secret of the Ruby Ring 153
Secret Passions 217
Seda, Jon 47
Sedgwick, Kimberley 140
Seduced By Evil 157
See How They Run 1
Seeber, Eckart 181
Seeberg, Ian 40
Segal, Amy 85
Segal, George 204
Segal, Jonathan 29, 65, 119
Segal, Philip Davis 57
Segall, Bernardo 125, 131
Segall, Don 78
Segall, Harry 14
Segall, Stu 22, 92
Sehayek, Isaac 113
Seid, Art 14, 79, 90, 109, 118, 157
Seidel, Art 176
Seidelman, Arthur Allan 61, 183
Seiden, Matthew 188
Seivwright-Adams, Troy 127
Seki, Dan 43
Sekia, Mamiya 110
Sekka, Johnny 18
Selbo, Jule 86
Selburg, David 80, 152
Selby, Darren 71
Selby, David 55, 79, 80, 211
Selinsky, Wladimir 162
Sellecca, Connie 23, 33, 186
Sellier, Charles E., Jr. 65, 113, 178
Sellier, Chuck 108
Selzer, Milton 43
Semel, Stephen 27
Senga, Ken 187
Sensation Comics 130
The Sentinel 93
Seppey, Robert P. 5
Ser, Randy 37
Sergei, Ivan 23, 166
Sergent, Glenna 38
Serling, Carol 188
Serling, Rod 130, 131, 179, 183, 188
Sertner, Robert M. 45, 99, 152, 194
Servais, James 181
Server, Eric 94
Severance, Joan 25, 26
Severn, Maida 129
Sexon, Ian 153
Seymour, Anne 14, 36
Seymour, Carolyn 41
Seymour, Jane 68, 84, 212
Seymour, Kenny 177
Sgarro, Nicholas 119

Shabazz, Attallah 29
Shackleford, Ted 61
Shadix, Glenn 133
Shadow on the Land 110, 213
Shadow Zone: My Teacher Ate My Homework 157, 217
Shadow Zone: Undead Express 158
Shadowhunter 214
Shadowplay Films 69
Shadowzone (book) 158
Shadyac, Tom 67
Shaff, Edmund L. 16
Shaffer, Nicholas 105
Shagan, Steve 161
The Shaggy D.A. 159
The Shaggy Dog 158
The Shaggy Dog (1959) 159
Shah, Ash R. 181
Shah, Kiran 102
Shah, Sundip R. 181
Shah, Sunil R. 181
Shail, Gary 102
Shaker, Errol 166
Shalet, Diane 132
Shamata, Chuck 167
Shane, Walter 55
Shaner, John Herman 46
Shaner, Madeleine 46
Shaner-Ramrus Productions 46
Shanklin, Douglas Alan 103
Shanks, Don 174
Shannon, Gregg 171
Shannon, Michael 42, 71
Shannon, Michael J. 177
Shannon, Polly 54
Shannon, Russell 46
Shannon, Vicellous Reon 120
Shanta, James 23
Shapiro, Alan 27
Shapiro, Esther 27
Shapiro, Marcia 10, 12
Shapiro, Melvin 170, 171
Shapiro, Paul 97
Shapiro, Richard 27
Shapiro, Stanley 154
Shapiro Entertainment 27
Shaps, Cyril 80
Sharbough, Theresa 166
Sharif, Omar 80
Sharma, Sandeep 80
Sharmhill Production, Inc. 138
Sharp, John 36
Sharp, Jon 42
Sharp, Saundra 130
Sharp, Todd 29, 174
Sharperson, George 115
Shatner, Melanie 11
Shatner, William 11, 88, 89, 141, 161, 214
Shattuck, Shari 78
Shaughnessy, Charles 47
Shavick, James 57, 141
Shavick, Lily 57
Shavick Entertainment 142
Shaw, David 126
Shaw, Joe-Norman 135
Shaw, Larry 190
Shaw, Stan 66, 114

Shaw, Steve 167, 174
Shawn, Wallace 135
Shaye, Lin 146
Shayne, Bob 149
She Waits 159
She-Wolf of London 43
Shea, Ann 186
Shea, Katt 110
Shear, Barry 131
Shearin, John 69
Sheats, Brittany 117
Sheedy, Ally 66, 70, 84
Sheehan, Doug 124
Sheen, Darryl 139
Sheen, Martin 19, 20, 146, 152
Sheffer, Jonathan 139
Sheffield, Jeremy 122
Sheffield, Raye 40, 46
Sheiner, David 46
Shelden, Jana 177
Sheldon, Linn 77
Sheldon, Rodney 31
Shelley, Dave 72
Shelley, Mary 55, 67, 68
Shelton, Abigail 90
Shen, Freda Foh 10
Shenar, Paul 72
Shengold, Nina 61
Shenken, Lionel 180
Shenken-Brin, Beverly 180
Shepard, Billie 137
Shepard, Keith 169
Sheppard, Hilary 110
Sheppard, Susan 25
Sheppard, Talula 122
Sherbanee, Maurice 160
Sheridan, Jamey 165
Sherman, Harry 163
Sherman, Jan-Michael 107
Sherman, Jim 183
Sherry, James 139
Sherwood, Anthony 82
Sherwood, Madeline 83
Sheslow, Stuart 75
Shick, Bill 92
Shields, Brent 117
Shields, Robert 199
Shigeta, James 148
Shimono, Sab 120, 144
Shingleton, Wilfred J. 68
The Shining 159
Shippey, William 134
Shipton, Susan 157
Shire, David 27, 40, 92, 106, 127
Shirley, John 102
Shock, Nina 82
Shoemaker, John Bruce 80
Sholder, Jack 73, 186
Shooting Gallery Productions 111
Short, Charles W. 150
Short, Martin 122
Short Circuit 183
Showcase Entertainment 111
Showtime 6, 7, 11, 12, 23, 24, 25, 26, 50, 55, 58, 66, 79, 82, 85, 90, 91, 93, 94, 95, 103, 110, 112, 122, 136, 146, 152, 153, 155, 157, 158, 161, 172, 173, 175, 176, 193, 196, 197, 198, 201, 202, 204, 206, 207, 211, 212, 214, 215
Shpetner, Stan 53, 173
Shragge, Lawrence 62, 70
Shriner, Kin 44
Shuck, Peter 11
Shugrue, Robert F. 72, 98, 100
Shulders, Jermaine 120
Shurman, Ira 47
Shuster, Rick 173
Shutan, Jan 178
Shuttleworth, Daryl 135
Shydner, Richard 119
Sibbett, Jane 66, 135
Sickle, Van 159
Sid Feders Productions 39
Siebert, Charles 94, 182
Siegel, Charles 15, 100
Siegel, Lionel E. 65
Siegel, Paul 123
Siegel, Randy T. 80
Siegler, Bill 51
Siemaszko, Casey 25
Sierra, Gregory 162
Siff, Helen J. 92
Sigel, Tom 47
The Sign of the Four 149
Sikking, James B. 21, 157
Silbley, Grey 188
Silla, Felix 58
Silliman, Drake 99, 187
Silva, Henry 25
Silver, Joel 196
Silver, Marc 91
Silver, Ron 114, 158
Silverback, Michael 181
Silverberg, Robert 12
Silverman, Jeff 19
Silverman, Jonathan 186
Silvers, Catherine 63
Silvers, Nancey 37, 57
Silverton Productions 98
Silvia, Mihai 112
Sim, Alistair 36
Simandl, Lloyd A. 49
Simmons, Chelan 100
Simmons, David A. 123
Simmons, Gene 107
Simmons, Grace 16
Simmons, James 178
Simmons, Richard Alan 67, 151
Simmons, Shane 71
Simms, Michael David 57
Simms, Philip
Simo-Maceo, Manny 108
Simon, Alex 11, 173
Simon, Josette 30
Simon, Mayo 118
Simon, Stacey 180
Simons, Frank 27
Simoun, Henri 65, 160
Simper, Julie 166
Simpson, Gary 22
Simpson, Sandy 78
Sims, Kelley 169
Sims, Robair 120
Sims, Warwick 78
Sims, William 34

Sincoff, Paul 168
Sindhul, Adelina 152
Singer, Alexander 179
Singer, Bruce Fanklin 47
Singer, Carla 93
Singer, Joan 93
Singer, Marc 22, 88, 189, 191, 192
Singer, Reuben 148
Singer, Robert 49, 59, 132, 136, 184, 192
Singer, Sheri 60, 82, 175
Singer-White Entertainment 82, 175
Singh, Parkie 147
Sinise, Gary 165
Sinise, Robert L. 18
The Sins of Dorian Gray 160
Siodmak, Curt 85
Sirianni, E.A. 53
Sissel, Sandi 70, 181
Sisto, Jeremy 158
Six, Sean 7–10
The Six Million Dollar Man 65, 160
The Six Million Dollar Man (series) 168
Skene, Rick 185
Skillen, Nancy 30
Skinner, Beverly 169
Skinta, George 21
Sklaroff, Jon 29
Skloff, Michael 87
Skodis, Bob 133
Skodis, Robert T. 133
Skotak, Dennis 11
Skotak, Robert 11
Slan, Jon 13
Slate, Jeremy 171
Slater, Helen 186
Slavin, Millie 151
Slavin, Randall 73
Slayton, Bobby 158
Sleete, Gena 111
Sliders 2, 57, 78, 97, 184
Sloan, Harry 106
Sloan, Michael 20, 23, 24, 150
Sloan, Sean 71, 91
Slovis, Michael 82
Slutske, Ronna 174
Small, Buddy (Budd) 53, 160
Small, Michael 111
Smalls, Clay 111
Smart, Patsy 20
Smart, Rebecca 58
Smerczak, Ron 146
Smiar, Brian 154
Smight, Jack 68
Smiley, Sam 152
Smillie, Bill 48
Smith, Allen E. 182
Smith, Andrew 112
Smith, Arjay 181
Smith, Caroline 29
Smith, Charles Martin 152
Smith, Cotter 30
Smith, Craig 161
Smith, Dean 180
Smith, Edgar D. 117
Smith, Forry 97

Smith, Francesca Marie 87
Smith, Frank T. 98
Smith, G. Warren 88
Smith, Gary 13
Smith, Gregory Edward 5, 112, 157
Smith, Howard A. 172
Smith, Howard K. 192
Smith, Irby 15
Smith, J.W. 89
Smith, Jack Martin 170
Smith, Jaclyn 117, 133
Smith, Jamie Renee 181
Smith, Jason D. 92
Smith, Jeffrey 190
Smith, Jim B. 32
Smith, Julie 196
Smith, Kavan 73
Smith, Keith C. 25, 171
Smith, Ken 104
Smith, Kent 34, 109, 131
Smith, Kreton 81
Smith, Kurtwood 123
Smith, Lane 10, 30, 60
Smith, Lewis 119
Smith, Liz 36
Smith, Marilyn 82
Smith, Mitty 27
Smith, Patricia 143
Smith, Rex 184
Smith, Roland 94
Smith, Roy Forge 83
Smith, Ryan 55
Smith, Scott 84, 128
Smith, Shawnee 28, 159, 165, 188
Smith, Shelley 142, 178
Smith, Taran Noah 62
Smith, Taylor 166
Smith, Thomas G. 64
Smith, Thorne 69, 182
Smith, Wallace E. 84
Smith, William 43
Smith, Yeardley 181
Smith-Hemion Productions 13
Smith-Sands, Lindsey 35
Smithie, Alan 138
Smits, Jimmy 169
The Smokey Mountain Christmas 214
The Smothers Brothers Show 38, 182
Smurl, Jack 83
Smurl, Janet 83
Smythe, Marcus 182
Snell, Richard 8
Snipes, Wesley 207
Snively, Robert 165
Snodgrass, Melinda 166, 167, 183
Snow, Mark 39, 92, 146, 163, 187
Snow White 214
Snow White: A Tale of Terror 161
Snowbeast 214
Snuffy, W.G. Walden 166
Snyder, John 97
Snyder, Rick 10
Sobel, Curt 33
Soden, Maura 67
Sofer, Rena 134
Sofron, Cristi 112
Sohl, Jerry 131
Sokoloff, Harvey 38

Sokoloff, Marla 68
Sokoloff, Philip 154
Solari, Camille 28
Solberg, Shayn 23
Sole, Alfred 82
Sole Survivor 161
Soles, P.J. 144
Solimine, Christopher 138
Solis, Christina 7, 26
Sollenberg, Lee 134
Solomon, George 79
Solomon, Ken 159
Solomon, Maribeth 50, 195
Solow, Herbert F. 106, 118
Solow Production Co. 118
Solowicz, Dick 163
Soltes, Elan 71
Somers, Suzanne 54, 117, 157
Something Evil 162
Something Is Out There 162
Sometimes They Come Back 163
Sometimes They Come Back Again 163
Sommer, Josef 24
Sondergaard, Gale 34
Sood, Veena 170
Soong, Lucille 201
Sopanen, Jeri 23
Soranson, Linda 12
Sorbo, Kevin 86
Sorcey, Juliet 124
Sorel, Theodore 55
Sorenson, Bob 115, 138
Sorenson, Heidi 172
Sorenson, January 200
Sori, Mireille 190
Soroor, Khan Agha 147
Sorrells, Bill 38, 145
Sorvino, Paul 36
Sosanya, Nina 86
Sosman, Pipo 18
Sosna, David 159, 166
Soto, Talisa 193
Sotriades, Phoebe 81
Soul, David 79, 156
Soule, Olan 160
South Pacific Pictures 38
Southcott, Fleet 43, 90
Southon, Mike 161
Southwick, Shawn 28
Soylent Green 110
Space: Above and Beyond 2
Space Marines 214
Space Rangers 137
Spacejacked 214
Spacek, Stephen 181
Spader, James 167
Spargo, Sheree 114
Sparks, Adrian 100
Sparrow, David 77
Speakman, Jeff 179
Specht, Robert 131
Special Report: Journey to Mars 163
Spectacor Films 54, 94, 104
Spectator Films/Academy Entertainment 13
Spectre 2, 148, 164, 217
Speer, Martin 65

272 Index

Speight, Richard, Jr. 12, 50, 121
Speirs, Steven 107
The Spell 164
Spellbreaker 112
Spelling Entertainment Group 98
Spelling Films 168
Spelling, Aaron 43, 90, 109, 118, 145
Spelman, Sharon 167
Spence, Bruce 128
Spence, Johnnie 165
Spence, Michael 113
Spence, Mindy 157
Spencer, James 104
Spencer, Norm 185
Spencer, Roy 59
Spencer-Phillips, Hugh 184
Sperdakos, George 65
Sperling, Milton 29
Spicer, Jerry 140
Spider-Man 2, 165
Spider-Man 56, 165
Spielberg, Steven 131, 162
Spier, Carol 79
Spies, Adrian 85
Spiliotopoulos, Evan 113, 140
Spillman, Darin 7, 71, 91, 96, 110, 175
Spindler, Vlado 16
Spinell, Joe 193
Spink, Philip 23
Spinner, Anthony 18
The Spirit 214
Spirit Productions 67
Spiro, Lev L. 7
Spirson, Leslie Lehr 85
Spohn, Carter Paul 10, 175
Sponsler, John 57
Spotts, Alli 28
Spradlin, G.D. 97
Sprague, Richard M. 160
Spraitley, Tom 182
Spring Creek Productions 39
Springfield, Rick 113, 130
Sprogis, Robert K. 191
Sprosty, Joe 175
Staahl, Jim 87
Stabenau, Erik F. 144
Stack, Elizabeth 96
Stack, Robert 214
Stack, Timothy 91
Stader, Peter 78
Stafford, Maire 90
Stafford, Shanghai 23
Stafford, Stephen T. 35
Stafford, Steven 23
Stagner, Rama Laurie 134
Staheli, Paul 65, 113, 178
Stahl, Richard 79, 87
Stahlbrand, Sandi 147
Staines, Christopher 153
Stainton, Michael 102
Stait, Brent 93
Staley, James 133, 167
Stalk the Wild Child 214
Stambler, Robert 144
Stamm, Raimund 84
Stamos, John 6

Stamp, Terence 177
The Stand 165
Standing, John 35, 80
Stanford, George Brown 105
Stanhill, Kimberly 22
Stanley, Paul 107, 161
Stanton, Todd 97
Stanwyck, Barbara 90
Staples, Sheryl 167
Stapleton, Brendon 81
Stapleton, Jean 74
Star Command 166
Star Portal 137
Star Trek 2, 21, 30, 74, 89, 108, 134, 141, 148, 171, 196
Star Trek: Deep Space Nine 97, 114, 135, 214
Star Trek: The Motion Picture 120
Star Trek: The Next Generation 12, 32, 45, 52, 74, 98, 119, 122, 120, 124, 167
Star Trek II: Wrath of Khan 143, 182
Star Trek: Voyager 21, 105, 119, 122, 211, 213
Star Wars 2, 61, 104
Starcrossed 167
Stardust International 169
Starflight: The Plane That Couldn't Land 214
Stark, Alan 166
Stark, Kimberleigh 30
Stark, Timothy 67
Starman 37, 65, 77, 96, 154, 167, 178
Starr, Adam 193
Starr, Don 192
Starr, Judy 137
Starr, Pat 16
Starr, Ringo 6
Starr, Robert 130
Starz! 5
Statham, Ellen 137
Statham, Patrick J. 194
Statt, Brent 139
Stauber, Carrie 29
Stavin, Mary 16
Stay, Richard 101
Steadham, John 171
Steadman, Ian 146
Steadman, Robert 114
Stearns, Craig 148, 159
Stears, John 121
Steckler, Len 53
Steedman, Tony 149
Steel, Brian 142
Steel, Don 107
Steel Justice 167
Steele, Peter 187
Steemson, Helen 86
Steemson, John 86, 169
Steenburgen, Mary 80
Stefaniuk, Rob 82, 195
Stefanovic, Jasna 190, 191
Stein, Ben 128
Steinberg, David A. 66
Steiner, Robert 155
Steinfeld, Jake 99, 101
Steinick, Lara 186
Steinmann, Danny 164

Stell, Aaron 43, 165
Stellar, James, Jr. 137
Stelzer, Peter A. 21
Stempel, Kyra 144
Stennett, Myra 55
Stensland, Athena 136, 173
Stenson, Alan 138
Stensvold, Alan 156
Step by Step 119
The Stepford Children 167
The Stepford Husbands 168
The Stepford Wives 151, 168
Stephen J. Cannell Productions 124, 176
Stephen King's "The Langoliers" 168
Stephen King's "The Night Flier" 169
Stephen King's "The Tommyknockers" 169
Stephens, Duane V. 48, 200
Stephens, Rod 41
Stephenson, Denise 79
Stephenson, Gary L. 158
Sterland, John 149
Sterling, John 111
Sterling, Mindy 136
Sterling, Philip 51, 56
Sterling, Tisha 131
Stern, Jamie 16, 52
Stern, Jenna 188
Stern, Kandy Berley 13
Stern, Mark 114, 142
Stern, Otto 85
Stern, Sandor 13, 16, 60, 197
Stern, Steven H. 137
Stern, Steven Hilliard 75
Sterne, Gordon 80
Sternhagen, Frances 147
Sternlake, Ian 183
Sternlight, Suzanne Chambre 19
Steve White Productions 47
Stevens, Andrew 182
Stevens, Craig 41, 106
Stevens, Damion 154
Stevens, David 122
Stevens, John Wright 111
Stevens, Leslie 72
Stevens, Mary Ann 191
Stevens, Morton 6, 89, 120, 144, 159, 179
Stevens, Neal 169
Stevens, Robert 66
Stevens, Scott 117
Stevens, Stella 129
Stevens, Tom 75
Stevens, William 72
Stevensen, Scott 194
Stevenson, Charles C., Jr. 92
Stevenson, Doug 80
Stevenson, Houseley 99, 101
Stevenson, Parker 113, 136, 139, 178
Stevenson, Robert Louis 102
Stevenson, Scott 118
Stewart, Amy 185
Stewart, Ashton 169
Stewart, Bobby L. 170
Stewart, Catherine Mary 15, 147

Stewart, Douglas 141, 151
Stewart, E.G. 65
Stewart, Fred Mustard 135
Stewart, Jamie 183
Stewart, John 135
Stewart, Lynne Marie 87
Stewart, Malcolm 62
Stewart, Mel 99
Stewart, Nils Allen 6
Stewart, Patrick 32, 139
Stewart, Paul 38
Stewart, Peg 171, 178
Stewart, Trish 179
Steyn, Jack 21
Stidder, Ted 84
Stier, Hans Martin 166
Still, Dana 139
Still Not Quite Human 138, 170
Stine, R.L. 158
Stitch, William B. 146
Stock, Barbara 91
Stock-Poynton, Amy 109
Stockdale, Gina 23
Stockwell, Dean 168
Stoddard, Malcolm 80
Stoica, Rares 112
Stoker, Austin 72
Stoker, Bram 59
Stokes, John 70, 71
Stone, Andy 116
Stone, Christopher 61, 128
Stone, Dee Wallace 93
Stone, Eric 154
Stone, Ezra 127
Stone, Fred 59
Stone, Jessica 29
Stone, Laurie 139
Stone, Oliver 199
Stone, Stephanie Ann 30
Stoneham, John, Jr. 191
Stoneham, John, Sr. 191
Stonehenge Productions 96, 121, 130, 164
Stonehouse, Marilyn 54, 195
Stoneman, John 83
Stoner, Ahmad 70
Stoner, Cara 117
Storch, Norma 65, 160
Storer, Stephen 117, 174
Storey, Howard 15
Storey, Michael 82, 94
Storke, Adam 114, 165
Storke, William F. 36
Storm, Elizabeth 8
Storm, James 165, 184
Storm, Wayne 142
Storyline Entertainment 37
Stotsky-Soloway, Trinka 97
Stover, Garreth 52
Stowaway to the Moon 214
Stowell, Rachel L. 110
Straczynski, J. Michael 18, 19, 20
Strader, Robert 128
Straight, Beatrice 28, 36
Stranded in Space 217
Strange, Sarah 5
The Strange and Deadly Occurrence 214

Strange New World 74, 143, 170
The Stranger 171, 217
Stranger in Our House 171, 217
The Stranger Within 1, 97, 172
Strangers in Town 217
Strangis, Sam 75
Stransky, Charles 80
Strasberg, Susan 85
Strasser, Michael 152, 180
Strassman, Marcia 29, 83
Stratton, David 149
Stratton, Hank 17, 119
Stratton, W.K. 163
Strauss, Kim 146
Strauss, Peter 14
Strauss, Stacey 50
Strawn, Amanda 198
Strawn, C.J. 5
Strawn, Mick 67, 86, 120
Strawn, Miq 5
Streethawk 184
Strickland, Amzie 182
Strickson, Mark 36, 37
Striglos, Bill 73
Strittmatter, Cyndi 66
Strobel, Al 35
Strohmaier, David 9–10, 135
Stromberg, Hunt, Jr. 68
Strong, Brenda 99
Strong, Dennis 75
Strong, James Lyle 178
Strong, Ken 176
Stroud, Don 11
Struthers, Sally 6
Struycken, Carel 64, 104
Stu Segall Productions 22, 92
Stuart, Gloria 189
Stuart, James 60
Stuart, James Patrick 19
Stuart, Jonathan 70
Stuart, Malcolm 75, 90
Stuart, Maxine 84
Stuart, Phyllis 110
Stuart-Phoenix Productions 75
Studios USA Pictures 29
Stummeyer, Cordula 166
Sturgeon, Theodore 106
Sturgeon, Wina 65
Sturges, Preston 194
Sturgis, Pat 186
Sturridge, Charles 81
Sturridge, Thomas 80
Stutman, Gary 15
Subliminal Seduction 214, 217
Subotsky, Milton 121, 163
Suchanek, Michal 135
Sucietto, Braden 110
Sudduth, Skipp 47
Sudeikis, Jason 7
Suggs, Steven 76
Sukman, Harry 73, 143, 156
Sullivan, Barry 130
Sullivan, Billy L. 166
Sullivan, Bonnie 151
Sullivan, Brett 60
Sullivan, Brian 200
Sullivan, Charlotte 112
Sullivan, D.J. 116

Sullivan, George 166
Sullivan, Ian 39
Sullivan, Jenny 191, 192
Sullivan, Liam 40
Sullivan, Stacy 126
Sullivan, Susan 94
Sultan, Arne 144
Summer, Josef 55
Summer, Robert 155
Summer of Fear 171, 217
Summerhays, Christie 48
Summers, Andy 140
Summers, Bob 65, 113
Summers, Caroline 99
Summers, Kerry 178
Sumner, John 169
Sumner, Joseph 166
Sunrise Studios 102
Sunset Films International 194
Supergirl 187
Superman II 181
Surovy, Nicolas 43, 55, 186
Susinni, Antonio 81
Susman, Todd 97
Suspect Device 48, 172
Susskind, Steve 201
Sussman, Peter 82, 145
Sutherland, Donald 114
Sutorius, James 147
Sutter, Randy 152, 194
Sutton, Raymond 143
Svanoe, Bill 157
Svenson, Bo 85
Swackhammer, E.W. 30, 165, 193
Swamp Thing 46
Swan, Michael 103
Swan, Socorro 150
Swanger, Claude 106
Swann, Dale 76
Swann, Nickolas 191
Swansburg, Jim 155
Swanson, Gloria 106
Swanson, Kristy 137
Swanson, Scott 100, 139
Swanson, Sterling 58
Swanson, Ted 58
Swanson, Ted Adam 45
The Swarm 106
Swaybill, Roger E. 111
Swayze, Don 103
Swedberg, Heidi 40, 188
Sweeney, Faye 60
Sweeney, Pepper 154
Sweeney, Warren 154
Sweet, Kristin 181
Sweet, Shane 91
Sweet Dreams 217
Sweet, Sweet Rachel 173
Sweeting, Dennis 74
Swensen, Edithe 176
Swenson, Inga 21, 61
Swerling, Tanya 37
Swetow, Joel 181, 195
Swierski, Sowri 108
Swift, Brenton 8
Swift, Jonathan 81
Swink, George E. 6, 38
Swinson, Howard 149

Switzer, Michael 115
Swofford, Ken 30, 33, 167
Sword of Justice 79
Sword of the Valiant 67
Sy, Jovanni 191
Syane, Toi 142
Sylbert, Anthea 77
Sylk, Ken 29
Sylos, Paul 109, 145, 173
Sylvester, Harry 114
Sylvester, William 58
Symphony Pictures 174
Synthetic Worlds 18
Syrgiannis, Maria 82
Szabo, Desiree 6
Szarabajka, Keith 133
Szkoda, Peter 191
Szoloy, Mariann 107
Szyma, Piotr 67

Tabet, Sylvio 22
Tabor, Margaret 134
Tabori, Kristoffer 29
Taborsky, Mikoslav 161
Taczanowski, Hubert 110
Taft Entertainment Television 167
Taft International Pictures 65, 113
Tager, Aron 185, 190, 191
Taggert, Brian 35, 130, 139, 164, 185, 192
Tait, Tristan 61
Takacs, Tibor 155
Takakjian, Glenn 140
Takeuchi, Warren 142
Talbiri, R.L. 109
Talbott, Michael 96
Tales from the Crypt 103, 197
Tales from the Darkside 3
Tales of the Gold Monkey 11
Talgorn, Frederick 15
Taliferro, Michael "Bear" 201
Tall, Alan 153
Tallman, Patricia 18, 20
Tanaki, Kenji 177
Tangorra, Karen 135
Tanju, Ceylan 43
Tanner, Peter 16, 36, 164, 177
Tanner, Richard 181
Tansey, Patrick-Alain 198
Tansik, David 85
Tanzini, Philip 118
Tapert, Robert 86, 120
Taplitz, Daniel 24, 133
Tapscott, Mark 173
Tarantula 67
Tarbuck, Barbara 51, 140
Target: Earth 2, 174
Tarkington, Rockne 96
Tarling, Bill 147, 158
Tarver, John 112
Tarver, Maggie 86
Tarver, Milt 154
Tarzan 203
Tarzan in Manhattan 214
Tarzan: The Epic Adventures 45, 214
Tasco, Rai 143
Tash, Max 5

Tassoni, Mark 35
Tate, Jacques 99
Tate, Larron 120
Tatum, Bradford 25, 201
Taub, Lori-Etta 154, 190
Tauro, Michael 128
Taurus Film 111
Tausik, David 29
Tauss, Tom 175
Tautu, Carina 112
Tayback, Vic 178
Taylor, Adele 55
Taylor, Augustus 163
Taylor, Bea 123
Taylor, Bill 84
Taylor, Brian 83
Taylor, Bruce A. 15
Taylor, Buck 180
Taylor, Christine 87, 181
Taylor, Courtney 40
Taylor, David 39, 86
Taylor, Deborah 83
Taylor, Dendrie 130
Taylor, Don 75
Taylor, Frank Hoyt 117
Taylor, Jason 128
Taylor, Jeffrey M. 111
Taylor, Jud 71, 157
Taylor, June Whitley 94
Taylor, Larry 146
Taylor, Lee 84
Taylor, Mark L. 75, 192
Taylor, Marlon 100
Taylor, Meshach 59
Taylor, Philip John 93
Taylor, Robert 167
Taylor, Rod 195
Taylor, Roderick 15
Taylor, Stan 61
Taylor, Valerie 20
Taylor, William 139
Taylor, Yvette 125
TBS 208
Teach 101 13
Teague, Marshall 35, 182
Team Knight Rider 108
Teaton, Kenneth 183
Technomagic 125
Tedrow, Irene 189
Teed, Jill 142
Teen Angel 156
Tefkin, Blair 191, 192
Teigh, Lila 144
Tejada-Flores, Miguel 147
Tekwar 214
Tekwar: Tek Justice 215
Tekwar: Teklab 215
Tekwar: Teklords 215
Televentures 162
Telvan Productions 5
The Tempest 174
Temple Street Productions 94
Tempting Fate 175
Ten-Four Productions 75
Tergesen, Lee 33
Teri, Millie 166
Terlesky, John 193
Terminal Virus 175

Terminator 52
Terrell, Cedrick 110
Terror on the Blacktop 217
Terry, Bridget 163, 176
Terry, Herbie 66
Terzo, Venus 100
Tessier, Christian 15
Tessite, Christian 81
Tevis, Walter 119
Tewes, Lauren 101
Tezcan, Michael 138
Thackery, Frank 36, 103
Thail, Benj 83
Thal, Tycho 198
Thaler, Jonas 12, 50
Thayer, Brynn 74
Thayer, Lorna 12
Theaker, Deborah 82
Theba, Iqbal 201
Theirse, Darryl 195
Them 176
Then Came Bronson 56
Theodore, Diana 157
"There Is No Such Thing as a Vampire" 49
Therrien, Gerry 134
They 176, 217
They Watch 217
Thicke, Alan 137, 138, 170
The Thief of Baghdad 177
Thiessen, Tiffani-Amber 31
Thinnes, Roy 25, 88, 89, 97, 135, 136
Thirloway, Gregory 23
Thirst 25
30-Years-to-Life 177
This House Possessed 178
Thomas, Alexis 81
Thomas, Brent 39
Thomas, Dave 74
Thomas, David C. 194
Thomas, Deborah 147
Thomas, Freida 83
Thomas, Gareth 123
Thomas, Henry 28
Thomas, Ian 74
Thomas, Jay 63
Thomas, John 74
Thomas, Kristin Scott 80
Thomas, Lee 55
Thomas, Maralyn 118
Thomas, Marlo 101
Thomas, Maureen 135
Thomas, Peter 125
Thomas, Richard 23, 97, 100
Thomas, Robin 69, 81, 83
Thomas Carter Company 190
Thomas-Costa, Anthony 104
Thomerson, Tim 95, 197
Thompson, Aidan 195
Thompson, Dar 22
Thompson, Erinn 180
Thompson, Fred Dalton 47
Thompson, Jody 141
Thompson, Kevin 64
Thompson, Robert E. 29
Thompson, Shawn Alex 177
Thompson, Stuart 138
Thompson, Susanna 8, 109

Thompson, Tara Chase 168
Thompson, Tiger 113
Thompson, Tommy 43
Thompson, Tracey 190
Thompson, Tyler 23
Thomson, Chris 185
Thomson, Kim 102
Thomson, R.H. 12
Thor 95
Thorburn, Jim 49
Thorley, Ken 33, 167
Thorne, Ken 149
Thornhill, Lisa 159
Thorns, Tricia 83
Thornton, Ann 16
Thornton, John 144
Thornton, Sigrid 183
Thorpe, Jerry 144
Thorson, Russell 131
Thrasher, Harold 74
Three Blind Mice Productions 27
Three Minutes to Impact 217
360 Entertainment 149, 201
Thrift, Michael 128
"Thriller" 124
Through the Looking Glass 6
Through the Magic Pyramid 178, 217
Thunder Bird Road Productions 75
Thurman, Sammy 105
Thurston, Robert 93, 170
Thurtell, Andrew 86
Tibbetts, Ed 23
Tibbs, Casey 126
Tichenor, Harold 62
Tidal Wave: No Escape 215
Tieche, Gary 12, 122
Tiernan, Andrew 161
Tierney, Brigid 198
Tierney, Jacob 198
Tierney, Kevin 198
Tighe, Kevin 63
Tihada, Lanny 43
Til, Roger 55
Tilche, Gary 50
Till, Eric 13, 38
Till, Paul 60
Tilton, Charlene 65
Time After Time 37, 199
The Time Machine 25, 54, 178
The Time Project 179
A Time to Remember 154
The Time Travelers 179
Time Trax 144, 182
Time Tunnel 3, 38, 179
Timecop 5
Timelock 179
Timescape 217
Timestalkers 180
Timm, Doug 119
Timothy Marx Productions 84
Tinder, Paul 78
Tingey, Cynthia 121
Tinted Venus 78
Tiny Ron 7, 9
Tippit, Wayne 154
Tipple, Gordon 57
Tipton, George Aliceson 53
Tipton, Vann 24

Tirelli, Aldo 81
Titus Productions 55
Tivers, Paul 67
TNT 19, 20, 67, 209, 216
To Catch a Yeti 180
To the Ends of Time 181
Tobban, Deborah 158
Tobey, Kenneth 75
Toby, Doug 106
Todd, Beverly 75
Todd, Erica 42
Todd, Tony 22, 176
Toji, Marcus 181
Tokuda, Marilyn 10
Tolbert, Belinda 41
Tolces, Todd 81
Toles-Bay, John 167
Tolkin, D. Garen 47
Tolkin, Stephen 47
Tolman, Conchetta 55
Tom, Lauren 54, 63
Tomb, Brooks 157
Tomita, Tamlyn 18
Tommasino, Tim 102
Tomney, Ed 71, 104
Tomorrow Entertainment, Inc. 72
Tomorrow's Child 215
Toothless 181
Tope, Joanna 153
Topol, Richard 154
Topolsky, Ken 21
Topper 182
Topper (novel) 182
Topper (series) 182
Torcellini, Jamie 126
Torday, Terry 16
Tordjmann, Fabien 106
Tordoff, John 122
Torme, Tracy 97
Tornatore, Joe 14
Torppe, Danil 105, 150
Torrenueva, Joe 188
Torres, Brunilda 47
Torres, Gina 120
Torres, Liz 126
Torres, Zarina 175
Torsek, Dierk 92
Tosh, A.V. 181
Totem Pictures 181
Toth, Richard 49
Toub, Shaun 140
Touched by an Angel 86
Touchstone TV 144
Tourist Trap 215
Toussaint, Beth 45
Touzie, Victor 154
Toven Productions 71
Tovey, Arthur 181
The Tower 215
Tower of Terror 182
Towey, John 10
A Town Has Turned to Dust 183
Towns, Colin 46
Townsend, Barbara 15
Trabucco, Candy 68, 181
Trachta, Jeff 87
Tract, Doug "Greaseman" 136
Tracy, Blumes 109

Tracy, Spencer 102
Traill, Robert 175
Transfilm 81
Transpacific Corporation 7
Trapped in Space 183
Travanti, Daniel J. 118, 196
Travis, Greg 91
Travis, Stacey 172
Travolta, Joey 75
Treas, Terry 7–10
Treat, Martin 140
Trejo, Danny 186
Tremblay, Anthony 84, 101, 128, 190
Trenchard-Smith, Brian 139
Trentini, Peggy 194
Treu, Blair 200
Trevan, Tim 11
Treveiler, Rob 174
Trevino, Jesus Salvador 20
Trewett, Richard 138
The Trial of the Incredible Hulk 51, 95, 184
Trickey, Paula 25
Trigo, Greg 91
Trikonis, Gus 46
Trilling, Zoe 13, 110
Trilogy Entertainment Group 114, 142
Trilogy of Terror 50, 184, 185
Trilogy of Terror II 50, 185
Trimark Pictures 5, 28, 186
Trimble, Jerry 71
Trimble, Tom 145
Trinidad, Arsenio "Sonny" 68
Tripe, Don 127
Tristan, Dorothy 150
TriStar Television 140
Trivas, Victor 106
Trompower, Max 152
Tron 199
Troncatty, Ron 154
Troscianiec, Hank 168, 188
Trotta, Edward 93
Trotter, Kate 38
Trowell, Katherine 81
Troy, Louise 43
Trucks 185
True, Jim 196
Trueblood, Guerdon S. 118, 161
Trujillo, Raoul 89, 97
Truly, Daniel 86
Truman, Tim 108
Trumbo, Karen 35
Tschernisch, Serge 62
Tso, Yee Jee 57
Tu, Francisca 166
Tuchner, Michael 177
Tuck, Jessica 114
Tucker, Burnell 121
Tucker, Forrest 180
Tucker, Hubert 149
Tucker, Jack 181
Tucker, Michael 94, 193
Tucker, Paul 35
Tucker's Witch 154
Tuckner, French 51
Tuerpe, Paul 8
Tufeld, Lynn 146, 201

Tunnicliffe, Gary J. 201
Tuntke, William H. 56
Turn Back the Clock 186
The Turn of the Screw 60, 83, 84
Turnabout 69
Turner, April 169
Turner, Cedric 66
Turner, Dennis 69
Turner, Frank C. 100
Turner, Jim 186
Turner, John 122
Turner, Leonard 172
Turner, Raymond D. 12
Turner, Tierre 120
Turner Pictures 67
Turville, Trace 175
Tut and Tuttle 217
TVA International 142
Twa, Kate 14
Twain, Mark 41, 107
Tweedle, Carolyn 180
12:01 186
12:01 PM (short film) 186, 187
20th Century Films 67
20th Century–Fox 28, 43, 79, 164
20th Century–Fox Television 38, 179
20th Television 8–10, 148
20,000 Leagues Under the Sea (1) 187
20,000 Leagues Under the Sea (2) 187
Twice Upon a Time 175, 188
Twiggy 103
Twilight of the Golds 215
The Twilight Zone 40, 77, 125, 131, 134, 159, 169, 172, 189, 211
The Twilight Zone: Rod Serling's Lost Classics 188
Twin Peaks 28, 93, 155, 167
Twister 165
Two-Fisted Productions 196
The Two Worlds of Jennie Logan 189
Twohy, David N. 55
The Twonky 1
Tyminski, Jery 75
Tyrell, Simon 80
Tyson, Cicely 30, 60, 127

Udenio, Fabiana 104
Udoffia, Atim 189
UFA Filmproduction Berlin 146
UFO Café 217
UFO Crash at Roswell 153
The UFO Incident 215
Uhl, Paul 118
Ui, Triona Chongaile 90
Ujlaki, Stephen 177
Ukda, Shoji 110
Ulee's Gold 175
Ulrich, Dave 49
Ulrich, Kim Johnston 27
The Ultimate Imposter 215
Umberger, Andy 175
Under Wraps 189
Underwood, Jay 137, 138, 166, 170
Underwood, Lana 33

Unforgettable 85
Unger, Bélo 107
Unger, Bertl 92
Unger, Gustaf 92
Unhappily Ever After 45
Unidentified Flying Oddball 107
The Uninvited 190
Unisol Productions 190
United Media Finance 146
Universal 21, 22, 23, 24, 33, 53, 56, 57, 59, 65, 67, 68, 72, 85, 88, 89, 95, 98, 99, 101, 106, 119, 120, 127, 131, 148, 150, 151, 167
Universal Soldier 190
Universal Soldier II (1999) 190
Universal Soldier II: Brothers in Arms 190
Universal Soldier III: Unfinished Business 191
Universal Television 15, 29, 86, 103, 108, 150, 160
Unlikely Angel 182, 215
Uno, Michael Toshiyuki 31
Unsolved Mysteries 205
UPN 60, 92, 93, 166, 176, 177, 195, 204, 209, 210, 213
Upton, Mike 136, 137
Upton, Morgan 27
Urich, Robert 99, 106
Uritescu, Bogdan 112
Ursoni, Lois 53
USA (network) 13, 35, 40, 44, 60, 61, 70, 84, 85, 88, 93, 114, 133, 147, 154, 157, 185, 204, 206, 208, 209, 211
USA Pictures 40, 185
Useldinger, Johnny 81
Ustinov, Pavla 177, 199
Ustinov, Peter 177
Utley, Scott 42
Uzzaman, Badi 80

V 43, 191
V (series) 24, 193
V: The Final Battle 192
Vacratis, Maria 77
Vail, Justina 104
Valenti, Mark 115, 122
Valentine, Chris 141
Valentine, Dick 156
Valentine, Nancy 131
Valentine, Scott 26
Valentine, Stephanie 141
Valentine Magic on Love Island 2, 215
Valenza, Tasia 163
Valk, Blair 50
Vallario, Lawrence J. 95
Vallejo, Herminio, III 47
Valverde, Mike 97
Vampire 193
Vampirella 193
Van, Alex 174, 188
Van, Casper Dien 22
Van, Jason 92
Van, John Dreelen 38
Van, Melvin Peebles 159
Van, Nicolas Burek 38

Van Ark, Joan 110
Vance, Marilyn 112
Van Cott, Jeanne M. 51
Vandegrift, Randy 141
Van Der Byl, Philip 146
Van Der Werff, Marius 153
Van Devere, Trish 22
Vandis, Titos 73
Van Dyke, Dick 74
Van Dyke, Philip 81
Van Eeghen, Henk 54, 181
Van Horn, Joan 63, 68, 116, 181
Van Norden, Peter 165
Van Nuys, Ed 55
Van Oostrum, Kees 76
Van Patten, Dick 123
Van Patten, Joyce 52, 83, 121, 172
Van Patten, Nels 75
Van Peebles, Mario 69
Van Rellim, Tim 161
Van Riesen, Wendy 139
Van Tongeren, John 142
Van Zandt, Ned 7, 45
Varela, Nanette 138
Vargas, Jacob 167
Vargas, John 157
Vargas, Jorge 134
Varsi, Diane 141
Vasels, Philip 175
Vasquez, Randy 125
Vassey, Liz 5
Vaughan, Betty 173
Vaughan, James 187
Vaughn, Robert 55, 63, 121, 194
Vaughn, Terri J. 25, 26
Vaught, Steve 201
Vavrovec, Karel 49
Vawter, Ron 144
Vega$ 106
Vejar, Mike 19, 144
Velez, Eddie 45, 103
Vella, Marlow 195
Vellani, Mishu 145
Vendress, Michael 78
Veneziano, Sandy 195
Venora, Diane 163
Venton, Harley 27
Ventura, Clyde 144
Ventura Entertainment 102
Venuti, Christina 87
Vera, Julia 97
Verbit, Helen 129
Verburg, Neil 180
Verea, John 69
Vereen, Ben 97
Veres, Jim 91
Verne, Jules 105, 187
Vernon, Gabor 177
Vernon, Glen 15, 197
Vernon, John 148
Vernon, Peter 30
Verrell, Cec 51, 130
Vesota, Bruno 162
Vestron Pictures 66
Viacom 155, 163, 176; Pictures 153
Vibar, Bon 175
Vickerman, Michael 48, 174
Vickers, Yvette 48

Vickrey, Scott 152
Victor, James 91
Victor, Ray 186
Victor, Stephani 174
Victor Television Productions 50, 54, 62, 168
Vidosa, Christian 66
Vieira, Asia 139
Vig, Tommy 106
Vilanch, Bruce 101, 117
Vilasuso, Jordi 111
Village of the Damned 172
Village Roadshow Pictures 70, 184, 187
Villela, Michael 79
Villiegas, Cristina 175
Villiers, James 164
Vince, Pruitt Taylor 66
Vincent, E. Duke 145
Vincent, Jan-Michael 156
Vincent, Jesse 125
Vincent, Virginia 99, 131
Vindeni, Dino 125
Vinson, Gary 127
"Vintage Season" 55
Vipond, Neil 21
Virgin 35
Virkler, Dennis 49
Virtual Obsession 194
Virtual Seduction 215, 217
Virtue, Tom 189
Visions... 215, 217
Visions of Death 217
Visions of Murder 207, 216
Visions of Terror 217
Visitor, Nana 214
The Visitor 196
Visitors of the Night 195
Vitale, Billi 47
Vitale, Thomas 1
Vitarelli, Joseph 98
Vitolo, F.X. 186
Vittes, Louis 92
Vlady, Marina 177
Vogel, Tony 138
Vogel, Virgil W. 41
Vogelsang, Judith 85
Voges, Danie 146
Voight, Dustin 176
Volokh, Ilia 95
Volton 155
Von Däniken, Erich 143
Von Detten, Erik 37, 63
Vonnegut, Kurt 82
Von Palleske, Heidi 66
von Sternberg, Nicholas 76
Von Zerneck, Frank 45, 99, 152, 194
Von Zerneck, Frank, Jr. 99
Von Zerneck, Peter 78
Von Zerneck/Sertner Films 45, 152, 194
Voyage to the Bottom of the Sea 38, 162, 179
Voyagis, Yorgo 138, 154
Voyce, Jonathan 76
Vozhenikov, Vladimir 85
V.R. 5 145

Vrana, Vlasta 114
Vukusic, Tom 16

Waagfjord, Berta 16
Wabe Inc. 62
Wade, Harker 43
Wagener, Christiaan 188
Waggoner, Lyle 129
Wagner, Bruce 198, 199
Wagner, Jack 183
Wagner, Jefferson 12
Wagner, Lindsay 23, 24, 69, 150, 189
Wagner, Mike 199
Wagner, Robert 37, 210
Wagner, Thomas 140
Wagrowski, Gregory 130
Wainwright, James 106
Waite, Ric 49, 96, 151
Waites, Thomas G. 179
Wakefield, David 21
Walberg, David 180
Walcott, Gregory 72
Wald, Malvin 113
Walden, Susan 144
Walden, W.G. "Snuffy" 80
Walker, Andrew 154, 190
Walker, Arnetia 33
Walker, Bill 109
Walker, Charles 42, 105
Walker, Clint 106
Walker, Eric 64
Walker, Greg 72
Walker, Justin 91
Walker, Matthew 59, 93, 134
Walker, Nancy 90
Walker, Rock 72
Walker, Saige 181
Walker, Scott 90
Walker, Shirley 5, 44, 84, 101, 116
Walkers 69
Wall, Christopher 66
Wall, Jared 190
Walla, Tom 84
Wallace, Art 159
Wallace, Chris 145
Wallace, Earl M. 44
Wallace, Elizabeth 40
Wallace, George 160
Wallace, Tommy Lee 45, 100
Wallach, Eli 204
Wallack, Kathryn 58, 155
Wallenstein, Joseph B. 42, 158, 186
Waller, Philip 167
Walling, Christopher 40
Wallis, Bill 31
Walos, Kari 141
Walsh, Bill 116, 158
Walsh, Chuck 65
Walsh, Dylan 35
Walsh, Helena 90
Walsh, M. Emmett 128
Walsh, Sydney 88
Walsh, Terry 102
Walston, Ray 65, 105, 146, 165
Walt DeFaria Productions 28
Walt Disney Co. 116, 170

Walt Disney Television 15, 47, 94, 107, 135, 181, 182
Walter, Barry 23, 110
Walter, Jessica 56, 193
Walter, Perla 36
Walter, Tracey 40, 54, 137, 180
Walters, Anne 141
Walters, Anthony 36
Walters, Melora 188
Walters, Susan 92
Waltman, Michael 182
Walton, Fred 88, 168
Walton, Janie 6
Waltz, Ken 115
Waltz, Lisa 114, 153
Walwin, Kent 114
Wanamaker, Sam 154
Wanberg, Victoria 55
Wanger, Karyn 22
War Eagle, John 157
Ward, Elaine 92
Ward, Fred 33
Ward, Kirk 198
Ward, Lyman 142
Ward, Rachel 24
Ward, Robert 51
Ward, Sandy 79
Ward, Sela 35
Ward, Simon 59
Ward, Tim 66
Warden, Jack 6, 182
Warden, Rachel 111
Wardlow, John 134
Ware, Herta 10
Ware, Peter V. 5, 57, 71
Ware, Susan 97
Warhol, Jordan Blake 158
The Warlord: Battle for the Galaxy 195, 217
Warner, David 22, 33, 36, 37, 103, 199
Warner, Marsha 99, 101
Warner, Natasha Gregson 158
Warner, Pam 83
Warner, Rick 37
Warner, Robert E. 55
Warner Bros. 17, 19, 20, 73, 129, 143, 144, 156, 157, 159, 170, 171; Television 59, 99, 192
Warren, Aimee 7
Warren, Dana 37
Warren, Danielle
Warren, Ed 53, 83
Warren, Gene, Jr. 89
Warren, Jennifer 96
Warren, Kiersten 79
Warren, Lorraine 53, 83
Warren, Marcie Jo 67
Warren, Michael 152
Warry-Smith, Daniel 74, 93, 112, 157
Warschilka, Edward A. 103
Washington, James E. 112
The Wasp Woman 17, 196, 217
Wass, Ted 31
Wasser, Ed 18
Wasserman, Jerry 134, 170
Wasson, Craig 183
Watanabe, Greg 189

Index

The Water Engine 216
Waterman, Stanton 23
Waters, Dana 148
Waters, Dionne 81
Waters, Ed 96
Watkins, Gary 198
Watkins, Michael 43
Watkins, Michael W. 167
Watson, Barry 16
Watson, Cameron 117
Watson, Carlton 82
Watson, James A., Jr. 106, 109
Watson, John 114, 142
Watson, Michael 43, 118
Watson, Mills 150
Watson, Scott 55
Watters, George 73, 143
Watts, Nigel 24
Waugh, Tamara 86
Waxman, Al 93
Way, Michael Ryan 67
Wayland, Len 72, 173
Wayne, David 12
Wayne, Ethan 28
Wayne, Michael 152
Wayne, Nina 132
Wayne, Patrick 161
Weatherly, Michael 5
Weatherred, Michael D. 101, 146, 166
Weathers, Carl 23
Weathington, Jesse 125
Weaver, Dennis 206
Weaver, Fritz 121
Weaver, Kevin 33
Weaver, Mary 84
Weaver, Rose 76
Weaver, Sigourney 161
Webb, Audrey 94
Webb, Brett 102
Webb, Bunny 74
Webb, Cynthia 117
Webb, Matt 169
Webb, Richard 179
Webb, Ryan 101
Webber, Robert 16, 85, 162
Webber, Tim 81, 122
Webber, Timothy 74
Weber, Dewey 109
Weber, Steven 159
Webner, Jules 177
Webster, Byron 144, 193
Webster, Diana 32, 61
Webster, Flip 83
Webster, Ion 82
Weddle, Vernon 39
Wedlock 205, 216
Wedlock II 217
Weeks, Danielle 91
Weezer, Lillian 192
Weill, Claudia 77
Wein, Dean 151
Weinger, Scott 158
Weinstein, Paula 39, 77
Weird Fantasy 196
Weird Science 196
W.E.I.R.D. WORLD 196
Weisbarth, Michael 93, 154

Weisberg, Ron 51
Weiser, Shari 18
Weisman, Howard 118
Weismuller, Johnny, Jr. 64
Weiss, D.B. 115
Weiss, David 7
Weiss, Don 127
Weiss, Peter 118
Weiss, Stuart 181
Weiss, Trudy 160
Weisser, Rene 12
Weissman, Benjamin A. 107, 130
Weist, Lucinda 84
Weitz, Barry 44, 118, 130
Welb Film Pursuits 197
Welch, Shannon 195
Welch, Tahnee 104
Welcome to Planet Earth 217
Weldon, Ann 150
Weldon, Michael 189
Weller, Craig 175
Weller, Rob 166
Welles, Orson 101
Wells, David 55, 136, 201
Wells, H.G. 98, 178
Wells, James D. 178
Wells, John 80
Wells, Kim 171
Welsh, Kenneth 81
Welsh, Richard 117
Welsman, John 94
Wen, Ming-Na 175
Wendel, J.C. 201
Wenderlich, Windy 169
Wendkos, Paul 67, 69, 79
Wendt, George 6–7
Wentworth, Alexandra 116
Werewolf 88
Werner, Peter 89, 175
Wert, Doug 85, 152, 196
Wertheimer, Bob 190, 191
Wertimer, Ned 36
Wescott, Bruce 197
Weselis, Danny 105
Wesley, John 180
West, Adam 144
West, Andy 200
West, Chandra 190, 191
West, Pamela 130
West, Roy 165
West, Tegan 97
Westburg, David 73
Westcott, Bruce 202
Westdal, Freya 81
Westenkow, Mike 166
Westgate, Murray 28
Westgate Productions 87
Westmore, Michael 15
Weston, Ann 23
Weston, Debora 149
Weston, Ellen 124, 148, 151
Weston, Larry 78
Weston, Whitney 69
Westwind 147
Wetherall, Virginia 59
Wettig, Patricia 168
Wexo, Alex 173
Whaley, Frank 28

Whaley, Michael 154, 188
Whalley, Joanne 36, 37
Wharmby, Tony 157
Wheat, Jim 64, 101, 168
Wheat, Ken 64, 101, 168
Wheaton, Wil 119
Wheel of Fortune 78
Wheeler, Charles F. 159
Wheeler, John 126, 199
Wheeler, John W. 144
Wheeler, Thomas 181
Whelan, Gerard 49
Whelan, Julia 37
When Dreams Come True 216
When Michael Calls 216
When Time Expires 197
Where Have All The People Gone? 197
Whipp, Joseph 36
Whipple, Sam 114
Whiskers 198
Whitaker, Brandlyn 176
Whitaker, Duane 201
Whitaker, Johnny 162
Whitaker, William 39
Whitcomb, Cynthia 62, 63
White, Al 127
White, Carol Ita 28
White, David 165
White, Deborah 150
White, DéVoreaux 67
White, J.B. 79, 89
White, John 112
White, John Sylvester 113
White, Kenneth 36, 188
White, Larry 78
White, Michael 78
White, Noni 69
White, Paul 55
White, Ron 82, 158
White, Scott 89
White, Steve 13, 60, 82, 175
White, Vanna 78
White Dwarf 198
"White Shark" 142
Whitefield, Anne 160
Whiteford, Steve 105
Whitehead, Bernedette 111
Whitehead, Paxton 35, 186
Whitehead, Robert 30
Whitelaw, Billie 122
Whitelow, Helen 125
Whitfield, David 99, 101
Whitford, Bradley 39
Whiting, Arch 171
Whiting, Leonard 68
Whitley, Patrick 94, 112
Whitman, Jack 92
Whitman, John 99, 101
Whitman, Rainer 83
Whitman, Stuart 34, 37
Whitmore, Brad 55
Whitmore, Hugh 83
Whitmore, James, Jr. 43, 90
Whitney, David 58
Whitten, Leslie H. 125
Whitting, Richard 24
Whittington, Gene 92
Who Is Julia? 216

Whorf, David 37
Wiard, William 77, 178
Wickes, David 67, 102
Wickware, Scott 54, 112
Wide World of Mystery 3, 60
Wiedlin, Jane 12
Wiesenfeld, Joe 107, 187
Wiest, Jeannine 186
Wiggins, Alfred 174
Wiggins, Chris 12
Wigman, Denis 81
Wigutow, Dan 24, 29, 133
Wihak, Marian 112
Wilbur, George P. 33
Wilcox, Richard 139
Wilcox, Steve 29
Wilcoxon, Henry 189
Wild Palms 199
Wild Street Pictures 55
The Wild, Wild West 16, 119, 200
Wild, Wild West Revisited 126, 199
Wilde, Cornel 72
Wilde, June B. 39
Wilde, Oscar 31, 32, 160
Wilding, Michael 68
Wilds, Rob 169
Wiley, David 197
Wilhoite, Benji 176
Wilkerson, George 7
Wilkes, Deborah 105
Wilkins, Mike 30
Wilkins, Richard 44
Wilkinson, M. Scott 183
Wilkinson, Scott 48, 178, 200
Will Success Spoil Rock Hunter? 1
Willard, Fred 156
Williams, Allen 189
Williams, Amir 47
Williams, Anthony 116
Williams, Ben 80
Williams, Bennett 29
Williams, Bret 142
Williams, Christian 86
Williams, Cindy 61, 168
Williams, Clarence, III 63, 116
Williams, Cress 142
Williams, David 189
Williams, Denalda 59, 170
Williams, Dick Anthony 29
Williams, Edward W. 94, 120
Williams, Ellis 10
Williams, Garfield 60
Williams, Greg Alan 146
Williams, Heathcote 138
Williams, Ian Patrick 137
Williams, J. Terry 78, 148
Williams, Jean 80
Williams, Jim Cody 7, 108
Williams, John 64
Williams, John Timothy 180
Williams, Johnny 151, 196
Williams, Joseph 112
Williams, Kelli 114
Williams, Ken 141
Williams, Larry 29
Williams, Mary Parker 200
Williams, Matt 60
Williams, Melanie F. 36
Williams, Mitchah 126
Williams, Natasha 41
Williams, Patrick 80, 107, 119
Williams, Paul 133, 199
Williams, Peter 61
Williams, Philip 38, 185, 191
Williams, R.J. 133
Williams, Stacey 140
Williams, Stephen (director) 157, 158
Williams, Steven 52
Williams, Trevor 49, 59, 131, 132, 136
Williams, Tricia 77
Williams, Vanessa 138, 207
Williamson, Scott 16
Willingham, Noble 197
Willis, Austin 51
Willis, Calvin 181
Willis, Donald 95
Willis, Mirron F. 29
Willoughby, Pat 137
Willows, Alec 79
Willrich, Rudolph 55
Wills, Terry 69, 73
Wilshire Court Productions 35, 60, 70, 88, 115, 127, 157, 184, 185
Wilson, Anthony 40, 42, 71, 88
Wilson, Barry M. 188
Wilson, Bridgette 194
Wilson, Dale 93
Wilson, Elizabeth 163
Wilson, Freddie 22
Wilson, Irv 30
Wilson, Jamie 123
Wilson, Keith 149
Wilson, Kelly 115
Wilson, Lambert 67
Wilson, Mark 82
Wilson, Nicky 123
Wilson, Patricia 171
Wilson, Richard 80
Wilson, Thick 75, 94
Wilson, Tom 128
Wiltse, David 151
Wiltshire, Miles 92
Wiltshire, Richard 35
Winans, Sam 76
Winchester, Maud 16
Winchester, Putu 58
Wincott, Jeff 190, 191
Windom, William 16
Windsor, Andrew 128
Windsor, Marie 103, 156
Windust, Penelope 191
Winfield, Dave 111
Winfield, Paul 88, 112, 198
Winfrey, Jonathan 25, 26
Wingreen, Jason 32, 109, 119
Winkler, Henry 12
Winkler, Mel 69
Winkless, Jeff 137
Winkless, Terence H. 137
Winley, Tony 128
Winn, Katherine 90
Winn, Timothy 175
Winner, Jeffrey 6
Winning, David 123
Winningham, Mare 97
Winslow, Kathryn 54
Winstead, Deborah 188
Winston, Adam 117
Winston, John 161
Winston, Stan 72, 142
Winter, Ralph 144
Winters, Dana 120
Winters, Jonathan 6, 126
Winters, Marc 107
Winters, Michael 109
Winters, Roland 124
Winters, Shelley 6, 96
Winters, Time 55, 97, 198
Winton, Colleen 23
Winzenried, Eric 190
Wirkkunen, Joel 57
Wise, David 22
Wise, Greg 89
Wise, Jonathan 67
Wise, Michael 181
Wise, Ray 41
Wiseman, Debra 126
Wiseman, Michael 25
Wiser, Linda 150
Wish Upon a Star 200
Wisman, Ron 13, 30, 54, 94, 138, 160
Witch Hunt 34, 200
Witherick, Arthur 164
Witherspoon, Dane 35
Within the Rock 201
Without Warning 216
Witkin, Stephen 118
Witt, Dan 134
Witt, Howard 151
Witt, Michael 113
Wittstein, Ed 55
Wixted, Michael-James 197
Wizan, Joe 139, 189
Wizards and Warriors 16
Wize, Tom 144
WNET-13 111
Wodoslawsky, Stefan 147
Wohlberg, Stanley 196
Wolcott, Jann Arrington 157
Wolf, Abby 39
Wolf, Gary 136
Wolf, Harry L. 29, 53, 127
Wolf, Laurie 169
Wolfe, Ian 129
Wolff, John Trevor 67
Wolff, Jurgen 59
Wolpe, Lenny 146
Wolsky, Albert 22
Wonder Woman 216
Wonder Woman 129
Wong, Helene 66
Wong, Janine 155
Wong, Kea 155
Wong, Roxanne 135
Wong, Vincent 177
Wood, Brett 128
Wood, Cynthia 170
Wood, Elijah 47
Wood, Ira David, IV 117
Wood, Janet 182
Wood, John Lisbon 107
Wood, Lana 33

Wood, Lynn 75
Woodard, Alfre 80, 163
Woodbury, Jamy 27
Woodfield, William Read 62
Woodford, John 123
Woodland, Lauren 7–10
Woodruff, Kurt 28
Woodruff Productions 12
Woods, Barbara Alyn 50
Woods, George J. 21
Woods, Kara 37
Woods, Leon 169
Woods, Lesley 58, 190
Woods, Michael 139
Woods, Richard 117
Woods, Robert S. 50
Woods, Tommy 115
Woodson, Julie 23
Woodthorpe, Peter 36, 122, 138
Woodville, Kate 67
Woodward, Edward 16, 36, 80
Woodward, Meredith 184
Woodworth, Daniel 106
Woolen, Thomas A. 68
Woolf, Jack 79, 106
Woollen, Susan 150
Woolnough, Jeff 190, 191
Woolrich, Cornel 93
Woolridge, Karen 83
Woolvett, Gordon Michael 112
Wooten, Andi 31
Worden, Hank 25
Wordsworth, Roy 160
Woren, Dan 99, 101
"A World of Difference" 134
World of Disney 3
The World, the Flesh and the Devil 198
Worldvision 168
Worldvision Enterprises 90
Worley, Jo Ann 178
Woronov, Mary 87, 128
Worth, Alison 16
Worth, Nicholas 50, 99, 179
Worthington, Wendy 182
Wrangler, Greg 50
Wright, Aloma 92
Wright, Ben 171
Wright, Bruce 91
Wright, David Grant 22
Wright, Ed 171
Wright, Herbert J. 178
Wright, J. Madison 195
Wright, Maggie 121
Wright, Max 47, 165
Wright, Michael 191, 192
Wright, Norton 83
Wright, Patrick 135
Wright, Wendell 41
Wu, Michael 196
Wyatt, Allan, Jr. 65
Wyatt, Dale 161
Wyatt, Jane 13
Wylie, Adam 189
Wyman, Bob 85, 116
Wynant, H.M. 72, 88, 171
Wynn, Paul 123
Wynne, Paul 28

Wynne/Pike Productions 28
Wynorski, Jim 194, 196
Wynter, Dana 148
Wyss, Amanda 178

The X-Files 108. 133, 153
X-Men 73
Xena: Warrior Princess 2, 87, 109, 121
Xuereb, Salvator 27, 149
X—The Man with the X-Ray Eyes 25, 49

Yacknin, Robert 84
Yagher, Jeff 24
Yancy, Emily 144
Yarmush, Michael 198
Yarnell, Lorene 199
Yates, Cassie 82
Yeager, Biff 75, 90
Yeager, Caroline 160, 195
Yeager, Derryl 166
Yearly, Robert 128
Yedidia, Mario 97, 189
Yee, Helena 61
Yellen, Sherman 22
Yerkes, Brayton 166
Yesterday's Target 201
Yip, Karen 139
Yoakam, Dwight 152
Yohn, Erica 79
Yohnka, Merritt 180
Yonis, Jeff 91
York, Francine 179
York, James 42
York, Michael 45, 107, 136, 141
York, Susannah 36
Yorke, Wayne Thomas 181
You Wish 156
Young, Aida 177
Young, Alan 61
Young, Blumen 8
Young, Buck 116, 171
Young, David 144
Young, Dennis 73
Young, Dey 76, 138
Young, Gig 164
Young, Harrison 91
Young, Jenna 174
Young, Jerry 39, 41, 42
Young, John Sacret 144, 145
Young, Keone 66, 87
Young, Ray 73
Young, Richard 163
Young, Robert Malcolm 63, 75
Young, Roger 107
Young, Roland 182
Young, Steen 81
Young, Victor A. 93, 195
Young Frankenstein 56
Youngblood, Rob 188
Youngfellow, Barrie 193
Youngs, Gail 180
Yount, Dell 146
Yuen, Galen 167

Zabel, Bryce 139
Zabka, William 181
Zabriskie, Grace 27, 54

Zacha, Charles 189
Zacha, W.T. 65
Zacharias, Steffen 77
Zachary, Bohdan 83
Zachary, John 45, 179
Zadan, Craig 37
Zadro, Louis E. 108
Zaharuk, Bill 28
Zale, Alexander 97
Zaloom, George 63, 68, 116, 158, 182
Zaloom-Mayfield Productions 63
Zambrano, David 159
Zamfirescu, Dan 112
Zand, Michael 8
Zane, Billy 154
Zann, Chara 141
Zapata, Joan 28
Zappa, Ahmet 146
Zarcoff, Mort 159
Zaremba, John 178
Zaremba, Kathryn 181
Zarnescu, Dana 112
Zastupnevich, Paul 6
Zateslo, George 31, 76, 77
Zavada, Ervin 123
Zavorak, Jack "JR" 193
Zednickova, Lucie 49
Zeek, Dawn 100
Zeitman, Jerome M. 53
Zeitman-Landers-Roberts Productions 53
Zelinger, Beatrice 184
Zelniker, Michael 201
Zeman, Richard 81
Zemanek, Timm 94
Zemeckis, Robert 196
Zenda, John 99
Zerbe, Anthony 107
Zeretzke, John 112
Zertuche, Kinta 196
Zetlin, Barry 182
Zidel, Bob 147
Ziegel, Roberta Becker 130
Ziembicki, Bob 24
Ziering, Nikki Schieler 19
Zigler, Scott 47
Zilah 7
Ziller, Paul 147
Zima, Yvonne 37, 48
Zimbalist, Stephanie 215
Zimmer, Constance 148
Zimmer, Diana 13
Zimmerman, Herman 96
Zimmerman, Joey 22, 81
Zindel, Paul 6, 18, 41
Zinyk, Allan 14
Zitner, Alan 128
Zlotoff, Inc. 144
Zlotoff, Lee David 144
ZM Productions 116, 158, 182
Zobel, Richard 120
Zohar, Rita 69
Zolotin, Adam 57
Zotter, Frank 54
ZPG 110
Zuckert, Bill 178
Zumwalt, Rick 8

www.ingramcontent.com/pod-product-compliance
Lightning Source LLC
Chambersburg PA
CBHW081544300426
44116CB00015B/2747